Fodor's® 99
The Best
Cruises

Previously published as Fodor's *Worldwide Cruises and Ports of Call*

Fodor's Travel Publications, Inc.
New York • Toronto • London • Sydney • Auckland
www.fodors.com

Copyright

ISBN 0–679–00169–7

Fodor's The Best Cruises '99

EDITOR: M. T. Schwartzman

Editorial Contributors: John Bigley, Carol Bareuther, Arline Bleecker, Sam Bleecker, Wendy Determan, David H. Jones, Lynda Lohr, Gordon Lomer, Karl Luntta, JoAnn Milivojevic, Laurence Miller, Jennifer Paull, Paris Permenter, Don Pitcher, Heidi Sarna, Theodore W. Scull, Jordan Simon, Jonathan Siskin, Jane Zarem
Editorial Production: Linda K. Schmidt
Maps: David Lindroth, *cartographer*; Robert Blake, *map editor*
Design: Fabrizio La Rocca, *creative director*; Guido Caroti, *associate art director*; Jolie Novak, *photo editor*
Production/Manufacturing: Mike Costa
Technical Illustration: Christopher A. Wilson
Illustrator: Karl Tanner
Cover Photograph: Harvey Lloyd/The Stock Market
Cover Design: John Olenyik

Special Sales

Contents

1 Best Cruise Lines and Ships 44

2 Special-Interest Cruises 169

3 Ports of Call 202

4 Itineraries 483

Index

Maps and Charts

At Sea with Fodor's

What makes one cruise line better than another? Why choose cruise line "A" instead of cruise line "B"? These are the questions we addressed in preparing *Fodor's The Best Cruises '99*. Only the 23 best cruise lines have been included in this book. To make our list, each cruise line had to be outstanding in some way. These are not necessarily the most expensive cruise lines or the newest, biggest cruise ships. Some specialize in giving you good value for your money. Others epitomize the tradition of luxury travel by sea. Some of the ships are quite small, while others are indeed among the biggest and most elaborate afloat. Some are brand-new, others quite old. But they all have one thing in common: Each delivers a consistently good cruise experience—which is the hallmark of a well-run cruise line.

About Our Writers

As they do every year, Fodor's cruise writers sailed the seven seas in search of their story. **Jon Siskin** put on his waterproof boots to make wet-landings in Antarctica aboard the *Explorer*. **Arline and Sam Bleecker** went to the Mediterranean aboard the *Pacific Princess* and Tahiti aboard the *Paul Gauguin*. **Heidi Sarna,** who wrote our new hints sections for honeymooners and sports enthusiasts, stayed a little closer to home as she sailed to Canada and New England aboard the *Silver Cloud*. **Ted Scull,** our leading ship buff, sailed Hawai'i on the classic *Independence*. And editor **M.T. Schwartzman** reviewed several new ships, including the *Enchantment of the Seas, Mercury, Rotterdam*, and *Grand Princess*.

New and Noteworthy

For ongoing updates of the most intriguing cruise itineraries, candid reviews of new vessels, and links to the best cruise sites, visit the Cruise News section of Fodor's Web site, www.fodor's.com/cruise.

Ship Delays New ships coming out late were the talk of the industry in late 1997 and early 1998. First the *Rotterdam VI* canceled three cruises, reportedly due to propulsion problems. Then the *Paul Gauguin* canceled several cruises due to noisy stabilizers, and the *Grand Princess* delayed its maiden voyage by one sailing because the ship wasn't ready. The biggest delay of all was for the *Disney Magic*, which postponed its debut from March 12 to July 30, 1998.

It's just a reminder that even in this age of cruise ship assembly lines, booking an inaugural cruise is—and has always been—risky business. Maiden voyages are glamorous, but never a sure thing.

Cruising 2000 The stampede to build new ships continues unabated. At press time, Holland America had announced plans for a sister to its new *Rotterdam,* scheduled to make its debut in the fall of the year 2000. Princess Cruises said it would build two more sisters to its 109,000-ton *Grand Princess*. The two ships will be deployed year-round in the Caribbean beginning in spring and fall 2001. Royal Caribbean announced plans to construct up to seven new ships (several for its sister line, Celebrity) through the year 2002.

Cruising on Credit Several cruise lines will now finance the cost of your cruise. Princess Cruises began the trend with its LoveBoat Loan cruise financing program. Royal Caribbean and Celebrity followed with their own CruiseLoan program. Interest rates vary considerably. Rates for past passengers can be as low as 12.5%. The average rate is about 14%.

On the agency front, Golden Bear Travel has branded credit cards with MasterCard and Visa. The MasterCard earns points redeemable for shipboard credits and cabin upgrades aboard 12 participating cruise lines. With the Visa card, passengers are automatically entitled to special offers that are determined by the cruise line.

Silly Awards It seems that virtually every travel publication has an awards program these days. But the awards frenzy reached new heights of self-congratulation when Seabourn Cruise Line *gave itself* an award. The line named the *Seabourn Legend* the best ship in its fleet.

Don't Forget to Write

You can use this book in the confidence that all prices and opening times are based on information supplied to us at press time; Fodor's cannot accept responsibility for any errors. Time inevitably brings changes, so always confirm information when it matters—especially if you're making a detour to visit a specific place.

Were the restaurants we recommended as described? Did you find a museum we recommended a waste of time? Keeping a travel guide fresh and up-to-date is a big job, and we welcome your feedback, positive *and* negative. If you have complaints, we'll look into them and revise our entries when the facts warrant it. If you've discovered a special place that we haven't included, we'll pass the information along to our correspondents and have them check it out. So send us your thoughts via e-mail at editors@fodors.com (specifying the name of the book on the subject line) or on paper in care of the *Best Cruises* editor at Fodor's, 201 East 50th Street, New York, New York 10022. In the meantime, have a wonderful trip!

Karen Cure
Editorial Director

Cruise Primer

Choosing Your Cruise

The right ship is one that makes you comfortable. Every ship has its own personality, depending upon whether it was built for ocean cruising, yachtlike cruising, coastal cruising, or expedition cruising. Big ships are more stable and offer a huge variety of activities and facilities. Smaller ships feel intimate, like private clubs. Each type of ship satisfies a certain type of passenger, and for every big-ship fan there is somebody who would never set foot aboard one of these "floating resorts."

Comparing Ships

In order to compare cruise ships, you need to speak "ship talk." Vessels are generally described according to their passenger capacity, gross registered tonnage, passenger-to-crew ratio, and space ratio. A ship's passenger capacity is usually based on double occupancy, meaning the normal cruise complement of the vessel with two passengers in each cabin. This does not include third or fourth passengers in a cabin, which on some ships can greatly increase the total passenger count. Gross registered tonnage is commonly used to measure a vessel's size. Technically, it is a measurement of the ship's volume, with 1 gross registered ton equal to 100 cubic ft. Passenger-to-crew ratio indicates the number of passengers served by each crew member—the lower the ratio, the better the level of service. Space ratio, the ship's tonnage divided by its passenger capacity, allows you to compare a ship's roominess. The higher the ratio, the more spacious a vessel will feel. The roomiest ships have ratios of 40:1 or better; ships with ratios of less than 28:1 may feel cramped.

But when choosing your cruise, the size of the ship isn't the only factor to consider. You also need to find out about the nature of the experience you will have—the lifestyle and activities available by day and after dark, the mealtime hours and dining-room dress codes, how roomy the ship is, and how good the service is apt to be. Equally important are your itinerary, the accommodations, and the cost of the cruise.

Types of Ships

Although all ocean liners are equipped with swimming pools, spas, nightclubs, theaters, and casinos, there are three distinct types: classic liners, cruise liners, and megaships. Many **classic liners,** ships constructed between 1950 and 1969 for transatlantic or other ocean crossings, are still sailing in the fleets of a few cruise lines. Beginning in the 1960s, ship lines began to create vessels specifically for cruising. Some of these **cruise liners** were brand new; others were converted ferries or freighters. Vessels known as **megaships,** the biggest cruise ships ever built, first appeared in the late 1980s and, with their immense proportions and passenger capacities, established a new standard of cruise-ship design.

Cruises are also available aboard a number of specialty ships: cruise yachts, expedition ships, motor-sailing ships, riverboats, and coastal cruisers.

Classic Liners With their long, sweeping hulls and stepped-back passenger decks, these vessels defined passenger-ship design for decades. Now serving cruise duty, they were originally configured to keep passengers happy during long ocean crossings. Typically, their cabins and closets are larger than those on vessels built for cruising. Deck space is sheltered, with fully or partially enclosed promenades that allow you to relax on deck even during foul weather. A few are still steam powered, without the vibrations sometimes associated with diesel power. Rich wood panels the walls, and fixtures may be the original brass. Smaller ships may feel cramped because of low ceilings in the lobby and corridors. But on the most opulent vessels, public spaces designed to inspire still do. There are balconies above the dining room, where musicians can serenade diners; stained glass graces the cinemas and other public spaces; and grand staircases lead from one deck to another. Such traditional features have proved so enduring they have been incorporated in the plans for some of today's newest vessels.

Although classic ships typically carry between 600 and 1,000 passengers and register between 20,000 and 30,000 tons, a couple of them are among the largest passenger ships afloat.

Cruise Liners When shipbuilders stopped constructing vessels for transportation and started designing them for vacationing, the cruise liner entered the scene. On these ships, outdoor deck space is plentiful; stateroom space is not. Many have a wraparound outdoor promenade deck that allows you to stroll or jog the perimeter of the ship. Older cruise liners resemble the transatlantic ships from which they are descended: Decks are stacked one atop the other in steps, and the hull amidships may appear to droop, so the bow and stern seem to curve upward. In the newest cruise liners, traditional meets trendy. You find atrium lobbies and expansive sun and sports decks, picture windows instead of portholes, and cabins that open onto private verandas. The smallest cruise liners carry 500 passengers and are no bigger than 10,000 tons, while the largest accommodate 1,500 passengers, exceed 50,000 tons, and are stuffed with diversions—almost like megaships.

Megaships The centerpiece of most megaships is a three-, five-, or seven-story central atrium. However, these giant vessels are most easily recognized by their boxy profile: The hull and superstructure rise straight out of the water, as many as 14 stories tall, topped out by a huge sun or sports deck with a jogging track and swimming pool, which may be Olympic size. Some megaships, but not all, also have a wraparound promenade deck. Like the latest cruise liners, picture windows are standard equipment, and cabins in the top categories have private verandas. From their casinos and discos to their fitness centers, everything is proportionally bigger and more extravagant than on other ships. Between 1,500 and 2,500 passengers can be accommodated, and tonnage ranges from 70,000 to 100,000 or more.

Cruise Yachts At the opposite end of the spectrum from the megaship is the tiny cruise yacht. These intimate vessels carry from 100 to 300 passengers, register between 4,000 and 15,000 tons, and are like miniature ocean liners, with big-ship amenities such as fitness centers, casinos, lounges, and swimming pools. What sets these yachts apart from typical ocean liners is that passengers are treated like royalty. Cabins are all outside suites equipped with every creature comfort on the high seas—from VCRs and stocked minibars to marble baths. Built into the stern of some of these vessels are retractable platforms, which are lowered for water sports when the ship is at anchor in calm waters.

Expedition Ships Vessels of this type are designed to reach into the most remote corners of the world. Shallow drafts allow them to navigate up rivers, close to coastlines, and into shallow coves. Hulls may be hardened for sailing in Antarctic ice. Motorized rubber landing craft known as Zodiacs, kept on board, make it possible for passengers to put ashore almost anywhere. However, because the emphasis during cruises aboard expedition ships tends to be on learning and exploring, the ships don't have casinos, showrooms, multiple bars and lounges, and other typical ocean-liner diversions. Instead, they have theaters for lectures, well-stocked libraries, and enrichment programs, led by experts, as entertainment. The smallest expedition ships carry fewer than 100 passengers and register just over 2,000 tons. The largest carries nearly 200 people and registers 9,000 tons.

Motor-Sail Vessels A number of cruise vessels were designed as sailing ships. With their sails unfurled, they are an impressive sight. But since they must keep to a schedule, they cannot rely solely on wind power. So all are equipped with engines as well. Usually they employ both means of propulsion, a technique known as motor sailing, to put on a good show and make the next port on time. These vessels range from small windjammers carrying a handful of passengers to rather large clipper-style ships that approach the size of a small ocean liner and accommodate almost 400 passengers.

Riverboats Most riverboats sailing in today's cruise fleet are replicas of those that sailed the nation's rivers in the 19th century. The feeling is definitely Victorian: Parlors are furnished with Tiffany lamps and leather wing chairs, and rocking chairs line the outer decks. Smaller riverboats offer just a lounge or two and a dining room. Bigger ones may add a small health club, theater, and a few other amenities, while still retaining their traditional character. But even the largest riverboat, which carries more than 400 passengers, registers only 3,000 tons.

Coastal Cruisers Closely related to the riverboat is its modern-day equivalent, the coastal cruiser. Designed more for exploring than entertaining, these yachtlike ships are able to sail to remote waterways and ports. Some have forward gangways for bow landings or carry a fleet of Zodiac landing craft. Unlike larger expedition ships, they do not have ice-hardened hulls. Registering no more than 100 tons and carrying only about 100 passengers, coastal cruisers offer few onboard facilities and public spaces—perhaps just a dining room and a multipurpose lounge.

The Cruise Experience

Your cruise experience will be shaped by several factors, and to determine whether a particular ship's style will suit you, you need to do a bit of research. Is a full program of organized activities scheduled by day? What happens in the evening? Are there one or two seatings in the dining room? If there is more than one, you will not be allowed to arrive and exit as the spirit moves you but instead must show up promptly when service begins—and clear out within a specified time. What kind of entertainment is offered after dark? And how often do passengers dress up for dinner? Some cruises are fancier than others.

Although no two cruises are quite the same, even aboard the same ship, the cruise experience tends to fall into three categories.

Formal Formal cruises embody the ceremony of cruising. Generally available on ocean liners and cruise yachts sailing for seven days or longer, formal cruises recall the days when traveling by ship was an event in itself. By day, shipboard lifestyle is generally unstructured, with few organized activities. Tea and bouillon may be served to the accompaniment of music from a classical trio in the afternoon. Ashore, passengers may be treated to a champagne beach party. Meals in the dining room are served in a single seating, and passengers enjoy the finest cuisine afloat. Jackets and ties for men are the rule for dinner, tuxedos are not uncommon, and the dress code is observed faithfully throughout the evening. Pianists, cabaret acts, and local entertainers provide nighttime diversion. Service is extremely attentive and personalized. Passenger-to-crew and space ratios are best. Because these cruises tend to attract destination-oriented passengers, shore excursions—such as private museum tours—sometimes are included in the fare, as are pre- or post-cruise land packages and sometimes even tips.

Semiformal Semiformal cruises are a bit more relaxed than their formal counterparts. Meals are served in two seatings on ocean liners or one seating on specialty ships, menu choices are plentiful, and the cuisine is on a par with that available in better restaurants. Men tend to wear a jacket and tie to dinner most nights. Adding a distinct flair to the dining room is the common practice of staffing the restaurant with waiters of one nationality. Featured dishes may be prepared table side, and you often are able, with advance notice, to order a special diet, such as kosher, low-salt, low-cholesterol, sugar free, or vegetarian (*see* Dining *in* On Board, *below*). There is a daily program of scheduled events, but there's time for more independent pursuits; passengers with similar interests are often encouraged to meet at appointed times for chess or checkers, deck games, and other friendly contests. Production-style shows are staged each evening, but the disco scene may not be too lively. Passenger-to-crew and space ratios assure good service and plenty of room for each passenger. Look for semiformal cruises aboard classic liners, cruise liners, megaships, and a few expedition ships on voyages of seven days or longer.

Casual Casual cruises are the most popular. Shipboard dress and lifestyle are informal. Meals in the dining room are served in two seatings on ocean liners and one seating on specialty ships; menus are usually not extensive, and the food is good but not extraordinary; your options may be limited if you have special dietetic requirements. Men dress in sport shirts and slacks for dinner most nights, in jackets and ties only two or three evenings of a typical seven-day sailing. Aboard casual ocean liners, activities are more diverse than on formal and semiformal ships, and there is almost always something going on, from bingo to beer-chugging contests. Las Vegas–style variety shows or Broadway revues headline the evening entertainment. Discos bop into the wee hours. Passenger-to-crew and space ratios are generally good, but service tends to be less personal. On the smallest ships, activities on board will be limited as indicated in Types of Ships, *above*.

Look for casual cruises aboard classic liners, cruise liners, and megaships sailing three- to seven-day itineraries to fun-and-sun destinations; expedition ships; motor-sailing ships; riverboats; and coastal cruisers calling on more unusual ports.

Theme Cruises These increasingly popular sailings highlight a particular activity or topic. Onboard lectures and other events are coordinated with shoreside excursions. There are photography cruises, square-dancing cruises, sports cruises, financial-planning cruises, wine-tasting cruises, and more. The most popular destinations for theme cruises are Europe and the Caribbean. To find out about theme cruises that might interest you, consult with the individual cruise lines or a travel agent. Lines that offer the greatest variety of theme cruises are **American Hawaii Cruises, Commodore Cruise Line, Delta Queen Steamboat Co., Holland America Line,** and **Norwegian Cruise Line.** Lines with occaisional theme cruises include **Cunard Line, Costa Cruise Lines, Crystal Cruises, Radisson Seven Seas, Silversea Cruises** and **Seabourn Cruise Line.** Theme cruises on several of these upscale lines usually emphasize food and wine.

For music cruises, food-and-wine cruises, and other cultural cruises, also try the **AnneMarie Victory Organization** (136 E. 64th St., New York, NY 10021, tel. 212/486–0353, fax 212/751–3149), **Dailey-Thorp Travel** (330 W. 58th St., Suite 610, New York, NY 10019, tel. 212/307–1555, fax 212/974–1420), or **IST Cultural Tours** (225 W. 34th St., New York, NY 10122, tel. 212/563–1202 or 800/833-2111, fax 212/594–6953). Theme cruises from these operators are often aboard a tall ship or riverboat.

How Long to Sail

After you choose the type of ship and cruise experience you prefer, you must decide on how long to sail: Do you want a two-day cruise to nowhere or a 100-day journey around the world? Two key factors to keep in mind are how much money you want to spend and how experienced are you at cruising—it probably wouldn't be a good idea to circumnavigate the globe your first time at sea.

Short cruises are ideal for first-time cruisers and families with children. In just two to five days you can get a quick taste of cruising. You'll have the chance to sail aboard some of the newest ships afloat, built exclusively for these runs. Short itineraries may include stops at one or two ports of call, or none at all. The most popular short cruises are three- and four-day sailings to the Bahamas or Key West and Cozumel out of Miami. From Los Angeles, three- and four-day cruises set sail for southern California and the Mexican Baja.

After you have experienced a long weekend at sea, you may want to try a **weeklong cruise.** With seven days aboard ship, you get twice as much sailing time and a wider choice of destinations—as many as four to six ports, depending on whether you choose a loop or one-way itinerary (*see* Ship Itineraries, *below*). Since cruises are priced by a per-diem rate multiplied by the number of days aboard ship (*see* Cost, *below*), a weeklong cruise probably costs twice as much as a short cruise.

For some people, seven days is still too short—just when you learn your way around the ship, it's time to go home. On **10- or 11-day sailings,** you get more ports as well as more time at sea, but you won't pay as much as on **two-week sailings.** Many experienced cruisers feel it's just not worth the effort to board a ship for anything less than 14 days, so they opt for either a single 14-day itinerary or sign up for two seven-day trips back-to-back, combining sailings to eastern and western Caribbean or Mediterranean ports of call, for example—and taking advantage of the discounts offered by some lines for consecutive sailings. Cruises that last longer than two weeks—**very long cruises**—require a lot of time and money and a love of cruising. If you have all these, then cruising can become more than a vacation—it can be a way of life.

Ship Itineraries

In choosing the best cruise for you, a ship's itinerary is another important factor. The length of the cruise will determine the variety and number of ports you visit, but so will the type of itinerary and the point of departure. Some cruises, known as **loop cruises,** start and end at the same point and usually explore ports close to one another; **one-way cruises** start at one port and end at another and range farther afield.

Most cruises to Bermuda, the Bahamas, the Mexican Riviera, and the Caribbean are loop cruises. On Caribbean itineraries, you often have a choice of departure points. Sailings out of San Juan, Puerto Rico, can visit up to six ports in seven days, while loop cruises out of Florida can reach up to four ports in the same time.

Cruises to Antarctica generally operate on one of two loop itineraries: most commonly from the tip of South America to the Antarctic Peninsula, but also from New Zealand or Australia to the Ross Sea. Because the latter itinerary covers much longer distances, you spend more time at sea and less on shore—though there is a stop at historic huts used by early Antarctic explorers.

The most common one-way itineraries are to Canada and New England or to South America. So-called Caribazon cruises combine a journey up or down the Amazon River with port calls in the Caribbean. Alaska sailings come as loop itineraries, generally only within the Inside Passage, and as one-way cruises, sailing across the Gulf of Alaska and giving you the chance to explore farther north on land before or after the cruise.

Many ships sailing the Caribbean or the Mexican Riviera in winter and spring move to Alaska or New England in summer and fall. Other ships spend part of the year in the Caribbean, part outside the Western Hemisphere. When a ship moves from one cruising area to another, it offers a **repositioning cruise,** which typically stops at less-visited ports and attracts fewer passengers. It often has a lower per diem than cruises to the most popular sailing destinations.

A handful of ships offer an annual one- to two-month **cruise around South America** or a three- to four-month **around-the-world cruise** that stops at dozens of fabulous ports. This continent-hopping itinerary typically costs from $20,000 per person for a small inside cabin to hundreds of thousands of dollars for a suite; partial segments, usually of 14 or 21 days, are also available.

Note: Cruise itineraries listed in Chapter 4 are for the late-1998 to mid-1999 cruise season but are subject to change. Contact your travel agent or the cruise line directly for up-to-the-minute itineraries.

Cost

For one price, a cruise gives you all your meals, accommodations, and onboard entertainment. The only extras are tips, shore excursions, shopping, bar bills, and other incidentals. The axiom "the more you pay, the more you get" doesn't always hold true: While higher fares do prevail for better ships, which have more comfortable cabins, more attractive decor, and better service, the passenger in the least-expensive inside cabin eats the same food, sees the same shows, and shares the same amenities as one paying more than $1,000 per day for the top suite on any given ship. (A notable exception is aboard the *Queen Elizabeth 2*, where your dining-room assignment is based on your cabin category.)

A handy way to compare costs of different ships is to look at the per diem—the price of a cruise on a daily basis per passenger, based on double occupancy. (For instance, the per diem is $100 for a seven-day cruise that costs $700 per person when two people share the same cabin.)

For each ship reviewed in Chapter 1, average per diems are listed for a standard outside cabin (*see* Accommodations, *below*). Rates are based on published brochure prices, in peak season, for itineraries as noted. Remember that these average per diems are meant for comparative purposes only—so you can see the relative costliness of one ship versus another. For actual cruise fares, which can vary wildly and are subject to widespread discounting, you'll need to contact your travel agent or cruise specialist. Of course, there will be additional expenses beyond your basic cruise fare. When you go to book a cruise, don't forget to consider these expenditures:

Pre- and post-cruise arrangements: If you plan to arrive a day or two early at the port of embarkation, or linger a few days for sightseeing after debarkation, estimate the cost of your hotel, meals, car rental, sightseeing, and other expenditures. Cruise lines sell packages for pre- and post-cruise stays that may or may not cost less than arrangements you make independently, so shop around.

Airfare: Be sure to check whether the price of your cruise includes air transportation to and from the ship. If it does not, you can purchase your airline tickets and transfers from the cruise line. This is known as an air-sea package. Air-sea packages generally are convenient and reasonably priced. However, the cruise line chooses your airline and flight. Lines sometimes give passengers who make their own arrangements an air transportation credit of $200 or more, depending on the destination. By arranging your own airfare, you may get a lower fare and a more convenient routing. If you have frequent-flyer miles, you may be able to get a free ticket.

Pre-trip incidentals: These may include trip or flight insurance, the cost of boarding your pets, airport or port parking, departure tax, visas, long-distance calls home, clothing, film or videotape, and other miscellaneous expenses.

Shore excursions and expenses: Costs for ship-organized shore excursions range from less than $20 for the cheapest city tour to almost $300 for the most expensive flightseeing packages. Review the descriptions of shore excursions in Chapter 3 to estimate how much you are likely to spend.

Amusement and gambling allowance: Video games, bingo, and gambling can set you back a bundle. If you plan to bet, budget for your losses—you'll almost certainly have them. You must be over 18 to gamble on a cruise ship.

Shopping: Include what you expect to spend for both inexpensive souvenirs and pricey duty-free purchases.

Onboard incidentals: Most cruise lines recommend that passengers tip their cabin steward, dining-room waiter, and assistant waiter a total of $8–$9 per person, per day. Tips for bartenders and others who have helped you will vary. Also figure in the bar tabs and the cost of wine with meals, laundry, beauty-parlor services, purchases in the gift shop, and other incidentals.

Accommodations

Cabins vary greatly depending upon the type of ship you choose. On every ship, though, there are different cabin categories priced according to their size, location, and amenities. Cruise brochures show the ship's layout deck by deck and the approximate location and shape of every cabin and suite. Use the deck plan to make sure the cabin you pick is not near public rooms, which may be noisy, or the ship's engines, which can vibrate at certain speeds, and make sure that you are near stairs or an elevator to avoid walking down long corridors every time you return to your cabin. Usually, the listing in the brochure of the ship's different cabin categories includes details on what kind of beds the cabin has, whether it has a window or a porthole, and what furnishings are provided. Brochures also usually show representative cabin layouts, but be aware that configurations within each category can differ. In Chapter 1, we have tried to indicate those outside cabins that may be partially obstructed by lifeboats or that overlook a public deck.

Cabin Size Compared with land-based accommodations, many standard ship cabins seem tiny. The higher you go in the ship, the larger the quarters tend to be; outside cabins are generally bigger than inside ones (*see* Location, *below*).

Suites are the roomiest and best-equipped accommodations, but even aboard the same ship, they may differ in size, facilities, and price. Steward service may be more attentive to passengers staying in suites; top suites on some ships are even assigned private butlers. Most suites have a sitting area with a sofa and chairs; some have two bathrooms, occasionally with a whirlpool bath. The most expensive suites may be priced without regard to the number of passengers occupying them.

Location On all ships, regardless of size or design, the bow (front) and stern (back) pitch up and down on the waves far more than the hull amidships (middle). Ships also experience a side-to-side motion known as roll. The closer your deck is to the true center of the ship—about halfway between the bottom of the hull and the highest deck and midway between the bow and the stern—the less you will feel the ship's movement. Some cruise lines charge more for cabins amidships; most charge more for the higher decks.

Outside cabins have portholes or windows (which cannot be opened); on the upper decks, the view from outside cabins may be partially obstructed by lifeboats or overlook a public deck. Because outside cabins are more desirable, newer ships are configured with mostly outside cabins or with outside cabins only. Increasingly, an outside cabin on an upper deck comes with a private veranda. Windows are mirrored in cabins that overlook an outdoor promenade so that passersby can't see in—at least by day; after dark, you need to draw your curtains.

Inside cabins on older vessels are often smaller and oddly shaped. On newer ships, the floor plans of inside cabins are virtually identical to those of outside cabins. Providing you don't feel claustrophobic without a window, inside cabins represent an excellent value.

Furnishings All cabins are equipped with individually controlled air-conditioning, limited closet space, and a private bathroom—usually closet-size, with a toilet, small shower, and washbasin. More expensive cabins, especially on newer ships, may have a bathtub. Most cabins also have a small desk or dresser, a reading light, and, on many ships, a TV and sometimes even a VCR. Except on some older and smaller ships, all cabins also come with a phone.

Depending upon the ship and category, a cabin may have beds or berths. The most expensive cabins usually have king- or queen-size beds. Cabins priced in the midrange often have doubles or twins. In cabins with twins, the beds may be positioned side by side or at right angles. On most newer ships, the twin beds in many cabins can be pushed together to form a double. If this is what you want, get written confirmation that your specific cabin number has this capability. Less expensive cabins and cabins on smaller or older ships, especially those that accommodate three or four people, may have upper and lower bunks, or berths; these are folded into the wall by day to provide more living space. Sofa beds replace upper berths on some newer ships.

Sharing Most cabins are designed to accommodate two people. When more than two share a cabin, such as when parents cruise with their children, the third and fourth passengers are usually offered a discount, thereby lowering the per-person price for the room for the entire group.

Sailing Alone Some ships, mostly older ones, have a few single cabins. But on most ships, passengers traveling on their own must pay a single supplement, which usually ranges from 125% to 200% of the double-occupancy per-person rate. On request, many cruise lines will match up two strangers of the same sex in a cabin at the standard per-person double-occupancy rate.

Hints for Passengers with Children

Children aboard cruise ships are a common sight these days. To serve this growing market, a number of cruise lines have expanded their facilities and programs aimed at children. Many offer reduced rates for younger cruisers.

Discounts While there may be free passage for children on special off-peak sailings, typically most cruise lines charge children under age 12 third and fourth passenger rates or special children's fares when traveling with two adults in the same cabin. These rates tend to be about half—sometimes even less than half—of the lowest adult fare. Some cruise lines, such as Celebrity Cruises, Norwegian Cruise Line, Premier Cruises and Royal Olympic Cruises, allow children under two to sail without charge; kids age 17 and younger sail free on American Hawaii Cruises. Airfares and shore excursions also are frequently discounted. For single parents sailing with their children, Premier Cruises offers a reduced single supplement of 25% (normally the charge is 100%).

Activities and Supervision Lines that frequently sail with children aboard may have costumed staff to entertain younger passengers. Premier Cruises has Looney Tunes favorites, such as Bugs Bunny and Daffy Duck, running around the *Oceanic*, the *Ocean Breeze*, and the *Sea Breeze*. Aboard Disney Cruise Line you can sail with Mickey Mouse or Donald Duck. Many other lines now have supervised play areas for children and teenagers, at least during summer vacation and holiday periods. Programs include arts and crafts, computer instruction, games and quizzes, kids' movies, swimming-pool parties, scavenger hunts, ship tours, magic shows, snorkeling lessons, kite flying, cooking classes, and teaching sessions on the history of the ports to be visited. Find out in advance whether there are special programs for your child's age group, how many hours of supervised activities are scheduled each day, whether meals are included, and what the counselor-to-child ratio is. Celebrity Cruises, Norwegian Cruise Line, Royal Caribbean International, and Carnival Cruise Lines divide their children's programs into four age groups. Premier Cruises divides its kids' program into five age groups. In Alaska, Holland America Line has shore excursions designed especially for kids.

Some ships provide day care and group baby-sitting for younger children at no extra charge, while most charge a nominal hourly rate. On many ships, private baby-sitting is by arrangement with crew members (at a negotiated price). If you plan to bring an infant or toddler, be sure to request a crib, high chair, or booster seat in advance and bring plenty of diapers and formula.

Ships with two dinner seatings routinely assign passengers with children to the earlier seating; some lines will not permit children to eat in the dining room on their own. If your kids are picky eaters, check ahead to see if special children's menus are offered; many lines offer them. (*See* Chapter 1 for specific information on each cruise line's policies and programs regarding children.)

Kids' Play and entertainment facilities for children and teens should be
Facilities separate. The newest ships have playrooms for younger kids and "clubs" for older children with nonalcoholic bars and their own high-tech disco. Among the lines with the best facilities for kids are Carnival, Celebrity, Royal Caribbean, and Premier Cruises' *Oceanic*; look especially into the latest, biggest vessels.

Hints for Honeymooners and Other Romantic Couples

It's no surprise that cruises attract honeymooners. By their very nature, cruises are romantic—moonlit nights on deck and the vast sea all around, elegant dining, dazzling entertainment, cozy cabins, private verandas, and a variety of ports. Many lines go out of their way to make a honeymoon cruise convenient and memorable. For example, Sunday departures. In recent years the honeymoon-friendly schedules have been introduced by nearly every line on at least some itineraries, so that couples who marry on Saturday can leave on a cruise the next day; in the past most sailings departed on Fridays or Saturdays, and newlyweds, who typically marry on Saturdays, had to wait almost a week to start their cruise.

Onboard, many big-ship lines offer honeymooners complimentary extras like a bottle of champagne in the cabin upon arrival, a special cake served in the dining room one night, and a private cocktail party for newlyweds. Norwegian Cruise Line, for example, treats honeymooners to breakfast in bed, hors d'oeuvres delivered to the cabin one evening, a free photograph, and the choice of dining at a special newlyweds-only table or a private table for two. Carnival offers a special champagne cocktail party and a honeymoon cake at dinner. To partake of the freebies, be sure to tell your travel agent or the cruise line reservation agent that you'll be celebrating your honeymoon on the cruise.

High-end small-ship lines, such as Windstar Cruises, Silversea Cruises and Radisson Seven Seas Cruises, don't offer special cocktail parties and the like, but their ultradeluxe amenities are especially pleasing to honeymooners. Guests are pampered with terrycloth bathrobes and slippers that await in walk-in closets; elegant in-cabin dining service complete with linens, china, crystal and silverware; whirlpool bathtubs; stocked mini-bars; and high

Selecting a Cabin*

Luxury Suite/Apartment

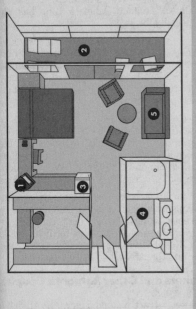

The largest accommodations on board, luxury suites have sitting areas, queen-size beds, vanity desks, and walk-in closets (with safes).

1. Although televisions are common, luxury suites often have VCRs (and access to a video library) and stereos as well.
2. Private verandas, connected by sliding doors, are on some ships.
3. Most luxury suites have refrigerators, often with stocked bars. Butler service is provided on some ships.
4. Twin sinks and Jacuzzi bathtubs (with shower) are typical.
5. The sofa can usually unfold into a bed for additional passengers.

Suite

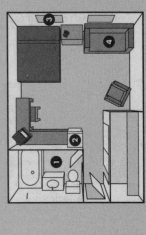

Though much more expensive than regular cabins, suites are also larger, featuring double beds, sitting areas, televisions, and comparatively large closets.

1. Bathrooms are likely to have single sinks and bathtubs (with showers).
2. Refrigerators are often included, although alcoholic beverages may not be complimentary.
3. Suites, which tend to be on upper decks, usually have large picture windows.
4. The sofa can be converted into a bed.

Outside Cabin

Outside cabins have showers rather than bathtubs and seldom have refrigerators. Most cabins have phones, and many have televisions.

1 Many cabins, especially those on lower decks, have portholes instead of picture windows. Cabins on newer ships, however, often have large windows.

2 Twin beds are common, although many ships now offer a double bed. Upper berths for additional passengers fold into the wall.

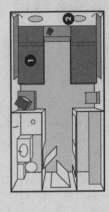

Inside Cabin

The least expensive accommodations, inside cabins have no portholes, tend to be tiny and oddly configured, have miniscule clothes closets, and bathrooms with showers only.

1 Almost all cabins have phones, but few have televisions.

2 Many inside cabins have upper and lower berths; the upper berth folds into the wall during the day, and the lower berth is made a couch.

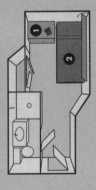

* Cruise lines offer a wide range of cabins, with a variety of names. This chart is intended as a general guide only.

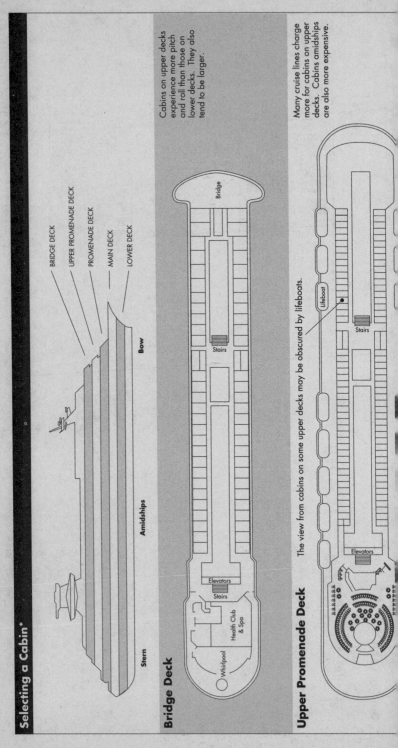

Selecting a Cabin*

14

BRIDGE DECK
UPPER PROMENADE DECK
PROMENADE DECK
MAIN DECK
LOWER DECK

Stern

Amidships

Bow

Bridge Deck

Cabins on upper decks experience more pitch and roll than those on lower decks. They also tend to be larger.

Bridge

Stairs

Elevators
Stairs

Health Club
& Spa

Whirlpool

Upper Promenade Deck

The view from cabins on some upper decks may be obscured by lifeboats.

Many cruise lines charge more for cabins on upper decks. Cabins amidships are also more expensive.

Lifeboat

Stairs

Elevators

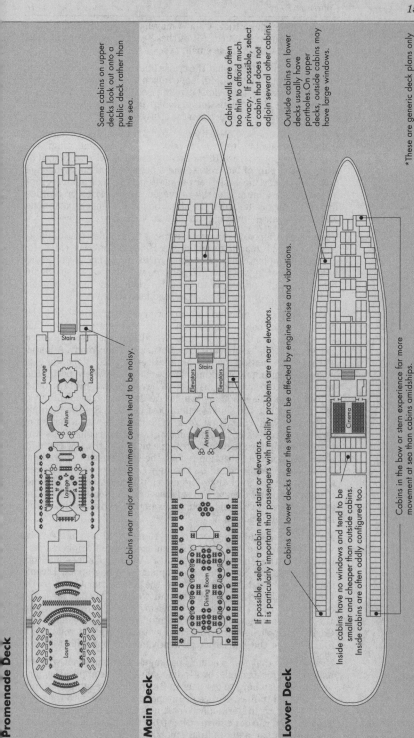

Promenade Deck

Lounge

Lounge

Lounge

Atrium

Lounge

Stairs

Some cabins on upper decks look out onto a public deck rather than the sea.

Cabins near major entertainment centers tend to be noisy.

Main Deck

Atrium

Stairs

Elevators

Elevators

Dining Room

Cabin walls are often too thin to afford much privacy. If possible, select a cabin that does not adjoin several other cabins.

If possible, select a cabin near stairs or elevators. It is particularly important that passengers with mobility problems are near elevators.

Lower Deck

Cinema

Outside cabins on lower decks usually have portholes. On upper decks, outside cabins may have large windows.

*These are generic deck plans only

Cabins on lower decks near the stern can be affected by engine noise and vibrations.

Inside cabins have no windows and tend to be smaller and cheaper than outside cabins. Inside cabins are often oddly configured too.

Cabins in the bow or stern experience for more movement at sea than cabins amidships.

crew-to-passenger ratios. Cabins may have private verandas, an especially romantic touch. All of these extra special touches are business as usual on these small, upscale ships.

If you want more than what the cruise lines offer for free, most also have a variety of wedding, honeymoon, anniversary, and vow-renewal packages that can be purchased before the cruise and start at about $50 to thousands of dollars per couple, with wedding-ceremony packages being the most costly.

For honeymooners, Celebrity Cruises' $119 package is typical; it includes breakfast in bed served with champagne, engraved champagne flutes, fresh floral arrangement, a red rose placed on the pillow, a pair of bathrobes, and a personalized honeymoon or anniversary certificate. Other packages may include a photograph and wedding album, chocolate-covered strawberries or truffles, limousine service between the ship and airport, shore excursions, and even a pair of massages at the spa.

Some lines offer vow-renewal packages for couples who'd like to celebrate their marriage again. On Holland America ships, for example, couples can renew their vows at a special ceremony while at sea or in port; the $95 package includes a corsage for the bride, printed invitations to send to friends on board, a photo album, music, wine or champagne, and hors d'oeuvres.

If you want to get married on board, you can legally do so on board many ships, although the captain hasn't been permitted to offici-ate weddings in U.S. ports since World War II. Instead, a local officiant is brought on board to perform a civil ceremony. A justice of the peace, notary public, or minister is used, depending on where the ceremony is taking place; sometimes where permitted, you're able to request or arrange to have a priest, rabbi or other official of your choice. Many couples tie the knot on the first day of the cruise, while the ship is still in port in the U.S.—for example, in Florida, California, New York, or San Juan—with a ceremony conducted on deck or inside in one of the public rooms. This way, friends and family are allowed to come on board for a few hours for a ceremony and a reception before the ship departs. A wedding chapel can even be found on the new *Grand Princess*, Princess Cruises' and the industry's biggest ship to date, and on Premier Cruises' *Seawind Crown*. Ceremonies can also sometimes be con-ducted in port, on a local beach, for example; each cruise line offers its own set of packages.

Many ships also offer opportunities to marry at one of the ports visited during the cruise, like Bermuda and the Caribbean. As a territory of the United States, the U.S. Virgin Islands—St. Croix, St. Thomas, and St. John—are popular wedding spots. License applications must be received by the Territorial Court in the USVI at least eight days prior to your wedding day (the fee is $50, contact the USVI Division of Tourism, 800/372–8784). In a non-U.S. or Canadian port, such as Bermuda and other islands of the Caribbean, policies vary from country to country and you need to find out what the rules are well in advance of your sailing date.

Cruise lines that sell wedding packages will assist you with the paperwork, for example, by sending you a license application form or telling you where to get one. In Bermuda, for example, couples are required to file a Notice of Intended Marriage with the office of the registrar in Bermuda at least a month in advance (the fee is $165 and you can get a form either from the cruise line or from the Bermuda Department of Tourism, 800/223–6106). You must be in the Bahamas for at least 24 hours before marrying there (the fee is $40; contact the Bahamas Tourist Office and 800/422–4262).

Remember, the cruise itinerary will limit where and when you can tie the knot; time spent in a given port generally ranges from three to 10 hours. No matter where you choose to wed, U.S. or foreign port, a wedding license must be obtained (or an application filed) in advance of the cruise and specific arrangements must be made for the wedding ceremony itself. At the time of booking, the cruise line or your travel agent can fill you in on the rules and regulations of the ports visited as well as offer you a selection of wedding packages for purchase; some lines, like Carnival, have a wedding department, while others handle wedding planning through the guest relations office or refer you to a wedding consultant.

The ceremony and reception packages sold include not only the services of a notary public or justice of the peace, but also things like floral arrangements, tuxedo and gown rental, wedding cake, photography, music, and hors d'oeurvres, and generally start at about $500 per couple, and like a wedding shore-side, can run into the thousands of dollars.

Hints for Sports Enthusiasts

Whether you prefer to play or watch, sports-related activities are increasingly common aboard cruise ships these days. Appealing to younger, more active passengers, the newest megaliners are the best equipped and have been built with sports-loving passengers in mind.

The newer megaships in the Carnival, Royal Caribbean, Celebrity, and Princess fleets have the greatest variety of options and the largest spaces in which to play. There are outdoor volleyball, basketball, and paddle tennis courts as well as outdoor jogging tracks, several pools for water-polo, volleyball, aqua-aerobics and swimming, and well-equipped fitness centers that rival those on shore (the biggest exceed 10,000 square ft). Workout options included daily aerobics classes. Certified instructors teach the classes, which offer an extensive schedule of exercises, from the traditional to the trendy. Among your choices may be high- and low-impact, funk, step, body sculpting, stretch and tone, abdominals, and spinning. Certified instructors teach the classes. To encourage and reward participation, several lines, like Holland America, Princess, Royal Caribbean and Celebrity, have fitness programs that award passengers who join in the activities with points redeemable at the end of the cruise for things like hats and T-shirts. (Keep in mind, older ships, usually those built before 1990, often do not devote nearly as much space and resources to sports and fitness.)

If golf is your bag, more and more cruises are offering the opportunity to tee off. The newest, technologically advanced ships, for example in the Celebrity and Princess fleets, have golf simulators—state-of-the-art virtual-reality machines that allow you to play the great courses of the world without ever leaving the ship. Full-sized clubs are used and a virtual reality video screen allows players to watch the path of an electronic ball they've actually hit soar high over the greens or land flat in a sand trap. Many more lines, including Norwegian Cruise Line, Crystal, Princess, Radisson Seven Seas, and Cunard, have outdoor golf cages—areas enclosed in netting where you can swing, putt, and whack at real golf balls. On Royal Caribbean's *Legend* and *Splendour of the Seas*, you'll find 18-hole miniature golf courses.

Land-and-sea golf programs are also very popular. These may include instruction and tips by golf pros who sail on board as well as scheduled tee times during port days at some of the best courses on earth. Among big-ship lines, Royal Caribbean (the official cruise line of the PGA Tour and Senior PGA Tour) offers passengers the chance to play golf at 31 courses from the Caribbean to Mexico and Hawaii as part of its "Golf Ahoy" program. Carnival offers one-on-one instruction on the ship and on the greens at courses in the Caribbean and Mexico. Sister line Holland America offers golf excursions on all of its Caribbean itineraries. Costa's "Golf Academy at Sea" features golfing packages throughout the Caribbean along with in-depth seminars and golf clinics during days at sea. Celebrity Cruises offers golf excursions when in port in Bermuda. American Hawaii can arrange for tee-time at courses on Oahu, the Big Island, Maui, and Kauai. Crystal Cruises offers onboard instruction as well as play at prestigious courses around the world.

Among small-ship lines, Radisson Seven Seas (the official cruise line of the PGA of America) offers onboard instruction by PGA-certified golf pros and golfing at some of Europe's best courses. Seabourn's "Signature Golf Cruises" offer play at renowned courses in the Orient, Europe, and the Caribbean. Silversea has golf instruction aboard ship and tee-time ashore. On the adventure side of things, Special Expeditions has "Expedition Golf" programs, which offer passengers the chance to play at popular courses throughout Europe. Typically, greens fees, cart, and transportation between the ship and course are included in the package price.

When it comes to water sports, small ships are tops. Windstar, Radisson Seven Seas, Cunard, and Seabourn have retractable water sports platforms that, weather-permitting, can be lowered from the stern into calm waters when the ship is anchored, allowing passengers to snorkel, windsurf, kayak, and swim near the ship. However, if waters are rough, as they often can be in the Mediterranean, the platforms cannot be used.

For those sports-loving couch potatoes, onboard sports bars are scoring big points these days. Norwegian Cruise Line's *Norwegian Wind* and *Norwegian Dream* and the *Carnival Destiny* have dedicated sports bars with large-screen televisions broadcasting live ESPN and NFL games. Holland America has a sports bar on the *Westerdam*, and the line recently added large-screen TVs to its ships and plans on creating sports bars fleetwide. During major sporting events, like the Super Bowl, many lines will outfit a public area or bar with televisions for game viewing. No need even to leave your cabin to enjoy a game on Royal Caribbean, Celebrity, Crystal and Princess ships: ESPN is available on all cabin televisions. For starstruck sports fans, NCL is well-known for its special sports theme cruises, where NFL, NBA, and NHL pros and past greats sail on board and mingle with passengers.

And the cruise lines are always looking for new ways to please the sports-crazed passenger, they are going to great lengths to do it. On the *Holiday*, Carnival has begun live simulcasts of horse racing via satellite from the world's top tracks. Royal Caribbean is planning an in-line skating rink, rock-climbing wall, and mega sports bar for its 136,000-ton Project Eagle ships, the first of which is due out in late 1999.

Hints for Passengers with Disabilities

The official position of the International Council of Cruise Lines, which is based in Washington, DC, and represents the cruise industry, is that the Americans with Disabilities Act does not apply to cruise ships. The council argues that most cruise ships, as foreign-flag vessels, are not subject to domestic U.S. laws governing construction and design. However, the council is working with the International Maritime Organization (IMO), which sets safety and design standards, to make cruise ships as accessible as possible. Nevertheless, disclaimers on every cruise brochure allow ships to refuse passage to anyone whose disability might endanger others. Most ships require that you travel with an able-bodied companion if you use a wheelchair or have mobility problems.

If you have a mobility problem, even if you do not use a wheelchair, tell your travel agent. Each cruise line sets its own policies; choose the line that is most accommodating. Also be careful to select a ship that is easy to get around. Ships vary even within the fleet of the same line. (*See* Chapter 1 for specific recommendations on which ships are suitable for passengers with mobility problems.) Follow up by making sure that the cruise line is fully informed of your disability and any special needs, and ask if the ship has a full-time physician on board. (Virtually all major cruise ships have a doctor on call.) Get written confirmation of any promises that have been made to you about a special cabin or transfers to and from the airport. The line may request a letter from your doctor stating that you need neither a wheelchair nor a companion, or that you will not require special medical attention on board.

If you have any type of chronic health problem that may require medical attention, notify the ship's doctor soon after you board so he or she will be prepared to treat you appropriately, if necessary.

Passengers Using Wheelchairs The latest cruise ships have been built with accessibility in mind, and many older ships have been modified to accommodate passengers using wheelchairs. The key areas to be concerned about are public rooms, outer decks, and, of course, your cabin. If you need a specially equipped cabin, book as far in advance as possible and ask specific questions of your travel agent or a cruise-line representative. Specifically, ask how your cabin is configured and equipped. Is the entrance level or ramped? Are all doorways at least 30 inches wide (wider if your wheelchair is not standard size)? Are pathways to beds, closets, and bathrooms at least 36 inches wide and unobstructed? In the bathroom, is there 42 inches of clear space in front of the toilet and are there grab bars behind and on one side of it and in the bathtub or shower? Ask whether there is a three-prong outlet in the cabin, and whether the bathroom has a handheld showerhead, a bath bench, or roll-in shower or shower stall with fold-down seat, if you need them. Are elevators wide enough to accommodate wheelchairs? For specific information about individual ships, *see* Accessibility *in* Chapter 1.

The best cruise ship for passengers who use wheelchairs is one that ties up right at the dock at every port, at which time a ramp or even an elevator is always made available. Unfortunately, it's hard to ascertain this in advance, for a ship may tie up at the dock at a particular port on one voyage and, on the next, anchor in the harbor and have passengers transported to shore via tender. Ask your travel agent to find out which ships are scheduled to dock on which cruises. If a tender is used, some ships will have crew members carry the wheelchair and passenger from the ship to the tender. Unfortunately, other ships point-blank refuse to take wheel-chairs on tenders, especially if the water is choppy. At some ports, ships always tender because docking facilities are unavailable. For more information about where and whether ships dock or tender, *see* Coming Ashore for each port *in* Chapter 3.

Passengers with Vision Impairments Some ships allow guide dogs to accompany passengers with vision impairments; however, if your cruise is scheduled to visit foreign ports (as most do), you may not be able to take a guide dog ashore, depending on the country. To avoid potential quarantine upon returning to the United States, guide dogs should have their shots updated within seven days of sailing, and owners should carry the dog's valid health and rabies certificates.

Hawaii is especially strict about importing animals. No dog, not even a guide dog, may step ashore without being quarantined for at least 30 days unless it arrives from an area recognized by the state as rabies-free. Guide dogs may remain aboard visiting ships during port calls for up to 48 hours. That period begins upon docking at the first Hawaiian port and includes all time spent in Hawaiian waters.

Pregnant Women Considering advanced pregnancy a disability, cruise lines may refuse passage to pregnant women. "Advanced" usually refers to the third trimester. If you are pregnant, check on the cruise line's policy before you book passage.

Travel Agencies and Tour Operators **Accessible Journeys** (35 W. Sellers Ave., Ridley Park, PA 19078, tel. 800/846–4537, fax 610/521–6959) arranges escorted trips for travelers with disabilities and provides licensed health-care professionals to accompany those who require aid. **Flying Wheels Travel** (143 W. Bridge St., Owatonna, MN 55060, tel. 800/535–6790) is a travel agency specializing in domestic and worldwide cruises for people with limited mobility.

Hints for Older Passengers

For older travelers, cruise vacations strike an excellent balance: They offer a tremendous variety of activities and destinations in one convenient package. You can do as much or as little as you want, meet new people, see new places, enjoy shows and bingo, learn to play bridge, or take up needlepoint—all within a safe, familiar environment. Cruises are *not* a good idea for those who are bedridden, have a serious medical condition that is likely to flare up on board, or are prone to periods of confusion or severe memory loss.

No particular rules apply to senior citizens on cruises, but certain freighter cruises do have an age limit (*see* Chapter 2). Those who want a leisurely, relaxed pace will probably be happiest on ships that attract a higher percentage of older passengers: luxury ocean liners, cruise yachts, and expedition ships on voyages of longer than seven days. Passengers who are less than spry should look for a ship where the public rooms are clustered on one deck and select a cabin near an elevator or stairway amidships. Do not book a cabin with upper and lower berths.

Several cruise lines, notably Carnival, Celebrity, Holland America, Premier, Royal Caribbean, and World Explorer have reduced rates for senior citizens (sometimes only on certain sailings), but seniors may be able to take advantage of local discounts ashore. When in port, showing proof of age often results in reduced admissions, half fares on public transportation, and special dining rates.

Quite a few cruise lines employ "gentleman hosts," who act as dancing and bridge partners for single ladies traveling alone. Look into Commodore Cruise Line, Cunard Line, Crystal Cruises, Delta Queen Steamboat Company, Holland America Line, Norwegian Cruise Line, Orient Lines, Premier Cruises, Royal Olympic Cruises, and Silversea Cruises.

Tour Operators **Saga International Holidays** (222 Berkeley St., Boston, MA 02116, tel. 800/343–0273) has its own ship for cruise passengers 50 and older (see Chapter 2). **SeniorTours** (508 Irvington Rd., Drexel Hill, PA 19026, tel. 800/227–1100) arranges cruises.

Hints for Gay and Lesbian Passengers

Some cruise lines are more gay-friendly than others, so consult one of the companies listed below.

Tour Operators and Travel Agencies Some of the largest agencies serving gay travelers are **Islanders/ Kennedy Travel** (183 W. 10th St., New York, NY 10014, tel. 212/ 242–3222 or 800/988–1181), **Now Voyager** (4406 18th St., San Francisco, CA 94114, tel. 415/626–1169 or 800/255–6951), **Pied Piper** (330 W. 42nd St., Suite 1804, New York, NY 10036, tel. 212/239–2412 or 800/874–7312), and **Yellowbrick Road** (1500 W. Balmoral Ave., Chicago, IL 60640, tel. 773/561–1800 or 800/642–2488). **R.S.V.P. Travel Productions** (tel. 800/328–7787) operates many gay cruises, and **Olivia Cruises & Resorts** (tel. 800/631–6277) provides the same service for lesbian travelers. You can also contact the **International Gay and Lesbian Travel Association** (4331 N. Federal Hwy., Suite 304, Ft. Lauderdale, FL 33308, tel. 800/448–8550), which has more than 1,500 travel-industry members.

Booking Your Cruise

Using a Travel Agent

A good travel agent is the secret to a good cruise. Since nearly all cruises are sold through travel agents, the agent you choose to work with can be just as important as the ship you sail on. So how do you know if an agent or agency is right for you? Talk to friends, family, and colleagues who have used an agency to book a cruise. The most qualified agents are members of CLIA (Cruise Lines International Association). Agents who are CLIA Accredited Cruise Counsellors or Master Cruise Counsellors have had extensive cruise and ship inspection experience. If you opt for a cruise-only agency (*see below*), they should also be a member of NACOA (National Association of Cruise-Only Agencies). These agents are also experienced cruisers. Finally, the most reputable agencies, both full-service and cruise-only, are members of ASTA (American Society of Travel Agents). *Remember, though: The best travel agent puts your needs first.*

The size of a travel agency tends to matter less than the experience of its staff. A good cruise agent will ask you many detailed questions about your past vacations, your lifestyle, and even your friends and your hobbies. Only by getting to know you can an agent successfully match you to a ship and a cruise. Never book a cruise with an agent who asks a few cursory questions before handing you a brochure.

Conversely, think of an agent as your travel consultant. Ask the agent any questions you may have about cruising. Most travel agents who book cruises have cruised extensively, and they can help you to decide on a cruise line and a ship. If you have a problem with the cruise line before, during, or after your cruise, they can act as an intermediary.

Of course, you want the best price. However, it's important not to make price your single greatest concern. Value—what you get for your money—is just as important as the dollar amount you pay. Keep in mind that the advertised prices you see in newspapers are usually for the lowest grade cabin. A better cabin—one with a window and maybe a private veranda—is likely to cost more. However, it pays to be wary of agencies that quote prices that are much higher than advertised. It's a bad sign when an agency's ads are blatant lies to get you in the door.

Perhaps the best way to shop for a cruise is to decide first on a cruise line and ship, and then to shop for an agency. Most agencies have "partnerships" with certain cruise lines, which can work to your advantage. By agreeing to sell a lot of cabins (and therefore, of course, by promoting certain cruise lines) the agency gets a better rate from the cruise line. The agency can then afford to offer a "discounted" price to the public.

When it comes down to it, the very top travel agencies can more or less get you the same price on most cruises, because they'll guarantee that if the cruise line lowers the price in a promotion, you'll get the better deal. Look for an agency that offers this guarantee. Remember, too, that agencies willing to go the extra mile for their clients are the best agencies. This means providing free cruise-discount newsletters, cabin upgrades, dollar-stretching advice, and, arguably most important of all, 24-hour service in case of a problem are your best bet.

Cruise-Only Travel Agents As the name implies, "cruise-only" travel agencies specialize in selling cruises. However, these agencies can sell you air tickets and other travel arrangements, too, as part of your cruise package. Sometimes, your choice may be limited to a package put together by the cruise line. Increasingly, though, cruise-only agencies are putting together their own custom-designed cruise vacations. Because they sell only cruises—and because they sell so many cruises—cruise-only agencies can generally get you the best deal.

Full-Service Travel Agents More and more, full-service agencies are focusing on cruising due to its growing popularity. And while many full-service agencies may not have the best cruise discounts at their fingertips, they may know where to look and how to negotiate with a cruise line for a good rate. When calling full-service agencies, look for one that has a "cruise" desk with agents who sell only cruises. Avoid agencies that try to steer you toward a land vacation instead of the cruise you really want.

Spotting Swindlers Although one is far more likely to encounter incompetent travel agents than scam artists, it's important to be on the lookout for a con. The best way to avoid being fleeced, if you don't have an established relationship with a travel agent, is to pay for your cruise with a credit card, from deposit to full payment. That way, if an agency goes out of business before your cruise departs, you can cancel payment on services not rendered. An agency may be a bad apple if it doesn't accept credit cards. Also be wary of any agency that wants an unusually high deposit (check the brochure). To avoid a disreputable agency, make sure the one you choose has been in business for at least five years. Check its reputation with the local Better Business Bureau or state consumer protection agency *before* you pay any deposits. If a cruise price seems too good to be true, it probably is. It could mean the agency is desperate to bring in money and may close its doors tomorrow. So be wary of agencies that claim they can beat any price.

Getting the Best Cruise for Your Dollar

By selecting the right agent, you have the greatest chance of getting the best deal. But having a basic knowledge of how and why cruises are discounted can only benefit you in the end. Since your vacation experience can vary greatly depending on the ship and its ports of call, it's best to pick your vessel and itinerary first, and then try to get the best price. Remember, it's only a deal if the cruise you book, no matter what the price, meets your expectations.

Like everything in retail, each cruise has a brochure list price. But like the sticker price on a new car, nobody actually pays this amount. These days, if you asked any 10 cruise passengers on any given ship what they paid, they would give you 10 different answers. Discounts from cruise lines and agencies can range from 5% on a single fare to 50% on the second fare in a cabin.

Approach deep discounts with skepticism. Fewer than a dozen cabins may be offered at the discounted price, they may be inside cabins, and the fare may not include air transportation or transfers between the airport and the ship. Finally, do the math. A promotion might sound catchy, but if you divide the price by the number of days you'll be cruising and include the cost of air and accommodations, you might find that the deal of the century is really a dud.

Deals and Discounts
Seasonal Discounts
Cruise-brochure prices are typically divided into three categories based on the popularity of sailing dates and weather: high season, shoulder season, and low-season. (Some lines divide their Alaska sailings into five seasons.) Obviously, prices will be higher for a Caribbean sailing in December than for the same sailing in August. Before you take advantage of a low-season rate, think about the pros and cons of off-season travel. It may be hotter (or colder) than you'd prefer—but it also may be less crowded.

Early-Bird Specials
More than ever, it's important to book early. This is especially true for the newest ships and for cabins with private verandas—both are selling out quickly. If you wait to book, you'll probably pay more even if you don't get shut out from the ship or cabin of your choice. That's because almost all cruise lines provide a discount for passengers who book and put down a deposit far in advance; an additional discount may be provided if payment is made in full at the time of booking. These discounts, given to passengers who book at least six months before departure, range from 10% to 50% off the brochure rate. (Brochures are usually issued a year or more in advance of sailing dates.) Cruises to some of the more exotic destinations such as Southeast Asia are sometimes sold on a two-for-the-price-of-one basis from the outset. Most early-booking discounts in the Caribbean include round-trip airfare.

As the sailing date approaches, the price of a cruise tends to go up. Not only that, but as the ship fills, the best cabins are no longer available and you'll be less likely to get the meal seating of your choice. So it certainly pays to book early.

Last-Minute Savings In recent years, cruise lines have provided fewer and fewer last-minute deals. However, if a particular cruise is not selling well, a cruise line may pick certain large cruise-only travel agencies to unload unsold cabins. Keep in mind that your choice of cabin and meal seating is limited for such last-minute deals. On older ships—those built before the 1980s—special deals may be limited to smaller cabins in undesirable areas of the ship. Last-minute deals may be available only to people living in certain cities. For example, people in Vancouver may get a break on a cruise to Alaska. People in Miami may get a deal on a cruise to the Bahamas. Or people who live in Kansas City may get a discount on a cruise to the Caribbean—because the cruise line booked too many plane tickets. Typically, these specials are unadvertised, but they may be listed in the agencies' newsletters and on their cruise telephone hot lines (*see* Agencies to Contact, *below*).

Mixed Bag Besides the major discounts mentioned above, agencies and cruise lines might attract passengers with price promotions such as "Sail for 12 Days and Pay for Only 10," "Free Hotel Stay with Your Cruise," and "Two Sail for the Price of One." Read the fine print before you book. The offer may be a bargain—or just slick advertising. How can you tell? Compare the advertised price to the standard early-booking discount, and check if the promotion includes airfare. Free or discounted air on cruise-only prices are common for Caribbean sailings. Also check on senior-citizen discounts and "cruise dollars" accrued on participating credit cards. Cruise lines that target families sometimes take on a third or fourth cabin passenger for free. Some of the best cruise prices are available on repositioning cruises, when, for example, ships are moving between Alaska or Europe and the Caribbean. (*see* Ship Itineraries, *above*).

Upgrades There are two types of cabin upgrades: One is guaranteed; the other is not. The first kind of upgrade is a promotional offer by the cruise line. For example, you may be offered a two-category upgrade if you book by a certain date. In this case, the cabin assignment that you receive with your documents prior to sailing should reflect your better accommodations. The second kind of upgrade is dispensed on board at the discretion of the cruise line. Like airlines, cruise lines overbook at their cheapest price in order to attract as many passengers as possible. When the number of bookings at these low rates exceeds the number of cabins available, some people are given better accommodations. How does the cruise line decide? Sometimes, those passengers who booked early get priority for upgrades. Other times, passengers who booked through top-selling travel agencies are at the top of the upgrade list—just two more reasons to book early and book with a cruise-only agency that does a lot of business with your line.

Payment

Once you have made a reservation for a cabin, you will be asked to put down a deposit. Handing money over to your travel agent constitutes a contract, so before you pay, review the cruise brochure to find out the provisions of the cruise contract. What is the payment schedule and cancellation policy? Will there be any additional charges before you can board your ship, such as transfers, port fees, or local taxes? If your air connection requires you to spend an evening in a hotel near the port before or after the cruise, is there an extra cost?

If possible, pay your deposit and balance with a credit card. This gives you some recourse if you need to cancel, and you can ask the credit-card company to intercede on your behalf in case of problems.

Deposit Most cruises must be reserved with a refundable deposit of $200–$500 per person, depending upon how expensive the cruise is; the balance is due 45–75 days before you sail. If the cruise is less than 60 days away, however, you may have to pay the entire amount immediately.

Cancellation Your entire deposit or payment may be refunded if you cancel your reservation between 45 and 75 days before departure; the grace period varies from line to line. If you cancel later than that, you will forfeit some or all of your deposit (*see* Protection, *below*). An average cancellation charge is $100 one month before sailing, $100 plus 50% of the ticket price between 15 and 30 days prior to departure, and $100 plus 75% of the ticket price between 14 days and 24 hours ahead of time. If you simply fail to show up when the ship sails, you will lose the entire amount. Many travel agents also assess a small cancellation fee. Check their policy.

Insurance Travel insurance is the best way to protect yourself against financial loss. The most useful plan is a comprehensive policy that includes coverage for trip cancellation-and-interruption, cruise line default, trip delay (including missed cruise connections), and medical expenses (with a waiver for preexisting conditions).

Without insurance you will lose all or most of your money if you cancel your trip, regardless of the reason. Should your cruise line go out of business, default protection will reimburse you for any payments you've made—or pay to get you home should you find yourself stranded. Another way to protect yourself is to book with a line that belongs to the United States Tour Operators Association (USTOA, 342 Madison Ave., Suite 1522, New York, NY 10022, tel. 212/599–6599 or 800/468–7862), which requires members to maintain $1 million each in an account to reimburse clients in case of default. A few cruise lines, such as Holland America Line and Special Expeditions, belong to this organization.

Trip-delay provisions will cover unforseen expenses that you may incur due to bad weather or sometimes mechanical delays. It's important to compare the fine print regarding trip-delay coverage when comparing policies.

For overseas travel, one of the most important components of travel insurance is its medical coverage. Supplemental health insurance will pick up the cost of your medical bills should you get sick or injured while traveling. U.S. residents should note that Medicare generally does not cover health-care costs outside the United States, nor do many privately issued policies.

Always buy travel insurance directly from the insurance company; if you buy it from a cruise line that goes out of business, your default coverage will be invalid.

Travel Insurers In the U.S., **Access America** (6600 W. Broad St., Richmond, VA 23230, tel. 804/285–3300 or 800/284–8300). **Travel Guard International** (1145 Clark St., Stevens Point, WI 54481, tel. 715/345–0505 or 800/826–1300). In Canada, **Mutual of Omaha** (Travel Division, 500 University Ave., Toronto, Ontario M5G 1V8, tel. 416/598–4083 or 800/268–8825).

Agencies to Contact The agencies listed below specialize in booking cruises, have been in business at least five years, and emphasize customer service as well as price.

Cruise Only **Cruise Fairs of America** (2029 Century Park E, Suite 950, Los Angeles, CA 90067, tel. 310/556–2925 or 800/456–4386, fax 310/556–2254), established in 1987, has a fax-back service for information on the latest deals. The agency also publishes a free quarterly newsletter with tips on cruising. Cruise Fairs can make independent hotel and air arrangements for a complete cruise vacation.

Cruise Holidays of Kansas City (7000 N.W. Prairie View Rd., Kansas City, MO 64151, tel. 816/741–7417 or 800/869–6806, fax 816/741–7123), a franchisee of Cruise Holidays, a cruise-only agency with outlets throughout the United States, has been in business since 1988. The agency mails out a free newsletter to clients every other month with listings of cruise bargains—its prices are among the best.

Cruise Line, Inc. (150 N.W. 168th St., N. Miami Beach, FL 33169, tel. 305/653–6111 or 800/777–0707, fax 305/653–6228), established in 1983, publishes *World of Cruising* magazine three times a year and a number of free brochures, including "Guide to First Time Cruising," "Guide to Family Cruises," "Guide to Exotic Cruising," and "Guide to Cruise Ship Weddings and Honeymoons." The agency has a 24-hour hot line with prerecorded cruise deals that are updated weekly.

Cruise Pro (2527 E. Thousand Oaks Blvd., Thousand Oaks, CA 91362, tel. 805/371–9884 or 800/222–7447; 800/258–7447 in CA; fax 805/371–9084), established in 1983, has special discounts listed in its one time per-month mailings to members of its Voyager's Club ($15 to join).

CruiseMasters (300 Corporate Pointe, Suite 100, Culver City, CA 90230, tel. 310/568–2040 or 800/242–9000, fax 310/568–2044), established in 1987, gives each passenger a personalized, bound guide to their ship's ports of call. The guides provide money-saving tips and advice on whether to opt for a prepackaged port excursion or strike out on your own.

Cruises, Inc. (5000 Campuswood Dr., E. Syracuse, NY 10357, tel. 315/463–9695 or 800/854–0500, fax 315/434–9175) opened its doors in 1981 and now has nearly 200 cruise consultants, including many CLIA Master Cruise Counsellors and Accredited Cruise Counsellors. Its agents are extensively trained and have extensive cruise experience. They sell a lot of cruises, which means the company gets very good prices from the cruise lines. Customer-service extras include complimentary accident insurance for up to $250,000 per cruise, a monthly bargain bulletin ($19 a yr), and a free twice-a-year cruise directory with cruise reviews, tips, and discounts.

Cruises of Distinction (2750 S. Woodward Ave., Bloomfield Hills, MI 48304, tel. 248/332–2020 or 800/634–3445, fax 248/333–9710), established in 1984, publishes a free 80-page cruise catalog four times a year. For no fee you can receive notification of unadvertised specials by mail or fax—just by filling out a questionnaire.

Don Ton Cruise Tours (3151 Airway Ave., E–1, Costa Mesa, CA 92626, tel. 714/545–3737 or 800/318–1818, fax 714/545–5275), established in 1972, features a variety of special-interest clubs, including a short-notice club, singles club, family cruise club, and adventure cruise club. Its "CruiseNet" magazine is filled with articles as well as price discounts six times a year.

Golden Bear Travel (16 Digital Dr., Novato, CA 94949, tel. 415/382–8900; 800/551–1000 outside CA; fax 415/382–9086) acts as general sales agent for a number of foreign cruise ships and specializes in longer, luxury cruises. Its Cruise Value club sends members free twice-a-month mailings with special prices on "distressed merchandise" cruises that are not selling well. The agency's Mariner Club (for past passengers) offers discounts on sailings and runs escorted cruises for people who would like to travel as part of a group.

Kelly Cruises (1315 W. 22nd St., Suite 105, Oak Brook, IL 60521, tel. 630/990–1111 or 800/837–7447, fax 630/990–1147), established in 1986, publishes a quarterly newsletter highlighting new ships and special rates. Passengers can put their name on a free mailing list for last-minute deals. Kelly is especially good if you're interested in the more expensive cruise lines.

National Discount Cruise Co. (1409 N. Cedar Crest Blvd., Allentown, PA 18104, tel. 610/439–4883 or 800/788–8108, fax 610/439–8086) is a five-year-old cruise division launched by GTA Travel, an American Express representative that has served travelers since 1967. The cruise division specializes in high-end cruises and includes shipboard credits, exclusive to American Express, on most of the sailings it books. A three-times-a-year newsletter highlights the agency's latest discounts.

Ship 'N' Shore Cruises (1160 S. McCall Rd., Englewood, FL 34223, tel. 941/475–5414 or 800/925–7447, fax 800/346–4119), an American Express representative founded in 1987, specializes in affordable cruise-tours around the world. In Alaska, the agency has its own fleet of motor coaches, and its land tours are custom-designed to complement the cruise itineraries of Alaska's major cruise lines.

Vacations at Sea (4919 Canal St., New Orleans, LA 70119, tel. 504/482–1572 or 800/749–4950, fax 504/486–8360), established in 1983, puts together its own pre- and post-cruise land packages and escorted land tours. The agency also publishes a free six-times-a-year newsletter with cruise reviews and discounts.

Full Service **Ambassador Tours** (717 Market St., San Francisco, CA 94103, tel. 415/357-9876 or 800/989–9000, fax 415/357-9667), established in 1955, does 80% of its business in cruises. Three times a year, the agency distributes a free 32-page catalog, which lists discounts on cruises and land packages, plus free monthly discount alerts.

Mann Travel and Cruises (6010 Fairview Rd., Suite 104, Charlotte, NC 28210, tel. 704/556–8311, fax 704/556–8303). established in 1975, does 65% of its business in cruises. The agency's cruise business has increased so much they recently added the word "cruises" to their name.

Prestige Travel (6175 Spring Mountain Rd., Las Vegas, NV 89102, tel. 702/248–1300, fax. 702/253–6316), established in 1981, does 60% of it business in cruises. The agency holds an annual trade show for all its local clients, publishes a quarterly travel catalog, and sends frequent mailings to past customers.

Time to Travel (582 Market St., San Francisco, CA 94104, tel. 415/421–3333 or 800/524–3300, fax 415/421–4857), established in 1935, does 90% of its business in cruises. It mails a free listing of cruise discounts to its clients three to five times a month. Time to Travel specializes in pre- and post-cruise land arrangements and claims its staff of 19 has been nearly everywhere in the world.

White Travel Service (127 Park Rd., West Hartford, CT 06119, tel. 860/233–2648 or 800/547–4790; 860/236–6176 prerecorded cruise hot line with discount listings; fax 860/236–6177), founded in 1972, does most of its business in cruises and publishes a free 40-page brochure listing the latest cruise discounts.

Before You Go

Tickets, Vouchers, and Other Travel Documents

After you make the final payment to your travel agent, the cruise line will issue your cruise tickets and vouchers for airport–ship transfers. Depending on the airline, and whether you have purchased an air-sea package, you may receive your plane tickets or charter-flight vouchers at the same time; you may also receive vouchers for any shore excursions, although most cruise lines issue these aboard ship. Should your travel documents not arrive when promised, contact your travel agent or call the cruise line directly. If you book late, tickets may be delivered directly to the ship.

Once aboard, you may be asked to turn over your passport for group immigration clearance (*see* Passports and Visas, *below*; Embarkation *in* Arriving and Departing, *below*) or to turn over your return plane ticket so the ship's staff may reconfirm your flight home. Otherwise, keep travel documents in a safe place, such as the safe in your cabin or at the purser's office.

Passports and Visas

Carrying a passport is always a good idea, and entry requirements do change, so read your cruise documents carefully to see what you'll need for embarkation. (You don't want to be turned away at the pier!)

U.S. Citizens In years past, cruise lines sailing from Florida ports to the Caribbean rarely asked to see passports from American passengers. That has changed recently, and it's now advisable to be prepared to show your passport. If you don't, you may be asked to fill out a citizenship form—delaying your embarkation.

If you are boarding a ship outside the United States, you'll need the appropriate entry requirements for that country. On cruises to or from some countries, you may be required to obtain a visa in advance. Check with your travel agent or cruise line about specific requirements. If you do need a visa for your cruise, your travel agent should help you obtain it, through a visa service by mail or directly from the consulate or embassy. (There may be a charge of up to $25 for this service, added to the visa charge.)

Passport Applications For information on obtaining or renewing a passport, contact the National Passport Information Center (tel. 900/225–5674).

Non-U.S. Citizens If you plan to embark, disembark, or call at ports in the United States, you may need a passport and possibly a visa, depending on your country of citizenship. Check with your cruise line or the U.S. embassy (*see below*) for the latest documentation requirements.

Passport Applications Canadian citizens should contact the Passport Office (tel. 819/994–3500 or 800/567–6868). Citizens of the United Kingdom interested in obtaining or renewing a passport should contact the London Passport Office (tel. 0990/21010).

What to Pack

Although you will naturally pack differently for the tropics than for an Alaska, certain packing rules apply to all cruises: Always take along a sweater in case of cool evening ocean breezes or over-active air-conditioning. A rain slicker usually comes in handy, too, and make sure you take at least one pair of comfortable walking shoes for exploring port towns.

Shorts or slacks are convenient for shore excursions, but remember that in Asia and Latin America women are expected to dress modestly and men to wear slacks. If you are going to Asia and plan to visit any holy places, both men and women will need a pair of slip-off shoes and garments that cover their knees (although these are usually available for rent at the site for a nominal charge). For European ports of call, pack as you would for any American city: casual clothes by day, dressier fashions for going out on the town at night. For visits to churches, cathedrals, and mosques, avoid shorts and other outfits that could be considered immodest. In Italy, women should cover their shoulders and arms (a shawl will do). In Turkey, women must have a head covering; a long-sleeve blouse and long skirt or slacks are also required.

In Chapter 1, we indicate how many formal evenings are typical on each ship—usually two per seven-day cruise. Men should pack a dark suit, a tuxedo, or a white dinner jacket. Women should pack one long gown or cocktail dress for every two or three formal evenings on board. Most ships have semiformal evenings, when men should wear a jacket and tie. On a few ships, men should wear a jacket and tie every evening (*see* The Cruise Experience *in* Choosing Your Cruise, *above*). A few lines have no dress codes or guidelines.

Generally speaking, plan on one outfit for every two days of cruising, especially if your wardrobe contains many interchangeable pieces. Ships often have convenient laundry facilities as well (*see* Shipboard Services *in* On Board, *below*). And don't overload your luggage with extra toiletries and sundry items; they are easily available in port and in the ship's gift shop (though usually at a premium price). Soaps, and sometimes shampoos and body lotion, are often placed in your cabin compliments of the cruise line.

Take an extra pair of eyeglasses or contact lenses in your carry-on luggage. If you have a health problem that requires a prescription drug, pack enough to last the duration of the trip or have your doctor write a prescription using the drug's generic name, because brand names vary from country to country. Always carry prescription drugs in their original packaging to avoid problems with customs officials. Don't pack them in luggage that you plan to check in case your bags go astray. Pack a list of the offices that supply refunds for lost or stolen traveler's checks.

Electricity Most cruise ships use U.S.-type 110V, 60-cycle electricity and grounded plugs, but others employ 220V, 50-cycle current and are fitted with European- or English-type outlets. In that case, to use U.S.-purchased electric appliances on board, you'll need an adapter plug. Unless the appliance is dual-voltage and made for travel, you'll also need a converter. (*See* Chapter 1 for details on each ship's voltage.) For a copy of the free brochure "Foreign Electricity is No Deep Dark Secret," send a stamped, self-addressed envelope to adapter-converter manufacturer Franzus

Company (Customer Service, Dept. B50, Murtha Industrial Park, Box 142, Beacon Falls, CT 06403, tel. 203/723–6664).

Luggage

Allowances On Board Ship Cruise passengers can bring aboard as much luggage as they like and are restricted only by the amount of closet space in their cabin. If you are flying to your point of embarkation, be aware of the airline's luggage policies. Because luggage is often tossed about and stacked as it is moved between ship and airport, take suitcases that can take abuse.

In Flight Free airline baggage allowances depend on the airline, the route, and the class of your ticket; ask in advance. In general, on domestic flights and on international flights between the United States and foreign destinations, you are entitled to check two bags. A third piece may be brought aboard, but it must fit easily under the seat in front of you or in the overhead compartment. In the United States, the Federal Aviation Administration gives airlines broad latitude to limit carry-on allowances and tailor them to different aircraft and operational conditions. Charges for excess, oversize, or overweight pieces vary.

If you are flying between two foreign destinations, note that baggage allowances may be determined not by piece but by weight; again, ask your airline about their specific restrictions. If your flight between two cities abroad *connects* with your transatlantic or transpacific flight, the piece method still applies.

Safeguarding Your Luggage When your cruise documents arrive, they will often include luggage tags bearing the name of your ship. Place one on each piece of luggage before leaving home: These tags will identify your luggage to cruise-line officials if there is an automatic luggage-pull service at the airport on arrival. Also tag your bags inside and out with your name, address, and phone number. (If you use your home address, cover it so that potential thieves can't see it.) Put a copy of your itinerary inside each bag, so you can easily be tracked, and itemize your bags' contents and their worth in case they go astray.

When you check in for your pre- or post-cruise flight, make sure that the tag attached by baggage handlers bears the correct three-letter code for your destination. If your bags do not arrive with you, or if you detect damage, immediately file a written report with the airline before you leave the airport.

Arriving and Departing

If you have purchased an air-sea package, you will be met by a cruise-company representative when your plane lands at the port city and then shuttled directly to the ship in buses or minivans. Some cruise lines arrange to transport your luggage between airport and ship—you don't have to hassle with baggage claim at the start of your cruise or with baggage check-in at the end. If you decide not to buy the air-sea package but still plan to fly, ask your travel agent if you can use the ship's transfer bus anyway; if you do, you may be required to purchase a round-trip transfer voucher ($5–$20). Otherwise, you will have to take a taxi to the ship.

If you live close to the port of embarkation, bus transportation may be available. If you are part of a group that has booked a cruise together, this transportation may be part of your package.

Another option for those who live close to their point of departure is to drive to the ship. The major U.S. cruise ports all have parking facilities.

Embarkation

Check-In On arrival at the dock, you must check in before boarding your ship. (A handful of smaller cruise ships handle check-in at the airport.) An officer will collect or stamp your ticket, inspect or even retain your passport or other official identification, ask you to fill out a tourist card, check that you have the correct visas, and collect any unpaid port or departure tax. Seating assignments for the dining room are often handed out at this time, too. You may also register your credit card to open a shipboard account, although that may be done later at the purser's office (*see* Shipboard Accounts *in* On Board, *below*).

After this you may be required to go through a security check and to pass your hand baggage through an X-ray inspection. These are the same machines in use at airports, so ask to have your photographic film inspected visually.

Although it takes only five or 10 minutes per family to check in, lines are often long, so aim for off-peak hours. The worst time tends to be immediately after the ship begins boarding; the later it is, the less crowded. For example, if boarding begins at 2 PM and continues until 4:30, try to arrive after 3:30.

Boarding the Before you walk up the gangway, the ship's photographer will
Ship probably take your picture; there's no charge unless you buy the picture (usually $6). On board, stewards may serve welcome drinks in souvenir glasses—for which you're usually charged between $3 and $5 cash.

You will either be escorted to your cabin by a steward or, on a smaller ship, given your key by a ship's officer and directed to your cabin. Some elevators are unavailable to passengers during boarding, since they are used to transport luggage. You may arrive to find your luggage outside your stateroom or just inside the door; if it doesn't arrive within a half hour before sailing, contact the purser. If you are among the unlucky few whose luggage doesn't make it to the ship in time, the purser will trace it and arrange to have it flown to the next port.

Visitors' Some cruise ships permit passengers to invite guests on board
Passes prior to sailing, although most cruise lines prohibit all but paying passengers for reasons of security and insurance liability. Cruise companies that allow visitors usually require that you obtain passes several weeks in advance; call the lines for policies and procedures.

Most ships do not allow visitors while the ship is docked in a port of call. If you meet a friend on shore, you won't be able to invite him or her back to your stateroom.

Disembarkation

The last night of your cruise is full of business. On most ships you must place everything except your hand luggage outside your cabin door, ready to be picked up by midnight. Color-coded tags, distributed to your cabin in a debarkation packet, should be placed on your luggage before the crew collects it. Your designated color will later determine when you leave the ship and help you retrieve your luggage on the pier.

Your shipboard bill is left in your room during the last day; to pay the bill (if you haven't already put it on your credit card) or to settle any questions, you must stand in line at the purser's office. Tips to the cabin steward and dining staff are distributed on the last night.

The next morning, in-room breakfast service is usually not available because stewards are too busy. Most passengers clear out of their cabins as soon as possible, gather their hand luggage, and stake out a chair in one of the public lounges to await the ship's clearance through customs. Be patient—it takes a long time to unload and sort thousands of pieces of luggage. Passengers are disembarked by groups according to the color-coded tags placed on luggage the night before; those with the earliest flights get off first. If you have a tight connection, notify the purser before the last day, and he or she may be able to arrange faster preclearing and debarkation for you.

Customs and Duties

U.S. Customs   Before your ship lands, each individual or family must fill out a customs declaration, regardless of whether anything was purchased abroad. If you have less than $1,400 worth of goods, you will not need to itemize purchases. Be prepared to pay whatever duties are owed directly to the customs inspector, with cash or check.

U.S. Customs now preclears a number of ships sailing in and out of Miami and other ports—it's done on the ship before you disembark. In other ports you must collect your luggage from the dock, then stand in line to pass through the inspection point. This can take up to an hour.

Allowances. You may bring home $400 worth of foreign goods duty-free if you've been out of the country for at least 48 hours and haven't already used the $400 exemption, or any part of it, in the past 30 days. Note that these are the *general* rules, applicable to most countries; passengers on certain Caribbean or Panama Canal itineraries may be entitled to bring back $600 worth of goods duty free, and if you're returning from a cruise that called in the U.S. Virgin Islands, the duty-free allowance is higher—$1,200.

Alcohol and Tobacco. Travelers 21 or older may bring back 1 liter of alcohol duty-free, provided the beverage laws of the state through which they reenter the United States allow it. In the case of the U.S. Virgin Islands, 5 liters are allowed. In addition, 100 non-Cuban cigars and 200 cigarettes are allowed, regardless of your age. From the U.S. Virgin Islands, 1,000 cigarettes are allowed, but only 200 of them may have been acquired elsewhere. Antiques and works of art more than 100 years old are duty-free.

Gifts. You may also send packages home duty-free: up to $200 worth of goods for personal use, with a limit of one parcel per addressee per day (and no alcohol or tobacco products or perfume worth more than $5); label the package PERSONAL USE, and attach a list of its contents and their retail value. Do not label the package UNSOLICITED GIFT, or your duty-free exemption will drop to $100. Mailed items do not affect your duty-free allowance on your return.

For More Information. For a copy of "Know Before You Go," a free brochure detailing what you may and may not bring back to the United States, rates of duty, and other pointers, contact the

U.S. Customs Service (Box 7407, Washington, DC 20044, tel. 202/927–6724).

U.S. Customs for Foreigners If you hold a foreign passport and will be returning home within hours of docking, you may be exempt from all U.S. Customs duties. Everything you bring into the United States must leave with you when you return home. When you reach your own country, you will have to pay appropriate duties there.

Canadian Customs **Allowances.** If you've been out of Canada for at least seven days, you may bring in C$500 worth of goods duty-free. If you've been away less than seven days but more than 48 hours, the duty-free exemption drops to C$200. You cannot pool exemptions with family members. Goods claimed under the C$500 exemption may follow you by mail; those claimed under the lesser exemption must accompany you.

Alcohol and Tobacco. Alcohol and tobacco products may be included in the seven-day and 48-hour exemption. If you meet the age requirements of the province or territory through which you reenter Canada, you may bring in, duty-free, 1.14 liters (40 imperial ounces) of wine or liquor *or* two dozen 12-ounce cans or bottles of beer or ale. If you are 16 or older, you may bring in, duty-free, 200 cigarettes, 50 cigars or cigarillos, and 400 tobacco sticks or 400 grams of manufactured tobacco. Alcohol and tobacco must accompany you on your return.

Gifts. An unlimited number of gifts valued up to C$60 each may be mailed to Canada duty-free. These do not count as part of your exemption. Label the package "Unsolicited Gift—Value Under $60." Alcohol and tobacco are excluded.

For More Information. For additional information, including details of duties on items that exceed your duty-free limit, contact Revenue Canada (2265 St. Laurent Blvd. S, Ottawa, Ontario K1G 4K3, tel. 613/993–0534 or 800/461–9999 in Canada) for a copy of the free brochure "I Declare/Je Déclare." For recorded information (within Canada only), call 800/461–9999.

U.K. Customs **Allowances.** If your cruise was wholly within European Union (EU) countries, you no longer need to pass through customs when you return to the United Kingdom. If you plan to bring back large quantities of alcohol or tobacco, check in advance on EU limits. When returning from cruises that called at countries outside the European Union, you may import duty-free 200 cigarettes, 100 cigarillos, 50 cigars or 250 grams of tobacco; 1 liter of spirits or 2 liters of fortified or sparkling wine or liqueur; 2 liters of still table wine; 60 milliliters of perfume; 250 milliliters of toilet water; plus £136 worth of other goods, including gifts and souvenirs.

For More Information. For further information or a copy of "A Guide for Travellers," which details standard customs procedures as well as what you may bring into the United Kingdom from abroad, contact HM Customs and Excise (Dorset House, Stamford St., London SE1 9NG, tel. 0171/202–4227).

On Board

Checking Out Your Cabin

The first thing to do upon arriving at your cabin or suite is to make sure that everything is in order. If there are two twin beds instead of the double bed you wanted, or other serious problems, ask to be moved *before* the ship departs. Unless the ship is full, you can usually persuade the chief housekeeper or hotel manager to allow you to change cabins. It is customary to tip the stewards who assist you in moving to another cabin.

Since your cabin is your home away from home for a few days or weeks, everything should be to your satisfaction. Take a good look around: Is the cabin clean and orderly? Do the toilet, shower, and faucets work? Check the telephone and television. Again, major problems should be addressed immediately. Minor concerns, such as not enough bath towels or pillows, can wait until the frenzy of embarkation has subsided.

Your dining-time and seating-assignment card may be in your cabin; now is the time to check it and immediately request any changes. The maître d' usually has set up shop in one of the public rooms specifically for this purpose.

Shipboard Accounts

Virtually all cruise ships operate as cashless societies. Passengers charge onboard purchases and settle their accounts at the end of the cruise with a credit card, traveler's checks, or cash. You can sign for wine at dinner, drinks at the bar, shore excursions, gifts in the shop—virtually any expense you may incur aboard ship. On some lines, an imprint from a major credit card is necessary to open an account. Otherwise, a cash deposit may be required and a positive balance maintained to keep the shipboard account open. Either way, you will want to open a line of credit soon after settling into your cabin if an account was not opened for you at embarkation. This easily can be arranged by visiting the purser's office, located in the central atrium or main lobby.

Tipping

For better or worse, tipping is an integral part of the cruise experience. Most companies pay their cruise staff nominal wages and expect tips to make up the difference. Most cruise lines have recommended tipping guidelines (*see* Chapter 1), and on many ships "voluntary" tipping for beverage service has been replaced with a mandatory 15% service charge, which is added to every bar bill. On the other hand, the most expensive luxury lines include tipping in the cruise fare and may prohibit crew members from accepting any additional gratuities. On most small adventure ships, a collection box is placed in the dining room or lounge on the last full day of the cruise, and passengers are encouraged to contribute anonymously.

Dining

Ocean liners serve food nearly around the clock. There may be up to four breakfast options: early-morning coffee and pastries on deck, breakfast in bed via room service, buffet-style breakfast in the cafeteria, and breakfast in the dining room. There may also be two or three choices for lunch, mid-afternoon hors d'oeuvres, and midnight buffets. You can eat whatever is on the menu, in any quantity, at as many of these meals as you wish. Room service is traditionally, but not always, free (*see* Shipboard Services, *below*).

Restaurants The chief meals of the day are served in the main dining room, which on most ships can accommodate only half the passengers at once. So meals are usually served in two sittings—early (or main) and late (or second) seatings—usually from 1½ to 2½ hours apart. Early seating for dinner is generally between 6 and 6:30, late seating between 8 and 8:30.

Most cruise ships have a cafeteria-style restaurant, usually near the swimming pool, where you can eat lunch and breakfast (dinner is usually served only in the dining room). Many ships provide self-serve coffee or tea in their cafeteria around the clock, as well as buffets at midnight.

Increasingly, ships also have alternative restaurants for ethnic cuisines, such as Italian, Chinese, or Japanese food. These are found mostly on newer vessels, although some older liners have been refitted for alternative dining. Other ships have pizzerias, ice-cream parlors, and caviar or cappuccino bars; there may be an extra charge at these facilities.

More and more lines are banning smoking in their main dining rooms. The policy of each line is noted in the individual cruise-line reviews in Chapter 1.

Seatings When it comes to your dining-table assignment, you should have options on four important points: early or late seating; smoking or no-smoking section (if smoking is allowed in the dining room); a table for two, four, six, or eight; and special dietary needs. When you receive your cruise documents, you will usually receive a card asking for your dining preferences. Fill this out and return it to the cruise line, but remember that you will not get your seating assignment until you board the ship. Check it out immediately, and if your request was not met, see the maître d'— usually there is a time and place set up for changes in dining assignments.

On some ships, seating times are strictly observed. Ten to 15 minutes after the scheduled mealtime, the dining-room doors are closed. On other ships, passengers may enter the dining room at their leisure, but they must be out by the end of the seating. When a ship has just one seating, passengers may enter at any time while the kitchen is open and are never rushed.

Seating assignments on some ships apply only for dinner. Several have open seating for breakfast or lunch, which means you may sit anywhere at any time. Smaller or more luxurious ships offer open seating for all meals.

Changing Tables Dining is a focal point of the cruise experience, and your companions at meals may become your best friends on the cruise. However, if you don't enjoy the company at your table, the maître d' can usually move you to another one if the dining room isn't completely full—a tip helps. He will probably be reluctant to comply with your request after the first full day at sea, however, because the waiters, busboys, and wine steward who have been serving you up to that point won't receive their tips at the end of the cruise. Be persistent if you are truly unhappy.

Cuisine Most ships reviewed in this book serve food geared to the American palate, but there are also theme dinners featuring the cuisine of a particular country. Some European ships, especially smaller vessels, may offer a particular cuisine throughout the cruise— Scandinavian, German, Italian, or Greek, perhaps—depending on the ship's or the crew's nationality. Aboard all cruise ships, the quality of the cooking is generally good, but even a skilled chef is hard put to serve 500 or more extraordinary dinners per hour. On the other hand, the presentation is often spectacular, especially at gala midnight buffets.

There is a direct relationship between the cost of a cruise and the quality of its cuisine. The food is very sophisticated on some (mostly expensive) lines, among them Crystal Cruises, Cunard Line, Seabourn Cruise Line, and Silversea Cruises. In the more moderate price range, Celebrity Cruises has gained renown for the culinary stylings of French chef Michel Roux, who acts as a consultant to the line.

Special Diets With notification well in advance, many ships can provide a kosher, low-salt, low-cholesterol, sugar-free, vegetarian, or other special menu. However, there's always a chance that the wrong dish will somehow be handed to you. Especially when it comes to soups and desserts, it's a good idea to ask about the ingredients.

Large ships usually offer an alternative "light" or "spa" menu based upon American Heart Association guidelines, using less fat, leaner cuts of meat, low-cholesterol or low-sodium preparations, smaller portions, salads, fresh-fruit desserts, and healthy garnishes. Some smaller ships may not be able to accommodate special dietary needs. Vegetarians generally have no trouble finding appropriate selections on ship menus.

Wine Wine at meals costs extra on most ships; the prices are usually comparable to those in shoreside restaurants and are charged to your shipboard account. A handful of luxury vessels include both wine and liquor.

The Captain's Table It is both a privilege and a marvelous experience to be invited to dine one evening at the captain's table. Although some seats are given to celebrities, repeat passengers, and passengers in the most expensive suites, other invitations are given at random to ordinary passengers. Any passenger can request an invitation from the chief steward or the hotel manager, although there is no guarantee you will be accommodated. The captain's guests always wear a suit and tie or a dress, even if the dress code for that evening is casual. On many ships, passengers may also be invited to dine at the other officers' special tables, or officers may visit a different passenger table each evening.

Bars

Ship's bars, whether adjacent to the pool or attached to one of the lounges, tend to be the social centers of a ship. Except on a handful of luxury-class ships where everything is included in the ticket price, bars operate on a pay-as-it's-poured basis. Rather than demand cash after every round, however, most ships allow passengers to charge drinks to their accounts. Prices are comparable to what you'd pay at home.

In international waters there are, technically, no laws against teenage drinking, but almost all ships require passengers to be over 18 or 21 to purchase alcoholic drinks. Many cruise ships have chapters of Alcoholics Anonymous (a.k.a "Friends of Bill W") or will organize meetings on request. Look for meeting times and places in the daily program slipped under your cabin door each night.

Entertainment

Lounges and Nightclubs
On ocean liners, the main entertainment lounge or showroom schedules nightly musical revues, magic acts, comedy performances, and variety shows. During the rest of the day the room is used for group activities, such as shore-excursion talks or bingo games. Generally, the larger the ship, the bigger and more impressive the productions. Newer ships have elaborate showrooms that often span two decks. Some are designed like an amphitheater while others have two levels—a main floor and a balcony. Seating is sometimes in clusters of armchairs set around cocktail tables. Other ships have more traditional theater-style seating.

Many larger ships have a second showroom. Entertainment and ballroom dancing may go on here late into the night. Elsewhere you may find a disco, nightclub, or cabaret, usually built around a bar and dance floor. Music is provided by a piano player, a disc jockey, or by small performing ensembles such as country-and-western duos or jazz combos.

On smaller ships the entertainment options are more limited, sometimes consisting of no more than a piano around which passengers gather. There may be a main lounge where scaled-down revues are staged.

Library
Most cruise ships have a library with anywhere from 500 to 1,500 volumes, including everything from the latest best-sellers to reference works. Many shipboard libraries also stock videotapes.

Movie Theaters
All but the smallest vessels have a room for screening movies. On older ships and some newer ones, this is often a genuine cinema-style movie theater. On other ships, it may be just a multipurpose room. The films are frequently one or two months past their first release but not yet available on videotape or cable TV. Films rated "R" are edited to minimize sex and violence. On a weeklong voyage, a dozen different films may be screened, each one repeated at various times during the day. Theaters are also used for lectures, religious services, and private meetings.

With a few exceptions, ocean liners equip their cabins with closed-circuit TVs; these show movies (continuously on some newer ships), shipboard lectures, and regular programs (thanks to satellite reception). Ships with VCRs in the cabins usually provide a selection of movies on cassette at no charge (a deposit is sometimes required).

Casinos
Once a ship is 12 mi off American shores, it is in international waters and gambling is permitted. (Some "cruises to nowhere," in fact, are little more than sailing casinos.) All ocean liners, as well as many cruise yachts and motor-sailing ships, have casinos. On larger vessels, they usually have poker, baccarat, blackjack, roulette, craps, and slot machines. House stakes are much more modest than those in Las Vegas or Atlantic City. On most ships the maximum bet is $200; some ships allow $500. Payouts on the slot machines (some of which take as little as a nickel) are generally much lower, too. Credit is never extended, but many casinos have handy credit-card machines that dispense cash for a hefty fee. Exceptions are the Caesars Palace at Sea casinos aboard the *Crystal Harmony* and *Crystal Symphony*, which are regulated by the Nevada Gaming Commission, offer the same gambling limits as in Las Vegas, and, by prior arrangement, will extend credit.

Children are officially barred from the casinos, but it's common to see them playing the slots rather than the adjacent video machines. Most ships offer free individual instruction and even gambling classes in the off-hours. Casinos are usually open from early morning to late night, although you may find only unattended slot machines before evening. In adherence to local laws, casinos are always closed while in port.

Game Rooms Most ships have a game or card room with card tables and board games. These rooms are for serious players and are often the site of friendly round-robin competitions and tournaments. Most ships furnish everything for free (cards, chips, games, and so forth), but a few charge $1 or more for each deck of cards. Be aware that professional cardsharps and hustlers have been fleecing ship passengers almost as long as there have been ships.

There are small video arcades on most medium and large ships. Family-oriented ships often have a computer learning center as well.

Bingo and The daily high-stakes bingo games are even more popular than
Other Games the casinos. You can play for as little as a dollar a card. Most ships have a snowball bingo game with a jackpot that grows throughout the cruise into hundreds or even thousands of dollars.

Another popular cruise pastime is the so-called "horse races": Fictional horses are auctioned off to "owners." Individual passengers can buy a horse or form "syndicates." Bids usually begin at around $25 and can top $1,000 per horse. Races are then "run" according to dice throws or computer-generated random numbers. Audience members bet on their favorites.

Sports and Fitness

Swimming All but the smallest ships have at least one pool, some of them
Pools elaborate affairs with water slides or retractable roofs; hot tubs and whirlpools are quite common. Pools may be filled with fresh water or salt water; some ships have one of each. While in port or during rough weather, the pools are usually emptied or covered with canvas. Many are too narrow or too short to allow swimmers more than a few strokes in any direction; none have diving boards, and not all are heated. Often there are no lifeguards. Wading pools are sometimes provided for small children.

Sun Deck The top deck is usually called the Sun Deck or Sports Deck. On some ships this is where you'll find the pool or whirlpool; on others it is dedicated to volleyball, table tennis, shuffleboard, and other such sports. A number of ships have paddle-tennis courts, and a few have golf driving ranges. (Skeet shooting is fast becoming a thing of the past on cruise ships; when available it's usually offered at the stern of a lower deck.) Often, at twilight or after the sun goes down, the Sun Deck is used for dancing, barbecues, limbo contests, or other social activities.

Exercise and Most newer ships and some older ones have well-equipped fitness
Fitness Rooms centers, many with massage, sauna, and whirlpools. An upper-deck fitness center often has an airy and sunny view of the sea; an inside, lower-deck health club is often dark and small unless it is equipped with an indoor pool or beauty salon. Many ships have full-service exercise rooms with bodybuilding equipment, stationary bicycles, rowing machines, treadmills, aerobics classes, and personal fitness instruction. Some ships even have structured,

cruise-length physical-fitness programs, which may include lectures on weight loss or nutrition. These often are tied in with a spa menu in the dining room. Beauty salons adjacent to the health club may offer spa treatments such as facials and mud wraps. The more extensive programs are often sold on a daily or weekly basis.

Promenade Deck Many vessels designate certain decks for fitness walks and may post the number of laps per mile. Fitness instructors may lead daily walks around the Promenade Deck. A number of ships discourage jogging and running on the decks or ask that no one take fitness walks before 8 AM or after 10 PM, so as not to disturb passengers in cabins. With the advent of the megaship (*see* Types of Ships, *above*), walking and jogging have in many cases moved up top to tracks on the Sun or Sports deck.

Shipboard Services

Room Service A small number of ships have no room service at all, except when the ship's doctor orders it for an ailing passenger. Many offer only breakfast (Continental on some, full on others), while others provide no more than a limited menu at certain hours of the day. Most, however, have certain selections that you can order at any time. Some luxury ships have unlimited round-the-clock room service. There usually is no charge for room service, other than for beer, wine, or spirits.

Minibars An increasing number of ships equip their more expensive cabins with small refrigerators or minibars stocked with snacks, soft drinks, and liquors, which may or may not be free.

Laundry and Dry Cleaning All but the smallest ships and shortest cruises offer laundry services—full-service, self-service, or both. Use of machines is generally free, although some ships charge for detergent, use of the machines, or both. Valet laundry service includes cabin pickup and delivery and usually takes 24 hours. Most ships also offer dry-cleaning services.

Hairdressers Even the smallest ships have a hairdresser on staff. Larger ships have complete beauty parlors, and some have barbershops. Book hairdressers well in advance, especially before such popular events as the farewell dinner.

Film Processing Many cruise ships have color-film processing and printing equipment to develop film overnight. It's expensive but convenient.

Photographer The staff photographer, a near-universal fixture on cruise ships, records every memorable, photogenic moment. The thousands of photos snapped over the course of a cruise are displayed publicly in special cases every morning and are offered for sale, usually for $6 for a 5″ 7″ color print or $12 for an 8″ × 10″. If you want a special photo or a portrait, the photographer is usually happy to oblige. Many passengers choose to have a formal portrait taken before the captain's farewell dinner—the dressiest evening of the cruise. The ship's photographer usually anticipates this demand by setting up a portable studio near the dining-room entrance.

Religious Services Most ships provide nondenominational religious services on Sundays and religious holidays, and a number offer daily Catholic masses and Friday-evening Jewish services. The kind of service held depends upon the clergy the cruise line invites on board. Usually religious services are held in the library, the theater, or one of the private lounges, although a few ships have actual chapels.

Communications
Shipboard   Most cabins have loudspeakers and telephones. Generally, the loudspeakers cannot be switched off because they are needed to broadcast important notices. Telephones are used to call fellow passengers, order room service, summon a doctor, leave a wake-up call, or speak with any of the ship's officers or departments.

Ship to Shore   Satellite facilities make it possible to call anywhere in the world from most ships. Most are also equipped with telex and fax machines, and some provide credit-card phones. It may take as long as a half hour to make a connection, but unless a storm is raging outside, conversation is clear and easy. On older ships, voice calls must be put through on shortwave wireless or via the one phone in the radio room. Newer ships are generally equipped with direct-dial phones in every cabin for calls to shore. Be warned: The cost of sending any message, regardless of the method, can be quite expensive—up to $15 a minute. (On some ships, though, it can be much cheaper, costing as little as $3.95 a minute.) If possible, wait until you go ashore to call home.

Safety at Sea

Fire Safety   The greatest danger facing cruise-ship passengers is fire. All of the lines reviewed in this book must meet certain international standards for fire safety. The latest rules, which went into effect in October 1997, require that ships have sprinkler systems, smoke detectors, and other safety features. However, these rules are designed to protect against loss of life. They do not guarantee that a fire will not happen; in fact, fire is a relatively common occurrence on cruise ships. The point here is not to create alarm, but to emphasize the importance of taking fire safety seriously.

Fire safety begins with you, the passenger. Once settled into your cabin, find the location of your life vests and review the emergency instructions inside the cabin door or near the life vests. Make sure your vests are in good condition and learn to secure the vest properly. Make certain the ship's purser knows if you or your companion has some physical infirmity that may hamper a speedy exit from your cabin. In case of a real emergency, the purser can quickly dispatch a crew member to assist you. If you are traveling with children, be sure child-size life jackets are placed in your cabin.

Within 24 hours of embarking your ship, you will be asked to attend a mandatory lifeboat drill. Do so and listen carefully. If you have any questions, ask them. If you are unsure of how to use your vest, now is the time to ask. Only in the most extreme circumstances will you need to abandon ship—but it has happened. The few minutes you spend learning the right procedure may serve you well in a mishap.

Health Care   Quality medical care at sea is another important safety issue. All big ships are equipped with medical infirmaries to handle minor emergencies. However, these should not be confused with hospitals. Unlike fire safety, there are no international standards governing medical facilities or personnel aboard cruise ships. The American Medical Association has recommended that such standards be adopted. If you have a preexisting medical condition, discuss your upcoming cruise with your doctor. Pack extra supplies of any medicines you might need. Once aboard, see the ship's doctor and alert him or her to your condition, and discuss treatments or emergency procedures before the situation arises. Passengers with potentially life-threatening conditions should seriously consider signing up with a medical evacuation service, and all passengers should review their health insurance to make sure they are covered while on a cruise.

If you become seriously ill or injured and happen to be near a modern major city, you may be taken to a medical facility shoreside. But if you're farther afield, you may have to be airlifted off the ship by helicopter and flown either to the nearest American territory or to an airport where you can be taken by charter jet to the United States. Many standard health insurance policies, as well as Medicare, do not cover these or other medical expenses incurred outside the United States. You can, however, buy supplemental health insurance to cover you while traveling.

The most common minor medical problems confronting cruise passengers are seasickness and gastrointestinal distress. Modern cruise ships, unlike their earlier transatlantic predecessors, are relatively motion-free vessels with computer-controlled stabilizers, and they usually sail in comparatively calm waters. If, however, you do feel queasy, you can always get seasickness pills aboard ship. (Many ships give them out for free at the front desk.)

Outbreaks of food poisoning happen from time to time aboard cruise ships. These episodes are random; they happen on ships old and new, big and small, budget and luxury. The Centers for Disease Control monitor cruise-ship hygiene and sanitation procedures, conducting voluntary inspections twice a year of all ships that sail regularly from U.S. ports (this program does not include ships that never visit the United States). For a free listing of all the latest ship scores, write the CDC's National Center for Environmental Health (Vessel Sanitation Program, 1015 North America Way, Room 107, Miami, FL 33132). You can also get a copy from the CDC's fax-back service at 888/232–3299. Request publication 510051. Another alternative is to visit the Centers' Web site at www.cdc.gov.

A high score on the CDC report doesn't mean you won't get sick. Outbreaks have taken place on ships that consistently score very highly; conversely, some ships score very poorly yet passengers never get sick. So use these scores as a guideline and factor them in with other considerations when choosing your ship.

World Time Zones

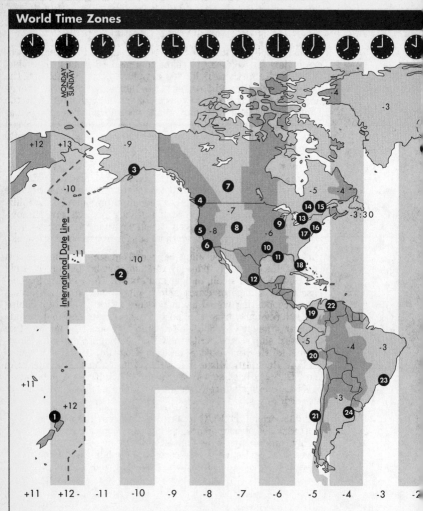

Numbers below vertical bands relate each zone to Greenwich Mean Time (0 hrs.).
Local times frequently differ from these general indications,
as indicated by light-face numbers on map.

Algiers, **29**	Berlin, **34**	Delhi, **48**	Istanbul, **40**
Anchorage, **3**	Bogotá, **19**	Denver, **8**	Jerusalem, **42**
Athens, **41**	Budapest, **37**	Djakarta, **53**	Johannesburg, **44**
Auckland, **1**	Buenos Aires, **24**	Dublin, **26**	Lima, **20**
Baghdad, **46**	Caracas, **22**	Edmonton, **7**	Lisbon, **28**
Bangkok, **50**	Chicago, **9**	Hong Kong, **56**	London
Beijing, **54**	Copenhagen, **33**	Honolulu, **2**	(Greenwich), **27**
	Dallas, **10**		Los Angeles, **6**
			Madrid, **38**
			Manila, **57**

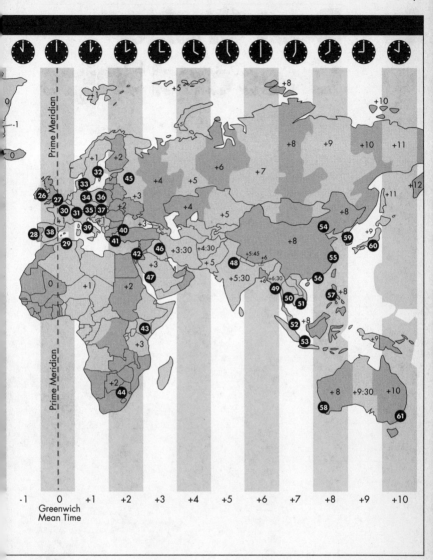

1 Best Cruise Lines and Ships

Abercrombie & Kent

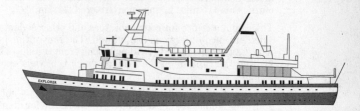

The Fleet MS *Explorer*

The *Explorer* has a long and illustrious history. In previous incarnations, it was the *Lindblad Explorer* and, later, the *Society Explorer*. When built in 1969, it incorporated many design features that set the standard for later expedition ships: It was the first to feature an ice-hardened hull, a relatively shallow draft, a small profile for entering otherwise inaccessible coves and harbors, and a fleet of Zodiacs. The *Explorer* was the first ship to offer adventure cruises to Antarctica and has sailed longer and farther than any other expedition ship. Its log book includes the first successful navigation of the Northwest Passage by a cruise ship and the first visit by a Western passenger ship to the Russian Far East. Its latest accomplishment was the first circumnavigation of James Ross Island in Antarctica in 1997.

Ship at a Glance

	Dining Rooms	Bars	Casino	Fitness Center	Pools	Average Per Diem
Explorer	1	1	○	●	1	$400–$500

Cruise Experience Abercrombie & Kent (A&K) is better known for its luxury safaris and land tours, but the company also runs a diverse program of cruises. In addition to the *Explorer*, A&K represents barges in Europe, Nile riverboats, and other vessels in Australia and elsewhere (*see* Chapter 2). As one of the industry's foremost advocates of environmentally sensitive travel, or ecotourism, A&K appeals to well-educated, sophisticated travelers looking to expand their horizons. Its cruises aboard the *Explorer* underline this commitment to ecology by emphasizing an environmentally friendly philosophy during lectures, shore excursions, and Zodiac explorations. Lecturers and staff are familiar with ecological issues and urge passengers to avoid damaging the environment and not to disturb, harass, or interfere with the wildlife.

Most passengers are extremely well traveled but may be first-time expedition cruisers. Frequently, passengers are A&K alumni, having traveled with the company on safari in Africa or elsewhere by land. While most passengers are couples 55 and older, there also are a few younger couples and a smattering of single passengers. On most Antarctica cruises, European passengers (primarily German and British) make up one-third to one-half the total. However, all lectures and announcements are give in English only.

Activities Once at anchor, the *Explorer* launches its fleet of Zodiacs, which can make landfall nearly anywhere as conditions allow. Naturalists lead these waterborne excursions, which frequently encounter penguins, seals, sea lions, humpback whales, and a host of other marine creatures and seabirds. Passengers should be in reasonably good physical condition and have a sense of adventure: The unpredictable Antarctic climate sometimes means rough seas, and land outings may require hiking on icy, rugged terrain.

This is not a cruise for couch potatoes and other sedentary types since onboard diversions are limited. The few options for those who stay aboard include reading a book from the ship's library or visiting the captain on the bridge, which is always open to passengers.

Dining Food is of the hearty, northern European variety—not bad, not gourmet. Menus are limited but there is a choice for dinner among appetizers, soups, and main dishes (usually meat or fish). Meals are served at a single seating at either 7:30 or 8. With no assigned seating arrangements, you can hop around from meal to meal to mingle with fellow travelers. This is no glamour cruise: The two semiformal evenings are frequently attended by casually dressed passengers who have wisely junked fancier duds to economize on packing space. There is no smoking in the dining room.

Other food service includes lunch and breakfast buffets and afternoon tea, cookies, and cake. Coffee and tea are available all day. Room service, too, is always available, but since there are no in-cabin phones, you must either find a steward or arrange delivery in advance.

Entertainment On most nights before dinner, passengers are invited to meet with the naturalists for an informal recap of the day's events and to preview the next day's agenda. After dinner, a movie is often shown in the lecture hall and drinks are served in the Explorer Lounge, where members of the crew and staff often mingle informally with passengers.

Service and Tipping Instead of deferential white-glove service, you'll find naturalists and lecturers eating with and moving about among the passengers—like members of the family. A service charge is included in the cruise fare in lieu of tips.

Destinations The ship that originally launched cruising to the "White Continent" spends November through mid-March, sailing there from southern tip of Australia. From April through June the ship calls along the Amazon and in the North Atlantic. (For seasonal itineraries, *see* Chapter 4.)

For More Information Abercrombie & Kent (1520 Kensington Rd., Oak Brook, IL 60521, tel. 708/954–2944 or 800/323–7308).

MS Explorer

Specifications *Type of ship:* Expedition
Cruise experience: Casual
Size: 2,398 tons
Number of cabins: 51
Outside cabins: 100%

Passengers: 96
Crew: 67 (European, American, and Filipino)
Officers: European
Passenger/crew ratio: 1.4 to 1
Year built: 1969

Ship's Log Compared with the newest generation of expedition ships, such as the *Clipper Adventurer* or *Hanseatic*, the *Explorer* is a bit small and spartan. The design is strictly practical, with narrow decks, exposed pipes, and cramped quarters. The *Explorer*'s compact size, however, enables all passengers to disembark onto Zodiacs more quickly than on larger vessels, allowing for additional landings per day and more time ashore. Despite the *Explorer*'s age and size, the ship, with its red hull, continues to be a beacon to adventure cruisers.

Cabins Cabins are tiny; each has a wooden desk and a view through a porthole or picture window. In the daytime, beds are converted into side-by-side sofas. Closet space is extremely limited; all accommodations have hair dryers. Cabins on the Boat Deck look onto the public promenade.

Outlet voltage: 220 AC.

Single supplement: 150%–200% of double-occupancy rate.

Discounts: You get a discount for booking early and for booking back-to-back cruises.

Sports and Fitness **Health club:** Reclining bike, exercycle, free weights, sauna.

Recreation: Small pool (not filled on Antarctica cruises).

Facilities **Public rooms:** Lounge, lecture hall; access to navigation bridge.

Shops: Small gift shop.

Health care: Doctor and nurse on call.

Child care: None.

Services: Laundry service.

Accessibility Because there is no elevator aboard, this ship is not recommended for wheelchair users.

Alaska Sightseeing/ Cruise West

The Fleet MV *Spirit of Alaska*   MV *Spirit of Endeavour*
MV *Spirit of Columbia*   MV *Spirit of Glacier Bay*
MV *Spirit of Discovery*   MV *Spirit of '98*

Alaska Sightseeing's philosophy is that smaller is better: Each vessel measures less than 210 ft in length, registers less than 100 tons, and carries no more than 107 passengers. Because they have shallow drafts, these small ships can hug the shoreline and explore narrow inlets, fjords, and rivers that bigger cruise ships must bypass. The *Spirit of Alaska, Spirit of Columbia,* and *Spirit of Discovery* have bow ramps that allow passengers to go ashore where docking or dropping anchor would otherwise be impossible.

Ships at a Glance

	Dining Rooms	Bars	Casino	Fitness Center	Pools	Average Per Diem
Spirit of Alaska	1	1	○	◑	0	$200–$300
Spirit of Columbia	1	1	○	◑	0	$300–$400
Spirit of Discovery	1	1	○	◑	0	$300–$400
Spirit of Endeavour	1	2	○	◑	0	$400–$500
Spirit of Glacier Bay	1	1	○	○	0	$300–$400
Spirit of '98	1	2	○	◑	0	$400–$500

Cruise Experience Alaska Sightseeing lets nature take center stage. Passengers are encouraged to spend their time out on deck, scanning the shore for wildlife. The captain may alter the ship's route or linger awhile when a foraging bear is sighted or a pod of whales is encountered. Guests may visit the wheelhouse anytime during daylight hours.

Alaska itineraries call for less time in port, and more time for shipboard touring, than is typical of cruises aboard large ocean liners. Passengers who sail this way are well-traveled nature lovers. Because there are so few people aboard, individual interests can be indulged, and sailing schedules are flexible enough to allow for extra time to watch a calving glacier or to photograph eagles. Upon request, crew members will awaken guests to view the northern lights.

California wine-country cruises are more port-oriented than Alaska sailings, and offer a unique short getaway. It's a pleasure to slow down and visit areas by ship that are two hours away from San Francisco by car. Excursions ashore include time spent exploring the restored historic district of Old Sacramento, where passengers can visit the California Railroad Museum, Sutters

Fort, the Crocker Art Museum, and the California State Capitol building. Another stop is made near the quaint town of Sonoma, renowned for its historic buildings and stylish boutiques. Highlights of a port call here include the Sonoma Mission and wineries such as Clos Pegase and Schramsberg for private tours and tastings. Complementing the shoreside experience are onboard wine and cheese tastings with local winery owners and history lectures.

Activities   There are no showgirls, no midnight buffets, and no aerobics classes. Talks given by park naturalists or the cruise director are the only organized activities aboard ship. In addition to wildlife watching, popular pastimes include checkers, cards, reading, and comparing notes on the day's events. Each ship except the *Spirit of Glacier Bay* is equipped with one or two pieces of workout equipment.

Dining   Food is plentiful and tasty; cuisine is classic American. Local catches and produce are often on the menu, as are home-baked breads and desserts. Meals are served in a single, open seating (dinner at 7 or 7:30). Passengers may choose from two entrées each evening. Like the rest of the Alaska Sightseeing cruise experience, dining is very informal, and food presentation is less important than the view outside. Service is more friendly than professional. Leave all your dress clothes at home: No one dons anything resembling high fashion—even blue jeans are just fine. Special dietary requests should be made at time of booking.

An early-riser Continental breakfast in the lounge is followed each morning by full breakfast in the dining room, where lunch also is served. Fresh fruit, coffee, tea, and other beverages are available throughout the day. Snacks are usually served around 4 and hors d'oeuvres at 6. There is no room service, except in the Owner's Suite on the *Spirit of '98*. However, since there is no cabin telephone, requests for in-suite meals must be made to the crew earlier in the day. Choices are limited to the day's menu.

Entertainment   Most Alaska Sightseeing passengers would rather rise early than revel late into the night. Except for an occasional movie, mingling in the lounge and discussing the day's wildlife sightseeing are the highlights of most evenings. On crew night, you may be treated to lighthearted skits and trivia games.

Service and Tipping   The mostly American crew is enthusiastic and informative. Even with myriad ship duties, these young hosts find time to form close friendships with their guests. Recommended tipping is $5–$10 per person, per diem. Passengers place their tips in an envelope on the last evening of the cruise and leave them, anonymously, in the lounge.

Destinations   Among the few American-flagged vessels sailing the Inside Passage, these are the only ships that have their home port in Seattle during the Alaska season. Spring and fall itineraries take in northern California's Napa Valley, Oregon's Columbia and Snake rivers, or the stretch of the Inside Passage that borders British Columbia. (For seasonal itineraries, *see* Chapter 4.)

For More Information   Alaska Sightseeing/Cruise West (4th & Battery Bldg., Suite 700, Seattle, WA 98121, tel. 800/426–7702).

MV Spirit of Alaska

Specifications   *Type of ship:* Coastal cruiser   *Passengers:* 82
                    Cruise experience: Casual   *Crew:* 21 (American/Canadian)

Size: 97 tons	*Officers:* American/Canadian
Number of cabins: 39	*Passenger/crew ratio:* 3.9 to 1
Outside cabins: 70%	*Year built:* 1980

Ship's Log Alaska Sightseeing's original overnight vessel epitomizes the concept of small-ship cruising. You are never by yourself in the lounge, and meals in the homey dining room resemble a family affair soon after the cruise has begun. Sleek and small, the *Spirit of Alaska* feels like a real yacht. A bow ramp adds to the sense of adventure, allowing passengers to put ashore at tiny islands and beaches where few other cruise travelers ever visit.

Cabins The *Spirit of Alaska* offers a wide variety of accommodations, from top-deck suites with two picture windows to claustrophobic lower-deck cabins with no windows. Most cabins are very small but tastefully decorated with colorful bedspreads and photographs of Alaskan wildlife. Toilets and showers are a combined unit (meaning that the toilet is inside the shower). Suites and some outside cabins have TVs, but only for watching videos.

Outlet voltage: 110 AC.

Single supplement: 125%–175% of double-occupancy rate.

Discounts: Four cabins (two Category AA, two Category A) are available as triples at reduced per diems. You get a discount for booking early and for paying early.

Fitness **Health club:** StairMaster, exercise bike, rowing machine.

Recreation: Unobstructed circuit for jogging.

Facilities **Public rooms:** Lounge; access to navigation bridge.

Shops: Souvenir items available.

Accessibility Four main deck cabins, the aft dining room, and the forward lounge are on a single level. There is no elevator.

MV Spirit of Columbia

Specifications

Type of ship: Coastal cruiser	*Passengers:* 81
Cruise experience: Casual	*Crew:* 21 (American/Canadian)
Size: 98 tons	*Officers:* American/Canadian
Number of cabins: 38	*Passenger/crew ratio:* 3.8 to 1
Outside cabins: 64%	*Year built:* 1979

Ship's Log Passengers who may have sailed aboard this ship during its days as ACCL's *New Shoreham II* will hardly recognize the vessel. After buying the ship in 1994, Alaska Sightseeing spent considerable money to gussy up its interiors, creating a more polished shipboard setting. Although cut from the same mold as Alaska Sightseeing's *Spirit of Alaska*, it has one notable feature: a unique bow ramp design that allows passengers to walk directly from the forward lounge onto shore. The *Spirit of Columbia*'s interior design was inspired by the national-park lodges of the American West; colors are drawn from a muted palette of rust, evergreen, and sand.

Cabins All cabins have modest-size closets and drawers between or under the beds. A watercolor print, depicting Pacific Northwest scenery, hangs in each cabin. Color schemes are similar to the shades found in the public rooms. Patterns were based on Native American designs from the desert Southwest. All suites and deluxe cabins have a mini-refrigerator, an armchair and a small desk. The

Owner's Suite stretches the width of the vessel; located just under the bridge, its row of forward-facing windows gives a captain's-eye view of the ship's progress. Suites and deluxe cabins have TVs, but only for watching videos.

Outlet voltage: 110 AC.

Single supplement: 125–175% of double-occupancy rate.

Discounts: You get a discount for booking early and for paying early.

Sports and Fitness   **Health club:** StairMaster, exercise bike, rowing machine.

Recreation: Unobstructed circuit (12 laps = 1½ km/1 mi) for jogging.

Facilities   **Public rooms:** Lounge; access to navigation bridge.

Shops: Souvenir items available.

Accessibility   Four main-deck cabins, the aft dining room, and the forward lounge are on a single level. There is no elevator.

MV Spirit of Discovery

Specifications   *Type of ship:* Coastal cruiser   *Passengers:* 84
Cruise experience: Casual   *Crew:* 21 (American/Canadian)
Size: 94 tons   *Officers:* American/Canadian
Number of cabins: 43   *Passenger/crew ratio:* 4 to 1
Outside cabins: 100%   *Year built:* 1976

Ship's Log   Floor-to-ceiling windows in the main lounge provide stunning views of glaciers, wildlife, and other passing scenery for passengers aboard this snazzy yacht. Blue-suede chairs, a wraparound bench sofa at the bow, and a mirrored ceiling make the chrome-filled lounge look extra swank. The lounge features a small library of paperbacks as well as nature and history books; the selection changes according to the itinerary. From the lounge, passengers have direct access to a large outdoor viewing deck, one of two aboard. This is especially convenient for those who don't want to trudge upstairs every time a whale is spotted.

Cabins   Although the cabins are small, their oversize picture windows keep the walls from closing in. Cream-color walls, contemporary-style furnishings, and Alaska wildlife photographs complement the ship's modern motif. All cabins have individual climate control, windows that open for fresh air, and a vanity desk with a chair. Deluxe cabins have mini-refrigerators. Two cabins are reserved for single travelers. Toilets and showers are a combined unit (meaning that the toilet is inside the shower). Suites and some outside cabins have TVs, but only for watching videos.

Outlet voltage: 110 AC.

Single supplement: 125–175% of double-occupancy rate. Two single cabins are available at no surcharge.

Discounts: You get a discount for booking early and for paying early.

Fitness   **Health club:** StairMaster, exercise bike, rowing machine.

Facilities   **Public rooms:** Bar/lounge; access to navigation bridge.

Shops: Souvenir items available.

Accessibility   This ship is not recommended for wheelchair users.

MV Spirit of Endeavour

Specifications   *Type of ship:* Coastal cruiser   *Passengers:* 107
Cruise experience: Casual   *Crew:* 26 (American/Canadian)
Size: 99 tons   *Officers:* American/Canadian
Number of cabins: 48   *Passenger/crew ratio:* 3.5 to 1
Outside cabins: 100%   *Year built:* 1983

Ship's Log   Originally built by Clipper Cruise Line, the *Spirit of Endeavour* is Alaska Sightseeing's flagship as well as its largest vessel. The *Endeavour*'s sleek lines and long, raked bow make it most similar in silhouette to the *Spirit of Discovery*. The only Alaska Sightseeing ship that stretches longer than 200 ft, the *Endeavour* has open, airy public rooms, with higher ceilings and wider corridors than those aboard its fleetmates. It also is the only Alaska Sightseeing ship with a full-size bridge, like those found on oceangoing liners. The lounge opens directly onto the outdoor viewing area. Teak decks, maple cabinets, and a covered outdoor service bar for picnics and parties are other distinguishing features. From an engineering standpoint the *Endeavour* is the quietest ship in the fleet because of its shrouded propellers (although it's still far from being noise-free). And unlike the line's other ships, the *Endeavour*'s cabins have phones for making cabin-to-cabin calls.

Cabins   The *Spirit of Endeavour*'s cabins have the largest picture windows in the Alaska Sightseeing fleet. Accommodations are comparable to those aboard the *Spirit of '98*—small but still the most spacious in the AS/CW fleet. Some cabins have connecting doors, which make them convenient for families traveling together. All cabins have TVs, but only for watching videos.

Outlet voltage: 110 AC.

Single supplement: 125–175% of double-occupancy rate.

Discounts: You get a discount for booking early and for paying early.

Fitness   **Health club:** StairMaster, exercise bike.

Recreation: Unobstructed circuit (17 laps = 1½ km/1 mi) for jogging.

Facilities   **Public rooms:** Lounge; access to navigation bridge.

Shops: Souvenir items available.

Accessibility   This ship is not recommended for wheelchair users.

MV Spirit of Glacier Bay

Specifications   *Type of ship:* Coastal cruiser   *Passengers:* 52
Cruise experience: Casual   *Crew:* 16 (American/Canadian)
Size: 98 tons   *Officers:* American/Canadian
Number of cabins: 27   *Passenger/crew ratio:* 3.4 to 1
Outside cabins: 52%   *Year built:* 1971

Ship's Log   Alaska Sightseeing's smallest overnight cruise vessel is nearly identical to the line's *Spirit of Alaska*, and its public rooms are even cozier. Wraparound couches and small table-and-chair groupings in the lounge create a living-room feel.

Cabins   Like the *Spirit of Alaska*, the cabins on the *Spirit of Glacier Bay*'s lowest deck are all inside and have no windows. Furnishings are minimal, but soft cream-color fabrics help brighten up the ship's tiny accommodations. All cabins have a hanging closet, minimal drawer space. Two outside cabins have a desk with a chair. Outside accommodations also have picture windows, and all have twin beds except two cabins, which instead have one double bed. Toilets and showers are a combined unit (meaning that the toilet is inside the shower). There are no TVs in any cabins.

Outlet voltage: 110 AC.

Single supplement: 125%–175% of double-occupancy rate.

Discounts: Two cabins (Category AA) can be booked as triples at reduced per diems. You get a discount for booking early and for paying early.

Fitness **Health club:** There are no exercise facilities aboard the *Spirit of Glacier Bay.*

Recreation: Unobstructed circuit (17 laps = 1½ km/1 mi) for jogging.

Facilities **Public rooms:** Bar/lounge; access to navigation bridge.

Shops: Souvenir items available.

Accessibility Four main deck cabins, the aft dining room, and the forward lounge are on a single level. There is no elevator.

MV Spirit of '98

Specifications

Type of ship: Coastal cruiser	*Passengers:* 101
Cruise experience: Casual	*Crew:* 24 (American)
Size: 96 tons	*Officers:* American/Canadian
Number of cabins: 49	*Passenger/crew ratio:* 4.2 to 1
Outside cabins: 100%	*Year built:* 1984

Ship's Log With its rounded stern and wheelhouse, old-fashioned smokestack, and Victorian decor, the *Spirit of '98* evokes the feel of a turn-of-the-century steamship, even though it was built in 1984. Second in size only to the *Spirit of Endeavour,* the *Spirit of '98* remains the line's most elegant vessel. Inside and out, mahogany adorns this ship, including the sculptured sideboard in its main lounge, where massive floral curtains conjure up the days of the cancan and the player piano is in constant demand. Overstuffed chairs upholstered in crushed velvet complete the gold-rush-era motif. For private moments, there are plenty of nooks and crannies aboard ship, along with the cozy Soapy's Parlor at the stern, with a small bar (open only occasionally during each cruise) and a few tables and chairs.

Cabins The small but comfortable cabins are appointed with mahogany headboards and Audubon prints. Each has a picture window that may be opened. All cabins have individual climate control, separate showers and toilet in the bathrooms, and excellent light for bedtime reading. Most have both closet and drawer space for storage. In addition, Deluxe cabins have a sitting area, and the single Owner's Suite comes with a living room; game/meeting room; separate bedroom; TV; VCR; fully stocked, complimentary wet bar; and oversize bathroom. All cabins have TVs, but only for watching videos.

Outlet voltage: 110 AC.

Single supplement: 125%–175% of double-occupancy rate.

Discounts: Two Category 1 cabins can be booked as triples at reduced per diems. You get a discount for booking early and for paying early.

Sports and Fitness **Health club:** StairMaster, exercise bike.

Recreation: Unobstructed circuit (12 laps = 1½ km/1 mi) for jogging.

Facilities **Public rooms:** Bar/lounge; access to navigation bridge.

Shops: Souvenir items available.

Accessibility Two cabins are accessible to wheelchair users. All public rooms and decks are accessible by elevator except the upper outdoor deck.

Alaska's Glacier Bay Tours & Cruises

The Fleet *Executive Explorer*
Wilderness Adventurer
Wilderness Discoverer
Wilderness Explorer

From their picture windows to their sea kayaks, Glacier Bay's small ships are designed to highlight the natural world and bring you closer to shore. Several of the line's ships have been previously owned by American Canadian Caribbean Line, so passengers who have sailed with that company will find the surroundings familiar.

Ships at a Glance

	Dining Rooms	Bars	Casino	Fitness Center	Pools	Average Per Diem
Executive Explorer	1	1	○	○	0	$400–$500
Wilderness Adventurer/ Wilderness Discoverer	1	1	○	○	0	$300–$400
Wilderness Explorer	1	1	○	○	0	$200–$300

Cruise Experience One passenger's comment best sums up the Glacier Bay experience: "When I saw the brochure, I said—That's it. The people in kayaks had gray hair." But the crowd isn't limited to seniors. You may find a honeymoon couple or young cruisers traveling with a grandparent. And while the Glacier Bay crowd is eco-oriented—searching for bear, eagles, and whales is No. 1 on their list—it's still very much a cruise crowd: After dinner, people are already talking about breakfast. Passengers come from across the United States and beyond—some from as far away as Australia.

Glacier Bay has two styles of cruising: What it calls "adventure cruising" and more conventional port-to-port itineraries. The "adventure cruises" spend all their time in wilderness areas, never visiting any towns. They are designed to be an escape from civilization. Not only don't you stop in any ports, but you're out of telephone range for most of the cruise. This is indeed a true wilderness experience, but one that requires no special experience.

Port-to-port itineraries, meanwhile, visit Alaska's most popular coastal communities. One ship, the *Executive Explorer*, is a high-speed catamaran capable of 18 knots, which allows it to stop at more ports than is typical on a seven-day cruise.

To its destination-intensive itineraries Glacier Bay adds several nice onboard touches. On most ships, a mint is placed on your pillow every night. And amenity packs in the bathrooms include a selection of Neutrogena products. Towels are only changed every other day, but as one purser noted, "You don't change your towels at home every day."

Activities On "adventure cruises," sea-kayaking excursions away from the ship are the highlight of each day. Soft-adventure cruises also offer shore-walking, while active-adventure cruises have hikes that involve a good deal of bushwhacking. Excursions last an hour to an hour and a half on soft adventure cruises, half the day on active cruises.

On all cruises, onboard activities are limited to talks on nature and native culture. There's a a selection of Alaska books and videos in the main lounge.

Dining You won't go hungry, but food is primarily fuel for the day's activities—basic fare with some flair served family style. There's a choice of entrée for dinner (except on the *Wilderness Explorer*), ranging from the hearty (rack of lamb, prime rib) to the light (salmon, scallops). There are never any formal occasions—even the Captain's dinner is come-as-you-are.

Throughout the day, coffee is always on (it's especially good, too), as are tasty, fresh baked cookies and brownies. Passengers may also help themselves at any time to complimentary soft drinks, ice tea, and lemonade.

In the morning, early-riser coffee and Continental breakfast precedes the full breakfast in the main dining room. Breakfast and lunch menus are more limited—usually salad, soup, and sandwiches for lunch—but if you ask for something different like eggs, they'll be cheerfully delivered to your table. Special dietary requests should be made at the time of booking, although they can be accommodated on shorter notice. There is no room service.

Entertainment Except for the occasional talk on nature and native culture mentioned above, there really is no scheduled entertainment. Most people spend the after-dinner hours socializing or out-on deck looking for wildlife. In Alaska, the long hours of sunlight allow wildlife watching to go on well into the night. By 11 or 12, though, the day—and the visible light—is spent, and virtually everyone is asleep.

Service and Tipping Service is truly exceptional: Enthusiastic and sincere. It is however, informal: The steward/waitresses are college students on summer vacation. Naturalists, too, have an irrepressible love of the environment, which quickly spreads among the passengers. Tips are pooled among the crew. The recommended amount is $12 per day per person.

Destinations From spring through fall, Glacier Bay roams Alaska's Inside Passage. In winter, the line heads south for cruises of Baja California as Voyager Cruise Line. (For seasonal itineraries, *see* Chapter 4.)

For More Information Alaska's Glacier Bay Tours & Cruises (520 Pike St., Suite 1400, Seattle, WA 98101, tel. 206/623–7110 or 800/451–5952).

Executive Explorer

Specifications

Type of ship: Coastal cruiser	*Passengers:* 49
Cruise experience: Casual	*Crew:* 18 (American)
Size: 98 tons	*Officers:* American
Number of cabins: 25	*Passenger/crew ratio:* 2.7 to 1
Outside cabins: 100%	*Year built:* 1986

Ship's Log As the name suggests, the *Executive Explorer* is a plush ship. Its appointments include rich wood-paneling throughout, deep-padded armchairs in the main lounge, and a gallerylike display of nearly 100 Alaskan prints. The main lounge has forward-facing observation windows; the dining room has color TV monitors. Even the stairwells have picture windows for views of the passing scenery. Outside observation areas include a partially covered sundeck, which gives a lofty perspective four decks above the water—an unusually high perch for such a small ship.

Cabins Cabins are all outside, and have even more artwork plus two big picture windows (also unusually large for a ship this size). Other cabin amenities include roomy closets, TVs, VCRs, minibars—another nice extra not often found in small-ship cabins. Sinks are located outside the bathroom. Five cabins can accommodate three passengers; one cabin can hold four.

Outlet voltage: 110 AC.

Single supplement: 175% of double-occupancy rate.

Discounts: A third or fourth passenger in a cabin pays reduced per diems. You get a discount for booking early.

Facilities **Public rooms:** Lounge.

Accessibility This ship is not recommended for wheelchair users.

Wilderness Adventurer and Wilderness Discoverer

Specifications *Type of ship:* Coastal cruiser
Cruise experience: Casual
Size: 89/98 tons
Number of cabins: 35/43
Outside cabins: 85%

Passengers: 74/86
Crew: 20 (American)
Officers: American
Passenger/crew ratio: 3.7 to 1/4.3 to 1
Years built: 1983/1992

Ship's Log These are friendly ships with the casual comforts of home. The coffee's always on and you'll never need a jacket and tie for dinner. Alaskan art enhances the otherwise simple surroundings. A library of books and videos has a nice selection of Alaska titles.

The ships carry a fleet of colorful kayaks, which are lowered into the water with an armlike crane seemingly adopted from the space shuttle. About four sea-kayaking excursions are scheduled during each six-night cruise. A floating dock allows passengers to get in and out of the kayaks safely and dryly.

But the most important asset of these ships are their naturalists, who put their hearts into their work. They lead the kayak excursions and shorewalks, and get as much of a thrill as the passengers do whenever wildlife is sighted. Since the *Wilderness Adventurer* and *Wilderness Discoverer* visit few ports and spends most of their time in the wild, you'll see things you're not likely to see on most other ships—like whales standing on their heads and flipping their tails above the water, a behavior known technically as "lobtailing." You'll also get to go ashore in places like Admiralty Island (the "Fortress of the Bears") and in Glacier Bay, where few other cruise passengers make landfall.

Cabins Cabins, like the rest of the ship, are and functional. (The toilet and sink are in the shower.) There are no TVs, but you can watch the tapes—or your own wildlife footage—on the community VCR in the main lounge. The color scheme is blue and beige, and surfaces are finished in a Formicalike material. There is, however, just enough varnished wood to imbue a nautical feel. The lowest category cabins have just a portlight (no window). Four cabins can accommodate up to three passengers. Avoid rear cabins on Deck 3 and especially Deck 2, which are prone to engine noise and vibration.

Outlet voltage: 110 AC.

Single supplement: 175% of double-occupancy rate.

Discounts: A third passenger in a cabin pays reduced per diems. You get a discount for booking early.

Sports and Fitness **Recreation:** Sea kayaks, unobstructed circuit for walking.

Facilities **Public rooms:** Lounge.

Accessibility This ship is not recommended for wheelchair users.

Wilderness Explorer

Specifications

Type of ship: Coastal cruiser	*Passengers:* 36
Cruise experience: Casual	*Crew:* 13 (American)
Size: 98 tons	*Officers:* American
Number of cabins: 18	*Passenger/crew ratio:* 2.7 to 1
Outside cabins: 78%	*Year built:* 1969

Ship's Log The Wilderness Explorer is billed as a "floating base camp" for "active adventure," and that's no exaggeration. Sea-kayak outings may last more than three hours (a 5-mi paddle). Discovery hikes cross dense thicket and climb rocky creek beds. You'll spend most of your time off the ship—which is a good thing, since you wouldn't want to spend much time on it. Decorwise, the ship is pleasing enough—mostly late 1960s mod with a dash of Old World leather and even Greek Revival accents. But the public spaces are very limited and the cabins are positively tiny. This ship is not for the typical cruise passenger, and should be considered only by the serious outdoor enthusiast.

Cabins Cabin accommodations are bunk-style with an upper and lower berth. Except for one spacious cabin on the top deck, they are very small. Avoid Cabins 106, 110, and 113, which are especially cramped due to their position underneath a stairwell. Most cabins do not have a window, just a small portlight.

Outlet voltage: 110 AC.

Single supplement: 175% of double-occupancy rate.

Discounts: You get a discount for booking early.

Sports and Fitness **Recreation:** Sea kayaks.

Facilities **Public rooms:** Lounge.

Accessibility This ship is not recommended for wheelchair users.

American Canadian Caribbean Line

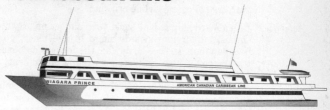

The Fleet *Grande Caribe*
Niagara Prince
Grande Mariner

ACCL's vessels are the personal creations of the line's owner, Luther H. Blount, who builds them in his Rhode Island shipyard. Their efficient layout and durability are the result of Blount's 45 years of shipbuilding experience—he has designed and constructed ferries, sightseeing boats, and small ships now operated by other cruise lines, such as Alaska Sightseeing/Cruise West and Glacier Bay Tours & Cruises. For ACCL, he has created a fleet of small, yachtlike vessels that are custom designed for cruising inland waterways and coastlines, with retractable pilothouses, shallow drafts, bow ramps, and rear swimming platforms.

Ships at a Glance

	Dining Rooms	Bars	Casino	Fitness Center	Pools	Average Per Diem
Grande Caribe *Grande Mariner*	1	0	○	○	0	under $200
Niagara Prince	1	0	○	○	0	under $200

Cruise Experience ACCL's passengers prefer a casual and simple shipboard environment to the glamour and luxury of pricier cruise lines. But some of the lowest rates in cruising mean that ACCL offers few traditional services and facilities—sheets and towels are changed every *other* day, and it's even suggested that you pack your own beach towel. These no-frills cruises are an excellent value, nevertheless. Everything is included in the base price except tips and certain shore excursions (*see* Activities, *below*). No alcohol is sold on board, although you are free to bring your own. At several ports, the crew can arrange to have liquor delivered directly to the ship. Mixers and other nonalcoholic drinks are available free from the bar at all hours.

New England charm and personal service make passengers feel like they're sailing on the family yacht. In a sense, they are, and Blount and his family personally send off every cruise that departs from the line's base in Warren, Rhode Island. Once underway, passengers find themselves on easy terms with one another as well as with the crew. The line is similar in its informal ambience and limited amenities to Alaska Sightseeing, but the latter's cabins and public spaces are decidedly more stylish. ACCL cruisers tend to be educated and older (63 on average), and children under 14 are not permitted. ACCL has inspired a loyal group of alumni passengers, and the number of repeaters aboard ship can be as high as 65%. On some Caribbean cruises you can board a day early and use the ship as a floating hotel for $50 per passenger, $100 per couple. In keeping with Blount's down-home hospitality, passengers embarking in Warren may park their cars in the ship-yard free of charge while cruising.

Activities Life aboard ship is laid-back, with almost no organized activities. Onboard diversions include bingo, bridge, chess, golf putting, and backgammon. In the Caribbean, the focus is on beachcombing and water sports. Two Sailfish, snorkeling equipment, and a 21-seat glass-bottom boat are available free to passengers; you can swim or sail from the stern platform. Fishing from ship or beach is encouraged; bring your own tackle. Shore excursions tend to be informative and extremely worthwhile; if the local tour guides don't meet ACCL standards, the ship supplies a guide. Passengers are charged for shore excursions only when ACCL itself incurs a cost, and the line charges no markup. The average price for these excursions is only $12; the most expensive (in Belize) costs $25.

Dining ACCL is one of the few lines that reserves its full-meal service for dinner and serves just a light lunch at midday—a policy that many passengers prefer. Lunchtime selections may be sandwiches on fresh-baked bread and classic pastas, and are interspersed with such gourmet treats as chilled gazpacho and crab-stuffed pastry. Dinner menus are full-course meals of well-prepared, standard American cooking. Many dishes use fresh seafood and produce picked up in ports along the way. Breakfast is buffet, lunch is family style, and an open-seating dinner is served at 6. There is only one choice of dinner entrée; the chef will prepare a special dish for passengers who want another option, but special diets, including low fat, kosher, sugar-free, and low salt, must be requested at least two weeks before departure. Passengers can help themselves at any time to tea, coffee, lemonade, and snacks, such as fruit and homemade cookies. There are no formal nights and no room service.

Entertainment Local musicians frequently come aboard during port calls, and there's an electric piano for those who want to make their own music. Every evening, movies are shown on a VCR in the main lounge. Otherwise most passengers pass the time socializing, playing cards, or reading.

Service and Tipping Service is quite casual. Tips are given anonymously via envelopes that you place in a basket in the lounge (tip $9–$12 per diem per passenger); the total is pooled among the crew.

Destinations Itineraries are as idiosyncratic as the line itself and take in offbeat islands in New England, the Caribbean, Central America, and the Bahamas; jungle rivers in Venezuela and Belize; the Panama Canal; the coastline of the Atlantic and the Gulf of Mexico; the Mississippi River system and the Great Lakes; and, in autumn, the Erie Canal, St. Lawrence Seaway, and Canadian sub-Arctic. (For seasonal itineraries, *see* Chapter 4.)

For More Information American Canadian Caribbean Line (Box 368, Warren, RI 02885, tel. 401/247–0955 or 800/556–7450).

Grande Caribe and Grande Mariner

Specifications *Type of ship:* Coastal cruiser *Passengers:* 100
Cruise experience: Casual *Crew:* 18 (American)
Size: 100 tons *Officers:* American

Number of cabins: 50   *Passenger/crew ratio:* 5.5 to 1
Outside cabins: 88%   *Years built:* 1997/1998

Ship's Log   ACCL touts the *Grande Caribe* and *Grande Mariner* as "the latest word" in small-ship cruising. Indeed, this new class of vessel
has some noticeable advantages over previous ACCL ships. The
most obvious benefit being their size—the ships are bigger inside
and out. Passengers will especially like the new observation
lounge, which is now located on the main deck rather than below
the hull line. This new vantage point allows for many entrance-
ways, giving better access to the bow and outdoor promenade.
Overall the ships feel roomier, from the Sun Deck up top to the
interior stairwells. The ships are also exceptionally quiet; there's
virtually no engine noise or vibration.

However, the "Grande Class" displays one less-desirable quality:
It's rather institutional, with little in the way of decor. This is
especially true in the spartan cabins, which lack the nautically
inspired wooden touches that distinguished such earlier ACCL
ships as the *Caribbean Prince* (now the *Wilderness Adventurer* of
Glacier Bay Tours & Cruises). Storage space is restricted to a blue
metal locker. Other furnishings are limited to two beds; a few
upper-category cabins have a tiny writing table. Some cabins open
onto the outdoor promenade, but unfortunately, these are smaller,
less desirable accommodations.

Ultimately, though, the sparse accommodations are of little consequence. ACCL passengers are not aboard for glitz and glamour.
They sign up for the casual, comfortable atmosphere that is the
hallmark of an ACCL cruise, and on the *Grande Caribe* or *Grande
Mariner*, they're sure to find that's one thing that hasn't changed.

Cabins   As noted above, the cabins are tiny. A few open onto an outside
deck; otherwise they are reached by an interior corridor. Inside
cabins include three on the Main Deck, aft, and six on the lower
deck. The latter have tiny port lights high in the cabin that provide some light but not much of a view; these accommodations
should not be booked by the claustrophobic. Storage space is limited to a few drawers, a locker, and some additional space beneath
the beds. Bathrooms have a curtain separating the sink and toilet
from the handheld shower. There are no keys to the cabins, but
valuables can be locked up in the ship's safe.

Outlet voltage: 110 AC.

Single supplement: 175% of double-occupancy rate (Cabins 20–22
only). The supplement is waived for passengers who agree to
share with another single traveler, even if one is not found by the
time of sailing.

Discounts: 15% per passenger when three passengers share a
cabin. You get a 10% discount when booking consecutive cruises.

Sports and   **Recreation:** Early-morning exercises, fishing, snorkeling, sailing,
Fitness   unobstructed circuit on Sun Deck (11 laps = 1½ km/1 mi) for jogging, swimming platform. The ship carries two aluminum 24-pas-
senger launches and a glass-bottom boat.

Facilities   **Public rooms:** Lounge.

Accessibility   An elevator provides access to all decks and two cabins are accessible to wheelchair-users. However, disembarking presents a
problem at ports where the ship does not dock.

Niagara Prince

Specifications *Type of ship:* Coastal cruiser
Cruise experience: Casual
Size: 99 tons
Number of cabins: 42
Outside cabins: 95%

Passengers: 84
Crew: 17 (American)
Officers: American
Passenger/crew ratio: 5 to 1
Year built: 1994

Ship's Log Although built just five years ago in 1994, the *Niagara* is actually ACCL's oldest and smallest ship. Like its fleetmates, it was built for both canal and ocean cruising, it has a retractable wheelhouse and a unique ballasting system, which submerges the vessel 10 inches so it can pass under the bridges of the Erie Canal. The dining room and lounge are connected on the main deck, with wraparound windows for good viewing. Both rooms are appointed in the standard ACCL furnishings: round tables in the dining room, a wraparound couch and overstuffed armchairs in the lounge, and mauve and teals upholstery and carpeting. Pastel prints and Caribbean scenes done in watercolor brighten the public rooms and corridors.

Cabins Cabins are small and storage space is limited, but the tweed teal carpeting and vibrant green and mauve trim are cheery. Prints and treasure maps depicting ports visited by ACCL add a nice finishing touch. In another plus, most staterooms have a chair and table. Along with quiet commodes, cabins have individual climate controls. Cabins with numbers in the 50s, 60s, and 70s have sliding picture windows. A few cabins have portholes. Beds in most cabins can be converted to doubles upon request. There are two inside cabins. There are no keys to the cabins, but valuables can be locked up in the ship's safe.

Outlet voltage: 110 AC.

Single supplement: 175% of double-occupancy rate (Cabins 20–22 only). The supplement is waived for passengers who agree to share with another single traveler, even if one is not found by the time of sailing.

Discounts: 15% per passenger when three passengers share a cabin. You get a 10% discount when booking consecutive cruises.

Sports and Fitness **Recreation:** Informal workouts, fishing, snorkeling, unobstructed circuit on Sun Deck for jogging, swimming platform.

Facilities **Public rooms:** Lounge.

Accessibility There is a stair lift for each deck, and all public areas are accessible to wheelchair users. Two cabins are accessible to wheelchair users as well.

American Hawaii Cruises

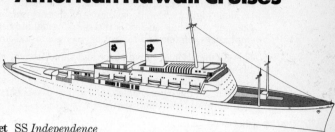

The Fleet SS *Independence*

Built in 1951, the *Independence* and its now departed sister, the *Constitution*, were the first modern liners to sail between New York and the Mediterranean; it was the *Constitution* that brought Grace Kelly and her wedding party to Monaco for her marriage to Prince Rainier in 1956. Other famous passengers have included Ernest Hemingway and Ronald Reagan. After nearly 50 years at sea, the *Independence* shows its age, although a $30 million makeover in late 1994 and $10 million more in 1997 did much to reverse the wear and added a tasteful Hawaiian motif to the cabins and many public rooms.

At press time, American Hawaii had announced its intention to buy another ship, giving the line two vessels by mid-1999.

Ship at a Glance

	Dining Rooms	Bars	Casino	Fitness Center	Pools	Average Per Diem
Independence	2	3	○	◑	2	$200–$300

Cruise Experience Travel on the *Independence* is really two cruise experiences in one. Fans of classic liners built for transatlantic travel will appreciate the finer points of this ship's design. Particularly noteworthy are the enclosed promenades, whose huge brass and glass doors open to the sea, letting in cool ocean breezes when the ship is docked or at anchor. Other "they don't make them like that anymore" qualities include heavy wooden doors with brass-rimmed portholes, which lead between inside and outside decks. Original cabin furnishings include light fixtures, medicine cabinets, bureaus, and Pullman-style folding beds.

For many other passengers, the attraction of this line is the chance to see Hawai'i's major islands at an affordable price. In all, the ship visits five ports on four islands in seven days, without the need to change hotels and to make intra-island plane connections. Because the ship sails solely within Hawai'i, the emphasis of the cruise, both aboard ship and ashore, is on the islands. The daily program of activities includes a full slate of Hawai'i crafts classes, storytelling, and other island traditions. You can learn to make jewelry from seashells or to play the ukulele. Whale-watching, too, is a big seasonal event, and local environmental representatives come aboard ship to lecture and point out the huge creatures. The line's shore-excursion booklet lists more than 50 choices, ranging from bus tours to rain-forest hikes.

Whether it's the classic style or the island ambience that appeals to you, make no mistake—this is not a luxury cruise. It is, however, a very good value. In fact, you'll find a number of nice touches aboard, such as complimentary bon-voyage mai-tais, free soft drinks, and no-charge laundry machines. Dramamine, aspirin, and acetaminophen are always available for free at the purser's office. On some higher priced lines, there's often a charge for all of these. Another appealing quality is the ship's casual atmosphere, which emphasizes comfort and relaxation over pomp and circumstance.

This combination of convenience and value attracts passengers in all age ranges. Aboard this liner you'll find everyone except younger couples. A typical mix includes families with younger children, middle-age couples, and older passengers celebrating their 50th wedding anniversary.

Activities   Shoreside activities are emphasized, and there are more than 50 excursions to choose from, including flightseeing by helicopter over an active volcano, bicycling down the slopes of a dormant volcano, or visiting Hawai'i Volcanoes National Park—you should be detecting a theme here. Also big are whale-watching, snorkeling, and kayaking.

Passengers who stay aboard by day will find plenty to do, from the usual cruise activities to ukulele, hula, lei making, palm weaving, and Hawaiian-language lessons. There are also such typical cruise diversions as line-dancing classes and, of course, bingo. Movies are screened daily in the ship's cinema-style theater. Be sure to see *An Affair to Remember*—the shipboard shots were filmed aboard the *Constitution*.

Dining   American cuisine—steaks, seafood, and lamb—dominates the daily menus, and although food is well prepared, some dishes are bland. An effort is made whenever possible to use local ingredients. The Kona coffee and Hawaiian pineapple are particularly noteworthy. Traditional Hawaiian "plate lunches" (combination platters of fish, meat, rice, and poi) top the menu in the dining room at the midday meal, and fresh local fish is always a selection at dinner. A Pu'uwai (Healthy Heart) program is available for low-fat, low-cholesterol entrées. The extensive wine list offers Californian, French, and German vintages.

On the *Independence*, passengers are assigned to one of two dining rooms at random. Although the dining rooms are below decks and lack panoramic windows, they are bright and colorful. There are two open seatings for dinner (6 and 8); breakfast and lunch are open seating. There is one semiformal/formal evening each cruise; otherwise, all dress is casual. On the first evening, dinner is a grand buffet. Passengers don Hawaiian fashions for the Polynesian dinner.

Breakfast and lunch are also served in a midships buffet. These are just as good as meals in the dining room, and taking your lunch or breakfast here has the added benefit of allowing you to sit outside on deck or in an enclosed promenade. Service also can be slow in the dining room for breakfast and lunch.

Other food service includes Continental breakfast of coffee, pastries, and fruit in one of the bars; afternoon hors d'oeuvres in the lounges; and complimentary brown-bag lunches for those going ashore for the day. A midnight buffet rounds out the day's food service. Coffee, soft drinks, and juices are available 24 hours, as is room service.

Entertainment   Passengers looking for a throbbing disco or casino will not find it here. (Because the *Independence* never leaves American waters, there is no gambling aboard.) Instead, you'll find pajama parties, 1950s sock hops, and karaoke nights, as well as traditional cruise-ship musical reviews in the main showroom and a piano player who takes requests in another lounge. There's also an orchestra for big-band dancing. Local Hawaiian entertainers sometimes come aboard while the ship is in port. All the entertainers, from the singers to the orchestra members, are accomplished musicians.

Service and Tipping The American crew is this line's great strength. Each member of the hotel staff—cabin stewards, waiters, waitresses, and bartenders—wears a badge identifying his or her name and home state, making for instant and easy conversation. Recommended tips per passenger, per diem are: dining-room waiter, $3.50; assistant waiter, $1.75; cabin steward, $3.50. A 15% gratuity is automatically added to bar and wine service.

Destinations As the name says, American Hawaii sails only in the Aloha state. (For year-round itineraries, *see* Chapter 4.)

For More Information American Hawaii Cruises (1380 Port of New Orleans Pl., New Orleans, LA 70130, tel. 504/586–0631 or 800/765–7000).

SS Independence

Specifications *Type of ship:* Classic liner
Cruise experience: Casual
Size: 30,090 tons
Number of cabins: 414
Outside cabins: 43%

Passengers: 828
Crew: 315 (American)
Officers: American
Passenger/crew ratio: 2.5 to 1
Year built: 1951

Ship's Log Age has its virtues, such as spacious cabins and enclosed, teak-lined promenades. A $30 million refit of the *Independence* in late 1994 created several new public rooms. The main lounge, often referred to as the ship's "living room," is a study in polished teak and rattan, with French doors that open onto the enclosed promenades. The adjoining bar is just as stylish, highlighted by an old-fashioned jukebox and Tiffany-style lamps. Not everything has been rejuvenated, though. There is still a fair amount of rot and rust on the outside decks—about what you'd expect on a ship that's been at sea for four decades. But there is another reason for the decay: You rarely see anybody painting and scraping as they should be. On the other hand, the improvements made during dry dock were expertly executed. Most impressive is a grand, outdoor staircase, which links the two pool decks and Promenade Deck for easy access.

Cabins Cabins come in 50 different configurations priced in 13 categories. Spaciousness can differ significantly even within the same category, so if roominess is most important to you, ask for a cabin configured to hold third and fourth passengers. If a double or queen-size bed is most important, emphasize that when booking.

Forty cabins, including six solarium suites on the Bridge Deck, were added to the *Independence* during the 1994 refit. The new suites are roomy and feature high ceilings and skylights, but they lack the traditional charm of these ships' original accommodations, which incorporate such classic hallmarks as in-the-round tiled showers and built-in half-moon sinks in the bathrooms. Decor in all cabins uses a kaleidoscope of colorful Hawaiian motifs. Patterns evoke a range of island imagery, from local flora to aloha shirts. Each cabin also has been given its own Hawaiian name.

Outlet voltage: 110 AC.

Single supplement: 200% of double-occupancy rate for suites, 160% for most other categories. Some inside cabins are available as singles for a $100 surcharge over the double-occupancy per diem.

Discounts: A third or fourth passenger in a cabin pays reduced per diems. Children 17 and under sail free.

Sports and Fitness

Health club: Exercise equipment including Lifecycles and Stair-Masters, saunas, massage (extra charge).

Recreation: Aerobics and stretch-and-tone classes, two freshwater pools, unobstructed circuit on wraparound promenade (7 laps = 1½ km/1 mi) for jogging.

Facilities

Public rooms: Three bars, main lounge, showroom, study, conference room, cinema.

Shops: Shopping arcade, beauty parlor/barbershop, photo gallery.

Health care: Doctor and nurse on call.

Child care: Supervised activities for children ages 5–16 during summer and holidays, youth recreation center, baby-sitting arranged privately with staff members.

Services: Self-service laundry, dry cleaning arranged off-ship, film processing.

Accessibility Although the *Independence* does not have designated cabins for wheelchair users, the line makes an effort to assign passengers with mobility problems to larger cabins off a main hallway on the Main Deck or on the decks above. Elevators are accessible to passengers using folding wheelchairs.

Carnival Cruise Lines

The Fleet
MS *Carnival Destiny*
MS *Carnival Triumph*
MS *Celebration*
MS *Ecstasy*
MS *Elation*
MS *Fantasy*
MS *Fascination*

MS *Holiday*
MS *Imagination*
MS *Inspiration*
MS *Jubilee*
MS *Paradise*
MS *Sensation*
MS *Tropicale*

Carnival ships are like floating theme parks, and all the line's vessels share this fun house aura to some degree. A real automobile, bus, or trolley car may be parked in one of the bars just as part of the decor. The effect is most exaggerated on the newer, bigger ships—especially the eight ships in the *Fantasy* series (*Fantasy* through *Paradise*). All were built from the same blueprint, but that's where the similarities end: Each has been given its own unique dreamscape. Carnival's older, smaller ships have their share of whimsy, too, but they're are a far cry from the latest mega-extravaganzas. Compared with Carnival's newer ships, the *Celebration, Holiday, Jubilee,* and *Tropicale* have lost a lot of their original luster: colors are faded, ceilings are lower, many public spaces are cramped, and overall the wear and tear can't be hidden.

Ships at a Glance

	Dining Rooms	Bars	Casino	Fitness Center	Pools	Average Per Diem
Celebration/Jubilee	3*	7	●	●	2	under $200
Carnival Destiny	3*	11	●	●	4	under $200
Ecstasy/Elation *Fantasy/Fascination* *Imagination/Inspiration* *Paradise/Sensation*	3*	9	●	●	2	under $200
Holiday	3*	7	●	●	2	under $200
Tropicale	2*	6	●	●	2	under $200

*includes alternative dining in the casual restaurant

Cruise Experience
Due to its success, Carnival is the standard by which all lower-priced cruise lines are measured. Not even its critics can deny that the line delivers what it promises: Brash and sometimes crass Carnival does throw a great party. Activities and entertainment are nonstop, food is plentiful, and cabins are spacious and comfortable. There's nothing exotic or genteel about it—beer and soda are served from a can rather than a bottle. Sometimes, the revelry gets out of hand, so uniform security guards patrol the ships to protect passengers from each other. Usually, it's just a prudent precaution. So if you're looking for a good tan, an island-hopping

itinerary, and pulsating nightlife, Carnival delivers a fun time at a reasonable price.

Passengers are young, or at least young at heart. More singles cruise on Carnival than on any other line, although the average passenger's age is 42, and you'll still find many cruisers older than 55. In many ways, Carnival is perfect for families, and the line continues to attract an ever-increasing number of parents who are cruising with their children. If you're lucky, your kids will develop friendships with children from all around the country, which sometimes last long after the cruise is over. However, parents should keep in mind that taking the kids on any mass-appeal cruise line is somewhat akin to taking them to Las Vegas. They'll love the glitz and glitter and nonstop fun of a Carnival cruise, but occasionally, the banter by cruise directors and passengers can get a little racy, and the scene at poolside can, at times, be described as a ruckus. Carnival has, however, taken steps to eliminate underage drinking and to discourage the rowdy "spring break" crowd. Passengers must be 21 to drink, and all minors are issued a specially marked onboard charge card—so they can't use the card to charge drinks to their parents' room. Passengers younger than 21 must be accompanied (in the same cabin) by a guardian 25 or older. There is a loophole, however: Youthful groups may still travel with a limited number of chaperons.

Activities Carnival vessels offer every activity that a cruise ship can: bingo, masquerade parties, pool games, water-balloon tosses, and trivia contests. No one can do it all, but many passengers try. Activity is centered around movement—from room to room and deck to deck. There are no lounges for curling up with a good book, except for the small libraries.

Dining The line has worked hard in recent years to shed its image as the McDonald's of the cruise industry, and current menus are healthier, more diverse, and better tasting. Seafood and poultry are served in light sauces, and specialties may include fajitas or blackened swordfish. Vegetarian dishes are available on all lunch and dinner menus, too.

Carnival's "Nautica Spa Selections" offer fare that is lighter in calories and lower in sodium, cholesterol, and fat. Salad bars serving an array of fruits, salads, and vegetables can be found in the indoor/outdoor bar and grill areas on all of the line's ships. Frozen yogurt is an alternative at the afternoon ice-cream bar and on dessert menus. Children's lunch and dinner menus offer favorites such as ravioli, hamburgers, and fish-and-chips. Meals are nothing less than feasts, with oversize but attractively arranged portions, noisy conversation, overly friendly waiters, and strolling musicians. French night, Spanish night, and other theme dinners feature special dishes and costumed waiters. The food quality is above average, and the quantity and hoopla associated with its presentation make it seem better than it is.

The dining room has two seatings per meal (dinner at 6 and 8). Tables are assigned, though you may ask to be placed at a table of your peers or with families traveling with children. Two formal evenings are held on cruises of four days or longer, one on three-day cruises. Requests for special diets should be made at the time of booking. Kosher food is not available. There is no smoking in the dining room.

Breakfast and lunch are also served in the buffet-style casual restaurant, which also serves as the ship's alternative restaurant for dinner. You can also get midmorning snacks and afternoon tea here. Coffee is on 24 hours a day; specialty coffees are available (at extra cost) on the newer ships. Every night there's a midnight buffet; some ships even offer a still-later buffet for those who party into the wee hours. All ships feature round-the-clock pizzerias and 24-hour room service from a limited menu.

Entertainment The action begins just after sunrise and continues well into the night. Disco music begins throbbing by midafternoon on deck and around the pool. At any given time you can choose from an abundance of contests, parties, classes, games, bar and lounge entertainers, and bands. In-cabin movies are limited to one film run several times a day. Carnival wants its passengers out and about its ships.

Carnival's performers are among the most diverse group at sea. There are musicians, magicians, dancers, comedians, jugglers, and other specialty acts. On the larger ships it's not unusual to have a country-and-western duo, a full-size dance band, a rock-and-roll group, a '40s swing band, a song stylist, a cocktail pianist, *and* a classical-music quartet, all performing simultaneously—in addition to the action in the disco and the teenage dance club. Even the smaller Carnival ships have more entertainment options than most cruise lines' largest. Fleetwide, the quality of the entertainment is often better than aboard higher-priced lines. Carnival's casinos are the largest afloat, and heavy emphasis is placed on gambling. Main lounge shows can be high-tech extravaganzas. On the newest ships, Carnival has taken these productions light years ahead of what used to be standard revues, with laser lighting, superior sound systems, and state-of-the-art stages.

Year-round children's programs in four age groups include "Coke-tail" parties, kite-flying contests, arts and crafts, bridge tours, and bingo. Baby-sitting is available in the playroom for a nominal charge. The newer ships have teen clubs with video games and music.

Service and Tipping In the past, the pressure to tip on Carnival ships has been considerable. Here, too, the line is working to bring a little more grace to its cruises. Tip the room steward and the waiter $3 each per passenger per diem; the busboy, $1.50. Bellboys, deck stewards, and room-service waiters expect to be tipped at the time of service; 15% is customary. Tip the maître d' and the headwaiter at your own discretion and whenever you request a special service, such as a change in your table assignment. A 15% service charge is automatically added to all bar bills.

Destinations True to its festive reputation, Carnival's ships call on sun-and-fun ports throughout the Caribbean, the Bahamas, and the Mexican Riviera, with one ship spending the summer in Alaska. Occasional cruises to Hawai'i and the Panama Canal are also scheduled. Land/sea packages combine a stay at Walt Disney World or Disneyland with a cruise. Itineraries run from three to 16 days. (For seasonal itineraries, *see* Chapter 4.)

For More Information Carnival Cruise Lines (Carnival Pl., 3655 N.W. 87th Ave., Miami, FL 33178, tel. 305/599–2600).

MS Carnival Destiny and MS Carnival Triumph

Specifications   *Type of ship:* Megaship   *Passengers:* 2,642
                     Cruise experience: Casual   *Crew:* 1,000
                     Size: 101,000 tons   *Officers:* Italian
                     Number of cabins: 1,321   *Passenger/crew ratio:* 2.6 to 1
                     Outside cabins: 60%   *Year built:* 1996

Ship's Log   The *Destiny* and *Triumph* carry 2,642 people based on double occupancy, but when all their third and fourth berths are filled, that number can balloon to 3,400. In keeping with their size, everything on these ships is big: The atrium spans nine decks, the spa sits on two decks, an outdoor water slide stretches 200 ft, and the casino covers 9,000 square ft. There's a two-level dance floor and a three-story theater for Las Vegas–style shows. In fact, among cruise ships in service or under construction today, only Princess Cruises' *Grand Princess* and Royal Caribbean's "Project Eagle" are larger. These are ships with all the bells and whistles—and then some.

The incredible deck area has four swimming pools and seven whirlpools. Two pools have swim-up bars; one has a retractable roof—a great advantage during the inevitable Caribbean rain showers. Inside, there are multiple venues for dining. In addition to the main dining rooms, serving breakfast, lunch, and dinner, and the standard Lido grill for casual fare, such as hamburgers and hot dogs, Carnival has embraced the trend toward alternative restaurants. Specialty foods available aboard the ship include Italian cuisine, served in the Trattoria; Chinese food, served in the Happy Valley restaurant; and a 24-hour pizzeria and patisserie.

In designing these ships, Carnival included plenty to keep children busy, too. Besides the above-mentioned mega–water slide, a Carnival trademark enjoyed by kids of all ages, there is a two-story indoor/outdoor children's play area with its own swimming pool. An arcade has the latest in virtual-reality and electronic games.

Cabins   More than 60% of the cabins have ocean views. Sixty percent of the standard outside cabins and all suites have private balconies. All outside cabins have a sitting area with a sofa and coffee table. Specially designed family staterooms, some with connecting cabins, are conveniently located near the ship's children's facilities.

Outlet voltage: 110 AC.

Single supplement: 150%–200% of double-occupancy rate. Carnival can match up to four same-sex adults in a cabin under its Guaranteed Share Program.

Discounts: A third or fourth passenger in a cabin pays reduced per diems. You get a discount for booking early.

Sports and   **Health club:** Two-level 15,000-square-ft fitness center with gym, aer-
Fitness   obics, massage, men's and women's steam rooms and saunas, fitness machines, two whirlpools, facial and body treatments, juice bar.

Recreation: Aerobics classes, shuffleboard, table tennis, trapshooting, four pools (one with water slide, one with retractable dome, and one children's pool), seven whirlpools, jogging track.

Facilities   **Public rooms:** Eleven bars and lounges, casino, disco, library.

Shops: Boutiques, drugstore, beauty salon/barbershop.

Health care: Doctor and nurse on call.

Carnival Cruise Lines 71

Child care: Two-level indoor/outdoor children's play area with children's pool. Youth programs in four age groups run by counselors, baby-sitting arranged privately with youth counselor. Video arcade with virtual-reality electronic games.

Services: Full- and self-service laundry, photographer, photo studio for portraits.

Accessibility Twenty-three cabins, on Upper, Empress, and Lido decks, are accessible to wheelchair users.

MS Celebration and MS Jubilee

Specifications *Type of ship:* Cruise liner   *Passengers:* 1,486
Cruise experience: Casual   *Crew:* 670 (international)
Size: 47,262 tons   *Officers:* Italian
Number of cabins: 743   *Passenger/crew ratio:* 2.2 to 1
Outside cabins: 61%   *Years built:* 1987/1986

Ship's Log Showy, brassy art; brightly colored walls; neon lights; spectacularly lighted ceilings and floors—when it comes to design and decor, there is nothing subtle about these ships. Just about every decorative material imaginable—wrought iron, stained glass, wood paneling, padded leather, Plexiglas—has been used. There's even a life-size trolley car in the *Celebration*'s Trolley Bar.

The result is overwhelming and is guaranteed to keep your adrenaline flowing from the moment you get up until you collapse into bed. But believe it or not, the *Celebration* and *Holiday* pale in comparison with Carnival's newer extravaganzas.

Cabins Cabins are of similar size, shape, and appearance. Eighty percent of the cabins are beige, with accents of red, black, and some wood tones. Accommodations could use a refurbishment to repair random broken drawers and stained carpeting. The Veranda Suite, however, has a whirlpool and a private balcony. Closed-circuit TV plays films all day and most of the night.

Outlet voltage: 110 AC.

Single supplement: 150%–200% of double-occupancy rate. Carnival can match up to four same-sex adults in a cabin under its Guaranteed Share Program.

Discounts: A third or fourth passenger in a cabin pays reduced per diems. You get a discount for booking early.

Sports and Fitness **Health club:** Tiny gym with exercise equipment; men's and women's spas with whirlpools, saunas, facial- and body-treatment center.

Recreation: Aerobics classes, shuffleboard, table tennis, trapshooting, two pools, children's wading pool, unobstructed circuit for jogging.

Facilities **Public rooms:** Seven bars, six entertainment lounges, casino, disco, library, card room, video-game room.

Shops: Gift shops, beauty salon/barbershop.

Health care: Doctor and nurse on call.

Child care: Playroom, youth programs in four age groups run by counselors, baby-sitting arranged privately with youth counselor.

Services: Full- and self-service laundry, photographer.

Accessibility Fourteen cabins on each ship are accessible to wheelchair users.

MS Ecstasy, MS Elation, MS Fantasy, MS Fascination, MS Imagination, MS Inspiration, MS Paradise, and MS Sensation

Specifications

Type of ship: Megaship
Cruise experience: Casual
Crew: 920 (international)
Officers: Italian
Outside cabins: 61%

Passengers: 2,040/2,044 (Fantasy)
Size: 70,367 tons
Number of cabins: 1,020/1,022 (Fantasy)
Passenger/crew ratio: 2.2 to 1
Years built: 1990–1998

Ship's Log

These eight ships, the mainstays of the Carnival fleet, appeal to the kind of crowd that loves Atlantic City and Las Vegas. They are identical in all but decor, although all share the marble, brass, mirrors, and electric lights that heighten Carnival's now-notorious hyperactivity. In addition to Olympic-size pools, the ships also have unique banked and padded jogging tracks with a special surface; their casinos and fitness centers are among the largest afloat. Each is built around a central, seven-story atrium.

Big, bright, bold, and brassy, the *Fantasy* lives up to its name, resembling a series of fantastic Hollywood sets rather than a cruise ship. Twenty-four kilometers (15 miles) of bright neon tubing snake through the ship. The public rooms are lavishly decorated in elaborate motifs; the Cats Lounge, for example, was inspired by the famous musical, and Cleopatra's Bar re-creates the interior of an Egyptian tomb.

The *Ecstasy* and *Sensation* are less futuristic and more elegant. The *Ecstasy*'s cityscape motif links the public areas: City Lights Boulevard evokes an urban street scene, the Rolls Royce Café is built around an antique Rolls, the Metropolis Bar is home to a skyscraperlike neon sculpture, and the entrance to the Chinatown lounge is guarded by twin lion-head foo dog sculptures reminiscent of ancient China. The *Sensation* takes a more subtle approach. Public rooms indulge the senses with lush greenery and carved wood in the Oak Room or a copy of the sculpture *David* in the Michelangelo Lounge. A portal of arched hands invites passengers to enter the Touch of Class piano bar, where passengers sit in the palms of still more hands.

The *Fascination* takes the movie-set theme quite literally: Public rooms evoke a Hollywood motif, and likenesses of Tinseltown legends populate its salons and lounges. Life-size figures portray Marilyn Monroe, James Dean, Bette Davis, Gary Cooper, John Wayne, and Humphrey Bogart—just to name a few.

The *Imagination*'s interior reaches deep into the past and peeks far into the future for its imagery. Symbols of antiquity—sphinxes, Medusas, and winged Mercury figures—evoke a classical ambience, while spaceships represent the dawn of the computer age. The casino is equipped with vintage slot machines from the 1930s and '40s, while the library creates a Victorian feel with its 19th-century European antiques. In the Candlelight Lounge, hundreds of electric candlesticks create a moody ambience for the room's late-night entertainment.

The *Inspiration* draws its decor from muses of the past, too. An avant-garde interpretation of the *Mona Lisa* and quotes from Shakespeare, painted on the library ceiling, are among the ship's more noteworthy design flourishes.

The mythical muses inspired the decor aboard the *Elation*. Symbols taken from Greek mythology appear throughout the ship, and real-life people who were inspired by the muses are celebrated in lounges such as the "Duke's," named in tribute to jazz great Duke Ellington.

The eighth and final ship in the Fantasy series, the *Paradise*, was at press time scheduled to make its debut in late 1998 as the world's first smoke-free cruise ship—even out on deck.

Cabins   Cabins are decorated in bright colors and wood tones. Each is quite spacious, with closed-circuit TV and private safes. Veranda Suites and Demi Suites have private balconies, wet bars, and VCRs. Veranda Suites have tubs with whirlpool jets. Some outside cabins on the Veranda Deck have partially obstructed views.

Outlet voltage: 110 AC.

Single supplement: 150%–200% of double-occupancy rate. Carnival can match up to four same-sex adults in a cabin under its Guaranteed Share Program.

Discounts: A third or fourth passenger in a cabin pays reduced per diems. You get a discount for booking early.

Sports and Fitness   **Health club:** Gym, aerobics room, massage room, women's and men's locker rooms with steam rooms and saunas, fitness machines, two whirlpools, facial and body treatments.

Recreation: Aerobics classes, shuffleboard, table tennis, trapshooting, two outdoor pools (one with slide), children's wading pool, four outdoor whirlpools, banked jogging track (11 laps = 1½ km/1 mi).

Facilities   **Public rooms:** Nine bars and lounges, casino, disco, card room, library.

Shops: Boutiques, drugstore, beauty salon/barbershop.

Health care: Doctor and nurse on call.

Child care: Two playrooms, teen center (with video games), youth programs in four age groups run by counselors, baby-sitting arranged privately with youth counselor.

Services: Full- and self-service laundry, photographer.

Accessibility   Twenty cabins, all on the Empress Deck of each ship, are accessible to wheelchair users.

MS Holiday

Specifications

Type of ship: Cruise liner	*Passengers:* 1,452
Cruise experience: Casual	*Crew:* 660 (international)
Size: 46,052 tons	*Officers:* Italian
Number of cabins: 726	*Passenger/crew ratio:* 2.2 to 1
Outside cabins: 62%	*Year built:* 1985

Ship's Log   One of the first generation of "superliners" built for Carnival, the *Holiday* was the forerunner of the line's megaships, although like the *Celebration* and *Jubiliee*, it's now almost quaint by Carnival standards. On the outside it ushered in the age of boxy hulls and superstructures that rise straight out of the water. Inside, it took Carnival's palatial, theme-park atmosphere to new extremes. A bar called the Bus Stop has red-top luncheonette stools, traffic signs, and an actual red-and-white bus from the 1930s. Another bar, Carnegie's, has the luxurious look of a private club, with overstuffed leather chairs and sofas and glass-door library shelves.

Rick's American Café is straight from *Casablanca*. The *Holiday* ushered in Carnival's first extra-wide, enclosed walkway that runs along the port side of the Promenade Deck. The teak passageway called Broadway connects the casino and all the bars and lounges on the deck. The main entertainment lounge, the Americana, is a six-level, curved room that accommodates more than 900 passengers. The Gaming Club Casino has more than 100 slot machines and 250 seats. For high-tech fun, there's a $1 million entertainment center, complete with the latest virtual-reality and video games.

Cabins The slightly larger-than-average cabins are appointed in bright colors and wood tones. The Veranda Suites have a sitting room, private balcony, and whirlpool. All cabins have wall safes.

Outlet voltage: 110 AC.

Single supplement: 150%–200% of double-occupancy rate. Carnival can match up to four same-sex adults in a cabin under its Guaranteed Share Program.

Discounts: A third or fourth passenger in a cabin pays reduced per diems. You get a discount for booking early.

Sports and Fitness **Health club:** Exercise equipment, spas with whirlpools, sauna, massage room, facial- and body-treatment center.

Recreation: Aerobics, shuffleboard, table tennis, trapshooting, two outdoor pools, wading pool, unobstructed circuit for jogging.

Facilities **Public rooms:** Seven bars, three entertainment lounges, casino, disco, library, virtual-reality and video-game room.

Shops: Boutique, gift shop, beauty salon/barbershop.

Health care: Doctor and nurse on call.

Child care: Playroom, youth programs in four age groups run by counselors, baby-sitting arranged privately with youth counselor.

Services: Full- and self-service laundry, photographer.

Accessibility Fifteen cabins are accessible to wheelchair users.

MS Tropicale

Specifications

Type of ship: Cruise liner	*Passengers:* 1,022
Cruise experience: Casual	*Crew:* 550 (international)
Size: 36,674 tons	*Officers:* Italian
Number of cabins: 511	*Passenger/crew ratio:* 1.9 to 1
Outside cabins: 63%	*Year built:* 1981

Ship's Log The *Tropicale* has been a very influential ship because of its resort-like qualities. Responding to passenger suggestions, Carnival created a vessel ideal for cruising, with plenty of open space; a good choice of bars, lounges, and play areas; and a spectacular swimming pool. From the outside, the *Tropicale* is recognizable by its clean lines; sloping superstructure; oversize portholes; and the raked, double-winged funnel near the stern. The interior is ultramodern and spans the entire spectrum of colors. The Exta-Z Disco's dance floor, for instance, is alive with red and yellow lights, the elaborate ceiling with blue, green, and red neon lights. Indirect lighting sets a more appetizing mood in the Riviera Restaurant, which, with its rattan furniture, resembles a tropical grand hotel.

Cabins Cabins are of similar size and appearance, comfortable and larger than average; the majority have twin beds that can be made into a king. Decor is a mix of bright colors and wood tones. Veranda

Suites have private balconies. Most outside cabins have large square windows rather than portholes.

Outlet voltage: 110 AC.

Single supplement: 150%–200% of double-occupancy rate. Carnival can match up to four same-sex adults in a cabin under its Guaranteed Share Program.

Discounts: A third or fourth passenger in a cabin pays reduced per diems. You get a discount for booking early.

Sports and Fitness

Health club: Exercise equipment, men's and women's saunas and massage rooms, facial- and body-treatment center.

Recreation: Aerobics classes, shuffleboard, table tennis, trapshooting, two pools, wading pool, small but unobstructed circuit for jogging.

Facilities

Public rooms: Six bars and lounges, casino, disco, card room, library, video-game room.

Shops: Gift shops, beauty salon/barbershop.

Health care: Doctor and nurse on call.

Child care: Playroom, youth programs in three age groups run by counselors, baby-sitting arranged privately with youth counselor.

Services: Full- and self-service laundry, photographer.

Accessibility Eleven cabins are accessible to wheelchair users.

Celebrity Cruises

The Fleet MV *Century*
MV *Galaxy*
MV *Horizon*
MV *Mercury*
MV *Zenith*

Celebrity likes to say that it doesn't build "cookie-cutter" ships, and indeed, each vessel has its own identity. Style and layout vary from ship to ship, lending each a distinct personality. This is especially true of the line's newer, bigger ships. Compared with sister line Royal Caribbean, the ships of Celebrity are decidedly more avante-garde. Yet they share the latest high-tech features, including interactive television systems and elaborate spas. Dining rooms and showrooms span two decks, and many cabins have private balconies.

Ships at a Glance

	Dining Rooms	Bars	Casino	Fitness Center	Pools	Average Per Diem
Century	2*	11	●	●	2/3/3	$200–$300
Galaxy/Mercury						
Horizon/Zenith	2*	9/7	●	●	2	$200–$300

*includes alternative dining in the casual restaurant

Cruise Experience Celebrity Cruises has made a name for itself based on sleek ships and superior food (*see* Dining, *below*). In terms of size and amenities, Celebrity's ships rival almost any in cruising, but with a level of refinement rare on bigger ships. Celebrity has in just a short time won the admiration of its passengers and its competitors—who have copied its nouvelle cousine, cigar clubs, and hired its personnel (a true compliment).

Celebrity attracts everyone from older couples to honeymooners. The summertime children's programs are among the best on board any upscale cruise line.

Activities Though not party ships, Celebrity packs plenty of fun. Activities include pool and card games, shuffleboard, snorkeling instruction, "horse racing," trapshooting, and golf putting. Passengers are not pressured to participate, and many choose to read or relax on their own in a lounge chair.

Dining Celebrity has risen nicely above typical cruise cuisine by hiring chef Michel Roux, proprietor of two of Britain's finest restaurants, as a consultant. Roux's experience in creating and cooking for large numbers of discriminating diners has been put to good use. Menus are creative; both familiar and exotic dishes have been customized to appeal to the mellow palate of American cruisers. To keep things fresh, the menus change frequently. At least one "lean and light" entrée is offered at every meal. A complete vegetarian menu is available for lunch and dinner. Dinner is at two assigned seatings (6:15 and 8:30). Two formal evenings are held each cruise. Special diets, such as kosher or salt-free, can be catered to when booked in advance or with the maître d' on the day of sailing.

There are no specialty restaurants for alternative dining aboard Celebrity's ships, but at press time, the line planned to add a second dinner option, served buffet-style, in its casual restaurants. On the *Century, Galaxy,* and *Mercury,* pizza is served poolside in the afternoons and late evening (it can also be delivered to your cabin in a pizzeria-style box); a frozen yogurt and ice-cream bar serves afternoon snacks, too. Celebrity has also put a new and typically stylish twist on the traditional midnight buffet. On two nights of every week at sea, dishes of "Gourmet Bites" are placed at strategic locations throughout the ship. The "Bites" include hot and cold buffets, carving stations, and pastry tables. White-gloved waiters circulate through the public rooms, serving from trays of selected delicacies. Limited room service is available 24 hours.

Entertainment Celebrity's ships present lavish, if predictable, variety shows, but there are innovative touches, too. At press time, the line was experimenting with roaming magicians and a cappella groups who float from lounge to lounge doing short performances before and after dinner. Smaller lounges offer low-key jazz and big-band music. Karaoke parties are popular, and the discos rock until 3 AM.

Service and Service is friendly and first class—rapid and accurate in the din-
Tipping ing room, but sometimes slower and uneven in the bars. Waiters, stewards, and bartenders are enthusiastic, take pride in their work, and try to please. Tip your room steward and your waiter $3 each per passenger per diem, the busboy $1.50. Bar stewards should be tipped 15% of the bill at the time of service.

Destinations Cruises to the Caribbean are scheduled year-round. Other destinations include Alaska, Bermuda, the Panama Canal, and South America. (For seasonal itineraries, *see* Chapter 4.)

For More Celebrity Cruises (5201 Blue Lagoon Dr., Miami, FL 33126, tel.
Information 800/437–3111).

MV Century, MV Galaxy, and MV Mercury

Specifications *Type of ship:* Megaship   *Passengers:* 1,750/1,870/1,888
Cruise experience: Semiformal   *Crew:* 858/909/909 (interna-
Size: 70,606 tons/77,713 tons/   tional)
77,713 tons   *Officers:* Greek
Number of cabins: 875/935/935   *Passenger/crew ratio:* 2.1 to 1
Outside cabins: 65%/68%/68%   *Years built:* 1995/1996/1997

Ship's Log The *Century* and its sisters are designed to appeal to both present-day and 21st-century cruisers. They have public rooms to satisfy virtually every taste, from the cozy to the trendy. Unlike their predecessors the *Horizon* and *Zenith,* the *Century*-class ships have glass-domed atrium lobbies. Other design departures from their fleetmates are a bilevel dining room whose ceilings rise two stories high and a two-deck theater with a stage large enough for full-scale musical productions. Elaborate spas are among the largest and best equipped in cruising. Known as the "Aqua Spa" they measure more than 10,000 square ft; each has a 15,000 gallon Thalassotherapy pool and the latest spa treatments. On the *Mercury,* exercise equipment includes virtual-reality stationary bikes and a roller-blading simulator. The ships'collections of modern art are among the most original (and strangest) at sea. Throughout the ships, video screens and "video wallpaper" present passengers with a constant array of visual images.

Passengers who have sailed aboard the *Horizon* or the *Zenith* will nevertheless find themselves in familiar surroundings. The main public lounges—the forward observation lounge/disco, cocktail lounge amidships, and cabaret lounge at the stern—are all based on similar rooms aboard the line's earlier ships.

The *Century*, first in this ship-of-the-future series, was designed with the most elaborate high-tech features. Monitors in the elevators tell passengers the time, date, and next stop. For kids of all ages, the *Century* has an arcade with 34 video games. Images, a lively "video bar," is as colorful as it sounds. In the disco, a space-age saucer rises to reveal the dance floor.

The *Galaxy*, meanwhile, has its share of high-tech touches, but more impressive is its aura of traditional elegance. In a way, the decor of the *Galaxy* takes Celebrity back to its original aesthetics: Greco-Roman imagery sprinkled liberally into a postmodern setting. It works especially well in the *Galaxy*'s Grand Foyer atrium, where a three-story-tall classic painting in a gilded frame can be electronically transformed into a patchwork of video screens. Another Celebrity trademark is to mix styles, and on the *Galaxy* this is done to great effect. Art deco dominates the showroom; art nouveau distinguishes the Savoy nightclub; and a Scandinavian style highlights the Stratosphere disco.

The *Mercury*, launched in late 1997, is the third and final ship in the Century-trilogy. Unlike its sisters, the *Mercury* displays more uniformity in its decor than do the *Century* and *Galaxy*. A Scandinavian mood ties links the major public rooms, creating a mood that's warm but sparse. In appointing the *Mercury*, the ship's designers drew upon a palette of alternating blond and dark woods, Nordic-style furnishings, and geometric shapes. Public rooms vary between earth tones and bold primary colors, but in either case the feeling of Northern European cool prevails. Following the theme begun with the *Century*, there's a smattering of "video art," but Celebrity has toned this down with each succeeding ship. On the *Mercury*, it's virtually inconspicuous.

Cabins Standard cabins are intelligently appointed and apportioned. Space is well used, making for maximum elbow room in the bathrooms and good storage space in the closets. The decor is clean and crisp, dispensing with fluff and frills. Private verandas are more numerous on the *Galaxy* and *Mercury* (34% of outside cabins) than on the *Century* (11% of outside cabins). Each deck on the *Century* has been given its own color scheme, and every cabin is decorated in corresponding colors. All categories have a built-in minibar and a recessed nook for a 20-inch TV. All outside cabins also have a small sitting area. Bathtubs in the Royal and Penthouse suites have whirlpool jets and large verandas.

Outlet voltage: 110/220 AC.

Single supplement: 150%–200% of double-occupancy rate.

Discounts: A third or fourth passenger in a cabin pays reduced per diems. Children 2–12 traveling with two full-paying adults pay reduced per diems. Children under two travel free. You get a discount for booking early.

Sports and Fitness

Health club: Aerobics, stationary bikes, weight machines, free weights, treadmills, rowing machines, saunas, massage rooms, steam rooms, spa treatments.

Recreation: Electronic golf simulator, shuffleboard, table tennis, trapshooting, swimming, volleyball, basketball, exercise classes, jogging track, two pools (three on *Galaxy* and *Mercury*).

Facilities

Public rooms: Eleven bars, four entertainment lounges, casino, cinema, card room, library, video-game room, conference center.

Shops: Atrium boutiques.

Health care: Doctor on call.

Child care: Playroom with interactive computer center, supervised children's program in four age groups, children's pool, baby-sitting arranged with crew member.

Services: Photographer, laundry service, dry cleaning, beauty shop/barber.

Accessibility

Elevators and eight cabins are accessible to wheelchair users.

MV Horizon and MV Zenith

Specifications

Type of ship: Cruise liner
Cruise experience: Semiformal
Size: 46,811 tons/47,255 tons
Number of cabins: 677/687
Outside cabins: 79%/84%

Passengers: 1,354/1,374
Crew: 642/657 (international)
Officers: Greek
Passenger/crew ratio: 2.1 to 1
Years built: 1990/1992

Ship's Log

Big when they were built but just midsize now, these sisters give passengers a somewhat more intimate alternative to Celebrity's expansive megaships. The interiors are indisputably gracious, airy, and comfortable. The design makes the most of natural light through strategically placed oversize windows. The nine passenger decks sport several bars and entertainment lounges, and ample deck space. Wide corridors, broad staircases, seven elevators, and well-placed signs make it easy to get around. Decor is contemporary and attractive, and the artwork is pleasant rather than memorable. The Zenith has a slightly different layout from that of its sister ship: There are two fewer bars—though some have been enlarged—more suites, a larger health club, more deck space, and a meeting room.

Cabins

The cabins are modern and quite roomy. Furnishings include a night stand, a desk, and a small glass-top coffee table. Closets are reasonably large, as are bathrooms. Bedtime readers will find the lone lamp on the night stand insufficient, especially in rooms with double beds. Every cabin is equipped with a television showing CNN and other broadcasts. The suites are enormous. They have large sitting areas, tubs with whirlpool jets, 24-hour room service, and a private butler. The view from many outside cabins on the Bermuda Deck is partially obstructed by lifeboats.

Outlet voltage: 110/220 AC.

Single supplement: 150%–200% of double-occupancy rate.

Discounts: A third or fourth passenger in a cabin pays reduced per diems. Children 2–12 traveling with two full-paying adults pay reduced per diems. Children under two travel free. You get a discount for booking early.

Sports and Fitness **Health club:** Bright, sunny upper-deck spa with sauna, massage, weight machines, stationary bicycles, rowing machine, stair climber, treadmill, separate mirrored aerobics area, massage, facial/body treatments.

Recreation: Exercise classes, putting green, shuffleboard, trap-shooting, table tennis, two pools, three whirlpools, unobstructed circuit (5 laps = 1½ km/1 mi) for jogging.

Facilities **Public rooms:** Nine bars and lounges (*Horizon*) or seven bars and lounges (*Zenith*), showroom, casino, disco, card room, library/reading room, video-game room.

Shops: Gift shop, boutique, perfume shop, cigarette/liquor store, photo shop.

Health care: Doctor and nurse on call.

Child care: Playroom, teen room on Sun Deck, youth programs in four age groups supervised by counselors in summer (*Zenith*), baby-sitting arranged with crew member.

Services: Photographer, laundry service, beauty shop/barber.

Accessibility Four cabins are accessible to wheelchair users. Specially equipped public elevators are 35½ inches wide, but certain public areas may not be wide enough for wheelchairs.

Clipper Cruise Line

The Fleet MV *Clipper Adventurer*
MV *Nantucket Clipper*
MV *Yorktown Clipper*

The yachtlike *Nantucket Clipper* and *Yorktown Clipper* are small, stylish coastal cruisers with a casual sophistication. With their shallow drafts and inflatable, motorized landing craft, they are well suited to exploring remote and otherwise inaccessible waters. Neither has an ice-hardened hull, so they stick to temperate or tropical waters. For true expedition cruising, Clipper was scheduled to add the *Clipper Adventurer* in April 1998. The ship, formerly a Russian vessel refitted to modern cruise standards, will be able to sail to the Arctic and Antarctica, and will include a library, a gym, and a sauna—facilities not found on the more intimate *Nantucket* and *Yorktown*.

Ships at a Glance

	Dining Rooms	Bars	Casino	Fitness Center	Pools	Average Per Diem
Clipper Adventurer	1	1/2	○	◑	0	$300–$400
Nantucket Clipper *Yorktown Clipper*	1	1/2	○	○	0	$200–$300

Cruise Experience Clipper Cruise Line's sailings come under the general category of "soft adventure," but these are adventures that don't sacrifice aesthetics. The vessels are nicely appointed, and the line emphasizes such shipboard refinements as fine dining, although the service is not of the white-glove variety.

Compared with other small ship lines, Clipper's Caribbean and East Coast experience is more sophisticated and service-oriented than life aboard an American Canadian Caribbean Line vessel. In Alaska, Clipper combines the creature comforts of Alaska Sightseeing with the educational emphasis of Special Expeditions. Passengers are older (typically in their mid-sixties), wealthier, and better educated than the average cruise passenger.

In the polar regions, the *Clipper Adventurer* is in the same league with Abercrombie & Kent's *Explorer* and Society Expedition's *World Discoverer*, but is less luxurious than the *Hanseatic*.

Activities Clipper is noted for its cultural bent, and on each cruise a naturalist, historian, or other expert leads lectures and field trips. All itineraries—whether inland or polar—include a full range of organized shore excursions. Apart from these occasional talks and outings, onboard organized activities are few. Board games and card games are popular, but reading and socializing are the main onboard activities. In the Caribbean, snorkeling off the side of the ship is popular.

The line provides excellent and thorough information to passengers prior to departure; once aboard, the knowledgeable crew offers advice as to what and what not to see in port.

Dining Clipper's American cuisine is quite good, with regional and vegetarian specialties. There is also a superb pastry chef aboard. Dinner (at 7:30) is served at one open seating. There are two "dressy" evenings per cruise, where a jacket but no tie is appropriate. Special dietary requests should be made in writing three weeks before departure; no kosher meals are available. Other food service includes an expanded Continental breakfast served in the Observation Lounge and freshly baked chocolate-chip cookies available in the afternoon. Fresh fruit can be had at any time; juice, coffee, tea, and hot chocolate are available 24 hours from a dispensing machine in the lounge. Specialty coffees, such as espresso and cappuccino, are available on request from lounge attendants or from the dining room staff at mealtimes, but there is no room service.

Entertainment There are no discos, casinos, or musical revues aboard Clipper's ships. Though local entertainers sometimes perform on board and movies may be shown after dinner on a retractable screen in the dining room, evenings are low-key; socializing in the lounge over drinks is about as rowdy as this crowd usually gets. Many passengers venture ashore to enjoy the nightlife or take evening strolls.

Service and Tipping It isn't unusual for Clipper's repeat passengers to choose the line for the extraordinary courtesies and care extended by the attentive staff and crew. Though small, the American staff (American and Filipino on the *Clipper Adventurer*) is young, energetic, and capable, working nicely together to provide good service without lobbying for tips. On the last evening passengers may leave tips in an envelope on the purser's desk (tip $9 per passenger per diem); these are pooled and distributed.

Destinations Clipper's coastal ships sail throughout the Americas. On the Atlantic coast, its programs stretch the length of the Eastern seaboard from New England and Canada to the Southeast's Intracoastal Waterway. Some sailings venture as far as the Caribbean or Central and South America. Midcontinental cruises explore the Great Lakes on both sides of the border. In western North America, the line has sailings from the Baja Peninsula to the California wine country and north to Alaska.

The *Clipper Adventurer* goes further afield: its itineraries range from Antarctica to the Canadian Arctic, and to Iceland, Greenland, and Northern Europe. (For seasonal itineraries, *see* Chapter 4.)

For More Information Clipper Cruise Line (7711 Bonhomme Ave., St. Louis, MO 63105, tel. 800/325–0010).

MV Clipper Adventurer

Specifications

Type of ship: Expedition	*Passengers:* 122
Cruise experience: Casual	*Crew:* 58 (American/Filipino)
Size: 4,364 tons	*Officers:* Scandinavian
Number of cabins: 61	*Passenger/crew ratio:* 2 to 1
Outside cabins: 100%	*Year built:* 1975 (rebuilt 1998)

Ship's Log Considerably larger than her coastal fleetmates, the *Clipper Adventurer* offers an observation lounge that seats all passengers for informal talks, a separate lounge bar on the same deck, and a serious library on the deck above. The single-seating dining room has windows on three sides, and the wide, wooden enclosed promenade deck is a big plus for cruising in cooler weather, such as found in Antarctica and the Canadian Arctic—two of the ship's primary destinations. An observation platform below the bridge and ahead of the superstructure gives unimpeded views forward. The ship also has laundry service—another nice plus.

Cabins The all outside cabins are located mostly amidships or slightly forward on all four passenger decks. Nine face the enclosed promenade, and the cabin windows, with shades, line up with the promenade deck windows. Three suites are up on the Boat Deck. None of the cabins have televisions, but all have hair dryers.

Outlet voltage: 220 AC.

Single supplement: 150%.

Discounts: Third passenger in cabin pays reduced per diem.

Sports and Fitness **Recreation:** Gym with weights, treadmill, stationary bicycle, sauna.

Facilities **Public rooms:** Observation lounge and bar, club lounge and bar, library.

Shops: Gift shop, beauty shop.

Health care: Doctor on call.

Child care: None.

Services: Laundry service.

Accessibility This ship is not recommended for wheelchair users.

MV Nantucket Clipper and MV Yorktown Clipper

Specifications *Type of ship:* Coastal cruiser
Cruise experience: Casual
Size: 95 tons/97 tons
Number of cabins: 51/69
Outside cabins: 100%

Passengers: 102/138
Crew: 32/40 (American)
Officers: American
Passenger/crew ratio: 3.2 to 1/3.5 to 1
Years built: 1984/1988

Ship's Log The *Clippers* look more like boxy yachts than cruise ships. Their signature design is dominated by a large bridge and large picture windows that ensure bright interior public spaces. As with all small ships, there are only two public rooms and deck space is limited. However, the cozy quarters engender a camaraderie and familiarity among passengers that you're unlikely to find on a big liner. The glass-walled Observation Lounge, for example, does double duty as the ship's bar and lecture room. Such close quarters can also seem claustrophobic at times, due to the lack of an alternative lounge. Get to dinner early and avoid tables at the rear of the dining room (nearest the engines). They tend to be noisy, even when the ship is in port, and since dinner is open seating, they're often the last seats left.

Cabins The all-outside cabins are small. How the designers stuffed two beds, a dresser, a desk, a bathroom, and a closet into such a tiny space is a great mystery. However, the larger top-deck staterooms are actually quite commodious. Nicely finished in pastel fabrics and accented with blond woods and prints on the walls, all the cabins make a comfortable home at sea. Most have a picture-window view; a few have portholes. Category 2 cabins open onto the public promenade.

Outlet voltage: 110 AC.

Single supplement: Single-occupancy cabins are available, depending on the itinerary.

Discounts: Third passenger in cabin pays reduced per diem.

Sports and Fitness **Recreation:** Snorkeling equipment and instruction, unobstructed circuit for walking; no organized deck sports or facilities.

Facilities **Public rooms:** Small lounge with TV serves as living room, bar, outdoor deck bar (*Yorktown* only), card room, and entertainment center.

Shops: Souvenir items available.

Health care: None.

Accessibility There are no facilities specifically equipped for wheelchair users. Access to Sun Deck cabins is by a heavy exterior fire door, which may present difficulties for passengers with mobility problems.

Crystal Cruises

The Fleet *Crystal Harmony*
Crystal Symphony

Counted among the world's most luxurious ocean liners, the Crystal fleet stands out for its modern design and amenities. The vessels were built to deliver the first-rate service of a luxury small ship with the onboard facilities of a big ship. This spaciousness, which includes two full ocean liner–size decks of public rooms, is Crystal's greatest strength.

Ships at a Glance

	Dining Rooms	Bars	Casino	Fitness Center	Pools	Average Per Diem
Crystal Harmony	3*	7	●	●	2	$400–$500
Crystal Symphony	3*	6	●	●	2	$600–$700

*includes two alternative restaurants

Cruise Experience Crystal is pure California: Based in Los Angeles, it has more panache and style than virtually any other cruise line. The ships are elegant, service is white glove, and the itineraries wide-ranging. Even the tenders that take passengers to shore are top-of-the-line, with air-conditioning and toilet facilities.

The atmosphere and attitude aboard ship is clubby, but clubby in the way the Beverly Hills Hotel is: If you're on the passenger list, you're an insider. Of course, membership in this exclusive circle does not come cheaply. However, Crystal has a rather reasonable single-supplement policy; most cabins are priced at a 20% to 25% surcharge over the standard double-occupancy rate.

About the only flaw in Crystal's finely conceived and executed concept lies in its dining-room arrangements (*see* Dining, *below*) and its tipping policy (*see* Service and Tipping, *below*).

Activities To the typical litany of ocean-liner diversions, Crystal adds destination-oriented lectures and talks on other subjects by scholars, political figures, and diplomats. The ships also carry fully equipped fitness centers and casinos, another advantage over Crystal's small-ship competitors. The casinos are operated under the auspices of Caesars Palace. A PGA golf instructor accompanies most cruises, as does an ACBL bridge instructor. On certain sailings, guest chefs and wine experts are aboard to give demonstrations, conduct tastings, and prepare a gala dinner one evening.

Dining Crystal offers very good dining for a cruise ship. It's better in the alternative dining rooms. Unlike other lines in this price category, Crystal seats passengers for dinner in two seatings (6:30 and 8:30). On any night passengers may also choose to dine in a Japanese restaurant on the *Harmony* or in a Chinese restaurant aboard the *Symphony*. A third choice, the Prego Italian restaurant, is found on both ships. Although the line promotes these restaurants as alternatives to dinner in the main dining room, in reality only about 300 passengers per ship can be accommodated in the main room on any given night. And while there is officially no extra charge for dining in one of the alternative restaurants, passengers do receive a tab of $5 per person at the end of the meal to cover "gratuities."

Meals in the main dining room tend to feature regionally inspired dishes with a contemporary twist. For example, the Chateau Brillon is accented with spices from the Pacific Rim. Great attention to detail is paid to every nuance of the dining experience: The place settings are perhaps the nicest in cruising. To complement dinner, each ship has an extensive wine cellar. Three formal nights are scheduled every seven to 10 days, but men wear a jacket to dinner virtually every night.

Other food-service options include the canopy-covered, indoor-outdoor Lido Cafe, which serves breakfast, bouillon, and lunch. The Trident Bar and Grill serves hot dogs, hamburgers, sandwiches, and pizza. The Bistro sells specialty coffees and wine and serves pâté and international cheeses. Room service is available 24 hours a day. Passengers can order from the full dining-room menu at lunch and dinner; a limited menu is served in-cabin at non-mealtimes.

Entertainment Here again, Crystal offers much more than its small-ship competitors with more refinement than many other big ships. There are cabarets and production-style revues in the main lounge that are more Broadway than Vegas. The handmade costumes are show-stoppers in their own right. In other lounges, a pianist or a classical trio from the Julliard School in Manhattan may be performing. Each ship has a theater for showing movies. And, of course, there are the casinos. Gentlemen hosts sail aboard the ship to act as dancing partners for single ladies traveling alone.

Service and Tipping Crystal's staff members are well trained, friendly, highly motivated, and thoroughly professional. However, tips are not included in the cruise fare, and the crew can be noticeably solicitous of gratuities. Recommended amounts are: Tip the steward and the waiter $4 each per passenger per diem, the assistant waiter $2.50

Destinations Although Crystal only has two ships, they cover a lot of ground. Destinations include the Caribbean, Europe, Alaska, Mexico, South America, Asia, and the Panama Canal. (For seasonal itineraries, *see* Chapter 4.)

For More Information Crystal Cruises (2121 Ave. of the Stars, Los Angeles, CA 90067, tel. 800/446–6620).

Crystal Harmony and Crystal Symphony

Specifications *Type of ship:* Cruise liner
Cruise experience: Formal
Size: 49,400 tons/51,044 tons
Number of cabins: 480
Outside cabins: 96%/100%

Passengers: 940
Crew: 545/530 (European)
Officers: Norwegian and Japanese
Passenger/crew ratio: 1.7 to 1
Years built: 1990/1995

Ship's Log The *Crystal Harmony*'s sleek and sophisticated exterior harbors a classy, uncluttered interior. About the best thing about this ship is its roominess: Never, ever is there a feeling of brushing shoulders with anyone, either in the public rooms or in the halls. Adding to the sense of space is the unobtrusive decor: Colors are pale, plants predominate, and here and there you'll find unobtrusive but interesting neoclassical sculptures. It's the type of ship where you'd expect to see a movie star—and sipping a cosmopolitan in the white-leather Vista Lounge, you might just feel like one yourself.

The *Crystal Harmony* has been kept fresh and up-to-date with several refurbishments since it was launched in 1990. The most recent, at the end of 1997, paid careful attention to lower deck cabins, which now sport the same decor as the more expensive upper-deck categories. Also included in the renovation was new equipment for the spa, a new sound-and-light system for the main showroom, and other refinements throughout the ship from the library to the piano bar.

The *Crystal Symphony*, meanwhile, is the biggest ship to be built with all outside cabins since the *Royal Princess* (*see* Princess Cruises). Inside, it differs from its sibling in a lighter color scheme for the decor and several larger public rooms. Repeat Crystal passengers will find that their favorite rooms, such as the Palm Court, alternative restaurants, casino, bistro, and Lido Cafe, have been expanded. The *Symphony*'s two-story atrium is twice the size of the same space aboard the *Harmony*.

Several years after it was launched, the *Symphony* still looks brand new. The inside and outside are meticulously maintained. There are few visible signs of rust; metal surfaces are newly painted and wood surfaces are freshly varnished—the way a ship should be. Carpeting and upholstery are obviously being replaced on a regular basis, which keeps the ship looking young.

Cabins Thanks to the skillful use of paneling and mirrors, the large accommodations appear even larger. Cabins are appointed similarly on both ships, although standard cabins on the newer *Symphony* are more conveniently arranged and have better storage space. The *Symphony* also has slightly more cabins with private verandah (58% versus 54%). Cabins in every category are beautifully decorated and equipped with 14-channel TVs (including CNN), VCRs, hair dryers, and robes. Other standard amenities and creature comforts include voice mail, goose-down pillows, fine linens, thick bath towels, and in-cabin safes. Penthouses have verandas and Jacuzzis (butler service is available). Some cabins on the Horizon and Promenade decks have obstructed views (Crystal's brochures clearly identify rooms with limited views). Cabins on the Promenade Deck look out onto a public walkway.

Outlet voltage: 110/220 AC.

Single supplement: 120%–200% of double-occupancy rate.

Discounts: A third passenger in a cabin pays the minimum per-person fare for that cruise. Children under 12 with two full-paying adults pay half the minimum per-person fare. You get a discount for booking early, paying early, and for booking a future cruise while on board. Repeat passengers get a 5% discount.

Sports and Fitness **Health club:** Fitness center with stationary bikes, rowing machines, stair climbers, treadmills, weight machines, free weights, saunas, steam rooms, massage, exercise classes, personal fitness trainers, weight-reduction regimens, body and facial care, makeup services.

Recreation: Aerobics, jazz-dance, exercise classes, paddle tennis, shuffleboard, golf driving, putting green, table tennis, two pools (one for laps), two whirlpools, unobstructed circuit for jogging.

Facilities **Public rooms:** Seven bars (*Harmony*), six bars (*Symphony*), six entertainment lounges, casino, disco, cinema, card room, library (books and videotapes), video-game room, smoking room.

Shops: Shopping arcade of boutiques, beauty salon/barbershop.

Health care: Doctors and nurses on call.

Child care: Youth programs with counselors during holidays or whenever a large number of children are on board, baby-sitting arranged privately with crew members.

Services: Concierge service, full- and self-service laundry, dry cleaning, photographer, video-camera rentals, film processing, secretarial and photocopying services, translation equipment for meetings.

Accessibility Two standard cabins on the *Harmony* and five standard cabins on the *Symphony* are accessible to wheelchair users. Two penthouses on both ships are also designed for travelers with disabilities.

Delta Queen Steamboat Company

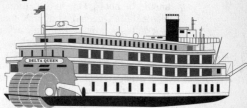

The Fleet *American Queen*
Delta Queen
Mississippi Queen

Evocative of the great floating palaces about which Mark Twain lovingly wrote, these boats (they're *not* ships) are among the few remaining overnight paddle-wheel riverboats in the country. They ply the Mississippi River system at 6–7 mph. The intimate, wooden *Delta Queen* is like a homey bed-and-breakfast. The *American Queen* and *Mississippi Queen* are steamboating's answer to megaships. The largest paddle wheelers ever built, they dwarf the size of the *Delta Queen*.

Ships at a Glance	Dining Rooms	Bars	Casino	Fitness Center	Pools	Average Per Diem
American Queen	1	4	○	●	1	$400–$500
Delta Queen	1	3	○	◐	0	under $200
Mississippi Queen	1	3	○	●	1	$400–$500

Cruise Experience Delta Queen preserves "Life on the Mississippi" with 19th-century charm, plus 20th-century air-conditioning and other newfangled doodads. These floating wedding cakes are outfitted in Victorian-style gingerbread trim, Tiffany-type stained glass, polished brass, crystal chandeliers, plush carpeting, and warm wood paneling. Public areas have cushy leather wing chairs and handsomely upholstered Chesterfield sofas. On deck, you can watch the country go by from oversize wooden rocking chairs, old-fashioned porch swings, and white-iron patio furniture—and you can do so while munching freshly made popcorn or a hot dog. Most passengers are well-heeled retirees, many of whom return time and again—the Paddlewheel Steamboatin' Society of America hosts a champagne-and-punch reception for repeat passengers. For single women passengers sailing alone, senior gentlemen act as hosts and social partners.

A "Riverlorian" (the steamboat company's term for river historian) gives lively talks about the river, explains how to find mile markers and read the river charts, answers questions, lends books, and provides free binoculars. The captain's lecture is a not-to-be-missed event. Passengers can try their hands at playing the calliopes. There's little pressure to participate in anything; you can do as little or as much as you like. Although riverboat gambling has become commonplace on the Mississippi, there are no casinos aboard.

Theme cruises are often scheduled. Topics may include sports, like the Kentucky Derby; American history, such as the Civil War; and various music cruises. Seasonal sailings highlight southern gardens in spring or the colors of fall foliage. Two special events should be noted: One is the annual Great Steamboat Race, which pits a Delta Queen boat against another steamboat challenger and re-creates a famous 19th-century race between the *Natchez* and the *Robert E. Lee*. For 11 nights, the two boats steam from New Orleans to St. Louis; the winner crosses the finish line on the Fourth of July. This is a wildly popular cruise: Crews challenge each other to tests of speed and maneuverability, and passengers gussy up for the annual Floozy Contest. With their flags flying and calliopes whistling away, the boats race at a dizzying 19 kph (12 mph) or so, while landlubbers line the shore and cheer them on. At Christmas, the bonfire cruises are also enormously popular. Replicating an age-old Cajun custom (the bonfires light the way for Papa Noel), a huge bonfire is lit along the levee, and there is a spectacular fireworks display. Shores and boat decks are lined with folks shouting Christmas greetings back and forth—and Papa Noel does pay a visit.

Most of all, a cruise aboard Delta Queen is a celebration of all things American, from cuisine to the sing-along.

Activities On the *AQ* or the *MQ* you can be as active or as relaxed as you want. On the leisurely side, you can do nothing more strenuous than write a letter in the card room or ladies' parlor, or sip a mint julep outside your cabin, by the railing. You can learn to read navigational charts and maps in the chart room, with help from the Riverlorian, or watch the world go by from a swing in the glass-enclosed Front Porch of America, where there's a soda fountain and a player piano. More active types can join their fellow passengers at bingo, bridge, and board games, plus dance lessons and sing-alongs.

In addition to these traditional cruise diversions, the *AQ* and *MQ* both are equipped with a small swimming pool and an equally small gym. Each ship also has a theater for showing movies (*Showboat* is frequently screened).

The *DQ*, meanwhile, is really not for type-A personalities, and a person can while away a fair amount of time just sitting on deck in a rocking chair or a swing. Bingo and bridge, quilting and hatmaking, trivia and kite-flying contests are about as hectic as things get. Tours of the pilothouse are conducted and passengers are encouraged to visit the engine room and have a cup of coffee with the crew, who will cheerfully show you how the engines and the 44-ton paddle operate.

Dining If bigger is better, then it shows most in *Delta Queen's* food: The food on the larger *AQ* and *MQ* is superior to that aboard the *DQ*, and the presentation on the bigger boats is more spectacular than on the *DQ* as well. Dinner on the *AQ* and *MQ* is a bit dressier than on the *DQ*, but formal wear is never never even considered. Dining rooms on the big twins offer better views; the only good river view in the low-lying *DQ* dining room is from a window seat.

Aboard all three boats, five meals are served daily. Dinner is scheduled in two seatings (5:30 and 8 on the *MQ* and *AQ*, 5:45 and 7 on the *DQ*). Menus mix American standards, southern dishes, and a hint of Cajun cooking. Every meal includes at least one "Heart Smart" selection and a vegetarian dish. "Theme" meals include an old-fashioned family-style picnic, with waiters in jeans passing around huge platters of fried chicken, barbecue ribs, corn bread, corn on the cob, potato salad, and such. Passengers with special dietary needs should notify the company a month in advance. The only room service is for Continental breakfast.

Entertainment   The evening's entertainment begins at dinner, when passengers are serenaded by a band playing antique musical instruments. The Grand Saloon is the main showroom for floor shows by night and lectures by day, and it's the venue for dancing to music that ranges from Dixieland to ragtime. (The *AQ* and *MQ* employ two "dance hosts," who dance with single female passengers.) The saloon on the *American Queen* is especially noteworthy: It was conceived as a miniature opera house, like the ones commonly found in small river towns during the 1880s. In the Engine Room Bar, entertainment on a smaller scale includes sing-alongs and recitals evocative of the Victorian era.

Entertainment on the *Delta Queen* is a bit less elaborate. Because the boat is small, the dining room has to do extra duty as a lecture and concert hall, a movie theater, and a nightclub. As a result, there is a great deal of moving about of chairs and tables between meals and during various functions. For nightly floor shows, seating is arranged as in a supper club; performances range from outstanding classical ragtime concerts to corny country hoedowns. Jokes and music are geared toward the older crowd. After the show, the orchestra plays music for dancing, while up in the Texas Lounge a pianist/vocalist entertains with standards and show tunes, mostly from the '40s and '50s, as she does during the cocktail hour. Sing-alongs are also popular, and the Texas Lounge features a great Dixieland band.

Service and   The staff and crew are extraordinarily friendly and helpful, and
Tipping   not at all intrusive. Dining-room service is superb. The night before debarkation, instructions and envelopes for tips are left in each stateroom. Tip waiters, waitresses, and cabin attendants $3.50 per person per diem; busboys $2.25 per person per diem; maître d's $5 per couple per cruise; porters $1.50 per bag. An automatic 15% is added to wine and bar purchases.

Destinations   Because the Delta Queen Steamboat Company's ports are not cov-
and Ports of   ered in Chapter 3, we've tried to give you a general idea of how
Call   time is spent ashore on a typical riverboat cruise. (For year-round itineraries, *see* Chapter 4.)

The boats rarely paddle for more than a day without putting into port, where they are usually docked for at least a half day. Shore excursions visit plantation homes, historic towns and Civil War battlefields, sleepy villages, and major metropolises. Tours are either by bus or on foot, and since there are scores of ports, there is a wide range available.

Shore excursions range from tours of riverside plantations to bus tours of Civil War military sites. About the most expensive is the Cajun Heritage tour from Baton Rouge (3½ hrs, $39). Casino boats are docked in several ports—but beware of boats that leave the pier, lest you gamble on missing your own.

In some ports the steamboat company provides a free shuttle into town. This is fine if you want to poke around on your own; however, the shore excursions are narrated and take you to plantation homes that you can't always reach on foot. In other ports, you can simply amble down the gangplank and walk to the sights.

For More Delta Queen Steamboat Co. (30 Robin St. Wharf, New Orleans,
Information LA 70130, tel. 504/586–0631 or 800/543–1949).

American Queen

Specifications *Type of boat:* Riverboat   *Passengers:* 436
Cruise experience: Casual   *Crew:* 165 (American)
Size: 4,700 tons   *Officers:* American
Number of cabins: 222   *Passenger/crew ratio:* 2.6 to 1
Outside cabins: 75%   *Year built:* 1995

Ship's Log The largest steamboat ever built for the Mississippi River system,
the *American Queen* is based on the great paddle wheelers of the
past. The *AQ*'s designers studied such famous river giants as the
J.M. White, the *Robert E. Lee*, and the *New Orleans*. At the *AQ*'s
stern, a huge, red paddle wheel works together with modern
thrusters to propel the boat forward. Two immense, black, fluted
smokestacks signify the presence of authentic steam engines salvaged from a 1930s river dredge. The retractable pilothouse was
modeled after the one on the turn-of-the-century *Charles Reb-
stock*, another famous riverboat; on its roof stands a 6-ft-high,
rooster-shape weather vane. Inside, the nostalgia continues. At
the bow, a sweeping grand staircase is based on the one once found
aboard the *J.M. White*. Bookcases in the gentlemen's card room
and ladies' parlor are stocked with firsthand accounts of exploration, how-to books, and novels from a century ago. More Victo-
riana can be found in the Mark Twain Gallery, a long, narrow room
overlooking the dining salon. Scattered throughout the boat's various public rooms are more than 200 pieces of artwork, most in
their original frames, from the 1860s to 1890s.

Cabins Cabins continue the Victorian theme with reproduction wallpaper,
floral carpeting, artwork, lighting fixtures, and period furnishings—some have authentic antique bureaus. Outside accommodations have private verandas, bay windows for panoramic views of
the river, or direct access to an outdoor promenade through windowed French doors. Top-category suites are furnished with
antique queen-size beds. Complimentary champagne, fresh fruit,
and cheese are provided to passengers in suites and upper-category
outside staterooms. Twenty-seven cabins have private verandas,
while six cabins have partially obstructed views due to exterior
staircases, which are shown clearly on the brochure deck plans.

Outlet voltage: 110 AC.

Single supplement: 150%–175% of double-occupancy rate.

Discounts: A third passenger in a cabin pays reduced per diems.
One child 16 or younger cruises free in some staterooms, when
sharing a cabin with two full-fare adults. You get a discount for
booking early.

Sports and **Health club:** StairMaster, stationary bikes, treadmills.
Fitness **Recreation:** Small swimming pool.

Facilities **Public rooms:** Four bars, showroom/lecture hall, theater, card
room, ladies' parlor, observation deck.

Shops: Victorian gift shop, beauty salon/barbershop.

Health care: None.

Child care: Passengers may make private baby-sitting arrangements with a staff or crew member.

Accessibility   Nine cabins, as well as elevators and wide hallways, are accessible to wheelchair users.

Delta Queen

Specifications   *Type of boat:* Riverboat   *Passengers:* 174
Cruise experience: Casual   *Crew:* 75 (American)
Size: 3,360 tons   *Officers:* American
Number of cabins: 87   *Passenger/crew ratio:* 2.3 to 1
Outside cabins: 100%   *Year built:* 1926

Ship's Log   If the *Delta Queen* were a song, she'd be "Up the Lazy River." This grande dame of America's most famous river first sailed the waters of the Sacramento River and served her country during World War II as a U.S. Navy ferry on San Francisco Bay. She began cruising the Mississippi River system after World War II. In the late '60s, due to federal legislation banning boats with wooden superstructures, she seemed doomed for demolition, but the hue and cry raised by preservationists and nostalgia buffs resulted in a congressional exemption, under which she still sails. This four-decker time capsule is now a designated National Historic Landmark and is listed on the National Register of Historic Places. Certain modifications have been made in the name of fire safety: The boat has a double hull and a sprinkler system and uses fire-retardant paint. But because the boat is made of wood, smoking is restricted to designated areas and forbidden in the cabins.

Cabins   One of the standard jokes aboard the *DQ* is, "You didn't realize that the brochure picture of your cabin was actual size, did you?" Most *are* quite small (baths are minuscule), but all cabins are outside. A slight disadvantage here is that in order to have any privacy it's necessary to keep your shades or shutters closed: There is a lot of activity on the wraparound decks. Accommodations on the Cabin Deck have inside entrances, while those on the Sun and Texas decks have outside entrances. The most charming aspect of these small accommodations is their original wood paneling. All also come with complimentary soap, shampoo, and body lotion, wall-to-wall carpeting, and there are no closets: just pipe-racks for hanging and a few drawers. Suites 307 and 308 are up front, on either side of the pilothouse. Superior Staterooms 117, 118, 121, and 122 on the Cabin Deck, and Staterooms 207, 208, 227, 228, and 230 on the Texas Deck have partially obstructed river views. Complimentary champagne, fresh fruit, and cheese are provided to passengers in suites and superior staterooms.

Outlet voltage: 110 AC.

Single supplement: 150%–175% of double-occupancy rate.

Discounts: No cabins accommodate third or fourth passengers. You get a discount for booking early.

Sports and Fitness   **Health club:** Stationary bike, rowing machine.
Recreation: Unobstructed circuits for jogging.

Facilities   **Public rooms:** Three lounges.

Shops: Gift shop.

Health care: None.

Child care: Passengers may make private baby-sitting arrangements with a crew member.

Accessibility The *Delta Queen* has no facilities for wheelchair users. However, passengers with mobility problems can travel aboard the boat provided they can traverse stairways, including a steep one down to the dining room.

Mississippi Queen

Specifications
Type of boat: Riverboat
Cruise experience: Casual
Size: 3,364 tons
Number of cabins: 207
Outside cabins: 64%

Passengers: 420
Crew: 165 (American)
Officers: American
Passenger/crew ratio: 2.5 to 1
Year built: 1976

Ship's Log The seven-deck *Mississippi Queen* combines the traditions of steamboating with resort-style facilities. She was built in 1976 at a cost of $27 million and refurbished in 1996 in a pleasing Victorian style. There is infinitely more space in public areas and in the cabins than aboard the *DQ*, but—ironically—less open deck space. Her huge calliope is the world's largest.

Cabins Although none of the staterooms is huge, and some are quite small, they're great places to settle in and contemplate the river in peace and quiet. A redecoration in early 1996 added some Victorian character through the use of period wall coverings, fabrics, and artwork. Closet and storage space, while not vast, is more generous than the *DQ's* limited hooks and rods. Of the outside cabins, 94 have private verandas. Inside cabins, however, are not for the claustrophobic. The four Victorian-style suites are another story entirely. Two are adjacent to the pilothouse, with windows facing forward and to the side for a captain's-eye view of the river; two are adjacent to the paddlewheel, with its lulling, sleep-inducing sounds. Staterooms 131, 132, 141, 220, 221, 327, and 328 have partially obstructed river views. Suites and some outside and inside staterooms can accommodate more than two passengers. Complimentary champagne, fresh fruit, and cheese are provided to passengers in suites and superior staterooms.

Outlet voltage: 110 AC.

Single supplement: 150%–175% of double-occupancy rate.

Discounts: A third passenger in a cabin pays reduced per diems. One child 16 or younger cruises free in some staterooms when sharing a cabin with two full-fare adults. You get a discount for booking early.

Sports and Fitness **Health club:** Stationary bike, treadmill, exercise classes, stair climber.

Recreation: Shuffleboard, sauna, whirlpool spa, pool.

Facilities **Public rooms:** Three bars, two lounges, showroom, lecture hall, theater/conference center, library, game room, activity center.

Shops: Gift shop, beauty salon/barbershop.

Health care: None.

Child care: Passengers may make private baby-sitting arrangements with a staff or crew member.

Accessibility Elevators, wide hallways, and one cabin are accessible to wheelchair users.

Disney Cruise Line

The Fleet *Disney Magic*
Disney Wonder

Neither the *Magic* nor the *Wonder* was available at press time for firsthand inspection because both were under construction. Scale models showed an impressive design, though, combining the classic lines of traditional cruise ships with advantages of today's modern megaships. However, there are always reminders that you're cruising with Disney—Mickey's silhouette graces the funnels and the fog horn bellows, "When You Wish Upon a Star."

Ships at a Glance

	Dining Rooms	Bars	Casino	Fitness Center	Pools	Average Per Diem
Disney Magic *Disney Wonder*	4	8	○	●	3	$400

Cruise Experience Who should consider a Disney Cruise? Based on what we know about the ships, they're not going to be just for families. Many areas, including one dining room and several bars and lounges, will be set aside for adults only. A special section of beach on Disney's private island will also be reserved for adult passengers. However, don't expect to gamble on these ships—there will be no casinos aboard—and don't expect raunchy humor from the late-night comedians, whose material will be "offbeat, but never off-color," according to the line.

Being an entertainment company, Disney should excel at this aspect of the cruise experience: The line is promising a different live production show every night of the cruise. And just as Celebrity Cruises made cuisine a priority in the early 1990s—and forced its competitors to pay more attention to their food service—Disney's entry into cruising may ultimately raise the standard of entertainment for all cruise passengers.

Dining Passengers will dine in a new restaurant every night aboard the ship so they can sample each of three theme restaurants—and their assigned waiter travels with them. A fourth restaurant is for adults only. With three seatings instead of the usual two, Disney hopes to create family seatings and an adult seating.

Activities While the kids are enrolled in their own programs, adults may take advantage of the adult-oriented diversions—spa treatments, table tennis, basketball, golf driving, and more.

Entertainment A whole new cast of characters has been created to star in what Disney bills as "Broadway-quality" productions. There will be a full-screen cinema showing Disney classics and first-run releases. Adults and kids will each have their own nightclubs.

Destinations   Disney sails from Port Canaveral in central Florida to the Bahamas. (For detailed itineraries, *see* Chapter 4.)

For More   Disney Cruise Line (Box 22804, Lake Buena Vista, FL 32830, tel.
Information   800/511–1333).

Holland America Line

The Fleet

MS *Maasdam*
MS *Nieuw Amsterdam*
MS *Noordam*
MS *Rotterdam*

MS *Ryndam*
MS *Statendam*
MS *Veendam*
MS *Westerdam*

Holland America emphasizes its nautical history more than any other line, and passengers will find themselves surrounded by imagery of Dutch exploration. Nautical antiques and memorabilia, from historic artifacts to nostalgic soap boxes, reflect the line's 100-year-plus seafaring heritage. All the line's vessels were originally built for Holland America except the *Westerdam*, which was purchased as the *Homeric* from Home Lines, stretched, and rechristened. The line's smaller ships, the *Nieuw Amsterdam* and *Noordam*, have a modern but classic appeal, while the newest ships, *Statendam, Maasdam, Ryndam, Veendam,* and *Rotterdam* are big without being too big, and have atriums, dining rooms, and showrooms that are the equal of any afloat. Two new sisters, the *Volendam* and *Zaandam*, are scheduled to make their debut in August 1999 and January 2000. A sister ship to the *Rotterdam* will join the fleet in the year 2000.

Ships at a Glance

	Dining Rooms	Bars	Casino	Fitness Center	Pools	Average Per Diem
Maasdam/Ryndam Statendam/Veendam	1	7	●	●	2	$200–$300
Nieuw Amsterdam Noordam	1	7	●	●	2	$200–$300
Rotterdam	2*	7	●	●	2	$400–$500
Westerdam	1	7	●	●	2	$200–$300

*includes alternative restaurant

Cruise Experience

Founded in 1873, Holland America is one of the oldest names in cruising. Steeped in the traditions of the transatlantic crossing, its cruises are conservative affairs renowned for their grace and gentility. Holland America is known throughout the industry for its devotion to safety, and its lifeboat drills are among the most serious at sea. Service, too, is taken seriously: The line maintains its own school (in Indonesia) to train staff members, rather than hiring them out of a union hall. Participation in shore excursions and special activities is emphasized, but passengers are otherwise left to their own devices.

Holland America passengers tend to be better educated, older, and less active than those traveling on sister line Carnival's ships, although the age difference is getting narrower. As its ships attract a more youthful clientele, the line has taken steps to shed its "old folks" image with a private island in the Bahamas, trendier cuisine, and a "Club HAL" children's program. Still, these are not party cruises. As the competition builds ever bigger ships, Holland America has chosen to build relatively smaller vessels. In doing so, it has managed to preserve the refined and relaxing qualities that have always been the hallmark of a Holland America cruise.

Activities   Holland America offers the full complement of organized group activities, such as poolside games, dance classes, trivia contests, and bingo, as well as the more offbeat karaoke machines, which allow passengers to sing along with orchestrated recordings. Nevertheless, relaxing in a deck chair and letting the world take care of itself while the ship's staff takes care of you is the prime attraction of a Holland America cruise.

Dining   Food is good by cruise-ship standards and served on Rosenthal china. In response to the challenge presented by its competitors, Holland America has gone "nouvelle" and introduced a lighter side to its menus, including many pastas and "heart-healthy dishes," as well as fresh fish from local markets. (However, it's sometimes hard to tell exactly what is lighter or healthier about some of these dishes.) At the same time, the line placed additional emphasis on "American-style dishes" to complement its trendy fare. In keeping with its ethnic traditions, the line continues to offer an occasional Dutch or Indonesian dish for variety. Special dinner menus are available for children. Breakfast and lunch are open seating; dinner is served at two assigned seatings (6:15 and 8:15). There are two formal evenings each week, three during a 10-day cruise. Special diets are catered to if requests are made one month in advance.

The menus for Holland America's breakfast and lunch buffets, served in the Lido, often outdo its dining-room selections. Once during each cruise there's an Indonesian lunch and an outdoor barbecue dinner. Every day there's a deck lunch of barbecued hot dogs and hamburgers, pasta, stir-fries, or make-your-own tacos. The Lido also features an ice-cream/frozen-yogurt bar. Other food service includes midmorning bouillon or iced tea, traditional afternoon tea served in an inside lounge, and hot hors d'oeuvres served during the cocktail hour. Passengers can help themselves to tea and coffee at any time; 24-hour room service is available from a limited menu.

Entertainment   Apart from a disco, Holland America's entertainment is still slanted toward an older audience. Shows in the main lounge, offered twice nightly, feature big-band sounds, comedy, magic and dance acts, and revues. Productions are now flashier than in the past, and what used to be rather subdued productions have been infused with higher-tech sets, zippier costumes, and jazzier music. Besides the main showroom acts, you'll also find dance orchestras, piano sing-alongs (very popular), string trios, and dance quartets. The Filipino and Indonesian crew put on a show once during each cruise, and there also is a passenger talent show one evening. Cabin TVs, standard on all ships, have superb closed-circuit service, including CNN broadcasts. Rare appearances are made by big-name performers and guest lecturers.

Service and Tipping   In the 1970s Holland America adopted a no-tips-required policy. Staff members perform their duties with great pride and professionalism. In turn, passengers don't feel the pressure or the discomfort of having crew members solicit tips. On the other hand, this is not a no-tipping policy, and most passengers give tips comparable to those recommended on other lines—but entirely at their own discretion. Perhaps that's because the crew seems to take a genuine, personal interest in passengers, learning not only their names but habits and personal preferences.

As Holland America absorbs its new ships, service has been spotty at times. Passengers may experience some momentary lapses, but they will also find the finer moments that Holland America has become known for—bartenders who make personalized bookmarks for guests and roll napkins into flowers for the ladies, for example.

Destinations Holland America offers Caribbean itineraries year-round. Seasonal sailings visit Alaska, Europe, and the Panama Canal. A world cruise is scheduled every year. (For seasonal itineraries, *see* Chapter 4.)

For More Information Holland America Line (300 Elliott Ave. W, Seattle, WA 98119, tel. 800/426–0327).

MS Maasdam, MS Ryndam, MS Statendam, and MS Veendam

Specifications *Type of ship:* Cruise liner
Cruise experience: Semiformal
Size: 55,451 tons
Number of cabins: 633
Outside cabins: 77%

Passengers: 1,266
Crew: 571 (Indonesian and Filipino)
Officers: Dutch
Passenger/crew ratio: 2.2 to 1
Years built: 1993–1996

Ship's Log These ships can best be described as classic revival, combining elements of the classic transatlantic liners with best of the new megaships in one neat package. From the outside, they look bigger than their 55,000 tons, thanks to their megaship profile. Inside, they dramatically express Holland America's past in a two-tier dining room, replete with dual grand staircases framing an orchestra balcony—the latter first introduced on the *Nieuw Amsterdam* of 1938.

Although these four ships are structurally identical, Holland America has given each its own distinct personality. Layout and decor of the public rooms differ from ship to ship; it is here that parent company Carnival's influence shows. For the first time, public rooms have whimsical themes. The Crow's Nest on the *Statendam* draws its inspiration from *Composition with Red, Blue, and Yellow* by Dutch abstract painter Piet Mondrian. The same room on the *Maasdam* evokes Alaska's northern lights; the theme on the *Ryndam* is the glaciers of Alaska. Aboard the *Veendam*, the Crow's Nest has not one but three different themes: a "Captain's Area," "Tea Area," and an unnamed bar area, decorated with various artifacts and nautical antiques.

The *Statendam* and *Ryndam* are more typical of Holland America than the *Maasdam* or *Veendam*. In a central three-story atrium, a fountain of bronze mermaids or fish, respectively, states the ships' connection to the sea. On the *Maasdam*, this space is occupied by a modern, green glass sculpture of no nautical significance. Similarly, a wall of televisions on the *Maasdam* displays computer-generated video art. The *Veendam's* atrium has *Jacob's Staircase* at its center—a blue and gold spiraling pillar made of steel and glass.

A big improvement on these ships over some previous Holland America cruise liners is the tiered showroom, where terraced seating creates good lines of sight all around. Aboard the *Maasdam*, notice the depictions of Henry Hudson's ship, the *Half Moon*, on the showroom light fixtures—a fitting reminder of Holland America's maritime heritage.

Cabins Every standard cabin comes with a small sitting area with a sofa; outside cabins have tubs in the bath, inside cabins have just showers. All have wall-mounted hair dryers. Closet space is excellent, but drawer space is limited. Color schemes are in muted blues, peaches, and grays, with plenty of wood paneling. A fruit bowl is refilled each day, and every passenger gets a canvas tote bag. Of the 633 cabins, 148 have private verandas. Suites also have verandas, whirlpool tubs, VCRs, and minibars.

Outlet voltage: 110 AC.

Single supplement: 200% of double-occupancy rates in suites and deluxe staterooms, 150% elsewhere.

Discounts: A third or fourth passenger pays reduced per diems. You get a discount for booking early.

Sports and Fitness **Health club:** Top deck, ocean-view facility with exercise equipment, massage, facials, aerobics studio, saunas, steam rooms.

Recreation: Fitness programs and classes, shuffleboard, two whirlpools, two pools (one with retractable glass roof), practice tennis courts (*Maasdam* and *Ryndam*), unobstructed circuit on wraparound promenade (4 laps = 1½ km/1 mi) for jogging, cushioned jogging track (14½ laps = 1½ km/1 mi; *Statendam* only).

Facilities **Public rooms:** Seven bars, five lounges, showroom, casino, disco, cinema, card and puzzle room, video-game room, meeting rooms.

Shops: Several boutiques and gift shops, beauty salon/barbershop.

Health care: Doctors and nurses on call.

Child care: Youth programs with counselors offered when demand warrants it, baby-sitting arranged privately with crew members.

Services: Full- and self-service laundry, dry cleaning, photographer, film processing.

Accessibility Six cabins are specially equipped for wheelchair users. Corridors are wide; elevators and public lavatories are accessible.

MS Nieuw Amsterdam and MS Noordam

Specifications *Type of ship:* Cruise liner *Passengers:* 1,214
Cruise experience: Semiformal *Crew:* 542 (Indonesian and
Size: 33,930 tons Filipino)
Number of cabins: 607 *Officers:* Dutch
Outside cabins: 68% *Passenger/crew ratio:* 2.2 to 1
Years built: 1983/1984

Ship's Log The N-ships, as they are sometimes called, evoke the days of Dutch exploration, from early New York to India. Dutch nautical antiques, scattered liberally throughout, give the vessels a sense of identity and history. Passengers will be struck by how conveniently laid out and comfortable the liners are (except for certain mazelike hallways). Although these ships are not particularly large, their designers managed to capture a sense of space with extra-wide teak promenades, oversize public rooms, and wide corridors. Of the public rooms, most noteworthy are the "Crow's Nest" observation lounges, which are rich in nautical ambience.

As older, midsize ships, the *Nieuw Amsterdam* and *Noordam* do have their drawbacks, and in certain ways compare less favorably with their larger, newer fleetmates. In particular, the single-level dining room, small pool decks, and tiny gym are far less elaborate.

Cabins Cabins are tidy, comfortable, and relatively large. Furnishings are meant to evoke the great steamship era of the past. A fruit bowl is refilled each day, and every passenger gets a canvas tote bag. Views from most cabins on the Boat and Navigation decks (including the Staterooms Deluxe) are partially obstructed.

Outlet voltage: 110/220 AC.

Single supplement: 200% of double-occupancy rate in Staterooms Deluxe, 150% elsewhere. Holland America can arrange for two same-sex adults to share a cabin at the double-occupancy rate.

Discounts: A third or fourth passenger in a cabin pays reduced per diems. You get a discount for booking early.

Sports and Fitness **Health club:** Ocean-view fitness center with jogging and rowing machines, stationary bicycles, barbells, isometric pulleys, massage, dual saunas, facials.

Recreation: Exercise classes, golf putting, paddle and deck tennis, shuffleboard, trapshooting, two pools, whirlpool, unobstructed circuit (5 laps = 1½ km/1 mi) for jogging.

Facilities **Public rooms:** Seven bars, three entertainment lounges, casino, disco, cinema, card room, library, video-game room.

Shops: Boutiques, gift shop, beauty salon/barbershop.

Health care: Doctor on call.

Child care: Children's activity room, youth programs with counselors offered when demand warrants it, baby-sitting arranged privately with crew member.

Services: Full- and self-service laundry, dry cleaning, photographer, film processing.

Accessibility Elevators and four staterooms on each ship are accessible to wheelchair users. They are Category-B cabins, which are Deluxe Outside Double rooms on the Navigation Deck.

MS Rotterdam

Specifications *Type of ship:* Cruise liner
Cruise experience: Semiformal
Size: 59,652 tons
Number of cabins: 658
Outside cabins: 82%

Passengers: 1,316
Crew: 630 (Indonesian and Filipino)
Officers: Dutch
Passenger/crew ratio: 2 to 1
Year built: 1997

Ship's Log After several delays, the *Rotterdam VI* made its debut in mid-December 1997. Essentially, this ship is a stretched version of the four *Statendam*-class vessels that preceded it, so passengers who have sailed on any one of these (*Statendam, Maasdam, Rydam,* and *Veendam*) will find much that is familiar in the way of layout and facilities. But as the new flagship of Holland America, and the heir to a name with a rich history, the *Rotterdam VI* also has some distinctive qualities. For starters, it's a little bigger and a little more spacious. Its itineraries are a little more exotic, including an annual world cruise, and it has a special lecture series, dubbed the "Flagship Forum," held aboard all European cruises and "Grand Voyages."

The *Rotterdam VI* also represents a couple of firsts for Holland America. It has the line's first alternative restaurant, the 88-seat Odyssey, which serves an Italian menu nightly for those who would prefer a change of pace from the main dining room. Another departure from Holland America's other ships is an exclusive deck of suites—accessible only to the those with a key. Passengers in these suites are entitled to the services of a concierge and private lounge. Passengers from this deck are also given priority in gaining reservations for the Odyssey Restaurant.

Which brings up an interesting question. Cruising has long been promoted as a "one-class" way to travel. Everyone eats in the same dining room, watches the same shows, and sunbathes around the same pool. But has Holland America created the first multi-class ship since the *Queen Elizabeth 2*, whose passengers are assigned to a dining room based on their cabin category? Most passengers will probably not feel like "second-class" citizens, since the exclusivity of the Concierge Deck applies only to the services of the concierge and the private lounge. However, when it comes to reservations for the Odyssey restaurant, all passengers should be treated equally.

Cabins The *Rotterdam*'s cabins were designed with world cruising in mind. All have phones and TVs. All suites and many outside cabins have sitting areas and mini-refrigerators. Suites and outside cabins also have tubs in the bathrooms. A concierge lounge serves passengers in suites.

Outlet voltage: 110 AC.

Single supplement: 200% of double-occupancy rate for penthouses and suites; 175% for deluxe staterooms; 130%–150% for all other outside cabins; 120% for all inside cabins.

Discounts: A third or fourth passenger in a cabin pays reduced per diems. You get a discount for booking early.

Sports and Fitness **Health club:** Ocean-view fitness center with exercise equipment, massage, facials, aerobics area, saunas, steam rooms.

Recreation: Exercise classes, shuffleboard, two whirlpools, two pools (one with retractable glass roof); practice tennis courts/volleyball courts; unobstructed circuit on wraparound promenade (3½ laps = 1½ km/1 mi) for jogging.

Facilities **Public rooms:** Five bars, three lounges, showroom, casino, disco, cinema, card room, library, video-game room, meeting rooms.

Shops: Several boutiques and gift shops; beauty salon/barbershop.

Health care: Doctor and nurses on call.

Child care: Children's activity room and youth programs with counselors when demand warrants it, baby-sitting arranged privately with crew member

Services: Full- and self-service laundry, dry cleaning, photographer, film processing.

Accessibility Elevators and 23 cabins are accessible to wheelchair users.

MS Westerdam

Specifications *Type of ship:* Cruise liner
Cruise experience: Semiformal
Size: 53,872 tons
Number of cabins: 747
Outside cabins: 66%

Passengers: 1,494
Crew: 620 (Indonesian and Filipino)
Officers: Dutch
Passenger/crew ratio: 2.4 to 1
Year built: 1986

Ship's Log Holland America set a record with this ship in 1989, when the line installed a 130-ft section into the midsection of the Westerdam—accomplishing the biggest stretch job in the history of cruising. This $84 million investment made the *Westerdam* into a bigger version of the *Nieuw Amsterdam* and *Noordam* and created a spacious, well-apportioned ship. Like its smaller siblings, the *Westerdam* carries a multimillion-dollar art collection that evokes Holland America's storied history. Perhaps most impressive is an antique bronze cannon, cast in Rotterdam, which is strategically positioned in the center of the ship. Also worthy of special note is the dining room. Unlike on many newer ships, where the restaurant occupies a strategic perch with expansive views, on the *Westerdam* it is located below decks. But Holland America has turned a negative into a positive and created a venue that is rich and inviting. The room is accented in wood and brass, and traditional portholes rather than picture windows line the walls.

Cabins Cabins are large, with plenty of storage space; all but the least expensive feature a sitting area with a convertible couch. The use of blond wood and ivory tones adds to the overall sense of airiness. A fruit bowl is refilled each day, and every passenger gets a canvas tote bag.

Outlet voltage: 110 AC.

Single supplement: 200% of double-occupancy rate for suites or staterooms deluxe, 150% elsewhere. Holland America will arrange for two same-sex adults to share a cabin at the double-occupancy rate.

Discounts: A third or fourth passenger in a cabin pays reduced per diems. You get a discount for booking early.

Sports and Fitness **Health club:** Hydro-fitness exercise equipment, dual saunas, massage, loofah scrubs, facials.

Recreation: Exercise classes, golf putting, paddle and deck tennis, shuffleboard, basketball, two pools (one with retractable glass roof), three whirlpools, unobstructed circuit (4 laps = 1½ km/1 mi) for jogging.

Facilities **Public rooms:** Seven bars, two entertainment lounges, casino, disco, cinema, card room, library, video-game room, meeting room.

Shops: Boutiques, drugstore, beauty salon/barbershop.

Health care: Doctor on call.

Child care: Youth programs with counselors when demand warrants it, baby-sitting arranged privately with crew member.

Services: Full- and self-service laundry, dry cleaning, photographer, film processing.

Accessibility Elevators and four cabins are accessible to wheelchair users.

Orient Lines

The Fleet MS *Marco Polo*

Like its namesake, the *Marco Polo* visits faraway lands on extended journeys. The vessel will appeal to ship buffs and world travelers alike. A former transatlantic liner, it first set sail as the *Alexandr Pushkin* in 1965 for the Soviet-flag Baltic Shipping Company. Completely rebuilt over a two-year period, the 850-passenger *Marco Polo* retains an ice-strengthened hull, a handsome profile, and smooth-running twin Sulzer diesel engines. The cabin accommodations and public rooms are decorated in understated good taste, and the deck spaces are generously proportioned.

Ship at a Glance

	Dining Rooms	Bars	Casino	Fitness Center	Pools	Average Per Diem
Marco Polo	2*	5	●	●	1	$200–$300

*includes alternative restaurant

Cruise Experience Since its inception in late 1993, Orient Lines has quickly established a reputation for its destination-intensive cruises. Moderate rates that include pre- or post-cruise land packages and exotic ports of call on six continents put this line in a niche with few competitors. The line already has its share of loyal repeaters, mostly 55 and older. American passengers predominate—especially on Mediterranean cruises, but in Asia and elsewhere there may be a sizable contingent of British passengers aboard and, to a lesser extent, Europeans and Australians.

Activities During days at sea, enrichment lectures are the most well-attended events. The daily program also lists bingo, "horse racing," bridge tournaments, fashion shows, food demonstrations, deck games, and exercise classes.

Dining Menus were developed by Wolfgang Puck, a southern California chef and restaurateur, but the menu selection goes far beyond this one region to please the ship's varied American and international clientele. There are four choices of entrées at dinner, plus healthy and vegetarian selections. From preparation to presentation, the quality is consistently good to excellent—above the standard expected from a midprice ship.

Dinner is served in two seatings (6:30 and 8:30) at assigned tables. Breakfast and lunch are open seating. Two formals are scheduled each week. Raffles, an attractive buffet restaurant, also serves a varied menu at breakfast and lunch. There's also an outdoor barbecue by the pool. On several nights, Raffles is transformed into a tranquil, reservations-only dining room serving from an Asian menu. You'll pay an extra $15 service charge, which includes unlimited wine and service charge. Room service is limited to breakfast.

Entertainment Two shows (one for each dining-room seating) are offered every night, featuring singers, dancers, and perhaps a magician or comedian. A small band provides dance music; in good weather, the band may play on deck. Local folkloric performers come aboard in some ports. A late-night disco generally attracts more officers and staff than passengers.

Service and Tipping The friendly and efficient hotel staff is Filipino. Tip the dining-room waiter $3.75 per person per day, $1.25 to the busboy, and $4 to the cabin steward. A 15% service charge is automatically added to your bar bill and to drinks in the dining rooms.

Destinations Cruise-tours of eight to 25 days concentrate on ports of call in Antarctica, Asia, Australia, Africa, and South America in the winter. The line switches its focus to Europe in the summer. (For seasonal itineraries, *see* Chapter 4.)

For More Information Orient Lines (1510 S.E. 17th St., Suite 400, Fort Lauderdale, FL 33316, tel. 954/527–6660 or 800/333–7300).

MS Marco Polo

Specifications

Type of ship: Classic liner	*Passengers:* 850
Cruise experience: Semiformal	*Crew:* 350 (Filipino)
Size: 22,080 tons	*Officers:* European
Number of cabins: 425	*Passenger/crew ratio:* 2.4 to 1
Outside cabins: 70%	*Year built:* 1965 (rebuilt 1993)

Ship's Log A handsome vessel with a raked profile, the *Marco Polo* is well suited to passengers who enjoy relaxing days at sea in preparation for an intensive itinerary of popular and exotic ports. Nearly all the cheerfully decorated public rooms are on one deck with an easy flow from the forward show lounge to the outdoor Lido surrounding the pool. The teak Promenade Deck offers wooden deck chairs and a wide, but not quite circular, walking track. The Upper Deck has a wraparound promenade but with narrow stretches alongside the lifeboats. The forward observation deck and tiered afterdecks are well designed for lounging and sightseeing. A helipad is used for reconnaissance and passenger flights in Antarctica.

Cabins Cabins are appointed with light-wood furniture trim and wainscoting, and those facing open decks have one-way glass for privacy. Furnishings include one or two chairs, a bedside table, and a chest of drawers—some doubling as writing desks. Closet space is adequate and suitcases may be stored under the beds. Bathrooms have hair dryers, complimentary toiletries, and a clothesline. Some cabins can accommodate a third and fourth person. Two deluxe and four junior suites have sitting areas and small refrigerators. TVs show feature films (some related to the destinations on your itinerary), documentaries, CNN, and taped lectures. Radios have two music channels. Cabins on Sky Deck and Cabins 712–727 have views partially obstructed by lifeboats.

Outlet voltage: 110/220 AC.

Single supplement: 125%–200% of double-occupancy rate. The supplement is waived for passengers who agree to share with another single traveler, even if one is not found by the time of sailing.

Discounts: A third or fourth passenger in a cabin pays the minimum fare. You get a discount for booking early and for booking back-to-back cruises. Repeat passengers get an additional discount.

Sports and Fitness

Health club: Fitness equipment, sauna, massage.

Recreation: Aerobics, table tennis, shuffleboard, pool, three Jacuzzis, two circuits (one unobstructed) for jogging.

Facilities

Public rooms: Five bars, two entertainment lounges, casino, disco, library, card room.

Shops: Two gift shops, beauty center/barbershop.

Health care: Doctor and nurse on call.

Child care: None.

Services: Laundry service, dry cleaning, photographer, film processing, post office and currency exchange in some ports.

Accessibility

Two cabins have wheelchair-accessible bathrooms; all others have 2-to 12-inch raised thresholds. Accessibility aboard local transportation and other facilities ashore varies greatly in the ports visited.

Princess Cruises

The Fleet
MV *Crown Princess*
MV *Dawn Princess*
MV *Grand Princess*   MV *Royal Princess*
MV *Island Princess*   MV *Sea Princess*
MV *Pacific Princess*   TSS *Sky Princess*
MV *Regal Princess*   MV *Sun Princess*

Princess proves that big can be classy aboard its increasingly huge, upscale megaships. Most of the ships in the Princess fleet are bigger than 70,000 tons and carry 1,500 or more passengers. In fact—for the time being—the *Grand Princess* holds the title of "World's Biggest Cruise Ship." At 109,000 tons, it's too big to fit through the Panama Canal, and it's taller than Niagara Falls. Yet Princess has made a conscious decision to design ships on a human scale by subdividing public areas into smaller, more intimate spaces.

Ships at a Glance

	Dining Rooms	Bars	Casino	Fitness Center	Pools	Average Per Diem
Crown Princess *Regal Princess*	2*	9	●	●	2	$300–$400
Dawn Princess *Sea Princess* *Sun Princess*	3*	7	●	●	5	$200–$300
Grand Princess	6*	12	●	●	5	$200–$300
Island Princess *Pacific Princess*	1	6	●	●	2	$400–$500
Royal Princess	2*	7	●	●	3	$400–$500
Sky Princess	1	7	●	●	2	$300–$400

includes bistro dining in the casual restaurant and alternative restaurants on Grand Princess.

Cruise Experience
Nearly everything about Princess is big, but the line doesn't sacrifice quality for quantity when it comes to building beautiful vessels. Decor and materials used to build the ships are top-notch, and service, especially in the dining rooms, is of a high standard. In short, Princess is refined without being pretentious.

Princess is less generous, however, when it comes to onboard amenities: The line charges for such "extras" as ice-cream served out on deck, soft-drinks in the dining room, and hot chocolate in the pizzeria. There's often a nominal charge for taking the shuttle bus into town when the ship pulls into port. It's a nickel-and-dime mentality. However, passengers in suite accommodations are given the royal treatment. They get butler service on European cruises and priority clearance at disembarkation.

Perhaps Princess Cruises' greatest strength is the wide range of choice you'll find aboard its vessels, especially the newer ones. On the *Dawn, Sea,* and *Sun,* there are five places to eat. On the *Grand,* there are eight dining and snacking options. Choices for activities and entertainment also abound, so you can do as much as you want—or nothing at all.

Princess also excels shoreside, where its people-handling skills and shore excursion program shine. Even on the biggest ships, getting ashore is a seamless experience. Passengers who want to book shore excursions rarely have to worry about being closed out from a popular trip, because the line will just add more departures. This is especially true in Alaska, where Princess and Holland America are the two major players. Shore excursion talks are replayed on in-cabin TVs throughout the day, and there are special rates for children (usually about 50% less than the adult price). Port materials even include telephone access numbers for passengers who want to phone home. Information is readily available for those who *don't* want to buy a tour. In fact, the line—unlike some others—never makes passengers feel like they *have* to take a tour to enjoy a port of call.

Activities Princess has all the expected ocean-liner activities—dance lessons, bingo, "horse racing," and bridge and backgammon tournaments. Fitness facilities include an exercise manager who can create a customized fitness program. On Caribbean sailings, passengers can earn PADI-sponsored scuba certification; classes are held in one of the pools.

For children, youth centers can be found on the *Dawn, Grand, Sea, Sky,* and *Sun.* These facilities have their own kids' pool and sundeck, and provide daily supervised activities year-round. The *Crown Princess* and *Regal Princess* have full-time children's programs but no dedicated youth centers. On the *Island Princess* and *Pacific Princess,* children's programs are offered only when enough children are aboard.

Dining Food lovers will likely be disappointed on a Princess cruise. While the line has tried to improve it's quality, the cuisine is still not up to the standard of many other lines. The food is best in the main dining room, where the menus are contemporary and sometimes innovative, and less recommendable in the casual dining areas, such as ship's buffet restaurant. Coffee throughout the ship is vapid and tastes like instant. Ironically, you often can't get regular coffee in the coffee bars and, conversely, you can't order espresso in the main dining room.

Princess does better at presentation. In the main dining room, the mostly Italian staff serves meals with élan and pride. Each night at dinner the headwaiter prepares a fresh pasta dish table-side. Continental cuisine is presented with flair and fanfare—the baked Alaska, in particular, is reason for a grand parade. The affable staff will memorize your name and your eating preferences, and they'll rarely refuse a special request. Meals are served at two assigned seatings (dinner at 6:15 and 8:15); breakfast and lunch may be open seating when the ship is in port. Two formal evenings are held on 7-day cruises, three on 9- to 16-day cruises. Alternative vegetarian, low-fat, low-cholesterol, and low-sodium selections are offered at every meal, and waiters rarely balk if you ask that an item on the menu be prepared a certain way. Special dietary requests are well handled, but they should be made in writing three weeks before sailing. There is no smoking in the dining room.

Like many other cruise lines, Princess is offering its passengers more dining choices than ever before. Seven ships have a 24-hour buffet restaurant, which at night doubles as a "bistro" alternative restaurant for dinner. The *Crown, Dawn, Grand, Regal, Royal, Sea, Sky,* and *Sun* have free pizza parlors open throughout the afternoon and evening. On the *Crown, Dawn, Grand, Regal, Royal, Sea,* and *Sun* a patisserie serves complimentary desserts and specialty coffees for an extra charge. Other food service includes midmorning bouillon, afternoon tea, and a midnight buffet; 24-hour room service is limited to sandwiches and beverages except during dinner, when a full menu is served.

Entertainment   Princess emphasizes entertainment suitable for the entire family, with a little more flair and flash than its chief rivals. In some cases, especially on the newer ships with their big stages, the Broadway-style shows are exceptional. Other evening diversions include musical revues, variety shows, cabarets, a piano bar, a dance orchestra and combo, and a disco. Local musicians sometimes come aboard to perform. In-cabin TV programming is among the most extensive you'll find on any ship; choices include movies, CNN, ESPN, the Discovery Channel, the BBC, and classic TV shows like *M*A*S*H*.

Enrichment programs are offered on all cruises outside of North America, but the speakers are as likely to discuss global economics as they are to discuss the next port of call.

Service and Tipping   Service is excellent and unobtrusive, thanks to a genuinely enthusiastic crew. The Italian dining-room staff is a great deal of fun, however, and the room service is exceptional. Service in the pizzerias can be inconsistent, though; perhaps it's because these waiters don't get a share of the tips from the dining room staff. Tip the room steward and waiter $3 each per passenger per diem, the waiter's assistant $1.75. A 15% gratuity is automatically added to bar and wine charges.

Destinations   The Princess fleet is like a small navy, sailing to virtually every cruise destination. Itineraries cover Alaska, the Caribbean, Europe, Hawai'i, the Mexican Riviera, New England and Canada, South America, Southeast Asia, the Panama Canal—virtually every cruise destination except Antarctica. The line also has "cruise-tours" in Alaska, where Princess owns its own chain of hotels, and safari "cruise-tours" in Africa. (For seasonal itineraries, *see* Chapter 4.)

For More Information   Princess Cruises (10100 Santa Monica Blvd., Los Angeles, CA 90067, tel. 310/553–1770 or 800/PRINCESS for brochures).

MV Crown Princess and MV Regal Princess

Specifications   *Type of ship:* Megaship
Cruise experience: Semiformal
Size: 70,000 tons
Number of cabins: 795
Outside cabins: 80%

Passengers: 1,590
Crew: 696 (international)
Officers: Italian
Passenger/crew ratio: 2.2 to 1
Years built: 1990/1991

Ship's Log   Supposedly modeled on the curves of a dolphin, these sister ships look more like oversize, seafaring versions of the Japanese bullet train. (A picture of the Crown is shown on the cover of this book.)

The unusual exteriors are a blend of the traditional (note the single, upright funnel) and the avant-garde. The ships are instantly recognizable for their most dramatic feature: a domed observation lounge/casino/entertainment area that sits atop the bridge. Other highlights include a million-dollar art collection and a three-story atrium foyer. And although the *Crown* and *Regal* are almost as large as Royal Caribbean Cruise Line's 74,000-ton megaship, *Majesty of the Seas*, they hold about 1,200 fewer passengers (counting upper and lower berths). The ships also have a high percentage of outside cabins, many of which have private verandas. These comfortable ships manage to avoid overwhelming passengers with their sheer size by creating a soft, warm interior, appointed with cozy couches and armchairs; art deco furnishings; light-wood panels; polished metals; and muted coral, blue, and aqua tones.

A small observation deck below the bridge provides great views and is a perfect perch for sailing through Alaska or the Panama Canal. You'll likely have it all to yourself: It's so well-hidden, it's not even on the deck plan.

Cabins Cabins are pleasantly appointed in contemporary wood and upholstered furnishings with framed prints on the walls. Each has a walk-in closet, a refrigerator, a separate dressing area, and a safe. Terry robes and fresh-fruit baskets are also found in each stateroom. Outside cabins have large picture windows. Most outside cabins on the Aloha and Baja decks (including all suites and minisuites) have private verandas. Even windowless inside cabins feel spacious. The view from the F-category outside cabins on the Dolphin Deck is obstructed.

Outlet voltage: 110 AC.

Single supplement: 150%–200% of double-occupancy rate.

Discounts: A third or fourth passenger in a cabin pays half the double-occupancy rate. You get a discount for booking early.

Sports and Fitness **Health club:** Sizable below-decks facility with aerobics room, steam room, sauna, weight machines, stationary bikes, other exercise equipment, massage, beauty parlor.

Recreation: Exercise classes, golf driving, table tennis, scuba and snorkeling lessons (scuba certification available), shuffleboard, skeet shooting, two pools (one with a waterfall, the other with a swim-up bar), two whirlpools, unobstructed jogging track (6 laps = 1½ km/1 mi).

Facilities **Public rooms:** Nine bars, five entertainment lounges, domed observation lounge, casino, disco, cinema/conference center, card room, library.

Shops: Two-level arcade of boutiques, gift shops, drugstore, hairdresser.

Health care: Two doctors and two nurses on call.

Child care: Children's program with youth counselor year-round.

Services: Laundry service, dry cleaning, self-service laundry, photographer, film processing.

Accessibility Ten cabins are accessible to wheelchair users.

MV Dawn Princess, MV Sea Princess, and MV Sun Princess

Specifications

Type of ship: Megaship	*Passengers:* 1,950
Cruise experience: Semiformal	*Crew:* 900 (international)
Size: 76,500 tons	*Officers:* Italian
Number of cabins: 975	*Passenger/crew ratio:* 2 to 1
Outside cabins: 62%	*Years built:* 1995/1998/1997

Ship's Log When the *Sun Princess* made its debut in December 1995, it was—for the time being—the largest cruise ship afloat. In fact, the captain's traditional welcome-aboard coctail party is likely to be held in the vast atrium instead of a lounge. The captain holds court four stories above the milling crowd, like the Pope at St. Peter's.

Yet despite its undeniable hugeness, the *Sun* and its sisters avoid the cumbersome lines and cavernous feeling that accompany many other megaships. Public areas have an intimacy that is unexpected on such a huge vessel. The main pool areas, with hundreds of deck chairs, seem more like private country clubs. The ships have two main dining rooms rather than one massive one, and again, the atmosphere is remarkably cozy, with clusters of two to four tables set between dividers of etched glass and arranged on three levels. The pleasant configuration results in a pleasantly quiet ambience. Adding to the sense of privacy is the decor, which uses generous amounts of burnished woods, leather, and paintings framed in brass.

Ironically, Princess may have solved the problem of megaship masses too well: There are so many options for where to spend your time and so much room to fan out that public spaces can feel empty. As a a consequence, some passengers say they miss the opportunity to mingle. Still, the ships are undeniably stunning, outfitted with generous doses of blond beechwood and a daunting attention to detail. Even the humblest metal screw is concealed with gleaming brass, and there's so much greenery that each ship has a full-time gardener aboard.

Cabins Nearly 70% of the outside accommodations have a private veranda, including all suites and minisuites and 372 outside cabins. But as on most vessels, cabins with balconies sacrifice interior space. So if a roomy cabin is important, keep in mind that a standard outside cabin with a picture window has more *interior* room than a cabin with a veranda. All cabins have refrigerators; standard amenities include terry cloth robes and hair dryers. Suite and minisuites have two TVs and bathrooms with a separate glass-enclosed shower and a tub with Jacuzzi jets. Some cabins on the Dolphin Deck have obstructed views. Cabins designed for families have upper berths. Lower-category cabins are small and have limited storage space.

Outlet voltage: 110 AC.

Single supplement: 150%–200% of double-occupancy rate.

Discounts: A third or fourth passenger in a cabin pays half the double-occupancy rate. You get a discount for booking early.

Sports and Fitness **Health club:** Top-deck facility with StairMasters, Lifecycles, treadmills, rowing machines, free weights, weight stations, saunas, massage, facial and body treatments.

Recreation: Aerobics and other exercise classes; four adult swimming pools and one children's splash pool; five whirlpool spas;

sports deck with volleyball, basketball, badminton, and paddle tennis; computerized golf simulator; unobstructed circuit (6 laps = 1½ km/1 mi) for jogging.

Facilities **Public rooms:** Seven bars and lounges, two showrooms, casino, disco, library, business center with phone, fax, and computers.

Shops: Seven duty-free shops.

Health care: Two doctors and two nurses on call.

Child care: Youth center and programs with counselors offered year-round.

Services: Full- and self-service laundry, dry cleaning, photographer, film processing.

Accessibility The *Sun Princess* and *Dawn Princess* are well suited to wheelchair users and have been designed with accessible elevators, wide corridors, and specially equipped public lavatories. Nineteen cabins meet the standards of the Americans with Disabilities Act.

MV Grand Princess

Specifications *Type of ship:* Megaship *Passengers:* 2,600
Cruise experience: Semiformal *Crew:* 1,100 (international)
Size: 109,000 tons *Officers:* Italian
Number of cabins: 1,300 *Passenger/crew ratio:* 2 to 1
Outside cabins: 71% *Year built:* 1998

Ship's Log The *Grand Princess* is indeed a stunning and impressive ship: It has five swimming pools, three showrooms, three dining rooms, three alternative restaurants, and more than 700 private verandas. But numbers are only the beginning. To get some perspective, consider this: The hull of the original "Love Boats," the *Island* and *Pacific Princess*, would fit inside the *Grand Princess* from the stern to the front of the funnel. And the *Grand Princess* isn't just big, it's dramatic: the Skywalkers Disco is suspended above the rear of the ship—15 decks above sea level. The view from inside spans a full 360 degrees.

There are some traditional touches: The rear of the ship is terraced with stepped-back decks reminiscent of more traditional cruise ships. And the Wheelhouse Bar evokes the 160-year history of P&O, Princess Cruises' parent company and one of the oldest names in passenger shipping.

Yet this vessel is very high-tech, too: A glass-enclosed "people mover" carries passengers from the sundeck to the disco and a virtual-reality ride simulates a high-speed submarine chase. There's also a golf simulator, an interactive television system in the cabins, a make-your-own-video studio, and a lap pool with a current that lets you swim against the tide.

The *Grand Princess* will spend its summers in the Mediterranean and winters in the Caribbean. But don't expect to see this ship in Alaska or elsewhere in the Pacific: it's 43 ft too wide to fit through the Panama Canal.

Cabins The *Grand Princess* has more private balconies than any other cruise ship—80% of the outside cabins have a veranda. Since the ship was already too wide to for the Panama Canal, balconies could be extended beyond the hull. So unlike on many other ships, having a veranda doesn't mean sacrificing interior cabin space. All cabins have terry cloth robes and hairdryers. Suites and minisuites have butler service; two Grand Suites have a fireplace and outdoor Jacuzzi.

Outlet voltage: 110 AC.

Single supplement: 150%–200% of double-occupancy rate.

Discounts: A third or fourth passenger in a cabin pays half the double-occupancy rate. You get a discount for booking early.

Sports and Fitness

Health club: Top-deck fitness center with waterfall and swim-against-the-tide lap pool, massage, aromatherapy treatments, stationary bikes, step machines, rowing machines, weight machines, juice bar, and beauty salon.

Recreation: Aerobics classes; four adult swimming pools and one children's splash pool; six whirlpool spas; sports deck with volleyball, basketball, and paddle tennis; computerized golf simulator and 9-hole putting green, jogging track and unobstructed circuit (3 laps = 1 mi) for walking.

Facilities

Public rooms: Twelve bars and lounges, three showrooms, disco, casino, libary, virtual-reality theater, video studio, wedding chapel, business center.

Shops: Gift shops and duty-free boutiques.

Health care: Two doctors and two nurses on call.

Child care: Youth center and programs with counselors offered year-round.

Services: Full- and self-service laundry, dry cleaning, photographer, film processing.

Accessibility

The *Grand Princess* is well suited to wheelchair users and have been designed with accessible elevators, wide corridors, and specially equipped public lavatories. Twenty-eight cabins meet the standards of the Americans with Disabilities Act.

MV Island Princess and MV Pacific Princess

Specifications

Type of ship: Cruise liner
Cruise experience: Semiformal
Size: 20,000 tons
Cabins: 305
Outside cabins: 78%

Passengers: 640
Crew: 350 (international)
Officers: British
Passenger/crew ratio: 1.8 to 1
Years built: 1972/1971

Ship's Log

The *Pacific Princess* and *Island Princess* were among the grandest ships at sea when they set sail nearly thirty years ago. Nowadays they seem less posh, but they remain impressive in other ways. They are intimate vessels, ideally suited to the exotic and longer itineraries on which they sail with a crew that has a distinctly familial style. And if they lack some of the glitz and glamour of Princess's newer ships, they are still impart a homey and intimate feel.

For their size (just 20,000 tons), they offer an impressive number of spacious public rooms. As for scale, everything is smaller: Don't expect a soaring atrium or monumental showlounge. Instead you'll find lots of nooks and crannies for private repose. In a short time you'll find some of the perennial hiding spaces—a few yards of deck just behind the bridge with half a dozen lounge chairs, a spot near the card room where two cozy chairs are framed by high windows, or the quieter second story of the cabaret lounge, with a panoramic view aft through a two-deck window.

Periodic makeovers have modernized both ships and updated patterns and fabrics throughout, but metal furnishings in the cabins and very modest fitness centers are enduring reminders that these ships were built in the early 1970s. And cabin keys are still the standard metal variety rather than the plastic cards now common on cruise ships. But in a way, that's part of the charm.

Cabins Other than suites and minisuites, cabins are tiny—especially those in the lower categories. None have private balconies. Decor on both ships is somewhat drab, and colors seem dimmed by time. On the *Island Princess*, it's a blend of blues, pinks, and greens; on the *Pacific Princess*, the palette draws from a mix of earth tones and blues. All cabins are outfitted with a color television, terry robes, and fresh-fruit baskets. There are no hair dryers, but you can request one from housekeeping. Deluxe outside cabins and suites have a refrigerator, but oddly, no bottle opener. Some cabins on the Promenade Deck look onto a public area or have partially obstructed views. Minisuites located at the rear of Promenade Deck should be avoided—they get a lot of noise from the nearby cabaret lounge.

Outlet voltage: 110 AC.

Single supplement: 160%–200% of double-occupancy rate.

Discounts: A third or fourth passenger in a cabin pays half the double-occupancy rate. You get a discount for booking early.

Sports and **Health club:** Lifecycles, rowing machines, weights, weight
Fitness machines, saunas, massage.

Recreation: Aerobics and other exercise classes, golf driving, table tennis, shuffleboard, skeet shooting, two pools, unobstructed circuit (18 laps = 1½ km/1 mi) for jogging.

Facilities **Public rooms:** Six bars, four entertainment lounges, casino, disco, cinema, card room, library/writing room.

Shops: Gift shop, beauty salon/barbershop.

Health care: Doctor and two nurses on call.

Child care: Daytime youth programs with counselors when 15 or more children on board.

Services: Laundry service, dry cleaning, photographer.

Accessibility Public lavatories and four cabins on each ship are equipped with wide toilet stalls and hand bars to accommodate passengers with mobility problems. All four elevators are accessible.

MV Royal Princess

Specifications *Type of ship:* Cruise liner   *Passengers:* 1,200
Cruise experience: Semiformal   *Crew:* 520 (international)
Size: 45,000 tons   *Officers:* British
Cabins: 600   *Passenger/crew ratio:* 2.4 to 1
Outside cabins: 100%   *Year built:* 1984

Ship's Log Although this ship dates back to the mid-1980s, you'd never know. The hull is bright and white, well painted and rust-free (except for a smattering of pitting and a streak by the anchor). Outdoor deck areas look equally good. Public rooms are well maintained, too, although corridors show signs of wear. Overall, though, this ship is immaculately maintained.

Compared with many ships, the *Royal Princess* is a conservative affair. Color schemes are mostly in pastels, and public rooms, from the dining room to the casino, are modest if very well apportioned. There are two showrooms, one for cabarets and the other for production shows, but again, it's not the double-decker extravaganza you'll find on the newest ships. The Horizon Bar and Lounge offers a 360 degree view of the sea from its position on the top deck, much like the Viking Crown Lounge on Royal Caribbean ships.

And while it may not be the most dramatic ship at sea, Princess has nonetheless kept the *Royal* up to date with a new Lido, which doubles as the ship's bistro and pizzeria—giving *Royal Princess* passengers the same dining alternatives that have become so popular on newer vessels.

Cabins   Cabins are all outside, and all standard staterooms are the same size. Each is finished in a different wood by category: oak veneers in the penthouses, teak in the suites, mahogany in the minisuites, and teak again in the standard cabins. Penthouses, suites, minisuites, and Aloha Deck outside cabins have private verandas. Even the smallest cabins are well equipped, with details and amenities not found in standard accommodations aboard many other ships, such as shower/bathtubs, refrigerators, and large windows. However, many cabins have one Pullman-style bed. Higher-priced cabins have wall safes, and penthouses have whirlpools. Terry robes and fresh-fruit baskets are found in each stateroom. Categories H, HH, I, J, JJ, and K are outside cabins with partially or entirely obstructed views.

Outlet voltage: 110 AC.

Single supplement: 200% of double-occupancy rate for suites or outside cabins with verandas, 150%–160% for other cabins.

Discounts: A third or fourth passenger in a cabin pays $132–$150 per diem. You get a discount for early booking and for arranging your own airfare.

Sports and Fitness   **Health club:** Stationary bikes, rowing machines, treadmills, free weights, various other exercise equipment.

Recreation: Aerobics and other exercise classes, golf driving, table tennis, pool sports, shuffleboard, skeet shooting, three pools (one for laps, a circular one surrounded by dipping pools, and another wading pool, all on Lido Deck), Jacuzzi, unobstructed circuit (3½ laps = 1½ km/1 mi) for jogging.

Facilities   **Public rooms:** Seven bars, four entertainment lounges, casino, disco, cinema, card room, library, video-game room.

Shops: Gift shop, beauty salon/barbershop.

Health care: Two doctors and two nurses on call.

Child care: Daytime youth programs with counselors when 15 or more children on board.

Services: Full- and self-service laundry, dry cleaning, photographer, film processing.

Accessibility   Four cabins and all public areas, except the self-service laundry room, are accessible to wheelchair users. Several public lavatories are grab bar–equipped. Raised thresholds leading to outside decks are especially high, but ramps are located at selected entrances.

TSS Sky Princess

Specifications

Type of ship: Cruise liner
Cruise experience: Semiformal
Size: 46,314 tons
Number of cabins: 600
Outside cabins: 64%

Passengers: 1,200
Crew: 535 (international)
Officers: International
Passenger/crew ratio: 2.2 to 1
Year built: 1984

Ship's Log The *Sky Princess* was the last major passenger *steamship* ever built. In keeping with this distinction, the vessel is rather traditional in its design. There is an outdoor promenade with its row of deck chairs shaded by the lifeboats (although the chairs are plastic rather than wooden), deck areas nicley sheltered from the wind, and a theater complete with balcony and plush seats. Most public rooms command good views of the sea. The Horizon Lounge, for example, offers floor-to-ceiling windows and a view directly over the bow—perfect for sailing in scenic waters. The two dining rooms are of intimate size, identical in docor, and have windows that provide a reasonably good view of the passing scene. And at roughly half the tonnage of the newest megaships, the *Sky* offers a comparatively cozy cruise experience with few lines and uncrowded public areas.

Cabins While the *Sky Princess* may have a traditional personality overall, cabins are modern and uniform in size. Many have two upper berths to accommodate third and fourth passengers. Only suites have verandas and tubs. Terry robes and fresh-fruit baskets are placed in each stateroom.

Outlet voltage: 110 AC.

Single supplement: 160%–200% of double-occupancy rate.

Discounts: A third or fourth passenger in a cabin pays half the double-occupancy rate. You get a discount for booking early.

Sports and Fitness **Health club:** Nautilus machines, sit-up board, three Lifecycles, two stationary bikes, ballet barre, sauna, massage room, large whirlpool.

Recreation: Aerobics and other exercise classes, paddle and table tennis, pool games, shuffleboard, skeet shooting, volleyball, three pools (one for children), scuba certification, jogging track (15 laps = 1½ km/1 mi).

Facilities **Public rooms:** Seven bars, four entertainment lounges, casino, disco, card room, library, video-game room.

Shops: Boutiques and gift shops, beauty salon/barbershop.

Health care: Two doctors and two nurses on call.

Child care: Youth center with separate rooms for teens and younger children (older than six months), games, video games, wide-screen TV, children's pool, sundeck, programs supervised by counselors when demand warrants.

Services: Full- and self-service laundry, dry cleaning, photographer, film processing.

Accessibility Ten cabins and all six elevators are accessible to wheelchair users.

Radisson Seven Seas Cruises

The Fleet MS *Hanseatic*   MS *Song of Flower*
MS *Paul Gauguin*   SSC *Radisson Diamond*

An expedition ship, a catamaran, a cruise liner, and a cruise yacht: This odd collection of ships couldn't be more different by design, but they share a level of luxury. The *Radisson Diamond* is the largest twin-hull ship ever built for cruising, while the *Hanseatic* claims the title of biggest expedition ship afloat. Both were built by the same Finnish shipyard and have space and passenger-to-crew ratios as good as any ship afloat. All four ships also offer all outside cabins.

Ships at a Glance

	Dining Rooms	Bars	Casino	Fitness Center	Pools	Average Per Diem
Hanseatic	2*	3	○	●	1	$600–$700
Paul Gauguin	3*	4	●	●	1	$400–$500
Radisson Diamond	2*	4	●	●	1	$500–$600
Song of Flower	2*	4	●	●	1	$400–$500

*includes alternative restaurant

Cruise Experience The *Hanseatic* and *Paul Gauguin* cruise Antarctica and French Polynesia, respectively, while the *Diamond* splits its time between the Caribbean and Europe and the *Song of Flower* concentrates mainly on Europe and Asia. Each ship delivers a different cruise experience. For that reason, details on dining, activities, entertainment, service and tipping, and destinations are covered individually under each Ship's Log.

For More Information Radisson Seven Seas Cruises (600 Corporate Dr., Suite 410, Fort Lauderdale, FL 33334, tel. 800/333–3333).

MS Hanseatic

Type of ship: Expedition
Cruise experience: Casual
Size: 9,000 tons
Number of cabins: 94
Outside cabins: 100%

Passengers: 188
Crew: 125 (Filipino and European)
Officers: European
Passenger/crew ratio: 1.5 to 1
Year built: 1993

Ship's Log The *Hanseatic* is the world's newest, biggest, and most luxurious expedition ship. It carries all the standard expedition features—a hardened hull for plowing through Antarctic ice and 14 Zodiac landing craft for exploring otherwise inaccessible shores—in a level of comfort unusual for an adventure ship. There's a small fitness center and spa, for instance, with a whirlpool, swimming pool, sauna, and massage therapy. The ship's passenger-to-crew ratio rivals the standards of the cruise world's most expensive ships. Because of its relatively large size, the *Hanseatic* is equipped with a more varied selection of public rooms than most expedition ships. There's a cruise-ship-style lounge for evening entertainment; a full-size lecture hall, which doubles as a cinema; and a top-deck observation lounge with 180-degree views of the sea. For warm-weather cruises, the ship also has a decent-size swimming pool and a glass-enclosed whirlpool. You can always visit the captain on the navigation bridge between the enrichment lectures and Zodiac excursions that are the hallmark of the expedition experience.

The *Hanseatic*'s very high standards of comfort, especially as compared with the earlier generation of expedition ships, attract people who might not otherwise take such a cruise. It also means that the hard-core adventure traveler with special interests will be sharing the experience with more mainstream, general-interest passengers. The *Hanseatic* draws a mix of Americans and German-speaking passengers, and the ratio may vary by destination and even departure. Some Antarctic sailings are almost entirely American, others less so. Expeditions to Northern Europe and the Canadian Arctic tend to carry a larger percentage of German-speaking passengers.

Activities   Zodiac explorations are the primary daytime event aboard the *Hanseatic*. In preparation for these shoreside explorations, a team of experts, such as naturalists, marine biologists, geologists, or anthropologists, brief passengers in the Darwin Lounge, a state-of-the-art facility with video and sound systems. (You can also watch the lectures in your cabin.) The experts then accompany passengers ashore. Hitting the beach in a Zodiac usually means a wet landing, but the *Hanseatic* also carries two cruise ship–style enclosed tenders.

Dining   Reflecting the ship's international clientele, menus are distinctly European, with an emphasis on central European cooking rather than the Continental cuisine more familiar to American cruise-ship passengers. This means excellent cream soups, very good salads, a game dish every night, and rich desserts—Americans may find the diet somewhat heavy-handed. A "light" menu is always available at dinnertime, though. The food is expertly presented, but portions are generally small by American standards.

The main restaurant is a spacious room, surrounded on three sides by windows. Meals are served in a single, open seating (dinner from 7 to 9:30). Breakfasts and lunches are hot and cold buffets or from a menu, while dinners are served from a menu only. The captain hosts a table several times during the cruise. A jacket and tie is standard attire for the welcome and farewell dinners, but otherwise, dress is "smart casual." Smoking is allowed in the dining room.

A second restaurant, the informal café, also serves three meals a day. Light breakfast and lunch menus are the standard buffets of salads, hot dogs, hamburgers, hot pastas, and soups; dinners are Asian cuisine—but the main dining room is so attractive that meals here become an afterthought. There are outside tables, though, for warm-weather alfresco dining.

Entertainment   Cabaret shows, orchestras, and dancing are nighttime staples in the Explorer Lounge, where a four-piece band plays at afternoon tea and for before- and after-dinner dancing. Throughout the day, documentary and feature films are shown in the Darwin Hall, as well as over closed-circuit television in the cabins. A resident pianist also performs pre- and post-dinner music in the Observation Lounge and may hold a classical-music evening.

Service and Tipping Service is excellent and the standard of English spoken by the crew is very high. The cabin staff is female, and the dining-room staff is male and female—all young, energetic Germans or northern Europeans. Tips are included in the *Hanseatic*'s cruise fares, but gratuities are allowed for special service. Still, additional tipping is not expected and is never solicited; there is no additional charge for dining in the alternative Asian restaurant, but reservations are necessary.

Destinations The *Hanseatic* sails from the Arctic to Antarctica, and along both coasts of North and South America. You're not likely to find a more comfortable ship going to these remote destinations. (For seasonal itineraries, *see* Chapter 4.)

Cabins Standard cabins are unusually spacious for an expedition ship, but storage space is only average. All accommodations are outside with ocean views, and come with a sitting area, marble bathroom with tubs and wall-mounted hair dryer, color television/VCR, and refrigerator stocked with complimentary nonalcoholic drinks. Beds are mostly twins that cannot be pushed together. Most cabins have picture windows; only the lowest-deck accommodations have portholes. Four suites are twice the size of standard cabins, with double sinks, walk-in closets, and twin or king beds. Private butler service is available for suites and some upper-category double staterooms.

Outlet voltage: 220 AC.

Single supplement: 150%–200% of the double-occupancy rate.

Discounts: A third passenger in a cabin pays 50% of the double-occupancy rate. You get a discount for booking early and for booking back-to-back cruises.

Sports and Fitness **Health club:** Top-deck facility with exercise equipment including stationary bikes, step machines, rowing machine, treadmill, and free weights; sauna; massage; and glass-enclosed whirlpool.

Recreation: Swimming pool.

Facilities **Public rooms:** Main lounge with dance floor and bar, observation lounge with bar, library (books and videos), cinema.

Shops: Boutique, beauty salon.

Health care: Doctor and nurse on call.

Child care: Baby-sitting arranged privately with crew member.

Services: Laundry service, dry cleaning, photographer, film processing.

Accessibility Two cabins are accessible to wheelchair users, as are all elevators and decks except Cinema Deck. Many voyages require Zodiac landings at all or most ports, which may make it difficult for passengers with mobility problems to go ashore.

MS Paul Gauguin

Type of ship: Cruise liner
Cruise experience: Casual
Size: 18,800 tons

Passengers: 320
Crew: 206 (international)
Officers: French

Number of cabins: 160 *Passenger/crew ratio:* 1.5 to 1
Outside cabins: 100% *Year built:* 1997

Ship's Log The Paul Gauguin was built specifically for South Pacific cruising and named after the French post-Impressionist painter, and you might naturally expect billowing white sails on his namesake ship. There are none, but otherwise this gracious cruise liner with a yachtlike feel strikes a perfectly harmonious note with its surroundings. An abundance of windows allows unobstructed views of the islands, and native Polynesian hostesses (known as "Gaugines,") bring a real touch of Tahiti to the ship. A generous amount of deck space and public rooms provides a wide array of retreats for privacy. All beverages aboard ship, except alcohol, are complimentary.

Despite no days at sea, the Paul Gauguin's overnights in three ports add a welcome pause for savoring the islands' distinctiveness and leisurely lifestyle. Towns may be no more than a few stores, and shore excursions rarely operate according to an on-the-dot schedule. But even Type A personalities go with the flow, and indeed by week's end many passengers have "gone native," parading around in pareus. Most passengers hail from the United States, but the French flag attracts French-speaking passengers and other European nationals, an appealing spectrum of experienced and sophisticated travelers.

Due to Tahiti's remoteness, air arrangements, particularly for East Coast passengers, can be strategically important: the line's regular Air New Zealand charters are comfortable; AOM Minerve flights, however, are abominable and should be avoided. Of necessity, passengers arriving on predawn flights will get a day room on Papeete. Conversely, the last night of the cruise often ends early, as passengers retire to their cabins to pack for predawn flight departures. So you may want to consider adding one of the line's three-day pre- or post-cruise vacation packages to the standard seven-day cruise. Carrying seasickness medication is also recommended: Even aboard a ship with stabilizers, island-to-island cruising can be choppy in the South Pacific.

Activities Cruises feature lectures on local history, nature, and culture. Activities emphasize water sports such as diving, snorkeling, and sailing. The ship even offers a certified dive program.

From the ship's retractable marina, passengers can launch a Windsurfer, sail a Sunfish, or go kayaking (but swimming from the marina is not permitted). Tours visit rain forests, tropical plantations, unexceptional archaeological sites, relics of World War II, and the bluest lagoons and coral reefs. The ship tenders passengers ashore in all ports except Papeete.

Most excursions ashore offer good value, especially the Jeep safaris and helicopter flights, and each day's excursion tickets thoughtfully remind passengers what to bring ashore. Complimentary bottled water and fluffy beach towels are distributed. Off Bora Bora, the *Paul Gauguin*'s version of a private island (a motu) affords an afternoon of snorkeling and sunbathing, complete with a champagne bar set in crystal-clear water.

Dining Even in the main dining room, men are never required to wear a jacket. Dinner is served in a single, open seating. Complimentary wines are offered at lunch and dinner. Cuisine is Continental, featuring French and seafood specialties. The daily luncheon buffets are imaginative and superb, especially the salads and pasta. Fresh island fruits, ferried directly from shore, are not to be missed.

Two alternative dining options are available. La Veranda serves from a fixed menu of outstanding French cuisine and so-so Italian food. The menu alternates between the two. Reservations must be made in advance, and they book up quickly. Another casual alternative for dinner is La Grille, an indoor-outdoor glass-partitioned bistro on the pool deck that can be hot, humid, and windy. Room service also is available 24 hours a day.

Entertainment As there are no days at sea, daytime diversions onboard tend to be prosaic, though pareu-tying lessons lend a nice island touch. Evening entertainment may include a magician, traditional Tahitian dancing and music, or cabaret shows presented in the main lounge.

The modest lecture program is hit or miss: some speakers are quite knowledgeable; others blow as much hot air as the trade winds. Because of local laws, the ship's casino levies a onetime $10 "club fee," and options may be limited to gaming tables.

There's also a film library with videos for the in-cabin VCRs. The selection is quite adequate, especially for a seven-day cruise.

Service and Tipping Service, although eager, often falls short of flawless—especially from the wait staff in the dining room. Room service, on the other hand, is stellar, delivering virtually instant response.

The international crew is directed by French officers, and English and French are the principal languages. All onboard gratuities are included in the fares. In general, tipping is not expected ashore in Polynesia.

Destinations The *Paul Gauguin* makes weekly seven-day cruises of French Polynesia, sailing round-trip from Papeete, Tahiti. Equatorial temperatures can be hot, hot, hot. (For year-round itineraries, *see* Chapter 4.)

Cabins All cabins are spacious outside accommodations with picture windows (except for Category F accommodations, which have portholes) and ample storage space. Half the ship's cabins have private verandas; suites have the largest verandas. All cabins offer a sitting area, individual temperature control, TV/VCR, refrigerator and minibar (stocked once for free with a charge for refills), personal safe, telephone, and marble bathroom with full-size bath and shower, hair dryer, terry cloth robes, generous bathroom amenities, including full-size soap. Curiously, though, cabins have no nightstands, although suites do. Cabins 409 and 411 should be avoided due to excessive engine noise.

Outlet voltage: 100/220 AC.

Single supplement: 125%–200% of double-occupancy rate.

Discounts: You get a discount for booking early.

Sports and Fitness **Health club:** Small fitness center with complete range of exercise equipment, spa with steam room, Jacuzzi, aromatherapy, thalassotherapy, massage, facials, and beauty salon.

Recreation: Retractable water-sports platform for launching Windsurfers and sea kayaks; snorkeling and diving gear; outdoor pool.

Facilities **Public rooms:** Four bars, entertainment/lecture lounge, disco, casino, library, card room.

Shops: Boutique, pharmacy, beauty salon/barbershop.

Health care: Doctor and nurse on call.

Child care: None.

Services: Laundry service, photographer, conference center.

Accessibility One Category E cabin and two sets of elevators are accessible to wheelchair users; elevators are not braille or audio-equipped.

SSC Radisson Diamond

Type of ship: Cruise liner	*Passengers:* 350
Cruise experience: Semiformal	*Crew:* 192 (international)
Size: 20,000 tons	*Officers:* Scandinavian
Number of cabins: 177	*Passenger/crew ratio:* 1.8 to 1
Outside cabins: 100%	*Year built:* 1992

Ship's Log As wide as an ocean liner but only as long as a yacht, the *Diamond* is the only cruise ship ever to receive a *Popular Mechanics* design and engineering award. The futuristic catamaran resembles a spider perched over the sea. While the twin-hull design actually does make the ship more stable and reduce the chance of causing seasickness, the difference in motion takes some getting used to. During a storm there is none of the normal pitch and roll, but stabilizers cause a very slight side-to-side jerking motion—which only becomes an issue if you are wearing high heels and trying to keep your balance. The *Diamond* was specifically built to stage meetings and conventions at sea, so in addition to being one of the most stable cruise ships afloat, it is also especially spacious. However, while the open-deck space is beautifully designed, the main bar is like a dark cave with no windows. The main showroom, meanwhile, is poorly designed, especially compared with most other ships. Most passengers cannot see the performers, except if seated in the front rows of each seating level.

On the other hand, outdoor deck space is especially well designed for sunbathers and shade-seekers alike. You can get your tan or find a wind-protected spot for curling up with a good book.

Activities In keeping with the ship's relaxed mood, there are few organized events on board. People gather at their leisure for such activities as dancing lessons, card games, backgammon, and shuffleboard. The *Diamond* also has an extensive book and videotape library. At least once a cruise (weather permitting), water activities are held off the large marina platform, which is built into the stern of the ship and lowers into the water. Passengers can swim in a small netted pool, ride on a Jet Ski, or snorkel.

A number of theme cruises are scheduled each year; the most popular are culinary and literary. The ship's lecture series headlines speakers on a wide range of topics from banking to Broadway musicals. Ashore, the *Diamond* offers some interesting alternatives to the usual shore excursions: In St. Maarten you can race on an "America's Cup" 12-meter sailboat.

Dining Dining aboard the *Diamond* reflects its elegant and exclusive demeanor. International cuisine is served in the Grand Dining Room—one of the prettiest dining rooms afloat—in one open seating, so you dine when and with whomever you want (dinner is served 7:30–10). Wine is complimentary at dinner. There's one formal night per seven-night cruise, with elegant casual attire the norm other evenings—a little more relaxed than on other ships in this price category.

A second dinner option is the intimate Italian restaurant, also with one seating at 8. Six wonderful courses are served from a fixed menu in a festive atmosphere. Reservations should be made as soon as you board, because the restaurant is very popular.

Breakfast and lunch buffets are served in the Grill (at night this is the Italian restaurant). The sumptuous lunch buffets, which feature a different theme menu each day, are among the best you'll find on any cruise ship. Early riser coffee is served daily beginning at 6:30 AM, and afternoon tea is served with rich pastries in the Windows Lounge or the Grill. Room service is available 24 hours a day from an extensive menu; in-room dinners are served complete with linen napery, crystal, china, and flowers.

Entertainment   Evening entertainment is generally mellow and consists of cabaret-style shows, a pianist, a small musical combo, and comedians. Partyers can stay as late as they like in the disco and the casino.

Service and   Cabin service is expertly provided by female Austrian, Swiss, and
Tipping   Scandinavian cabin stewardesses; the dining-room staff is mostly female as well. The *Radisson Diamond* has a no-tipping policy.

Destinations   The *Diamond* gives passengers a choice of wintertime Caribbean itineraries lasting 3, 4, 7, or 10 days, as well as Panama Canal transits. Summer and fall are spent cruising the Mediterranean. (For seasonal itineraries, *see* Chapter 4.)

Cabins   Cabins are all outside on three upper decks; most (70%) have a private veranda, others have a large bay window. The balconies are very well designed to ensure privacy. None have obstructed views. Soothing mauve, sky-blue, or sea-green fabrics are accented by birch wood, and each cabin has a stocked minibar and refrigerator. (Your initial allotment of drinks is free; refills are provided for a fee.) Bathrooms are spacious, with marble vanities, tubs, and hair dryers. In-cabin TVs show CNN and feature films. No third or fourth berths are available.

Outlet voltage: 110 AC.

Single supplement: 125% of double-occupancy rate.

Discounts: You get a discount for booking early and for booking back-to-back cruises on selected itineraries.

Sports and   **Health club:** Aerobics studio, weight room, Lifecycles, Lifesteps,
Fitness   Liferowers, Jacuzzi, and body-toning spa with massage and herbal-wrap treatments.

Recreation: Golf driving range with nets, putting green, minigolf; shuffleboard; water sports, including snorkeling, windsurfing, jet skiing, and swimming; jogging track.

Facilities   **Public rooms:** Four bars, entertainment lounge/disco, casino, library, conference center and boardroom.

Shops: Boutique, drugstore, beauty salon/barbershop.

Health care: Doctor and nurse on call.

Child care: None.

Services: Laundry service, photographer, film-developing service, business center with software library, fax, publishing facilities, personal computer hookups.

Accessibility   Elevators, public lavatories, and two cabins are accessible to wheelchair users.

MS Song of Flower

Type of ship: Cruise yacht	*Passengers:* 180
Cruise experience: Semiformal	*Crew:* 144 (international)
Size: 8,282 tons	*Officers:* Norwegian
Number of cabins: 100	*Passenger/crew ratio:* 1.3 to 1
Outside cabins: 100%	*Year built:* 1986

Ship's Log   Like its fleetmates, the *Song of Flower* is designed to appeal to upscale cruisers. Although the ship is luxurious, it is also quite small, with limited public space, mostly at the rear of the ship. (Cabins are all located amidships and forward.) The few public rooms include a tiered, theaterlike main lounge with a bar and good views of the water, a nightclub with a bar and a small casino (blackjack) to one side, a book-and-video library, a boutique, and a small gym with sauna. Up high and overlooking the bow is an attractive observation lounge, which serves as a popular venue for pre-dinner drinks. Inside the observation lounge are charts and a world globe; outside is a good viewing deck.

Passengers may visit the bridge at any time while the ship is at sea in good weather. For sunbathing and swimming, there's a pool and a Jacuzzi on the Sun Deck; an ample supply of lounge chairs can also be found on the two decks above, one sheltered. The *Song of Flower* has no wraparound deck for walking or jogging, only a narrow open deck down each side. The main purpose of this vessel is to provide a stylish home base for visiting exotic ports of call.

Activities   There are few of the usual cruise games and demonstrations on the *Song of Flower*'s daily schedule. Other than exploring in port, the main activities are lectures given by an expert speaker who accompanies every cruise. Topics may include art, history, and local culture—usually two a day when the ship is at sea.

Dining   The food is excellent in all the ship's dining venues, and complimentary red and white wines are offered at lunch and dinner.

The Galaxy Dining Room accommodates all passengers in one seating (dinner served from 7 to 9:30), but when the ship is completely full, there may be a wait at the peak dinner hour of 8 PM. The nightly menu features six entrées; a standard daily menu offers steak, roast chicken, and other dishes.

Dinner is also served in A Taste of Italy, an attractive alternative restaurant seating 30 (reservations are required). Except for three entrées, the menu changes nightly, and the entire meal, 13 items, is presented one dish at a time (thus the name "A Taste of Italy"). A pianist accompanies dinner; after the main course, two Italian waiters join in with song. It makes for a spirited evening—but you'll probably only want to do it once each cruise.

Other meal venues include an outdoor café and grill on the Sun Deck, which is somewhat marred by engine noise when the ship is traveling at full speed. Buffet breakfast and lunch are served here, with cook-to-order entrées also available. The lunch buffets here and in the main restaurant are theme affairs that may highlight Italian, Asian, or Mexican dishes. Room service is available 24 hours a day.

Entertainment   Entertainment is low-key. There are nightly cabaret shows, a five-piece orchestra for dancing, a small disco, and a pianist, who plays during dinner in the alternative Italian restaurant. The ship's library stocks 2,000 books and 400 videos for use on in-cabin VCRs.

Service and Tipping	Service is excellent throughout. Scandinavian stewardesses keep staterooms stocked with fresh flowers and fruit. All beverages, alcoholic and otherwise, are complimentary throughout the ship—in the bars, dining room, and cabins. The *Song of Flower* has a no-tipping policy.

Destinations The *Song of Flower* sails to Europe, Arabia, India, Southeast Asia, and the Far East. Pre- and post-cruise land packages are an integral part of the journey. All shore excursions are included, but the ship offers concierge service for those who prefer to tour independently. (For seasonal itineraries, *see* Chapter 4.)

Cabins All cabins are roomy and outside; the Category B veranda rooms are the most popular. Every room is equipped with TV/VCR, complimentary stocked minibar, hair dryer, bathrobes, and two locked drawers. The half tubs are awkwardly placed in a corner and difficult to step out of. Closet and drawer storage is more than adequate.

Outlet voltage: 110/220 AC.

Single supplement: 125% of double-occupancy rate.

Discounts: You get a discount for booking early and for booking back-to-back cruises on selected itineraries.

Sports and Fitness **Health club:** Lifecycles, StairMaster, free weights, Jacuzzi, sauna, massage.

Recreation: Swimming pool; Windsurfers and snorkeling equipment available when in port.

Facilities **Public rooms:** Four bars, observation lounge, showroom, casino, disco, library.

Shops: Gift shop, beauty salon/barbershop.

Health care: Doctor and nurse on call.

Child care: None.

Services: Laundry and dry-cleaning service, photographer, business center, concierge.

Accessibility Elevators, public lavatories, and two cabins are accessible to wheelchair users.

Royal Caribbean International

The Fleet

MS *Enchantment of the Seas*	MS *Rhapsody of the Seas*
MS *Grandeur of the Seas*	MS *Song of America*
MS *Legend of the Seas*	MS *Sovereign of the Seas*
MS *Majesty of the Seas*	MS *Splendour of the Seas*
MS *Monarch of the Seas*	MS *Viking Serenade*
MS *Nordic Empress*	MS *Vision of the Seas*

Imagine if they took the Mall of America and sent it to sea. Then you have a pretty good idea of what Royal Caribbean's huge megaships are all about. These giant vessels are indoor/outdoor wonders, with atrium lobbies, shopping arcades, elaborate spas, and expansive sundecks. Two Royal Caribbean ships have 18-hole miniature-golf courses; another vessel has two movie theaters. And as the year 2000 approaches, these mammoth ships are fast replacing the smaller vessels in Royal Caribbean's fleet. The line is currently engaged in the industry's most ambitious shipbuilding program, making cruising's biggest fleet even bigger. Just over the horizon is "Project Eagle"—two 136,000-ton ships carrying 3,100 passengers. The first is due out in late 1999 and the second in the fall of the year 2000, each at a cost of $500 million. A third Eagle-class ship may be ordered for delivery in 2001.

Royal Caribbean passengers have three generations of megaships to choose from including the prototype, the *Sovereign of the Seas*. Each shares certain design qualities, but each successive generation improves upon the basic design. The centerpiece of all these ships is the Centrum atrium, a Royal Caribbean hallmark that many other cruise lines have adopted. The brilliance of this layout is that all the major public rooms radiate from this central focus point, so you'll learn your way around these huge ships within minutes of boarding. The latest ships, known as the "Vision" series (the *Legend of the Seas* and *Splendour of the Seas*, *Enchantment of the Seas* and *Grandeur of the Seas*, and *Rhapsody of the Seas* and *Vision of the Seas*) are not just big but airy: Views of the sea always seem to be all around.

The main problem with these otherwise well-conceived vessels is that Royal Caribbean still packs too many people aboard, especially if all upper berths are filled, making for an exasperating experience at embarkation, while tendering, and at disembarkation. However, the range of facilities is unparalleled and the ships maintain a sense of ocean liner tradition.

Ships at a Glance

	Dining Rooms	Bars	Casino	Fitness Center	Pools	Average Per Diem
Grandeur of the Seas *Enchantment of the Seas*	1	8	●	●	2	$200–$300

Legend of the Seas Splendour of the Seas	1	7	●	●	2	$200–$300
Majesty of the Seas Monarch of the Seas	2	8	●	●	2	$200–$300
Nordic Empress	1	5	●	●	1	$200–$300
Rhapsody of the Seas Vision of the Seas	1	8	●	●	2	$200–$300
Song of America	1	6	●	●	2	$200–$300
Sovereign of the Seas	2	8	●	●	2	$200–$300
Viking Serenade	2	4	●	●	1	$200–$300

Cruise Experience Royal Caribbean is one of the best-run and most popular cruise lines. While the fleet comprises ships both big and small, the company's philosophy remains consistent: Offer every imaginable activity in a resortlike atmosphere between port calls at a variety of destinations. Royal Caribbean draws customers from every age group and economic bracket. While the line competes directly with Carnival (*see above*) for passengers, there are distinct differences of ambience and energy. Royal Caribbean is a bit more sophisticated and subdued, while delivering a good time on a grand scale.

Activities Life on board is similar to that on the party ships run by Carnival, but slightly more sophisticated and conservative. Among the many activities offered are cash bingo (plus free poolside bingo for prizes), board and card games, arts and crafts, pool games, dance classes, golf driving and putting, and "horse racing." Gaming lessons will teach you how to play the games of chance in the casino. Following current fitness trends, the ships also feature numerous exercise activities and well-equipped gyms. Most Caribbean cruises have daylong beach parties at Labadee, Haiti, or CocoCay, a private Bahamian island. The line's Golf Ahoy program includes greens time at private courses in Florida, the Caribbean, Bermuda, the Bahamas, and Baja, Mexico.

Dining Food is Royal Caribbean's weakness—although the dining rooms on the newer ships are indeed beautiful, the food and service often doesn't measure up to it surroundings. While dishes are adequately prepared, they are just not as tasty as they should be. Dinner is served at two assigned seatings per meal (dinner at 6:15 and 8:30). Two formal evenings are held on each seven-day cruise, one on three- and four-day cruises. The line's *Monarch* and *Majesty* sisters have two dining rooms—the closest you get to intimate aboard these huge vessels.

Health-conscious eaters or those just watching their diet will find an extensive vegetarian menu, low-fat choices, and low-cholesteral optons, but Royal Caribbean is not equipped to handle individual dietary requests such as kosher meals. There is no smoking in the dining room.

The buffet-style indoor-outdoor café serves early-morning coffee, breakfast and lunch. At night it becomes the ship's alternative restaurant for casual dinners (except on the *Song of America*).

Other food service includes afternoon tea (with a make-your-own sundae bar), a midnight buffet, and late-night sandwich service in the lounges. Room service is available 24 hours from a limited menu. In-cabin multicourse dinners can be ordered from a selection of dishes off the evening's dining-room menu.

Entertainment This is one of Royal Caribbean's strong suits. The company follows the established formula for cruise-ship entertainment, but with a dash of pizzazz and professionalism. Nightly variety shows, late-night comedy and solo cabaret acts, steel-drum combos, passenger talent shows, and theme parties are staged on each cruise.

Service and Tipping The crew is generally enthusiastic and personable, although service can be slow—not surprising given the number of passengers that must be served on the larger ships. Royal Caribbean does the big things very well, the smaller things less well, and it's those small annoyances that add up. Service is often programmed rather than personal; individual requests are not easily handled. Generally, the staff is friendly if not overly proficient.

Tip the room steward and the waiter each $3 per passenger per diem, the busboy $1.50; the headwaiter gets $2.50 per passenger per cruise (for excellent service only). Tips for bar staff should be given at the time of service.

Destinations Royal Caribbean still calls its namesake home, but the line also sails on 73 itineraries to 145 destinations in Alaska, Asia, Bermuda, Europe, Hawai'i, Mexico, and the Panama Canal. (For seasonal itineraries, *see* Chapter 4.)

For More Information Royal Caribbean International (1050 Caribbean Way, Miami, FL 33132, tel. 305/539-6000 or 800/255-4373 for brochures).

MS Enchantment of the Seas and MS Grandeur of the Seas

Specifications *Type of ship:* Megaship
Cruise experience: Casual
Size: 73,817 tons
Number of cabins: 975
Outside cabins: 58%

Passengers: 1,950
Crew: 760 (international)
Officers: International
Passenger/crew ratio: 2.5 to 1
Years built: 1997/1996

Ship's Log With touches of Jazz Age opulence, the *Grandeur of the Seas* may be the line's most elegant (and impressive) ship. In fact, it has few rivals at sea from any line. This big boat has it all: a seven-story atrium, bilevel health club, balconied show room, and more. Unfortunately, it doesn't have an 18-hole miniature golf course like the *Legend of the Seas* and *Splendour of the Seas*. Maybe that's because the line has designed the *Grandeur* so that passengers spend less time at sea: It's a fast ship, and passengers will get four full days in port during a weeklong Caribbean cruise.

From its gilded showroom to its soaring atrium, the *Enchantment of the Seas* bears a striking resemblance to its sister, the *Grandeur*. Of course, the *Enchantment* has its own design flourishes, especially in the key public spaces. Themes here include an Asian motif in the Solarium and Spa and a Victorian formality in the colonnaded dining room—all done up in wedding-cake white. There's a little whimsy—a plundering pirate keeps an eye on his booty in the casino—and there's a little history—Viking imagery complements the Viking Crown Lounge, while ropes and rigging in the Schooner Bar evoke the olden days of seafaring.

This eclectic mix of styles makes the *Enchantment* something of a bridge between its sister the *Grandeur* and the other ships in the "Vision-class" series. And while the *Enchantment's* isn't quite as rich as the *Grandeur*, it's still an elegant ship, and along with its sister, the cream of the crop. These two are the nicest ships in the Royal Caribbean fleet.

Cabins The *Enchantment* and *Grandeur* have relatively large cabins and more balconies than Royal Caribbean's previous megaships. Of the total cabins aboard, about one quarter have private verandas. The ships also have specially designed family suites with separate bedrooms for parents and children.

Standard cabins are pretty, with a small sitting area. Each is appointed in light woods and brass accents. Draperies draw from colors schemes in peach, mauve, and turquoise. Bathrooms are small and have pink towels to match the cabin decor. However, like the other ships in the "Vision" series, the *Enchantment* and *Grandeur* have no built-in hair dryers, an odd oversight for such well-equipped vessels.

Outlet voltage: 110/220 AC.

Single supplement: 150% of double-occupancy rate; however, less expensive singles are available if you are willing to wait until embarkation time for your cabin assignment.

Discounts: A third or fourth passenger in a cabin pays reduced per diems. You get a discount for booking early.

Sports and Fitness
Health club: Two-level spa with Lifecycles, Lifesteps, exercise equipment, Jacuzzis, sauna, and massage.

Recreation: Two pools, shuffleboard, table tennis, unobstructed circuit for jogging.

Facilities
Public rooms: Eight bars, three entertainment lounges, casino, disco, library, card room, video-game room, conference center.

Shops: Gift shop and boutiques, beauty salon/barbershop.

Health care: Doctor and three nurses on call.

Child care: Playroom, teen center, youth counselors, children's programs in four age groups year-round, baby-sitting arranged privately with crew member, cribs available but must be requested at time of booking.

Services: Laundry service, dry cleaning, photographer.

Accessibility Fourteen staterooms are designed to meet the standards of the Americans with Disabilities Act. Elevators, extra-wide corridors, and public lavatories are also designed to be accessible to wheelchair users. Crew members will carry passengers and their wheelchairs onto the ship's tenders if conditions permit.

MS Legend of the Seas and MS Splendour of the Seas

Specifications

Type of ship: Megaship	*Passengers:* 1,804/1,800
Cruise experience: Casual	*Crew:* 732 (international)
Size: 69,130 tons	*Officers:* International
Number of cabins: 902/900	*Passenger/crew ratio:* 2.4 to 1
Outside cabins: 65%	*Years built:* 1995/1996

Ship's Log These may not be the biggest ships afloat, but they are state of the art in every other respect. Aboard the *Legend* and *Splendour* you'll find everything one would expect on a cruise ship and more: There's an indoor/outdoor spa reminiscent of a Roman bath, and the cruise world's first 18-hole miniature-golf courses, landscaped to imitate real links with greens, sand traps, and water hazards. The Solarium, an indoor-outdoor public space set around the pool, uses a new design that increases the amount of glass in the retractable roof and minimizes the need for steel supports. The Solarium's Roman-inspired decor uses lightweight plastics and plaster to simulate a setting of marble and stone. Each ship also has a stargazing platform on the highest forward deck.

The dining rooms aboard the *Legend* and *Splendour* are two-level extravaganzas, flanked on either side by 20-ft walls of glass. In the center, a revolving platform supports a grand piano. A grand staircase connects the upper and lower dining levels. Main show-rooms span two decks as well, but rather than a balconied design, there is a single, sloping, amphitheater-style floor. At the stage, a real orchestra pit can be raised and lowered. Unlike many other showrooms, passengers sit in real theater seats rather than in groupings of lounge chairs and couches.

Cabins The *Legend* and *Splendour* have larger cabins than Royal Caribbean's earlier megaships and more have balconies (231 compared with 60). All cabins have a sitting area—even inside cabins—and are appointed in pretty pastels, with brass accents and wood moldings. Many cabins are family-friendly, with upper berths for a third or fourth person. Bathrooms lack hair dryers, an odd omission on a ship otherwise so well equipped. The Royal Suite, largest on the ship, has a bedroom, a dining room, and a living room with a baby grand piano. Other suites have separate sleeping and living quarters, too, but no piano. Standard equipment does include refrigerators, bars, and real bathtubs.

Outlet voltage: 110/220 AC.

Single supplement: 150% of double-occupancy rate; however, less-expensive singles can be had if you're willing to wait until embarkation time for your cabin assignment.

Discounts: A third or fourth passenger in a cabin pays reduced per diems. You get a discount for booking early.

Sports and Fitness **Health club:** Rowing machines, treadmills, stationary bikes, massage, men's and women's saunas, outdoor whirlpools.

Recreation: Aerobics and fitness program, miniature golf, table tennis, shuffleboard, snorkeling lessons, two pools, jogging track.

Facilities **Public rooms:** Seven bars, four entertainment lounges, casino, disco, theater, card room, library, video-game room.

Shops: Five boutiques and gift shops, beauty salon/barbershop.

Health care: Two doctors and three nurses on call.

Child care: Teen center, children's playroom, year-round supervised youth programs in four age groups, baby-sitting privately arranged with crew member, cribs available but must be requested at time of booking. Two family cabins with a parent's bedroom, children's bedroom, two bathrooms, living area, and private balcony.

Services: Laundry service, dry cleaning, photographer, film processing.

Accessibility These ships are well suited to wheelchair users, with accessible elevators, wide corridors, and specially equipped public lavatories. Seventeen cabins are designed for passengers with mobility problems. Crew members will carry passengers and their wheelchairs onto the tenders if conditions permit.

MS Majesty of the Seas and MS Monarch of the Seas

Specifications

Type of ship: Megaship	*Passengers:* 2,354
Cruise experience: Casual	*Crew:* 822 (international)
Size: 73,941 tons	*Officers:* Norwegian
Number of cabins: 1,177	*Passenger/crew ratio:* 2.8 to 1
Outside cabins: 63%	*Years built:* 1992/1991

Ship's Log *Majesty of the Seas* and *Monarch of the Seas*, identical sister ships, are two of the largest vessels built specifically for cruising. Each is as tall as the Statue of Liberty and three football fields long. The glass-enclosed Viking Crown Lounge is 14 stories above sea level. Given such enormous dimensions, these ships are often described in superlatives. Their immense size, however, also means that you can spend seven days on board and never feel that you're really at sea. Lines, too, can be long, and the service, although efficient, sometimes lacks a personal touch. Nevertheless, these are excellent ships for first-time passengers because they have everything a cruise was ever meant to have.

The heart of each ship is a dramatic five-story atrium accented with brass railings and curving stairways as well as signature glass elevators. An arcade with 10 shops sells everything from fur coats to jewelry. During mealtimes and in the afternoon, passengers are serenaded with music. The dining room serves a different international menu each evening; waiters dress accordingly, and musicians stroll among the tables playing music to match the cuisine.

Cabins Standard cabins on the *Majesty* and *Monarch* are appointed in either nautical blues or shades of pink. Cabins on the Promenade Deck look onto a public area. Concierge service is provided for passengers in suites. Many cabins have one or two upper berths in addition to beds. In-cabin TVs show CNN broadcasts.

Outlet voltage: 110/220 AC.

Single supplement: 150% of double-occupancy rate; however, less expensive singles can be had if you're willing to wait until embarkation time for your cabin assignment.

Discounts: A third or fourth passenger in a cabin pays reduced per diems. You get a discount for booking early.

Sports and Fitness **Health club:** Rowing machines, treadmills, stationary bikes, massage, men's and women's saunas, outdoor whirlpool.

Recreation: Aerobics and fitness program, basketball, table tennis, shuffleboard, snorkeling lessons, two pools, unobstructed circuits for jogging.

Facilities **Public rooms:** Eight bars, seven entertainment lounges, casino, disco, cinema, card room, library, video-game room.

Shops: Ten boutiques and gift shops, beauty salon/barbershop.

Health care: Two doctors and three nurses on call.

Child care: Playroom, teen centers, youth counselors, children's programs in four age groups year-round, baby-sitting privately arranged with crew member, cribs available but must be requested at time of booking. Each ship has a family cabin (No. 1549) with a parent's bedroom, children's bedroom, two bathrooms, living area, and private balcony.

Services: Laundry service, dry cleaning, photographer, film processing.

Accessibility   These ships are well suited to wheelchair users, with 18 accessible elevators, wide corridors, and specially equipped public lavatories. Four cabins, two inside and two outside, are designed for passengers with mobility problems. Crew members will carry passengers and their wheelchairs onto the ship's tenders if conditions permit; Coco Cay is all sand, however, which makes moving about in a wheelchair difficult.

MS Nordic Empress

Specifications   *Type of ship:* Cruise liner   *Passengers:* 1,600
Cruise experience: Casual   *Crew:* 671 (international)
Size: 48,563 tons   *Officers:* International
Number of cabins: 800   *Passenger/crew ratio:* 2.3 to 1
Outside cabins: 60%   *Year built:* 1990

Ship's Log   The *Nordic Empress*—a distinctive-looking ship with huge rear bay windows—was specifically designed for the three- and four-day cruise market. Much thought was put into making it easy for passengers to learn their way about the ship on such a short voyage. The result includes the innovative idea of a single main corridor running down only one side of the ship, on the decks where the public rooms are located.

The interior, filled with large and festive public rooms, is a glittering combination of art deco and futuristic designs. At the center of the ship is a six-story atrium, which dazzles with light, glass, chrome, and even cascading waterfalls. Vying for attention is cruising's only triple-level casino and a spacious double-decker dining room with a sensational view of the sea. The commodious showroom and the disco also rise two decks. Because of the stern windows, the *Empress*'s Windjammer Café is forward rather than aft, where most Lidos are traditionally situated. The unusually configured and decorated Sun Deck is more like a private club, with its sail-like canopies, gazebos, and fountains.

Cabins   Cabins and closets are average in size and comtemporary in their appointments. Fabrics are light pastels; furnishings are beige Formica with light wood trim. Bathrooms are bright, compact, and intelligently laid out. In-cabin TVs show CNN broadcasts. Some cabins are not well insulated against noise. Views from some cabins on the Mariner Deck are obstructed by lifeboats. Suites have private verandas.

Outlet voltage: 110/220 AC.

Single supplement: 150% of double-occupancy rate; however, less expensive singles can be had if you're willing to wait until embarkation time for your cabin assignment.

Discounts: A third or fourth passenger in a cabin pays reduced per diems. You get a discount for booking early.

Sports and Fitness   **Health club:** Gym with treadmills, step machines, rowing machine, stationary bicycles, free weights, sauna, steam room, and massage.

Recreation: Aerobics and other exercise classes, table tennis, shuffleboard, pool, children's pool, four whirlpools, unobstructed circuit (5 laps = 1½ km/1 mi) for jogging.

Facilities   **Public rooms:** Five bars, three entertainment lounges, casino, disco, video-game room, conference center.

Shops: Gift shop, beauty salon/barbershop.

Health care: Doctor and two nurses on call.

Child care: Kid/Teen Center playroom on Sun Deck has supervised programs in four age groups year-round, baby-sitting arranged privately with crew member, cribs available but must be requested at time of booking.

Services: Laundry service, photographer.

Accessibility The *Nordic Empress* is well suited to wheelchair users, although official company policy requires that an able-bodied traveling companion accompany wheelchair users. Four cabins are accessible, with wide doors, level floors, and oversize bathrooms with rails. Most elevators accommodate standard-size wheelchairs. Crew members will carry passengers and their wheelchairs onto the ship's tenders if conditions permit.

MS Rhapsody of the Seas and MS Vision of the Seas

Specifications   *Type of ship:* Megaship   *Passengers:* 2,000
Cruise experience: Casual   *Crew:* 760 (international)
Size: 78,491 tons   *Officers:* International
Number of cabins: 1,000   *Passenger/crew ratio:* 2.5 to 1
Outside cabins: 58%   *Year built:* 1997

Ship's Log The *Rhapsody of the Seas* has a cooler personality than other ships in the "Vision" series. This difference in temperament is most evident in the art nouveau–inspired dining room, where the etched glass and crystal accents are a clear departure from the rich wood and deep hues found aboard the *Grandeur.* An industrial feel prevails in the main shopping corridor, with its brushed metal and overhead lighting panels—much like an underground passageway. In fact, the *Rhapsody* has a more enclosed feeling than the other ships in the "Vision" series. Even around the pool, the canopied areas seem more closed in than similar spaces do aboard the *Grandeur* (perhaps this is because the *Rhapsody* was designed to spend part of the year in Alaska). On the other hand, Royal Caribbean has become increasingly creative at inventing themes for its Solarium Spas. The *Legend of the Seas'* was Greco-Roman, the *Grandeur*'s was Moorish, and now the *Rhapsody*'s is ancient Egyptian. It's by far the most imaginative part of the ship.

The *Vision of the Seas* was scheduled to make its European debut in May of 1998. As the sixth and final ship in Royal Caribbean's "Vision" series, it should look a lot like its sister, the *Rhapsody,* meaning that lighter touches, like etched glass and crystal, are likely to dominate its decor. Of course, the *Vision* is sure to incorporate many of the standard design features of its fleetmates. A dramatic balconied dining room and tiered showroom are sure to be among the highlights of the ship. The Schooner Bar—a standard feature of every Royal Caribbean ship—will evoke seafaring days of the past. And the Viking Crown Lounge, with its wraparound glass, will be the crowning touch of the seven-story atrium. The Solarium Spa will certainly have a whimsical theme. The only question is, "what?"

Cabins The *Rhapsody* and *Vision* have relatively large cabins and more balconies than Royal Caribbean's previous megaships. Of the total cabins aboard, about one quarter have private verandas. The ships also have specially designed family suites with separate bedrooms for parents and children.

Standard cabins are pretty, with a small sitting area. Each is appointed in light woods and brass accents. Draperies draw from colors schemes in peach, mauve, and turquoise. Bathrooms are small and have pink towels to match the cabin decor. However, like the *Rhapsody* and *Vision* have no built-in hair dryers, an odd oversight for such well-equipped vessels.

Outlet voltage: 110/220 AC.

Single supplement: 150% of double-occupancy rate; however, less expensive singles are available if you are willing to wait until embarkation time for your cabin assignment.

Discounts: A third or fourth passenger in a cabin pays reduced per diems. You get a discount for booking early.

Sports and Fitness

Health club: Two-level spa with Lifecycles, Lifesteps, exercise equipment, Jacuzzis, sauna, and massage.

Recreation: Two pools, shuffleboard, table tennis, unobstructed circuit for jogging.

Facilities

Public rooms: Eight bars, three entertainment lounges, casino, disco, library, card room, video-game room, conference center.

Shops: Gift shop and boutiques, beauty salon/barbershop.

Health care: Doctor and three nurses on call.

Child care: Playroom, teen center, youth counselors, children's programs in four age groups year-round, baby-sitting arranged privately with crew member, cribs available but must be requested at time of booking.

Services: Laundry service, dry cleaning, photographer.

Accessibility

Fourteen staterooms are designed to meet the standards of the Americans with Disabilities Act. Elevators, extra-wide corridors, and public lavatories are also designed to be accessible to wheelchair users. Crew members will carry passengers and their wheelchairs onto the ship's tenders if conditions permit.

MS Song of America

Specifications

Type of ship: Cruise liner	*Passengers:* 1,402
Cruise experience: Casual	*Crew:* 535 (international)
Size: 37,584 tons	*Officers:* Norwegian
Number of cabins: 701	*Passenger/crew ratio:* 2.6 to 1
Outside cabins: 57%	*Year built:* 1982

Ship's Log

With its bold colors, ample chrome, and period decor, the *Song of America* exudes a 1980s flashiness. Guests enter into a traditional lobby appointed in warm earth tones, which contrast sharply with the halogen brightness of Royal Caribbean's megaships. Like the lobby, the magenta-themed main showroom is a far cry from the two-deck facilities on the line's biggest ships, but it stands out nonetheless for its early 1980s glass-bubble chandeliers and Victorian table lamps. A small gym has windows, but lighting is more florescent than natural. Things get a little brighter in the Oklahoma Lounge, the ship's cabaret, where in-the-round couches and groups of swivel chairs provide a visual extravaganza of red, orange, and yellow. A similar scheme prevails in the Guys and Dolls Lounge, the ship's disco. In fact, three large entertainment lounges are a lot for a ship this size.

The sunniest spot on the ship, at least indoors, is the Viking Crown Lounge, a study in turquoise, chrome, and some badly stained carpeting. The highlight of the ship's public rooms is without a doubt the Schooner Bar, a nautical tour de force of brown leather, brass accents, and maritime imagery. Moving outside, the

Song of America has an expansive sundeck with plenty of chaise lounges and two well-apportioned swimming pools. Seating at the Verandah Cafe, the ship's buffet restaurant, is all outside, but this really isn't a problem since the vessel sails exclusively to warm-weather destinations.

As a middle-age liner in its second decade of service, the *Song of America* is in basically good repair. There's no rust to be seen, but worn fabrics and furniture, and dented wall and ceiling panels in some areas of the ship, are in need of refurbishment.

Cabins Cabins are on the small side; bathrooms are tiny, too. A high percentage of cabins are inside, and many accommodations have Pullman-style lower berths, particularly in standard outside cabins. Suites however, are especially nice, with the bed at the far end of the cabin and the sitting area forward, closest to the door. It's the perfect arrangement for entertaining. Standard outside cabins are done in a soft blue; inside cabins are finished in peach. In-cabin TVs show CNN broadcasts. Suites on the Promenade Deck look onto a public area.

Outlet voltage: 110/220 AC.

Single supplement: 150% of double-occupancy rate; however, less expensive singles are available if you are willing to wait until embarkation time for your cabin assignment.

Discounts: A third or fourth passenger in a cabin pays reduced per diems. You get a discount for booking early.

Sports and Fitness **Health club:** Rowing machines, treadmills, stationary bikes, massage, men's and women's saunas.

Recreation: Aerobics, table tennis, ring toss, snorkeling lessons, shuffleboard, two pools, unobstructed circuits for jogging.

Facilities **Public rooms:** Six bars, four entertainment lounges, casino, disco, cinema, card room.

Shops: Gift shop, drugstore, beauty salon/barbershop.

Health care: Doctor and two nurses on call.

Child care: Youth counselors, children's programs in four age groups during holidays and in summer, baby-sitting arranged privately with crew member, cribs available but must be requested at time of booking.

Services: Laundry service, dry cleaning, photographer, film processing.

Accessibility Accessibility aboard this ship is limited. Doorways have lips, and public bathrooms are not specially equipped. Crew members will carry passengers and their wheelchairs onto the ship's tenders if conditions permit.

MS Sovereign of the Seas

Specifications *Type of ship:* Megaship
Cruise experience: Casual
Size: 73,192 tons
Number of cabins: 1,138
Outside cabins: 63%

Passengers: 2,276
Crew: 808 (international)
Officers: Norwegian
Passenger/crew ratio: 2.8 to 1
Year built: 1988

Ship's Log It seems like decades ago, but when the brand-new *Sovereign of the Seas* sailed into the Port of Miami in 1988, it dwarfed the ships around it. The *Sovereign* was the first of Royal Caribbean's ships to have an atrium, which the line called the Centrum. An architectural tour de force, this five-deck lobby featured a dazzling display of glass elevators, curving stairways, and boutiques for shopping. The Viking Crown Lounge, a standard on every Royal Caribbean ship, was perched an amazing 14 stories above sea level.

It's still big by today's standards, but no longer the giant it once seemed, as other ships have surpassed the *Sovereign* in size (with even bigger vessels yet to come). Still, the *Sovereign* was definitely a trendsetter. It established the standards for big-ship design, and ushered in some of the facilities that are now commonplace. And while Royal Caribbean has modeled its other megaships on this one, certain features of the *Sovereign* remain one of a kind. Its Viking Crown Lounge is the only one where passengers can sit at the bar and have a direct view forward of the ship stretching out to the sea. Its walk-around outdoor promenade is traditionally styled, and an expansive outdoor lido amidships is shielded from the wind on four sides.

Originally built for seven-day cruises, the ship is now deployed on three- and four-day sailings and has been refitted to accommodate more active passengers—many families traveling with children—who frequent these shorter cruises. Changes include the addition of 194 upper berths, a new video arcade, an arts-and-crafts center for kids, and a teen disco. For adults, there's a new nightclub-style disco.

Cabins Cabins on the *Sovereign* are decorated in shades of nautical blues and pink. Like other ships in the *Sovereign* series, cabins are compact and it pays to upgrade if your budget permits. Inside accommodations with two upper berths are a claustrophobe's nightmare—fit for sleeping and changing only. On the other hand, outside cabins serve as comfortable sitting rooms by day in spite of their relatively small size. Cabins on the Promenade Deck look onto a public area.

Outlet voltage: 110/220 AC.

Single supplement: 150% of double-occupancy rate; however, less expensive singles are available if you are willing to wait until embarkation time for your cabin assignment.

Discounts: A third or fourth passenger in a cabin pays reduced per diems. You get a discount for booking early.

Sports and **Health club:** Rowing machines, stationary bikes, treadmills, sauna,
Fitness   massage, outdoor whirlpool.

Recreation: Aerobics and other exercise classes, table tennis, shuffleboard, basketball, snorkeling lessons, two pools, unobstructed circuit (8 laps = 1½ km/1 mi) for jogging.

Facilities **Public rooms:** Eight bars, seven entertainment lounges, casino, disco, two cinemas, card room, library, video-game room.

Shops: Shopping arcade with boutiques and gift shops, beauty salon, barbershop.

Health care: Doctor and three nurses on call.

Child care: Playroom, youth counselors, children's programs in four age groups year-round, baby-sitting arranged privately with crew member, cribs available but must be requested at time of booking.

Services: Laundry service, dry cleaning, photographer, film processing.

Accessibility   The *Sovereign* doesn't have any cabins specifically equipped for wheelchair users, but 10 cabins have extra-wide doors. Crew members will carry passengers and their wheelchairs onto the ship's tenders if conditions permit.

MS Viking Serenade

Specifications   *Type of ship:* Cruise liner   *Passengers:* 1,512
Cruise experience: Casual   *Crew:* 612 (international)
Size: 40,132 tons   *Officers:* International
Number of cabins: 756   *Passenger/crew ratio:* 2.4 to 1
Outside cabins: 63%   *Year built:* 1982 (rebuilt 1991)

Ship's Log   Formerly Admiral Cruises' *Stardancer*, the *Viking Serenade* was originally designed as the world's only cruise ship/car ferry, which explains why it looks more like a barge than a cruise ship. However, Royal Caribbean spent $75 million to convert the car deck into cabins, add a three-story atrium, renovate the existing cabins and public rooms, and add the company's signature observation deck, the glass-enclosed Viking Crown Lounge. Other features are a much-enlarged casino, a shopping arcade, a teen disco, and a state-of-the-art fitness center. Designs and furnishings are bright and contemporary. Brass, glass, mirrors, and stainless steel are used extensively.

Cabins   Standard outside cabins are pretty, with frilly window treatments; standard inside cabins feature murals in the window's place. In-cabin TVs show CNN broadcasts. The larger outside staterooms on Club Deck have partially obstructed views.

Outlet voltage: 110/220 AC.

Single supplement: 150% of double-occupancy rate; however, less expensive singles are available if you are willing to wait until embarkation time for your cabin assignment.

Discounts: A third or fourth passenger in a cabin pays reduced per diems. You get a discount for booking early.

Sports and Fitness   **Health club:** Top-deck spa with rowing machines, stationary bikes, free weights, sauna.

Recreation: Aerobics and other exercise classes, table tennis, shuffleboard, pool with retractable dome, unobstructed circuit (8 laps = 1½ km/1 mi) for jogging.

Facilities   **Public rooms:** Four bars, four entertainment lounges, casino, disco, card room/library.

Shops: Gift shop, beauty salon/barbershop.

Health care: Doctor and two nurses on call.

Child care: Playroom; teen club with soda bar, video games, and dance floor; youth counselors; children's programs in four age groups year-round; cribs available but must be requested at time of booking.

Services: Laundry service, dry cleaning, photographer.

Accessibility   Four cabins and all public areas are accessible to wheelchair users. Crew members will carry passengers and their wheelchairs onto the ship's tenders if conditions permit.

Royal Olympic Cruises

The Fleet	MS *Odysseus*
The Blue	MS *Stella Oceanis*
Fleet	TSS *Stella Solaris*
	MS *World Renaissance*
The White	MS *Olympic Countess*
Fleet	MS *Orpheus*
	MS *Triton*

Royal Olympic Cruises is the name adopted by two well-known Greek cruise lines, Sun Line Cruises (the blue fleet) and Epirotiki (the white fleet). While the ships in both fleets are nearly identically priced, each line sails with a distinctly different style—so choose your ship carefully.

Ships at a Glance

	Dining Rooms	Bars	Casino	Fitness Center	Pools	Average Per Diem
Odysseus	1	4	●	●	1	$200–$300
Stella Oceanis	1	3	◑	○	1	$200–$300
Stella Solaris	1	4	●	●	1	$300–$400
World Renaissance	1	3	●	●	2	$200–$300
Olympic Countess	1	4	●	●	1	$200–$300
Orpheus	1	2	●	○	1	$200–$300
Triton	1	5	●	●	1	$200–$300

The individual review of each ship is organized according to the table above. Sun Line's blue-fleet ships come first, in alphabetical order, followed by Epirotiki's white-fleet ships, also in alphabetical order.

Cruise Experience Although both lines offer a distinctive Greek flavor, Sun Line remains more elegant, traditional, and low-key, while Epirotiki has more activities and entertainment and is less formal. Historically, Sun Line has largely catered to Americans. Some Europeans join the line's Mediterranean cruises, but U.S. passengers are in the great majority during winter sailings to the Caribbean and Amazon. Epirotiki's individual passengers are mostly European, although tour groups, a large part of the line's business, come from both North America and Europe.

Mediterranean itineraries on both lines are port-intensive, and these Greek ships are completely at home there, providing comfortable and convenient conveyance. The *Stella Solaris* is equally well suited to an oceangoing experience on its twice-yearly transatlantic crossings and long "Caribazon" cruises.

Activities Lectures, to prepare passengers for the trips ashore to ancient sites, are key elements of the cruise. Of particular note for the *Stella Solaris*'s Amazon itineraries are talks by Captain Loren McIntyre, who is credited with discovering the source of the Amazon and who helped Sun Line pioneer Amazon cruising in 1983.

Traditional cruise activities, such as bingo, card tournaments, board games, and trivia contests, are scheduled, as are classes in bridge, arts and crafts, and ballroom and Greek dancing.

Dining Cuisine is essentially Continental, with Greek specialties featured at lunch and on Greek Night. Expect more careful preparation and presentation from Sun Line ships. The wine lists feature inexpensive Greek and Italian choices as well as more pricey French selections. Dinner is served in two seatings (6:30 and 8:30) with assigned tables. Sun Line passengers dress more formally on the longer cruises, and men tend to wear a jacket and tie on most nights, while Epirotiki is more casual—with a jacket and tie requested on two nights a week.

All Royal Olympic ships offer buffet dining at breakfast and lunch, formal afternoon tea, and 24-hour room service from a limited menu. Special dietary requests can be accommodated if furnished in writing two weeks prior to sailing.

Entertainment Epirotiki passengers tend to stay up later, so the line offers more elaborate after-dinner shows, while Sun Line emphasizes cabaret acts such as a singer, comedian, or magician. All the ships have late-night discs and bands for dancing, and Greek Night is an exuberant affair on every vessel.

Gentlemen host, who act as dancing and card partners for single women traveling alone, are aboard the *Stella Solaris*. Both the *Olympic Countess* and *Stella Solaris* have cinemas for showing documentaries and feature films.

Service and Longevity of employment is the norm, and it is not unusual to find
Tipping cabin and dining stewards who have 20 or more years of service with the line. Tips of $8–$9 per person per day are pooled among the crew according to the Greek Stewards' Union, and individual tipping is discouraged.

Destinations The Mediterranean is home water for both these lines, and from spring through fall up to six ships sail to the Greek Islands, Turkish coast, Egypt, Israel, and elsewhere.

The *Stella Solaris* crosses the Atlantic before Christmas to spend the winter on long Amazon-Caribbean voyages and shorter Panama Canal and Caribbean cruises. The *Olympic Countess*, meanwhile, cruises the Caribbean and Orinoco River. (For seasonal itineraries, *see* Chapter 4.)

For More Royal Olympic Cruises (1 Rockefeller Plaza, Suite 325, New York,
Information NY 10020, tel. 212/397–6400 or 800/872–6400; 800/368–3888 in Canada).

MS Odysseus

Specifications

Type of ship: Cruise liner	*Passengers:* 400
Cruise experience: Semiformal	*Crew:* 190 (mostly Greek)
Size: 12,000 tons	*Officers:* Greek
Number of cabins: 226	*Passenger/crew ratio:* 2.1 to 1
Outside cabins: 81%	*Year built:* 1962 (rebuilt 1988)

Ship's Log A transfer from the Epirotiki fleet, the *Odysseus* has a most pleasing profile and once sailed as a Brazilian coastal liner. Its airy and bright public rooms run the length of the Jupiter Deck, then open onto a spacious Lido. Four decks offer open side promenades for constitutional walks or for watching as the ship arrives in port and departs. The dining room, located on a lower deck, is a bit crowded. Apart from short, standard eastern Mediterranean cruises, the Odysseus offers a unique winter Red Sea itinerary.

Cabins The great majority of cabins are outside, with double, parallel, or L-shape bed configurations, and are attractively furnished with wood and cane chairs. Some have third and fourth upper berths. All, apart from the two top suites, have showers only. Every cabin has a radio and phones, but none have televisions.

Outlet voltage: 110 AC.

Single supplement: 150% of double-occupancy rate; 200% for suites. Guaranteed share rates are available at no surcharge.

Discounts: First through fourth passengers in a cabin pay 15% less than the double-occupancy rate. Passengers who book early get a 10% discount on Mediterranean cruises. Children pay reduced per diems; kids under two sail free.

Sports and Fitness **Health club:** Gym, sauna, massage.

Recreation: Pool, four whirlpools, shuffleboard, table tennis, partially obstructed circuits for jogging.

Facilities **Public rooms:** Four bars, entertainment lounge, casino, disco, card room, library/reading room, solarium.

Shops: Two shops, beauty salon/barbershop.

Health care: Doctor and nurse call.

Child care: Children's playroom

Services: Laundry service, ping service, photographer, film processing.

Accessibility: No cabins are ded for wheelchair users.

MS Stella Oceanis

Specifications

Type of ship: Cruise liner	*Passengers:* 300
Cruise experience: Semiformal	*Crew:* 140 (mostly Greek)
Size: 5,500 tons	*Officers:* Greek
Number of cabins: 150	*Passenger/crew ratio:* 1.9 to 1
Outside cabins: 75%	*Year built:* 1965

Ship's Log With its Mediterranean-style atmosphere, the *Stella Oceanis* is a professionally run veteran of Greek Island cruising. Public rooms are few, limited to a large lounge for lectures and entertainment, a small annex, and a dark tavern forward on the deck above. By contrast, the attractive restaurant has windows on three sides and offers a very good Continental menu. A variety of Greek specialty dishes are available at the lunch buffet. During days at sea, the deck chairs are in limited supply. To avoid the crowded Lido, many passengers retreat to the open promenade below.

Cabins The average-size cabins are plainly furnished and come with limited storage space, but these warm-weather cruises do not require an elaborate wardrobe. Cabins in the top three categories have twin portholes and bathtubs, and except for the 10 suites, they are located on a lower, but stable, passenger deck. The largest cabins are on a higher deck. These accommodations have windows rather than portholes; some face an open promenade deck through one-way glass.

Outlet voltage: 220 AC (razors only).

Single supplement: 150% of double-occupancy rates; 200% for suites. Guaranteed share rates are available at no surcharge.

Discounts: First through fourth passengers in a cabin pay 15% less than the double-occupancy rate. Passengers who book early get a 10% discount on Mediterranean cruises. Children pay reduced per diems; kids under two sail free.

Sports and Fitness	**Health club:** None.
	Recreation: Outdoor pool, partially obstructed circuit for jogging.
Facilities	**Public rooms:** Three bars, entertainment lounge, casino (slot machines only).
	Shops: Boutique.
	Health care: Doctor and nurse.
	Child care: None.
	Services: Laundry service, pressing service, photographer, film processing.
	Accessibility: No cabins are designed for wheelchair users.

TSS Stella Solaris

Specifications

Type of ship: Cruise liner	*Passengers:* 620
Cruise experience: Semiformal	*Crew:* 310 (Greek and Filipino)
Size: 18,000 tons	*Officers:* Greek
Number of cabins: 329	*Passenger/crew ratio:* 2 to 1
Outside cabins: 76%	*Year built:* 1953 (rebuilt 1973)

Ship's Log This former French passenger liner once sailed as the *Cambodge* on long ocean voyages between France, Indochina, and the Far East. It was completely rebuilt in 1973 as a cruise liner, so that only the graceful hull and quiet steam engines remain from the original ship. An attractive vessel with curving lines, teak decks, and hardwood railings, the *Solaris* today is a homey ship with a friendly atmosphere. Spacious, with relatively few passengers aboard, it's designed for easy mixing. The centrally located foyer serves as a village green of sorts, where several times a day, everyone pauses or passes through on their way to the restaurant, one of the lounges, a favorite bar, or the completely new spa that was added during a 1995 refurbishment. The boat deck, the prime outdoor gathering area, attracts sizable numbers of early-morning walkers (not many joggers on this ship) doing their constitutional rounds. As the day wears on, many take to the sheltered deck chairs that line both sides of the wide promenade.

Cabins Cabins come in either green, salmon, or gold, and most are well apportioned; storage space is especially generous. Many can be connected as adjoining staterooms. Each is equipped with a lockable drawer for valuables. Suites on the Boat Deck (Category 1) look out onto a public promenade through one-way glass and have a large walk-in closet and a sitting area with coffee table, sofa, and chairs. Superior inside and standard outside cabins have upper berths for third and fourth passengers. A third passenger may also be accommodated in a sofa bed in the deluxe suites.

Outlet voltage: 110/220 AC.

Single supplement: 150%–200% of double-occupancy rate. Guaranteed share rates are available at no surcharge.

Discounts: First through fourth passengers in a cabin pay 15% less than the double-occupancy rate. Passengers who book early get a 10%–35% discount. Children pay reduced per diems; kids under two sail free.

Sports and Fitness

Health club: Fitness equipment, sauna, massage.

Recreation: Aerobics, table tennis, shuffleboard, pool, unobstructed circuit (7 laps = 1½ km/1 mi) for jogging.

Facilities

Public rooms: Four bars, three entertainment lounges, casino, disco, cinema, card room, library/writing room.

Shops: Gift shop, beauty salon/barbershop.

Health care: Doctor and two nurses on call.

Child care: Playroom, youth programs with counselors when demand warrants it, baby-sitting arranged privately with crew member.

Services: Laundry service, pressing service, photographer, film processing, shoe shines.

Accessibility

All public areas except the disco are accessible to wheelchair users. No cabin is specially equipped, and cabin and bathroom entrances have raised thresholds. Bathroom entries are 21½ inches wide.

MS Olympic Countess

Specifications

Type of ship: Cruise liner
Cruise experience: Casual
Size: 18,000 tons
Number of cabins: 423
Outside cabins: 66%

Passengers: 840
Crew: 350 (mostly Greek)
Officers: Greek
Passenger/crew ratio: 2.4 to 1
Year built: 1975

Ship's Log

The Olympic Countess serves its purpose as an efficient and comfortable ship for port-intensive Mediterranean itineraries, and it's a midsize alternative to the newer, bigger ships in the Caribbean—where it formerly sailed as the *Cunard Countess.* A wide variety of public rooms with good views of the sea are spread over three decks, and the dining room has good viewing too.

Cabins

Cabins are small but convert to sitting rooms during the day, giving them a slightly roomier feel. Some beds are in an L-shaped arrangement which gives even more floor space. But mainly, they're meant for sleeping, and most passengers will be ashore or in the public rooms on most days.

Outlet voltage: 110 AC.

Single supplement: 150% of the double-occupancy rate, 200% for suites.

Discounts: First through third passengers in a cabin pay 15% less than the double-occupancy rate. On Mediterranean cruises, passengers who book early get a 10% discount. Children pay reduced per diems; kids under two sail free.

Sports and Fitness

Health club: Gym with weight machines, rowing machines, stationary bicycles, massage, sauna and exercise classes.

Recreation: Golf driving range, paddle tennis, table tennis, shuffleboard, outdoor pool, whirlpools.

Facilities **Public rooms:** Four bars, three entertainment lounges, disco, casino, cinema, library, card room.

Shops: Gift shop, beauty salon/barbershop.

Health care: Doctor and nurse on call.

Child care: No special facilities.

Services: Laundry service, photographer, film processing.

Accessibility No cabins are designed for wheelchair users.

MS Orpheus

Specifications		
Type of ship: Cruise liner	*Passengers:* 290	
Cruise experience: Casual	*Crew:* 110 (mostly Greek)	
Size: 6,000 tons	*Officers:* Greek	
Number of cabins: 152	*Passenger/crew ratio:* 2.6 to 1	
Outside cabins: 77%	*Year built:* 1948 (rebuilt 1969)	

Ship's Log For nearly two decades, the *Orpheus* did yeoman charter service for the British firm Swan Hellenic, sailing on intensive enrichment cruises of the Mediterranean and northern Europe. Rebuilt from an Irish Sea overnight ferry, the *Orpheus* has been well maintained, although the ship is now considered rather elderly and lacks a variety of onboard amenities; it has, for example, just two bars. Mediterranean decor and Greek artifacts enhance the large, functional multipurpose lounge and the much more attractive lounge and adjacent bar one deck above. Although the deck space around the aft pool is limited, the parallel boat deck promenades are spacious and attractive for lounging and walking.

Cabins Cabins are plain and functional with adequate storage space. Most have parallel beds and private facilities with showers. Eight suites are located toward the front of the ship, on the same deck as the main lounge. Perhaps the most desirable cabin location on the ship is the small cluster of doubles that face the Promenade Deck, affording easy access to the open deck.

Outlet voltage: 220 AC.

Single supplement: 150% of double-occupancy rates. Guaranteed share rates are available at no surcharge.

Discounts: First through fourth passengers in a cabin pay 15% less than the double-occupancy rate. Children pay reduced per diems; kids under two sail free.

Sports and **Recreation:** Outdoor pool, shuffleboard, table tennis, unobstructed
Fitness circuit for jogging.

Facilities **Public rooms:** Two bars, two entertainment lounges, casino, library.

Shops: Gift shop, beauty salon/barbershop.

Health care: Doctor and nurse.

Child Care: None.

Services: Laundry service, pressing service, photographer, film processing.

Accessibility No cabins are designed for wheelchair users, and this ship has no elevator.

MS Triton

Specifications *Type of ship:* Cruise liner   *Passengers:* 620
Cruise experience: Casual   *Crew:* 285 (mostly Greek)
Size: 14,110 tons   *Officers:* Greek
Number of cabins: 377   *Passenger/crew ratio:* 2.2 to 1
Outside cabins: 67%   *Year built:* 1971

Ship's Log First serving Cunard (as the *Cunard Adventurer*), then Norwegian Cruise Line (*Sunward II*), the *Triton* is well equipped for warm-weather Greek Island cruises. A variety of public rooms are located on three consecutive decks, each one offering a special atmosphere or activity. After dark, an outdoor disco is very popular. Deck space becomes crowded during the few half days at sea.

Cabins The great majority of cabins are small outside rooms with decent storage capacity for a casual cruise. Deluxe cabins are on the same deck as the dining room. Many cabins have third and fourth upper berths.

Outlet voltage: 110/220 AC.

Single supplement: 150% of the double-occupancy fare. Guaranteed share rates are available at no surcharge.

Discounts: First through fourth passengers in a cabin pay 15% less than the double-occupancy rate. Children pay reduced per diems; kids under two sail free.

Sports and Fitness **Health club:** Gym, massage.

Recreation: Outdoor pool, shuffleboard, table tennis, unobstructed circuit for jogging.

Facilities **Public rooms:** Five bars, two entertainment lounges, observation lounge/disco, casino, cinema.

Shops: Gift shop, beauty salon/barbershop.

Health care: Doctor and nurse on call.

Child care: None.

Services: Laundry and pressing service, photographer, film processing.

Accessibility No cabins are designed for wheelchair users.

MS World Renaissance

Specifications *Type of ship:* Cruise liner   *Passengers:* 457
Cruise experience: Semiformal   *Crew:* 235 (mostly Greek)
Size: 12,000 tons   *Officers:* Greek
Number of cabins: 242   *Passenger/crew ratio:* 2 to 1
Outside cabins: 74%   *Year built:* 1966

Ship's Log With its traditional lines and fine wood paneling, the World Renaissance reflects its origins as a French-owned Mediterranean liner, then full-time cruise ship. Ironically, Epirotiki bought the ship in 1977 then sold it to Indonesian owners and in 1997 took it back again. The ship's abundant deck space and two outdoor pools (unusual for a ship this size) will make her once again a popular ship for warm-weather itineraries, and the high standard of accommodations allows the ship to join the blue fleet.

Cabins The majority of the cabins, arranged over no less than seven of the eight decks, are outside and the higher categories are roomy for a ship of this size. If they are lacking in some of the standard amenities, they make up for it with charm including fine wood paneling in some rooms.

Outlet voltage: 110 AC.

Single supplement: 150% of the double-occupancy rate, 200% for suites.

Discounts: First through third passengers in a cabin pay 15% less than the double-occupancy rate. On Mediterranean cruises, passengers who book early get a 10% discount. Children pay reduced per diems; kids under two sail free.

Sports and Fitness

Health club: Gym with sauna, massage.

Recreation: Two outdoor pools.

Facilities

Public rooms: Three bars, one entertainment lounge, theater, disco, casino, library.

Shops: Gift shop.

Health care: Doctor and nurse on call.

Child care: No special facilities.

Services: Laundry service, photographer, film processing.

Accessibility

No cabins are designed for wheelchair users.

Seabourn Cruise Line

The Fleet *Seabourn Legend*
Seabourn Pride
Seabourn Spirit

Almost futuristic in appearance, the streamlined Seabourn ships always attract attention when they pull into port. As on all cruise yachts, every cabin is an outside suite (but there are few private verandas). A platform at the stern lowers for water sports, but it is used sparingly and only in the calmest waters.

However, Seabourn's strengths lie not in its ships, which have been surpassed by the line's archrival, Silversea Cruises. Instead, Seabourn offers what many consider to be the best cruise experience at sea, which accounts for Seabourn's high rate of repeat passengers (53%).

Ships at a Glance

	Dining Rooms	Bars	Casino	Fitness Center	Pools	Average Per Diem
Seabourn Legend	2*	3	●	●	1	$600–$700
Seabourn Pride						
Seabourn Spirit						

*includes alternative restaurant

Cruise Experience As noted above, Seabourn is most often compared with Silversea. While the Seabourn ships are only half as big as Silversea's, passengers who have sailed with both lines tend to give Seabourn the advantage in food and service. When deciding between Seabourn and Silversea, veteran cruise passengers often make their choice based on destination and price, since both lines offer a top of the line experience.

With per diems averaging $600–$700 per person in the Mediterranean, Seabourn remains one of the most expensive lines in cruising. What do passengers get for this princely sum? Pretty much anything they want. Most drinks are free throughout the ship, champagne and caviar are delivered on request, meals can be served course-by-course in your cabin, and there is no tipping allowed.

Activities Seabourn lets passengers enjoy the ship's facilities at their own pace, and there are few organized activities. There's a small casino, a library with a good selection of books and videos, and a card room. Water sports are popular on cruises to warm-weather destinations. Anchored in the calm waters of a cove or bay, the ship can lower its stern to create a platform with a central swimming area protected by wire netting; from this platform passengers can swim, sail, waterski, or ride banana boats—weather permitting.

The few scheduled events include a diverse series of enrichment lectures. Well-known personalities talk about everything from cruising to cuisine. Speakers include renowned chefs, editors of major travel and lifestyle publications, and celebrities. Headliners during the past year included newsmen David Brinkley and Walter Cronkite, astronauts Wally Schirra and Walter Cunningham, and actors Ernest Borgnine and Robert Stack. The line's "Signature Series" of shore excursions include invitations to private golf clubs of championship caliber. Some cruises also have onboard golf seminars led by a pro. Other unique excursions on past cruises have included a reception with an Ottoman princess and a visit to a family-run château and winery.

Dining Dining aboard a Seabourn ship compares favorably with the best restaurants ashore. The dining room is pretty but modest, refined but restrained compared with the two-level extravaganzas of today's late-model megaships. Meals are prepared to order, and passengers are free to ask for dishes not on the menu. The complimentary wine selection is limited, however, and may not match the cuisine. If you want something better, there's a charge. Dinner is served in a single, open seating (tables are unassigned), and passengers may dine at any time during meal hours (dinner is from 7 to 9:30). Three formal nights are held on a typical ten-day cruise, but men are expected to wear a jacket to the dining room each evening.

The formality of the dining room, which works so successfully for dinner, seems stuffy at breakfast and lunch. So most passengers eat breakfast and lunch in the Veranda Café, which at night doubles as the ship's alternative restaurant, serving mostly Italian but sometimes Indian or Oriental cuisine. The Cafe is a delightful spot. With its rattan furniture and tightly packed tables, it is the ship's cheeriest room. On the same deck as the pool, the café serves opulent buffet breakfasts and lunches, as well as a few items cooked to order, such as eggs, hot dogs, hamburgers, and fresh pastas.

Room service is superb and available 24 hours. At least once during your cruise, be sure to have dinner in your cabin; it's a romantic affair, with personal service and beautifully prepared cuisine served course by course. Breakfast in the cabin is also presented with grace and panache.

Entertainment If dining is Seabourn's strong suit, entertainment is a weaker link in the chain. The small showroom means little space for full-scale productions shows. Instead you'll find cabarets, classical artists, and comedians. One highlight of Seabourn's entertainment is the line's practice of choosing artists from the countries being visited. In-cabin diversions include watching movies on TV or one chosen from the ship's video library.

Service and Tipping The passenger-to-crew ratio is among the best of any ship. No tipping is allowed, yet the European service crew is professional, personable, and eager to accommodate virtually any personal request.

Destinations Seabourn ships call at nearly 300 ports of call in 78 countries. The line's cruising regions include the Caribbean, Europe and the Mediterranean, Asia, and elsewhere. (For seasonal itineraries, *see* Chapter 4.)

For More Information Seabourn Cruise Line (55 Francisco St., San Francisco, CA 94133, tel. 415/391–7444 or 800/929–9595).

Seabourn Legend, Seabourn Pride, and Seabourn Spirit

Specifications

Type of ship: Cruise yacht	*Passengers:* 204 (212 *Legend*)
Cruise experience: Formal	*Crew:* 140 (international)
Size: 10,000 tons	*Officers:* Norwegian
Number of cabins: 106	*Passenger/crew ratio:* 1.5 to 1
Outside cabins: 100%	*Years built:* 1992/1988/1989

Ship's Log Outwardly, the Seabourn ships may be the most striking small ships afloat. With their sleek lines and twin funnels that resemble airfoils, they look like they were meant to fly as much as to cruise. Inside, they foster a sense of community that encourages passengers to socialize. And while you'll never feel crowded aboard a Seabourn ship, there is a certain sense of confinement due to the lack of sea views and the overall smallness of the ship. On the other hand, the surroundings are refined: The color schemes are soft hues of peach, blue, and beige, complemented by subtle touches of glass, brass, and marble.

Cabins Here, as in the rest of the ship, glass, blond woods, and mirrors are nicely used. Five-foot-wide picture windows, a sitting area, TV (including CNN and ESPN) and VCR, large marble bath (with hair dryers provided upon request) are among the creature comforts of every suite. However, only a few top-category cabins have private verandas. Refrigerators/bars are stocked with a large selection of liquors, beer, and soft drinks; there's no charge for refills except for premium brands of liquor. All cabins have coffee tables that convert to dinner tables for course-by-course in-cabin dining. The Owner's Suites at the front of the ship have curved bow windows that make you feel as though you're on your own yacht, but midship Owner's Suites are larger. Cabins amidships also will experience less motion than cabins forward or aft—an important consideration on a ship this small.

Outlet voltage: 110/220 AC.

Single supplement: 110%–150% of double-occupancy rate if you let Seabourn choose the cabin; 175%–200% if you select a specific category.

Discounts: A third passenger in a suite pays reduced per diems. You get a discount for paying early and—on selected cruises—for booking more than one cabin with family or friends. A frequent-cruiser program offers reduced rates to passengers who sail 45–120 days in a 36-month period.

Sports and Fitness **Health club:** Aerobics rooms, exercise equipment (including Nautilus), weight-training classes, massage, steam room, sauna, health and beauty treatments (herbal wraps, facials, dietary counseling, personalized fitness programs).

Recreation: Aerobics and other exercise classes, shuffleboard, small pool, three whirlpools, sailing, windsurfing, waterskiing, snorkeling, unobstructed circuit for jogging.

Facilities **Public rooms:** Three bars, two lounges, casino, card room, library (books and videos), business center.

Shops: Clothing boutique, gift shop, beauty salon/barbershop.

Health care: Doctor on call.

Child care: Baby-sitting arranged with purser's office.

Services: Full- and self-service laundry, dry cleaning, overnight shoe-shine service, photographer, film processing.

Accessibility Four Seabourn Suites (Type A) are laid out for easier access by wheelchair users. All elevators and public areas are accessible, and public lavatories are specially equipped. In small ports to which passengers must be ferried by tender, wheelchair users may have trouble getting ashore.

Silversea Cruises

The Fleet MV *Silver Cloud*
MV *Silver Wind*

Silversea straddles the line that separates ocean-liner and luxury yacht cruising. On the one hand, its ships have full-size show-rooms, domed dining rooms, and a selection of bars and shops. On the other hand, accommodations are all outside suites, and space and passenger-to-crew ratios are among the best at sea. The line hopes to build two new ships that will be even bigger than the *Silver Cloud* and *Silver Wind*, but they will preserve the spaciousness that has made Silversea one of cruising's most acclaimed lines.

Ships at a Glance

	Dining Rooms	Bars	Casino	Fitness Center	Pools	Average Per Diem
Silver Cloud *Silver Wind*	2*	3	●	●	1	$600–$700

*includes alternative Italian restaurant

Cruise Experience Larger ships mean more facilities and room for passengers. For example, the Silversea ships have larger swimming pools and more deck space than other cruise yachts. Most of the all-suite cabins (75%) have private verandas—an important consideration if you're deciding among Silversea, Seabourn, and Cunard's *Sea Goddess*. And since Silversea is a relative newcomer to the luxury cruise scene, there's a lack of clubbiness among passengers, who may be aboard for the first time. On any given cruise about a third of the passengers may be European; so the ambience is international.

Another of the line's selling points is its all-inclusive packaging, which includes gratuities, port charges, transfers, selected shore excursions, and all beverages aboard ship. These complimentary drinks include alcoholic and nonalcoholic beverages—in suites, in the dining room, and in the public lounges. House wines are available at lunch and dinner. Not included are some special-vintage wines, champagnes, and spirits, which may be ordered from a separate menu. Each air-sea package comes with round-trip economy airfare and a complimentary pre-cruise hotel room for passengers who arrive early. A unique, personalized stock market report by fax allows passengers to follow their investments back home. But, depending on the itinerary, Silversea may still cost less than its competitors.

Perhaps more compelling than its price, however, is the line's flair for originality. Events like disco night, when a member of the staff breaks out his personal collection of CDs, set these ships apart. The pasta chef's daily creation, presented with panache, is always a passenger favorite. Another memorable event is the Galley

Lunch, held just once each cruise, when the galley is transformed into a buffet restaurant and the tools of cooking only add to the culinary ambience.

Activities With its more extensive facilities, Silversea offers passengers a little more to do aboard ship than does Seabourn or *Sea Goddess*. Passengers can join the morning aerobics classes, work out in small fitness center, swim in the tile-lined pool, or jog on the Promenade Deck. For the less athletically inclined, there are card and board games, celebrity speakers, foreign-language classes, chess and bridge competitions, and a large library stocked with books, videotapes, and compact discs. The library has an IBM-compatible computer with CD-ROM drive. On selected cruises (about eight to 11 a year), National Geographic Society photographers and journalists sail aboard ship to give talks and lead shore excursions related to their on-assignment experiences.

Dining Continental, American, and regional specialties tied to the itinerary top Silversea's wide-ranging menus. The line's executive chef has been trained at Le Cordon Bleu cooking school in Paris. A dish from an original Le Cordon Bleu recipe is featured at every meal, and there are specially highlighted Le Cordon Bleu theme cruises as well. In keeping with recent eating trends, "Light and Healthy" choices and vegetarian entrées are available at all meals.

Panoramic windows line the domed dining room, which accommodates all passengers in a single, open seating (dinner is from 7:30 to 9:30). Meals are served amidst candlelight and fresh flowers. Table settings are an international affair: There's German crystal, Norwegian china, French silverware, and Italian table linens. Two formal nights are scheduled on every seven-day cruise; three on cruises of eight to 14 days. Longer cruise combinations will have additional formal nights, depending on the itinerary and number of days at sea. However, passengers tend to primp for dinner every evening. Special dietary requests should be submitted well in advance.

Another room with a view for dining is the elegant Terrace Cafe, which overlooks an open deck. Breakfast and lunch are served in this more casual setting. Seating is mostly indoors, with a few outdoor tables. And although the Terrace Cafe is designed for buffet meals, the tables are nevertheless set with linens, china, silver, and crystal—just as they are in the main dining room. Waiters take orders for drinks and hot entrées. Certain dishes, such as eggs and pizzas, may be prepared to order.

The Terrace Cafe also doubles as the ship's alternative restaurant. Dinner is served here several nights a week. Menus are usually regional Italian but sometimes French or Asian. With its low lighting and tables for two, it's more romantic and intimate than the main dining room. Reservations must be made in advance—by 4 PM on the day you want to dine.

Room service is available 24 hours from a limited menu, and passengers may choose to have the dining room's lunch and dinner menu served course-by-course in their suites. Complimentary caviar is available upon request at any time during the cruise.

Entertainment Production-style shows are staged a few nights a week in the balconied Venetian Lounge showroom, featuring resident performers as well as local talent. A variety of other acts and entertainers take the stage on other evenings. Films and lectures are presented in the main showroom as well.

However, in the tradition of small-ship cruising, many passengers bypass the main show for more intimate socializing in one of the bars. After dinner, a pianist or jazz quartet often performs in the mellow Panorama Lounge. And age notwithstanding, one of the most popular evening events is disco night, when a member of the ship's staff assumes the role of disc jockey. There's also a small casino for gaming. For in-cabin entertainment, films are broadcast over the ship's closed-circuit television system, and an array of videotapes is available in the library.

Service and Tipping Silversea's staff has been recruited from some of the finest lines in cruising, such as Crystal and Seabourn. Cabin service is exceptional, but the poolside wait staff is limited. Tipping is included in the cruise fare, and no additional gratuities are accepted.

Destinations Silversea cruises throughout the world on itineraries of seven to 14 days. Itineraries can be combined for longer cruises. (For seasonal itineraries, *see* Chapter 4.)

For More Information Silversea Cruises (110 E. Broward Blvd., Fort Lauderdale, FL 33301, tel. 954/522–4477 or 800/722–9955).

MV Silver Cloud and MV Silver Wind

Specifications
Type of ship: Cruise yacht
Cruise experience: Formal
Size: 16,800 tons
Number of cabins: 148
Outside cabins: 100%

Passengers: 296
Crew: 196 (International)
Officers: Italian
Passenger/crew ratio: 1.5 to 1
Year built: 1994

Ship's Log The *Silver Cloud* and *Silver Wind* have taken the cruise-yacht category to a new scale of size and spaciousness. The additional space their tonnage allows has been put to use in the public rooms, particularly in the two-tier showroom, where a movable stage makes full-scale productions possible. Unlike Cunard's *Sea Goddess* and Seabourn ships, there is no retractable marina at the stern for water sports. They do, however, have larger pools, more open deck space, and private verandas in 75% of the all-suite cabins.

The sleek, Italian decor aboard the Silversea ships is subtle yet distinctive and meant to evoke the great steamships of the past. Brass sconces, wood paneling, and brass-ringed portholes in the dining room deliver the desired effect. Soft suedes in muted tones and tile mosaics are also part of the rich interiors. Throughout the ship, there is an obvious attention to detail. Note, for instance, the inlaid designs in the dining room's hardwood floor, glazed marble frescoes peppered throughout the ship, and lace doilies that line the bottom of the waste cans.

Public rooms on the *Silver Wind* and *Silver Cloud* are well designed, and, except for the forward observation lounge, are congregated at the rear of the ship. Cut off from the ship's passenger flow, the forward lounge seems more like an afterthought than an integrated part of the design. Passengers must go outside to reach the lounge, which is sparsely furnished—just some simple tables, chairs, plants, and an array of navigation equipment that gives passengers a captain's-eye view of the ship's course. However, this room is one of the few flaws in these otherwise well-executed vessels. Simply put, these are among the nicest cruise ships afloat.

Cabins As with other luxury cruise yachts, each warmly appointed cabin is an outside suite. Large picture windows, walk-in closets, and marble bathrooms with robes, slippers, makeup mirrors, and a hair dryer (as well as a generous supply of Bulgari bath products) are among the many amenities, along with a writing table stocked with personalized stationery, a basket of fresh fruit replenished daily, and flowers and champagne upon arrival. The creature comforts extend to bedding (pure-cotton Frette linens and down pillows); the large umbrellas placed in each room and the complimentary shoe-shine service are evidence of the attention to detail. Other standard equipment includes remote-control television (placed oddly low to the floor, making bedtime viewing difficult) with closed-circuit and satellite broadcasts (including CNN), a VCR, refrigerator (stocked with complimentary beverages of your choice), and large wall safe. Except for Vista Suites, all accommodations open onto a teak veranda with floor-to-ceiling glass doors.

Outlet voltage: 110/220 AC.

Single supplement: 110%–150% of the double-occupancy rate.

Discounts: A third or fourth passenger in a suite pays reduced per diems. You get a discount for booking early and for booking back-to-back cruises.

Sports and Fitness

Health club: Fitness center with exercise equipment, aerobics area, spa treatments, sauna, and massage rooms.

Recreation: Pool, two whirlpools, unobstructed circuit for jogging.

Facilities

Public rooms: Three bars, observation area, showroom, casino, library/computer center, card/conference room.

Shops: Boutique, Bulgari shop (*Silver Cloud*), beauty salon/barbershop, photo shop.

Health care: Doctor and nurse on call.

Child care: None.

Services: Laundry service, dry cleaning, photographer, film processing, fax.

Accessibility

Two cabins are accessible to wheelchair users on the *Silver Wind*.

Special Expeditions

The Fleet MS *Caledonian Star*   MV *Sea Bird*
MS *Polaris*   MV *Sea Lion*

Like other small-ship lines, Special Expeditions operates a collection of shallow-draft vessels designed to explore nature and visit remote ports. The *Sea Bird* and *Sea Lion* are tiny, the *Polaris* is among the smallest of expedition ships, and even the *Caledonian Star* carries only 110 passengers. While all carry Zodiacs for wet landings almost anywhere, only the *Caledonian Star* has an ice-hardened hull for Antarctic sailings. It's also the only Special Expeditions ship with stabilizers.

Ships at a Glance

	Dining Rooms	Bars	Casino	Fitness Center	Pools	Average Per Diem
Caledonian Star	1	1	○	○	●	$400–$500
Polaris	1	1	○	◐	○	$300–$400
Sea Bird/Sea Lion	1	1	○	○	○	$300–$400

Cruise Experience Special Expeditions cruises attract a slightly younger, less affluent, more easygoing crowd than other adventure lines. Unlike guest experts on some ships, who are treated either as employees or celebrities, specialists on Special Expeditions cruises eat and socialize with passengers. This informal atmosphere prevails at all times, on the ship and off.

Special Expeditions' primary vessels, the *Sea Bird* and *Sea Lion*, are neither as plushly appointed as Clipper's similar ships nor as roomy as Alaska Sightseeing's larger vessels. Where Special Expeditions excels is in its staff, especially the lecturers. In fact, Special Expeditions sails with more top experts aboard than any other small-ship line. The line has also earned numerous awards for its longstanding commitment to environmentally responsible tourism.

Activities These are truly active cruises. Most passengers have come to explore off the ship as much as possible, and the daily schedule of events is centered around one or two Zodiac excursions. More may be arranged if time, weather, and sea conditions permit. The captain and expedition leader work closely together, occasionally diverting from the planned route to get a closer look at wildlife or some natural phenomenon. As with any cruise, certain activities, such as lectures, are run according to a published schedule. But spontaneity and unpredictability are important elements of any

Special Expeditions cruise, and the anticipation of unexpected wildlife sightings are a key part of the expedition experience.

Shipboard activities consist mainly of numerous lectures given by the staff of naturalists and historians. Topics usually examine the wildlife or culture in the next port of call. In keeping with similar programs on other expedition lines, there are recap sessions in the lounge just before dinner. During these nightly get-togethers, passengers can ask questions of the naturalists and other experts and compare notes on the day's events. In tropical waters, more emphasis is placed upon individual leisure activities, such as snorkeling and sailing.

Dining Hearty meals draw on fresh ingredients available in ports along the way and are influenced by North American and European cooking traditions. The diet, more homey than gourmet, is somewhat heavy (especially if you help yourself to seconds), but with all the adventure activity you will quickly burn off the calories. Breakfast and lunch are served buffet-style with some hot dishes cooked to order; dinner is sit-down service from a menu of seafood, meat, or poultry for a main course. Meals are served in a single, open seating (dinner from about 7 to 8:30). The dress code is always casual. There is no smoking in the dining room.

Mealtimes on Special Expeditions' ships are more social than ceremonial. There are no dress-up nights, and passengers can help themselves to coffee and cookies at any time. Special dietary requests are not easily handled. Room service is available only if you are ill.

Entertainment Although there is no organized entertainment, the captain will occasionally invite local performers to dinner and have them play or sing in the lounge afterward. Otherwise, passengers play cards or board games at night or read. Most passengers hit the sack early to rest up for the next day's adventures.

Service and Tipping Besides the sheer adventure of a Special Expeditions cruise, it is the warmth, competence, and intelligence of the crew that passengers remember. Crew members are very special; they engender trust, respect, and friendship. Tips are given anonymously by placing cash (or not-so-anonymous personal checks) in an envelope at the purser's office, where they're then pooled and divided among the crew. Tip $7 per passenger per diem.

Destinations The *Sea Bird* and *Sea Lion* cruise primarily along the West Coast of the Americas, from Alaska to Baja California. The *Caledonian Star* divides its time between Europe and Antarctica. The *Polaris* spends most of the year in the Galápagos. (For seasonal itineraries, *see* Chapter 4.) Special Expeditions also represents ships on the Nile (*see* Chapter 2).

For More Information Special Expeditions (720 5th Ave., New York, NY 10019, tel. 212/265–7740 or 800/762–0003).

MS Caledonian Star

Specifications *Type of ship:* Expedition
Cruise experience: Casual
Size: 3,095 tons
Number of cabins: 62
Outside cabins: 100%

Passengers: 110
Crew: 63 (Filipino)
Officers: Scandinavian
Passenger/crew ratio: 2 to 1
Year built: 1966

Ship's Log The *Caledonian Star* began operation as an oceangoing trawler named the *North Star*. For nearly 20 years, it plied the stormy waters of the North Sea. The ship was converted for passenger service in 1983–86 and was completed rebuilt and outfitted for expedition cruising in 1990. In 1998 Special Expeditions spent another $3 million on the ship to prepare it for cruising to Antarctica. Besides reinforcing the hull, the line enlarged and remodeled the dining room and added a fitness center.

An informal ambience characterizes this sturdy vessel. Like other Special Expeditions ships, it attracts a well-traveled group of passengers who are looking more for the spirit of adventure than for pampering or opulence.

Cabins   All 62 cabins face the sea and are above the waterline. Each is simply furnished: two lower beds (one converts to a sofa for day use), a desk/dresser with a chair, and a refrigerator/minibar. Cabins are also equipped with a VCR. The largest accommodations are three suites with separate sleeping and sitting areas.

Outlet voltage: 110 AC.

Single supplement: 150% of double-occupancy rate subject to availability.

Discounts: Third or fourth passenger in a cabin pays half the per-person rate for that category.

Facilities   **Public rooms:** Main lounge/bar, lecture lounge/library; navigation bridge open to passengers.

Shops: Gift shop, hair salon.

Health care: Doctor on call.

Services: Laundry service.

Accessibility   This ship is not recommended for passengers with mobility problems.

MS Polaris

Specifications   *Type of ship:* Expedition   *Passengers:* 80
Cruise experience: Casual   *Crew:* 44 (Ecuadorian)
Size: 2,214 tons   *Officers:* Swedish
Number of cabins: 41   *Passenger/crew ratio:* 1.8 to 1
Outside cabins: 100%   *Year built:* 1960

Ship's Log   The *Polaris* began its life as a Scandinavian ferry and was later converted for expedition service. It lacks a wealth of amenities, but is well suited for adventure cruises. The main public room is more like an oversize living room than a cruise-ship lounge. As with many smaller ships, it serves many purposes: as a bar, theater, and auditorium for slide shows and lectures. Before dinner, passengers gather here to recap the day's events and hear informal talks by the naturalists. Passengers then adjourn for dinner, which is served in an upper-deck dining room with wraparound views. After dinner, videos are shown. Serving as the ship's library is an even smaller room at the stern—well stocked with reference books, best-sellers, and atlases. The dining room commands a magnificent view of the sea. For views below the waterline, the vessel is stocked with snorkeling equipment and carries a glass-bottom boat.

Cabins   Cabins are small, but they provide sufficient comfort; all have sea views through windows or portholes. Stylistically speaking, the furnishings are purely practical.

Outlet voltage: 220 AC (bathrooms 110 AC).

Single supplement: 140% of double-occupancy rate.

Discounts: A third passenger in a cabin pays half the double-occupancy rate.

Facilities   **Public rooms:** Lounge/bar, library; navigation bridge open to passengers.

Shops: Small gift shop.

Health care: Doctor on call.

Services: Laundry service.

Accessibility   This ship is not recommended for passengers with mobility problems.

MV Sea Bird and MV Sea Lion

Specifications   *Type of ship:* Coastal cruiser   *Passengers:* 70
Cruise experience: Casual   *Crew:* 21 (American)
Size: 99.7 tons   *Officers:* American
Number of cabins: 37   *Passenger/crew ratio:* 3.3 to 1
Outside cabins: 100%   *Years built:* 1982/1981

Ship's Log   The lilliputian *Sea Lion* and *Sea Bird* look like hybrids of ferries and riverboats. While technically oceangoing vessels, they mostly sail on rivers and protected waterways. Their shallow drafts allow them to enter waters that would ground larger ships, even the *Polaris*.

Homey and very friendly, the *Sea Lion* and the *Sea Bird* carry almost the same number of passengers as the *Polaris*, despite their smaller size. The ships' storage capacity, the size of the crews, and the number of public areas have been cut back as a result. Lectures, films, and other entertainment are held in the single lounge/bar, which also holds the ship's small reference library. While cruising, the partially covered Sun Deck is the most comfortable public space for watching the passing scenery. Another favorite perch is the bow area on the upper deck, which is an excellent vantage point for whale-watching. However, these ships are not for claustrophobics, or for those who easily become seasick. They rock noticeably in rough waters. Packets of Dramamine are available from the purser.

Cabins   The cabins are among the smallest afloat, so form follows function to maximize space and minimize waste. Upper deck cabins are the biggest on the ship, and these have either a double bed or twins, a sitting area, and a large picture window. Although all cabins technically are outside accommodations, the lower deck accommodations (Numbers 400–404 in Category 1) have portlights (very small portholes) rather than windows.

Outlet voltage: 110 AC.

Single supplement: 150% of double-occupancy rate subject to availability.

Discounts: No cabins are available for third or fourth passengers.

Facilities   **Public rooms:** Lounge/bar, library; navigation bridge open to passengers.

Shops: Gift shop.

Health care: Doctor on call only on Baja California cruises; otherwise, the ship, never far from land, will dock in a U.S. or Canadian port if care is required.

Services: Laundry service.

Accessibility These ships are not recommended for passengers with mobility problems.

Star Clippers

The Fleet *Star Clipper*
Star Flyer

Taller, faster, and bigger than the original clippers, these sister ships re-create the 19th-century vessels that supplied the California gold rush. First-time sailors and seasoned yachtsmen alike will appreciate Star Clippers' attention to sailing's finer details. The ships rely chiefly on sail power—36,000 square ft of billowing Dacron polyester on four masts. A single engine is used to augment the wind and to maneuver in tight harbors. Some concessions have been made to modern technology: The ships are equipped with antirolling systems that keep them upright at high speeds and prevent rocking while at anchor.

Ships at a Glance

	Dining Rooms	Bars	Casino	Fitness Center	Pools	Average Per Diem
Star Clipper *Star Flyer*	1	2	○	○	2	$200–$300

Cruise Experience Old-fashioned sailing is the key to Star Clippers' appeal. Guests can pitch the sails, help steer the ship, and learn about navigational techniques from the captain. Most, however, opt to take in the nautical ambience as they lounge on the upper deck. While Star Clippers' laid-back philosophy is similar to a windjammer cruise (*see* Chapter 2), the vessels' facilities were designed with a more upscale passenger in mind: They have greater public space and larger cabins, with hair dryers, televisions, and telephones, plus two swimming pools aboard. As cruise ships, their amenities fall somewhere in-between the authentic *Sea Cloud* (*see* On Board Tall Ships *in* Chapter 2) and the high-tech, computer-controlled vessels of Club Med and Windstar, but at a more affordable price. However, the differences are more than a matter of creature comforts: The Star Clippers are true sailing vessels, albeit with motors, while Club Med and Windstar vessels are ocean liners with masts and sails.

Star Clippers' crowd is an international one: About half the 170 passengers are European (French, German, and Swedish). With all the nautical ambience, the Star Clippers are among the most romantic of ships, so it's not surprising that nearly all passengers are couples, from honeymooners to well-traveled retirees. The ships' officers mix socially with passengers and eat with passengers during dinner.

Activities Passengers do their own thing. The only organized activities are daily exercise classes, scuba-diving excursions, talks on ports of call, knot-tying lessons, and captain's tales—a daily briefing and storytelling session by your commander. Scrabble, checkers, and other board games are played in the library. Snorkeling, windsurfing, waterskiing, and sailing are available whenever the ship is at anchor; the ship carries its own banana boat and four Zodiacs for wet landings, dive excursions, and waterskiing. Night dives are particularly popular. All passengers can pick up snorkeling equipment free of charge for the duration of the cruise. Scuba diving is available at $40 per dive, including equipment. Divers must be certified or take classroom and pool instruction on board ($78 plus $35 per dive)—which allows even noncertified passengers to dive all week. It's great for people who want to sample the sport.

Dining   Star Clippers' weakness is its food, which can be hit or miss. If you're expecting gourmet dining, these are not the ships for you. The chef does a great job with buffet breakfasts, and pastas cooked to order at lunch everyday are a nice touch. But dinner entrées can be uninspired—too much emphasis on meats in heavy sauces. The wine list, however, is excellent. Passengers are charged for all nonalcoholic drinks except coffee, tea, and iced tea during breakfast, dinner, and some lunches. Tables and booths seat six to 10, so dining tends to be a family-style event. Dinner is served at an open seating from 7:30 to 10. Formal attire is never required in the dining room; collared shirts for men is about as dressy as it gets. Special dietary requests, with the exception of vegetarian meals, are not easily accommodated.

Other food service includes Continental breakfast in the piano bar and a buffet breakfast, with omelets cooked to order, served in the dining room. Lunchtime beach barbecues are a favorite among passengers. Lunch buffets are also served on deck or in the dining room, followed by hors d'oeuvres in the afternoon. Midnight sandwiches in the piano bar conclude the eating day. There is no room service.

Entertainment   The piano bar, with its friendly piano player/singer, and the Tropical Bar, an adjacent outdoor covered bar, are the main gathering spots for low-key evening diversion. Passengers often request songs and join the show, especially on crew-passenger talent night. Local musical groups board the ship at happy hours for short but colorful performances. Dancing at night under the covered Tropical Bar can be a nightly affair, depending on the crowd. Traditional crab races, as practiced by the sailors of yesteryear, are another evening highlight. Several movies play throughout the night on in-cabin televisions.

Service and Tipping   Cabin service is excellent; dining-room service is a bit harried. The genial international crew works well together and is generally helpful, if not overly attentive. Tip the room steward $3 per diem and dining-room staff $5 per diem.

Destinations   Stopping at ports rarely visited by larger ships, the *Star Flyer* and *Star Clipper* cruise the Caribbean, Mediterranean, and Southeast Asia. Transatlantic crossings are also available. (For seasonal itineraries, *see* Chapter 4.)

For More Information   Star Clippers (4101 Salzedo Ave., Coral Gables, FL 33146, tel. 800/442–0551).

Star Clipper and Star Flyer

Specifications   *Type of ship:* Motor-sail   *Passengers:* 170
Cruise experience: Casual   *Crew:* 72 (international)
Size: 2,298 tons   *Officers:* International
Number of cabins: 85   *Passenger/crew ratio:* 2.3 to 1
Outside cabins: 83%   *Years built:* 1992/1991

Ship's Log These long, slender white ships have sharp, pointed bows to cut quickly through the water, narrowly curved steel hulls, teak decks and trim, and four tapered steel masts rigged with 16 sails. Two small, saltwater swimming pools are surrounded by sunning areas on the aft and sundecks. The pool on the latter has a glass bottom, so patrons of the piano bar can view swimmers from below. Most social activity takes place on the Tropical Deck, either outside at the bar or inside the brass-finished piano bar. Here, passengers gather to chat and relax on leather-cushioned stools and semicircular booths. Navy blue and beige lend a nautical air to the room. A winding grand stairway leads from the bar to the dining room, appointed in the same blue/beige decor, teak-and-marble trim, and handsome nautical art.

Cabins Accommodations are somewhat small but closets are adequately roomy. Each cabin has a vanity and a tiny corner sitting area with a built-in seat and an upholstered stool. Outside cabins have portholes; only a very few have picture windows. Showers and sink faucets are the push type and require constant pressing to maintain water flow. Ten cabins have an additional berth that folds out of the wall for a third passenger. The top accommodations (Category 1) have minibars and whirlpool tubs. All cabins have in-room safes for stowing valuables.

Outlet voltage: 110/220 AC.

Single supplement: 150% of double-occupancy rate.

Discounts: A third passenger in a cabin pays reduced per diems. You get a discount for booking early and for booking back-to-back cruises.

Sports and Fitness **Recreation:** Four fitness instructors, water-sports equipment, scuba gear for certified divers.

Facilities **Public rooms:** Two bars, one lounge, library.

Shops: Gift shop.

Health care: Nurse on call.

Child care: There are no organized children's programs or provisions for young children, but older children are welcome.

Accessibility These ships are not recommended for passengers with mobility problems.

Windstar Cruises

The Fleet
Wind Song
Wind Spirit
Wind Star
Wind Surf

In creating Windstar's vessels, the designers crossed a 19th-century sailing ship with a 20th-century yacht. They took the latest in hull technology and put four masts on top, then added computers to control the six sails. At the touch of a button, thousands of feet of canvas unfurl—a spectacular sight to see. Diesel engines help to propel the ships when the wind does not provide enough sail power, although in 1992, the *Wind Star* achieved 14.8 knots—a world record for a ship this size under sail. Inspired as much by today's luxury cruise liners as yesterday's clippers, Windstar celebrates the new as well as the old.

Ships at a Glance

	Dining Rooms	Bars	Casino	Fitness Center	Pools	Average Per Diem
Wind Song Wind Spirit Wind Star	1	2	◗	◗	1	$500–$600
Wind Surf	2	3	◗	●	2	$500–$600

Cruise Experience
Few modern vessels capture the feeling of being at sea the way a Windstar ship does. But although the ship's design may be reminiscent of sailing vessels of yore, the amenities and shipboard service are among the best at sea. Life on board is unabashedly sybaritic, attracting a sophisticated crowd happy to sacrifice bingo and masquerade parties for the attractions of remote islands and water sports. While the cruise experience is casual, the daily rates aren't cheap: Average per diems put these sailings in the upper echelon of cruising.

Due to the romantic nature of the Windstar cruise experience, these ships are especially popular with honeymooners, and there are usually several newlyweds aboard. On the other hand, you won't find many singles or children aboard. Most passengers tend to be well-heeled couples in their thirties to fifties; average age is 48. Windstar inspires a loyal following of alumni passengers, and it's likely that up to a third of those aboard any given cruise may be repeaters.

Activities
Shipboard life is unregimented and unstructured. No group activities are held; passengers pursue their own interests. Chief among these is water sports. In calm waters, the ship lowers a platform built into the stern, creating a water-level deck for swimming and sunning. Snorkels, masks, and fins are distributed to passengers, free of charge, at the beginning of the week and are theirs to use

for the duration of the cruise. Other water sports include water-skiing, kayaking, windsurfing, sailing, scuba diving, and even fishing. Banana-boat rides are always popular (the banana boat is a large, yellow inflatable craft that sits up to five people as it's pulled at a rapid rate of speed by another boat). There is a small casino on board, but gambling is not a priority for most Windstar passengers.

For passengers who prefer to go ashore, land excursions include nature hikes, helicopter flightseeing, horseback riding, and wine tasting.

Dining Windstar's food is among the best served by any cruise line. The menus have been created by award-winning chef Joachim Splichal of Los Angeles. Complementing Splichal's signature cuisine is a healthy menu including vegetarian selections developed by noted light-cooking expert Jeanne Jones.

Dinner is open seating, and passengers can wander in any time between 7:30 and 9:30. Elaborate formal wear is not considered appropriate; men generally do not wear a tie or jacket to dinner. A weekly barbecue dinner is held on deck (weather permitting) to the accompaniment of a local band.

Breakfast and lunch are served in the glass-enclosed Veranda Lounge, or on an outside deck, weather permitting. Other food service includes early-morning coffee, croissants, and pastries, plus afternoon tea served poolside. Room service, available 24 hours a day, may be ordered from the ship's regular dining-room menu. Special dietary requests should be made four weeks before sailing.

Entertainment The little entertainment that is planned is strictly low-key. Every evening the ship's band or local musicians play in the lounge; there is also a piano bar and nightly dancing. The library has a selection of videotapes for use in the cabins. When the ship is in port, many passengers go ashore to sample the local nightlife. An enrichment series brings experts aboard to talk about wine tasting, cooking, art appreciation, and other lifestyle topics. Theme cruises feature guest hosts, who in the past have included Galloping Gourmet Graham Kerr, wine expert Marcia Mondavi, and ice-cream moguls Ben and Jerry.

Service and Tipping Service is comprehensive, competent, and designed to create an elite and privileged ambience. Tipping is not expected.

Destinations The Windstar ships sail the Mediterranean during summer and either Costa Rica or the Caribbean in winter. (For seasonal itineraries, *see* Chapter 4.)

For More Information Windstar Cruises (300 Elliott Ave. W, Seattle, WA 98119, tel. 800/258–7245).

Wind Song, Wind Spirit, and Wind Star

Specifications *Type of ship:* Motor-sail
Cruise experience: Casual
Size: 5,350
Number of cabins: 74
Outside cabins: 100%

Passengers: 148
Crew: 88 (Indonesian and Filipino)
Officers: British
Passenger/crew ratio: 1.6 to 1
Years built: 1987/1988/1986

Ship's Log Inspired by the great sailing ships of a bygone era, the Windstar ships are white, long, and lean, with bow masts and brass-rimmed portholes. To satisfy international safety regulations, the hulls are steel, not wood; the interiors, however, glow with wood paneling and teak trim—a look rare among modern cruise ships. Instead of the chrome-and-glass banisters so popular on other ships, Windstar vessels feature white-painted iron ones with teak handrails. Although the ships are narrow—a necessity for sail-powered vessels—the interiors are unusually spacious, mainly because there are so few passengers. The sense of space is heightened by skylights and huge glass windows that allow plenty of light into the public rooms.

Cabins   Windstar cabins represent the height of sailing luxury. Every cabin is an outside suite, appointed in burled maple veneer and outfitted with plentiful closet space and mirrors. Portholes are trimmed in brass, the white laminated cabinetwork is accented with rich wood moldings, and bathroom floors are made of teak. All are outside suites with stocked refrigerators, sitting areas, safes, CD players, and VCRs. In-cabin TVs show CNN broadcasts. Other creature comforts include hair dryers and terry robes. The larger Owner's Suite costs 30% more. Some cabins can accommodate a third passenger, and some side-by-side cabins can be joined by a private door.

Outlet voltage: 110 AC.

Single supplement: 175% of double-occupancy rate; 200% for Owner's Suite.

Discounts: A third passenger in a cabin pays reduced per diems. You get a discount for booking early.

Sports and Fitness   **Health club:** Exercise equipment, sauna, massage, hot tub, spa treatments including aromatherapy, facials, and manicures.

Recreation: Exercise classes, sailing, scuba diving (for certified divers), snorkeling, waterskiing, windsurfing, swimming platform, pool, hot tub, scheduled morning walks on unobstructed circuit.

Facilities   **Public rooms:** Two bars, entertainment lounge, small casino (slots and blackjack), disco, library (books and videotapes).

Shops: Boutique, sports shop, hairstylist.

Health care: Doctor on call.

Child care: Bringing children on board is discouraged; no provisions are made for them.

Services: Laundry service.

Accessibility   The lack of an elevator makes moving through the ship almost impossible for wheelchair users. Tenders are used to transport passengers from ship to shore in most ports.

Wind Surf

Specifications   *Type of ship:* Motor-sail
Cruise experience: Casual
Size: 14,745 tons
Number of cabins: 156
Outside cabins: 100%

Passengers: 312
Crew: 163 (Indonesian and Filipino)
Officers: British
Passenger/crew ratio: 1.9 to 1
Year built: 1990

Ship's Log   It used to be the *Club Med 1*, one of the biggest sailing ships afloat. Now it's the *Wind Surf*, and while it's still just as big, it carries fewer passengers than before in more spacious accommodations. In making this ship part of the Windstar fleet, the line reduced passenger capacity to 312 and combined several standard cabins to create 31 new suites—the first on a Windstar ship. Perhaps most significantly, the company also added a new 10,000-ft spa that equals any similar shipboard facility.

Cabins All cabins are outside and are equipped with a TV/VCR, CD player, queen or twin beds, safe, minibar/mini-refrigerator, hair dryer, and terry cloth robes. Suites have separate sleeping and living/dining areas and his and her bathrooms, except Suite 501, which has just one bathroom.

Outlet voltage: 110 AC.

Single supplement: 175% of double-occupancy rate; 200% for suites.

Discounts: A third passenger in a cabin pays reduced per diems. You get a discount for booking early.

Sports and Fitness **Health club:** 10,000-square-ft fitness center with spa with exercise equipment, massage, spa treatments including aromatherapy and facials.

Recreation: Exercise classes, sailing, scuba diving (for certified divers), snorkeling, waterskiing, windsurfing, kayaking, swimming platform, 2 pools, 2 hot tubs, scheduled morning walks on unobstructed circuit.

Facilities **Public rooms:** Three bars, entertainment lounge, small casino (slots, blackjack, craps, and roulette), library (books, CDs, and videotapes), conference center.

Shops: Boutique.

Health care: Doctor on call.

Child care: Bringing children on board is discouraged; no provisions are made for them.

Services: Laundry service.

Accessibility The *Wind Surf* has an elevator, but no cabins are specifically designed for wheelchair users. Tenders are used to transport passengers from ship to shore in most ports.

World Explorer Cruises

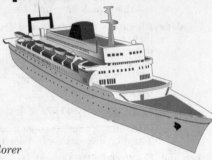

The Fleet SS *Universe Explorer*

The *Universe Explorer* has sailed under more names than any other passenger ship. It was built in 1957 as the *Brasil*, an ocean-crossing liner. Later it became Holland America's *Volendam*, Bermuda Star Line's *Queen of Bermuda*, and most recently, Commodore Cruise Line's *Enchanted Seas*—just to name a few. In its latest incarnation as the *Universe Explorer*, the ship has been modified to serve as a floating classroom. Rather than the disco and casino typically found on a cruise ship, the *Universe Explorer* has a 15,000-volume library—the largest at sea. Repeat passengers should note that the *Universe Explorer* has replaced the old *Universe*.

Ship at a Glance

	Dining Rooms	Bars	Casino	Fitness Center	Pools	Average Per Diem
Universe Explorer	1	4	○	●	1	$200–$300

Cruise Experience World Explorer's strong suit is education, and passengers should not expect the glitz and glamour of some newer ships. Instead, the line emphasizes an onboard enrichment program that is one of cruising's best. On any given sailing, you may travel in the company of four or five experts in history, art, geology, marine life, music, or geography. The *Universe Explorer*'s itineraries incorporate long port stays and an excellent array of shore excursions. Evening entertainment is by noted classical artists. Gentlemen hosts sail on certain cruises. Cabins are spacious and there are several public rooms, including a forward observation lounge, for watching the passing scenery. If you want to learn about the ports you visit, and don't need the amenities associated with a luxury cruise, this ship is comfortable and a good value.

Activities Days at sea and time en route to a port are packed with classes, slide shows, video presentations, and educational films. In keeping with the latest trends, World Explorer recently added computer instruction to its list of enriching options. Much time is spent observing passing scenery and wildlife, but bridge, table tennis, board games, and jigsaw puzzles are popular pastimes, too. Typical cruise-ship activities include bingo, trivia contests, and other competitions. Feature films are occasionally screened in the ship's theater.

Activities ashore include a special bike-touring option on selected departures. Passengers who choose this program, which costs extra, go on 19- to 24-km (12- to 15-mi) rides in each port of call. There's also a hiking option for passengers who want to add plant specimens to the ship's herbarium. On all cruises, World Explorer offers a wide-ranging choice of more than 40 shore excursions.

Dining World Explorer's mostly Filipino dining room staff are top-notch—not only are they unfailingly professional and congenial, they sing. Diners look forward to their tablemates's birthdays and anniversaries as waiters appear with guitars to serenade those celebrating special occasions with a mix of cheery Filipino and familiar American songs. Food, however, is uneven. First-time cruisers especially enjoy the food, but experienced cruisers often find it institutional when compared with the cuisine of other lines. A variety of options is always available and dishes are often chosen to reflect the itinerary. Cuisine is mostly American, with Asian, Italian, and Latin American dishes frequently on the menu. Vegetarian selections are available every evening. Breakfast and lunch are served in a single, open seating. Dinner is served in two assigned seatings (6 and 8). Two semiformal evenings are held each cruise. Make special diet requests in writing 30 days prior to sailing.

Other mealtime options include self-serve breakfast and lunch in the cafeterialike Harbour Grill, where you'll also find afternoon tea and late-night snacks. Self-serve beverages such as coffee, tea, water, and juices are available at all times here as well. Room service is available 24 hours from a limited menu.

Entertainment Lecturers become the daytime entertainment on these cruises; you can attend the talks in person in the main lounge or watch them on TV in your cabin. Two movies are also shown daily—one a recent release and the other often related to the next port of call. In the evening, you'll find outstanding classical and folk performances by singers, cabarets, string quartets, a pianist or violinist, a harp-and-dulcimer duo, or perhaps a flamenco guitarist. There's also a smattering of more traditional cruise fun: dancing, passenger talent competitions, and costume shows.

Service and Tipping Crew members are friendly, but service is not of the pampering kind usually associated with cruise ships. The ship's waiters, bartenders, and cabin stewards receive consistently high marks from passengers. Some staff members may have been with the line for years; others may be college students aboard just for the summer. Tip the room steward and the waiter $3 each per passenger per diem and the assistant waiter $2 per passenger per diem.

Destinations In summer, the *Universe Explorer* has two-week cruises to Alaska (for itineraries, *see* Chapter 4). The rest of the year, the ship becomes a floating university as students and some adult passengers travel the world during the Semester at Sea program (*see* For a Semester at Sea *in* Chapter 2).

For More Information World Explorer Cruises (555 Montgomery St., San Francisco, CA 94111, tel. 415/393–1565 or 800/854–3835).

SS Universe Explorer

Specifications *Type of ship:* Cruise liner   *Passengers:* 739
Cruise experience: Casual   *Crew:* 220 (international)
Size: 23,500 tons   *Officers:* International
Number of cabins: 290   *Passenger/crew ratio:* 3.4 to 1
Outside cabins: 80%   *Year built:* 1958

Ship's Log The *Universe Explorer*, with its emphasis on learning, is noteworthy mostly for its facilities that contribute to the cultural experience: the library, a herbarium with samples collected over 10 years in Alaska, and the ship's artwork. Frank Townsley, the artist responsible for the lovely Alaskan watercolors on board, teaches art classes on many sailings.

The library is well used, probably much more so than on other cruise ships. It's packed with reference books, field guides, and clippings of magazine and newspaper articles on the ports of call. In fact, you'll sometimes have to wait your turn to get a look at the files. The expert speakers are available to passengers outside of scheduled lecture times. When not delivering formal talks, they're just fellow passengers watching the world go by from the rail.

The educational nature of a World Explorer cruise tends to attract like-minded people, many of whom are repeaters. So you'll probably get to know your fellow passengers well during the course of your two weeks, and maybe even get a Christmas card or two.

Cabins As with most ships built for transatlantic travel, cabins are larger than average. All accommodations have television and telephones, but few other amenities.

Outlet voltage: 110 AC.

Single supplement: 130% of double-occupancy rate.

Discounts: A third or fourth passenger in a cabin pays reduced per diems. AARP members get a discount on selected sailings.

Sports and Fitness **Health club:** Exercise equipment, aerobics classes, massage.

Recreation: Table tennis, unobstructed circuit for jogging.

Facilities **Public rooms:** Four bars, five lounges, cinema, card room, library, computer room.

Shops: Gift shops, beauty salon/barbershop.

Health care: Doctor and nurses on call.

Child care: Youth center, supervised children's programs.

Services: Self-service and valet laundry.

Accessibility Several cabins are accessible to wheelchair users and should be requested at the time of booking.

2 Special-Interest Cruises

Finding Your Special Interest

We call the cruises in this chapter "special interest" because they appeal to a certain type of traveler. Perhaps it's someone looking for an international experience. Maybe it's an explorer type, looking for a tour of hidden towns and coastlines. Or it could be a cerebral sort of person, who wants to learn as much as to cruise.

Destinations are worldwide, and the types of ships are as varied as the ports they call on. Icebreakers sail to the Canadian Arctic and Antarctica. Tall ships visit secluded harbors and idyllic islands. Old-fashioned steamboats ply the Columbia River and St. Lawrence Seaway. Riverboats explore deep up the Amazon, the Irrawaddy, and the Nile. Barges travel a network of inland canals and rivers in France, Belgium, and Holland, while ferries crisscross the waterways of coastal Europe.

Many of the cruises described below fall under the broad and often-used label of "educational cruises." The term refers not to formal education, but to the tradition of expanding your horizon as part of the cruise experience. Most of the education that takes place on or off the ship is relatively casual—nothing more than a scheduled lecture or slide show. Remember, however, that although some big lines reviewed in Chapter 1 carry lecturers, putting one expert aboard a 1,000-passenger ship does not make a learning experience. The most highly regarded educational cruises limit their passenger capacity to 150 or less, and their experts are available not just during scheduled enrichment talks but on deck, at meals, and during trips ashore.

Along America's Waterways

Cruises in sheltered American and Canadian waters have become increasingly popular in recent years. The Inside Passage from Vancouver or Seattle north to Alaska remains the most popular and best-known protected North American waterway. Lesser-known choices include Oregon's Columbia and Snake rivers, California's Sacramento Delta, and the East Coast's Intracoastal Waterway.

Cruise Experience Ever since Robert Fulton invented the steamboat, traveling up and down America's inland waters and along its coastline has been fashionable. In many respects, that tradition remains unchanged. Ships stop at historic ports—although not to board passengers but to disembark those already aboard for shore excursions. Cuisine may also capture the flavor of America and take advantage of local specialties—such as Cajun in the South, fresh seafood in the Pacific Northwest, and local wines in the Napa Valley.

The Fleet Most ships traveling America's waterways are yachtlike in their design, while a few are typical but comfortable ferries, capable of carrying both passengers and motor vehicles. Some riverboats re-create the steamships of a century ago.

Down the St. Lawrence Seaway

When to Go Cruises run along the St. Lawrence River and Seaway from May to October. Spring is warm but relatively uncrowded. Summer means long hours of daylight and warm temperatures. Fall is especially popular for its colorful foliage.

Operators and Itineraries **St. Lawrence Cruise Lines** (253 Ontario St., Kingston, ON K7L 2Z4, Canada tel. 613/549–8091 or 800/267–7868, fax 613/549–8410) operates the 64-passenger *Canadian Empress* on five-, six-, and seven-day cruises. Voyages are one way by ship and the other way by VIA Rail express train. The ship attracts mainly older Americans and Canadians, who come for relaxed sightseeing on the river and to learn about Canadian history. The compact cabins are all outside, and the one public room serves as the restaurant, lounge, and bar. This is a very personal, well-organized, family-owned operation aimed at middle-income North Americans. Ports of call include Kingston, Montréal, Ottawa, and Québec City, depending on your itinerary. Scenic cruising areas include the locks of the international seaway, the 1,000 islands region, and the Ottawa River.

American Canadian Caribbean Line and **Clipper Cruise Line** both pass through the St. Lawrence on their way to and from the Sageunay Fjord and the Great Lakes. For detailed descriptions of both lines, *see* Chapter 1.

Following Arctic Arteries

When to Go Inland water cruises of Canada's Northwest Territories operate only during the warmest summer months—mid June to late August. Daytime highs reach 85°F, and with 20 hours of daylight, nights are cool but short.

Operators and Itineraries **N. W. T. Marine Group** (17 England Crescent, Yellowknife, NWT X1A 3N5, Canada, tel. 403/873–2489) has been a family-run operation for two generations. The company operates the 20-passenger *Norweta*, a former river supply boat, along thousands of miles of the fast-flowing MacKenzie River. Downriver trips embark at Yellowknife and take nine days to reach Inuvik. Upriver trips against the current require 10 days. Both itineraries include numerous stops at isolated communities. A six-day Great Slave Lake cruise goes in search of wildlife, flora, and archaeological sites; fishing and canoeing are regular activities. The boat has small cabins, a lounge, a dining saloon that seats all passengers at once, and a sundeck. All cabins have private heads.

In the California Wine Country

When to Go Wine country cruises have a very short season. Springtime cruises are scheduled mostly in March, with a few in April and May. Fall departures are available in October and November.

Operators and Itineraries **Alaska Sightseeing/Cruise West** and **Clipper Cruise Line** both have itineraries that visit Sonoma and Napa valleys. These cruises travel California's inland waterways round-trip from San Francisco, stopping at Sausalito and Sacramento. Some cruises may have shore excursions to the redwood forests. For detailed descriptions of both lines, *see* Chapter 1.

Inland Through Ontario

When to Go Cruises of Ontario's waterways operate from the middle of May until the middle of October; fall colors usually begin to show around the last week of September.

Operators and Itineraries **Ontario Waterway Cruises** (Box 6, Orilla, ON L3V 6H9, Canada, tel. 705/327–5767 or 800/561–5767, fax 705/327–5304) is a family-owned company that runs the 107-ft, 38-passenger *Kawartha Voyageur* along the rivers and canals and across the lakes of southern Ontario, tying up each night at small towns and water-front parks.. The leisurely five-day, one-way trips negotiate between 19 and 39 locks, depending on the itinerary. Passengers, who are mostly retirees, can choose from among three routes: Peterborough to Big Chute (a marine railway just in from the Georgian Bay), Peterborough to Kingston, or Kingston to Ottawa. The air-conditioned boat has 19 cabins, each with a sink and toilet; showers are shared. The dining room serves straightforward Canadian cooking—dishes like baked ham with candied yams, chicken breast in melted Swiss cheese, or farm sausages with sauerkraut and cabbage—and seats all passengers in a single sitting. Other public areas include a forward observation lounge, a library alcove, covered fore and aft outdoor decks, and a top sundeck. An elevator links the two enclosed public decks—so all decks, except the sundeck, are accessible to passengers with disabilities.

North to Alaska

When to Go June through August are the most popular months to cruise Alaska. Spring, especially May, is less crowded and drier than summer, which gets rainier as fall approaches. Autumn is a fleeting time of colorful foliage and cooler temperatures in Alaska, where fall reaches its peak in early to late September along the Inside Passage. The state ferry system runs year-round, but other boat operators may sail only during the warm-weather months.

Operators and Itineraries The **Alaska Marine Highway** (Box 25535, Juneau, AK 99802, tel. 800/642–0066, fax 907/277–4829) has cabins aboard several ferries that serve the communities of southeast and south-central Alaska. Dining is cafeteria-style with good American-style food. Public rooms include an observation lounge, a bar, and a solarium. Many passengers are RV travelers transporting their vehicles (no roads connect the towns within the Inside Passage). Time spent in port is short—often just long enough to load and unload the ship. A weekly departure leaves from Bellingham, Washington, north of Seattle. Service to Alaska is also available from Prince Rupert, British Columbia, where the marine highway system connects with Canada's **BC Ferries.** Cabins on the Alaskan ferries book up as soon they become available, but a number of tour operators sell packages that include accommodations. One of the oldest and largest is **Knightly Tours** (Box 16366, Seattle, WA 98116, tel. 206/938–8567 or 800/426–2123).

Alaska Yacht Safaris (1724 W. Marine View Dr., Everett, WA 98201, tel. 800/325–6722) is a relative newcomer to the Alaska scene. Since 1997, it has welcomed up to 12 passengers at a time aboard its 120-ft "megayachts," which look like something out of a James Bond movie with their streamlined design and louvered windows. Itineraries explore the nooks and crannies of the Inside Passage and include a stop at a native village.

Discovery Voyages (tel. 907/424–7602) sails solely within Prince William Sound on the 12-passenger, 65-ft *Discovery*, which was built in the 1950s as a Presbyterian mission boat. To carry guests, the vessel has been completely renovated by owners Dean and Rose Rand, who live aboard the ship year-round. Passenger facilities include six cabins with shared baths and a main lounge/dining room. The ship is also equipped with inflatable skiffs and kayaks for off-ship excursions. Sailings are round-trip from Whittier.

Another option for cruising Prince William Sound is the four-passenger *Arctic Tern III*, which is one of the smallest overnight vessels sailing in Alaska. Longtime Sound residents Jim and Nancy Lethcoe operate the boat under the name **Alaska Wilderness Sailing Safaris** (tel. or fax 907/835–5175) and charter the 40-ft sloop to small parties of two to four passengers, generally for three days of sailing and kayaking.

A number of interesting and unorthodox cruise vessels travel the Inside Passage, too. For a cruise aboard a former minesweeper, contact **The Boat Company** (tel. 360/697–5454). The 12-passenger *Observer* and 20-passenger *Liseron* were commissioned by the Navy in the 1940s and '50s, but are now in service to the conservation movement. In the past, organizations such as the Sierra Club have brought groups aboard, and all sailings are designed to raise awareness of environmental issues. The vessels themselves are constructed of wood and finished with brass and bronze fittings, so dismiss any thoughts of boats painted battleship gray.

Raising environmental awareness also is the mission of the 16-passenger *Island Roamer*, a 68-ft sailboat operated by **Bluewater Adventures** (tel. 604/980–3800), which has been in business for more than 20 years. The vessel is sometimes chartered by Oceanic Society Expeditions, an affiliate of Friends of the Earth. Bluewater Adventures also has the 12-passenger *Snow Goose*, a 65-ft, steel-hulled motor yacht. Built in 1973, it, too, has served time as a research vessel. For leisure cruising, the *Snow Goose* has a Zodiac, two kayaks, and a natural-history library.

For something even smaller, **Dolphin Charters** (tel. 510/527–9622) uses the *Delphinus* (eight passengers), a 50-ft motor yacht, to explore uncharted coves in Glacier Bay. This vessel is popular with professional photographers, who often hire it for their photographic workshops.

Equally intimate is the eight-passenger *Steller* from **Glacier Bay Adventures** (tel. 907/697–2442). The vessel was built as a research vessel for the Alaska Department of Fish and Game and is staffed by a crew of trained naturalists.

Outside of Glacier Bay, another cozy cruise for just six passengers at a time can be booked from **All Aboard Yacht Charters** (tel. 360/898–7300). Cruises sail from Seattle to Ketchikan, from Ketchikan to Juneau, and on loops round-trip from Juneau.

Alaska Sea Adventures (tel. 206/284–7648) caters to sportfishing enthusiasts, photography buffs, and amateur naturalists aboard the Alaska Adventurer. The ship holds up to 10 passengers and was built in 1980 specifically for cruising the Inside Passage.

Stopping on the Labrador Coast

When to Go Cruises of coastal Labrador operate seasonally between early July and late October from a port in Newfoundland.

Operators and Itineraries **Marine Atlantic** (100 Cameron St., Moncton, NB E1C 5Y6, Canada, tel. 506/851–3600, fax 506/851–3615) runs the *Northern Ranger* along the coast of Labrador on one of the most unusual cruise-ferry experiences in North America. It's similar to that of the Alaska Marine Highway or the Norwegian Coastal Voyage, but much less traveled. The ship sails northward from St. Anthony, Newfoundland, making dozens of passenger and cargo calls on its 2,500-mi round-trip route. The *Northern Ranger* was built in 1986 and accommodates 131 passengers in standard cabins with private facilities or economy berths with shared showers. Meals are taken in a cafeteria, and a cruise director of sorts arranges activities and shore excursions. TravLtips (*see* On Board Freighters, *below*) also handles bookings.

Through the American South

When to Go   Cruises operate year-round, but summers are hot and humid while winters are chilly and rainy. Spring and fall are the best. Several theme cruises are scheduled throughout the year, including Mardis Gras, music cruises, fall foliage, and Christmas cruises.

Operators and Itineraries   **RiverBarge Excursion Lines** (201 Opelousas Ave, New Orleans, LA 70114, tel. 504/365-0022 or 888/650-5041, fax 504/362-6531) was expected to begin service in late summer 1998 with a 200-passenger American-built, flagged, and crewed hotel barge. The *River Explorer*—actually twin barges tied together and propelled by a tug—travels along the Mississippi, Ohio, and Cumberland rivers, the Atchafalaya Basin, and along the Intracoastal Waterway in Louisiana and Texas. Cruises last 4 to 10 days.

Cruises of America's heartland are also available from the **Delta Queen Steamboat Company** (*see* Chapter 1).

Up the Columbia and Snake Rivers

When to Go   Ships ply the Columbia and Snake rivers in the spring, summer, and fall—first departures are scheduled in March with the final cruises in late December.

Operators and Itineraries   The **American West Steamboat Company** (601 Union St., Suite 4343, Seattle, WA 98101, tel. 206/292–9606 or 800/434–1232, fax 206/340–0975) is the latest entry on the Columbia and Snake rivers. The company's sole ship, the 165-passenger stern-wheeler *Queen of the West*, was built in 1995 to modern standards of comfort with a turn-of-the-century decor. The meat-and-potatoes menu is very good, the atmosphere low-key, the entertainment musical and the shore excursions unambitious. These seven-night cruises, scheduled March through December, sail the full navigable length of the river as far as Lewiston, Idaho—1,000 mi round-trip.

Among the major lines (reviewed in Chapter 1) that offer these itineraries are **Alaska Sightseeing/Cruise West** and **Special Expeditions.**

Along Central America

The longest barrier reef in the Western Hemisphere parallels the coast of Belize, while nearby Costa Rica offers two coasts with awesome rain forests and national parks, some only accessible by sea. Off the coast of Panama are the San Blas Islands, home to the Kuna Indians—the oldest indigenous culture in the region.

When to Go   High season for cruises along the Belize, Costa Rica, and Panama coasts is late November to March, but one line offers departures year-round.

Cruise Experience   Cruising the coast, the ships are never out of sight of beaches, the rain forest, or the mountains. Passengers go ashore in small groups aboard inflatable landing craft, accompanied by naturalists. Excursions include jaunts up the coastal rivers and other natural waterways and walks on deserted beaches and jungle paths in search of birds, wildlife, and unusual plants and flowers. Dress aboard ship is always casual, and most activities take place during the day. An international crowd is found aboard the ships run by Temptress Adventure Cruises (*see* Operators and Itineraries, *below*), while the other seasonal operators attract mainly North Americans.

The Fleet The ships that sail along the coastlines of Belize and Costa Rica are small but nonetheless diverse: You can choose from a motor yacht, a coastal cruiser, or a tall ship.

Operators and **Temptress Adventure Cruises** (351 N.W. LeJeune Rd., Penthouse 6,
Itineraries Miami, FL 33126, tel. 305/643–6404 or 800/336–8423, fax 305/643–6438) has two ships exploring these pristine cruising areas. On the Caribbean coast, the 63-passenger *Temptress Voyager* cruises to the barrier reef, islands, rain forests, and Mayan temples of Belize. Another itinerary takes the *Temptress Voyager* through the Panama Canal. On the Pacific coast, the larger and newly renovated 99-passenger *Temptress Explorer* calls at small towns, national rain-forest parks, and offshore islands. These itineraries are three, four, or seven days. Temptress operates nearly year-round (the only months when cruises aren't scheduled are June and September) and attracts an international crowd, while other seasonal operators (*see below*) cater mainly to North Americans.

For a luxury sailing experience, **Tauck Tours** (Box 5027, Westport, CT 06881, tel. 203/226–6911 or 800/468–2825, fax 203/221–6828) operates the sleek *Le Ponant* (*see* On Board Tall Ships, *below*), carrying 60 passengers along the Belize coast. Four-night cruises are combined with a land-and-air package to Guatemala. Departures are scheduled in March and April. *Le Ponant* also cruises the Pacific coast between Costa Rica and Panama, including the Panama Canal and San Blas Islands. These six-day voyages are scheduled from late December through February.

Special Expeditions (*see* Chapter 1) also sends its 80-passenger *Polaris* and a staff of naturalists to the Panama and Costa Rica coasts on eight-day cruises. The enrichment programs on these cruises, scheduled from January to March, are tops.

Clipper Cruise Line (*see* Chapter 1) sends its 138-passenger *Yorktown Clipper* on several voyages along the coasts of Costa Rica and Panama, which include a full transit of the Panama Canal and a call in the Darien Jungle. These nine-day, one-way cruises depart December to April.

Windstar Cruises (*see* Chapter 1) explores the Pacific coast of Costa Rica, sailing round-trip from Puerto Caldera and calling at national parks and a wildlife refuge.

Along the Great Barrier Reef

Cruising Australia's Great Barrier Reef (the longest barrier reef in the world), puts you on the water's surface for some of the best snorkeling and scuba diving anywhere. Shoreside excursions visit resort islands, national parks, and the Queensland coast.

When to Go Great Barrier Reef cruises operate year-round, and the waters are always warm enough for swimming and snorkeling. Queensland's weather gets very hot in the Australian summer (December through March), although it's more uncomfortable ashore than afloat.

Cruise Experience Although most people visit the Barrier Reef on a day trip from the mainland, a longer cruise gives you the opportunity to truly appreciate this unique environment. On one side lies the Pacific Ocean; on the other side lie calm waters sheltered by the reef. Days are spent exploring the marine life on diving and snorkeling excursions—some operators organize fishing and sailing for passengers, too. Menus aboard ship offer some of the best seafood in the world, featuring barramundi, tuna, oysters, shrimp, and Moreton Bay bugs, a flavorful crayfish.

The Fleet Several Australian operators use small catamarans or single-hull vessels to explore the reef. These boats provide an intimate experience for an international clientele in a thoroughly relaxed Aussie setting.

Operators and Itineraries **Captain Cook Cruises** (Qantas Vacations, tel. 800/682–6025; or ATS Tours, 2381 Rosecrans Ave., Suite 325, El Segundo, CA 90245, tel. 800/423–2880) operates the largest of the local vessels: the 168-passenger *Reef Endeavour*. The ship departs from Cairns on three-, four-, and seven-day trips. Cruises are comparable to a sailing aboard Clipper Cruise Line (*see* Chapter 1), with excellent seafood meals, a friendly young staff, all outside cabins, a lounge, a bar, and good open and covered deck space.

Coral Princess Cruises (520 Monterey Dr., Rio Del Mar, CA 95003, tel. 800/441–6880) has two upscale 114-ft catamarans: the 54-passenger Coral Princess and the 50-passenger *Coral Princess II* (formerly the P&O *Spice Islander*). Both make four-day, one-way Barrier Reef cruises between Cairns and Townsville. **Abercrombie & Kent** (1520 Kensington Rd., Oak Brook, IL 60521, tel. 630/954–2944 or 800/323–7308, fax 630/954–3324) also includes a coastal voyage aboard the Coral Princess pair as part of its Wonders of Australia tour.

Roylen Cruises, which can be booked through **ATS Tours** (*see* Captain Cook Cruises, *above*), uses a pair of 114-ft, 50-passenger catamarans, the *Roylen Endeavor* and *Roylen Endeavor II*, on Barrier Reef cruises from Mackay. This company has been in business longer than any of the other companies operating along the Great Barrier Reef. Another advantage is the ships' southerly departure point, which is closer to international resort islands.

For a Semester at Sea

As noted above, many cruises in this chapter can legitimately be considered educational cruises, but aboard only one cruise can you actually earn college credits. The **Semester at Sea** (University of Pittsburgh, 811 William Pitt Union, Pittsburgh, PA 15260, tel. 412/648–7490 or 800/854–0195, fax 412/648–2298) is a bona fide educational experience, sponsored by the University of Pittsburgh, for undergraduate students to gain college credit while seeing the world and for a growing number of adults who would like to share this experience on a more informal basis. Sailings are aboard the *Universe Explorer* (formerly Commodore Cruise Line's *Enchanted Seas);* "semesters" last 100 days, but shorter summer and winter programs are also available. Destinations include the Pacific Rim, the coast of Africa, and South America. The staff, students, and adults mix freely aboard ship and on visits ashore to hosting universities, cultural venues, cities, and villages.

In the Galápagos

Ecuador's "Enchanted Isles," the Galápagos archipelago, include 13 major islands and dozens of islets. This 3-million-year-old cluster of volcanic islands is home to giant tortoises (after which the Galápagos Islands are named); marine iguanas; sea lions; and such rare birds as cormorants, albatross, and blue-footed boobies. The islands, while no longer pristine, still captivate amateur naturalists, who come to see species described by Charles Darwin—some of which exist nowhere else in the world.

When to Go The Galápagos climate is subtropical, and cruises operate throughout the year. December to May is warm and sunny; June to November is cool and breezy. Most birds nest year-round.

Cruise Experience Passengers on larger ships go ashore in groups of about 20. For a more personal experience, there are a number of converted motor-sailing vessels and yachts.

The Fleet The government of Ecuador (which governs the Galápagos) has banned foreign cruise ships from calling directly at the islands. All visitors, therefore—even ones sailing on foreign-ship itineraries billed as Galápagos sailings—must arrive aboard a local boat that carries no more than 100 passengers. These include the *Ambassador I* (86 passengers), a spacious but older ship. Newer is the *Santa Cruz* (90 passengers), built in 1979 specifically to cruise the Galápagos. Smaller are the *Corinthian* (48 passengers) and the *Isabella II* (38 passengers). The latest addition to the Galápagos fleet is the *Polaris* (80 passengers), an expedition ship from Special Expeditions (*see* Chapter 1) with an excellent reputation among experienced cruisers.

Operators and Itineraries Local Galápagos cruises are available in three-, four-, and seven-day packages. Many operators sell these vacations, and many ships are sold by more than one operator. Shop around for the best air, land, and cruise combination. Among the companies to contact are:

Abercrombie & Kent (1520 Kensington Rd., Oak Brook, IL 60523, tel. 630/954–2944 or 800/323–7308, fax 630/954–3324).

Adventure Associates (Metropolitan Touring, 13150 Coit Rd., Suite 110, Dallas, TX 75240, tel. 972/907–0414 or 800/527–2500, fax 972/783–1286).

Galapagos Network (7200 Corporate Center Dr., Miami, FL 33126, tel. 305/592–2294 or 800/633–7972, fax 305/592–6394).

International Expeditions (One Environs Park, Helena, AL 35080, tel. 800/633–4734).

Marco Polo Vacations (16776 Bernardo Center Dr., San Diego, CA 92128, tel. 619/451–8406 or 800/421–5276, fax 619/451–8472).

Mountain Travel-Sobek (6420 Fairmount Ave., El Cerrito, CA 94530, tel. 510/527–8100 or 888/687–6235, fax 510/525–7710).

OdessAmerica Cruises (170 Old Country Rd., Suite 608, Mineola, NY 11501, tel. 516/747–8880 or 800/221–3254, fax 516/747–8367).

Special Expeditions (720 5th Ave., New York, NY 10019, tel. 212/765–7740 or 800/762–0003).

Tauck Tours (Box 5027, Westport, CT 06811, tel. 203/226–6911 or 800/468–2825, fax 203/221–6828).

In Southeast Asia

Southeast Asia has long been regarded as the next big destination in cruising. Slowly, the large cruise lines are offering more and more itineraries. In the meantime, you can book a cruise with a local operator that specializes in a specific area, such as Singapore and Malaysia, the Indonesian archipelago, and New Guinea.

When to Go The waters of Southeast Asia straddle the equator, so temperatures change very little from month to month; it's generally hot and humid.

Cruise Experience Due to the wide variety of ships in service in this region, there is a great range of onboard amenities. Big ships may have ocean-liner-type facilities, while the smallest vessels emphasize the destinations, offering intimate quarters and little in the way of shipboard diversions. Ashore, the region offers large cities and international resorts in Malaysia and Thailand, as well as more remote and less-visited landfalls in the Indonesian Islands and along the coast of New Guinea. Most people combine a Southeast Asia cruise with a land itinerary.

The Fleet Ships in service in Southeast Asia can be small or huge, and they range from a catamaran to ferries that once operated on the Baltic Sea. Some are cruise liners once familiar to North Americans under other names. There are even sailing vessels. Some lines cater to the local population, especially passengers from Singapore, Hong Kong, Thailand, and Malaysia, while others carry both Eastern and Western passengers. As a result, the cruise experience will vary considerably.

Operators and Itineraries By far the largest local operator is **Star Cruise** (391B Orchard Rd., 13-01 Ngee Ann City, Tower B, Singapore 0923, tel. 011/65–733–6988, fax 011/65–733–3622), with seven ships based in Singapore plus additional cruises from Hong Kong. Most interesting are two huge ships, the 1,900-passenger *Star Aquarius* and the 1,900-passenger *Star Pisces*, both former Baltic cruise ferries. Experienced cruisers may recognize the *SuperStar Capricorn* (formerly the *Royal Viking Sky)*, the *SuperStar Gemini* (formerly the *Crown Jewel)* and *SuperStar Sagittarius* (formerly the *Sun Viking)*. The line, the largest in Asia, is now being promoted in Europe and will soon become more familiar in the United States.

The 330-passenger *Andaman Princess* of **Siam Cruise Line** (33/10-11 Chaiyod Arcade, Sukhumvit Soi 11, Sukhumvit Rd., Bangkok 10110, Thailand, tel. 011/66–2–255–4563, fax 011/66–2–255–8961) operates from Thai ports along both coasts depending on the season. The food and most of the passengers are Thai, so it's a true ethnic experience on a very handsome, older ship, built in 1960 for Baltic service.

For a luxury cruise of the Indonesian Archipelago from Sumatra to Irian Jaya (Indonesian New Guinea), the 120-passenger *Oceanic Odyssey* (built as the *Oceanic Grace* in Japan in 1989) offers a wide varieties of itineraries, almost year-round. For a short Indonesian cruise from Bali that includes Komodo Island, home of the famous dragons, the *Bali Sea Dancer* (formerly Classical Cruises' *Illiria*) offers a very high standard of accommodations for 150 passengers. These ships are represented in the United States by **Esplanade Tours** (581 Boylston St., Boston, MA 02116, tel. 617/266–7465 or 800/426–5492, fax 617/262–9829).

International Expeditions (One Environs Park, Helena, AL 35080, tel. 800/633–4734) operates the 124-ft motorized sailing vessel *Adelaar,* built in Holland in 1902, on 13-night island cruises from Bali eastward to Lombok, Sumbawa, Komodo, and Rinca. The *Adelaar* accommodates 14 passengers in air-conditioned cabins. Once used as a private yacht, it has a single seating for dinner and private facilities for all passengers.

Farther east, the *Melanesian Discoverer,* a 42-passenger catamaran, operates four-, five-, and seven-night cruises calling at the coastal villages and islands of Papua New Guinea. up the Sepik River and amongst the Bismarck and Solomon islands. The ship can be booked in the United States through **Melanesian Tourist Services** (302 W. Grand Ave., El Segundo, CA 90245, tel. 310/785–0370 or 800/776–0370, fax 310/785–0314).

Abercrombie & Kent (1520 Kensington Rd., Oak Brook, IL 60523, tel. 630/954–2944 or 800/323–7308, fax 630/954–3324) has a cruise-tour program in Papua New Guinea aboard the 20-passenger *Sepik Spirit.*

On Board Hotel Barges

In Britain and Europe, rivers have served as arteries of commercial transportation for centuries, while canals have been in service for the past 200 years. For cruise passengers, this network of waterborne transportation offers numerous choices, at many different price levels, in the United Kingdom, Ireland, France, Belgium, and the Netherlands.

Cruise Experience Boat and barge travel is about as far removed from deep-sea cruising as you can get. About the only shared factor is the water flowing beneath the hull as you cruise along at the pace of a fast walk.

In England, an active 2,000-mi canal system stretches from London to Yorkshire. The canals, 18th- and 19th-century equivalents of automobile freeways, cut right through city centers, cross valleys on aqueducts, and climb hills using a stepladder of locks. Today, the network is used almost exclusively by pleasure craft, and in many places, the lock operations are self-service. Popular rivers are the Thames between London, Windsor, and Oxford, and the Shannon in Ireland.

Across the English Channel in France, Belgium, and the Netherlands, the canals and rivers are broader and the barges are larger, and most waterways still see commercial traffic.

The most popular barges feature beautifully decorated, wood-paneled accommodations, gourmet food and wines, and a shared social experience for three to six nights. Besides the chance to drift leisurely through the countryside, canal and barge cruises may offer the opportunity for excursions by van, bike, foot, and hot-air balloon to medieval villages, châteaus, and wineries.

Hotel boats, with crew and food provided, are mid-priced at about $650 per person for a week. At the top of the scale are luxury barges. Six nights, including a crew and all food and drinks, will range from about $1,400 to $3,500 per person.

The Fleet Within this varied fleet, there are substantial differences in accommodations.

Luxury barges, stretching from 100 to 200 ft in length and carrying up to 50 people, may have one or two decks of interior space that includes roomy outside cabins and suites with private facilities, a dining room, and a separate lounge with a bar. The sundeck is usually open with lounge seating, umbrellas for shade, and space to store bicycles. Some are air-conditioned, and all have central heating.

In Britain and Ireland

When to Go Most hotel barges operate between the end of April and the beginning of October. However, the weather is highly unpredictable, so be prepared to spend at least some time cooped up inside. Boats are not air-conditioned—not normally a problem—but cabins do get stuffy in persistently hot weather.

Operators and Itineraries **Abercrombie & Kent** (1520 Kensington Rd., Oak Brook, IL 60523, tel. 630/954–2944 or 800/323–7308, fax 630/954–3324) represents the 100-ft, 12-passenger *Actief* on three- and six-night cruises between Windsor and Oxford in the Upper Thames Valley. This barge has two suites, three twins, and two singles. All are outside accommodations with private facilities.

European Waterways (140 E. 56th St., Suite 4C, New York, NY 10022, tel. 212/688–9489 or 800/217–4447, fax 212/688–3778 or 800/296–4554) represents several interesting vessels:

In Scotland, the eight-passenger *Vertrouwen*, Dutch-built in 1931 and converted to a hotel barge in 1992, makes six-night voyages along the Caledonian Canal, which slices diagonally through the Highlands between Inverness and Ft. William. Excursions ashore visit Loch Ness, castles, and wilderness areas. Optional activities include golf, salmon fishing, and deer tracking.

In Ireland, European Waterways has the 10-passenger *Bon Spes* on six-night cruises of the Upper Shannon River and Ballinamore Canal. Stops along the way are made at stately homes and gardens, castles, a monastery, and Irish pubs. Accommodations are in bunk-style cabins with private facilities.

In England, European Waterways books the *Actief* on the Thames; the company also represents barges in France and Holland (*see* On the Continent, *below*).

Highland Steamboat Holidays (c/o Nick Walker, The Change House, Lochgilphead, Argyll, PA31 8QH, Scotland, tel. 011/44–1546–510–232, fax 011/44–1546–510–249) operates a unique 12-passenger, coal-fired coastal steamboat on five- and six-day cruises in the sheltered waters off the west coast of Scotland and along the Caledonian Canal. Known as *Clyde Puffer*, the former cargo carrier was built in 1943 and, for the last 20 years, has operated passenger cruises. Cabin bunks are tiny—basic twins or doubles with shared shower and toilet facilities—and there's a small dining lounge.

For More Information The **British Tourist Authority** (551 5th Ave., New York, NY 10176, tel. 212/986–2200 or 800/462–2748) has information on individual operators as well as the useful booklet "Inland Waterways."

On the Continent

When to Go In France, Belgium, and the Netherlands, the barging season stretches from early March into December, though the best chance of warm weather begins in late April and ends in the early autumn. Some itineraries highlight tulip time in Holland, gardens in bloom in England, and the grape harvest in France.

Operators and Itineraries **Abercrombie & Kent** (*see* In Britain and Ireland, *above*) has no less than 11 barges in France, plus two in Holland and Belgium. The barges in this top-of-the-line fleet accommodate from six to 51 passengers; all cabins have private facilities. Newest are the *Lorraine* and *Marjorie II*, both launched in 1998. Three- to six-night cruises travel the Loire, Soane, Seine, Rhône, and other rivers and canals in France, and the canals of Belgium and Holland.

European Waterways (*see* In Britain and Ireland, *above*) markets eight barges, carrying from six to 12 passengers, on six-night cruises throughout France. Waterways include the Upper Loire and Canal du Midi. Regions visited include Burgundy, Champagne, Alsace-Lorraine, Gascogny, and Provence. In addition, the eight-passenger *Stella* cruises Dutch waterways in tulip season (March through mid-May).

French Country Waterways (Box 2195, Duxbury, MA 02331, tel. 617/934–2454 or 800/222–1236, fax 617/934–9048) operates four eight- to 18-passenger luxury barges on six-night trips through Burgundy. Cabins have twin or double beds with private facilities. All cruises include a dinner at a Michelin three-star restaurant. A fifth barge, refitted in 1997 with spacious suites, cruises on various itineraries through France, Germany, and Luxembourg.

On Board European Ferries

Combining the amenities and comforts of an ocean liner with the point-to-point service of a bus or train, a trip on a European ferry makes for a very attractive short cruise. In northern and southern Europe, these ferries form major links with the highway and railway system. In fact, a ferry cruise can be combined with a driving or Eurailpass itinerary.

Some routes, especially in Scandinavia, thread through forested archipelagoes and sail into scenic fjords, and the relaxing onboard ambience encourages visitors to meet local people. In the Mediterranean, large ferry liners link Italy with Greece. Feeder routes continue on to the Greek Islands, Turkey, Cyprus, and Israel.

Along the Coast of Norway

Like Alaska's Inside Passage, the Norwegian coastline boasts spectacular scenery and the advantage of cruising in calm waters. And as in southeast Alaska, the coastal waters serve as a "marine highway," where a network of mail ferries provides transportation for local travelers and visitors alike.

When to Go Again like Alaska, Norway has its period of nearly continuous daylight from mid-May to July, and this is, of course, the most popular time to travel. Although the summer season books up early, space may nevertheless be available at short notice. Cabins may be easier to find during the less-traveled spring and fall.

Cruise Experience Most of the route is protected from the open sea, but short open-water stretches can be rough. Passengers may elect to take the entire 11-day, 2,500-mi round-trip journey, book a one-way voyage going northbound or southbound, or get on and off at any one of 35 stops in between. Time in port ranges from 15 minutes to several hours. Optional overland shore excursions leave the ship in one port and rejoin it in another.

Travelers hail from the United States, Britain, and the rest of Europe, particularly Germany and, of course, Norway. As a result, menus aboard ship are mainly Continental, with Norwegian specialties. Breakfast and lunch are served buffet style, while dinner is a sit-down affair at reserved tables. Daily activities include watching the scenery pass by, watching the ship's cargo operations, and socializing with fellow passengers. Newer ships may have a band aboard during summer sailings.

The Fleet Three generations of vessels operate on Norwegian coastal cruises. The newest, built since 1993, have modern cruise-ship amenities such as cocktail lounges, library/card rooms, a restaurant, a cafeteria, a sauna, and an observation lounge. They carry 490 passengers in comfortable outside cabins, and register about 11,000 tons.

A little older are the ferries built in 1982–83. These ships, which were enlarged in 1988–89, carry 325 passengers. Cabins are smaller than in the newest ships, but the vessels have restaurant facilities and two observation lounges—one of which is glass-enclosed.

The two oldest ships in the Norwegian coastal fleet—the *Harald Jarl* and *Lofoten*—were built in the 1960s. They carry 170 to 225 passengers in small cabins—some without private facilities. What they lack in amenities they make up for in historical appeal. Their onboard ambience reflects Norway's maritime heritage, with wood-paneled lounges, local artwork, and teak decks. Public rooms are limited to two forward-facing lounges, a restaurant, and a cafeteria used by deck passengers. Cargo is crane-loaded the old-fashioned way, an endless delight to watch.

Operators and Cruises of Norway travel nearly the entire length of the coastline
Itineraries from the North Sea to the Arctic Ocean. In the south, the terminus is Bergen, Norway's second-largest city and most important seaport. In the north, Kirkenes, near the border with Finland and Russia, is the end of the line. Eleven ships are marketed by **Bergen Line** (405 Park Ave., New York, NY 10022, tel. 212/319–1300 or 800/323–7436, fax 212/319–1390). Departures are scheduled daily.

Elsewhere in Scandinavia and the North Sea

Like a spider's web connecting the cities of Scandinavia and its offshore islands, overnight ferry routes crisscross the Baltic and North seas. Many routes are designed to feed into the well-developed northern European rail system, allowing passengers to create their own rail-sea itineraries.

When to Go Most of these ferry services operate on a year-round basis. Ships may shift from route to route depending on the season.

Cruise Most passengers are British, German, and Scandinavian. Dining
Experience varies by the size of the ship. Meals may be served by waiters in sit-down restaurants, at elaborate buffet-style smorgasbords, or in inexpensive cafeterias. One ship even has a McDonald's. Like a typical cruise liner, some ferries offer passage with prepaid meals. Cruise ship–style entertainment is equally varied: There may be cabarets, dancing, and gambling, again, depending upon the size of the ship.

The Fleet The largest ships resemble oceangoing cruise liners and are equally sophisticated. Some are bigger than 30,000 tons and have such onboard facilities such as theaters, saunas, and duty-free shops. There may also be playrooms and video arcades for children. Cabins range from outside accommodations with picture windows to inside cabins designed for families.

Operators and The following lines operate some of the most popular northern
Itineraries European ferry routes:

The Norwegian-based **Color Line** sails across the North Sea, connecting Norway, Germany, Denmark, and England. Routes include Bergen–Newcastle, Stavanger–Newcastle, Oslo–Kiel; Kristiansand–Hirtshals, and Oslo–Hirtshals.

Danish-owned **Scandinavian Seaways** operates between England and Denmark, Sweden, Germany, and the Netherlands, and also between Norway and Denmark. Routes include Copenhagen–Oslo and Harwich (England)–Esbjerg (Denmark).

Silja Line operates the world's largest cruise ferries, registering up to 60,000 tons and carrying almost 3,000 passengers. Routes include Stockholm–Helsinki, Stockholm–Turku (Finland), and Helsinki–Travemunde (Germany).

Silja Line's main competitor is **Viking Line,** which offers equally large ships. Routes include Stockholm–Helsinki or Stockholm–Turku with a daytime stop in the pretty Aland Islands. Two principal U.S. agencies can book passages and combination tours with the lines described above and others not specifically listed here, such as short-duration Baltic Sea cruises from Scandinavian ports to Russia, Estonia, and Latvia and longer sea routes to the Shetland Islands, Faroes, Iceland, and Spitzbergen.

Bergen Line (405 Park Ave., New York, NY 10022, tel. 212/319–1300 or 800/323–7436, fax 212/319–1390) books one-way and round-trip cruises and cruise-tour packages for more than half a dozen lines.

EuroCruises (303 W. 13th St., New York, NY 10014, tel. 212/691–2099 or 800/688–3876) represents more than 20 European-based cruise lines and 60 ships sailing throughout Scandinavia, the Baltic states, and Russia.

For More National tourist offices can supply connecting rail and ferry sched-
Information ules. **Rail Europe** (tel. 800/438–7245) is the main source of rail passes; some are valid for certain ferry routes at no extra cost or at a discount. None, however, include cabin accommodations.

Through Southern Europe

Like the northern European ferry system described above, the Mediterranean abounds with unusual cruise options. But unlike the northern European ferry routes, which link mainly coastal cities, southern European ferries principally connect vacation islands with the Continent.

Italy is the main gateway for ferry cruises to points in Greece, Turkey, Cyprus, Israel, and Egypt. Ports of embarkation include Venice, Ancona, Bari, and Brindisi. Most runs to Greece take about 24 hours, but longer one-way and round-trip voyages are available to the eastern Mediterranean ports of Izmir (Turkey), Limassol (Cyprus), Haifa (Israel), and Alexandria (Egypt).

To island-hop through Greece, ferry travel is not only affordable but it may be the only way to go. Once in Aegean waters, a short crossing to the Turkish coast—or beyond—becomes a natural extension to a Greek-island itinerary.

When to Go Although some of the most popular routes have frequent service and schedules that change little from year to year, other destinations may see only seasonal access. Summertime travel can be crowded with backpackers. Determining specific departure times for Greek-island ferries has always been problematic, but there are some reliable and fairly comprehensive sources for those who like to plan ahead.

Cruise Experience From the deck of your ferry, anticipation runs high at the first sighting of Corsica's rugged north coast, the swirling waters known as Charybdis off Sicily, the Grand Harbor at Malta, or the whitewashed towns of the Aegean Islands. Generally, these ships are meant for basic transportation. They are less luxurious and offer fewer cruise-style services than the cruise-ferries found in northern Europe.

Operators and Itineraries From Spanish ports, the state-owned **Trasmediterranea Line** operates high-standard ferries on overnight runs. Routes include Cadiz–Canary Islands, Barcelona–Balearic Islands (Palma de Majorca, Ibiza, and Mahon), and Valencia–Balearic Islands. Shorter day ferries run from southern Spain to North Africa.

From French ports, **SNCM** uses the embarkation points of Toulon, Marseilles, or Nice for day and overnight cruises. Routes include service to Corsica, Sardinia, and North Africa.

From Italian ports, there are dozens of state-run and privately owned lines sailing from points on Italy's west coast. Routes service Corsica, Sardinia, Sicily, Malta, Tunisia, and coastal islands such as Elba, Ischia, and Capri. From Italy's east-coast ports of Venice, Ancona, Bari, and Brindisi, passengers can sail to the Greek island of Corfu and the coastal ports of Igoumentisa and Patras, the principal entry point for connecting buses to Athens and the port of Piraeus. Major lines sailing on these routes include **Adriatica** (also service to Alexandria), **Hellenic Mediterranean, Marlines** (also to Crete and Kuşadası, Turkey), **Minoan** (also to Crete and Cesme, Turkey), **Poseidon** (also to Limassol and Haifa), **Strintzis, SuperFast Ferries,** and **Vergina Cruises** (also to Limassol and Haifa). **Turkish Maritime Lines** uses Venice and Brindisi, but bypasses Greek ports for Antalya, Cesme, and I zmir.

From Greek ports, many ships that originated in Italy may be boarded en route to destinations on the Turkish coast, Cyprus, Israel, and Egypt. Most domestic services leave from Piraeus, the port of Athens, and northern routes depart from Thessaloniki.

From Turkish ports, **Turkish Maritime Lines** operates summer sailings of several days' duration that make an inexpensive cruise along the Black Sea coast. The route sails from Istanbul to Samsun and Trabzon. Other year-round routes include an overnight run from southern Turkey to Cyprus and service between Izmir and Istanbul.

For More Information Unlike Scandinavian operators, most Mediterranean ferry services do not have representatives in the United States, and unfortunately some lines do not think it worthwhile to answer queries. However, national tourist offices for Spain, France, Italy, Greece, Turkey, Cyprus, Israel, and Egypt can often supply ferry information, along with handy timetables (sometimes photocopies only) and overseas addresses, telephone numbers, and fax numbers for specific lines. Some Italy–Greece ferry operators are participants in the Eurailpass. Fares are included, but cabin accommodations are always extra.

Another excellent source of information is the "Thomas Cook European Timetable" (Forsythe Travel Library, 9154 W. 57th St., Box 2975, Shawnee Mission, KS 66201, tel. 913/384–3440 or 800/367–7984), a monthly guide to major rail and ferry schedules that includes a section of useful route maps.

On Board European Liners

The cruise ships detailed in Chapter 1 carry primarily North American passengers. Other liners serve mostly British, German, or Italian passengers. Generally speaking, these ships are for experienced cruisers. If the idea of cruising with people from other countries sounds appealing, you may find the experience extremely satisfying.

When to Go The best months for the Mediterranean are April, May, September, and October, when the weather is comfortable and summer crowds are absent. In northern Europe, where it's typically much cooler, June through August are the optimum sailing months due to the weather and the long hours of daylight.

Cruise Experience The experience of sailing on a European ship can be quite different from that encountered on the North American lines. Cuisine and entertainment are geared for British and European tastes. Ethnic dishes in the dining room and folkloric dancing in the showroom frequently reflect the origin of the ship's crew and passengers. Announcements may be made in a language other than English, and shipboard performers may entertain in their native tongue as well. Also, many Europeans have very different ideas about smoking and there are fewer restrictions. However, almost half the lines listed here cater primarily to the British market where language won't be a problem, though social customs may be quite different.

The Fleet European ships tend to be smaller and older than those sold primarily to North American passengers, and you may find several old favorites among them. Most ships listed here will have English-language information and English-speaking personnel. However, the mother tongue aboard ship will reflect the line's country of origin.

Operators and Itineraries **Airtours** (011/44–1706–240–033, fax 011/44–1706–212–144), a **British Liners** British firm owned partly by Carnival Cruise Lines, operates a fleet of four ships for British and European passengers, sailing mainly in the Mediterranean and the Caribbean. They are the 1,062-passenger *Carousel* (former *Nordic Prince)*, 752-passenger *Seawing* (formerly *Southward)* and 1,004-passenger *Sundream* (formerly *Song of Norway)*. At press time, the company also had acquired Royal Caribbean's 1,402-passenger *Song of America.*

The 50-passenger *Hebridean Princess*, from **Hebridean Island Cruises** (Acorn Park, Skipton, North Yorkshire, DB23 2UE, England, tel. 011/44–1756–701338, fax 011/44–1756–701455), is comparable to a five-star country hotel and quite unlike any other ship afloat. It puts to sea mostly from Oban and other Scottish ports, sailing to the Inner and Outer Hebrides, Orkney and Shetland islands, Ireland, and the coast of Norway. Each day includes one or two calls, and the ship anchors or docks at night. Cabins and lounges are beautifully decorated; the restaurant is outstanding. The *Hebridean Princess* caters to an upper-income British clientele. An increasing number of Americans have discovered this gem, but generally no more than four to six are aboard at any one time.

Another English firm that caters to a British clientele, **Noble Caledonia** (Esplanade Tours, 581 Boylston St., Boston, MA 02116, tel. 617/266–7465 or 800/426–5492, fax 617/262–9829) books the expedition ship *World Discoverer* (*see* Society Expeditions in Chapter 1) and Russian icebreakers for voyages up the Amazon and to Antarctica. Other possibilities include riverboats in Europe, Russia, and Myanmar.

British **P&O**, the parent company of Los Angeles–based Princess Cruises (tel. 310/553–1770), has one of Europe's newest and biggest vessels: the 67,000-ton, 1,760-passenger *Oriana*. It carries mostly British passengers on cruises from England to northern Europe, the Atlantic Islands, the Mediterranean, and the Caribbean. Many more Americans (and Australians) are aboard for the round-the-world cruises, which call at U.S. ports, such as Los Angeles and San Francisco. Other ships in P&O's fleet include the 714-passenger *Victoria* (formerly *Sea Princess*), a newly refitted classic liner with a lovely wood-paneled Scandinavian interior, and the 63,564-ton *Arcadia*, a megaship which for many years served Princess Cruises as the *Star Princess*. The trio operates with British officers and a British and Indian hotel staff. P&O also operates year-round cruises from Australia aboard the *Fair Princess*. Yet another Princess Cruises alumnus, this 1957 liner now sails from Sydney to other ports Down Under, as well as to New Zealand and the South Pacific islands. Most passengers are Australians. They're a lively bunch, and the shorter the itinerary, the more festive the cruise.

Another venerable British institution, **Swan Hellenic Cruises** (*see* P&O, *above*) has offered educationally oriented cruises for more than 40 years. Professors from British universities accompany every cruise, giving 45-minute lectures and providing leadership ashore. As educational cruises have become more popular, the line's long-standing reputation has attracted an increasing number of Americans. Many are aboard as part of an alumni or museum group. In 1996, the line, owned by P&O, introduced a new, more upscale ship, the 388-passenger Minerva, built specifically for enrichment cruises and far more spacious and better equipped than its previous vessel, *Orpheus*, which now sails for Royal Olympic Cruises (*see* Chapter 1). The *Minerva*'s summer destinations include ports in Europe and the Mediterranean; winter voyages sail to destinations in the Indian Ocean and Southeast Asia. Swan Hellenic also charters a riverboat in Europe and another on the Nile (*see below*).

Saga Holidays (222 Berkeley St, Boston, MA 02116, 617/262–2262 or 800/343–0273, fax 617/375–5950) now operates its own ship, the 25,147-ton, 580-passenger *Saga Rose* (formerly Cunard's *Sagafjord*), on 14- to 16-day northern European and Mediterranean cruises departing England and a round-world cruise. The passengers on this fine older ship will mainly be British, and all are age 50 and above (*see* Hints for Older Passengers *in* Cruise Primer).

Thomson Cruises (011/44–171–707–9000, fax 011/44–171–387–8451) operates three ships for British and European passengers. Operating mainly in the Mediterranean and Caribbean, they are 968-passenger *Emerald* (formerly the *Regent Rainbow* of Regency Cruises), the 573-passenger *Sapphire* (formerly *Ocean Princess* of Ocean Cruise Lines), the 975 passenger *Topaz* (formerly the *Olympic* of Royal Olympic Cruises), and the 1,432-passenger *IslandBreeze* (on charter from Premier Cruises for eight months of the year).

Scandinavian Liners New York–based **EuroCruises** (303 W. 13th St., New York, NY 10014, tel. 212/691–2099 or 800/688–3876, fax 212/366–4747) represents several European cruise ships, including the traditional 9,846-ton, 424-passenger *Funchal* on a wide variety of cruises to the Baltic, Norwegian fjords, Greenland, and to southern Europe. One of the agency's specialties is summer Baltic cruises aboard the Finnish registered *Kristina Regina* (200 passengers) and *Kristina Brahe* (80 passengers). The *Kristina Regina* also sails on special opera cruises and makes expedition-style trips north to the Russian White Sea calling at Murmansk and Archangel.

Fred. Olsen Cruise Lines's 450-passenger *Black Prince* is Norwegian-owned with a Filipino crew. The vessel caters to middle-income British passengers with year-round cruises from southern England to Iberia, Madeira, the Canary Islands, Morocco, the western Mediterranean, and, in summer, northern Europe. Built in 1966, this well-maintained, professionally run ship has built a very loyal following over many years. Another Fred. Olsen ship with a record of distinguished service—and the latest addition to the fleet—is the *Black Watch* (built as the *Royal Viking Star* in 1972 and later known as Royal Cruise Line's *Star Odyssey)*. Now refitted to accommodate 832 passengers, the *Black Watch* sails on Canary Island itineraries and extended voyages to the eastern Mediterranean, Scandinavia, the Caribbean, Africa, and the Far East. Both ships are represented in the United States by Euro-Cruises (*see above*).

Italian Liners **Italian Costa Cruise Lines** is reviewed in Chapter 1 for its ships that cater to North Americans, but the line is also one of the best-known names among Europeans for cruising. The ships sail in European waters in summer and in South America or the Caribbean in winter. Transatlantic crossings are scheduled in fall and spring. All Costa ships may be booked through the line's U.S. headquarters (tel. 800/462–6782).

The Italian-based company **Mediterranean Shipping Cruises** (420 5th Ave., New York, NY 10018, tel. 212/764–4800 or 800/666–9333, fax 212/764–8592) caters to Europeans—and more and more Americans—on northern European, Mediterranean, Black Sea, and Caribbean cruises. The fleet consists of the 35,143-ton, 972-passenger *Melody* (formerly Premier Cruise Lines's *Star/Ship Atlantic*) which spends the winter in the Caribbean and carries the highest percentage of Americans passengers; the American-built, 21,051-ton, 600-passenger *Monterey;* the 17,495-ton, 800-passenger *Rhapsody* (formerly the Cunard *Princess);* and the 16,495-ton, 775-passenger *Symphony* (formerly Costa Cruise Lines' *EnricoCosta)*, which is permanently stationed in the Indian Ocean.

French Liners **Paquet French Cruises** (1510 S.E. 17th St., Fort Lauderdale, FL 33316, tel. 305/764–3500 or 800/556–8850, fax 305/764–2888) is another name that longtime American cruisers may remember well. The line's sole ship, the 13,691-ton, 533-passenger *Mermoz* offers a sophisticated classic-ship experience on cruises in northern and southern Europe in the summer and in the Caribbean and along the South American coast in winter. These cruises draw mostly French passengers, along with others who speak French or are Francophiles.

Greek Liners **First European Cruises** (95 Madison Ave, Suite 1203, New York, NY 10016, tel. 212/779–7168 or 888/983–8767, fax 212/779–0948), a new North American booking agency, can put you aboard the 16,107-ton, 802-passenger *Bolero* (formerly Norwegian Cruise Line's *Starward);* the 17,503-ton, 784-passenger *Flamenco;* or the 15,000-ton, 720-passenger *Azur* for a variety of four- to 14-day cruises in the Mediterranean and northern Europe. The officers are Greek, chefs are Italian, the food Continental, and the ships are a good value for the money. Packages include hotel accommodations, airfare, and transfers. EuroCruises (*see above*) also books these ships.

Swiss Liners **OdessAmerica Cruises** (170 Old Country Rd., Suite 608, Mineola, NY 11501, tel. 516/747–8880 or 800/221–3254, fax 516/747–8367) represents the African Safari Club's 220-passenger *Royal Star* on Indian Ocean cruises. Embarking from Mombasa, Kenya, it sails to Zanzibar, the Seychelles, the Comores, and Madagascar. Occasional long cruises extend to Mauritius, Reunion, and ports in South Africa. Most of the passengers are German speaking or British; a popular option is to combine a cruise with an East African beach and safari package.

On Board Freighters

To embark on a freighter cruise is to join a tiny floating community that roams the high seas in a world of its own. Freighter travelers are a special breed; most are retired yet active people who like a leisurely pace, lots of time at sea, considerable comfort, and moderate rates averaging about $100 per day.

When to Go Many North Americans book during the cold winter months, but many routes are attractive year-round—except for the North Atlantic in winter.

Cruise Experience Unlike most cruise ships, which have precisely scheduled port calls, freighters stay in port as long as it takes to load or unload their cargo. This can be measured in hours or in days—depending upon how modern the ship is. Itineraries, too, are sometimes subject to change. Flexibility is the key word as there may be delays.

Passengers tend to be older than the typical cruiser, and the complement of passengers aboard a freighter is considerably smaller than that aboard a standard cruise ship. Cargo ships that take from two to 12 passengers do not carry a doctor and have age limits that vary from 75 to 82. Larger passenger freighters have no age restrictions and may employ a physician.

The Fleet Most cargo liners carry up to 12 passengers, although the biggest accommodates 88. Because most of the space aboard ship is devoted to freight, passenger facilities are more limited than they are on ocean liners and usually consist of a dining room, a small lounge, and an exercise room. Outdoor deck space for passengers is provided at the stern, where there may be a small pool and a whirlpool. Often, passengers share these facilities with the ship's officers. Cabins are larger than those on a typical cruise ship, but they're much more modestly decorated. There usually is no room service.

Operators and Itineraries

Passenger-carrying cargo ships depart the United States from ports on the East Coast, West Coast, and Gulf Coast. Some also travel the St. Lawrence River from ports on the Great Lakes and in Canada. Round-trip journeys last from four weeks to four months. Shorter one-way passages may also be available.

The list of passenger-carrying freighter companies included below is a small but varied selection of ships sailing from North America and elsewhere. Some lines have years of service while others, dependent on sufficient cargo inducement, may appear and disappear at fairly short notice. A few of these operators may be contacted directly, as noted; otherwise, contact one of the two freighter-cruise agencies listed under For More Information, *below*.

Bank Line (British and Indian officers) operates the eight-passenger semicontainer ship *Olivebank* from Savannah, Georgia, on a 70- to 75-day round-trip voyage to the Canary Islands, Africa, and South America. From Hull, England, this venerable British company also runs 120- to 130-day around-the-world freighter cruises, which depart on a monthly basis.

Blue Star runs two services with high standards, using six ships (British officers) that take 10 to 12 passengers. The East Coast Service, about 66 days round-trip, embarks in Savannah, Georgia, for ports in Australia and New Zealand and returns to Philadelphia. The West Coast Service, about 49 days round-trip, departs Los Angeles, also bound for Australia and New Zealand, and returns via Fiji to Seattle, Oakland, and Los Angeles.

Niederelbe Schiffahrtsgesellschaft Buxtehude (NSB) operates German-owned and registered container ships that accommodate seven to 10 passengers. Three services are offered: Around-the-world cruises depart from the East Coast cities of New York, Norfolk, and Charleston (about 101 to 104 days round-trip). From the Gulf Coast, there's a 42-day round-trip departing Houston and New Orleans for the Mediterranean and returning by way of Mexico. From the West Coast there are sailings from Los Angeles to Australia and New Zealand (about 46 days round-trip).

Columbus Line (German officers) operates two top-notch services: The East Coast (Boomerang Service) sails from Savannah, Georgia, and usually Houston, Texas, by way of the Panama Canal to Australia and New Zealand, and returns to Philadelphia. The round-trip voyage takes about 66 days. Ships carry eight to 12 passengers. The West Coast (Kiwi Service) departs Los Angeles for Australia and New Zealand and returns to Los Angeles. This round-trip lasts about 49 days. Three newly refurbished ships carry eight passengers.

Compagnie Polynesienne de Transport Maritime (2028 El Camino Real S, Suite B, San Mateo, CA 94430, tel. 415/574–2575 or 800/972–7268) provides the lifeline for French Polynesia with the 77-passenger cargo ship *Aranui II* on a 16-day round-trip voyage from Papeete, Tahiti, to the Society Islands and Marquesas, calling at Ua Pou, Nuku Hiva, Hiva Oa (where French painter Gauguin lived), Fatu Hiva, Ua Huka, and Rangiroa. The ship carries local passengers on deck and international passengers in cabins. The accommodations are simple, and some do not have private facilities. Tours, included in the fare, are organized in each port, and although there is no age limit, clambering into small boats and landing through the surf requires some agility.

Curnow Shipping Ltd. (c/o Golden Bear Travel, 16 Digital Dr., Suite 100, Navato, CA 94949, tel. 415/382–8900 or 800/551–1000) of Cornwall, England, operates the world's most remote passenger and cargo service with the Royal Mail Ship *St. Helena*, sailing from Cardiff in South Wales to the beautiful South Atlantic island of St. Helena, a British dependency that does not have an airport. The ship carries up to 132 islanders and adventure-seeking tourists in a wide variety of cabins. Most trips call at Tenerife and Ascension and may also call at Banjul, The Gambia. Passengers continuing on to Cape Town, South Africa, enjoy a week ashore on St. Helena and a warm welcome at a small hotel or guest house while the ship unloads cargo and makes a shuttle run to Ascension and back. The one-way passage between Britain and South Africa takes about four weeks. Passengers then have the option of sailing or flying back. Once a year, the *St. Helena* departs from Cape Town on a two-week round-trip voyage, always a sellout, to even more remote Tristan da Cunha.

Ivaran Lines (111 Pavonia Ave., Jersey City, NJ 07310, tel. 201/798–5656 or 800/451–1639, fax 201/798–7304) has the distinction of operating the world's largest and most luxurious container ship, the *Americana*, carrying 88 passengers in cruise ship–style accommodations. Cabins consist of singles, doubles, and suites, some with sitting areas and private verandas. Passenger facilities include a piano bar and lounge, library/card room, dining room, exercise room, sauna, outdoor pool, whirlpool, ample deck space, and an infirmary with a Scandinavian doctor and nurse. The service, by a South American staff, and the food, which includes Norwegian delicacies, are both excellent. A purser/cruise director arranges excursions ashore. A 21-day round-trip voyage departs Houston, setting sail for Mexico, Costa Rica, Colombia, Venezuela, Barbados, Puerto Rico, and the Dominican Republic. Ivaran also operates a smaller freighter, the 12-passenger *San Antonio*. Built in 1994, this 12-passenger ship embarks in New Orleans, and makes calls at Houston, Rio, Santos and Buenos Aires before returning to Louisiana by way of Brazil, Venezuela, and Mexico. The entire journey takes 48 or 49 days.

Mineral Shipping operates two seven- to 12-passenger ships (Croatian officers) from Savannah, Georgia, to Dutch ports, with several days' stay ashore, before returning to the U.S. East Coast. Voyages last 32 to 40 days round-trip. Sailings from Savannah to the Mediterranean are also available aboard 12-passenger ships. The round-trip voyages take about 70 days and ports change at short notice.

Windjammer Barefoot Cruises (Box 120, Miami Beach, FL 33119, tel. 800/327–2601), best known for its fleet of tall ships (*see* On Board Tall Ships, *below*), operates the 100-passenger *Amazing Grace* as a supply vessel for its Caribbean ships. Built in 1955 as a Scottish lighthouse tender, the ship has wood-paneled accommodations, including original cabins with shared facilities and more recently added rooms with private showers. The onboard atmosphere is low-key, and the food is thoroughly American. Sailing from Freeport, the Bahamas, the ship makes 13-day one-way trips and 26-day round-trips to 20 islands as far south as Grenada.

For More Information The following agencies have booked freighter travel for many years, and they may act as general sales agents (GSA) for individual lines. Both agencies offer useful though very different publications.

Freighter World Cruises (180 S. Lake Ave., Suite 335, Pasadena, CA 91101, tel. 818/449–3106, fax 818/449–9573) publishes the "Freighter Space Advisory" every two weeks. This is the bible of freighter cruises, listing itineraries, cabin availability, and special fares. Brief descriptions detail the accommodations aboard the various ships. Most of the freighters listed have been inspected by the agency's staff.

TravLtips (Box 580188, Flushing, NY 11358, tel. 718/939–2400 or 800/872–8584) publishes a bimonthly magazine ($20 a year) with black-and-white photos and reports on freighter trips by passengers. The magazine also lists special cruise-ship offers.

On Board Research Vessels

Perhaps the most adventurous endeavor in cruising is to book yourself aboard an icebreaker on a scientific research mission.

When to Go Cruises aboard research vessels sail to the Arctic and Antarctic in the summer—June through September in the Northern Hemisphere and December through March in the Southern Hemisphere. At these times of year, days are generally sunny and temperatures are relatively warm (at least above freezing), but wind and cloud cover can create bundle-up conditions.

Cruise Experience Sailing to the polar regions and elsewhere, the "shore excursions" aboard these ships may include standing beside the ship on the Arctic pack ice or taking a helicopter flight to scout the route ahead. The research opportunities these unique vessels present attract top-echelon lecturers, too.

The Fleet Most passenger-carrying research vessels are Russian, Ukrainian, or Estonian, under charter to tour agencies. They usually accommodate up to 100 passengers, sometimes less. Cabins are typically all outside with private facilities, although some may have shared baths. Shipboard amenities can be surprisingly good, as some of these vessels were designed to spend extended time at sea. One even has an indoor swimming pool. Some are actual icebreakers, while others are ice-rated, meaning they have hardened hulls for pushing through the ice. Any one ship may be sold by more than one operator. Rates vary enormously, depending on the itinerary's remoteness and the degree of competition. When comparing different packages, look carefully at what's included and what's not.

Operators and Itineraries Canadian-based **Marine Expeditions** (13 Hazelton Ave., Toronto, Ontario M5R 2EI, tel. 416/964–9069 or 800/263–9147, fax 416/964–2366) charters four research vessels for affordable expedition cruises to Antarctica and the Arctic, the coast of Norway, and repositioning trips that call at mid-Atlantic islands from the Falklands northward. Although officially the ships are Russian- and Estonian-owned, they carry "marine" aliases such as *Marine Adventurer* and *Marine Spirit*. The vessels vary in size, carrying from 44 to 80 passengers. The 92-passenger *Disko*, rebuilt from a coastal passenger ship, makes summer cruises along Greenland's West Coast.

Mountain Travel-Sobek (6420 Fairmount Ave., El Cerrito, CA 94530, tel. 510/527–8100 or 800/227–2384, fax 510/525–7710), one of the oldest adventure-travel companies, charters the 38-passenger ice-rated *Livonia* for a December to February Antarctic program.

Noble Caledonia (*see* On Board European Liners, *above*) uses the 48-passenger research vessel *Professor Molchanov*, with one of the smallest passenger complements, on 11-night cruises from the tip of South America to Antarctica. The company also books space on other research ships to the North Pole, the Northeast Passage, and the Spitsbergen and Arctic islands.

Quark Expeditions (980 Post Rd., Darien, CT 06820, tel. 203/656–0499 or 800/356–5699, fax 203/655–6623) has one of the most extensive and innovative research-vessel programs available. In the Arctic region, the 98-passenger icebreaker *Yamal* crashes through the Russian ice to the North Pole, while the 106-passenger *Kapitan Dranitsyn* pounds its way along the Northeast Passage above Siberia to Greenland, Spitsbergen, and remote islands within the Arctic Circle. At the other end of the globe, cruises to the Antarctic Peninsula, the Falklands, and South Georgia use the 79-passenger *Akademik Ioffe* and other research ships.

TCS Expeditions (2025 1st Ave., Seattle, WA 98121, tel. 206/727–7300 or 800/727–7477, fax 206/727–7309) also charters the *Yamal* and the 108-passenger *Kapitan Khlebnikov* for voyages to the North Pole. The icebreakers, originally designed to spend months away from home, offers such luxuries as an indoor swimming pool, a sauna, a gym, and a basketball/volleyball court.

On Board Riverboats

Cruises on the rivers of the world are as varied as the rivers themselves. The Rhine's castles and cathedrals look down onto a busy commercial waterway, while the mighty Amazon surges through the rain forest, and the Nile forms a green ribbon in the desert. The Yangtze is best known for the Three Gorges and Australia's Murray River is hardly known at all. In Russia, the Volga leads to small villages closed to the outside world less than a decade ago. And in Myanmar, the Irrawaddy—Kipling's "Road to Mandalay"—has become the newest river-cruise destination.

Cruise Experience Some waterways are high on scenery, while others offer more in the way of cultural interest. All explore deep inland at a leisurely pace, visiting remote villages and attractions both natural and man-made.

The Fleet Riverboats may be plain or fancy, and the leisurely pace might suit some and bore others. Most have all outside cabins, private facilities, a restaurant for dining, and perhaps a single lounge/bar for entertainment. Some rivers, such as the Amazon, the Niger in West Africa, the Upper Nile in the Sudan, and the Congo, maintain scheduled daily or weekly services, but these boats are only suitable for the hardy. The boats and river trips listed here meet international standards for comfort, safety, and expert guidance.

In Europe

When to Go European river cruises generally operate from April through October, but the best times to go are late spring and early fall, when the Continent is less crowded. Discounts are often available at the very beginning and very end of the season.

Operators and Itineraries **KD River Cruises of Europe** (2500 Westchester Ave., Purchase, NY 10577, tel. 914/696–3600 or 800/346–6525, fax 914/696–0833) is the largest and oldest passenger line in Europe; its Rhine River voyages date from 1827. The modern era began in 1960, with the first cruise vessel sailing between Rotterdam and Basel, Switzerland. Nowadays, 450 annual departures, mostly three to seven days, operate on the Rhine, Main, Moselle, Neckar, Elbe, Danube, Saar, Seine, Soane, and Rhône rivers in Germany, Holland, France, Switzerland, Austria, Hungary, and the Czech Republic. There are 32 different itineraries. Eleven riverboats carry between 100 and 184 passengers, generally in windowed cabins with twin beds (one converting to a daytime sofa) and private facilities.

Peter Deilmann/EuropAmerica Cruises (1800 Diagonal Rd., Suite 170, Alexandria, VA 22314, tel. 703/549–1741 or 800/348–8287, fax 703/549–7924) markets six high-standard riverboats that carry 68 to 207 passengers on mostly seven-day cruises of the Danube, Elbe, Rhine, Main, Moselle, Rhône, and Soane. These vessels are geared toward German tastes: Food is German and Continental; dinner runs to six courses and lunch to five. However, English-speaking passengers will find the staff easy to communicate with, and the shore excursion program and other printed matter is fully bilingual. Itineraries through Germany provide a good setting for meeting local residents traveling in their own country.

Elegant Cruise & Tours (31 Central Dr., Port Washington, NY 11050, tel. 516/767–9302 or 800/683–6767, fax 516/767–9303) specializes in European river cruises in all price ranges, from budget to upscale. At the economy end of the scale lies the comfortable *Delta Star* on the Danube. At the high end, the 1996-built *River Cloud* is brought to you by the same owners as the luxury *Sea Cloud* (*see* On Board Tall Ships, *below*), cruising between Dietfurt in southeastern Germany and Budapest by way of the Main-Danube Canal. Also new is the *Amadeus*, launched in 1997, which cruises four German rivers and operates special departures from Vienna down the Danube to the Black Sea. Other riverboats in Elegant Cruise's portfolio ply the waterways of Holland and France.

EuroCruises (303 W. 13th St., New York, NY 10014, tel. 212/691–2099 or 800/688–3876, fax 212/366–4747) represents the *Rhine Princess* (120 passengers), with twin- or double-bedded outside cabins, making eight-day cruises between Amsterdam and Basel via a beautiful section of the Moselle. The *Blue Danube I* (148 passengers) and *Blue Danube II* (144 passengers) sail between Berching near Nuremburg and Budapest via the Main-Danube Canal, an eight-day cruise making stops at Regensburg, Passau, Linz, Vienna, and Bratislava. The *Cezanne* travels the Rhône through Provence, between Avignon and Lyon, while the *Normandie* cruises the Seine between Paris and Honfleur.

Both **Bergen Line** (405 Park Ave., New York, NY 10022, tel. 212/319–1300 or 800/323–7436, fax 212/319–1390) and **EuroCruises** (*see above*) market three classic 60-passenger riverboats—the *Diana* (1931), *Wilhelm Tham* (1912), and *Juno* (1874)—which sail on four- and six-day voyages along Sweden's Gota Canal between Stockholm and Gothenburg. The sheltered and sometimes forested route passes islands, forts, palaces, churches, villages, and 65 locks. These are not luxury vessels, and the compact cabins have upper and lower berths, while toilets and showers are in the hallways. The smorgasbord, however, is among the best in Sweden.

In Russia and the Ukraine

When to Go   Cruising in Russia is a summer pastime, while the season in the more southerly Ukraine extends into the spring and fall.

Operators and **EuroCruises** (*see above*) uses the large 424-ft, 250-passenger
Itineraries *Sergei Kirov* for its 12- and 13-day program of cruises between
Moscow and St. Petersburg. The five-deck vessel is Swiss-man-
aged, ensuring high standards, and it acts as a hotel for two nights
in both terminal cities. The Svir and Volga River route crosses
lakes and reservoirs and calls at cities, towns, cathedrals, and
monasteries. One of the most remote inland cruises in the world
takes place on the Yenisey River in Siberia aboard the 184-pas-
senger Anton Chekhov. The 9- or 10-day cruise operates, at the
north end, above the Arctic Circle.

OdessAmerica Cruise Line (170 Old Country Rd., Suite 608, Mineola, NY 11501, tel. 516/747–8880 or 800/221–3254, fax 516/747–
8367) is another source of Moscow–St. Petersburg cruises, but
its vessels—the 270-passenger *Andropov*, *Lenin*, and *Litvinov*—
are not Western-managed. Accommodations on all three riverboats are outside, with picture windows and private facilities. A
wide variety of configurations are available, including cabins
designed for two passengers, four passengers, and even 12 single
cabins for passengers traveling alone. There are two suites as
well. Itineraries are 15 days. Better yet is the 210-passenger *Lev
Tolstoy*—considered to be the flagship of the Russian fleet and
once used to carry high officials and visiting foreign dignitaries
on holidays. Itineraries are 11 or 12 days.

In the Ukraine, OdessAmerica has 11- and 12-day cruises on board
the 270-passenger *Victor Glushkov*. The boat sails the Dnieper
River and the Black Sea between Kiev and Odessa, visiting the
Cossack region as well as Sevastopol and Yalta in the Crimea, and
some distance up the Danube running between Bulgaria and
Romania.

General Tours (53 Summer St., Keene, NH 03431, tel. 800/221–
2216, fax 603/357–4548) also books passengers aboard the
Andropov, *Lenin*, *Litvinov*, and *Furmanov* as well as the superior
Kirov on Russian waterways cruises between Moscow and St.
Petersburg and the Guschkov and the Dneiper.

On the Amazon

It's nearly impossible to comprehend the Amazon Basin without
taking a river cruise of at least several days. Oceangoing ships
cruise the Amazon, but just the lower portion from the mouth of
the river to Manaus, Brazil—a mere 1,000 mi upriver. For the
real flavor of the steamy jungle, head for the Upper Amazon or
the Solimoes (a tributary of the Amazon that meets the river at
Manaus).

When to Go Oceangoing ships visit the Amazon during the dry season (which
coincides with the northern winter months between December
and March), but local cruises run year-round. Even during the dry
season, it's hot ashore in villages and during rain-forest walks, but
quite pleasant when under way on the river.

Operators and **Amazon Tours & Cruises** (8700 W. Flagler St., Miami, FL 33174,
Itineraries tel. 305/227–2266 or 800/423–2791, fax 305/227–1880) will bring you
up the river and into the jungle for a true taste of the rain forest.
Three- to six-night trips operate between Iquitos, Peru, and Leti-
cia, Colombia, or Tabatinga, Brazil. Aboard these small riverboats, which aren't always air-conditioned, you can scan the water
for pink dolphins and watch for birds from a deck chair. Excursions off the boat include jungle walks and visits to Indian villages.

The *Rio Amazonas* is the largest of ATC's fleet, carrying 44 passengers in 21 air-conditioned cabins with private baths. The dining room is air-conditioned, too. The *Arca* has 16 air-conditioned cabins (upper and lower berths) with private baths, an air-conditioned dining room and lounge. The *Amazon Explorer* (also available from Mountain Travel-Sobek, 6420 Fairmount Ave., El Cerrito, CA 94530, tel. 510/527–8100 or 800/227–2384, fax 510/525–7710) has 16 air-conditioned cabins with private facilities and an air-conditioned lounge. For really roughing it, the *Delfin* (20 passengers) and *Amazon Discoverer* (16 passengers) have non-air-conditioned cabins with shared facilities.

Other local riverboats with upper Amazon adventures are the *Flotel Orellana* (Adventure Associates/Metropolitan Touring, 13150 Coit Rd., Suite 110, Dallas, TX 75240, tel. 972/907–0414 or 800/527–2500, fax 972/783–1286), with fans only in cabins for 48 passengers; and *La Esmeralda* (International Expeditions, One Environs Park, Helena, AL 35080, tel. 800/633–4734), with air-conditioned cabins for 16 passengers.

Still another local boat with short cruises of the Rio Negro, a tributary of the Amazon, is the *Desafio* (16776 Bernardo Center Dr., San Diego, CA 92128, tel. 619/451–8406 or 800/421–5276, fax 619/451–8472), fully air-conditioned for 24 passengers. The vessel makes three- and four-day ecological cruises year-round from Manaus.

Among the major cruise ships with upper Amazon sailings is **Abercrombie & Kent**'s *Explorer* (*see* Chapter 1). **Marine Expeditions** (*see* On Board Research Vessels, *above*) has rather affordable Amazon adventures aboard the *Marine Discovery*.

On the Irrawaddy

In the country now called Myanmar but formerly known as Burma, a relatively new riverboat links Pagan and its field of 5,000 temples with the northern river city of Mandalay. The boat, originally from the Rhine, has been renamed *The Road to Mandalay* and accommodates 139 passengers and a crew of 70. Beyond Mandalay, another riverboat, the *Myat Thanda*, sails even farther north—well beyond the tourist circuit to the start of navigation in upper Myanmar. River travel does not get more exotic than this.

When to Go Myanmar is a year-round destination with high temperatures and humidity that vary little from month to month.

Operators and Itineraries Cruises on *The Road to Mandalay* last three days and include a stay in Yangon (Rangoon), with optional extensions to Thailand, Laos, and Cambodia and a two-night ride on the Eastern & Oriental Express, a luxury train operating between Bangkok, Penang, Kuala Lumpur, and Singapore. **Abercrombie & Kent** (1520 Kensington Rd., Oak Brook, IL 60523, tel. 630/954–2944 or 800/323–7308, fax 630/954–3324) offers complete tours. The riverboat and train agent is **Orient-Express Trains & Cruises** (tel. 800/524–2420).

Cruises on the 20-passenger *Myat Thanda*, built in 1995, sail deeper into Myanmar and spend more time on the river, visiting remote areas not easily reached any other way. The complete trip is 12 nights, including overnights in Rangoon. The *Myat Thanda* can be booked through **Esplanade Tours** (581 Boylston St., Boston, MA 02116, tel. 617/266–7465 or 800/426–5492, fax 617/262–9829).

On the Murray

Cruising Australia's Murray River closely parallels a lazy trip on the Mississippi, if on a much more intimate scale. The 1,609-mi Murray divides New South Wales and Victoria, and exits through South Australia into the sea. In the 19th century it served as an important water highway for the farms and mines in the developing interior.

When to Go The austral spring and fall (October and November or April and May) are the most pleasant seasons. Summers can be quite hot and dry in the river valley. Victorian winters are mild compared with those of the northeastern United States, but they can still be damp and rainy.

Operators and Itineraries Two- to five-night cruises embark year-round from Murray Bridge, Mannum, and Blanchetown. The 120-passenger *Murray Princess* is fashioned after a Mississippi-style stern-wheeler and operated by **Captain Cook Cruises** (Qantas Vacations, tel. 800/682–6025; or ATS Tours, 2381 Rosecrans Ave., Suite 325, El Segundo, CA 90245, tel. 800/423–2880)—the same company that runs the *Reef Endeavor* and *Reef Escape* (*see* Along the Great Barrier Reef, *above*).

Also contact the *Proud Mary* (Proud Australia Cruises, 33 Pirie St., Adelaide, SA 5000 Australia, tel. 011/61–8–231–9472, fax 011/61–8–212–1520).

On the Nile

Without the Nile, there would be no Egypt—no Aswan, Luxor, Thebes, Valley of the Kings, or Valley of the Queens—all stops on most Nile cruises. The Nile River fleet numbers over 200 boats, and with each flotilla catering to a special market, the quality of onboard enrichment programs, facilities, and service varies enormously. Although the cruising portion will be relaxing, shore excursions can get very crowded, especially in the cooler high-season months. The best operators get you up early to be among the first at the tomb entrance and to have everyone back on the boat during the midday heat.

When to Go Boats sail the Nile year-round, but late fall, winter, and spring are the most comfortable times. The Nile Valley gets extremely hot in summer, when nothing much takes place in the middle of the day.

Operators and Itineraries Nearly all Nile cruises are three to seven days long and are packaged with hotel stays in Cairo, Luxor, or Aswan. Group travel in Egypt is almost de rigueur, but the numbers need not be large. The Nile operators listed here run boats that have all outside cabins and private facilities, open and covered top-deck seating, a tiny pool, a lounge, a bar, a dining room with Western and Middle Eastern menus, and a comprehensive lecture program.

Abercrombie & Kent (1520 Kensington Rd., Oak Brook, IL 60521, tel. 708/954–2944 or 800/323–7308, fax 708/954–3324) has two boats, the 40-passenger *Sun Boat III* and the new 84-passenger *Sun Boat IV,* which are among the most spacious on the Nile. Upper Nile cruises of five to eight days are part of an Egyptian tour package, with a limit of 24 passengers.

Esplanade Tours (581 Boylston St., Boston, MA 02116, tel. 617/266– 7465 or 800/426–5492) sells the top-rated *Regency*, with 49 large double cabins and two suites. Its one-week year-round cruises from Luxor are part of a 14-day tour.

Hilton International Nile Cruises (c/o Misr Travel, 630 5th Ave., New York, NY 10111, tel. 212/582–9210 or 800/223–4978) uses the *Isis* and *Osiris*, each carrying 96 passengers, and the 120-passenger *Nephtis* on four- and six-day cruises between Luxor and Aswan.

Nabila Nile Cruises (605 Market St., Suite 1310, San Francisco, CA 94105, tel. 415/979–0160 or 800/443–6453) operates a fleet of five boats—*Queen Nabila I, Queen Nabila III, Queen of Sheba, Ramses of Egypt,* and *Ramses King of the Nile.* The boats carry 72 to 156 passengers on four- and six-day trips between Luxor and Aswan.

Special Expeditions (720 5th Ave., New York, NY 10019, tel. 212/765–7740 or 800/762–0003) puts only 30 passengers aboard its Nile boat, the *Hapi,* for seven-day cruises between Luxor and Aswan. These cruises are part of longer land-and-air tour packages from the United States.

Swan Hellenic (Classical Cruises & Tours, 132 E. 70th St., New York, NY 10021, tel. 212/794–3200 or 800/252–7745), a British operator with top lecturers (*see* On Board European Liners, *above*) and one of the best choices on the river, combines the riverboat *Vittoria* on the Nile and a small cruise ship known as the *Nubian Sea* on Lake Nasser as part of a 14-day cruise-tour package from the United States.

On the Yangtze

The Yangtze is 4,000 mi long and with much of it navigable, the river is central China's main artery for moving freight, produce, and passengers. Most travelers embark in either Chongquin or Wuhan to see the magnificent Three Gorges and village life along the river. Itineraries usually include a look at the controversial Three Gorges Dam, which will be the largest dam in the world when it's finished.

When to Go Cruises operate year-round, but spring and fall are best. Summer months are very hot. Winter is very cold, and fog may prevent navigation during the season. In about 10 years, rising waters behind the Three Gorges Dam, now under construction, will begin to submerge some of the archaeological sites and diminish the natural grandeur of the region.

Operators and Itineraries The two operators listed below, both Sino-American joint ventures, are the largest operators on the Yangtze River. Both aim for international standards of accommodations, service, and Chinese and Western food. Their riverboats have all outside cabins and river views, restaurants with a single seating for dinner, several lounges and bars, a gift shop, a beauty salon, and a fitness center. Cruises to the Three Gorges are four, five, or six days, and are usually part of a longer China tour.

Regal China Cruises (57 W. 38th St., New York, NY 10018, tel. 212/768–3388 or 800/808–3388, fax 212/768–4939) operates three German-built boats: *Princess Jeannie, Princess Elaine,* and *Princess Sheena.* All three were launched in 1993; each carries 258 passengers.

Victoria Cruises (57–08 39th Ave., Woodside, NY 11377, tel. 212/818–1680 or 800/348–8084, fax 212/818–9889) operates four Chinese-built boats, *Victoria I* through *IV*. The boats were launched between 1994 and 1997; each accommodates 154 passengers.

Several other tour operators, such as **Abercrombie & Kent** (1520 Kensington Rd., Oak Brook, IL 60523, tel. 630/954–2944 or 800/ 323–7308, fax 630/954–3324), **General Tours** (53 Summer St., Keene, NH 03431, tel. 800/221–2216, fax 603/357–4548), Maupintour (1515 St. Andrews Dr., Lawrence, KS 66047, tel. 913/843– 1211 or 800/255–4266, fax 913/843–8351), and **Uniworld** (16000 Ventura Blvd., Suite 200, Encino, CA 91436, tel. 818/382–7820 or 800/ 366–7831, fax 818/382–7829), include these and other high-quality riverboats in their China packages.

On Board Tall Ships

Unfurling their sails for part of each day and night (and motor powered the rest of the time), windjammers differ only in size and amenities from the big motor-sailing cruise ships reviewed in Chapter 1, such as those from Star Clippers, Club Med, or Windstar. What these windjammers lack in terms of swimming pools or in-room televisions, they make up for in romance and intimacy. People come aboard for the genuine experience of sailing before the wind and to join an informal seagoing community where handling the lines is entirely optional.

When to Go Tall-ship cruises operate year-round in the Caribbean, although some vessels are redeployed to the Mediterranean for the late spring, summer, and early fall. Summer in the Caribbean and the Mediterranean is very pleasant, but the south coast of Turkey can be beastly hot in July and August. Between seasons, transatlantic repositioning cruises are available. Maine windjammers operate only in the summer, and even then, expect some rain and somewhat cool water temperatures.

Cruise Experience Most tall ships cruise between nearby ports, then anchor so that passengers can swim, snorkel, scuba dive, sun, or even take the rudder of something smaller, such as a Sunfish (a little sail boat). Itineraries include part of the day under sail, but for those desirous of ocean cruising, a repositioning voyage between the Caribbean and the Mediterranean offers the truest experience under sail.

The Fleet The tall-ship cruises listed here come under the broad term of windjammers, which includes historic ships plus a new breed of sleek, modern sailing yachts. Windjammer cruises appeal to nature lovers, photographers, sailors, and those who just want to get away from it all. Some are family oriented, while others are designed for adults or for singles. Bunk accommodations are simple, and don't expect private facilities—the rates are moderate.

Operators and Itineraries
Historic Ships
The four-masted *Sea Cloud* (Sea Cloud Cruises, Ballindamm 17, D-20095 Hamburg, Germany, tel. 49–40–3690272, fax 49–40– 373047), perhaps the most beautiful bark afloat, is a vision of maritime grace and elegance. Every inch of this classic sailing yacht is finely polished and crafted. It's truly a sight to watch crew members scamper up the 20-story masts to unfurl the ship's 30 billowing sails (which cover 32,000 square ft). When it was built, as the *Hussar V*, for the heiress Marjorie Merriweather Post and financier E. F. Hutton, it was the world's largest privately owned yacht. It has led a colorful life since then: as a naval weather station during World War II, as the yacht of Dominican dictator

Molina Trujillo, and as the carrier of numerous Hollywood stars and even the Duke and Duchess of Windsor. Every attempt has been made to keep the Sea Cloud true to its origins, an artifact of a grander, more glamorous era. Many of the original wood panels, desks, antiques, and other furnishings have been meticulously restored. From its companionways to its salons, the ship evokes the air of a millionaire's mansion. In the United States, the Sea Cloud is bookable through **Abercrombie & Kent** (1520 Kensington Rd., Oak Brook, IL 60523, tel. 630/954–2944 or 800/323–7308, fax 630/954–3324) and **Elegant Cruises & Tours** (31 Central Dr., Port Washington, NY 11050, tel. 516/767–9302 or 800/683–6767, fax 516/767–9303). The *Sea Cloud* also is used by nonprofit groups and cultural institutions, such as the American Museum of Natural History and the Smithsonian Institution.

The **Maine Windjammer Association** (Box 1144P, Blue Hill, ME 04614, tel. 207/374–2955 or 800/807–9463) represents 10 vessels, many with interesting former lives as private yachts, lighthouse tenders, or cargo carriers. In their present incarnations, they sail the coast and islands of Maine, departing from Camden, Rockport, and Rockland.

Out O' Mystic Schooner Cruises (7 Holmes St., Box 487, Mystic, CT 06355, tel. 203/536–4218 or 800/243–0416) has the 100-ft, 44-passenger *Mystic Whaler* and the 125-ft, 56-passenger *Mystic Clipper.*

Tall Ship Adventures (1389 S. Havana St., Aurora, CO 80012, tel. 303/755–7983 or 800/662–0090, fax 303/755–9007) operates the 30-passenger *Sir Francis Drake,* a three-masted schooner with an 80-year history and a good standard of accommodations. The ship sails on seven-day Caribbean itineraries.

Windjammer Barefoot Cruises (Box 190120, Miami Beach, FL 33119, tel. 800/327–2601, fax 305/674–1219) has the largest single fleet and a name that says it all about informality. Based in the Caribbean since 1947, the six vessels, with between 64 and 128 berths, possess intriguing histories equal to those of the Maine windjammers. Although the standard of accommodations varies from ship to ship, most cabins have a private head and shower. Island-hopping cruises last from six to 13 days. For information on the company's supply ship, the *Amazing Grace, see* On Board Freighters, *above.*

Newly Built Tall Ships In addition to the restored vessels described above, a new class of modern-day tall ships has hit the scene in recent years. These vessels offer a uniformly high standard of accommodations, food, and service, and they have smaller passenger capacities.

For a private yacht experience, **Classical Cruises** (132 E. 70th St., New York, NY 10021, tel. 212/794–3200 or 800/252–7745, fax 212/774–1545) operates the three-masted *Panorama* on Red Sea itineraries in winter and Greek Island and Turkish coastal voyages in summer. Built in Greece in 1994, the 175-ft ship carries up to 45 passengers in 23 well-appointed outside cabins with private facilities. Seven-day sailings are combined with pre- or post-cruise hotel stays on land for an in-depth travel experience.

Peter Deilmann (1800 Diagonal Rd., Suite 170, Alexandria, VA 22314, tel. 703/549–1741 or 800/348–8287, fax 703/549–7924) owns the stylish *Lili Marleen,* a three-masted barkentine. In winter, the ship operates on seven- and eight-day Caribbean cruises. In summer, it cruises the Baltic, western Europe, the Canary

Islands, and the Mediterranean. Transatlantic crossings are scheduled in spring and fall. This technically advanced 250-ft ship entered service in 1994 and takes on 50 passengers in considerable comfort; cabins have private facilities. The *Lili Marleen* was built in Germany, and the officers and most of the crew are German.

The 64-passenger *Le Ponant*, a three-master with a French flavor built in 1991, is now mostly under charter to tour operators in Europe and Central America. Cabins are outside and upscale with private facilities. **Tauck Tours** (Box 5027, Westport, CT 06811, tel. 203/226–6911 or 800/468–2825, fax 203/221–6828) has a 13-day cruise-tour program between Nice and Malta. The cruise segment is seven days. For information on Tauck's Central America cruises, *see* Along the Belize and Costa Rica Coasts, *above*.

Through the Chilean Fjords

The waterways and fjords that line the coast of Chile are more remote and much less traveled than the fjords of Norway. Large cruise ships—which frequent the more famous Norwegian fjords—can only duck in and out, while small expedition ships can make the full voyage from Puerto Montt south to the Strait of Magellan.

When to Go Cruises of coastal Chile operate in the Southern Hemisphere's spring, summer, and fall (October through May). The farther south you sail, the colder and windier it's likely to get. Unexpected gusts may come racing down the mountains and glaciers, quickly depressing temperatures—but the scenic rewards are unparalleled.

Cruise Experience Passengers will probably be an international mix, drawn from all over the world to see the stunning scenery of rugged mountains, massive glaciers, uninhabited islands, and deep fjords. The short stretches of open sea can get rough. Shore excursions tend to emphasize the area's natural beauty, and apart from the embarkation ports, towns and villages are minor and secondary.

The Fleet With the exception of a few oceangoing expedition ships, which make seasonal calls in the Chilean fjords, local vessels are relatively small but adequately comfortable.

Operators and Itineraries Two Chilean-based companies specialize in these cruises.

The 100-passenger *Terra Australis* (formerly an American coastal ship known as the *Savannah*) makes weekly cruises into the Beagle Channel and along the coast of Tierra del Fuego. The ship has all outside cabins, two lounges, and good food in a noisy dining room. Departures are scheduled about seven months of the year, from September to April. The ship can be booked in the United States through **OdessAmerica** (Cruceros Australis, c/o OdessAmerica, 170 Old Country Rd., Suite 608, Mineola, NY 11501, tel. 516/747–8880 or 800/221–3254, fax 516/747–8367) or **Adventure Associates** (Metropolitan Touring, 13150 Coit Rd., Suite 110, Dallas, TX 75240, tel. 972/907–0414 or 800/527–2500, fax 972/783–1286).

OdessAmerica also represents the 74- to 160-passenger *Skorpios I*, *II*, and *III* fleet, which sail to the spectacular San Rafael Lagoon and Glacier on their Chilean fjord cruises, scheduled September to May.

The *Terra Australis* and *Skorpios* ships may also be booked through **Meg Tours** (tel. 800/579–9731).

Abercrombie & Kent's *Explorer,* **Society Expedition**'s *World Discoverer,* **Radisson Seven Seas**' *Bremen* and *Hanseatic* (*see* Chapter 1), and other major expedition ships heading to Antarctica often make several voyages that thread through Chilean coastal waters as well.

3 Ports of Call

Going Ashore

Traveling by cruise ship presents an opportunity to visit many different places in a short time. The flip side is that your stay will be limited in each port of call. For that reason, cruise lines invented shore excursions, which maximize passengers' time by organizing their touring for them. There are a number of advantages to shore excursions: In some destinations, transportation may be unreliable, and a ship-packaged tour is the best way to see distant sights. Also, you don't have to worry about being stranded or missing the ship. The disadvantage is that you will pay more for the convenience of having the ship do the legwork for you. Of course, you can always book a tour independently, hire a taxi, or use foot power to explore on your own.

Disembarking

When your ship arrives in a port, it either ties up alongside a dock or anchors out in a harbor. If the ship is docked, passengers just walk down the gangway to go ashore. Docking makes it easy to go back and forth between the shore and the ship.

Tendering If your ship anchors in the harbor, however, you will have to take a small boat—called a launch or tender—to get ashore. Tendering is a nuisance. When your ship first arrives in port, everyone wants to go ashore. Often, in order to avoid a stampede at the tenders, you must gather in a public room, get a boarding pass, and wait until your number is called. This continues until everybody has disembarked. Even then, it may take 15–20 minutes to get ashore if your ship is anchored far offshore. Because tenders can be difficult to board, passengers with mobility problems may not be able to visit certain ports. The larger the ship, the more likely it will use tenders. It is usually possible to learn before booking a cruise whether the ship will dock or anchor at its ports of call. (For more information about where and whether ships dock, tender, or both, *see* Coming Ashore for each port, *below*.)

Before anyone is allowed to walk down the gangway or board a tender, the ship must first be cleared for landing. Immigration and customs officials board the vessel to examine passports and sort through red tape. It may be more than an hour before you're actually allowed ashore. You will be issued a boarding pass, which you must have with you to get back on board.

Returning to the Ship

Cruise lines are strict about sailing times, which are posted at the gangway and elsewhere as well as announced in the daily schedule of activities. Be certain to be back on board at least a half hour before the announced sailing time or you may be stranded. If you are on a shore excursion that was sold by the cruise line, however, the captain will wait for your group before casting off. That is one reason many passengers prefer ship-packaged tours.

If you are not on one of the ship's tours and the ship does sail without you, immediately contact the cruise line's port representative, whose name and phone number are often listed on the daily schedule of activities. You may be able to hitch a ride on a pilot boat, though that is unlikely. Passengers who miss the boat must pay their own way to the next port of call.

Alaska

Alaska, it would seem, was made for cruising. The traditional route to the state is by sea, through a 1,000-mi-long protected waterway known as the Inside Passage. From Vancouver in the south to Skagway in the north, the Inside Passage winds around islands large and small, past glacier-carved fjords, and along hemlock-blanketed mountains. This great land is home to breaching whales, nesting eagles, spawning salmon, and calving glaciers. Most towns here can be reached only by air or sea; there are no roads. Juneau, in fact, is the only water-locked state capital in the United States. Beyond the Inside Passage, the Gulf of Alaska leads to Prince William Sound—famous for its marine life and more fjords and glaciers—and Anchorage, Alaska's largest city.

Natural beauty is just one reason why so many cruise passengers now set sail for Alaska. The peak season falls during summer school vacation, so kids are now a common sight aboard ship. Cruise lines have responded with programs designed specifically for children, and some discount shore excursions for kids under 12.

For adults, too, the cruise lines now offer more than ever before. Alaska is one of cruising's hottest destinations, so the lines are putting their newest, biggest ships up here. These gleaming vessels have the best facilities at sea. Fully equipped, top-deck health spas give panoramic views of the passing scenery. Some ships feature onboard broadcasts of CNN and ESPN or sports bars showing live televised events. New itineraries give passengers more choices than ever before, too—from Bering Strait cruises, which include a crossing to the Russian Far East, to 10-, 11-, and 14-day loop cruises of the Inside Passage, round-trip from Vancouver. Shorter cruises focus on Glacier Bay or equally scenic Prince William Sound.

You will still find all the time-honored diversions of a vacation at sea aboard Alaska-bound ships. Daily programs schedule bingo and bridge tournaments, deck games, and various contests, demonstrations, and lectures. You'll also find trendier pursuits: Some lines have stress-management seminars and talks on financial planning.

Food remains a major reason to visit Alaska aboard a cruise ship. On the big ocean liners, you can eat practically all day and night. Along with prime rib now comes a selection of healthful choices for nutrition-conscious eaters. Some ships offer a "spa menu," which ties your dining-room meals together with your exercise program in the health club.

Nearly every day, your ship will make a port call. With the exception of Anchorage, Alaskan port cities are small and easily explored by foot. For those who prefer to be shown the sights, ship-organized shore excursions are available. These range from typical city bus tours to Alaska's most exciting excursion adventure: helicopter flightseeing with a landing on a glacier. Other choices include charter fishing, river rafting, and visits to Native American communities. To satisfy the interest of their ever-younger and more active passengers, Alaska's cruise lines constantly refine their shore-excursion programs, adding new educational and adventure-oriented choices. The programs change annually, as the lines search for just the right mix of leisure and learning (*see* Shore Excursions, *below*).

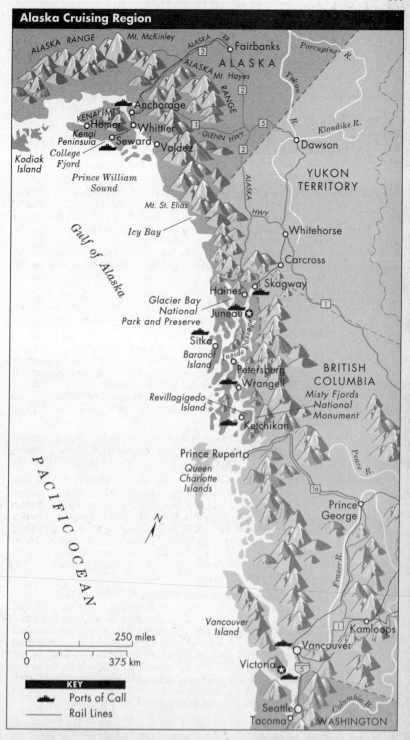

Alaska Cruising Region

ALASKA RANGE   Mt. McKinley
ALASKA 3   RR   Fairbanks
ALASKA   ALASKA
RANGE   Mt. Hayes
2
Anchorage   1
KENAI MTS   Whittier   GLENN HWY
Homer   5
Kenai   Seward   Valdez   2
Peninsula   College
Fjord
Kodiak   Prince William
Island   Sound
Mt. St. Elias
Icy Bay
Gulf of Alaska
Porcupine R.
Yukon R.
Klondike R.
Dawson
YUKON
TERRITORY
ALASKA   HWY.
Whitehorse
Carcross
Haines   Skagway
Glacier Bay   1
National   Juneau ★
Park and Preserve
Inside Passage
Sitka
Baranof
Island   Petersburg
Wrangell
Revillagigedo   BRITISH
Island   COLUMBIA
Ketchikan   Misty Fjords
National
Monument
PACIFIC OCEAN
Prince Rupert
Queen
Charlotte   Peace R.
Islands
16
Prince
George
Fraser R.
N
Vancouver   Kamloops
Island
250 miles   Vancouver
375 km   Victoria ★   5
KEY   Seattle   Columbia R.
Ports of Call   Tacoma   WASHINGTON
Rail Lines

Itineraries About a dozen major cruise lines deploy ships in Alaska. Sailings come chiefly in two varieties: round-trip Inside Passage loops or one-way Inside Passage–Gulf of Alaska cruises. Both itineraries are typically seven days. However, if you want to combine a land tour with your Inside Passage loop, you can only spend three or four days aboard ship. On the other hand, Inside Passage–Gulf of Alaska cruises allow you to spend a full week aboard ship and still take a pre- or post-cruise land tour. A few lines schedule longer one-way or round-trip sailings from Vancouver or San Francisco.

Whether you sail through the Inside Passage or along it will depend upon the size of your vessel. Smaller ships can navigate narrow channels, straits, and fjords. Larger vessels must sail farther from land, so don't expect to see much wildlife from the deck of a megaship.

Cruise Tours Most cruise lines give you the option of an independent, hosted, or fully escorted land tour before or after your cruise. Independent tours allow maximum flexibility. You have a preplanned itinerary with confirmed hotel reservations and transportation arrangements, but you're free to follow your interests and whims in each town. A hosted tour is similar, but tour company representatives are available along the route to help out should you need assistance.

On fully escorted tours, you travel with a group, led by a tour director. Activities are preplanned (and typically prepaid) so you have a good idea of how much your trip will cost (not counting incidentals) before you depart.

Modes of tour transportation range from plane to bus, rail to ferry. Most cruise tour itineraries include a ride aboard the Alaska Railroad in a private, glass-domed railcar. Running between Anchorage, Denali National Park, and Fairbanks, Holland America Westours' *McKinley Explorer* and Princess Tours' *Midnight Sun Express Ultra Dome* offer unobstructed views of the passing land and wildlife.

In addition to full-length cruise-tours, cruise lines usually sell pre- or post-cruise packages lasting one to three days. Hotel accommodations and some sightseeing in port cities are generally included.

When to Go The Alaska cruise season runs from spring through fall, but mid-summer departures are the most popular. Cruise lines schedule first sailings in mid-May and final sailings in late September. May and June are the driest summer months, but you should still come prepared for rain, especially in Southeast Alaska. At least two cruise lines price sailings by six "seasons," with spring and fall departures the least expensive and midsummer sailings the most costly. Virtually every line offers early-booking discounts to passengers for advance deposits.

There are plenty of advantages besides discounted fares to cruising in the low seasons. Availability of ships and particular cabins is greater in the low and shoulder seasons and the ports are almost completely empty of tourists. In spring, wildflowers are abundant. You're apt to see more wildlife along the shore, because the animals have not yet gone up to higher elevations. Alaska's early fall brings the splendor of autumn hues and the first snow falls in the mountains. The animals have returned to low ground, and shorter days bring the possibility of seeing the northern lights. Mosquitoes are also not as thick in the fall, a decided plus.

Temperatures along the Southeast Alaska cruise routes are in the 50s and 60s in May, June, and September. In July and August averages are generally in the 60s and low 70s. Southcentral Alaska has warmer temperatures, with many midsummer days in the mid-70s. For passengers opting to take a cruise-tour (a combination of cruising and land touring that is popular in Alaska), the Interior section of the state—where you'll find Mt. McKinley—often reaches into the 80s, with occasional days topping 90 degrees.

Shore Excursions Shore excursions in Alaska give cruise passengers a chance to get closer to the state's natural beauty. For this reason, active or adventure-oriented tours are usually the best choices. Not all shore excursions are offered by every ship. However, you can book any excursion directly; try calling one of the ground operators listed below (*see* Independent Touring, *below*).

Aerial Tours Anyone unwilling to hike or boat in the backcountry should take at least one small-plane or helicopter tour to see the state in its full glory. The aircraft fly over glaciers and waterways, with floatplanes landing on wilderness lakes. Some helicopter tours actually land on a glacier and let passengers out to do some brief exploring.

Fishing The prospect of bringing a trophy salmon or halibut to net is one reason many people choose an Alaskan cruise. Every ship offers optional fishing excursions on charter boats.

Hiking Trekking through woods and mountains and along the beaches is a popular pastime in Southeast Alaska. Some trails are abandoned mining roads; others are natural routes or game trails that meander over ridges, through forests, and alongside streams and glaciers. Many ships offer hiking excursions, but every port is within easy access of at least some hiking. Trails go through real wilderness, so check with local public information centers for current conditions, and leave your intended itinerary with someone on the ship. Look under the hiking section for each port to find trails and paths convenient to cruise passengers.

Salmon Bake Alaska is famous for outdoor salmon barbecues, called salmon bakes. Fresh fish is grilled on an open fire and served with plenty of fixings. Quality varies, so ask locals for advice on which bake to attend. Juneau has one of the best: the Gold Creek Salmon Bake, which is sold as a shore excursion by virtually every cruise line.

Whale-Watching Whales are plentiful in these waters, and several small-boat excursions offer excellent opportunities to see them up close. Humpback whales are often seen in the waters near Glacier Bay National Park, but you may also see the smaller minke whales and killer whales (orcas). Beluga whales are frequently observed in Cook Inlet near Anchorage—but few ships sail that far north.

Independent Touring As noted below, not all shore excursions recommended in this chapter are offered by all cruise lines. Some passengers may also choose to make arrangements on their own to avoid the cruise-line markup. To book shore excursions directly, contact these companies:

In Anchorage For flightseeing or fly-in fishing trips contact **Rust's Flying Service** (tel. 907/243–1595 or 800/544–2299), **Regal Air** (tel. 907/243–8535), or **Ketchum Air Service** (tel. 907/243–5525 or 800/433–9114). For a glacier and wildlife viewing tour in Prince William Sound, contact **Phillips Cruises and Tours** (tel. 907/276–8023 or 800/544–0529), **Renown Charters and Tours** (tel. 907/272–1961 or 800/655–3806), or **Major Marine Tours** (tel. 907/274–7300 or 800/764–7300). For a trip north to Talkeetna or south to Seward, contact the **Alaska Railroad** (tel. 907/265–2494 or 800/544–0552). For historic walking tours of downtown, contact **Anchorage Historic Properties** (tel. 907/ 274–3600); **Anchorage City Trolley Tours** (tel. 907/257–5603) offers the motorized version.

In Haines Try **Mountain Flying Service** (tel. 907/766–3007) or **Haines Airways** (tel. 907/766–2646) for flightseeing tours. For local bike tours contact **Sockeye Cycle** (tel. 907/766–2869), and for float trips down the Chilkat River contact **Chilkat Guides** (tel. 907/ 766-2491).

In Homer Contact **Homer Air** (tel. 907/235–8591 or 800/235–8591), **Southcentral Air** (tel. 907/235–6172 or 800/478–6172), or **Bald Mountain Air Service** (tel. 907/235–7969 or 800/478–7969) for flightseeing tours. For local sightseeing contact **Homer Tours** (tel. 907/235–6200). For wildlife watching contact **Rainbow Tours** (tel. 907/235–7272) or **Alaska Maritime Tours** (tel. 907/235-2490 or 800/478–2490). The **Homer Chamber of Commerce** (tel. 907/235–7740) has a complete list of fishing charter boats.

In Juneau For flightseeing contact two longtime favorites: **Ward Air** (tel. 907/ 789–9150) or **Alaska Coastal Airlines** (tel. 907/789–7818). Other air taxi operators include **Wings of Alaska** (tel. 907/789–0790) and **L.A.B. Flying Service** (tel. 907/789–9160 or 800/426–0543). Both **Era Helicopters** (tel. 907/586–2030 or 800/843–1947) and **Temsco Helicopters** (tel. 907/789–9501) offer tours that include a glacier landing. For local sightseeing contact **Alaska Native Tours** (907/463–3231). For Mendenhall River float trips call **Alaska Discovery** (tel. 907/780–6226 or 800/586–1911).

In Ketchikan For flightseeing contact **Taquan Air** (tel. 907/225–9668 or 800/770–8800), **Island Wings Air Service** (tel. 907/225–2444 or 888/854–2444), or **ProMech Air** (tel. 907/225–3845). For on-the-water adventures contact **Southeast Exposure** (tel. 907/225–8829), **Outdoor Alaska** (tel. 907/225–6044), or **Southeast Sea Kayaks** (tel. 907/225–1258). Native cultural tours are offered by **Saxman Native Village** (tel. 907/225–5163) and the **Ketchikan Indian Corporation** (tel. 907/ 225–5158 or 800/252–5158).

In Petersburg Contact **Pacific Wing** (tel. 907/772–9258), **Nash West** Aviation (tel. 907/772–3344), or **Kupreanof Flying Service** (tel. 907/772–3396) for flightseeing. For a kayak trip up Petersburg creek, contact **Tongass Kayak Adventures** (tel. 907/772–4600). The **Petersburg Visitors Center** (tel. 907/772–4636) has a complete list of local fishing boats and operators for other activities.

In Seward For flightseeing contact **Scenic Mountain Air** (tel. 907/224–7277). **Kayak and Custom Adventures Worldwide** (tel. 907/276–8282 or 800/ 288–3134) offers kayak rentals and sea-kayak day trips. For fishing charters contact **Fish House** (tel. 907/224–3674 or 800/257–7760).

In Sitka For flightseeing contact **Mountain Aviation** (tel. 907/966–2288). For sightseeing and historical walking tours, contact **Tribal Tours** (907/747–7290 or 888/270–8687). For soft adventure, sea kayaking trips contact **Baidarka Boats** (tel. 907/747–8996).

In Skagway Contact **Skagway Air** (tel. 907/983–2218), **Wings of Alaska** (tel. 907/ 983–2442), **L.A.B. Flying Service** (tel. 907/789–9160 or 800/426–0543), or **Temsco Helicopters** (tel. 907/789–9501) for flightseeing. For local sightseeing contact **Skagway Street Car Company** (tel. 907/983–2908).

In Valdez For flightseeing contact **BMH Aviation** (tel. 907/255–8359) or **Era Helicopters** (tel. 907/835–2595 or 800/843–1947). For local sightseeing contact **Valdez Tours** (tel. 907/835–2686) or **Sentimental Journeys** (tel. 907/835–4988). For soft-adventure tours contact **Anadyr**

Seakayaking Adventures (tel. 907/835–2814), **Northern Magic Charters** (tel. 800/835–4433), or **Stan Stephens Charters** (tel. 907/835–4731 or 800/992–1297).

Saloons Socializing at a bar or saloon is an old Alaska custom, and the towns and cities of the Southeast Panhandle are no exception. Listed under the individual ports of call are some of the favorite gathering places in these parts.

Sea Kayaking More adventurous travelers will enjoy paddling sea kayaks in the protected waters of Southeast and Southcentral Alaska. Ketchikan, Homer, Juneau, Seward, Sitka, and Valdez all have companies that rent sea kayaks, with lessons and short kayak tours available. Gear is usually provided.

Shopping Alaskan Native American handicrafts range from Tlingit totem poles—a few inches high to several feet tall—to Athabascan beaded slippers and fur garments. Many other traditional pieces of art are found in gift shops up and down the coast: Inupiat spirit masks and intricately carved ivory, Yupik dolls and dance fans, Tlingit button blankets and silver jewelry, and Aleut grass baskets and carved wooden items. To ensure authenticity, buy items tagged with the state-approved AUTHENTIC NATIVE HANDCRAFT FROM ALASKA "Silverhand" label. Better prices are found in the more remote villages where you buy directly from the artisan, in museum shops, or in craft fairs such as Anchorage's downtown Saturday Market.

Salmon, halibut, crab and other seafood are very popular with both locals and visitors. Most towns have a local company that packs and ships seafood.

Dining Not surprisingly, seafood dominates most menus. In summer, salmon, halibut, crab, cod, and prawns are usually fresh. Restaurants are uniformly informal; jeans and windbreakers are the norm.

Category	Cost*
$$$	over $40
$$	$20–$40
$	under $20

per person for a three-course meal, excluding drinks, service, and sales tax

Anchorage

A local newspaper columnist once dubbed Anchorage "a city too obviously on the make to ever be accepted in polite society." And for all its cosmopolitan trappings, this city of 240,000 people does maintain something of an opportunistic, pioneer spirit. Its inhabitants hustle for their living in the retail, transportation, communications, medical, oil, and education fields.

Superficially, Anchorage looks like any other sprawling western American city, with WalMarts and shopping malls, but sled-dog races are as popular here as surfing is in California, and moose occasionally roam along city bike trails. This is basically a modern, relatively unattractive city, but the Chugach Mountains form a striking backdrop, and spectacular Alaskan wilderness is found just outside the back door. Few people come to Alaska to see

Anchorage, but almost everybody passes through sometime during their trip, and the city does have almost anything you may want, from Starbucks espresso to Native handicrafts.

Anchorage took shape with the construction of the federally built Alaska Railroad (completed in 1923), and traces of the city's railroad heritage remain. With the tracks laid, the town's pioneer forefathers actively sought expansion by hook and—not infrequently—by crook. City fathers, many of whom are still alive, delight in telling how they tricked a visiting U.S. congressman into dedicating the site for a federal hospital that had not yet been approved.

Boom and bust periods followed major events: an influx of military bases during World War II; a massive buildup of Arctic missile-warning stations during the Cold War; and more recently, the discovery of oil at Prudhoe Bay and the construction of the trans-Alaska pipeline.

Anchorage today is the only true metropolis in Alaska. There's a performing-arts center, a diversity of museums, and a variety of ethnic eateries for cruise passengers to sample.

Shore Excursions Other than a typical city bus tour, few shore excursions are scheduled in Anchorage. Most cruise passengers are only passing through the city as they transfer between the airport and the ship or a land tour and their cruise. For passengers who arrive early or stay later, independently or on a pre- or post-cruise package, there is much to see and do (*see* Exploring Anchorage, *below*).

The following is a good choice in Anchorage. It may not be offered by all cruise lines. All times and prices are approximate.

Anchorage Highlights. This motor-coach tour visits the Museum of History and Art, then moves on to see the bears, moose, wolves, bald eagles, and other Alaskan wildlife at the city zoo. Before returning to the ship, the tour climbs the Chugach Mountains for panoramic views of Anchorage and then passes by the downtown historic area. *4 hrs. Cost: $29.*

Coming Ashore Cruise ships visiting Anchorage most often dock at the port city of Seward, 125 mi to the south on the Kenai Peninsula; from here passengers must travel by bus or train to Anchorage. Ships that do sail directly to the city dock just beyond downtown. A tourist information booth is right on the pier. The major attractions are a 15- or 20-minute walk away; turn right when you disembark and head south on Ocean Dock Road. The main tourist district of downtown Anchorage is very easy to navigate on foot. If you want to see some of the outlying attractions, like Lake Hood (*see* Exploring, *below*), you'll need to hire a taxi. Taxis are expensive: Rates start at $2 for pickup and $1.50 for each mile (1½ km). Most people in Anchorage telephone for a cab, although it is not uncommon to hail one. Contact **Alaska Cab** (tel. 907/563–5353), **Anchorage Taxicab** (tel. 907/278–8000), **Checker Cab** (tel. 907/276–1234), or **Yellow Cab** (tel. 907/272–2422).

If you have the time and want to explore further afield, such as Girdwood and points south on the Kenai Peninsula, Anchorage is a great place to rent a car.

Exploring Anchorage *Numbers in the margin correspond to points of interest on the Downtown Anchorage map.*

❶ A marker in front of the **Log Cabin Visitor Information Center** shows the mileage to various world cities. Fourth Avenue sus-

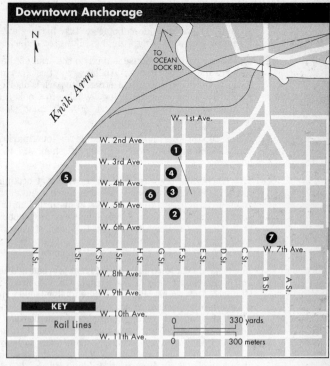

Downtown Anchorage

tained heavy damage in the 1964 earthquake. The businesses on this block withstood the destruction, but those a block east fell into the ground as the earth under them slid toward Ship Creek. Most of these buildings have since been rebuilt. *Corner of 4th Ave. and F St., tel. 907/274–3531. Open summer, daily 7:30–7; spring and fall, daily 8–6.*

2 Anchorage's real centerpiece is the distinctively modern **Performing Arts Center** at 5th Avenue and G Street. A diversity of musical, theatrical, and dance groups perform here throughout the year. Out front is flower-packed **Town Square**, a delightful place to relax on a sunny day.

3 The Art Deco **Fourth Avenue Theater** (4th Ave., between F and G Sts.) has been restored and put to new use as a gift shop, cafe, and gallery. Note the lighted stars in the ceiling that form the Big Dipper against a field of blue—it's the Alaska state flag.

4 Displays about Alaska's national parks, forests, and wildlife refuges can be seen at the **Alaska Public Lands Information Center**. The center also shows films highlighting different regions of the state and sells natural history books. *4th Ave. and F St., tel. 907/271–2737. Open daily 9–5:30 in summer.*

Resolution Park, a cantilevered viewing platform dominated by a monument to Captain Cook, looks out toward Cook Inlet and the mountains beyond. Mt. Susitna (known as the Sleeping Lady) is the prominent low mountain to the northwest. To her north, Mt. McKinley is often visible 125 mi away. (Most Alaskans prefer the traditional name for this peak, Denali.)

The paved **Tony Knowles Coastal Trail** runs along Cook Inlet for about 10 mi (16 km), and is accessible from the west end of 2nd Avenue. This is a wonderful place to take in the view, or to join the throngs of folks walking, running, biking, or rollerblading.

❺ The **Oscar Anderson House** is next to the trail at the north end of Elderberry Park. It was Anchorage's first permanent frame house, built in 1915. Tours are free. The park is also a good place to watch for porpoise-sized beluga whales in Cook Inlet. *Near 5th Ave. between L and N Sts., tel. 907/274–2336. Open Tues.–Sat. noon–4.*

❻ A fun stop for kids and adults alike is the **Imaginarium,** an interactive science museum with a great gift shop. *725 W. 5th Ave., tel. 907/276–3179. Admission: $5. Open Mon.–Sat. 10–6, Sun. noon–5.*

❼ The **Anchorage Museum of History and Art** occupies the whole block at 6th Avenue and A Street, with an entrance on 7th Avenue. It houses a fine collection of historical and contemporary Alaskan art, displays on Alaskan history, and a special section for children. One gallery is devoted to views of Alaska, as seen by early explorers, painters, and contemporary artists. *121 W. 7th Ave., tel. 907/343–4326. Admission: $5. Open daily 9–6.*

The new **Alaska Native Heritage Center** is scheduled to open in 1999 on the northeast side of Anchorage. On a 26-acre site facing the Chugach Mountains, this $15-million dollar facility includes a spacious Welcome House, where you are introduced to the Native peoples of Alaska through displays, artifacts, photographs, demonstrations, performances, and films. You can also circle a small lake and explore five recreated village sites to learn more about Alaska's diverse Native cultures. There's a cafe and Native arts gift shop as well. *Glenn Hwy. and Muldoon Rd., tel. 907/263–5170.*

If you have the time, take a taxi to the **Lake Hood floatplane base,** where colorful aircraft come and go almost constantly in the summer months. The best vantage point is from the patio of the lounge at the Regal Alaskan Hotel. *4800 Spenard Rd., tel. 907/243–2300.*

Shopping The **Alaska Native Arts and Crafts Association** sells items from all Alaskan Native American groups and carries the work of the best-known carvers, silversmiths, and bead workers, as well as the work of unknown artists. *333 W. 4th Ave., tel. 907/274–2932. Open weekdays 10–7, Sat. 10–6, Sun. noon–5.*

The best buys on Native Alaskan artists' work are found at the gift shop inside the **Alaska Native Medical Center.** *Tudor Centre Dr. off East Tudor Rd., tel. 907/729–1122. Open weekdays 10–2, 1st Sat. of month 10–2.*

Artwork created by Alaskan artists, both Native and non-Native, can be found at **Artique Ltd.** (314 G St., tel. 907/277–1663). The work of better-known Alaskan artists can be seen at the **Decker/Morris Gallery** (corner of 7th Ave. and G St. in the Performing Arts Center, tel. 907/272–1489). For "wearable art" and one-of-a-kind designs in polar fleece apparel, stop in at designer **Tracy Anna Bader's** boutique, (416 G St., tel. 907/272–6668). Another option for warm wear is the **Oomingmak Musk Ox Producers Co-op** (corner of 6th Ave. and H St., tel. 907/272–9225). Native Alaskan villagers hand knit scarves and hats from the soft-as-cashmere underwool of the musk ox into traditional designs. Another place for distinctive garments and parkas is **Laura Wright Alaskan Parkys** (343 W. 5th Ave., tel. 907/274–4215). The parkas are available off-the-rack or by custom order. Not far from here is

Cook Inlet Book Company (415 W. 5th Ave., tel. 907/258–4544), with a huge selection of Alaskan titles.

Wolf aficionados will enjoy a stop at **Wolf Song** (corner of 6th Ave. and C St., tel. 907/274–9653), a nonprofit gift shop with wildlife art and educational material. The **Alaska General Store** (715 W. 4th Ave., tel. 907/272–1672) gift shop is a browsers' delight, with an old fashioned ambience and a diverse collection of items, both old and new.

Anchorage's best places to buy fresh, frozen, or smoked seafood are not far from the center of town: **10th and M Seafoods** (1020 M St., tel. 907/272–6013), and **New Sagaya's City Market** (900 W. 13th Ave., tel. 907/274–6173). Both places will also ship seafood for you.

Entertainment Take a goofy, off-kilter romp across Alaska at the "Whale Fat Follies" Tuesday through Saturday evenings in the **Fly By Night Club** (3300 Spenard Rd., tel. 907/279–7726). Mr. Whitekeys is the master of ceremonies for this musical extravaganza of bad taste and Spam jokes.

Jogging/ Walking The Coastal Trail (*see* Exploring Anchorage, *above*) and other trails in Anchorage are used by cyclists, runners, and walkers. The trail from Westchester Lagoon at the end of 15th Avenue runs 2 mi (3 km) to Earthquake Park and, beyond that, 8 mi (13 km) out to Kincaid Park. For bike rentals, contact **Adventure Cafe** (K St. between 4th and 5th Aves., tel. 907/276–8282 or 800/288–3134) or **Downtown Bicycle Rental** (corner of 5th Ave. and C St., tel. 907/279–5293).

Dining **Club Paris.** It's dark and smoky up front in the bar, where for
$$–$$$ decades old-time Anchorage folks have met to drink and chat. Halibut and fried prawns are available, but the star attractions are the big, tender, flavorful steaks. If you have to wait for a table, have a drink at the bar and order the hors d'oeuvres tray—a sampler of steak, cheese, and prawns that could be a meal for two people. *417 W. 5th Ave., tel. 907/277–6332. AE, D, DC, MC, V.*

$$–$$$ **Marx Bros. Cafe.** Fusion cuisine served by chef Jack Amon shows that frontier cooking is much more than a kettle in the kitchen. Among the multicultural specialties of the house is baked halibut with a macadamia crust served with coconut curry and mango chutney. Reservations are essential—you might even want to call before you reach Anchorage. *627 W. 3rd Ave., tel. 907/278–2133. AE, MC, V, DC. No lunch.*

$$–$$$ **Sacks Cafe.** The downtown business crowd favors this bright little café. Delightfully creative soups, sandwiches, and salads fill the lunch menu, and for dinner, the kitchen produces such entrées as lamb braised in a spicy red curry sauce, and baked penne pasta with sun-dried tomatoes, spinach, roasted peppers, and three cheeses. Be sure to check out the daily specials, which are usually extraordinary. The salads are large enough for a light meal, but be sure to leave room for dessert, especially the decadent chocolate gâteau. *625 W. 5th Ave., tel. 907/276–3546. AE, MC, V.*

$$–$$$ **Simon & Seaforts Saloon and Grill.** This is the place to enjoy a great view across Cook Inlet while dining on consistently fine Alaskan seafood or rock salt-roasted prime rib. The bar is a good spot for appetizers, including beer-batter halibut and potatoes Gorgonzola, but you can also order from the full menu. *Corner of 4th Ave. and L St., tel. 907/274–3502. AE, MC, V.*

$–$$ **Thai Cuisine Too.** The menu here is a welcome change from Alaska's ubiquitous seafood and steak houses; you'll find all the

Thai standards on the menu, including fresh rolls, Pad-Thai, and a wonderful Tom Khar Gai soup. The food is dependably good, and the atmosphere is quiet. Thai Cuisine Too is right in the center of town and is especially popular for lunch. *328 G St., tel. 907/277–8424. AE, MC, V.*

Brew Pubs Brew pubs, along with a multitude of espresso stands, have arrived in Anchorage. For visitors limited to touring the city by foot, the downtown area has several breweries/restaurants within easy walking distance from downtown hotels:

Alaska Glacier Brew House Restaurant. Tasty food, such as wood-fired pizza, fresh seafood, and rotisserie-grilled meats, complement the home-brewed beer in a stylish setting with high ceilings and a central fireplace. *737 W. 5th Ave., tel. 907/274–2739. AE, MC, V.*

Humpy's Great Alaskan Alehouse. This immensely popular restaurant and bar has more than 40 draught beers on tap, and cranks out huge plates halibut tacos, health-nut chicken, and smoked-salmon Caesar salad. Humpy's has live music most evenings, so don't expect quiet (or a smoke-free atmosphere) in this hopping nightspot. *610 W. 6th Ave., tel. 907/276–2337. MC, V, DC, D, AE.*

Railway Brewing Company. The historic Alaska Railroad depot provides a trackside setting for train buffs and beer enthusiasts alike. Sandwiches, burgers, pizzas, and pastas are the mainstays of the menu. A small deck is opened in the summer months for those who want to enjoy the midnight sun. Brewery tours are available. *421 W. 1st Ave., tel. 907/277–1996. AE, D, MC, V.*

Snowgoose Restaurant and Sleeping Lady Brewing Company. The latest addition to the Anchorage brew-pub scene stands out for its large deck with a view of Cook Inlet, Mt. Susitna (the Sleeping Lady), and—on a clear day—Mt. McKinley. The menu includes burgers and pasta, along with seafood specials each evening. Unfortunately, smoke from the upstairs pub (where cigars are allowed) sometimes drifts down to patrons below. *717 W. 3rd Ave., tel. 907/277–7727. MC, V, AE.*

Glacier Bay National Park and Preserve

Cruising Glacier Bay is like revisiting the Little Ice Age, when glaciers covered much of the Northern Hemisphere. This is one of the few places in the world where you can get within a ¼ mi (½ km) of tidewater glaciers, which have their base at the water's edge. Twelve of them line the 60 mi (96 km) of narrow fjords at the northern end of the Inside Passage. Huge chunks of ice break off the glaciers and crash into the water, producing a dazzling show known as calving.

Although the Tlingit Indians have lived in the area for 10,000 years, the bay was first popularized by naturalist John Muir, who visited in 1879. Just 100 years before, the bay was completely choked with ice. By 1916, though, the ice had retreated 65 mi (105 km)—the most rapid glacial retreat ever recorded. To preserve its clues to the world's geological history, Glacier Bay was declared a national monument in 1925. It became a national park in 1980. Today, several of the glaciers in the west arm are advancing again, but very slowly.

Competition is fierce among cruise ships for entry permits into Glacier Bay. To protect the humpback whale, which feeds here in

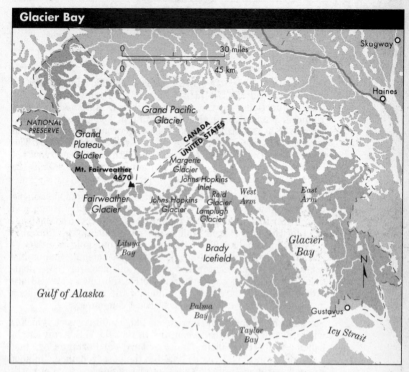

Glacier Bay

summer, the Park Service limits the number of ships that can call. Check your cruise brochure to make sure that Glacier Bay is included in your sailing. Most ships that do visit spend at least one full day exploring the park. There are no shore excursions or landings in the bay, but a Park Service naturalist boards every cruise ship to provide narration on its history and scientific importance. It is often misty or rainy, so rain gear is essential. The average summer temperature is 50° F. As always in Alaska, be prepared for the cold. Also, be sure to bring binoculars, extra film, and a telephoto lens.

The glaciers that most cruise passengers see are in the west arm of Glacier Bay. Ships linger in front of five glaciers so passengers may view their stunning appearance. Most ships stop briefly at **Reid Glacier** before continuing on to **Lamplugh Glacier**—one of the bluest in the park—at the mouth of Johns Hopkins Inlet. Next is **Johns Hopkins Glacier** at the end of the inlet, where cruise passengers are likely to see a continuous shower of calving ice. Sometimes there are so many icebergs in the inlet that ships must avoid the area. Moving farther north, to the end of the western arm, **Margerie Glacier** is also quite active. Adjacent is **Grand Pacific Glacier,** the largest glacier in the park.

Your experience in Glacier Bay will depend partly on the size of your ship. Ocean liners tend to stay midchannel, while small yachtlike ships spend more time closer to shore. Passengers on smaller ships may get a better view of the calving ice and wildlife—such as brown and black bears, mountain goats, moose, and seals with their pups—but big-ship passengers, on vessels with much higher decks, get a loftier perspective. Both types of vessels come within ¼ mi (½ km) of the glaciers themselves.

Haines

Unlike most other cities in Southeast Alaska, Haines can be reached by road; the 152-mi (245-km) Haines Highway connects at Haines Junction with the Alaska Highway. Missionary S. Hall Young and famed naturalist John Muir picked the site for this town in 1879 as a place to bring Christianity and education to the natives. They could hardly have picked a more beautiful spot. The town sits on a heavily wooded peninsula with magnificent views of Portage Cove and the Coastal Mountain Range. It lies 80 mi (129 km) north of Juneau via fjordlike Lynn Canal.

The town has two distinct personalities. On the north side of the Haines Highway is the portion of Haines founded by Young and Muir. After its missionary beginnings the town served as the trailhead for the Jack Dalton Trail to the Yukon during the 1897 gold rush to the Klondike. The following year, when gold was discovered in nearby Porcupine (now deserted), the booming community served as a supply center and jumping-off place for those goldfields as well. Today things are quieter; the town's streets are orderly, its homes are well kept, and for the most part it looks a great deal like any other Alaska seacoast community.

South of the highway, the town looks like a military post, which is what it was for nearly half a century. In 1903 the U.S. Army established a post—Ft. William Henry Seward—at Portage Cove just south of town. For 17 years (1922–39) the post (renamed Chilkoot Barracks to avoid confusion with the city of Seward, farther north in the southcentral part of the state) was the only military base in the territory. That changed with World War II, when the army built both the Alaska Highway and the Haines Highway to link Alaska with the other states.

After the war, the post closed down, and a group of veterans purchased the property from the government. They changed its name to Port Chilkoot and created residences, businesses, and a Native American arts center from the officers' houses and military buildings that surrounded the old fort's parade ground. Eventually Port Chilkoot merged with the city of Haines. Although the two areas are now officially one municipality, the old military post with its grassy parade ground is referred to as Ft. Seward.

The Haines–Ft. Seward community today is recognized for the Native American dance and culture center at Ft. Seward, as well as for the superb fishing, camping, and outdoor recreation at Chilkoot Lake, Portage Cove, Mosquito Lake, and Chilkat State Park on the shores of Chilkat Inlet. The last locale, one of the small treasures of the Alaska state park system, features views of the Davidson and Rainbow glaciers across the water.

Shore Excursions The following are good choices in Haines. They may not be offered by all cruise lines. All times and prices are approximate.

Adventure **Glacier Bay Flightseeing.** If your cruise doesn't include a visit to Glacier Bay, here's a chance to see several of its tidewater glaciers during a low-altitude flight. *1-hr flight plus transfers. Cost: $125.*

Mountain Biking. Ride through historic Ft. William Henry Seward and view the impressive architecture of this turn-of-the-century

U.S. army facility. After the fort, the guide will lead riders through the natural beauty of the Chilkat River estuary. Bikes and equipment are included. *2 hrs. Cost: $45.*

City Sights | **Haines Cultural and Natural Wonders Tour.** This excursion tours Ft. Seward, the Sheldon Museum and Cultural Center, and the Alaska Indian Arts Center and includes time to browse through the downtown galleries. *2½–3 hrs. Cost: $40.*

Native Cultural | **Chilkat Dancers.** A drive through Ft. William Henry Seward includes a dance performance by the Chilkat Dancers, noted for their vivid tribal masks, and a stop at the American Bald Eagle Interpretive Center. Some lines combine this tour with a salmon bake (*see below*). *3 hrs, including 1-hr performance. Cost: $41.*

Salmon Bake | **Chilkat Dancers and Salmon Bake.** The narrated tour of Haines and Ft. Seward and a Chilkat Dancers performance are combined with a dinner of salmon grilled over an open fire. *2½–3 hrs. Cost: $55.*

Wildlife Up Close | **Chilkat River by Jet Boat.** A cruise through the Chilkat Bald Eagle Preserve reveals some eagles and—if you're lucky—perhaps a moose or a bear. It is a smooth, rather scenic trip, but in summer, you'll see little wildlife. Come October, though, imagine the trees filled with thousands of bald eagles. *3½ hrs. Cost: $80.*

Coming Ashore | Cruise ships dock in front of Ft. Seward, and downtown Haines is just a short walk away (about ¾ mi). You can pick up walking-tour maps of both Haines and Ft. Seward at the visitor center on 2nd Avenue (tel. 907/766–2234 or 800/458–3579). Most cruise lines provide a complimentary shuttle service to downtown. Taxis are always standing by; hour-long taxi tours of the town cost $10 per person. A one-way trip between the pier and town costs $5. If you need to call for a pickup, contact **The Other Guys Taxi** (tel. 907/766–3257) or **Haines Taxi** (tel. 907/766–3138).

Exploring Haines | *Numbers in the margin correspond to points of interest on the Haines map.*

❶ The **Sheldon Museum and Cultural Center,** near the foot of Main Street, houses Native American artifacts—including famed Chilkat blankets—plus gold-rush memorabilia such as Jack Dalton's sawed-off shotgun. *25 Main St., tel. 907/766–2366. Admission: $3. Open daily 1–5 and whenever cruise ships are in port.*

❷ The building that houses **Chilkat Center for the Arts** was once Ft. Seward's recreation hall, but now it's the space for Chilkat Indian dancing. Some performances may be at the tribal house next door; check posted notices for performance times. *Ft. Seward, tel. 907/766–2160. Admission: $10. Performances scheduled when cruise ships are in port.*

❸ At **Alaska Indian Arts,** a nonprofit organization dedicated to the revival of Tlingit Indian art forms, you'll see Native carvers making totems, metalsmiths working in silver, and weavers making blankets. *Between Chilkat Center for the Arts and Haines parade ground, tel. 907/766–2160. Admission free. Open weekdays 9–noon and 1–5, and whenever cruise ships are in port.*

Celebrating Haines's location in the "Valley of the Eagles" is the ❹ **American Bald Eagle Foundation Natural History Museum.** The name is a bit grandiose for this collection of stuffed eagles and other dead animals. A video documents the annual "Gathering of the Eagles," when thousands of (live) bald eagles converge on the Alaska Chilkat Bald Eagle Preserve just north of town (*see Shore Excursions, above*). *2nd Ave. and Haines Hwy., tel. 907/766–3094.*

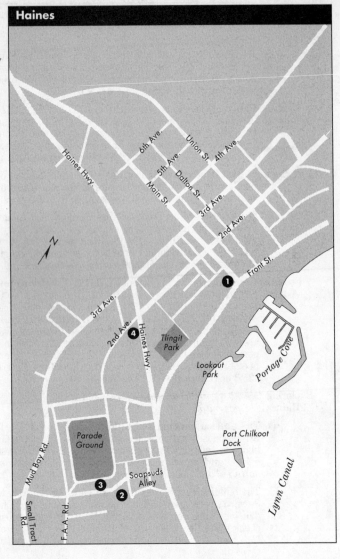

Admission free; donations accepted. Open when cruise ships are in port.

Sports
Hiking One of the most rewarding hikes in the area is to the north summit of **Mt. Ripinsky,** the prominent peak that rises 3,610 ft behind the town. Be warned: It's a strenuous trek and requires a full day, so most cruise passengers will want to only try a partial summit. (Make sure you leave plenty of time to get back to your ship.) The trailhead lies at the top of Young Street, along a pipeline right-of-way. For other hikes, pick up a copy of "Haines Is for Hikers" at the visitor center.

Dining
$–$$
Lighthouse Restaurant. You get a great view of Lynn Canal from this restaurant at the foot of Main Street next to the boat harbor. Steaks, seafood, and barbecued ribs are the standards here. Save room for a slice of their famous buttermilk pie. *Front St. on the harbor, tel. 907/766–2442. AE, MC, V.*

$
Mountain Market & Deli. This spot is a bit out of the way, but it's a great place to have a mocha or latte and get in synch with Haines's outdoorsy-artist crowd. The fare includes fresh baked goods, soups, and sandwiches. *3rd Ave. at Haines Hwy., tel. 907/766–3340. MC, V.*

$–$$
Commander's Room. Stop here for fresh seafood, fish and chips, burgers, and more. Facing Ft. Seward's parade ground, this restaurant in Hotel Halsingland is a good place to soak up atmosphere. *At Ft. Seward, tel. 907/766–2000 or 800/542–6363. AE, DC, MC, V.*

$–$$
Chilkat Restaurant and Bakery. Family-style cooking is served in a homelike, no-smoking setting with lace curtains. Seafood, steaks, and sandwiches are cooked to order; Friday is all-you-can-eat night. The bakery has tasty pastries to go. *5th Ave. near Main St., tel. 907/766–2920. AE, MC, V. Closed Sun., winter hrs vary.*

Saloons
Harbor Bar (Front St. at the Harbor, tel. 907/766–2444). Commercial fishermen gather nightly at this circa 1907 bar next to the Lighthouse Restaurant. Sometimes there's live music. It's colorful but can get a little loud at night.

Homer

Of the hundreds of thousands of cruise passengers who visit Alaska each year, only a very few get to see Homer. It's a shame. In a state of beautiful places, Homer has emerged as its premier artists colony. Those travelers who do arrive by ship are usually beginning or ending an expedition cruise to the Arctic or traveling aboard an Alaska Marine Highway ferry (*see* Chapter 2). Fortunately, Homer is easily reached from Seward, where all Gulf of Alaska cruises start or finish. If you rent a car, Homer is just 173 mi (278 km) down the Sterling Highway—practically next door by Alaskan standards. Direct bus connections are also available from both Anchorage and Seward; contact **Homer Stage** (tel. 907/272–8644).

The city of Homer lies at the base of a long sandy spit that juts into Kachemak Bay. It was founded just before the turn of the century as a gold-prospecting camp and later became a coal-mining headquarters. Today the town is a funky fishing port with picturesque buildings, good seafood, and beautiful bay views. It's a favorite weekend spot of Anchorage residents who need a change of scene and weather. Halibut fishing is especially good in this area.

Shore
Excursions
The following are good choices in Homer. They may not be offered by all cruise lines. All times and prices are approximate.

Above the Spit. See the sights from a flightseeing plane, including nearby Seldovia. Longer flights visit area glaciers; other tours may focus on wildlife spotting. *1 hr. Cost: $145.*

Sights of the Spit. See the unique Homer Spit from the ground, as well as other area sights and attractions. *3 hrs. Cost: $45.*

Wildlife-Watching. Board a local boat for Halibut Cove, Seldovia, or the nearby seabird colonies. *1½ hrs. Cost: $35–$47.*

Coming Ashore   Cruise ships dock at the Homer Spit. Fishing charters, restaurants, and shops line the spit, or passengers can take a taxi to town, where local galleries and additional dining are found. Look for **Day Breeze Shuttle and Tours** (tel. 907/399–1168), which charges $2 per person to the main drag. For door-to-door service, call **Chuck's Cab** (tel. 907/235–2489). A ride from the spit into town will set you back $14 one-way for the first person and $1 for each additional passenger. Taxi tours of Homer are available for around $35 an hour.

Exploring Homer   For an introduction to Homer's history, visit the **Pratt Museum** with three saltwater aquariums and exhibits on pioneers, Native Americans, and the 1989 Prince William Sound oil spill. Outside is a wildflower garden and a ⅛-mi (½-km) nature trail. The museum also leads 1½-hour walking tours of the harbor for $10 per person. *Bartlett St., just off Pioneer Ave., tel. 907/235–8635. Admission: $4. Open daily 10–6.*

Kachemak Bay abounds in wildlife. Shore excursions or local tour operators take visitors to bird rookeries in the bay or across the bay to gravel beaches for clam digging. Many Homer visitors come to fish for salmon or halibut. Most fishing charters will include an opportunity to view whales, seals, sea otters, porpoises, and seabirds close-up. A walk along the docks on Homer Spit at the end of the day is a pleasant chance to watch commercial fishing boats and charter boats unload their catch. The bay supports a large population of puffins and eagles.

Directly across Kachemak Bay from the end of the Homer spit, **Halibut Cove** is a small community of people who make their living on the bay or by selling handicrafts. The Central Charter (tel. 907/235–7847 or 800/478–7847) booking agency runs frequent boats to the cove from Homer. Halibut Cove has an art gallery and a restaurant that serves local seafood. The cove itself is lovely, especially during salmon runs, when fish leap and splash in the clear water. There are also several lodges on this side of the bay, on pristine coves away from summer crowds.

Seldovia, isolated across the bay from Homer, retains the charm of an earlier Alaska. The town's Russian bloodline shows through in its onion-dome church and its name, derived from a Russian place-name meaning "herring bay." Those who fish use plenty of herring for bait, catching salmon, halibut, and king or Dungeness crab. You'll find excellent fishing whether you drop your line into the deep waters of Kachemak Bay or cast into the surf for silver salmon on the shore of Outside Beach, near town. Self-guided hiking or berry picking in late July are other options. Seldovia can be reached from Homer by boat, and the dock of the small boat harbor is in the center of town—allowing for easy exploration. For a guided historical tour, contact South Shore Tours (tel. 907/234–8000).

Shopping   The galleries on and around Pioneer Avenue, including **Ptarmigan Arts** (471 E. Pioneer Ave., tel. 907/235–5345), a local cooperative, are good places to find works by the town's residents. For contemporary art pieces, head to **Bunnell Street Galley** (106 W. Bunnell St., tel. 907/235–2662)—it's next to Two Sisters (*see below*).

Dining   **Homestead Restaurant.** Eight miles (13 kilometers) from town, this
$$$ log roadhouse overlooking Kachemak Bay is where locals take guests for a night out. The fare here includes Caesar salads, steak, prime rib, and fresh seafood; the flavors are rich and spicy, with splashes of mango, macadamia nuts, and garlic. *Mile 8.2 East End Rd., tel. 907/235–8723. AE, MC, V. Closed Jan.–Feb.*

$$$ **The Saltry in Halibut Cove.** Exotically prepared local seafood
dishes, including curries and pastas, and a wide selection of
imported beers are served here. The deck overlooks the boat dock
and the cove. It's a good place to while away the afternoon or
evening, meandering along the boardwalk and visiting galleries.
Dinner seatings are at 6 and 7:30. *Take the* Danny J *ferry ($17.50
round-trip) from Homer harbor; tel. 907/235–7847. Reservations
essential. MC, V. Open summer only.*

$ **Café Cups.** With microbrewery beer on tap and local artists' works
on the walls, this renovated house offers more than just great
food, fresh-baked breads, and desserts. Locals and visitors alike
crowd into the cozy dining room for coffee and conversation in the
morning or later in the day for fresh pasta, local seafood, and an
eclectic but reasonably priced wine selection. Desserts include a
triple decadent cheesecake and black-bottom almond cream pie.
The outside deck is a fine place to enjoy a lazy morning while
savoring your eggs Florentine. *162 W. Pioneer Ave., tel. 907/235–
8330. MC, V.*

$ **Two Sisters.** For a delightful taste of the real Homer, visit this tiny
coffeehouse-bakery housed in a historic building. The funky,
mixed crowd here includes fishermen, writers, and local business-
people drinking perfectly brewed espresso, talking politics, and
sampling pastries that are to die for. Two Sisters gets crowded on
weekend mornings—you'll see folks overflowing out to the porch.
106 W. Bunnell St., tel. 907/235–2280. No credit cards. No dinner.

Saloon   **Salty Dawg Saloon** (tel. 907/235–9990) is famous all over Alaska.
Fishermen, cannery workers, and carpenters have been holding
court here for decades in this friendly and noisy pub. Today
they're joined by college kids working in the gift shops, retirees,
and tourists. Near the end of the spit, the Salty Dawg is easy to
find; just look for the "lighthouse."

Tastes of   **Alaska Wild Berry Products** (528 Pioneer Ave., tel. 907/235–8858 or
Alaska   800/280–2927) manufactures jams, jellies, sauces, syrups, choco-
late-covered candies, and juices made from wild berries hand-
picked on the Kenai Peninsula; shipping is available. Alaska Wild
Berry also has a big confectionery kitchen and gift shop in Anchor-
age at 5225 Juneau Street.

Juneau

Juneau owes its origins to a trio of colorful characters: two pio-
neers, Joe Juneau and Dick Harris, and a Tlingit chief named
Kowee, who discovered rich reserves of gold in the stream that
now runs through the middle of town. That was in 1880, and
shortly after the discovery a modest stampede led first to the for-
mation of a camp, then a town, then the Alaska district (now state)
capital.

For nearly 60 years after Juneau's founding, gold remained the
mainstay of the economy. In its heyday, the Alaska Juneau gold
mine was the biggest low-grade-ore mine in the world. Then, dur-
ing World War II, the government decided it needed Juneau's
manpower for the war effort, and the mines ceased operations.
After the war, mining failed to start up again, and the government
became the city's principal employer.

Juneau is a charming, cosmopolitan frontier town. It's easy to nav-
igate, has one of the best museums in Alaska, is surrounded by
beautiful (and accessible) wilderness, and has a glacier in its back-

yard. To capture the true frontier ambience, stop by the Red Dog Saloon or the Alaskan Hotel. Both are on the main shopping drag, just a quick walk from the cruise ship pier.

Shore Excursions The following are good choices in Juneau. They may not be offered by all cruise lines. All times and prices are approximate.

Adventure **Mendenhall Glacier Helicopter Ride.** One of the best helicopter glacier tours, including a landing on an ice field for a walk on the glacier. Boots and rain gear provided. *2¼ hrs, including 30-min flight. Cost: $165.*

Mendenhall River Float Trip. A rafting trip down the Mendenhall River passes through some stretches of gentle rapids. Experienced oarsmen row the rafts; rubber boots, ponchos, and life jackets are provided. The minimum age is six. An excellent first rafting experience for those in good health, it's great fun. *3½ hrs. Cost: $80–$100.*

Salmon Bakes **Gold Creek Salmon Bake.** This all-you-can-eat outdoor meal includes Alaskan king salmon barbecued over an open alder-wood fire. After dinner, walk in the woods, explore the abandoned mine area, or pan for gold. *1½–2 hrs. Cost: $25–$30.*

Taku Glacier Lodge Flightseeing and Salmon Bake. Fly over the Juneau Ice Field to Taku Glacier Lodge. Dine on barbecued salmon, then explore the virgin rain forest or enjoy the lodge. It's expensive, but this trip consistently gets rave reviews. *3 hrs. Cost: $180–$200.*

Coming Ashore Most cruise ships dock or tender passengers ashore at **Marine Park** or at the old **Ferry Terminal.** Princess ships (and some others) tie up at the **South Franklin Dock.** Ask aboard your ship exactly which facility you'll be using. Both Marine Park and the Ferry Terminal are within easy walking distance of the downtown shops and attractions. The South Franklin Dock is about a fifth of a mile, or an eight-minute walk, from the edge of downtown and the new Mt. Roberts tram. For those who prefer not to walk, a shuttle bus ($1 round-trip) runs from the dock to town whenever ships are in town.

For visitor information, there's a small kiosk on the pier at Marine Park filled with tour brochures, bus schedules, and maps (staffed according to cruise ship arrivals). There is a tourist information center at the old ferry terminal as well. The downtown shops along South Franklin Street are just minutes away.

You won't need to hire a taxi in Juneau unless you are heading to the glacier. In that case, taxis will be waiting for you at Marine Park. Another option is the city bus that stops on South Franklin Street. For $1.25, it'll take you within 1¼ mi (3½ km) of the Mendenhall Visitor Center. The **Glacier Express** (tel. 907/789–0052 or 800/478–0052) provides direct bus service between downtown and the glacier for $10 round-trip.

Exploring Juneau *Numbers in the margin correspond to points of interest on the Juneau map.*

❶ A block east of the cruise ship docks at Marine Park is **South Franklin Street.** The buildings here and on Front Street, which intersects South Franklin several blocks north, are among the oldest and most interesting in the city. Many reflect the architecture of the 1920s and '30s; some are even older.

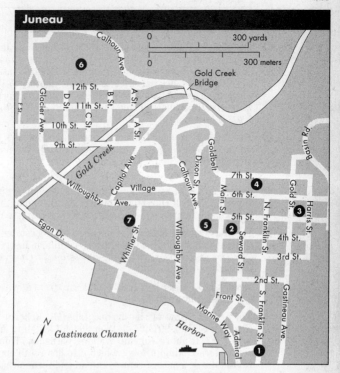

At No. 278 South Franklin Street is the **Red Dog Saloon.** With a sawdust-covered floor, a stuffed bear, and big-game heads mounted on the walls, this is Alaska's most famous saloon.

Just down the street from the Red Dog Saloon is the small **Alaskan Hotel** (167 S. Franklin St.), which was called "a pocket edition of the best hotels on the Pacific Coast" when it opened in 1913. Owners Mike and Betty Adams have restored the building with period trappings. The barroom's massive, mirrored oak bar, accented by Tiffany lamps and panels, is a particular delight.

Also on South Franklin Street is the **Alaska Steam Laundry Building,** a 1901 structure with a windowed turret. It now houses a great collection of photos from Juneau's past, a popular espresso shop (Heritage Coffee Co., tel. 907/586–1752), and several stores.

Across the street from the Steam Laundry Building, the equally venerable **Senate Building Mall** (175 S. Franklin St.) contains one of the two Juneau Christmas stores, a fine jewelry shop, a place to buy Russian icons, and even a shop with goods from Ireland.

② At the corner of Seward Street is the **Alaska State Capitol,** constructed in 1930, with pillars of southeastern-Alaska marble. The structure now houses the governor's office and other state agencies, and the state legislature meets here January through May each year. *Tel. 907/465–2479. Tours weekdays 8:30–4:30 in summer. Call for hours of weekend tours.*

③ At the top of the hill on 5th Street is little **St. Nicholas Russian Orthodox Church,** built in 1894. Here you can see icons that date from the 1700s. *326 5th St., off N. Franklin St., tel. 907/586–1023. Donation requested. Open daily 9–6 in summer.*

❹ The **House of Wickersham,** the 1899 residence of James Wickersham, a pioneer judge and delegate to Congress, houses memorabilia from the judge's travels, ranging from rare Native American basketry and ivory carvings to historic photos, 47 diaries, and a Chickering grand piano that came "round the horn" to Alaska when the Russians still ruled the region. *213 7th St., tel. 907/586–9001. Admission: $2.50. Tours Mon.–Sat. noon–5.*

❺ Two fine totem poles flank the entrance to Juneau's **City Museum.** Inside, the city's history is relayed through memorabilia, gold-mining exhibits, and videos. *4th and Main Sts., tel. 907/586–3572. Admission: $2. Open weekdays 9–5, weekends 10–5.*

❻ **Evergreen Cemetery** is where many Juneau pioneers (including Joe Juneau and Dick Harris) are buried. At the end of the gravel lane is the monument to Chief Kowee, who was cremated on this spot.

❼ The **Alaska State Museum** is one of Alaska's best, with exhibits on the state's history, Native cultures, wildlife, industry, and art. *395 Whittier St., tel. 907/465–2901. Admission: $3. Open weekdays 9–6, weekends 10–6.*

Mendenhall Glacier is only 13 mi (21 km) from downtown, and you can walk right up to it.

For a great view of the harbor, take **Mt. Roberts Tram** (490 S. Franklin St., tel. 907/463–3412 or 800/461–8726) to an observation deck 2,000 ft above Juneau. Walking paths lead from the visitors center (*see* Hiking, *below*), which also has retail shops, a restaurant and bar, a nature center, and an auditorium that shows films on native culture and bears. You can catch the tram from the base terminal downtown—it's within walking distance of the cruise ship piers. For $17.75, you get unlimited rides for the day

Shopping South Franklin Street is the place in Juneau to shop. The variety of merchandise is good, though some shops offer an abundance of Made-in-China Alaskan keepsakes. You'll pay high prices for authentic native handicrafts or handknitted sweaters. One of the better galleries is **Mt. Juneau Artists** (211 Front St., tel. 907/586–2108), an arts and crafts cooperative.

In the Senate Building Mall on South Franklin Street is the **Russian Shop** (tel. 907/586–2778), a repository of icons, samovars, lacquered boxes, nesting dolls, and other items that reflect Alaska's 18th- and 19th-century Russian heritage.

For a souvenir from one of Alaska's most famous saloons, stop by the gift shop at the **Red Dog Saloon** (*see* Exploring Juneau, *above*).

Knowledgeable locals frequent the **Rie Munoz Gallery** (2101 N. Jordon Ave., tel. 907/789–7411) for fine art. Munoz is one of Alaska's favorite artists, and her stylized, colorful design technique is much copied. Other artists' works are also on sale, including woodblock prints by nationally known artist Dale DeArmond. Another fun place to browse is the **Wm. Spear Designs Gallery** (165 S. Franklin St., tel. 907/586–2209). His colorful enameled pins are witty, creative, amusing, and sometimes simply perverse.

Sports More than 30 charter boat operators offer fishing trips in the
Fishing Juneau area; stop by the **Davis Log Cabin** (3rd and Seward Sts., tel. 907/586–2201) for a complete listing.

Hiking   Surrounded by the **Tongass National Forest,** Juneau is a hiker's paradise. For trail maps, information, and advice, stop by Centennial Hall on Willoughby at Egan Drive (tel. 907/586–8751).

The Davis Log Cabin (3rd and Seward Sts., tel. 907/586–2201) sells two useful booklets, "90 Short Walks Around Juneau" ($5) and "Juneau Trails" ($4). Good trails for cruise passengers begin just behind the **Mendenhall Glacier Visitor Center** (*see* Exploring Juneau, *above*).

For guided walks, the **Juneau Parks and Recreation Department** (tel. 907/586–5226) sponsors Wednesday- and Saturday-morning group hikes. On Saturday, there's free car-pool pickup at the docks.

Gastineau Guiding (tel. 907/586–2666) leads guided hikes from the nature center at the top of Mt. Roberts Tram. A one-hour hike costs $30 including the tram ride; a four-hour hike costs $50.

Kayaking   **Alaska Discovery** (tel. 907/780–6226 or 800/586–1911) offers escorted day tours for $95 per person. Lunch and rain gear are included. Trips leave around 9:30 AM and return about 5 PM, so participation is practical only for passengers whose ships make day-long calls.

Dining   **Fiddlehead Restaurant and Bakery.** Definitely a favorite with
$–$$$ Juneau locals, this delightful place decorated with light wood, stained glass, and historic photos, serves generous portions of healthy fare. How about a light dinner of black beans and rice? Or pasta Greta Garbo (locally smoked salmon tossed with fettuccine in cream sauce). Their bakery always has delicious breads, croissants, and sweets. Upstairs, the Fireweed Room features a more diverse menu, along with folk and jazz music most nights. *429 W. Willoughby Ave., tel. 907/586–3150. AE, D, DC, MC, V.*

$ **Armadillo Tex-Mex Cafe.** A devoted clientele of locals wait in line to order border eats at this bustling, boisterous café. Check the daily specials, or if you aren't too hungry, order a big bowl of homemade chili and cornbread. *431 S. Franklin St., tel. 907/586–1880. MC, V.*

Saloons   Juneau is one of the best saloon towns in all of Alaska. Try stopping in one of the following:

Alaskan Hotel Bar (167 S. Franklin St., tel. 907/586–1000). This spot is popular with locals and distinctly less touristy. If live music isn't playing, an old-fashioned player piano usually is.

Bubble Room (127 N. Franklin St., tel. 907/586–2660). This comfortable lounge off the lobby in the Baranof Hotel is quiet—and the site (so it is said) of more legislative lobbying and decision making than in the nearby state capitol building. The music from the piano bar is soft.

Red Dog Saloon (278 S. Franklin St., tel. 907/463–3777). This pub carries on the sawdust-on-the-floor tradition, with a mounted bear and other game animal trophies on the walls and lots of historic photos. There's live music, and the crowd is raucous, particularly when cruise ships are in port.

Tastes of   When you're "shopping" the bars and watering holes of Southeast
Alaska   Alaska, ask for Alaskan Amber, Frontier Beer, or Pale Ale. All are brewed and bottled in Juneau. If you'd like to see how this award-winning brew is crafted, visit the **Alaskan Brewing Company.** *5429 Shaune Dr., Juneau, tel. 907/780–5866. Open Tues.–Sat. 11–4:30.*

Kenai Peninsula

Salmon fishing, scenery, and wildlife are the standouts of the Kenai Peninsula, which thrusts into the Gulf of Alaska south of Anchorage. Commercial fishing is important to the area's economy, and the city of Kenai, on the peninsula's northwest coast, is the base for the Cook Inlet offshore oil fields.

The area is dotted with roadside campgrounds, and you can explore three major federal holdings on the peninsula—the western end of the sprawling **Chugach National Forest,** along with **Kenai National Wildlife Refuge,** and **Kenai Fjords National Park.**

Portage Glacier, 50 mi (80 km) southeast of Anchorage, is one of Alaska's most frequently visited tourist destinations. A 6-mi (10-km) side road off the Seward Highway leads to the Begich-Boggs Visitor Center (tel. 907/783–2326) on the shore of Portage Lake. The center houses impressive displays that will tell you all you need to know about glaciers. Boat tours of the face of the glacier are conducted aboard the 200-passenger *Ptarmigan.* Unfortunately, the glacier is receding rapidly, and is no longer pushing so many icebergs into the lake, so the views are not what they once were.

The mountains surrounding Portage Glacier are covered with smaller glaciers. A short hike to Byron Glacier Overlook, about a mile (1½ km) west, is popular in the spring and summer. Twice weekly in summer, naturalists lead free treks in search of microscopic ice worms. Keep an eye out for black bears in all the Portage side valleys in the summer.

Ketchikan

At the base of 3,000-ft Deer Mountain, Ketchikan is the definitive Southeast Alaska town. Houses cling to the steep hillsides and the harbors are filled with fishing boats. Until miners and fishermen settled here in the 1880s, the mouth of Ketchikan Creek was a summer fishing camp for Tlingit Indians. Today the town runs on fishing, tourism, and logging.

Ketchikan is Alaska's totem-pole port: At the nearby Tlingit village of Saxman, 2½ mi (5 km) south of downtown, there is a major totem park, and residents still practice traditional carving techniques. The Ketchikan Visitors Bureau on the dock can supply information on getting to Saxman on your own, or you can take a ship-organized tour. Another excellent outdoor totem display is at Totem Bight State Historical Park, a coastal rain forest 10 mi (16 km) north of town. The Totem Heritage Center preserves historic poles, some nearly 200 years old.

Expect rain at some time during the day, even if the sun is shining when you dock: Average annual precipitation is more than 150 inches.

Shore Excursions The following are good choices in Ketchikan. They may not be offered by all cruise lines. All times and prices are approximate.

Adventure **Misty Fjords Flightseeing.** Aerial views of granite cliffs rising 4,000 ft from the sea, waterfalls, rain forests, and wildlife lead to a landing on a high wilderness lake. *2 hrs, including 65-min flight. Cost: $155–$180.*

Sportfishing. You're almost sure to get a bite in the "Salmon Capital of the World." Charter boats hold up to 16 passengers; fish can be butchered and shipped home for an additional charge. *4–5 hrs, including 3–4 hrs of fishing. Cost: $160.*

Native Culture
Saxman Village. See 27 totem poles and totem carvers at work at this Native community. The gift shop is among the best for Alaska Native crafts. *2½ hrs. Cost: $45.*

Totem Bight Tour. This look at Ketchikan's native culture focuses on Tlingit totem poles in Totem Bight State Historical Park. Guides interpret the myths and symbols in the traditional carvings. *2½ hrs. Cost: $30.*

Coming Ashore
Ships dock or tender passengers ashore directly across from the Ketchikan Visitors Bureau on Front and Mission streets, in the center of downtown. Here you can pick up brochures and maps.

The impressive **Southeast Alaska Visitor Center** has exhibits on native culture, wildlife, logging, recreation, and the use of public lands. You can also watch their award-winning film, "Mystical Southeast Alaska." *50 Main St., tel. 907/228–6214. Admission: $4.*

Ketchikan is easy to explore, with walking-tour signs to lead you around the city. Most of the town's sights are within easy walking distance. A new paved bike-and-foot path leads to the city of Saxman, for those who wish to walk to the Native village—but remember it's 2½ mi (5 km) from downtown Ketchikan.

To reach the sights outside downtown on your own, you'll want to hire a cab or ride the local buses. Metered taxis meet the ships right on the docks and also wait across the street. Rates are $2.10 for pickup, 23¢ each ⅒ mi.

Exploring Ketchikan
Numbers in the margin correspond to points of interest on the Ketchikan map.

❶ You can learn about Ketchikan's early days of fishing, mining, and logging at the **Tongass Historical Museum and Totem Pole.** *In the library building at Dock and Bawden Sts., tel. 907/225–5600. Admission: $2. Open daily 8–5 in summer.*

❷ For a great view of the harbor, take curving Venetia Avenue to the **Westmark Cape Fox Lodge.** Not only are the views stunning at the lodge, but the dining is excellent. You can also take a tramway ride ($1) down the mountainside to popular Creek Street (*see below*).

❸ Every visitor to Ketchikan should stop by the **Totem Heritage Center,** which has a fascinating display of weathered, original totem carvings. *Woodland Ave. at corner of Deermont St., tel. 907/225–5900. Admission: $4. Open daily 8–5 during cruise season.*

❹ **Creek Street,** formerly Ketchikan's infamous red-light district, remains the picturesque centerpiece of town. Its small houses, built on stilts over the creek, have been restored as trendy shops. The street's most famous brothel, **Dolly's House** (tel. 907/225–5900, admission: $3.50), has been preserved as a museum, complete with original furnishings and a short history of the life and times of Ketchikan's best-known madam. There's good salmon viewing in season at the Creek Street footbridge. You can catch the tram here for a ride up to the Westmark Cape Fox Lodge, if you missed it before (*see above*).

Shopping
Because artists are local, prices for Native American crafts are better in Ketchikan than at most other ports. The **Saxman Village** gift shop has some Tlingit merchandise, along with less expensive mass-produced souvenirs. A better bet is to head a block downhill

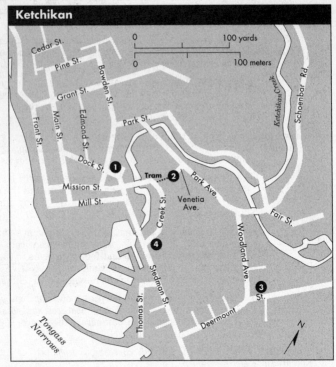

to **Saxman Arts Co-op** (tel. 907/225–4166) where the crafts are all locally made.

Creek Street has several attractive boutiques. At **Parnassus Bookstore** (5 Creek St., tel. 907/225–7690), you can browse through an eclectic collection of books. The same building houses two fine arts and crafts shops: **Alaska Eagle Arts** (tel. 907/225–8365) and **Soho Coho** (tel. 907/225–5954). The latter is headquarters for artist Ray Troll, Alaska's famed producer of all things weird and fishy.

Salmon, Etc. (322 Mission St., tel. 907/225–6008) sells every variety of Alaskan salmon, which can be sent, frozen and processed, to your home.

Sports Salmon are so plentiful in these waters that the town has earned
Fishing the nickname "Salmon Capital of the World." Contact **Chinook Charters** (tel. 907/225–9225), **Ketchikan Charter Boats** (tel. 907/ 225–7291), **Chip Port Charters** (tel. 907/225–2447), or **Knudson Cove Marina** (tel. 907/247–8500). The **Ketchikan Convention & Visitors Bureau** (tel. 907/225–6166 or 800/770–2200) has a full list of other charter companies; they will send you a vacation planner as well.

Hiking Check at the visitors bureau on the dock for trail maps and advice. If you're a tough hiker with sturdy shoes, the trail from downtown (starting at the end of Fair Street) to the top of **Deer Mountain** will repay your effort with a spectacular panorama of the city below and the wilderness behind. It's 6 mi (10 km) round-trip. The **Ward Lake Area,** about 6 mi (10 km) north of town, offers easier hiking along lakes and streams and beneath towering spruce and hemlock trees.

The Southeast Alaska Visitor Center (*see* Coming Ashore, *above*) has trail maps detailing these and other U.S. Forest Service trails.

Kayaking and Canoeing Both **Southeast Exposure** (507 Stedman St., tel. 907/225–8829) and **Southeast Sea Kayaks** (tel. 907/225–1258) offer sea kayak rentals, instruction, and tours. Three-hour tours (all gear included) cost around $70.

Dining **Annabelle's Keg and Chowder House.** In the Gilmore Hotel, this
$$–$$$ seafood restaurant takes you back to the 1920s. The walls are covered with photos and paintings depicting the Ketchikan of years past. Specials include steamers, oysters on the half shell, delicious clam chowder, steaks, and pasta. Afterwards, be sure to order a slice of peanut butter pie. *326 Front St., tel. 907/225–6009. AE, D, DC, MC, V.*

$ **Five Star Cafe.** One of Creek Street's old bordellos is now a trendy café serving espresso coffees and an earthy selection of breakfast and lunch choices—sandwiches, soups, salads, pastries—that are always well-prepared. This is where you'll meet young Ketchikan business folk and post-hippie funksters. *5 Creek St., tel. 907/247–7827. No credit cards.*

Saloons **Annabelle's Keg and Chowder House** (326 Front St., tel. 907/225–6009). This restaurant-lounge with a jukebox in the Gilmore Hotel blends old and new Alaska in a semiformal atmosphere. There's no pretense of formality at the **Potlatch Bar** (tel. 907/225–4855) in Thomas Basin, where local fishermen and cannery workers play pool and tip back cans of Rainier Beer.

Misty Fjords National Monument

In the past, cruise ships used to bypass Misty Fjords on their way up and down the Inside Passage. But today more and more cruise passengers are discovering its unspoiled beauty. Ships big and small, from the yachtlike vessels of Alaska Sightseeing to the liners of Crystal, Cunard, Norwegian Cruise Line, and others, now feature a day of scenic cruising through this protected wilderness. At the southern end of the Inside Passage, Misty Fjords usually lies just before or after a call at Ketchikan. The attraction here is the wilderness—3,500 square mi of it—highlighted by waterfalls and cliffs that rise 3,000 ft.

Petersburg

Getting to Petersburg is an experience. Only ferries and the smallest cruise ships can squeak through Wrangell Narrows with the aid of more than 50 buoys and markers along the 22-mi (35-km) crossing. At times the channel seems too narrow for ships to pass through, making for a nail-biting—though safe—trip. The inaccessibility of Petersburg is part of its off-the-beaten-path charm. Unlike at several other Southeast communities, you'll never be overwhelmed by the hordes of cruise passengers here.

At first sight of Petersburg you may think you're in the old country. Neat, white, Scandinavian-style homes and storefronts with steep roofs and bright-colored swirls of leaf and flower designs (called rosemaling) and row upon row of sturdy fishing vessels in the harbor invoke the spirit of Norway. No wonder. This prosperous fishing community was founded by Norwegian Peter Buschmann in 1897.

The Little Norway Festival is held here each year on the third full weekend in May. If you're in town during the festival, be sure to partake in one of the fish feeds that highlight the Norwegian Independence Day celebration. The beer-batter halibut is delectable, and you won't find better folk dancing outside of Norway.

Shore Excursions The following are good choices in Petersburg. They may not be offered by all cruise lines. All times and prices are approximate.

Adventure **LeConte Flightseeing.** One of the best flightseeing tours in Alaska takes you to the southernmost calving glacier in North America. *45-min flight. Cost: $123.*

Petersburg by Bus. Here's a chance to get outside of town and see the scenery. The tour also includes Norwegian refreshments and a performance of Norwegian dance at the Sons of Norway Hall. *2 hrs. Cost: $26.*

Walking Tour. A guide will relate the history and fishing heritage of Petersburg as you explore the old part of town on foot. *1½ hrs. Cost: $10.*

Coming Ashore Ships small enough to visit Petersburg dock in the South Harbor, which is about a ½-mi (1-km) walk to downtown. Everything in Petersburg is within easy walking distance of the harbor. Renting a bicycle is an especially pleasant way to see the sights. A good route is to ride along the coast on Nordic Drive, past the lovely homes, to the boardwalk and the city dump, where you might spot some bears. Coming back to town, take the interior route and you'll pass the airport and some pretty churches before returning to the waterfront. Bicycles are available for rent from **Northern Bikes** (110 N. Nordic Dr., tel. 907/772–3978) at the Scandia House Hotel.

Passengers who want to learn about the local history, the commercial fishing industry, and the natural history of the Tongass National Forest can book a guided van tour. Contact **See Alaska Tours and Charters** (tel. 907/772–4656).

Exploring Petersburg *Numbers in the margin correspond to points of interest on the Petersburg map.*

One of the most pleasant things to do in Petersburg is to roam among the fishing vessels tied up at dockside. This is one of Alaska's busiest, most prosperous fishing communities, and the variety of seacraft is enormous. You'll see small trollers, big halibut vessels, and sleek pleasure craft as well. Wander, too, around the fish-processing structures (though beware of the pungent aroma). Just by watching shrimp, salmon, or halibut catches being brought ashore, you can get a real appreciation for this industry and the people who engage in it.

Overlooking the city harbor there are great viewing and picture-taking vantage points. The peaks of the Coastal Range behind the town mark the border between Canada and the United States; the most striking is **Devils Thumb** at 9,077 ft (2,767 m). About 25 mi (40 km) east of Petersburg lies spectacular **LeConte Glacier,** the continent's southernmost tidewater glacier and one of its most active. Oftentimes so many icebergs have calved into the bay that the entrance is carpeted bank-to-bank with floating bergs. The glacier is accessible only by water or air.

❶ For a scenic hike closer to town, go north on Nordic Drive to **Sandy Beach,** where there's frequently good eagle viewing and access to one of Petersburg's favorite picnic and recreation locales.

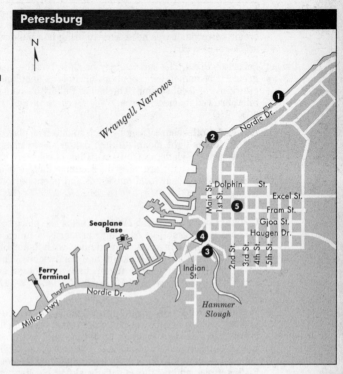

Petersburg

② The best place to watch for America's national bird is the appropriately named **Eagle's Roost Park,** along the shore north of the Petersburg Fisheries cannery. At low tide you may see more than two dozen eagles here.

③ Still another photo opportunity lies in the center of town at **Hammer Slough,** where houses built on stilts make for a postcard-perfect picture. The large, white, barnlike structure on stilts that
④ borders the slough is the **Sons of Norway Hall,** where locals work to keep alive the traditions and culture from the old country.

⑤ Those wanting to do some sightseeing in town should head northeast up the hill from the visitor center to the **Clausen Museum** and the bronze *Fisk* (Norwegian for "fish") sculpture at 2nd and Fram streets. The museum—not surprisingly—devotes a lot of its space to fishing and processing. There's an old "iron chink," used in the early days for gutting and cleaning fish, as well as displays that illustrate the workings of several types of fishing boats. A 126½-pound king salmon, the largest ever caught, came out of a fish trap on Prince of Wales Island in 1939 and is on exhibit, as is the world's largest chum salmon—a 36-pounder. Also here are displays of Native artifacts. *203 Fram St., tel. 907/772–3598. Admission: $2. Open Mon.–Sat. 10–4, Sun. 1–4 in summer.*

Three **pioneer churches**—Catholic, Lutheran, and Presbyterian—are nearby at Dolphin and 3rd streets, Excel and 5th streets, and on Haugen Street between 2nd and 3rd streets, respectively. Of the three, the 50-year-old Lutheran edifice is the oldest. It is said that boys would bring dirt by the wheelbarrow load for landscaping around the foundation. Their compensation? Ice-cream cones. The enticement was so successful that, after three years of ice-cream rewards, it was necessary to bring in a bulldozer to scrape off the excess dirt.

Dining **Pellerito's Pizza.** The service may be slow, but the pizzas here are
$–$$ great. Recommended toppings include Canadian bacon and pineapple or local shrimp. The bar at Pellerito's pours all sorts of microbrewed beers. *Across from ferry terminal, tel. 907/772–3727. MC, V.*

$ **AlasKafe Coffeehouse.** Looking for a smoke-free place to hang out? AlasKafe has light meals all day: panini sandwiches, homemade soups, pastas, salads, and desserts. Plus, of course, coffee. The outdoor balcony seats are nice on a sunny day, and on Saturday evenings you'll hear local musicians and poets perform. *Upstairs at the corner of Nordic and Excel, tel. 907/772–5282. No credit cards.*

$ **Coastal Cold Storage Fish Market.** This is the place to go for fresh seafood in Petersburg. Although primarily a lunch eatery, they are also open for breakfast and dinner, with fish chowders, beer-batter halibut, shrimp cocktail, and sandwiches. They also ship fresh, smoked, canned, or frozen fish, or process any that you catch. *Corner of Excel and Main Sts., tel. 907/772–4171. No credit cards.*

$ **Helse.** Natural foods, including enormous vegetable-laden sandwiches, are a specialty in this homey cross between a diner and a restaurant. Helse, a favorite lunchtime spot with locals, is filled with plenty of plants and works by local artists. You'll find soups, chowders, home-baked breads, and salads on the menu. Espresso makes a nice ending to a meal. Breakfast consists only of coffee and pastries. *Sing Lee Alley and Harbor Way, tel. 907/772–3444. No credit cards.*

$ **The Homestead.** There's nothing at all fancy here, just basic American fare: steaks, local prawns, and halibut, a salad bar, and especially generous breakfasts. Rhubarb pie is the fastest-selling item on the menu. This 24-hour joint is popular with chain-smoking locals. *217 Main St., tel. 907/772–3900. DC, MC, V.*

Saloons **Harbor Bar** (Nordic Dr. near Dolphin St., tel. 907/772–4526). The name suggests the decor here—ship's wheels, ship pictures, and a mounted red snapper.

Kito's Kave (on Sing Lee Alley, tel. 907/772–3207). A colorful, authentic Alaskan bar of regional fame, Kito's serves Mexican food in a pool-hall atmosphere. It's not for the timid or faint-hearted. Beer drinkers are really better off heading to the bar at Pellerito's Pizza (described above), or getting a pitcher of draught from **Harbor Lights Pizza** (tel. 907/772–3424), overlooking the harbor on Sing Lee Alley.

Tastes of One of the Southeast's gourmet delicacies is "Petersburg shrimp."
Alaska Small (they're seldom larger than half your pinky finger), tender, and succulent, they're much treasured by Alaskans, who often send them "outside" as thank-you gifts. You'll find the little critters fresh in meat departments and canned in gift sections at food stores throughout the Panhandle. You can buy fresh vacuum-packed Petersburg shrimp in Petersburg at **Coastal Cold Storage Fish Market,** downtown on Main Street, or by mail-order (tel. 907/772–4177).

Prince William Sound

Every Gulf of Alaska cruise visits Prince William Sound. The sound made worldwide headlines in 1989, when the *Exxon Valdez* hit a reef and spilled 11 million gallons of North Slope crude. The oil has sunk into the beaches below the surface, however, and vast parts of the sound appear pristine, with abundant wildlife. What lasting effect this lurking oil—which is sometimes uncovered after storms and high tides—will have on the area is still being studied.

Numbers in the margin correspond to points of interest on the South Central Alaska map.

❶ A visit to **Columbia Glacier,** which flows from the surrounding Chugach Mountains, is included on many Gulf of Alaska cruises. Its deep aquamarine face is 5 mi (8 km) across, and it calves new icebergs with resounding cannonades. This glacier is one of the largest and most readily accessible of Alaska's coastal glaciers.

The major attraction in Prince William Sound on most Gulf of
❷ Alaska cruises is the day spent in **College Fjord.** Dubbed "Alaska's newest Glacier Bay" by one cruise line, this deep finger of water is ringed by 16 glaciers, each one named after one of the colleges that sponsored early exploration of the fjord.

Of the three major Prince William Sound communities—Valdez,
❸ Whittier, and Cordova—only **Valdez** (pronounced val-*deez*) is a major port of call for cruise ships. For more information on visiting Valdez, *see below.*

Seward

On the southeastern coast of the Kenai Peninsula, Seward is surrounded by four major federal landholdings—**Chugach National Forest, Kenai Wildlife Refuge, Kenai Fjords National Park,** and the **Alaska Maritime National Wildlife Refuge.** The entire area is breathtaking, and you should not miss it in your haste to get to Anchorage.

Seward is one of Alaska's oldest and most scenic communities, set between high mountain ranges on one side and Resurrection Bay on the other. The city was named for U.S. Secretary of State William H. Seward, who was instrumental in arranging the purchase of Alaska from Russia in 1867. Resurrection Bay was named in 1791 by Russian fur trader and explorer Alexander Baranof. The town was established in 1903 by railroad surveyors as an ocean terminal and supply center. The biggest event in Seward's history came after the 1964 Good Friday earthquake—the strongest ever recorded in North America. The tidal wave that followed the quake devastated the town; fortunately, most residents saw the harbor drain almost entirely, knew the wave would follow, and ran to high ground. Since then the town has relied heavily on commercial fishing, and its harbor is important for shipping coal to Asia.

For cruise ship passengers, historic downtown Seward retains its small-town atmosphere; many of its buildings date back to the early 1900s. Modern-day explorers can enjoy wildlife cruise, sportfishing, sailing, and kayaking in the bay, or investigate the intricacies of marine biology at the $52 million **Alaska SeaLife Center,** which opened its doors in 1998.

South Central Alaska

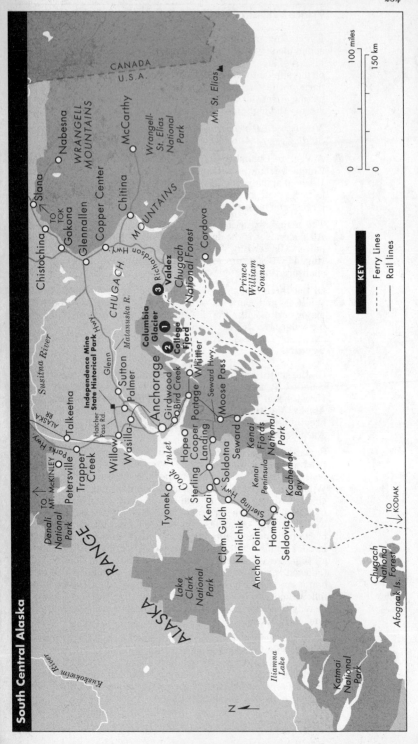

If you're in Seward on the 4th of July, you'll have the chance to see—and perhaps join—the second oldest footrace in North America. Each year participants race straight up the 3,022-ft trail on Mt. Marathon from downtown. (*See* Hiking, *below.*)

Shore Excursions Seward is where most passengers taking a Gulf of Alaska cruise get on or off the ship—so most people don't hang around for long. If your ship is one that calls here for the day, or if you're planning to linger a bit longer in town, the following excursions are a good choice. They may not be offered by all cruise lines. All times and prices are approximate.

Adventure **Alaska Railroad Day-Tour.** Take a scenic ride on the Alaska Railroad round-trip from Seward to Portage through what the railroad calls "the most scenic part of our route." Food and beverages are sold on board. Trains depart Saturday and Sunday from Seward at noon and return at 5:30 PM. Make reservations in advance by calling 800/544–0552. *Cost: $50.*

IdidaRide Sled-Dog Tours. Seward was the start of the original Iditarod Trail, used to bring medicine to Nome during an epidemic in 1925. Visitors can experience this piece of history by taking a summer sled-dog ride with modern-day Iditarod musher Mitch Seavey. For reservations call 907/224–8607 or 800/478–3139. *1¼ hrs. Cost: $27.50.*

Mt. McKinley Flightseeing. From Anchorage, fly to Denali National Park (filled with bears, wolves, caribou, and moose) to see North America's highest peak. The trip is often canceled due to cloudiness. *3 hrs, 2 hrs flying time. Cost: $288.*

Coming Ashore Cruise ships dock within a ½ mi (1 km) of downtown. The Seward Chamber of Commerce has a visitor information center at the cruise ship dock that is staffed when ships are in port. The Kenai Fjords National Park visitor center (tel. 907/224–3175) is within walking distance: Turn left as you leave the pier, then left again onto 4th Avenue; the center is two blocks ahead. It's open daily, 8 AM to 7 PM. Ask here about visiting scenic Exit Glacier, which is 13 mi (21 km) northwest of Seward. The Alaska National Historical Society operates a book and gift store in the Park Service center. The Chugach National Forest Ranger District office is at 334 4th Avenue.

The **Seward Trolley** (tel. 907/224–8051) stops at the cruise ship dock every half hour and heads to Seward's various points of interest. The cost is $1.50 one-way or $3 round-trip.

Exploring Seward Seward's newest attraction, is the **Alaska SeaLife Center,** right in town at the south end of Fourth Avenue. Funded largely by money from the 1989 Exxon Valdez oil spill settlement, this facility covers a 7-acre site facing Resurrection Bay. Inside, you can watch scientists as they study everything from the genetics of herring to Steller sea lion telemetry. The emphasis is on wildlife research, rehabilitation, and education. No leaping killer whales here, but the centerpieces are the re-created sea and shore habitats—complete with underwater viewing windows—that house seals, sea lions, marine birds, salmon, and other animals. *Tel. 907/224–3080. Admission: $12.50. Open daily in summer.*

Although most cruise-ship passengers head into Anchorage, there's a great deal to be seen in the Seward area. Don't miss the fjords in Resurrection Bay, with their bird rookeries and sea-lion haulouts. There are numerous tours to choose from—just check out the boardwalk area adjacent to the docks. **Kenai Fjords Tours** (tel. 907/

224–8068 or 800/478–8068) has a very good half-day cruise of the bay with a stop for a salmon bake on Fox Island ($59 for a 4-hour dinner cruise, or $74 for a 5-hour lunch cruise). Other tour companies include **Mariah Charters** (tel. 907/243–1238 or 800/270–1238), **Kenai Coastal Tours** (tel. 907/224–8068 or 800/770–9119), **Alaska Renown Charters** (tel. 907/224–3806), **Fresh Aire Charters** (tel. 907/272–2755), and **Major Marine Tours** (tel. 907/224–8030 or 800/764–7300).

Thirteen miles (21 kilometers) northeast of Seward, **Exit Glacier** is the only road-accessible part of Kenai Fjords National Park. It's an easy ½ mi (1 km) hike to Exit Glacier from the parking lot; the first ¼ mi (½ km) is paved, which makes it accessible to those using wheelchairs.

If you're looking for history rather than scenery and wildlife, check out the **Seward Museum,** which has exhibits on the 1964 earthquake, the Iditarod, and Native history. *Corner of 3rd and Jefferson, tel. 907/224–3902. Admission: $2. Open daily 9–5.*

Across from the museum is the **1916 Rail Car Seward.** Once part of the Alaska's Railroad's rolling stock, it today is permanently parked here as an information center. Displays inside detail the 1964 Good Friday earthquake and how it devastated the town of Seward.

Shopping   Local gift and souvenir shops include the **Alaska Shop** (210 4th Ave., tel. 907/224–5420), **Bardarson Studio** (Small Boat Harbor, tel. 907/224–5448), and the **Treasure Chest** (Small Boat Harbor, tel. 907/224–8087). One of the best options is **Resurrect Art Coffee-house Gallery** (320 3rd Ave., tel. 907/224–7161, *see* Food, *below*), where you'll find jewelry, pottery, books, prints, and paintings by local artisans.

Ranting Raven Bakery (228 4th Ave., tel. 907/224–2228) has a gift shop stocked with Russian and Ukrainian imports. Don't forget to try the home-baked breads, pastries, and cakes.

Sports   Every August the **Seward Silver Salmon Derby** attracts hundreds
Fishing   of folks who compete for the $10,000 top prize. For fishing, sight-seeing, and drop-off/pickup tours, contact **Fish House** (tel. 907/224–3674 or 800/257–7760), Seward's oldest operator.

Hiking   The strenuous **Mt. Marathon** trail starts at the west end of Lowell Canyon Road and runs practically straight uphill. An easier and more convenient hike for cruise passengers is the **Two Lakes Trail,** a loop of footpaths and bridges on the edge of town. A map is available from the Seward Chamber of Commerce (tel. 907/224–8051).

Dining   **Ray's Waterfront.** When it comes to seafood, Ray's is the place. The
$$ walls are lined with trophy fish, and the windows front the busy harbor. It's a favorite place to grab a bite to eat while waiting for your tour boat, or to relax with a cocktail as the sun goes down. The menu includes delicious mesquite-grilled salmon, plus clam chowder, crab, and other fresh-from-the-sea specialties. *On the Small Boat Harbor, tel. 907/224–5632. AE, DC, MC, V.*

$–$$ **Harbor Dinner Club & Lounge.** Stop at this spot in Seward's his-toric downtown district for solid lunch fare including burgers, sandwiches, and clam chowder. The outside deck is a good place to dine on a sunny summer afternoon. You'll find prime rib, steaks, and seafood on the dinner menu. *220 5th Ave., tel. 907/224–3012. AE, D, DC, MC, V.*

$ Built in 1916-17, the **Resurrect Art Coffeehouse Gallery** served for many years as a Lutheran church. Today, locals and tourists come to worship the espresso coffee and pastries on rainy days, or for live music and poetry on summer evenings. *320 3rd Ave., tel. 907/ 224–7161. No credit cards.*

Sitka

For hundreds of years before the 18th-century arrival of the Russians, Sitka was home to the Tlingit people. But Sitka's protected harbor, mild climate, and economic potential caught the attention of outsiders. Russian Territorial Governor Alexander Baranof saw in the island's massive timbered forests raw materials for shipbuilding, and its location suited trading routes to California, Hawaii, and the Orient. In 1799 Baranof established an outpost that he called Redoubt St. Michael, 6 mi (10 km) north of the present town, and moved a large number of his Russian and Aleut fur hunters there from Kodiak Island.

The Tlingits attacked Baranof's people and burned his buildings in 1802, but Baranof returned in 1804 with a formidable force, including shipboard cannons. He attacked the Tlingits at their fort near Indian River (site of the present-day, 105-acre Sitka National Historical Park) and drove them to the other side of the island. The Tlingits and Russians made peace in 1821, and, eventually, the capital of Russian America was shifted to Sitka from Kodiak.

Sitka today is known primarily for its onion-dome Russian Orthodox church, one of Southeast Alaska's most famous landmarks, and the Alaska Raptor Rehabilitation Center, a hospital for injured bald eagles and other birds of prey. But don't miss the 15 totem poles scattered throughout the grounds of the national historical park.

Shore Excursions   The following is a good choice in Sitka. It may not be offered by all cruise lines. All times and prices are approximate.

Adventure   **Kayak Adventure.** Get down to sea level to search for marine and land wildlife in two-person sea kayaks. Sightings of eagles, seals, bears, and deer are likely. If your ship doesn't offer this excursion, contact Baidarka Boats (*see* Kayaking, *below*). *3 hrs, includes 1½ hrs of kayaking. Cost: $78.*

Dance   The 40 members (all women) of the **New Archangel Dancers** perform Russian dances at Centennial Hall when cruise ships are in port. Call 907/747–5940 for details.

Coming Ashore   Only the smallest excursion vessels can dock at Sitka. Ocean liners must drop anchor in the harbor and tender passengers ashore near Centennial Hall, with its big Tlingit war canoe. Inside is the Sitka Visitors Bureau information desk, which provides maps and brochures.

Sitka is hilly, but the waterfront attractions are an easy walk from the tender landing. You may, however, want to consider a taxi if you're heading all the way to the other side of the harbor.

Exploring Sitka   *Numbers in the margin correspond to points of interest on the Sitka map.*

❶   To get one of the best views in town, turn left on Harbor Drive and head for **Castle Hill,** where Alaska was handed over to the United States on October 18, 1867, and where the first 49-star U.S. flag was flown on January 3, 1959, signifying the spirit of Alaska's statehood. Take the first right off Harbor Drive, then look for the entrance to Baranof Castle Hill State Historic Site. Make a left on

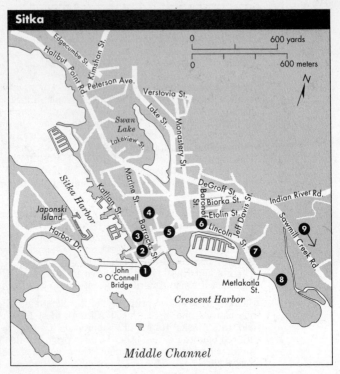

the gravel path that takes you to the top of the hill overlooking
Crescent Harbor.

② The **Sitka State Pioneers' Home** was built in 1934 as the first of several state-run retirement homes and medical-care facilities. The
statue, symbolizing the state's sourdoughs (as old-timers are nicknamed), was modeled after an authentic pioneer, William "Skagway Bill" Fonda. It portrays a determined prospector with pack,
pick, rifle, and supplies, headed for gold country.

Three old anchors, believed to be from 19th-century British ships,
mark **Totem Square.** Notice the double-headed eagle of czarist
Russia on the park's totem pole. Just up the street from the Pio-
③ neers' Home is the **Shee'ka Kwaan Naa Kahidi Performing Arts Center,** with demonstrations and performances by members of the
Sitka tribe. A small museum here houses historic prints and displays on edible plants.

④ The most distinctive grave in the **Russian and Lutheran cemetery**
marks the final resting place of Princess Maksoutoff, one of the
most famous members of the Russian royal family buried on
Alaskan soil.

⑤ Sitka's most photographed sight, **St. Michael's Cathedral** had its
origins in a frame-covered log structure built in the 1840s. In 1966
the church burned in a fire that swept through the business district. Using original blueprints, an almost-exact replica of St.
Michael's was built and dedicated in 1976. *Lincoln St., tel. 907/747–
8120. Admission: $1 donation requested. Open daily 7:30 AM–5:30
PM and when cruise ships are in port.*

❻ Several blocks past St. Michael's Cathedral on Lincoln Street and facing the harbor is the **Russian Bishop's House.** Constructed in 1842, this is one of the few remaining Russian log homes in Alaska. The Park Service has carefully restored the building, using original Russian furnishings and artifacts. In one room a portion of the house's structure has been peeled away to expose 19th-century building techniques. *Lincoln St., tel. 907/747–6281. Donation requested. Open daily 9–1 and 2–5.*

❼ The octagonal **Sheldon Jackson Museum,** built in 1895, contains priceless Native American items collected by Dr. Sheldon Jackson from the remote regions of Alaska. Carved masks, Chilkat blankets, dogsleds, kayaks—even the helmet worn by Chief Katlean during the 1804 battle between the Sitka Tlingits and the Russians—are displayed here. *Lincoln St., tel. 907/747–8981. Admission: $3. Open daily 8–5.*

❽ **Sitka National Historical Park Visitor Center** is at the far end of Lincoln Street. Audiovisual programs and exhibits, including native and Russian artifacts, give an overview of Southeast Alaskan cultures, both old and new. Native artists and craftspeople are on hand to demonstrate and interpret traditional crafts of the Tlingit people, such as silversmithing, weaving, and basketry. A self-guided trail (maps available at the visitor center) to the site of the Tlingit Fort passes by some of the most skillfully carved totem poles in the state; some of these 15 poles date back more than nine decades. *Tel. 907/747–6281. Admission free. Open daily 8–5.*

❾ One of Sitka's most interesting attractions is the **Alaska Raptor Rehabilitation Center,** where injured birds of prey are nursed back to health. A visit to this unusual nature center rarely disappoints. *1101 Sawmill Creek Rd., tel. 907/747–8662. Admission: $10. Open daily 8–5, and when cruise ship passengers are in port.*

Shopping Several local shops sell quality crafts and gifts, including **Sitka Rose Gallery** (419 Lincoln St., tel. 907/747–3030) and the **Sitka Crafters Mall** (110 American St., tel. 907/747–6544). Native jewelry and other handicrafts are available from the **Sitka National Historical Park Visitor Center** (*see* Exploring Sitka, *above*).

A few stores, such as the **Russian-American Company** (407 Lincoln St., tel. 907/747–6228) and the **New Archangel Trading Co.** (335 Harbor Dr., across from Centennial Hall, tel. 907/747–8181), sell Russian items, including the popular *matruchka* nesting dolls.

For books on Alaska, stop by **Old Harbor Books** (201 Lincoln St., tel. 907/747–8808).

Sports
Fishing Fishing is excellent here. Contact **Steller Charters** (tel. 907/747–6167) or see the information desk in Centennial Hall for a list of other charter operators.

Hiking Sitka's easiest hiking can be done along the 2 mi (3 km) of trails in **Sitka National Historical Park.** Here you can find some of the most dramatically situated totem poles in Alaska, relax at the picnic areas, and watch spawning salmon during the seasonal runs on the Indian River.

Sea Kayaking Several local companies offer guided sea-kayak trips, but you won't go wrong with **Baidarka Boats** (above Old Harbor Books at 201 Lincoln St., tel. 907/747–8996). Half-day trips are $50 for a double kayak. Be sure to make arrangements in advance so that your guide and/or kayak is waiting for you at the harbor.

Dining   **Backdoor Cafe.** For a dose of Sitka's caffeine-fueled hip side, scoot
$ on through Old Harbor Books to this cozy latte joint. Good pas-
tries and bagels, too. *201 Lincoln St., tel. 907/747–8856. No credit
cards.*

$ **Bay View Restaurant.** Conveniently located for passengers touring
the historic waterfront, the Bay View has Russian specialties that
reflect Sitka's colonial heritage. Gourmet burgers (including one
with caviar) and deli sandwiches are also available, as is beer and
wine. *407 Lincoln St., tel. 907/747–5440. AE, MC, V.*

Saloons   **Pilot House** (713 Katlean St., tel. 907/747–4707) is a dance spot with
a waterfront view.

Pioneer Bar (212 Katlean St., tel. 907/747–3456), across from the
harbor, is a hangout for local fishermen. Tourists get a kick out of
its authentic Alaskan ambience; the walls are lined with pictures
of local fishing boats.

Skagway

The early gold-rush days of Alaska, when dreamers and hooligans
descended on the Yukon via the murderous White Pass, are preserved in Skagway. Now a part of the Klondike Gold Rush
National Historical Park, downtown Skagway was once the picturesque but sometimes lawless gateway for the frenzied stampede to the interior goldfields.

Local park rangers and residents now interpret and re-create that
remarkable era for visitors. Old false-front stores, saloons, broth-
els, and wood sidewalks have been completely restored. You'll be
regaled with tall tales of con artists, golden-hearted "ladies,"
stampeders, and newsmen. Such colorful characters as outlaw Jefferson "Soapy" Smith and his gang earned the town a reputation
so bad that, by the spring of 1898, the superintendent of the
Northwest Royal Mounted Police had labeled Skagway "little better than a hell on earth." But Soapy was killed in a duel with sur-
veyor Frank Reid, and soon a civilizing influence, in the form of
churches and family life, prevailed. When the gold played out just
a few years later, the town of 20,000 dwindled to its current population of just over 700 (twice that in the summer months).

Shore   The following are good choices in Skagway. They may not be
Excursions   offered by all cruise lines. All times and prices are approximate.

Adventure   **Bike the Klondike.** By van, travel to the top of the 3,000-ft Klondike
Pass. Then by mountain bike, coast 15 mi (24 km) down a moder-
ate grade, enjoying the spectacular views of the White Pass along
the way. Great photo opportunities, including the waterfalls,
glaciers, and coastal mountains, abound. All equipment is
included. *2 hrs. Cost: $70.*

Glacier Bay Flightseeing. If your ship doesn't sail through Glacier
Bay—or even if it does—here's your chance to see it from above. *2
hrs, including 90-min flight. Cost: $110–$135.*

Gold Rush Helicopter Tour. Fly over the Chilkoot Gold Rush Trail
into a remote mountain valley for a landing on a glacier. Special
boots are provided for walking on the glacier. *2 hrs, including 50-
min flight. Cost: $150–$220.*

Gold Rush   **White Pass and Yukon Railroad.** The 20-mi (32-km) trip in vintage
History   railroad cars, on narrow-gauge tracks built to serve the Yukon
goldfields, runs past the infamous White Pass, skims along the

edge of granite cliffs, crosses a 215-ft-high steel cantilever bridge over Dead Horse Gulch, climbs to a 2,865-ft elevation at White Pass Summit, and zigzags through dramatic scenery—including the actual Trail of '98, worn into the mountainside a century ago. A must for railroad buffs; great for children. *3 hrs. Cost: $80–$90.*

Coming Ashore Cruise ships dock just a short stroll from downtown Skagway. From the pier you can see the large yellow-and-red White Pass & Yukon Railroad Depot, now the National Park Service Visitor Center. Inside is an excellent photographic exhibit and a superb documentary film. Ask the rangers about nearby hiking trails and exploring the gold rush cemetery. Information on local history and attractions is also available from the **Skagway Visitor Information Center** (333 5th Ave., ½ block off Broadway, tel. 907/983–2855).

Virtually all the shops and gold rush sights are along Broadway, the main strip that leads from the visitor center through the middle of town, so you really don't need a taxi. Horse-drawn surreys, antique limousines, and modern vans pick up passengers at the pier and along Broadway for tours. The tracks of the White Pass and Yukon Railway run right along the pier; train departures are coordinated with cruise ship arrivals.

Exploring Skagway *Numbers in the margin correspond to points of interest on the Skagway map.*

Skagway is perhaps the easiest port in Alaska to explore on foot. Just walk up and down Broadway, detouring here and there into the side streets. Keep an eye out for the humorous architectural details and advertising irreverence that mark the Skagway spirit.

❶ From the cruise ship dock, follow the road into town to the **Red Onion Saloon,** where a lady-of-the-evening mannequin peers down from the former second-floor brothel, and drinks are still served on the original mahogany bar. *Broadway and 2nd Ave., tel. 907/983–2222.*

❷ You can't help but notice the **Arctic Brotherhood Hall/Trail of '98 Museum,** with its curious driftwood-mosaic facade. *Broadway between 2nd Ave. and 3rd Ave., tel. 907/983–2420. Open when cruise ships are in port.*

❸ A small, almost inconsequential shack on 2nd Avenue was **Soapy's Parlor**—named after the notorious, gold-rush con man—but it's not open to tourists. *Off Broadway.*

You'll find down-home sourdough cooking at the **Golden North Hotel.** Founded in 1898, it bills itself as the oldest hotel in Alaska. *Broadway and 3rd Ave., tel. 907/983–2451.*

❹ A rip-roaring revue, "Skagway in the Days of '98," is staged at the **Eagles Hall.** *Broadway and 6th Ave., tel. 907/983–2545. Admission: $15. Performances scheduled when cruise ships are in port.*

Shopping Broadway is filled with numerous curio shops selling unusual merchandise. Although prices tend to be high as a general rule, good deals can be found, so shop around and don't buy the first thing you see.

David Present's Gallery (Broadway and 3rd Ave., tel. 907/983–2873) has outstanding but pricey art by Alaskan artists.

Dedman's Photo Shop (Broadway between 3rd and 4th Aves., tel. 907/983–2353) has been a Skagway institution since the early days; here you'll find unusual historical photos, guidebooks, and old-fashioned newspapers.

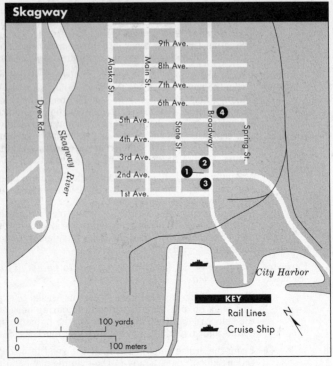

242

Arctic Brotherhood Hall/Trail of '98 Museum, **2**

Eagles Hall, **4**

Red Onion Saloon, **1**

Soapy's Parlor, **3**

Kirmse's (Broadway and 5th Ave., tel. 907/983–2822) has a large selection of expensive, inexpensive, and downright tacky souvenirs. On display is the world's largest, heaviest, and most valuable gold-nugget watch chain.

Sports
Hiking Real wilderness is within a stone's throw of the docks, which makes this an excellent hiking port. Try the short jaunt to beautiful **Lower Dewey Lake.** Start at the corner of 4th Avenue and Spring Street, go toward the mountain, cross the footbridge over Pullen Creek, and follow the trail uphill.

A less strenuous hike is the trip through **Gold Rush Cemetery,** where the epitaphs offer strange but lively bits of social commentary. To get there, keep walking up Broadway, turn left onto 8th Avenue, then right onto State Street. Go through the railroad yards and follow the signs to the cemetery, which is 1½ mi (3 km), or a 30- to 45-minute walk, from town. To reach 300-ft-high **Reid Falls,** continue through the cemetery for ¼ mi (½ km). The National Park Service Visitor Center offers trail maps, advice, and the helpful brochure, *Skagway Gold Rush Cemetery Guide.* Trail maps also are available at the **City Visitor Center** (333 5th Ave., ½ block off Broadway, tel. 907/983–2855).

Dining **Lorna's at the Skagway Inn.** This is Skagway's upmarket restau-
$$$ rant, with a French-trained chef who specializes in artfully prepared Alaskan seafood. Guaranteed to please your palate, though your wallet will be a bit worse for the experience. Lorna's also has a great wine and dessert selection. *7th Ave. and Broadway, tel. 907/983–3161. MC, V.*

$–$$ **Golden North Restaurant.** To eat in the Golden North Hotel's dining room is to return to the days of gold-rush con man Soapy Smith, heroic Frank Reid, and scores of pioneers, stampeders, and dance-hall girls. The decor is authentic and has been tastefully restored. Try the sourdough pancakes for breakfast. *3rd Ave. and Broadway, tel. 907/983–2294. AE, DC, MC, V.*

Saloons **Moe's Frontier Bar** (Broadway, between 4th and 5th Sts., tel. 907/983–2238). A longtime fixture on the Skagway scene, Moe's is a bar much frequented by the local folk.

Red Onion (Broadway at 2nd St., tel. 907/983–2222). You'll meet at least as many Skagway people here as you will visitors. There's live music on Thursday nights, ranging from rock and jazz to folk and acoustic. The upstairs was a gold-rush brothel.

Tracy Arm

Like Misty Fjords (*see above*), Tracy Arm and its sister fjord, Endicott Arm, have become staples on many Inside Passage cruises. Ships sail into the arm just before or after a visit to Juneau, the state capital, 50 mi (80 km) to the north. A day of scenic cruising in Tracy Arm is a lesson in geology and the forces that shaped Alaska. The fjord was carved by a glacier eons ago, leaving behind sheer granite cliffs. Waterfalls continue the process of erosion that the glaciers began. Very small ships may nudge their bows under the waterfalls, so crew members can fill pitchers full of glacial runoff. It's a uniquely Alaskan refreshment. Tracy Arm's glaciers haven't disappeared, though, they've just receded, and at the very end of Tracy Arm you'll come to two of them, known collectively as the twin Sawyer Glaciers.

Valdez

Valdez, with its year-round ice-free port, was an entry point for people and goods going to the interior during the gold rush. Today that flow has been reversed, and Valdez Harbor is the southern terminus of the Trans-Alaska pipeline, which carries crude oil from Prudhoe Bay and surrounding oil fields nearly 800 mi (1,287 km) to the north.

Much of Valdez looks new because the business area was relocated and rebuilt after being destroyed by the devastating Good Friday earthquake in 1964. A few of the old buildings were moved to the new town site.

Many Alaskan communities have summer fishing derbies, but Valdez may hold the record for the number of such contests, stretching from late May into September for halibut and various runs of salmon. The Valdez Silver Salmon Derby begins in late July and runs the entire month of August. Fishing charters abound in this area of Prince William Sound, and for a good reason, too: These fertile waters provide some of the best saltwater sport-fishing in all of Alaska.

Shore Excursions The following are good choices in Valdez. They may not be offered by all cruise lines. All times and prices are approximate.

Adventure **Columbia Glacier Floatplane Sightseeing.** Enjoy aerial views of Valdez and Shoup Glacier, a section of the pipeline, and its terminus. The highlight is touching down in the water for a close-up view of the massive Columbia Glacier. *1½ hrs, including 1-hr flight and 15-min landing on glacier. Cost: $179.*

Columbia Glacier Helicopter Flightseeing. The flight over the huge Columbia Glacier includes a landing near the face of Shoup Glacier and aerial views of Valdez Bay, the pipeline terminus, and the old Valdez site. *1¼ hrs, including 45-min flight. Cost: $150–$200.*

Keystone River Rafting. This 1½-hour raft trip goes down the Lowe River, through a scenic canyon, and past the spectacular Bridal Veil Falls, which cascades 900 ft down the canyon wall. The bus trip from the ship is narrated. *2¼ hrs. Cost: $60–$70.*

Sea-kayaking Adventures. Get down on the water's surface for a guided tour of the port of Valdez or Robe Lake. See a seabird rookery and seals up close or float across the mirrorlike surface of a freshwater lake tucked against the bottom of the Chugach Mountains. *4–6 hrs. Cost: $52–$185.*

Trans-Alaska **Pipeline Story.** Tour the pipeline terminus and hear tales of how
Pipeline the pipeline was built. This is the only way to get into this high-security area. *2¼ hrs. Cost: $24.*

Coming Ships tie up at the world's largest floating container dock. About 3
Ashore mi (5 km) from the heart of town, the dock is used not only for cruise ships, but also for loading cargo ships with timber and other products bound for markets "outside" (that's what Alaskans call the rest of the world).

Ship-organized motor coaches meet passengers on the pier and provide transportation into town. Cabs and car-rental services will also provide transportation from the pier. Several local ground and adventure-tour operators meet passengers as well.

Once in town, you'll find that Valdez is a very compact community. Almost everything is within easy walking distance of the Valdez Convention and Visitors Bureau in the heart of town. Motor coaches drop passengers at the Visitor Information Center. Taxi service is available and individualized tours of the area can be arranged with the cab dispatcher.

Exploring Other than visiting the oil-pipeline terminal, which must be done
Valdez on a tour, sightseeing in Valdez is mostly limited to gazing at the 5,000-ft mountain peaks surrounding the town or visiting the **Valdez Museum.** It depicts the lives, livelihoods, and events significant to Valdez and surrounding regions. Exhibits include a 1907 steam fire engine, a 19th-century saloon, and a model of the pipeline terminus. *217 Egan Ave., tel. 907/835–2764. Admission: $3. Open daily 8–8.*

Dining **Mike's Palace.** This busy restaurant with typical Italian-diner
$–$$ decor serves great pizzas, lasagna, beer-batter halibut, and Greek specialties, including gyros. *On the harbor, 201 N. Harbor Dr., tel. 907/835–2365. MC, V.*

Vancouver, British Columbia

Cosmopolitan Vancouver, Canada's answer to San Francisco, enjoys a spectacular setting. Tall fir trees stand practically downtown, rock spires tower close by, the ocean laps at your doorstep, and people from every corner of the earth create a youthful and vibrant atmosphere.

Vancouver is a young city, even by North American standards. It was not yet a town in 1870, when British Columbia became part of the Canadian confederation. The city's history, such as it is, remains visible to the naked eye: Eras are stacked east to west along the waterfront like some century-old archaeological dig—from cobblestoned, late-Victorian Gastown to shiny postmodern glass cathedrals of commerce grazing the sunset.

Shore Excursions Unless you're on a longer cruise that begins in Los Angeles or San Francisco, Vancouver will likely be your first or last stop. If you're sailing round-trip, you'll get on and off the ship in Vancouver (*see* Itineraries, *above*). Because most passengers are busy transferring between the airport and the ship, few shore excursions are scheduled. If you plan to stay in Vancouver before or after your cruise, most lines sell pre- or post-cruise city packages.

For cruise passengers on longer cruises, a call in Vancouver will be much like any other port call: You'll disembark just for the day and have the option of taking a ship organized tour or exploring independently.

The following are good choices in Vancouver. They may not be offered by all cruise lines. Times and prices are approximate.

City Tour. If this is your first visit to Vancouver, a city tour is a convenient way to see all the sights of this cosmopolitan city—the largest you'll visit on an Alaska cruise. Highlights include the Gastown district, Chinatown, and Stanley Park. *3 hrs. Cost: $29.*

Vancouver Pre- or Post-Cruise Package. Cruise-line land packages are an easy way to extend your cruise vacation without making separate arrangements. Usually, you'll have a choice of one, two, or three nights in town. Often, you'll also have a choice of hotels (in different price ranges). Most packages include sightseeing tours and transfers between the ship and the hotel. Meals are generally extra unless noted in the brochure; transfers between the airport and hotel may be included only for air-sea passengers. Check with your cruise line or travel agent for the exact terms of your Vancouver package.

Coming Ashore Most ships dock downtown at the Canada Place cruise-ship terminal—instantly recognizable by its rooftop of dramatic white sails. A few vessels tie up at the nearby Ballantyne cruise terminal. Both are within minutes of the city center. Stop off at Tourism Vancouver Infocentre across the street (next door to the Waterfront Centre Hotel) to pick up brochures on other Vancouver attractions and events before leaving the pier area.

Many sights of interest are concentrated in the hemmed-in peninsula of Downtown Vancouver. The heart of Vancouver—which includes the downtown area, Stanley Park, and the West End high-rise residential neighborhood—sits on this peninsula bordered by English Bay and the Pacific Ocean to the west; by False Creek, the inlet home to Granville Island, to the south; and by Burrard Inlet, the working port of the city, to the north, past which loom the North Shore mountains. The oldest part of the city—Gastown and Chinatown—lies at the edge of Burrard Inlet, around Main Street, which runs north–south and is roughly the dividing line between the east side and the west side. All the avenues, which are numbered, have east and west designations.

It is difficult to hail a cab in Vancouver; unless you're near a hotel, you'd have better luck calling a taxi service. Try **Yellow** (tel. 604/681–3311) or **Black Top** (tel. 604/681–2181).

Exploring Vancouver *Numbers in the margin correspond to points of interest on the Downtown Vancouver map. Prices are given in Canadian dollars.*

❶ At **Canada Place,** walk along the promenade on the pier's west side for fine views of the Burrard Inlet harbor and Stanley Park.

❷ The **Canadian Craft Museum,** which opened in 1992, is one of the first national cultural facilities dedicated to crafts—historical and contemporary, functional and decorative. Examples here range from elegantly carved utensils with decorative handles to colorful hand-spun and handwoven garments. *639 Hornby St., tel. 604/687–8266. Admission: $4. Open Mon.–Sat. 10–5, Sun. and holidays noon–5.*

❸ **Gastown** is where Vancouver originated after Jack Deighton arrived at Burrard Inlet in 1867 with his Indian wife, a barrel of whiskey, and few amenities and set up a saloon to entertain the scattered loggers and trappers living in the area. When the transcontinental train arrived in 1887, Gastown became the transfer point for trade with the Orient and was soon crowded with hotels and warehouses. The Klondike gold rush encouraged further development until 1912, when the "Golden Years" ended. From the 1930s to the 1950s hotels were converted into rooming houses, and the warehouse district shifted elsewhere. The neglected area gradually became run-down. However, both Gastown and Chinatown were declared historic districts in the late 1970s and have been revitalized. Gastown is now chockablock with boutiques, cafés, and souvenir shops.

The Chinese were among the first inhabitants of Vancouver, and
❹ some of the oldest buildings in the city are in **Chinatown.** There was already a sizable Chinese community in British Columbia because of the 1858 Cariboo gold rush in central British Columbia, but the greatest influx from China came in the 1880s, during construction of the Canadian Pacific Railway, when 15,000 laborers were imported. It is best to view the buildings in Chinatown from the south side of Pender Street, where the Chinese Cultural Center stands. From here you'll see important details that adorn the upper stories. The style of architecture in Vancouver's Chinatown is patterned on that of Canton and won't be seen in any other Canadian cities.

Stanley Park is a 1,000-acre wilderness park just blocks from the downtown section of the city. An afternoon in Stanley Park gives you a capsule tour of Vancouver that includes beaches, the ocean, the harbor, Douglas fir and cedar forests, and a good look at the North Shore mountains. The park sits on a peninsula, and along the shore is a pathway 9 km (5½ mi) long, called the seawall. You can drive or bicycle all the way around. Bicycles are for rent at the foot of Georgia Street near the park entrance. Cyclists must ride in a counterclockwise direction and stay on their side of the path.

The totem poles you'll see in Stanley Park were not made in the Vancouver area; these, carved of cedar by the Kwakiutl and Haida peoples late in the last century, were brought to the park from the north coast of British Columbia. There's also an aquarium (tel. 604/682–1118) within the park grounds, where you can see the sealife of coastal British Columbia, the Canadian arctic, and other areas of the world.

Shopping Unlike many cities where suburban malls have taken over, Vancouver has a downtown that is still lined with individual boutiques and specialty shops. Stores are usually open daily and on Thursday and Friday nights, and Sunday noon to 5.

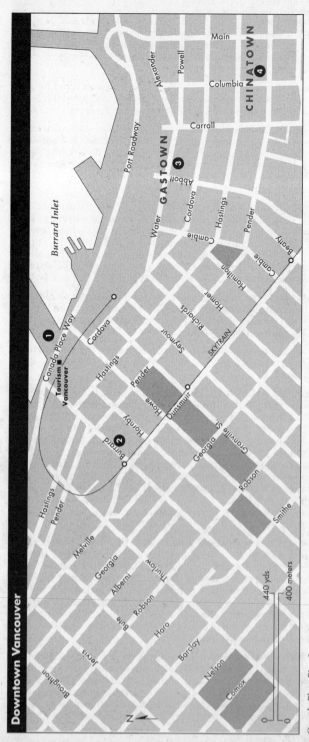

Downtown Vancouver

Burrard Inlet

CHINATOWN
Main
Powell
Alexander
Columbia
Carrall
GASTOWN
Port Roadway
Abbott
Water
Cordova
Cambie
Hastings
Pender
Beatty
Cambie
Hamilton
Homer
Richards
Seymour
SKYTRAIN
Canada Place Way
Cordova
Hastings
Pender
Howe
Dunsmuir
Georgia
Granville St.
Robson
Smithe
Tourism
Vancouver
Burrard
Hornby
Hastings
Pender
Melville
Georgia
Thurlow
Alberni
Burrard
Robson
Haro
Barclay
Nelson
Comox
Jervis
Broughton

N

440 yds
400 meters

0

Canada Place Pier, **1**
Canadian Craft
Museum, **2**
Chinatown, **4**
Gastown, **3**

Robson Street, stretching from Burrard to Bute streets, is chock-ablock with small boutiques and cafés. Vancouver's liveliest street is not only for the fashion-conscious; it also provides many excellent corners for people-watching and attracts an array of street performers.

Chinatown (*see* Exploring Vancouver, *above*)—centered on Pender and Main streets—is an exciting and animated place for restaurants, exotic foods, and distinctive architecture.

For books, **Duthie's** (919 Robson St., tel. 604/684–4496) downtown is a favorite in Vancouver. Fashion is big business in Vancouver, and there are clothing boutiques on almost every corner downtown. If your tastes are traditional, don't miss **George Straith** (900 W. Georgia St., tel. 604/685–3301) in the Hotel Vancouver, offering tailored designer fashions for both sexes.

Want something special to take home from British Columbia? One of the best places in Vancouver for good-quality souvenirs (West Coast native art, books, music, jewelry, and so on) is the **Clamshell Gift Shop** (Vancouver Aquarium, tel. 604/685–5911) in Stanley Park. In Gastown, Haida, Inuit, and Salish, native art is available at **Images for a Canadian Heritage** (164 Water St., tel. 604/685–7046), as is a selection of fine Canadian crafts.

Sports

Biking **Stanley Park** (*see* Stanley Park, *above*) is the most popular spot for family cycling. Rentals are available here from Bayshore Bicycles (745 Denman St., tel. 604/688–2453) or Stanley Park Rentals (1798 W. Georgia, tel. 604/681–5581).

Golf One of the finest public courses in the country is **Peace Portal** (6900 4th Ave., tel. 604/538–4818), near White Rock, a 45-minute drive from downtown.

Dining

$$ **Five Sails.** On the fourth floor of the Pan Pacific Hotel, this special-occasion restaurant affords a stunning panoramic view of Canada Place, Lions Gate Bridge, and the lights of the north shore across the bay. Austrian chef Ernst Dorfler has a special flair for presentation, from the swan-shape butter served with breads early in the meal to the chocolate ice-cream bonbon served at the end. The broad-reaching, seasonally changing Pacific Rim menu often includes caramelized swordfish, spicy Mongolian-style chicken, and such old favorites as medallions of British Columbia salmon or lamb from Salt Spring Island. *Pan Pacific Hotel, 300–999 Canada Pl., tel. 604/662–8211. Reservations essential. AE, DC, MC, V. No lunch.*

$$ **Imperial Chinese Seafood.** This elegant Cantonese restaurant in the art deco Marine Building offers stupendous views through two-story floor-to-ceiling windows of Stanley Park and the North Shore mountains across Coal Harbour. Any dish featuring lobster, crab, or shrimp from the live tanks is recommended, as is the dim sum served every day from 11 to 2:30. Portions tend to be small and pricey (especially the abalone, shark's fin, and bird's-nest delicacies) but never fail to please. *355 Burrard St., tel. 604/688–8191. Reservations essential. AE, MC, V.*

$$ **Joe Fortes Seafood House.** Reserve a table on the second floor balcony at this Vancouver seafood hot spot to take in the view of the broad wall murals and the mounted blue marlins. The signature panfried Cajun oysters, clam and corn fritters, salmon with smoked apple and cider chutney, and seared sea scallops in sesame and oyster glaze are tasty and filling, but often overlooked in favor

In case you want to see the world.

At American Express, we're here to make your journey a smooth one. So we have over 1,700 travel service locations in over 120 countries ready to help. What else would you expect from the world's largest travel agency?

do more

http://www.americanexpress.com/travel

Travel

In case you want to be welcomed there.

We're here to see that you're always welcomed at establishments everywhere. That's why millions of people carry the American Express® Card – for peace of mind, confidence, and security, around the world or just around the corner.

do more

Cards

In case you're running low.

We're here to help with more than 118,000 Express Cash locations around the world. In order to enroll, just call American Express before you start your vacation.

do more

Express Cash

And just in case.

We're here with American Express® Travelers Cheques and Cheques *for Two*.® They're the safest way to carry money on your vacation and the surest way to get a refund, practically anywhere, anytime.

Another way we help you...

do more

Travelers Cheques

of the reasonably priced daily special. *777 Thurlow St., tel. 604/ 669–1940. Reservations essential. AE, D, DC, MC, V.*

$ **Olympia Fish Market and Oyster Co. Ltd.** Owner Carlo Sorace fries up some of the city's best fish-and-chips in this tiny shop behind a fish store in the middle of the Robson Street shopping district. The choice is halibut, cod, prawns, calamari, and whatever's on special in the store, served with homemade coleslaw and genuine—never frozen—french fries. It's funky and fun. *1094 Robson St., tel. 604/685–0716. Reservations not accepted. DC, MC, V.*

Bars and Lounges The **Gérard Lounge** (845 Burrard St., tel. 604/682–5511) at the Sutton Place Hotel, with its Old World ambiance, is probably the nicest in the city. For spectacular views, head up to the **Roof Lounge** (900 W. Georgia St., tel. 604/684–3131) in the Hotel Vancouver, where a band plays contemporary dance music nightly. The **Bacchus Lounge** (845 Hornby St., tel. 604/689–7777) in the Wedgewood Hotel is stylish and sophisticated. The **Garden Terrace** (791 W. Georgia St., tel. 604/689–9333) in the Four Seasons is bright and airy with greenery and a waterfall, plus big soft chairs you won't want to get out of; a pianist plays here on the weekends.

Microbreweries have finally hit Vancouver. At **Steam Works** (375 Water St., tel. 604/689–2739) on the edge of bustling Gastown, they use an age-old steam brewing process and large copper kettles (visible through glass walls in the dining room downstairs) to whip up six to nine brews; the espresso ale is interesting. The **Yaletown Brewing Company** (1111 Mainland St., tel. 604/681–2739) is based in a huge renovated warehouse with a glassed-in brewery turning out eight tasty microbrews; it also has a darts and billiards pub and a restaurant with an open-grill kitchen.

Victoria, British Columbia

Though Victoria is not in Alaska, it is a port of call for many ships cruising the Inside Passage. Just like the communities of Southeast Alaska, Victoria had its own gold rush stampede in the 1800s, when 25,000 miners flocked to British Columbia's Cariboo country. Today the city is a mix of stately buildings and English traditions. Flower baskets hang from lampposts, shops sell Harris tweed and Irish linen, locals play cricket and croquet, and visitors sightsee aboard red double-decker buses or horse-drawn carriages. Afternoon tea is still held daily at the city's elegant Empress Hotel. No visit to Victoria is complete without a stroll through Butchart Gardens, a short drive outside the city.

Shore Excursions The following are good choices in Victoria. They may not be offered by all cruise lines. All times and prices are approximate.

Grand City Drive and Afternoon High Tea. This is a good choice for Anglophiles and others with an interest in Victoria's British heritage. The drive through downtown, past Craigdarroch Castle and residential areas, finishes with a British-style high tea at a hotel. A variation of this excursion takes visitors on a tour of the castle in lieu of high tea. *3¼ hrs. Cost: $35.*

Short City Tour and Butchart Gardens. Drive through key places of interest, such as the city center and residential areas, on the way to Butchart Gardens—a must for garden aficionados. *3¼ hrs. Cost: $39.*

Coming Ashore Only the smallest excursion vessels can dock downtown in the Inner Harbour. Ocean liners must tie up at the Ogden Point Cruise Ship Terminal, a C$4–C$5 cab ride from downtown.

Metered taxis meet the ship. The tourist visitor information center (812 Wharf St., tel. 250/953–2033) is in front of the Empress Hotel, midway along the Inner Harbour.

Most points of interest are within walking distance of the Empress Hotel. For those that aren't, public and private transportation is readily available from the Inner Harbour. The public bus system is excellent as well. Pick up route maps and schedules at the tourist information office.

By Taxi Rates are C$2.15 for pickup, C$1.30 per km (½ mi). Contact **Bluebird** (tel. 250/382–2222) or **Victoria Taxi** (250/383–7111).

Exploring *Numbers in the margin correspond to points of interest on the*
Victoria *Inner Harbour, Victoria, map. Prices are given in Canadian dollars.*

❶ Victoria's heart is the **Inner Harbour,** always bustling with ferries, seaplanes, and yachts from all over the world. The ivy-covered Empress Hotel (721 Government St., tel. 250/384–8111), with its well-groomed gardens, is the dowager of Victoria. High tea in this little patch of England is a local ritual: Recline in deep armchairs and nibble on scones or crumpets with honey, butter, jam, and clotted cream while sipping blended tea.

❷ The **Crystal Gardens** were built in 1925 under a glass roof as a public saltwater swimming pool. They have been renovated into a tropical conservatory and aviary, with flamingos, parrots, fountains, and waterfalls. *Douglas St. behind the Empress Hotel, tel. 250/381–1213. Admission: $7. Open spring and summer, daily 8–8; fall, daily 9–6.*

❸ **Thunderbird Park** displays a ceremonial longhouse (a communal dwelling) and the finest collection of replicated totem poles outside Alaska. *Belleville St.*

❹ Next to Thunderbird Park is **Helmcken House,** the province's oldest residence, which has a display of antique medical instruments. *10 Elliot St. Sq., tel. 250/361–0021. Admission: $4. Open daily 10–5.*

❺ The superb **Royal British Columbia Museum** will require at least an hour of your time: Its exhibits encompass 12,000 years of natural and human history. *675 Belleville St., tel. 250/387–3014. Admission: $5.35. Open summer, daily 9–7.*

❻ The stately, neo-Gothic **British Columbia Parliament Buildings** (501 Belleville St.) were constructed of local stone and wood and opened in 1898. Atop the central dome is a gilded statue of Captain George Vancouver, for whom Vancouver Island is named.

❼ Prints by Emily Carr, who was a member of the "Canadian Group of Seven," adorn the walls at the **Emily Carr House,** the beautifully restored residence of the famous early 20th-century painter. *207 Government St., tel. 250/383–5843. Admission: $4.50. Open May–Oct., daily 10–5.*

❽ You can descend beneath the water for a live scuba show with Armstrong, the Pacific octopus, at the **Pacific Underseas Gardens,** a natural aquarium with more than 5,000 species from the area. *490 Belleville St., tel. 250/382–5717. Admission: $7. Open summer, daily 9–9.*

❾ Just a short walk from the Inner Harbour is **Bastion Square.** Follow Government Street to Humboldt Street. With the water to your left, bear left onto Wharf Street, and look for the square on

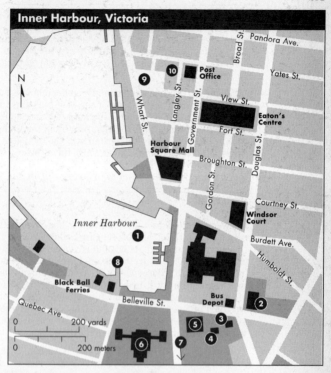

Inner Harbour, Victoria

your right. Established in 1843 as the original site of Ft. Victoria, it now boasts several restored buildings open for viewing.

On the far side of Bastion Square, the old courthouse is now the ⑩ **Maritime Museum of British Columbia.** It has a collection of artifacts—including a 38-ft Native American dugout canoe and the 20-ft ketch *Trekka*, which has sailed around the world. In the Captain Cook gallery, nautical maps and other tools of 17th-century exploration are on display. *28 Bastion Sq., tel. 250/385–4222. Admission: $5. Open daily 9:30–4:30.*

Take a taxi (or a shore excursion) to **Butchart Gardens.** In a city of gardens, these 50 acres rank among the most beautiful in the world. In July and August, a fireworks display is held every Saturday evening. *22 km (14 mi) north of Victoria on Hwy. 17, tel. 250/652–4422. Admission: $15.50. Open daily at 9 AM–10:30 PM in summer.*

Shopping Save your receipts to receive a 7% GST tax refund from the Canadian government when you leave Canada; ask for a form at customs. Victoria stores specializing in English imports are plentiful, though Canadian-made goods are usually a better buy for foreigners. Look for Hudson's Bay Co. blankets and other woolens. From the Empress Hotel walk along Government Street to reach **Piccadilly Shoppe British Woolens** and **Sasquatch Trading Company,** both of which sell high-quality woolen clothing.

Turn right onto Fort Street and walk four blocks to **Antique Row,** between Blanshard and Cook streets. The **Connoisseurs Shop** and **David Robinson, Ltd.** offer a wide variety of 18th-century pieces.

Dining **Bengal Lounge.** Buffet lunches in the elegant Empress Hotel
$$ include curries with extensive condiment trays of coconut, nuts,
cool *raita* (yogurt with mint or cucumber), and chutney. Popular
with cabinet ministers and bureaucrats, the Bengal Lounge offers
splendid garden views. *721 Government St., tel. 250/384–8111. AE,
D, DC, MC, V.*

$$ **La Ville d'Is.** This cozy and friendly seafood house, run by Brittany
native Michel Duteau, is one of the best bargains in Victoria. The
chef's strong suit is seafood, including lobster soufflé and *perche
de la Nouvelle Aelande* (orange roughy in muscadet with herbs),
rabbit, lamb, and beef tenderloin are also available. The wine list
is limited but imaginative. On warm days there's seating outside.
*26 Bastion Sq., tel. 250/388–9414. AE, DC, MC, V. Open for lunch
and dinner Mon.-Fri., and for dinner only on Sat., closed Sun.*

Wrangell

Between Ketchikan and Petersburg lies Wrangell, on an island
near the mouth of the fast-flowing Stikine River. The town is off
the typical cruise-ship track and is visited mostly by lines with an
environmental or educational emphasis, such as Alaska Sightseeing or World Explorer Cruises. A small, unassuming timber and
fishing community, it has lived under three flags since the arrival
of the Russian traders. Known as Redoubt St. Dionysius when it
was part of Russian America, the town was renamed Fort Stikine
after the British took it over. The name was changed to Wrangell
when the Americans purchased it in 1867.

Shore   The following are good choices in Wrangell. They may not be
Excursions offered by all cruise lines. All times and prices are approximate.

Island Sights **City Tour.** Explore Native history at Shakes Island, the Wrangell
Museum, and Petroglyph Beach. *2 hrs. Cost: $26.*

Stikine River Tour. Experience a thrilling jet-boat ride to the
Stikine River. Visit Shakes Glacier, traveling in and around the
icebergs, explore the back-slough and clear-water tributaries and
listen to tales of gold-mining and fur trapping. *4 hrs. Cost: $140–
$150.*

Coming   Cruise ships calling in Wrangell dock downtown, within walking
Ashore   distance of the museum and gift stores. Greeters welcome passengers and are available to answer questions. The chamber of commerce visitor center is next to the dock inside the Stikine Inn.

Wrangell's few attractions—most notably its totem park—is
within walking distance of the pier. To get to Petroglyph Beach
(*see* Exploring, *below*), where you find rocks marked with mysterious prehistoric symbols, you'll need to take a shore excursion or
hire a cab. Call **Porky's Cab Co.** (tel. 907/874–3603) or **Star Cab** (tel.
907/874–3622).

Exploring *Numbers in the margin correspond to points of interest on the
Wrangell Wrangell map.*

❶ Walking up Front Street will bring you to **Kiksadi Totem Park,** a
pocket park of Alaska greenery and impressive totem poles. This
is the spot for a pleasant stroll.

On your way to Wrangell's number-one attraction—Chief Shakes
❷ Island—stop at **Chief Shakes's grave site,** uphill from the Wrangell
shipyard on Case Avenue. Buried here is Shakes VI, the last of a
succession of chiefs who bore that name. He led the local Tlingits

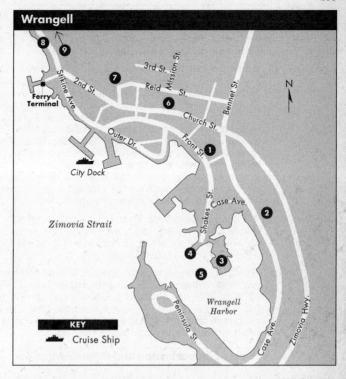

during the first half of the 19th century. Two killer-whale totems mark the chief's burial place.

❸ On **Chief Shakes Island,** reached by a footbridge off the harbor dock, you can see some of the finest totem poles in Alaska, as well as a tribal house constructed in the 1930s as a replica of one that was home to many of the various Shakes and their peoples. You'll see six totems on the island, two of them more than 100 years old. The original corner posts of the tribal house are in the museum. The house is open for visitors when ships are in port. *Tel. 907/874–2023 or 907/874–3747. Admission: $1 donation requested.*

After your visit to Chief Shakes Island, wander out to the end of the dock for the view and for picture taking at the **seaplane float** ❹ ❺ and **boat harbor.**

❻ The **Wrangell City Museum's** historical collection includes totem fragments, petroglyphs, and other Native artifacts; a bootlegger's still; a vintage 1800s Linotype and presses; and a cedar-bark basket collection. *318 Church St., tel. 907/874–3770. Admission: $2. Open summer weekdays 10–5, Sat. 1–5, and, when cruise ships are in port.*

❼ Outside the **public library** (124 2nd Ave., tel. 907/874–3535) are a couple of ancient petroglyphs. It's worth seeing if you don't plan to make the trip to Petroglyph Beach (*see below*).

❽ To some, the artifacts that make up **"Our Collections"** by owner Elva Bigelow constitute less a museum than a garage sale waiting to happen. Still, large numbers of viewers seem quite taken by the literally thousands of unrelated collectibles (clocks, animal traps, waffle irons, tools, etc.) that the Bigelows have gathered in a half century of Alaska living. *Evergreen Ave., tel. 907/874–3646. Donations accepted. Call before setting out to visit.*

⑨ **Petroglyph Beach** is undoubtedly one of the more curious sights in Southeast Alaska. Here, scattered among other rocks along the shore, are three dozen or more large stones bearing designs and pictures chiseled by unknown ancient artists. No one knows why the rocks were etched the way they were. Perhaps they were boundary markers or messages; possibly they were just primitive doodling. Because the petroglyphs can be damaged by physical contact, the state discourages visitors from creating a "rubbing" off the rocks with rice paper and crayons. Instead, you can photograph the petroglyphs or purchase a rubber-stamp duplicate of selected petroglyphs from the city museum. Do not, of course, attempt to move any of the petroglyph stones.

Shopping A unique souvenir from Wrangell is a natural garnet, gathered at Garnet Ledge, facing the Stikine River. The semiprecious gems are sold on the streets by the children of Wrangell for 50¢ to $50, depending on their size and quality.

Dining Wrangell's dining options are limited, with no real standouts. Sev-
$ eral local restaurants, including the **Stikine Inn** (107 Front St., tel. 907/874–3388) and **Diamond C Cafe** (214 Front St., tel. 907/874–3677), offer standard fill-you-up American fare. The best bet for visitors is probably **Waterfront Grill** (214 Front St., tel. 907/874–2353) for homemade pizzas, salads, and burgers.

Ports of Embarkation and Disembarkation

San Francisco The entire dock area of San Francisco is a tourist neighborhood of entertainment, shops, and restaurants called the Embarcadero. There's plenty to see and do within easy walking distance of the cruise ship terminals. With your back to the cruise pier, turn right to get to Fisherman's Wharf, Ghirardelli Square, and the Maritime Museum. If you don't want to walk, Bus 32 travels along the Embarcadero. You can also pick up a ferry to Alcatraz at Pier 41.

Long-Term A five-story public garage is one block from the cruise terminal at
Parking Pier 35. Parking is $8 per day.

From the San Francisco International Airport, one of the busiest in the
Airport country, is about 14 mi (22 km) from the cruise pier. A cab ride from the airport to the cruise pier costs a flat rate of $34 and takes 25–30 minutes, depending upon traffic. Less expensive ($12 per person) shuttle buses and shared stretch limousines can be picked up curbside at the airport, but they take longer. Make sure the shuttle or limousine will drop you off at the cruise pier.

Vancouver Many travelers consider British Columbia's Vancouver one of the most beautiful cities in the world, so it is only appropriate that its cruise ship terminal is also one of the most convenient and attractive. Right on the downtown waterfront, the Canada Place terminal is instantly recognizable by its rooftop of dramatic sails. Inside are shops and restaurants. Porters are courteous and taxis plentiful.

If you are early, consider visiting historic Gastown just a couple of blocks away (to the left if you have your back to the water).

Long-Term Parking at **Citipark** (tel. 604/684–2251 for reservations) at Canada
Parking Place costs C$14 per day for cruise ship passengers who pay in advance. Cheaper rates (less than C$10 a day) are available at cer-

tain hotels near the terminal, but you will need to take a cab between your car and the ship.

From the Airport Vancouver International Airport is approximately 17½ km (11 mi) away from Canada Place, but the road weaves through residential neighborhoods instead of highways. A taxi from the airport costs about C$25 and takes about 25 minutes.

Cruise-line bus transfers from the Vancouver and Seattle airports are the most convenient, providing baggage handling and, for those with flights into Seattle, customs clearance. If for some reason you cannot connect with one of these buses, **Vancouver Airporter Service** (tel. 604/244–9888 or 800/668–3141) provides fast, frequent bus service between the Vancouver airport and the Pan Pacific Hotel at Canada Place for C$10 one-way, C$17 round-trip. From Seattle's SeaTac Airport, **Quick Shuttle** (tel. 604/244–3744 or 800/665–2122) makes the four- to five-hour bus trip for $35 one-way, $63 round-trip.

Caribbean and the Bahamas

Nowhere in the world are conditions better suited to cruising than in the Caribbean Sea. Tiny island nations, within easy sailing distance of one another, form a chain of tropical enchantment that curves from Cuba in the north all the way down to the coast of Venezuela. There's far more to life here than sand and coconuts, however. The islands are vastly different, with their own cultures, topographies, and languages. Colonialism has left its mark, and the presence of the Spanish, French, Dutch, Danish, and British is still felt. Slavery, too, has left its cultural legacy, blending African overtones into the colonial/Indian amalgam. The one constant, however, is the weather. Despite the islands' southerly position, the climate is surprisingly gentle, due in large part to the cooling influence of the trade winds.

The Caribbean is made up of the Greater Antilles and the Lesser Antilles. The former consists of those islands closest to the United States: Cuba, Jamaica, Hispaniola (Haiti and the Dominican Republic), and Puerto Rico. (The Cayman Islands lie south of Cuba.) The Lesser Antilles, including the Virgin, Windward, and Leeward islands and others, are greater in number but smaller in size, and constitute the southern half of the Caribbean chain.

More cruise ships ply these waters than any others in the world. There are big ships and small ships, fancy ships and party ships. In peak season, it's not uncommon for thousands of passengers to disembark from several ships into a small town on the same day—a phenomenon not always enjoyed by locals. With such an abundance of cruise ships in this area, however, you can choose an itinerary that suits you best. Cruises of the western Caribbean often include port calls in Key West, in Cozumel, and sometimes in Guatemala. Eastern Caribbean itineraries usually stop at Nassau in the Bahamas. (For seasonal itineraries, *see* Chapter 4.)

When to Go Average year-round temperatures throughout the Caribbean are 78°F–85°F, with a low of 65°F and a high of 95°F; downtown shopping areas always seem to be unbearably hot. High season runs from December 15 to April 14; during this most fashionable, most expensive, and most crowded time to go, reservations up to a year in advance are necessary for many ships. A low-season (summer) visit offers certain advantages: Temperatures are virtually the same as in winter (even cooler on average than in parts of the U.S. mainland), island flora is at its peak, and the water is smoother and clearer. Some tourist facilities close down in summer, however, and many ships move to Europe, Alaska, or the northeastern United States.

Hurricane season runs from June 1 through November 30. Although cruise ships stay well out of the way of these storms, hurricanes and tropical storms—their less-powerful relatives—can affect the weather throughout the Caribbean for days, and damage to ports can force last-minute itinerary changes.

Currency Currencies vary throughout the islands, but U.S. dollars credit cards are widely accepted. Don't bother changing more than a few dollars into local currency for phone calls, tips, and taxis.

Passports and Visas American citizens boarding ships in the United States usually need neither a passport nor visas to call at ports in the Caribbean.

However, carrying a passport is always a good idea. Citizens of Canada and the United Kingdom should consult with their travel agent or cruise line regarding any documentation they may need for a Caribbean cruise.

Shore Excursions Typical excursions include a bus tour of the island or town, a visit to a local beach or rum factory, boat trips, snorkeling or diving, and charter fishing. As far as island tours go, it's always safest to take a ship-arranged excursion, but it's almost never cheapest. You also sacrifice the freedom to explore at your own pace and the joys of venturing off the beaten path.

If you seek adventure, find a knowledgeable taxi driver or tour operator—they're usually within a stone's throw of the pier—and wander around on your own. A group of four to six people will find this option more economical and practical than will a single person or a couple.

Renting a car is also a good option on many islands—again, the more people, the better the deal. But get a good island map before you set off, and be sure to find out how long it will take you to get around. The boat will leave without you unless you're on a ship-arranged tour.

Conditions are ideal for water sports of all kinds; scuba diving, snorkeling, windsurfing, sailing, waterskiing, and fishing excursions abound. Your shore-excursion director can usually arrange these activities for you individually if the ship offers no formal excursion.

Many ships throw beach parties on a private island or an isolated beach in the Bahamas, the Grenadines, or (depending on the current political climate) Haiti. These parties are either included in your fare, with snorkeling gear and other water-sports equipment extra, or offered as an optional tour for which you pay.

Golf is popular among cruise passengers. For more information, *see* the section on Hints for Sports Enthusiasts *in* the Cruise Primer.

Dining Cuisine on the Caribbean's islands is hard to classify. The region's history as a colonial battleground and ethnic melting pot creates plenty of variety. The gourmet French delicacies of Martinique, for example, are far removed from the hearty Spanish casseroles of Puerto Rico and even farther from the pungent curries of St. Lucia.

The one quality that defines most Caribbean cooking is its essential spiciness. Seafood is naturally quite popular. Some of it is even unique to the region, such as Caribbean lobster: Clawless and tougher than other types, it is more like crawfish than Maine lobster. And no island menu is complete without at least one dish featuring conch—a mollusk served in the form of chowders, fritters, salads, and cocktails. Dress is generally casual, though throughout the islands beachwear is often inappropriate.

Category	Cost*
$$$	over $30
$$	$15–$30
$	under $15

*per person for a three-course meal, excluding drinks, service, and sales tax

The Caribbean

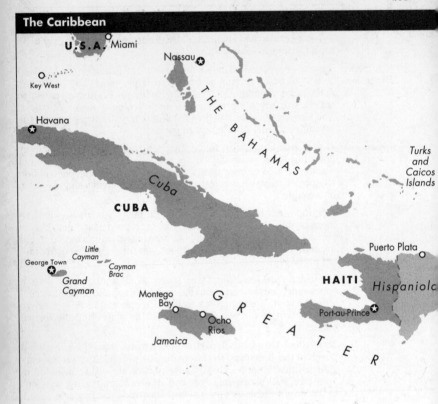

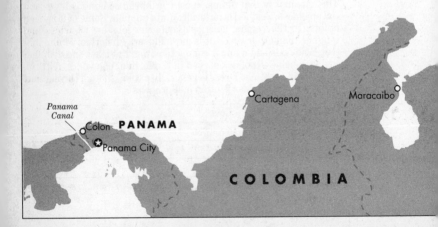

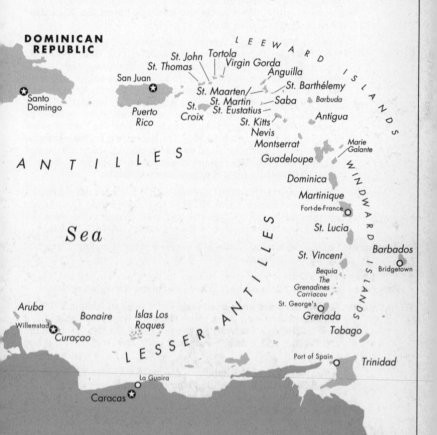

ATLANTIC OCEAN

DOMINICAN
REPUBLIC

LEEWARD ISLANDS

St. John Tortola
St. Thomas Virgin Gorda
San Juan Anguilla
Santo St. Maarten/ St. Barthélemy
Domingo St. Martin Saba Barbuda
Puerto St. St. Eustatius Antigua
Rico Croix St. Kitts
ANTILLES Nevis
Montserrat Marie
Guadeloupe Galante

Sea Dominica

Martinique
Fort-de-France

St. Lucia

WINDWARD ISLANDS

St. Vincent Barbados
Bequia Bridgetown
The
Grenadines
Aruba Carriacou
Bonaire Islas Los St. George's
Willemstad Roques Grenada
Curaçao Tobago

LESSER ANTILLES

Port of Spain Trinidad

La Guaira

Caracas

VENEZUELA

0 ——— 200 miles
0 ——— 300 km

Antigua

Some say Antigua has so many beaches that you could visit a different one every day for a year. Most have snow-white sand, and many are backed by lavish resorts that offer sailing, diving, windsurfing, and snorkeling.

The larger of the British Leeward Islands, Antigua was the headquarters from which Lord Horatio Nelson (then a mere captain) made his forays against the French and pirates in the late 18th century. A decidedly British atmosphere still prevails, underscored by a collection of pubs that will raise the spirits of every Anglophile. If you have a taste for history you'll want to explore English Harbour and its carefully restored Nelson's Dockyard, as well as tour an 18th-century Royal Naval base, old forts, historic churches, and tiny villages. If you like to hike, you can wander through a tropical rain forest lush with pineapples, bananas, and mangoes. If you have an interest in archaeology you can head for the megaliths of Greencastle and explore some of the 30 excavations of ancient Indian sites.

About 4,000 years ago Antigua was home to a people called the Ciboney. They disappeared mysteriously, and the island remained uninhabited for about 1,000 years. When Columbus sighted the 173-square-km (108-square-mi) island in 1493, the Arawaks had already set up housekeeping. The English moved in 130 years later, in 1623. Then a sequence of bloody battles involving the Caribs, the Dutch, the French, and the English began. Africans had been captured as slaves to work the sugar plantations by the time the French ceded the island to the English in 1667. On November 1, 1981, Antigua, with Barbuda, its sister island 48 km (30 mi) to the north, achieved full independence. The combined population of the two islands is about 70,000—only 1,200 of whom live on Barbuda.

Currency Antigua uses the Eastern Caribbean (EC) dollar, commonly known as beewees. Figure about EC$2.70 to U.S.$1. While U.S. dollars are generally accepted, you may get your change in beewees. All prices given below are in U.S. dollars except where indicated.

Telephones Calling the United States is a simple matter of dialing 1 to reach AT&T's USADirect.

Shore Excursions The following are good choices in Antigua. They may not be offered by all cruise lines. Times and prices are approximate.

Island Sights **Nelson's Dockyard and Countryside.** Get a sense of Antigua's British Colonial history with great views along the way. The highlight is a visit to Nelson's Dockyard, a gem of Georgian British maritime architecture and a must for history buffs and Anglophiles. *3 hrs. Cost: $35.*

If you want to feel like Indiana Jones, opt for a tour with **Tropikelly** (tel. 809/461–0383). You'll be given an insider's look at the whole island by four-wheel drive, complete with deserted plantation houses, rain-forest trails, ruined sugar mills and forts, and even a picnic lunch with drinks. The highlight is the luxuriant tropical forest around the island's highest point, Boggy Peak. *5 hrs. Cost: $60.*

Coming Ashore Though some ships dock at the deep-water harbor in downtown St. John's, most use the town's Heritage Quay, a multimillion-dollar complex with shops, condominiums, a casino, and a food court. Most St. John's attractions are an easy walk from Heritage Quay; the older part of the city is eight blocks away. A tourist information booth is in the main docking building.

If you intend to explore beyond St. John's consider hiring a taxi driver-guide. Taxis meet every cruise ship. They're unmetered; fares are fixed, and drivers are required to carry a rate card. Agree on the fare before setting off, and plan to tip drivers 10%.

Exploring Antigua *Numbers in the margin correspond to points of interest on the Antigua map.*

❶ St. John's is home to about 40,000 people (more than half the island's population). The city has seen better days, but there are some notable sights. At the far south end of town, where Market Street forks into Valley and All Saints roads, locals jam the marketplace every Friday and Saturday to buy and sell fruits, vegetables, fish, and spices. Be sure to ask before you aim a camera, and expect the subject of your shot to ask for a tip.

If you have a serious interest in archaeology, see the historical displays at the **Museum of Antigua and Barbuda.** The colonial building that houses the museum is the former courthouse, which dates from 1750. *Church and Market Sts., tel. 268/462–1469. Admission free. Open weekdays 8:30–4, Sat. 10–1.*

Two blocks east of the Museum of Antigua and Barbuda on Church Street is the Anglican **St. John's Cathedral,** which sits on a hilltop, surrounded by its churchyard. At the south gate are figures said to have been taken from one of Napoléon's ships. A previous structure on this site was destroyed by an earthquake in 1843, so the interior of the current church is completely encased in pitch pine to forestall heavy damage from future quakes. *Between Long and Newcastle Sts., tel. 268/461–0082. Admission free.*

❷ A favorite car excursion is to follow Fort Road northwest out of town. After 3 km (2 mi) you'll come to the ruins of **Ft. James,** named for King James II. If you continue on this road, you'll arrive at Dickenson Bay, with its string of smart, expensive resorts on one of many beautiful beaches.

❸ In the opposite direction from St. John's, 13 km (8 mi) south on All Saints Road is **Liberta,** one of the first settlements founded by freed slaves. East of the village, on Monk's Hill, are the ruins of Ft. George, built in 1669.

❹ Falmouth, 2¼ km (1½ mi) farther south, sits on a lovely bay, backed by former sugar plantations and sugar mills. St. Paul's Church, dating from the late 18th and early 19th centuries, held services for the military in Nelson's time; it has been restored and is now used for Sunday worship.

❺ English Harbour, the most famous of Antigua's attractions, lies on the coast just south of Falmouth. The Royal Navy abandoned the station in 1889, but it has been restored as Nelson's Dockyard, which epitomizes the colonial Caribbean. Within the compound are crafts shops, hotels, a marina, and restaurants. The Admiral's House Museum has several rooms displaying ship models, a model of English Harbour, and various artifacts from Nelson's days. *Tel. 268/463–1053. Admission: $2. Open daily 8–6.*

The English Harbor area has a number of other attractions. On a ridge overlooking Nelson's Dockyard is Clarence House, built in 1787 and once the home of the duke of Clarence (unfortunately, tours are no longer given to the public). As you leave the dockyard, turn right at the crossroads in English Harbour and drive up to **❻** Shirley Heights for a spectacular harbor view. Nearby, the **Dows Hill Interpretation Center** chronicles the island's history and culture

Antigua

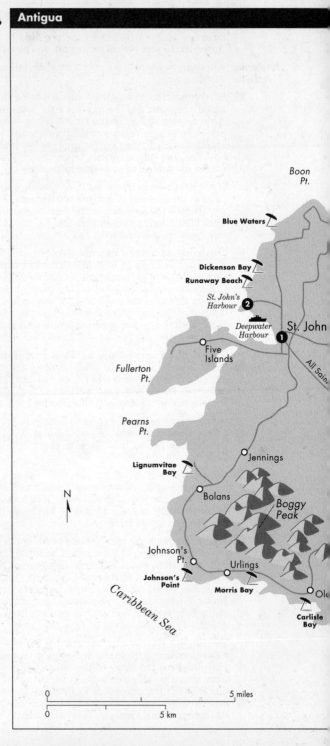

Boon
Pt.

Blue Waters

Dickenson Bay
Runaway Beach

St. John's
Harbour **2**

Deepwater
Harbour **1**

St. John

All Sain

○ Five
Islands

Fullerton
Pt.

Pearns
Pt.

○ Jennings

Lignumvitae
Bay

○ Bolans

Boggy
Peak

N

Johnson's
Pt. ○

○ Urlings

Johnson's
Point

Morris Bay

○ Old

Caribbean Sea

Carlisle
Bay

0 — 5 miles

0 — 5 km

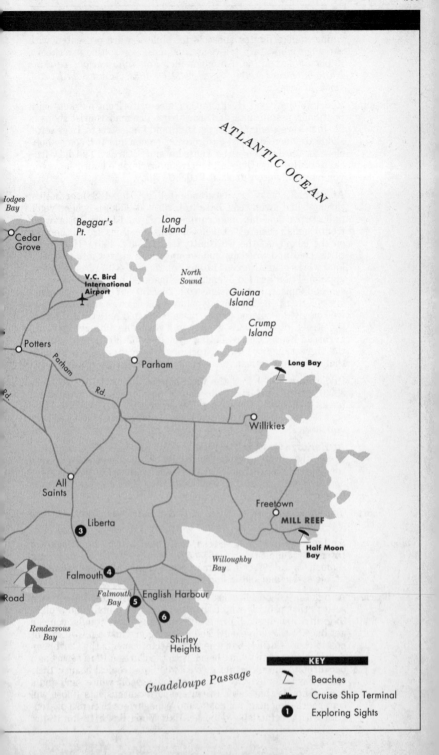

from Amerindian times to the present. A highlight of the center is its multimedia presentation in which illuminated displays, incorporating lifelike figures and colorful tableaux, are presented with running commentary, television, and music—resulting in a cheery, if bland, portrait of Antiguan life. *For information, call the National Parks Authority, tel. 268/460–1053. Admission: EC$15. Open daily 9–5.*

Shopping   Redcliffe Quay and Heritage Quay are waterfront markets with boutiques, restaurants, and snack bars. The main tourist shops in St. John's are along St. Mary's, High, and Long streets. In general, shops are open Monday–Saturday 8:30–noon and 1–4; some shops close for the day at noon on Thursday and Saturday. The duty-free shops of Heritage Quay often have more flexible hours; however, you may find better deals at Redcliffe Quay.

At Redcliffe Quay, try **Jacaranda** (tel. 268/ 462–1888) for batiks, sarongs, and swimwear. **Base** (tel. 268/460–2500) is where you'll find striped and hip monochrome cotton-and-Lycra resortwear from English designer Steven Giles; his creations are all the rage on the island. At the **Goldsmitty** (tel. 268/462–4601), Hans Smit turns gold and precious and semiprecious stones into one-of-a-kind works of art. **Noreen Phillips** (tel. 268/462–3127) creates glitzy appliqued and beaded eveningwear inspired by the colors of the sea and sunset. **Kate Designs** (tel. 268/460–5971) sells acclaimed artist Kate Spencer's flowing painted silk scarves and sarongs, as well as vividly colored prints, place mats, and note cards. Across the street, down a narrow alley in a charming 19th-century gingerbread house, **Coates Cottage** (tel. 268/462–3636) sells some of the highest-quality local artwork at the lowest prices—a bonus is that artists and artisans often use the space as a temporary studio.

In downtown St. John's, the **Map Shop** (St. John's St., tel. 268/462–3993) has a wonderful collection of antique maps and nautical books and charts. **CoCo Shop** (St. Mary's St., tel. 268/462–1128) sells Sea Island cotton designs, Daks clothing, and Liberty of London fabrics.

At Heritage Quay, **La Casa Habana** (tel. 268/462–2677) has Cuban cigars (though these cannot be legally brought back with you into the United States.) You'll also find a wide range of duty-free shops and factory-outlet stores, from **Body Shop** and **Benetton,** to **Polo** to **Gucci.**

Sports   You'll find an 18-hole course at **Cedar Valley Golf Club** (tel. 268/
Golf   462–0161).

Scuba Diving   Antigua has plenty of wrecks, reefs, and marine life. **Dockyard Divers** (St. Johns, tel. 268/464–8591), run by British ex–merchant seaman Captain A. G. Finchman, is one of the oldest and most reputable diving and snorkeling outfits on the island.

Beaches   Antigua's 366 beaches are public, and many are dotted with resorts that provide water-sports equipment rentals and a place to grab a cool drink. Since most hotels have taxi stands, you can get back to the ship easily. The following are just a few excellent possibilities: **Carlisle Bay,** where the Atlantic meets the Caribbean Sea, is a long, snow-white beach with the Curtain Bluff resort as a backdrop. A large coconut grove adds to its tropical beauty. **Dickenson Bay** has a lengthy stretch of powder-soft white sand and a host of hotels that cater to water-sports enthusiasts (most will rent snorkeling gear, sailboats, and Windsurfers to cruise passengers with a refundable deposit). **Half Moon Bay,** a 1½-km (¾-mi) crescent of shell-pink sand, is another great place for snorkeling and windsurfing. **Johnson's Point** is a deliciously deserted beach of bleached white sand on the southwest coast.

Dining   In restaurants a 10% service charge and 7% tax is usually added to the bill.

$$ **Admiral's Inn.** Known simply as "the Ads" to yachtsmen around the world, this historic inn in the heart of English Harbour is a must for Anglophiles and mariners. Dine on velvety pumpkin soup, fresh snapper with lime, or lobster thermidor while taking in the splendid harbor views. *Nelson's Dockyard, tel. 268/460–1027. Reservations essential. AE, MC, V.*

$$ **Redcliffe Tavern.** Set amid the courtyards of Redcliffe Quay, on the second floor of a colonial warehouse, this appealing restaurant has an inventive menu that's part northern Italian, part Continental, part Creole, and all fresh. Antique water-pumping equipment, salvaged from all over the island, adds to the unusual dining experience. *Redcliffe Quay, St. John's, tel. 268/461–4557. AE, MC, V.*

Aruba

Though the "A" in the ABC (Aruba, Bonaire, Curaçao) Islands is small—only 31 km (19 mi) long and 10 km (6 mi) at its widest—the island's national anthem proclaims "the greatness of our people is their great cordiality," and this is no exaggeration. Once a member of the Netherlands Antilles, Aruba became independent within the Netherlands in 1986, with its own royally appointed governor, a democratic government, and a 21-member elected parliament. Long secure in a solid economy—with good education, housing, and health care—the island's population of nearly 89,000 treats visitors as welcome guests. Waiters serve you with smiles and solid eye contact. English is spoken everywhere.

The island's distinctive beauty lies in the stark contrast between the sea and the countryside: rocky deserts, cactus jungles, secluded coves, and aquamarine panoramas with crashing waves. It's famous mostly, however, for its duty-free shops, the glorious 11.3-km (7-mi) strand of Palm and Eagle beaches, and casinos.

Currency   Arubans accept U.S. dollars, so you need only exchange a little money for pocket change. Local currency is the Aruban florin (AFl). At press time, the exchange rate was AFl 1.77 to U.S.$1. Note that the Netherlands Antilles florin used in Bonaire and Curaçao is not accepted on Aruba. All prices given below are in U.S. dollars except where indicated.

Telephones   International calls are placed at the phone center in the cruise ship terminal. To reach the United States, dial 001, the area code, and the local number.

Shore Excursions   The following are good choices on Aruba. They may not be offered by all cruise lines. Times and prices are approximate.

Island Sights   **Aruba Town and Countryside Drive.** A comprehensive town-and-country bus tour takes in the major island sights, including the breathtaking limestone Natural Bridge; the California Lighthouse, set amid vanilla sand dunes; the desolate Alto Vista Chapel; boulder formations that resemble abstract sculptures; and various caves stippled with petroglyphs and fanciful stalactites and stalagmites shaped like the Madonna or a jaguar. After the tour, passengers may stay in town, on the beach, or at the casino. *3 hrs. Cost: $28.*

Undersea   **Atlantis Submarine.** Aboard a 65-ft submarine, passengers dive
Creatures   50–90 ft below the surface along Aruba's Barcadera Reef. *2 hrs.
             Cost: $72.*

             Glass-Bottom Boat Tour. The view of undersea creatures is less
             dramatic than aboard the *Atlantis* submarine, but the price is less
             expensive, too. *2 hrs. Cost: $40.*

Coming   Ships tie up at the Aruba Port Authority cruise terminal; inside
Ashore   are a tourist information booth and duty-free shops. From here,
             you're a five-minute walk from various shopping districts and
             downtown Oranjestad. Just turn right out of the cruise-terminal
             entrance.

             The "real" Aruba—what's left of its wild, untamed beauty—can
             only be experienced on a drive through the countryside (though
             be aware that, except for those in a few restaurants, there are no
             public bathrooms). Since car rental agencies are friendly but slow
             and roads aren't always clearly marked, your best bet is to hire a
             taxi (you can flag one in the street). Rates are fixed (i.e., there are
             no meters), so confirm the fare before setting off—whether your
             journey is across town or farther afield. It should cost about $25 an
             hour for up to four people.

Exploring   *Numbers in the margin correspond to points of interest on the
Aruba   Aruba map.*

❶   Aruba's charming capital, **Oranjestad,** is best explored on foot. If
             you're interested in Dutch architecture, begin at the corner of
             Oude School Straat and walk three blocks toward the harbor to
             Wilhelminastraat, where some of the buildings date from Oranjes-
             tad's 1790 founding. Walk west and you'll pass old homes, a gov-
             ernment building, and the Protestant church. When you reach
             Shuttestraat again, turn left and go one block to Zoutmanstraat.

             The small **Archaeology Museum** in Oranjestad has two rooms of
             Indian artifacts, farm and domestic utensils, and skeletons. *Zout-
             manstraat 1, tel. 297/8–28979. Admission free. Open weekdays 8–
             noon and 1–4.*

             Ft. Zoutman, the island's oldest building, was built in 1796 and used
             as a major fortress in skirmishes between British and Curaçao
             troops. The Willem III Tower was added in 1868. The fort's
             museum displays island relics and artifacts in an 18th-century
             Aruban house. *Oranjestraat, tel. 297/8–26099. Admission: $1.15.
             Open weekdays 9–noon and 1:30–4:30.*

             Just behind the St. Francis Roman Catholic Church is the **Numis-
             matic Museum,** displaying coins and paper money from more than
             400 countries. *Zuidstraat 7, tel. 297/8–28831. Admission free.
             Open weekdays 7:30–noon and 1–4:30.*

❷   The 541-ft peak of **Hooiberg** (Haystack Hill) is mid-island; you can
             climb 562 steps to the top for an impressive view. To get there
             from Oranjestad, turn onto Caya C. F. Croes (shown on island
             maps as 7A) toward Santa Cruz; the peak will be on your right.

             For a shimmering panorama of blue-green sea, drive east on L. G.
             Smith Boulevard toward San Nicolas. Turn left where you see the
             drive-in theater. At the first intersection, turn right, then follow
❸   the curve to the right to **Frenchman's Pass,** a dark, luscious stretch
             of highway arbored by overhanging trees. Legend claims the
             French and native Indians warred here during the 17th century
             for control of the island.

❹ Near Frenchman's Pass are the cement and limestone ruins of the **Balashi Gold Mine** (follow the directions to Frenchman's Pass, *above*, and then take the dirt road veering to the right), a lovely place to picnic, listen to the parakeets, and contemplate the towering cacti. A gnarled divi-divi tree stands guard at the entrance.

❺ The area called **Spanish Lagoon** is where pirates once hid to repair their ships (follow L. G. Smith Boulevard, which crosses straight over the lagoon). It's a picturesque place for a picnic or to enjoy the island scenery.

❻ **San Nicolas** is Aruba's oldest village. In the 1980s, the town, with its oil refinery, was a bustling port with a rough-and-tumble quality; now it's dedicated to tourism, with the Main Street promenade full of interesting kiosks. Charlie's Bar (Zeppenfeldstraat 56) on the main street is a popular tourist lunch spot; while you eat your "jumbo and dumbo" shrimp, you can gawk at the thousands of license plates, old credit cards, baseball pennants, and hard hats covering every inch of the walls and ceiling.

Shopping Caya G. F. Betico Croes in Oranjestad is Aruba's chief shopping street. Several malls—gabled, pastel-hued recreations of traditional Dutch colonial architecture—house branches of such top names as Tommy Hilfiger, Little Switzerland, Nautica, and Benetton; the ritziest are the Royal Plaza and Seaport Village Malls, both right near the cruise ship pier. The stores are full of Dutch porcelains and figurines, as befits the island's Netherlands heritage. Also consider the Dutch cheeses (you're allowed to bring up to 1 pound of hard cheese through U.S. Customs), hand-embroidered linens, and any product made from the native aloe vera plant (sunburn cream, face masks, and skin fresheners). There's no sales tax, and Arubans consider it rude to haggle.

Artesania Aruba (L. G. Smith Blvd. 178, tel. 297/8–37494) has charming home-crafted pottery and folk objets d'art. **Aruba Trading Company** (Caya G. F. Betico Croes 12, tel. 297/8–22602) discounts brand-name perfumes and cosmetics (first floor), and jewelry and men's and women's clothes (second floor) up to 30%. **Gandelman Jewelers** (Caya G. F. Betico Croes 5–A, tel. 297/8–34433) sells jewelry as well as full line of watches. **Wulfsen & Wulfsen** (Caya G. F. Betico Croes 52, tel. 297/8–23823) is one of Holland's best stores for fine-quality clothes and shoes.

Sports Contact **De Palm Tours** in Oranjestad (tel. 297/8–24400 or 800/766–
Fishing 6016) for information on fishing charters.

Golf The Robert Trent Jones–designed, 18-hole, par-71 course, **Tierra del Sol** (Malmokweg, tel. 297/8–67800), sits on the northwest coast near the California Lighthouse. It combines Aruba's native beauty—the flora and rock formations—with the lush greens of the world's best courses. The $120 greens fee includes a golf cart. Club rentals are $25–$45. The **Aruba Golf Club** near San Nicolas (tel. 297/8–42006) has a nine-hole course with 20 sand and five water traps, roaming goats, and lots of cacti. Greens fees are $7.50 for nine holes, $10 for 18. Caddies and rental clubs are available.

Hiking **De Palm Tours** (tel. 297/8–24400 or 800/766–6016) offers a guided three-hour trip to remote sites of unusual natural beauty that are accessible only on foot. The fee is $25 per person, including refreshments and transportation; a minimum of four people is required.

Horseback At **Rancho El Paso** (tel. 297/8–63310), one-hour jaunts ($25) take
Riding you through countryside flanked by cacti, divi-divi trees, and aloe

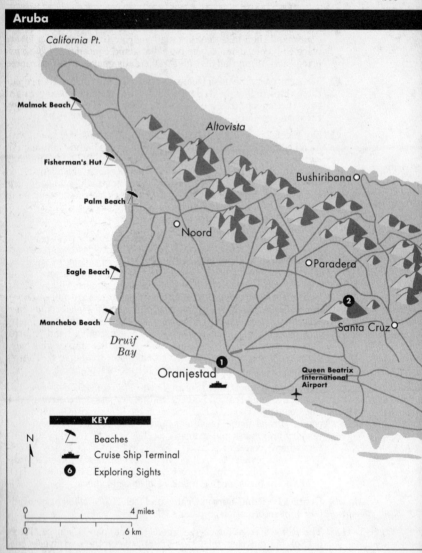

Aruba

California Pt.

Malmok Beach

Fisherman's Hut

Palm Beach

Noord

Altovista

Bushiribana

Paradera

Eagle Beach

Manchebo Beach

Santa Cruz

Druif Bay

Oranjestad

Queen Beatrix
International
Airport

KEY

N

Beaches

Cruise Ship Terminal

6 Exploring Sights

0 — 4 miles

0 — 6 km

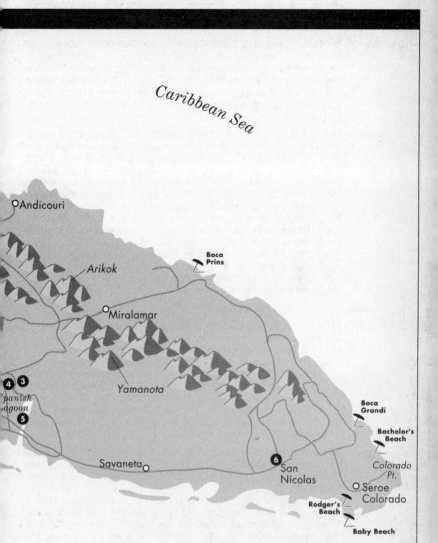

vera plants; two-hour trips ($35) go to the beach as well. Wear lots of sunblock.

Water Sports **De Palm Tours** (tel. 297/8–24400 or 800/766–6016) has a near monopoly on water sports, including equipment and instruction for scuba diving, snorkeling, and windsurfing. However, **Pelican Watersports** (tel. 297/8–63600 or 297/8–31228) and **Red Sail Sports** (tel. 297/8–61603) may offer cheaper rates on water-sports packages, including those for snorkeling, sailing, windsurfing, fishing, and scuba diving.

Beaches Beaches in Aruba are not only beautiful but clean. On the north side the water is too choppy for swimming, but the views are great. **Palm Beach**—which stretches behind the Americana, Aruba Palm Beach, Holiday Inn, Hyatt, Radisson, and Wyndham hotels—is the center of Aruban tourism, offering the best in swimming, sailing, and fishing. In high season, however, it's packed, and you might prefer the adjoining Eagle Beach, which is anchored by the minivillage of La Cabana Suite Resort and is even closer to town. **Manchebo Beach,** by the Bucuti Beach Resort, is an impressively wide stretch of white powder and Aruba's unofficial topless beach. On the island's eastern tip, tiny **Baby Beach** is as placid as a wading pool and only 4 or 5 ft deep—perfect for tots and bad swimmers. Thatched shaded areas provide relief from the sun. You'll see topless bathers here from time to time as well.

Dining Restaurants usually add a 10%–15% service charge.

$$$ **Chez Mathilde.** This elegant, romantic restaurant, occupies one of the last surviving 19th-century houses on the island. Dine either in the light-filled greenhouse atrium or a more intimate, swooningly romantic, antiques-filled room. The French-style menu is continually being re-created. Feast on the likes of artfully presented baked escargots with herbs and garlic, braised monkfish in watercress and vermouth sauce, or filet mignon in a signature pepper sauce prepared table-side. Then, too, there are crêpes suzettes and profiteroles to tempt the taste buds. *Havenstraat 23, Oranjestad, tel. 297/8–34968. Reservations essential. AE, MC, V. No lunch Sun.*

$–$$ **Boonoonoonoos.** The name—say it just as it looks!—means extraordinary, which is a bit of hyperbole for this Austrian-owned Caribbean bistro in the heart of town. The specialty here is Pan-Caribbean cuisine: The roast chicken Barbados is sweet and tangy, marinated in piña colada sauce. The Jamaican jerk ribs (a 300-year-old recipe) are tiny but spicy, and the satin-smooth hot pumpkin soup drizzled with cheese and served in a pumpkin shell may as well be dessert. Avoid the place if it's crowded, since the service and the quality of the food deteriorate. *Wilhelminastraat 18A, Oranjestad, tel. 297/8–31888. AE, MC, V. No lunch Sun.*

$ **Le Petit Café.** The motto here is "Romancing the Stone"—referring to tasty cuisine cooked on hot stones. The low ceiling and hanging plants make this an intimate lunch spot for shoppers. Alfresco dining in the bustling square lets you keep an eye on things, but fumes from nearby traffic tend to spoil the meal. Jumbo shrimp, sandwiches, ice cream, and fresh fruit dishes are light delights. *Emmastraat 1, Oranjestad, tel. 297/8–26577. AE, DC, MC, V. No lunch Sun.*

Barbados

Barbados is a sophisticated island with a lifestyle of its own that continues long after cruise passengers have packed up their suntan oils and returned to their ships. A resort island since the 1700s, Barbados has cultivated a civilized attitude toward tourists.

Under uninterrupted British rule for 340 years—until independence in 1966—Barbados retains a very British atmosphere. Afternoon tea is a ritual, and cricket is the national sport. The atmosphere, though, is hardly stuffy.

Beaches along the island's south and west coasts are spectacular, and all are open to cruise passengers. On the rugged east coast, where Bajans (as people in Barbados are called) themselves have vacation homes, the pounding Atlantic attracts world-class surfers. The northeast is dominated by rolling hills and valleys; the interior of the island is covered by impenetrable acres of sugarcane and dotted with small villages. Historic plantations, a stalactite-studded cave, a wildlife preserve, rum factories, and tropical gardens are among the island's more pleasing attractions, but Bridgetown, the capital, is a busy city with more traffic than charm.

Currency One Barbados dollar (BDS$) equals about U.S.50¢. Either currency is accepted everywhere on the island, as are major credit cards and travelers checks. Always ask which currency is being quoted. All prices given below are in U.S. dollars except where indicated.

Telephones Public pay phones and phone cards are available at the cruise ship terminal. Use the same direct-dialing procedure as in the United States, or dial for assistance with collect and credit-card calls. To charge international calls to a major credit card at direct-dialing rates, dial 800/877–8000.

Shore Excursions The following are good choices on Barbados. They may not be offered by all cruise lines. Times and prices are approximate.

Island Sights **Harrison's Cave and Island Tour.** After a bus tour of the island, passengers board an electric tram for a one-hour tour of this series of limestone caves. A highlight is the 40-ft underground waterfall that plunges into a deep underground pool. *4 hrs. Cost: $52.*

Undersea Creatures **Atlantis Submarine.** A 50-ft sub dives as deep as 150 ft below the surface for an exciting view of Barbados's profuse marine life. Most passengers find this trip to the depths to be a thrilling experience. *1½ hrs. Cost: $82.*

Coming Ashore Up to eight ships at a time can dock at Bridgetown's Deep Water Harbour, on the northwest side of Carlisle Bay. The cruise ship terminal has duty-free shops, handicraft vendors, a post office, a telephone station, a tourist information desk, and a taxi stand. To get downtown, follow the shoreline to the Careenage. On foot, it will take you about 15 minutes; you could also take a cab for $1.50 each way.

Taxis await ships at the pier. The fare to Brighton Beach, just north of Bridgetown, runs $3–$5; to Paynes Bay or Holetown, it's $7. Drivers accept U.S. dollars and appreciate a 10% tip. Taxis operate at a fixed hourly rate of $17.50 per carload (up to three passengers fit comfortably) and will cheerfully narrate an island tour.

Exploring Barbados *Numbers in the margin correspond to points of interest on the Barbados map.*

Bridgetown The narrow strip of sea known as the Careenage made early
❶ **Bridgetown** a natural harbor. In the old days, this is where working schooners were careened (turned on their sides), scraped of bar-

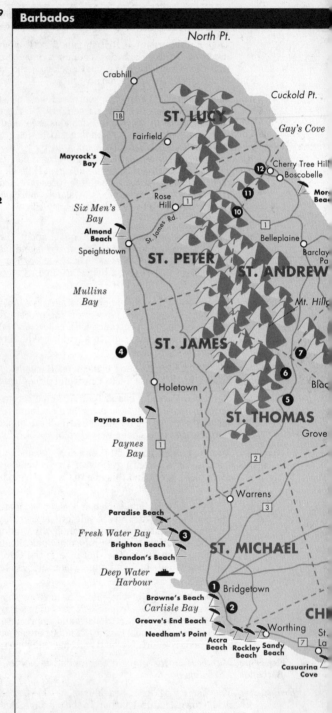

Barbados

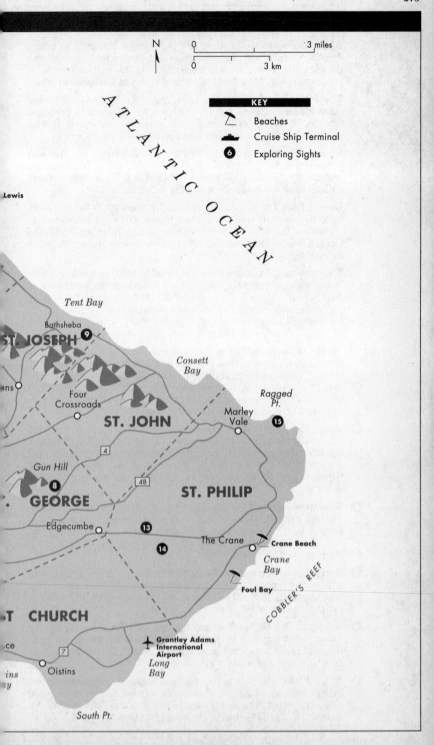

N

0 | 3 miles
0 | 3 km

KEY

Beaches
Cruise Ship Terminal
6 Exploring Sights

ATLANTIC OCEAN

Lewis

Tent Bay

Bathsheba

ST. JOSEPH **9**

Consett Bay

Ragged Pt.

Four Crossroads

Marley Vale

15

ST. JOHN

4

Gun Hill

8

4B

ST. PHILIP

GEORGE

Edgecumbe

13

The Crane

Crane Beach

14

Crane Bay

COBBLER'S REEF

Foul Bay

T CHURCH

7

Grantley Adams International Airport

Oistins

Long Bay

South Pt.

nacles, and repainted. Today, the Careenage serves mainly as a marina for pleasure yachts and excursion boats.

At the center of the bustling city is **Trafalgar Square.** The monument to Lord Nelson predates its London counterpart by about two decades. Also here are a war memorial and a three-dolphin fountain commemorating the advent of running water in Barbados in 1865.

The **Parliament Buildings** (c. 1870) house the third-oldest parliament of the British Commonwealth and are adjacent to Trafalgar Square. A series of stained-glass windows depicting British monarchs adorns these Victorian Gothic buildings.

George Washington is said to have worshiped at **St. Michael's Cathedral** on his only trip outside the United States. The structure was nearly a century old when he visited in 1751; destroyed twice by hurricanes, it was rebuilt in 1784 and again in 1831.

Queen's Park, northeast of downtown Bridgetown, is the site of an immense baobab tree more than 10 centuries old. The historic Queen's Park House, former home of the commander of the British troops, has been converted into a theater and a restaurant (open daily 9–5).

The intriguing **Barbados Museum** (about 1½ km/1 mi south of downtown Bridgetown on Highway 7) has artifacts dating from Arawak days (around 400 BC), mementos of military history and everyday life in the 19th century, wildlife and natural history exhibits, a well-stocked gift shop, and a good café. *Garrison Savannah, tel. 246/427–0201. Admission: $5 Open Mon.–Sat. 9–5, Sun. 2–6.*

Central Barbados/ West Coast **Tyrol Cot Heritage Village,** just south of Bridgetown, is a historic home constructed in 1854 and now the centerpiece of an outdoor "living" museum: colorful chattel houses all have a traditional artisan or craftsman at work inside. The crafts are for sale, and refreshments are available at the "rum shop." *St. Michael, tel. 246/424–2074 or 246/436–9033. Admission: $5. Open weekdays 9–5.*

③ **Mount Gay Rum Visitors Centre,** just 5 minutes north of the port, offers a 45-minute tour where you'll learn the story behind the world's oldest rum and the rum-making process. It concludes with a tasting, and you can buy still more rum at the gift shop. *Spring Garden Hwy., St. Michael, tel. 246/425–8757. Admission: $5. Open daily 9–4.*

④ **Folkestone Marine Park** has a museum of marine life and a snorkeling trail around Dottin's Reef. Nonswimmers can ride in a glass-bottom boat. A barge sunk in shallow water is home to myriad fish. *Hwy. 1, north of Holetown, St. James, tel. 246/422–2314. Admission: 50¢. Closed Mon.*

⑤ **Harrison's Cave,** a series of beautiful limestone caverns, complete with subterranean streams and a 40-ft waterfall, is toured by electric tram. *Hwy. 2, St. Thomas, tel. 246/438–6640. Admission: $7.50. Open daily 9–6.*

⑥ **Welchman Hall Gully** offers another opportunity to commune with nature, with acres of labeled flowers, the occasional green monkey, and great peace and quiet. *Hwy. 2, tel. 246/438–6671. Admission: BDS$10. Open daily 9–5.*

⑦ At the **Flower Forest,** you can meander through 8 acres of fragrant bushes, canna and ginger lilies, puffball trees, and more than 100 other species of flora in a tranquil setting. *Hwy. 2, Richmond, St. Joseph, tel. 246/433–8152. Admission: $6. Open daily 9–5.*

8 The view from **Gun Hill Signal Station** is so pretty it seems unreal. Fields of green and gold extend all the way to the horizon, and brilliant flowers surround a picturesque gun tower. The white limestone lion behind the garrison is a famous landmark. *St. George, tel. 246/429–1358. Admission: $4.. Open Mon.–Sat. 9–5.*

Northern The small but fascinating **Andromeda Gardens,** set into the cliffs
Barbados/ that spill into the Atlantic Ocean on the east coast, are planted
East Coast with unusual specimens from around the world. *Bathsheba, St.*
9 *Joseph, tel. 246/433–9384. Admission: $5. Open daily 9–5.*

10 At **Farley Hill,** a national park, you can roam through the imposing ruins of a once-magnificent plantation house and its surrounding gardens, lawns, and towering royal palms. From the back of the estate, there's a sweeping view of the area of Barbados called Scotland owing to its rugged landscape. *St. Peter, no phone. Admission: $1.50 per car, walkers free. Open daily 8:30–6.*

You'll encounter herons, land turtles, screeching peacocks, innumerable green monkeys, geese, brilliantly colored parrots, a kan-
11 garoo, and a friendly otter at the **Barbados Wildlife Reserve.** The fauna roam freely, so step carefully and keep your hands to yourself. *Farley Hill, St. Peter, tel. 246/422–8826. Admission: $10. Open daily 10–5.*

12 **St. Nicholas Abbey** is the oldest house on the island (c. 1650) and worth visiting for its stone and wood architecture in the Jacobean style. *Near Cherry Tree Hill, St. Lucy, tel. 246/422–8725. Admission: $2.50. Open weekdays 10–3:30.*

Southern **Sunbury Plantation House & Museum** has been lovingly rebuilt
Barbados after a 1995 fire destroyed everything but its 2½-ft thick walls.
13 This 300-year-old plantation house is once again an elegant representation of life on a Barbados sugar estate in the 18th and 19th centuries. A Bajan buffet lunch is served on the back patio. *St. Philip, tel. 246/423–6270. Admission: $5 tour only, $12.50 with lunch. Open daily 10–5.*

14 The **Rum Factory & Heritage Park** is a theme park that combines an operating high-tech rum distillery, the first to be built in Barbados in this century, with activities that showcase Bajan art, skills, and talents. Vendor carts and shops display local products, crafts, and foods. *Foursquare Sugar Plantation, St. Philip, tel. 246/423–6669. Admission: $12. Open Sun.–Thurs. 9–5, Fri.–Sat. 9–9.*

15 The appropriately named **Ragged Point Lighthouse** is where the sun first shines on Barbados and its dramatic Atlantic seascape.

Shopping Duty-free shopping is found in Bridgetown's Broad Street department stores and boutiquesand their branches at the cruise ship terminal. (Note that to purchase items duty-free, you must show your passport). Stores are generally open weekdays 8:30–4:30 and Saturdays 8:30–1.

For antiques and fine memorabilia, try **Greenwich House Antiques** (Greenwich Village, Trents Hill, St. James, tel. 246/432–1169). **Antiquaria** (Spring Garden Hwy., St. Michael's Row next to Anglican cathedral, Bridgetown, tel. 246/426–0635) is another good place to search for antiques.

Colours of the Caribbean (On the Wharf, Bridgetown, tel. 246/436–8522) is worth visiting for its original—and expensive—handmade clothing and accessories.

At Bridgetown's **Pelican Village Handicrafts Center** (Princess Alice Hwy. near Cheapside Market, tel. 246/426–4391) you can watch Bajan goods and crafts being made before you purchase them; woven straw rugs and mats are particularly good buys.

There are two **Chattel House Village** complexes (St. Lawrence Gap and Holetown), each a cluster of shops in brightly colored chattel houses. At **Best of Barbados** (tel. 246/436–1416), you'll find local products. Other shops sell rums and liqueurs, hand-designed clothing, beachwear, and souvenirs.

Sports *Fishing*	***Billfisher II*** (tel. 246/431-0741), a 40-ft. Pacemaker, accommodates up to 6 people for full- or half-day fishing trips. **Blue Jay Charters** (tel. 246/422–2098) has a 45-ft., fully equipped fishing boat with a knowledgeable crew; four fishermen can be accommodated, and each can invite, free of charge, a spouse or guest.
Golf	Several courses are open to cruise passengers:**Club Rockley Barbados** (tel. 246/435–7873), where there are 9 holes and the greens fee is $22.50, and **Royal Westmoreland Golf Club** (tel. 246/422–4653), which has 18 holes and a greens of $145. **Sandy Lane Golf Club** (tel. 246/432–1145), has only 9 of its 18 holes open until October 1999, while the property undergoes extensive renovations.
Horseback Riding	**Brighton Stables** (Black Rock, St. Michael, tel. 246/425–9381) offers one-hour rides along beaches and palm groves for $27.50, including transportation. The **Caribbean International Riding Center** (St. Joseph, tel. 246/433–1246) offers scenic trail rides, beginning at $40 for a 1-hour trail ride, including transportation.
Water Sports	Waterskiing, snorkeling, and parasailing are available on most beaches along the west and south coasts. Windsurfing is best at **Silver Sands Beach,** near the southern tip of the island, where the winds are strongest.. For scuba divers, Barbados is a rich and varied underwater destination. Reputable dive operators include the **Dive Shop Ltd.** (Aquatic Gap, St. Michael, near Grand Barbados Beach Resort, tel. 246/426–9947), **Dive Boat Safari** (Barbados Hilton, St. Michael, tel. 246/427–4350), and **Hightide** (Sandy Lane Hotel, St. James, tel. 246/432–0931).
Beaches	All beaches in Barbados are open to cruise ship passengers. The west coast has the stunning coves and white-sand beaches dear to the hearts of postcard publishers, plus calm, clear water for snorkeling, scuba diving, and swimming. **Paynes Bay,** south of Holetown, is the site of several fine resorts; public access to the beach is easiest opposite the Coach House Pub. **Greave's End Beach,** south of Bridgetown at Aquatic Gap, is convenient and good for swimming. On the south coast, **Sandy Beach**, in Worthing, has shallow, calm waters and a picturesque lagoon; it's ideal for families. **Accra Beach,** in Rockley, is a popular beach with water-sports equipment rental and snacks available. If you don't mind a drive across the island along Highway 7, **Crane Beach,** where the Atlantic meets the Caribbean, is a great find. Waves pound in, the sand is golden, and a reef makes swimming safe—but for strong swimmers only. For refreshment, the Crane Beach Hotel dining room is on the cliff above.
Dining	A 15% VAT (value-added tax) has been instituted in Barbados. Check restaurant menus to see whether the prices are VAT-inclusive or subject to the additional tax. A 10% service charge is added to most restaurant bills; if no service charge is added, tip waiters 10%–15%.

$–$$ **Waterfront Cafe.** A sidewalk table overlooking the Careenage is the perfect place to enjoy a drink, snack, burger, or Bajan meal. This popular bistro is a gathering place for locals and tourists alike. *Bridge House, Bridgetown, tel. 246/427–0093. MC, V.*

$ **Atlantis Hotel.** When you tour the rugged east coast, plan to arrive in Bathsheba at lunchtime and stop here for the enormous Bajan buffet, with pumpkin fritters, fried flying fish, roast chicken, pepper-pot stew, and more—along with a spectacular view of the pounding Atlantic surf—all for about $12.50 per person (slightly more on Sundays). *Bathsheba, St. Joseph, tel. 246/ 433–9445. AE.*

$ **Bomba's Beach Bar & Restaurant.** On the beach at Paynes Bay, Bomba's serves Bajan specialties, veggie food (fabulous avocado salad), and drinks made with fresh fruit juice—all whipped up by a Scottish chef and his Rasta partner. All dishes are less than $10. *Paynes Bay, St. James, tel. 246/432–0569. MC, V.*

$ **Sunbury Plantation House.** In the patio behind the restored great house, luncheon is served to visitors as part of the house tour. The Bajan buffet includes baked chicken and fish, salads, rice and peas, steamed local vegetables, and dessert. Sandwiches and other items are available, too. *St. Philip, tel. 246/423–6270 AE, MC, V.*

Cozumel, Mexico

Sun-saturated Cozumel, its ivory beaches fringed with coral reefs, fulfills the tourist's vision of a tropical Caribbean island. More Mexican than Cancún and less developed, Cozumel surpasses its better-known, fancier neighbor to the north in several ways. It has more—and lovelier—secluded beaches, superior diving and snorkeling, more authentically Mexican cuisine, and a greater diversity of handicrafts at better prices.

However, since Cozumel has become a mainstay for ships sailing on western Caribbean itineraries, the island has grown more commercial. Waterfront shops and restaurants have taken on a more glitzy appearance—gone are the hole-in-the-wall craft shops and little diners, replaced by high-dollar duty-free shops, gem traders, and slick eateries. There are also no fewer than half a dozen American fast-food chains and a Hard Rock Cafe and Planet Hollywood.

Life on this flat jungle island centers on the town of San Miguel. The duty-free shops stay open as long as a ship is in town, and most of the salespeople speak English. With the world-renowned Palancar Reef nearby, San Miguel is also a favorite among divers.

Cruise ships visiting just for the day normally call only at Cozumel; ships staying for two days usually call at Cozumel on one day and anchor off Playa del Carmen, across the channel on the Yucatán Peninsula, on the other. From here, excursions go to Cancún or to the Mayan ruins at Tulum, Cobá, and Chichén Itzá.

Currency In Mexico, the currency is the peso, indicated by a MX$ sign. At press time, the exchange rate was about $8.50 to US$1. To avoid confusion, when a price is given in dollars, "US$" precedes the amount. Most prices given below are in U.S. dollars.

U.S. dollars and credit cards are accepted at most restaurants and large shops. Most taxi drivers take dollars as well. There is no advantage to paying in dollars, but there may be an advantage to paying in cash. To avoid having to change unused pesos back to dollars, change just enough to cover what you'll need for public transportation, refreshments, phones, and tips. Use up your Mexican coins; they can't be changed back to dollars.

Telephones The best place to make long-distance calls is at the Calling Station (Av. Rafael E. Melgar 27 and Calle 3 S, tel. 987/2–14–17), where you'll save 10%–50%. You can also exchange money here. It is open mid-December–April, daily 8 AM–11 PM; the rest of the year, it's open Monday–Saturday 9 AM–10 PM and Sunday 9–1 and 5–10.

Shore Excursions The following are good choices in Cozumel. They may not be offered by all cruise lines. Times and prices are approximate.

Archaeological Sites **Chichén Itzá.** This incredible and awe-inspiring ruin of a great Mayan city is a 45-minute flight from Cozumel or a 12-hour round-trip bus ride from Playa del Carmen. A box lunch is included. *Full day. Cost: $200 (by plane), $85 (by bus).*

San Gervasio and Cozumel Island. If you want to see Mayan ruins but don't want to spend a full day on a tour, this excursion to a local archaeological site is a good alternative. Time is also allotted for swimming and snorkeling at the Playa Sol beach. *4 hrs. Cost: $36.*

Tulum Ruins and Xel-ha Lagoon. An English-speaking guide leads a tour to this superbly preserved ancient Mayan city, perched on the cliffs above a beautiful beach. A box lunch is usually included. A stop is made for a swim in the glass-clear waters of Xel-ha. The tour leaves from Playa del Carmen. *6 hrs. Cost: $80.*

Undersea Creatures **Glass-Bottom Boat.** For those who don't dive, a tour boat with a see-through floor takes passengers to the famed Paraiso and Chankanaab sites to view schools of tropical fish. *2 hrs. Cost: $37.*

Snorkeling. This region has been acknowledged by experts from Jacques Cousteau to *Skin Diver* magazine as one of the top diving destinations in the world. If your ship offers a snorkeling tour, take it. Equipment and lessons are included. *3 hrs. Cost: $29.*

Coming Ashore As many as six ships call at Cozumel on a busy day, tendering passengers to the downtown pier in the center of San Miguel or docking at the international pier 6 km (4 mi) away. From the downtown pier you can walk into town or catch the ferry to Playa del Carmen. Taxi tours are also available. Sample prices are $7 to the Chankanaab Nature Park, $12 to the Playa Sol beach, and $35 to the Mayan ruins at San Gervasio. An island tour, including the ruins and other sights, costs about $60. The international pier is close to many beaches, but you'll need a taxi to get into town. Fortunately, cabs meet incoming ships, so there's rarely a wait. Expect to pay $4 for the ride into San Miguel from the pier.

Once in town, you can find a tourist information directory on the main square, immediately across from the downtown pier, and an information office upstairs in the Plaza del Sol mall, at the east end of the square; open weekdays 9 AM–2:30 PM.

To get to Playa del Carmen from Cozumel, you can take a ferry or a jetfoil from the downtown pier. It costs about $10 round-trip and takes 30–40 minutes each way. Ferries depart every hour or two; the last ferry back to Cozumel leaves around 8:30 PM, but be sure to double-check because the schedule changes frequently.

Exploring Cozumel San Miguel is tiny—you cannot get lost—and best explored on foot. The main attractions are the small eateries and shops that line the streets. Activity centers on the ferry and the main square, where the locals congregate in the evenings. The lovely **Museo de le Isla de Cozumel,** with exhibits devoted to the island environment and to the ecosystem of the surrounding reefs and water, is on the main coastal drag, near the ferry dock. On the second floor are displays on Mayan and colonial life and on modern-day Cozumel. *Av. Melgar and Calle 4 N, tel. 987/2–14–75. Admission: $3. Open daily 10–6.*

To see the largest Mayan and Toltec site on Cozumel, head inland to the jungle. The ruins at **San Gervasio** once served as the island's capital and probably its ceremonial center, dedicated to the fertility goddess Ixchel. What remains today are numerous ruins scattered around a plaza and a main road leading to the sea (probably a major trade route). There's no interpretive signage, so you'll need to hire a guide in order to get much out of your visit. Guides charge $12 for groups of up to six, so try to get a group together aboard ship. *Admission: $1 to private road, $3.50 for ruins. Open daily 8–5.*

To sample Cozumel's natural beauty, head south out of town on Avenida Melgar; after 11 km (6½ mi) your first stop will be the **Chankanaab Nature Park.** The natural aquarium has been designated an underwater preserve for more than 50 species of tropical fish, as well as crustaceans and coral. Snorkeling and scuba equipment can be rented, and instruction and professional guides are available, along with gift shops, snack bars, and a restaurant serving fresh seafood. You'll also find reproductions of Mayan ruins and a botanical garden with 350 species of plant life from 20 countries. *No phone. Admission: $7. Open daily 6–5:30; restaurant open daily 10–5.*

Shopping   San Miguel's biggest industry—even bigger than diving—is selling souvenirs and crafts to cruise-ship passengers. The primary items are ceramics, onyx, brass, wood carvings, colorful blankets and hammocks, reproductions of Mayan artifacts, shells, silver, gold, sportswear, T-shirts, perfume, and liquor. Keep an eye out for Mexican pewter; it's unusual, affordable, and attractive. Almost all stores take U.S. dollars.

The shopping district centers on the Plaza del Sol—which is off Avenida Melgar, across from the ferry terminal—and extends out along Avenida Melgar and Avenida 5 South and North. A **crafts market** is at Calle 1 S, behind the plaza. Good shops for Mexican crafts are **Los Cinco Soles** (Av. Melgar N 27) and **Unicornio** (Av. 5a S 1, just off the Plaza del Sol). The most bizarre collection of shops on the island is the **Cozumel Flea Market**, on Avenida 5 N between Calles 2 and 4, which sells reproductions of erotic Mayan figurines, antique masks, rare coins, and *Xtabentún*, the local anise-and-honey liqueur. Down the street at **Na Balam** (Av. 5 N, 14) there are high-quality Mayan reproductions, jewelry, batik clothing, and a typical array of curios. For atmosphere, fresh fruit, and other foods, go to the **Municipal Market** (Av. 25 S and Calle Salas).

Passengers whose ships dock at the International Pier can shop dockside at a complex selling T-shirts, handicrafts, trinkets, and more.

Sports   In Cozumel contact **Yucab Reef Diving and Fishing Center** (tel. 987/
Fishing   2–41–10) or **Club Náutico Cozumel** (tel. 987/2–01–18; 800/253–2701 in the U.S.).

Scuba Diving   Cozumel is famous for its reefs. In addition to **Chankanaab Nature**
and   **Park** (*see* Exploring, *above*), another great dive site is **La Ceiba**
Snorkeling   **Reef,** in the waters off La Ceiba and Sol Caribe hotels. Here lies the wreckage of a sunken airplane that was blown up for a Mexi-

can disaster movie. Cozumel's dive shops include **Aqua Safari** (tel. 987/2–01–01), **Blue Angel** (tel. 987/2–16–31), **Dive Paradise** (tel. 987/2–10–07), **Fantasia Divers** (tel. 987/2–28–40; 800/336–3483 in the U.S.), and **Michelle's Dive Shop** (tel. 987/2–09–47).

Dining *Although it is not common in Mexico, a 10%–15% service charge may be added to the bill. Otherwise, a 10%–20% tip is customary.*

$$ **La Choza.** Some of the best home-cooked Mexican food on the island is found in this family-run restaurant with thick white walls and wooden windows that open onto the street. Specialties include chicken *mole* (a chile-chocolate sauce), red snapper, grilled lobster, and stuffed peppers. *Calle Rosada Salas 198 at Av. 10a S, tel. 987/2–09–58. AE, MC, V.*

$$ **Pancho's Backyard.** A jungle of greenery, trickling fountains, ceiling fans, and leather chairs set the tone at this inviting restaurant, located on the cool patio of Los Cincos Soles shopping center. The menu highlights local standards such as black-bean soup, *carmone al carbon* (grilled prawns), and fajitas. Round out your meal with coconut ice cream in Kahlua. This is a good, convenient choice for cruise passengers shopping the main drag. *Av. Rafael Melgar N 27 at Calle 8 N, tel. 987/2–21–41. AE, MC, V. Closed Sun. No lunch Sat.*

$ **Prima Pasta.** Since Texan Albert Silmai opened this northern Italian diner just south of the plaza, he's attracted a strong following of patrons, who come for the hearty, inexpensive pizzas, calzones, sandwiches, and pastas. The breezy dining area, on a second-floor terrace above the kitchen, smells heavenly and has a charming Mediterranean mural painted on two walls. *Calle Rosada Salas 109, tel. 987/2–42–42. MC, V.*

Nightlife After 10 PM, **Carlos 'n' Charlie's** (Av. Melgar 11 between Calles 2 and 4 N, tel. 987/2–01–91) and **Chilly's** (Av. Melgar near Av. Benito Juarez, tel. 987/2–18–32) are the local equivalent of college fraternity parties. The **Hard Rock Cafe** (Av. Rafael Melgar 2A near Av. Benito Juarez, tel. 987/2–52–71) is similarly raucous. A favorite with ships' crews is **Scaramouche** (Av. Melgar at Calle Rosada Salas, tel. 987/2–07–91), a dark, cavernous disco with a crowded dance floor surrounded by tiered seating.

Curaçao

Try to be on deck as your ship sails into Curaçao. The tiny Queen Emma Floating Bridge swings aside to open the narrow channel. Pastel gingerbread buildings on shore look like dollhouses, especially from the perspective of a large cruise ship. Although the gabled roofs and red tiles show a Dutch influence, the riotous colors of the facades are peculiar to Curaçao. It's said that an early governor of the island suffered from migraines that were irritated by the color white, so all the houses were painted in wild hues from magenta to mauve.

Fifty-six kilometers (35 miles) north of Venezuela and 67 km (42 mi) east of Aruba, Curaçao is, at 61 km (38 mi) long and 5–12 km (3–7½ mi) wide, the largest of the Netherlands Antilles. Although always sunny, it's never stiflingly hot here because of the constant trade winds. Water sports attract enthusiasts from all over the world, and the reef diving is excellent.

History books still don't agree as to whether Alonzo de Ojeda or Amerigo Vespucci discovered Curaçao, only that it happened

BONUS MILES MAKE GREET SOUVENIRS.

Earn Miles With Your MCI Card.

Take the MCI Card along on this trip and start earning miles for the next one. You'll earn frequent flyer miles on all your calls and save with the low rates you've come to expect from MCI. Before you know it, you'll be on your way to some other international destination.

Sign up for MCI by calling 1-800-FLY-FREE

Earn Frequent Flyer Miles.

Is this a great time, or what? :-)

Easy To Call Home.

1. To use your MCI Card, just dial the WorldPhone access number of the country you're calling from.
2. Dial or give the operator your MCI Card number.
3. Dial or give the number you're calling.

American Samoa	633-2MCI (633-2624)
# Antigua	1-800-888-8000
(Available from public card phones only)	#2
# Argentina (CC)	0-800-5-1002
# Aruba ⬦	800-888-8
# Bahamas	1-800-888-8000
# Barbados	1-800-888-8000
# Belize	557 from hotels
	815 from pay phones
# Bermuda ⬦	1-800-888-8000
# Bolivia ♦(CC)	0-800-2222
# Brazil (CC)	000-8012
# British Virgin Islands ⬦	1-800-888-8000
# Cayman Islands	1-800-888-8000
# Chile (CC)	
To call using CTC ■	800-207-300
To call using ENTEL ■	800-360-180
# Colombia (CC) ♦	980-16-0001
Collect Access in Spanish	980-16-1000
# Costa Rica ♦	0800-012-2222
# Dominica	1-800-888-8000
# Dominican Republic (CC) ⬦	1-800-888-8000
Collect Access in Spanish	1121
# Ecuador (CC) ⬦	999-170
El Salvador	800-1767
# Grenada ⬦	1-800-888-8000
Guatemala (CC) ♦	9999-189
Guyana	177
# Haiti ⬦ Collect Access	193
Collect Access in French/Creole	190
Honduras ⬦	8000-122
# Jamaica ⬦ Collect Access	1-800-888-8000
(From Special Hotels only)	873
From payphones	★2
# Mexico (CC)	
Avantel	01-800-021-8000
Telmex ▲	001-800-674-7000
Mexico Access in Spanish	01-800-021-1000
# Netherlands Antilles (CC) ⬦	001-800-888-8000
Nicaragua (CC)	166
(Outside of Managua, dial 02 first)	
Collect Access in Spanish from any public payphone	★2
# Panama	108
Military Bases	2810-108
# Paraguay ⬦	00-812-800
# Peru	0-800-500-10
# Puerto Rico (CC)	1-800-888-8000
# St. Lucia ⬦	1-800-888-8000
# Trinidad & Tobago ⬦	1-800-888-8000
# Turks & Caicos ⬦	1-800-888-8000
# Uruguay	000-412
# U.S. Virgin Islands (CC)	1-800-888-8000
# Venezuela (CC) ⬦ ♦	800-1114-0

You've read the book. Now book the trip.

For all the best deals on flights, hotels, rental cars, and vacation packages, book them online at www.previewtravel.com. Then click on our Destination Guides featuring content from Fodor's and more. You'll find hotels, restaurants, attractions, and things to do around the globe. There are even interactive maps, videos, and weather forecasts. You'll have everything you need to make your vacation exactly what you want it to be. All it takes is a trip online.

preview travel ℠

Travel on Your Terms™
www.previewtravel.com
aol keyword: previewtravel

around 1499. In 1634 the Dutch came and promptly shipped off the Spanish settlers and the few remaining Indians to Venezuela. To defend itself against French and British invasions, the city built massive ramparts, many of which now house unusual restaurants and hotels.

Today, Curaçao's population, which comprises more than 50 nationalities, is one of the best educated in the Caribbean. The island is known for its religious tolerance, and tourists are warmly welcomed and almost never pestered by vendors and shopkeepers. Although there's plenty to see and do in Willemstad, the rest of the island features rugged natural beauty in the form of cramped champagne coves shadowed by gunmetal cliffs and a remarkable, beautifully preserved collection of *landhuisen,* or plantation land houses, all distinctively colored and many open to the public.

Currency U.S. dollars are fine, so don't worry about exchanging money, except for pay phones or soda machines. The local currency is the guilder or florin, indicated by "fl" or "NAf" on price tags. At press time, the exchange rate was NAf 1.77 to U.S.$1.

Telephones The telephone system is reliable, and there's an overseas phone center in the cruise ship terminal. Dialing to the United States is exactly the same as dialing long distance within the United States.

Shore Excursions The following are good choices in Curaçao. They may not be offered by all cruise lines. Times and prices are approximate.

Island Sights **Country Drive.** This is a good tour if you'd like to see Westpunt and Mt. Christoffel but don't want to risk driving an hour there yourself. Other stops are made at a land house, Hato Caves, and the Curaçao Museum. *3 hrs. Cost: $32.*

Willemstad Trolley Train. Although there are several walking tours of the charming capital, Willemstad, they're lengthy and detailed. The trolley visits such highlights as the Floating Market, Synagogue, Fort Amsterdam, and Waterloo Arches. *75 minutes. Cost: $21.*

Undersea Creatures **Sharks, Stingrays, and Shipwrecks.** Curaçao's seaquarium, a marine park, and two sunken ships reached by a 30-minute submarine trip highlight this tour of the island's marine environment. *3 hrs. Cost: $39.*

Coming Ashore Ships dock at the terminal just beyond the Queen Emma Bridge, which leads to the floating market and the shopping district. The walk from the berth to downtown takes less than 10 minutes. Easy-to-read maps are posted dockside and in the shopping area. The terminal has a duty-free shop, a telephone office, and a taxi stand. Taxis, which meet every ship, aren't metered, so confirm the fare before setting out. A taxi for up to 4 people will cost about $30 an hour.

Exploring Curaçao *Numbers in the margin correspond to points of interest on the Curaçao map.*

Willemstad **Willemstad** is small and navigable on foot; you needn't spend more
❶ than two or three hours wandering around here, although the narrow alleys and various architectural styles are enchanting. English, Spanish, and Dutch are widely spoken. Narrow Santa Anna Bay divides the city into the Punda, where the main shopping district is, and the Otrabanda (literally, the "other side"), where the cruise ships dock. The Punda is crammed with shops, restaurants, monuments, and markets. The Otrabanda has narrow

Curaçao

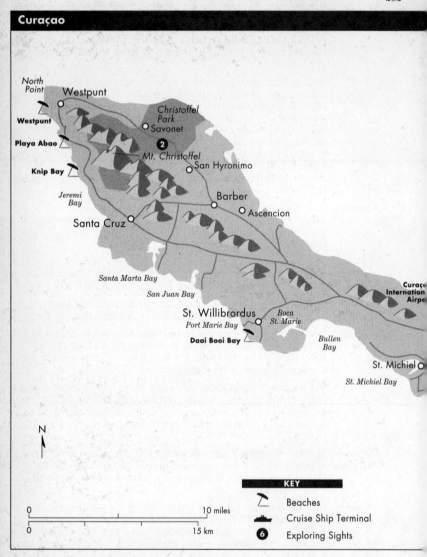

North
Point

Westpunt

Westpunt

Playa Abao

Knip Bay

Jeremi
Bay

Santa Cruz

Christoffel
Park
Savonet

2

Mt. Christoffel

San Hyronimo

Barber

Ascencion

Santa Marta Bay

San Juan Bay

St. Willibrordus

Port Marie Bay

Daai Booi Bay

Boca
St. Marie

Bullen
Bay

Curaçao
International
Airport

St. Michiel

St. Michiel Bay

N

0   10 miles

0   15 km

KEY

Beaches

Cruise Ship Terminal

6 Exploring Sights

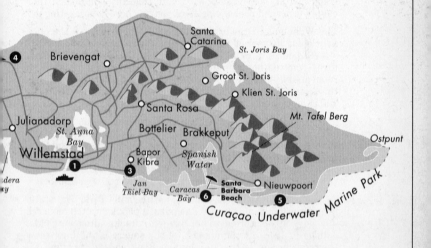

winding streets full of colonial homes notable for their gables and Dutch-influenced designs.

You can cross from the Otrabanda to the Punda in one of three ways: Walk over the Queen Emma Pontoon Bridge; ride the free ferry, which runs when the bridge swings open (at least 30 times a day) to let seagoing vessels pass; or take a cab across the Juliana Bridge (about $7). The first landmark that cruise passengers come upon is the **Queen Emma Bridge,** which the locals call the Lady. The toll to cross the original bridge, built in 1888, was 2¢ per person if wearing shoes and free if barefoot. Today it's free, regardless of what's on your feet.

On the Punda side of the city, **Handelskade** is where you'll find Willemstad's most famous sights—the colorful colonial buildings that line the waterfront. The original red roof tiles came from Europe on trade ships as ballast.

The bustling, colorful, noisy **floating market** is on Sha Caprileskade. Each morning, dozens of Venezuelan schooners arrive laden with tropical fruits and vegetables. (Note that any you should thoroughly wash and peel any produce you buy here before eating it).

The Wilhelmina Drawbridge connects the Punda with the once-flourishing district of **Scharloo.** The early Jewish merchants built stately homes in Scharloo, and many of these intriguing structures (some dating from the 17th century) have been meticulously renovated by the government. If you cross the bridge to admire the architecture along Scharlooweg, steer clear of the waterfront end (Kleine Werf), which is now a red-light district.

The Punda's **Mikveh Israel-Emmanuel Synagogue** was founded in 1651 and is the oldest temple still in use in the Western Hemisphere. It draws 20,000 visitors a year. Enter through the gates around the corner on Hanchi Snoa. A museum in the back displays Jewish antiques and fine Judaica. *Hanchi Di Snoa 29, tel. 5999/ 461–1067. Admission: $2. Open weekdays 9–11:45 and 2:30–5.*

At the end of Columbusstraat lies **Wilhelmina Park.** The statue keeping watch is of Queen Wilhelmina, a popular Dutch monarch, who gave up her throne to her daughter Juliana after her Golden Jubilee in 1948. At the far side of the square is the impressive Georgian facade of the McLaughlin Bank and, to its right, the courthouse with its stately balustrade.

Guarding the waterfront at the foot of the Pontoon Bridge are the mustard-color walls of **Ft. Amsterdam;** take a few steps through the archway and enter another century. In the 1700s the structure was actually the center of the city and the most important fort on the island. Now it houses the governor's residence, the Fort Church, the ministry, and several other government offices. Outside the entrance, a series of gnarled wayaka trees have small, fanciful carvings of a dragon, a giant squid, and a mermaid.

Western Curaçao The road that leads to the northwest tip of the island winds through landscape that Georgia O'Keeffe might have painted— towering cacti, flamboyant dried shrubbery, aluminum-roof houses. In these parts you may see fishermen hauling in their nets, women pounding cornmeal, and donkeys blocking traffic. You can often glimpse land houses—large estate homes—from the road.

❷ **Christoffel Park** is a good hour from Willemstad (so watch your time) but worth a visit. This fantastic 4,450-acre garden and wildlife preserve with Mt. Christoffel at its center consists of three former plantations. As you drive through the park, watch for tiny deer, goats, and other small wildlife that might suddenly dart in front of your car. If you skip everything else on the island, it's possible to drive to the park and climb 1,239-ft Mt. Christoffel, which takes from two to three strenuous hours. The island panorama you get from the peak is amazing—on a clear day you can even see the mountain ranges of Venezuela, Bonaire, and Aruba. *Savonet, tel. 5999/864-0363. Admission: $9. Open Mon.-Sat. 8-4, Sun. 6-3.*

Eastern Curaçao

❸ At the **Curaçao Seaquarium,** more than 400 varieties of exotic fish and vegetation are displayed. Outside is a 1,623-ft-long artificial beach of white sand, well-suited to novice swimmers and children. There's also a platform that overlooks the wreck of the steamship SS *Oranje Nassau* and an underwater observatory where you can watch divers and snorkelers swimming with stingrays and feeding sharks. *Tel. 5999/461-6666. Admission: $13.25. Open daily 9-6 PM.*

❹ Near the airport are the **Hato Caves,** where you can take an hour-long guided tour into water-pool chambers, a voodoo chamber, fruit bats' sleeping quarters, and Curaçao Falls—where a stream of silver joins a stream of gold. Hidden lights illuminate the limestone formations and gravel walkways. This is one of the better Caribbean caves open to the public. (Passengers with mobility problems should note that a series of steep steps lead to the cabin entrance.) *Tel. 5999/868-0379. Admission: $6.25. Open 9:30-5; closed Mon.*

❺ **Curaçao Underwater Marine Park** (*see* Sports, *below*) is the best spot for snorkeling—though the seabed is sadly litter-strewn in places. The park stretches along the southern shore, from the Princess Beach Hotel in Willemstad to the eastern tip of the island.

❻ Along the southern shore, several private yacht clubs attract sports anglers from all over the world for international tournaments. Stop at Santa Barbara Beach, especially on Sunday, when the atmosphere approaches party time. **Caracas Bay** is a popular dive site, with a sunken ship so close to the surface that even snorkelers can view it clearly.

Shopping

Curaçao has some of the best shops in the Caribbean, but in many cases the prices are no lower than in U.S. discount stores. Hours are usually Monday–Saturday 8–noon and 2–6. Most shops are within the six-block area of Willemstad described *above*. The main shopping streets are Heerenstraat, Breedestraat, and Madurostraat, where you'll find **Bamali** (Waterfort Arches, tel. 5999/461-2258) for Indonesian batik clothing and leather. **Fundason Obra di Man** (Bargestraat 57, tel. 5999/461-2413) sells native crafts and curios, including marvelous posters and metal or ceramic renderings of typical landhuisen. If you've always longed for Dutch clogs, tulips, delftware, Dutch fashions, or chocolate, as well as, incongruously enough, craftwork from Latin America, try **Clog Dance** (De Rouvilleweg 9B, tel. 5999/462-3280).

Arawak Craft Products (Mattheywerf 1, tel. 5999/462-7249), between the Queen Emma Bridge and the cruise ship terminal, is open whenever ships are in port. You can buy a variety of tiles, plates, pots, and tiny land house replicas here.

Julius L. Penha & Sons (Heerenstraat 1, tel. 5999/461–2266), in front of the Pontoon Bridge, sells French perfumes; Hummel figurines; linen from Madeira; delftware; and handbags from Argentina, Italy, and Spain. The store also has an extensive cosmetics counter. **Boolchand's** (Heerenstraat 4B, tel. 5999/461–2262) handles an interesting variety of merchandise behind a facade of red-and-white-check tiles. Stock up here on French perfumes, British cashmere sweaters, Italian silk ties, Dutch dolls, Swiss watches, and Japanese cameras. **Little Switzerland** (Breedestraat 44, tel. 5999/461–2111) is the place for duty-free shopping; here you'll find perfumes, jewelry, watches, crystal, china, and leather goods at significant savings. Try **New Amsterdam** (Gomezplein 14, tel. 5999/461–2469) for hand-embroidered tablecloths, napkins, and pillowcases.**La Casa Amarilla** (Breedestraat 46, tel 5999/461–3222) purveys premier perfumes and cosmetics from Poison to Passion.

Sports
Hiking **Christoffel Park** (*see* Exploring Curaçao, *above*) has a number of challenging trails.

Scuba Diving and Snorkeling The **Curaçao Underwater Marine Park** (tel. 5999/461–8131) is about 21 km (12½ mi) of untouched coral reef that has been granted national park status. Mooring buoys mark the most interesting dive sites. If your cruise ship doesn't offer a diving or snorkeling excursion, contact **Curaçao Seascape** (tel. 5999/462–5000, ext. 6056), **Peter Hughes Divers** (tel. 5999/736–7888), or **Underwater Curaçao** (tel. 5999/461–8131).

Beaches Curaçao doesn't have long, powdery stretches of sand. Instead you'll discover the joy of inlets: tiny bays marked by craggy cliffs, exotic trees, and scads of interesting pebbles and washed up coral. **Westpunt,** on the northwest tip of the island, is rocky, with very little sand, but shady in the morning and with a bay view worth the one-hour trip. On Sunday watch the divers jump from the high cliff. **Knip Bay** has two parts: Groot (Big) Knip and Kleine (Little) Knip. Both have alluring white sand, but Kleine Knip is shaded by (highly poisonous) manchineel trees. Take the road to the Knip Landhouse, then turn right; signs will direct you.

Dining Restaurants usually add a 10%–15% service charge to the bill.

$$$ **Bistro Le Clochard.** This romantic gem is built into the 18th-century Rif Fort and is suffused with the cool, dark atmosphere of ages past. The use of fresh ingredients in consistently well-prepared French and Swiss dishes makes dining a dream. Try the fresh fish platters or the tender veal in mushroom sauce. Save room for the chocolate mousse. *On Otrabanda Rif Fort, tel. 5999/462–5666. AE, DC, MC, V. Closed Sun. No lunch Sat.*

$–$$ **Mambo Beach.** This beach bar at the Seaquarium's artificial strand offers a lively, nonstop, party atmosphere and surprisingly creative seafood. You may try the dish named after Marlin Monroe (smoked marlin in sundried-tomato sauce) or the salmon fried in couscous with tomato and saffron; you could also opt for pastas and burgers. *Seaquarium Beach, tel 5999/461–8999. AE, MC, V.*

Grand Cayman

The largest and most populous of the Cayman Islands, Grand Cayman is also one of the most popular cruise destinations in the western Caribbean, largely because it doesn't suffer from the ailments afflicting many larger ports: panhandlers, hasslers, and crime. Instead, the Cayman economy is a study in stability, and residents are renowned for their courteous behavior. Though cacti and

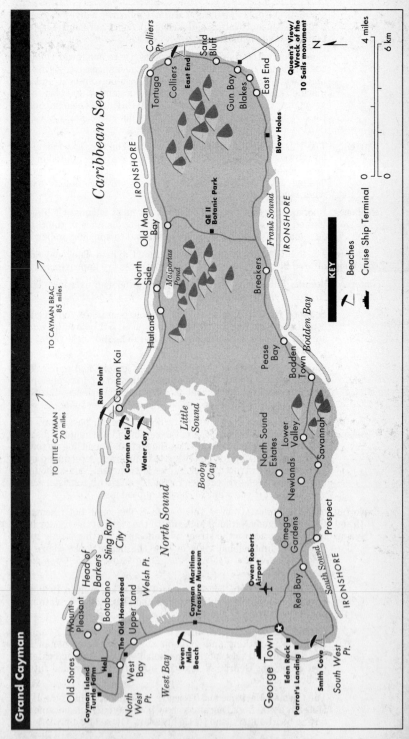

Grand Cayman

Caribbean Sea

TO CAYMAN BRAC
85 miles

TO LITTLE CAYMAN
70 miles

Old Stores
Mount Pleasant
Hell
Cayman Island Turtle Farm
Botabano
The Old Homestead
Upper Land
Welsh Pt.
North West Pt.
West Bay
Head of Barkers
Sting Ray City
North Sound
Welsh Pt.
Cayman Maritime Treasure Museum
Owen Roberts Airport
Omega Gardens
Newlands
North Sound Estates
Lower Valley
Little Sound
Booby Cay
Water Cay
Cayman Kai
Rum Point
Hutland
North Side
Mastportus Pond
Old Man Bay
QE II Botanic Park
Breakers
Frank Sound
Tortuga
Colliers
East End
Sand Bluff
Gun Bay
Blakes
East End
Queen's View/Wreck of the 10 Sails monument
Blow Holes
Colliers Pt.
Pease Bay
Bodden Town
Bodden Bay
Savannah
Prospect
South Sound
Red Bay
Eden Rock
Parrot's Landing
George Town
Smith Cove
South West Pt.
Seven Mile Beach
IRONSHORE

KEY
Beaches
Cruise Ship Terminal

N

0 4 miles
0 6 km

scrub fill the dusty landscape, Grand Cayman is a diver's paradise, with translucent waters and a colorful variety of marine life protected by the government.

Compared with other Caribbean ports, there are fewer things to see on land; instead, the island's most impressive sights are underwater. Snorkeling, diving, and glass-bottom-boat and submarine rides top every ship's shore-excursion list and also can be arranged at major aquatic shops. Grand Cayman is also famous for the 554 offshore banks in George Town; not surprisingly, the standard of living is high, and nothing is cheap.

Currency The U.S. dollar is accepted everywhere. The Cayman Island dollar (CI$) is worth about U.S.$1.20. Prices are often quoted in Cayman dollars, so make sure you know which currency you're dealing with. All prices given below are in U.S. dollars except where indicated.

Telephones Phone service is better here than on most islands. Calling the United States is the same as calling long distance in the States: Just dial 01 followed by the area code and telephone number.

Shore Excursions The following are good choices in Grand Cayman. They may not be offered by all cruise lines. Times and prices are approximate.

Undersea Creatures **Atlantis Submarine.** A real submarine offers an exciting view of Grand Cayman's profuse marine life. *1½ hrs. Cost: $79.*

Seaworld Explorer Cruise. A glass-bottom boat takes you on an air-conditioned, narrated voyage where you sit 5 ft below the water's surface and see sunken ships, tropical fish, and coral reefs. *1 hr. Cost: $29.*

Snorkeling Adventure. Novices can take lessons and experienced snorkelers will find good adventure on this boat trip to one or two snorkeling sites. For a once-in-a-lifetime experience, the Sting Ray City tour is highly recommended. *2½ hrs. Cost: $34.*

Coming Ashore Ships anchor in George Town Harbor and tender passengers onto Harbour Drive, placing you in the center of the shopping district. A tourist information booth is on the pier, and taxis line up for disembarking passengers. Note that taxi fares are determined by an elaborate rate structure set by the government, and although it may seem expensive, cabbies rarely try to rip off tourists. Ask to see the chart if you want to check a quoted fare.

Exploring Grand Cayman You can explore George Town on foot. The small but fascinating **Cayman Islands National Museum,** to the right of the tender landing and just across the street, is well worth visiting if only to see the three-dimensional view of how the island looks above and below the sea. *Tel. 345/949–8368. Admission: CI$5. Open weekdays 9–5, Sat. 10–2.*

On Cardinal Avenue is the **General Post Office,** built in 1939, with strands of decorative colored lights and about 2,000 private mailboxes (island mail is not delivered).

Behind the general post office is **Elizabethan Square,** a complex that houses clothing and souvenir stores. At the corner of Fort and Edward streets, notice the small clock tower dedicated to Britain's King George V and the huge fig tree pruned into an umbrella shape.

The **Cayman Maritime and Treasure Museum,** in front of the Hyatt Hotel, is a real find. Dioramas show how Caymanians became seafarers, boatbuilders, and turtle breeders. Owned by a professional treasure-salvaging firm, the museum displays an assortment of artifacts from shipwrecks. A shop offers excellent buys on authentic ancient coins and jewelry. *W. Bay Rd., tel. 345/947–5033. Admission: $5. Open Mon.–Sat. 9–5.*

The **Old Homestead,** formerly known as the West Bay Pink House, is probably the most photographed home in Grand Cayman. This picturesque pink-and-white cottage was built in 1912 of wattle and daub around an ironwood frame. Tours are led by Mac Bothwell, a cheery guide who grew up in the house. *W. Bay Rd., tel. 345/949– 7639. Admission: $5. Open Mon.–Sat. 8–5.*

Near the Old Homestead is the tiny village of **Hell,** which is little more than a patch of incredibly jagged rock formations called ironshore. The big attractions here are a small post office, which sells stamps and postmarks cards from Hell (the postcard of bikini beauties emblazoned "When Hell Freezes Over" gives you the idea), and lots of T-shirt and souvenir shops.

The **Cayman Island Turtle Farm** is the most popular attraction on the island. Here you'll see turtles of all ages, from day-old hatchlings to huge 600-pounders that can live to be 100. In the adjoining café, sample turtle soup or turtle sandwiches. *W. Bay Rd., tel. 345/ 949–3893. Admission: $5. Open daily 8:30–5.*

At **Bodden Town**—the island's original capital—you'll find an old cemetery on the shore side of the road. Graves with A-frame structures are said to contain the remains of pirates. A curio shop serves as the entrance to what's called the Pirate's Caves, partially underground natural formations that are more hokey than spooky, with fake treasure chests and mannequins in pirate garb.

Queen Elizabeth II Botanic Park is a 60-acre wilderness preserve that showcases the variety of habitats and plants native to the Caymans. Interpretive signs identify the flora along the 1½-km-long (1-mi-long) walking trail. Halfway along the route is a walled compound housing the rare blue iguana—it's found only in remote sections of the islands. *Frank Sound Rd., tel. 345/947–9462. Admission: $3. Open daily 7:30–5:30.*

The Mastic Reserve and Trail is part of the largest contiguous area of untouched old growth woodland remaining on the island. It passes through black mangrove, abandoned agricultural land, and ancient dry woodlands. The trail is 2 mi long and the guided tour takes about 2½ to 3 hours. Note though this is not a rigorous hike, it's a lengthy walking tour so be sure you're in adequate shape to take it. *North side, tel. 345/949-1996. Reservations essential. Open Mon.–Sat.; two tours daily.*

On the way to the East End are the **Blow Holes,** a great photo opportunity as waves crash into the fossilized coral beach, forcing water into caverns and sending geysers shooting up through the ironshore.

Beyond the Blow Holes is the village of **East End,** the first recorded settlement on Grand Cayman. Farther on, as the highway curves north, you'll come to Queen's View lookout point. There's a monument commemorating the legendary Wreck of the Ten Sails, which took place just offshore.

Pedro St. James Castle is the oldest stone building in the Cayman Islands, estimated to have been built in 1780. Though still in restoration at press time, you can still visit the site which sits atop a 30 ft bluff in Savannah.

Shopping Fort Street and Cardinal Avenue are the main shopping streets in George Town. On Cardinal Avenue is Kirk Freeport Plaza, with lots of jewelry shops. The **Tortuga Rum Company's** (tel. 345/949–7701) scrumptious rum cake makes a great souvenir; most shops on Grand Cayman carry it.

Be sure to visit **Out of Africa** (tel. 345/945–1147), next to the Kirk Freeport Plaza, for exotic handicrafts from Kenya, Tanzania, and Zaire. **Heritage Craft** (tel. 345/945–6041) opposite the National Museum has a large selection of wind chimes, hammocks, handmade dolls, wood carvings, and local arts.

A short drive down South Church Street will take you to **Pure Art Gallery & Gifts** (tel. 345/949–9133) which has a fine selection of unique local paintings, prints, artsy frames, mugs, and handmade Caribbean collectibles.

Sports
Fishing For fishing enthusiasts, Cayman waters are abundant with blue and white marlin, yellowfin tuna, sailfish, dolphinfish, bonefish, and wahoo. If your ship doesn't offer a fishing excursion, about 25 boats are available for charter. Ask at the tourist information booth on the pier.

Scuba Diving and Snorkeling Contact **Bob Soto's Diving Ltd.** (tel. 345/949–2022 or 800/262–7686), **Don Foster's Dive Grand Cayman** (tel. 345/945–5132 or 800/833–4837), and **Parrot's Landing** (tel. 345/949–7884 or 800/448–0428). The best snorkeling is off the **Ironshore Reef** (within walking distance of George Town on the west coast) and in the reef-protected shallows of the north and south coasts, where coral and fish are much more varied and abundant.

Beaches The west coast, the island's most developed area, is where you'll find the famous **Seven Mile Beach.** This white, powdery stretch is free of both litter and peddlers, but it's also Grand Cayman's busiest vacation center, and most of the island's resorts, restaurants, and shopping centers are along this strip. The Holiday Inn rents Aqua Trikes, Paddle Cats, and Banana Rides.

Dining Many restaurants add a 10%–15% service charge.

$$$ **Lantana's.** Try the American-Caribbean cuisine at this fine eatery, where the decor is as imaginative and authentic as the food, and both are of top quality. Lobster quesadillas, blackened king salmon over cilantro linguine with banana fritters and cranberry relish, incredible roasted garlic soup, and apple pie are favorites from the diverse menu. *Caribbean Club, W. Bay Rd., Seven Mile Beach, tel. 345/947–5595. AE, D, MC, V. No lunch weekends.*

$$ **Cracked Conch by the Sea.** If you visit the Turtle Farm, this restaurant is right next door and worth a visit for lunch. Patio diners will enjoy a panoramic view of the sea. Specialties include conch fritters, conch chowder, spicy Cayman-style snapper, turtle steak, and other seafood offerings. A collection of antique diving equipment makes the place something of a diver's museum. *West Bay Rd. near Turtle Bay Farm, tel. 345/947–5217. MC, V.*

$$$ **Crow's Nest.** With the ocean as its backyard, this secluded seafood restaurant, about a 15-minute drive south of George Town, is a great spot for snorkeling as well as lunching. The shark du jour, herb-crusted dolphinfish with lobster sauce, and the shrimp and conch dishes are excellent, as is the chocolate-fudge rum cake. *S. Sound Rd., tel. 345/949–9366. AE, MC, V. No lunch Sun.*

$$ **Hog Sty Bay Cafe.** For a beer and a bite to eat with a view of the sea, this colorful café is just a few minutes walk from the tender

landing. Ask for a table on the outdoor deck that overlooks the beach and try a Stingray on draft—a British-style, Cayman-brewed pilsner. To get here, make a left as you exit the dock and stroll down Harbor Road. *Harbor Rd. on waterfront, tel. 345/949–6163. AE, MC, V.*

$ **Breadfruit Tree Garden.** This spot is a favorite with locals, and the price is certainly right. The jerk chicken may just be the best on the island, and the menu also has curry chicken and stewed pork, oxtail, rice and beans, and homemade soups; drinks include breadfruit, mango, passion fruit, and carrot juices. The interior has an island-country kitsch look with silk roses, white porch swings, straw hats, empty bird cages and fake ivy crawling along the ceiling. It's less than a five-minute cab ride from town. *Eastern Ave. George Town, 345/945–2124.*

Grenada/Carriacou

Nutmeg, cinnamon, cloves, cocoa . . . the aroma fills the air and all memories of Grenada (pronounced gruh-*nay*-da). Only 33½ km (21 mi) long and 19½ km (12 mi) wide, the Isle of Spice is a tropical gem of lush rain forests, green hillsides, white-sand beaches, secluded covers, and exotic flowers.

Until 1983, when the U.S.–Eastern Caribbean intervention catapulted this little nation into the headlines, Grenada was a relatively obscure island hideaway for lovers of fishing, snorkeling, or simply lazing in the sun. Grenada has been back to normal for years; it's a safe and secure vacation spot with enough good shopping, restaurants, historic sites, and natural wonders to make it a popular port of call. Tourism is growing each year, but the expansion of tourist facilities is carefully controlled. New construction on the beaches must be at least 165 ft back from the high-water mark, and no building can stand taller than a coconut palm. As a result, Grenada continues to retain its distinctly West Indian culture and identity.

Nearby Carriacou (pronounced *car*-ree-a-coo) is visited mostly by sailing ships, such as the Club Med vessels and Windjammer Barefoot Cruises's tall ship, *Yankee Clipper.* Part of the three-island nation of Grenada (Petit Martinique, a tiny island 3 km (2 mi) north of Carriacou, is the third), the 21-square-km (13-square-mi) island is 37 km (23 mi) north of the island of Grenada. Carriacou is the largest and southernmost island of the Grenadines, an archipelago of 32 small islands and cays that stretch northward from Grenada to St. Vincent.

The colonial history of Carriacou parallels Grenada's, but the island's small size has restricted its role in the nation's political history. Carriacou is hilly not lush like Grenada. In fact, it's quite arid in some areas. A chain of hills cuts a wide swath through the center, from Gun Point in the north to Tyrrel Bay in the south. The island's greatest attraction for cruise passengers is its diving and snorkeling opportunities.

Currency Grenada uses the Eastern Caribbean (EC) dollar. The exchange rate is officially EC$2.70 to U.S.$1, although taxi drivers, stores, and vendors will frequently calculate at a rate of EC$2.50. U.S. dollars are readily accepted, but always ask which currency is referred to when asking prices. All prices given below are in U.S. dollars except where indicated.

Telephones U.S. and Canadian telephone numbers can be dialed directly. Pay phones and phone cards are available at the welcome center, on the Carenage in St. George's, where cruise ship passengers come ashore.

Shore Excursions The following are good choices in Grenada. They may not be offered by all cruise lines. Times and prices are approximate.

Island Sights **City and Spice Tour.** Tour St. George's, then ride north along the spectacular west coast, through small villages and lush greenery. Stop along the way to see how nutmegs are processed. *3 hrs. Cost: $34.*

Nature Tours **Spice and Rum Tour.** Visit the cottage industries of Grenada, including a nutmeg factory (Grenada is the world's largest nutmeg producer), a small soap-and-perfume factory, and a rum factory. Purchase samples, and see how the products are made. *3 hrs. Cost: $34.*

Island Sights and Grand Étang. Tour the capital, then travel north through Grenada's central mountain range to the rain forest, Crater Lake, and Grand Étang National Park. *3¼ hrs. Cost: $38.*

Coming Ashore Large ships anchor outside St. George's Harbour and tender passengers to the east end of the Carenage, a thoroughfare that surrounds the horseshoe-shape harbor. Smaller ships can dock beside the welcome center. You can easily tour the capital on foot, but be prepared to climb up and down steep hills. At the welcome center, you can hire a walking-tour guide ($5 an hour), a taxi to take you around the Carenage to Market Square ($3 one-way), or a hand-rowed water taxi (50¢ one-way) across the harbor.

To explore areas outside St. George, hiring a taxi or arranging a guided tour is more sensible than renting a car. Taxis are plentiful, and fixed rates to popular island destinations are posted at the welcome center. Cab drivers charge $15 per hour; island tours generally cost $40–$55 per person for a full day of sightseeing.

Water taxis are the most picturesque way to get from the welcome center to the beach; the fare is $5 one-way to Grand Anse, $10 to Morne Rouge. Minibuses are the least expensive (and most crowded) way to travel between St. George's and Grand Anse. Catch one just outside the welcome center, pay EC$1 (37¢), and hold onto your hat!

Exploring Grenada *Numbers in the margin correspond to points of interest on the Grenada (and Carriacou) map.*

St. George's **St. George's** is one of the most picturesque and authentic West
❶ Indian towns in the Caribbean. Pastel-painted buildings with orange-tile roofs line the Carenage, facing the harbor. Small, rainbow-color houses rise up from the waterfront and disappear into steep green hills. On weekends, a windjammer is likely to be anchored in the harbor, giving the entire scene a 19th-century appearance.

Ft. George, built by the French in 1708, rises high above the entrance to the harbor. The first shots fired from the fort occurred in October 1983, when Prime Minister Maurice Bishop and some of his followers were assassinated in the courtyard. The fort now houses Grenada's police headquarters but is open to the public. The 360-degree view from here is magnificent. *Admission free. Open daily during daylight hrs.*

A couple of blocks from the harbor, the **National Museum** has a small, interesting collection of archaeological artifacts and colonial items. You'll find such things as the young Josephine Bonaparte's marble bathtub, old rum-making equipment, and recent political memorabilia documenting the intervention. *Young and Monckton Sts., tel. 473/440–3725. Admission: $1. Open weekdays 9–4:30, Sat. 10–1:30.*

On the bay side of St. George's, facing the sea and separated from the harbor by the Sendall Tunnel, the **Esplanade** is the location of the open-air meat and fish markets. At high tide, waves sometimes crash against the sea wall.

Don't miss picturesque **Market Square,** a block from the Esplanade on Granby Street. It's open weekday mornings but really comes alive every Saturday from 8 AM to noon. The atmosphere is colorful, noisy, and exciting. Vendors sell baskets, spices, fresh produce, clothing, and other items.

The West Coast
② Concord Falls, up the Coast Road about 13 km (8 mi) north of St. George's, is really three beautiful cascades and a great spot for hiking. There's a small visitors center at the first waterfall. It's a 3-km (2-mi) hike through tropical rain forest to get to the others. The farthest one thunders down 65 ft onto huge boulders, creating a natural pool. It's smart to use a guide for this hike, which can be slippery and tricky in places. *No phone. Admission: $1. Open daily 9–4.*

③ Dougaldston Spice Estate is a historic plantation where they still process cocoa, nutmeg, mace, cloves, cinnamon, and other spices the old-fashioned way. You'll see them laid out on giant rolling trays to dry in the sun. A worker will be happy to explain the process—you can sniff, taste, and even buy some spices. *Coast Rd. just south of Gouyave. No phone. Admission: $1. Open weekdays 9–4.*

④ The ½-hour tour of the **Nutmeg Processing Cooperative,** in the center of Gouyave, is fragrant and fascinating. Workers in the three-story plant, which turns out 3 million pounds per year of Grenada's most famous export, sort nutmegs by hand and pack them in burlap bags for shipment around the world. *Coast Rd., Gouyave (center of town), tel. 473/444–8337. Admission: $1. Open weekdays 10–1 and 2–4.*

Central Grenada
⑤ In the center of this lush, mountainous island is **Grand Étang National Park,** a bird sanctuary and forest reserve where you can fish in mountain streams, hike on miles of trails, and take a refreshing swim. Crater Lake, in the crater of an extinct volcano, is a 13-acre expanse of cobalt-blue water 1,740 ft above sea level. *Main Interior Rd., between Grenville and St. George's, tel. 473/440–6160. Admission: $1. Open weekdays 8:30–4.*

⑥ Grenville, on the Atlantic coast and Grenada's second-largest city, retains its historical identity as a French market town; Saturday is market day. The local spice-processing factory, the largest on the island, is open to the public.

⑦ At the rustic, picturesque **River Antoine Rum Distillery,** you can see rum produced by the same methods used since the mid-1700s. The process begins with the crushing of sugarcane from adjacent fields. The result is a potent, overproof rum that will knock your socks off. *River Antoine Estate, St. Patrick's. Admission: $1. Guided tours daily 9–4.*

⑧ Westerhall, a residential area about 8 km (5 mi) east of St. George's, is known for its beautiful villas, gardens, and panoramic views. A great deal of residential development is happening here. European and North American retirees and local businesspeople are building

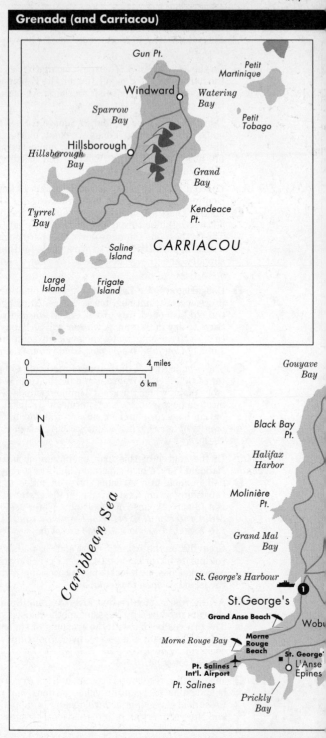

Grenada (and Carriacou)

Gun Pt.

Petit Martinique

Windward

Watering Bay

Sparrow Bay

Petit Tobago

Hillsborough

Hillsborough Bay

Grand Bay

Tyrrel Bay

Kendeace Pt.

Saline Island

CARRIACOU

Large Island

Frigate Island

0   4 miles
0   6 km

N

Caribbean Sea

Gouyave Bay

Black Bay Pt.

Halifax Harbor

Molinière Pt.

Grand Mal Bay

St. George's Harbour

St.George's **1**

Grand Anse Beach

Wobu

Morne Rouge Bay

Morne Rouge Beach

Pt. Salines Int'l. Airport

St. George'

L'Anse Epines

Pt. Salines

Prickly Bay

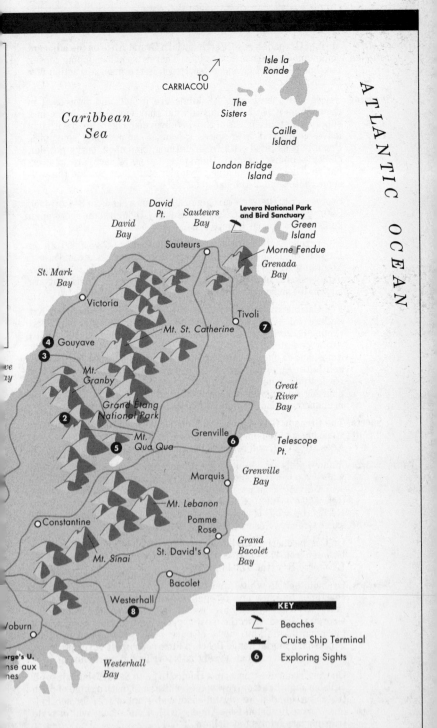

Isle la Ronde

TO CARRIACOU

The Sisters

Caille Island

Caribbean Sea

London Bridge Island

Atlantic Ocean

David Pt.

David Bay

Sauteurs Bay

Levera National Park and Bird Sanctuary

Green Island

Sauteurs

Morne Fendue

Grenada Bay

St. Mark Bay

Victoria

Tivoli

7

Mt. St. Catherine

4 Gouyave

3

ve y

Mt. Granby

Great River Bay

2

Grand Étang National Park

Grenville

6

Telescope Pt.

5 *Mt. Qua Qua*

Marquis

Grenville Bay

Mt. Lebanon

Constantine

Pomme Rose

Grand Bacolet Bay

St. David's

Mt. Sinai

Bacolet

Westerhall

8

Voburn

rge's U.

nse aux
nes

Westerhall Bay

KEY

Beaches

Cruise Ship Terminal

6 Exploring Sights

elegant homes with striking views of the sea at prices that compare with those in expensive communities in the United States.

Grand Anse/ South End Most of Grenada's resort activity is in Grand Anse or the adjacent community of L'Anse aux Epines. There's a small shopping center, too, but beautiful Grand Anse Beach is the main attraction (*see* Beaches, *below*).

Shopping Spices are a best buy. All kinds are grown and processed in Grenada and cost a fraction of what they would back home in a supermarket. Six-packs of tiny handwoven baskets lined with bay leaves and filled with spices (about $8) make good souvenirs. Small bottles filled with fresh nutmeg, cinnamon, curry powder, cloves, peppercorns, and other spices (about $2 each) are an alternative. These are available at vendor stalls just outside the welcome center and at the market.

Stores in St. George's are generally open weekdays 8–4 or 4:30, Saturday 8–1. Most are closed on Sunday, though some shops open and vendors appear if ships are in port.

For native handicrafts, **Grenada Craft Center** (473/440–9512), on Lagoon Road south of the Carenage, is both a workshop and store. You can watch artisans create jewelry, pottery, batik, wood carvings, baskets, screen-printed T-shirts, and woven items that are all sold in the shop next door.

For Caribbean art and antique engravings, visit **Yellow Poui Art Gallery** (tel. 473/444–3001), on Cross Streetin St. George's. **Tikal** (Young St., tel. 473/440–2310) is a long-established boutique with exquisite handicrafts, baskets, artwork, jewelry, carvings, batik items, and fashions—both locally made and imported from Africa and Latin America. **Art Fabrik** (Young St., tel. 473/440–0568) is a batik studio where you can watch artisans create the designs by painting fabric with hot wax. You can buy batik by the yard or fashioned into clothing and other items.

Sports
Golf The **Grenada Golf & Country Club** (tel. 473/444–4128) near Grand Anse has a nine-hole golf course and is open to cruise passengers. Fees are EC$7, and rental clubs are available.

Water Sports Major hotels on Grand Anse Beach have water-sports centers where you can rent small sailboats, Windsurfers, and Sunfish. For scuba diving, contact **Dive Grenada** at Allamanda Beach Resort (tel. 473/444–1092), **Grand Anse Aquatics, Ltd.** at Coyaba Beach Resort (tel. 473/444–1046), or **Sanvics Scuba Watersports** at Renaissance Grenada Resort (tel. 473/444–4371, ext. 638).

On Carriacou, try **Carriacou Silver Diving** on Main Street in Hillsborough (tel. 473/443–7882) or **Tanki's Watersport Paradise, Ltd.** on L'Esterre Bay (tel. 473/443–8406).

Beaches Grenada has 45 white-sand beaches along its 128 km (80 mi) of coastline. Beaches are all open to cruise passengers, and some great stretches of sand are just 10 minutes from the dock in St. George's. **Grand Anse,** the most spectacular and most popular, is a gleaming 3-km (2-mi) curve of pure white sand lapped by clear, gentle surf. **Morne Rouge Beach,** a little southwest of Grand Anse, is less crowded and has a reef that's terrific for snorkeling.

On Carriacou, don't pass up a chance to go to **Sandy Island,** just off Hillsborough. It's a narrow spit of white sand, with a ridge of palm trees, surrounded by crystal-clear water and a reef for snorkeling—a true deserted isle. Anyone with a motorboat will provide transportation for a few dollars.

Dining   Restaurants usually add a 10% service charge to your bill. If not, tip 10%–15% for a job well done.

$$ **Coconut Beach, The French Creole Restaurant.** Take local seafood, add butter, wine, and Grenadian herbs, and you have excellent French Creole cuisine. Throw in a beautiful setting right on Grand Anse Beach, and this West Indian cottage becomes a delightful spot for lunch. Lobster is prepared in a dozen different ways. You can approach the restaurant from the sand, hardly interrupting your day in the sun. *Grand Anse Beach, Grenada, tel. 473/444–4644. AE, D, MC, V.*

$ **The Nutmeg.** Fresh seafood, homemade West Indian dishes, great hamburgers, and the view of the harbor draw residents and visitors alike. The Nutmeg is on the second floor, and you peer through large open windows as you eat. *The Carenage, St. George's, Grenada, tel. 473/440–2539. AE, D, MC, V.*

$ **Rudolf's.** This busy English-style pub offers fine West Indian fare—crab back, *lambi* (conch), and delectable nutmeg ice cream—along with fish-and-chips, sandwiches, burgers, and the best gossip on the island. *The Carenage, St. George's, Grenada, tel. 473/440–2241. MC, V. Closed Sun.*

$ **Callaloo Restaurant and Bar (Carriacou).** This quaint second-floor restaurant has extraordinary views of Hillsborough Bay and Sandy Island. Excellent seafood dishes, including lobster thermidor, are reasonably priced. Be sure to sample the callaloo soup. *Main St., Hillsborough, Carriacou, tel. 473/443–8044. AE, MC, V. Closed Sept.*

Guadeloupe

On a map, Guadeloupe looks like a giant butterfly resting on the sea between Antigua and Dominica. Its two wings—Basse-Terre and Grande-Terre—are the two largest islands in the 1,054-square-km (659-square-mi) Guadeloupe archipelago. The Rivière Salée, a 6-km (4-mi) channel between the Caribbean and the Atlantic, forms the "spine" of the butterfly. A drawbridge over it connects the two islands.

If you're seeking a resort atmosphere, casinos, and white sandy beaches, your target is Grande-Terre. On the other hand, Basse-Terre's Natural Park, laced with mountain trails and washed by waterfalls and rivers, is a 74,100-acre haven for hikers, nature lovers, and anyone yearning to peer into the steaming crater of an active volcano.

This port of call is one of the least touristy (and least keen on Americans). Guadeloupeans accept visitors, but their economy does not rely on tourism. Pointe-à-Pitre, the port city, is a kaleidoscope of smart boutiques, wholesalers, sidewalk cafés, produce markets, barred and broken-down buildings, little parks, and bazaarlike stores. Though not to everyone's liking, the city has more character than many other island ports.

French is the official language, and few locals speak English—although Guadeloupeans are very similar to Parisians in that if you make an attempt at a few French words, they will usually open up. (It's sensible to carry a postcard of the ship with the name of where it's docked written in French.) Like other West Indians, many Guadeloupeans do not appreciate having their photographs taken. Always ask permission first, and don't take a

refusal personally. Also, many locals take offense at short shorts
or swimwear worn outside bathing areas.

Currency Legal tender is the French franc, composed of 100 centimes. At
press time, the rate was 5.65F to U.S.$1. All prices given below
are in U.S. dollars except where indicated.

Telephones To call the United States from Guadeloupe, dial 001-191, the area
code, and the local number. For calls within Guadeloupe, dial the
six-digit number.

Shore The following is a good choice in Guadeloupe. It may not be offered
Excursions by all cruise lines. Time and price are approximate.

Pointe-à-Pitre/Island Drive. Explore both of Guadeloupe's islands—
Grande-Terre and Basse-Terre. The tour includes a walk through
the lush national park and a stop at a rum factory. If you're not
going to explore the island on your own, this tour is highly recommended. *3 hrs. Cost: $40.*

Coming Ships dock at the Maritime Terminal of Centre St-John Perse in
Ashore downtown Pointe-à-Pitre, about a block from the shopping district. To get to the tourist information office, walk along the quay
for about five minutes to the Place de la Victoire. The office is
across the road at the top of the section of the harbor—called La
Darse—just a few blocks from your ship. There's also a small
information booth in the terminal, a branch of the main office.

The most interesting area in Pointe-à-Pitre, with food and clothing stalls, markets, pastry shops, and modern buildings, is compact and easy to see on foot. If you want to use a taxi driver as a
guide, make sure you speak a common language. Taxi fares (more
expensive here than on other islands) are regulated by the government and posted at taxi stands. If your French is good, you can
call for a cab (tel. 590/82–21–21, 590/83–90–00, or 590/20–74–74).
Tip drivers 10%.

Exploring *Numbers in the margin correspond to points of interest on the*
Guadeloupe *Guadeloupe map.*

❶ Pointe-à-Pitre, a city of some 100,000 people, lies almost on the
"backbone" of the butterfly, near the bridge that crosses the Salée
River. With its narrow streets, honking horns, and traffic jams, it's
full of pulsing life.

The **Musée St-John Perse** is dedicated to the Guadeloupean poet
who won the 1960 Nobel Prize in literature. Inside the restored
colonial house is a complete collection of his poetry, as well as
many of his personal effects. *Corner rue Noizières and Achille
René-Boisneuf, tel. 590/90–07–92. Admission: 10F. Open Thurs.–
Tues. 8:30–12:30 and 2:30–5:30.*

In the cacophonous, colorful **marketplace,** locals bargain for
papayas, breadfruit, christophenes, tomatoes, and a vivid assortment of other produce. Saturday mornings are particularly bois-
terous. *Between rues St-John Perse, Fré-bault, Schoelcher, and
Peynier.*

The **Musée Schoelcher** honors the memory of Victor Schoelcher,
the 19th-century Alsatian abolitionist who fought slavery in the
French West Indies. Exhibits trace his life and work. *24 rue
Peynier, tel. 509/82–08–04. Admission: 10F. Open weekdays 8:30–
11:30 and 2–5.*

Place de la Victoire, surrounded by wood buildings with balconies
and shutters and lined by sidewalk cafés, was named in honor of

Victor Hugues's 1794 victory over the British. The sandbox trees in the park are said to have been planted by Hugues the day after the victory. During the French Revolution a guillotine here lopped off the heads of many an aristocrat.

The imposing **Cathedral of St. Peter and St. Paul** has survived havoc-wreaking earthquakes and hurricanes. Note the lovely stained-glass windows. *rue Alexandre Isaac.*

Basse-Terre High adventure can be yours on a drive across Basse-Terre to the **❷ Parc National de la Guadeloupe.** For the ecologically minded, this is the place to come. The park is bisected by the Route de la Traversée (Rte. D23), a 26-km-long (16-mi-long) paved road lined with masses of thick tree ferns, shrubs, flowers, tall trees, and green plantains. If you plan to do any exploring, wear rubber-sole shoes and pack a picnic lunch as well as both a swimsuit and a sweater. Once you've reached the coast, head north on route N2 toward Grand Anse. The road twists and turns up steep hills smothered in tropical vegetation, skirts deep blue bays, and drops to colorful little seaside towns. Constantly changing light, towering clouds, and frequent rainbows add to the beauty.

Shopping For serious shopping in Pointe-à-Pitre, browse the boutiques and stores along rue Schoelcher, rue Frébault, and rue Noizières. The market square and stalls of La Darse are filled mostly with vegetables, fruits, and housewares, but you will find some straw hats and dolls.

There are dozens of shops in and around the cruise ship terminal, Centre St-John Perse. Many stores here offer a 20% discount on luxury items purchased with traveler's checks or major credit cards. You can find good buys on anything French—perfume, crystal, wine, cosmetics, and scarves. As for local handcrafted items, you'll see a lot of junk, but you can also find island dolls dressed in madras, finely woven straw baskets and hats, *salako* hats made of split bamboo, madras table linens, and wood carvings.

The following shops are all in Pointe-à-Pitre: For Baccarat, Lalique, Porcelaine de Paris, Limoges, and other upscale tableware, check **Rosebleu** (5 rue Frébault, tel. 590/82–93–43). Guadeloupe's exclusive purveyor of Orlane, Stendhal, and Germaine Monteil is **Vendôme** (8–10 rue Frébault, tel. 590/83–42–44). The largest selection of perfumes is at **Phoenicia** (8 rue Frébault, tel. 590/83–50–36). You many also want to try **Au Bonheur des Dames** (49 rue Frébault, tel. 590/82–00–30).

Other shopping can be found in Ste-Anne. **La Case à Soie** (tel. 590/88–11–31) creates flowing silk dresses and scarves in Caribbean colors. The **Centre Artisanat** offers a wide selection of local crafts.

Sports Contact **Caraibe Peche** (Marina Bas-du-Fort, tel. 590/90–97–51),
Fishing **Fishing Club Antilles** (Bouillante, tel. 590/98–70–10), or **Le Rocher de Malendure** (Pigeon, Bouillante, tel. 590/98–28–84).

Golf **Golf Municipal Saint-François** (St-François, tel. 590/88–41–87) has an 18-hole Robert Trent Jones course, an English-speaking pro, and electric carts for rent.

Hiking Basse-Terre's **Parc National** is abundant with trails, many of which should be attempted only with an experienced guide. Before heading out, pick up a *Guide to the National Park* from the tourist office (*see* Coming Ashore, *above*), which rates the hiking trails according to difficulty. (Note: The majority of mountain trails are in the southern half.) If you want to do a light hike, head for the

Guadeloupe

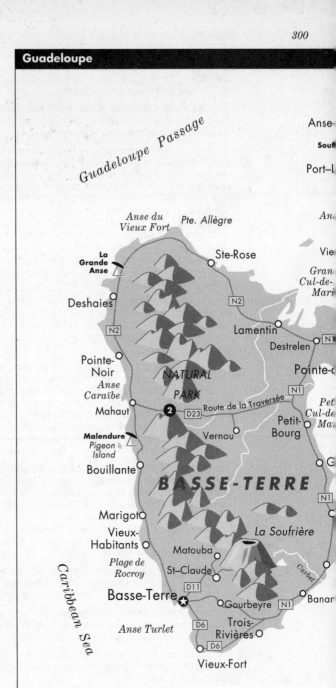

Guadeloupe Passage

Anse-

Souf

Port–L

Anse du
Vieux Fort

Pte. Allègre

An

La
Grande
Anse

Ste-Rose

Vie

Gran
Cul-de-
Mari

Deshaies

N2

N2

Lamentin

Pointe-
Noir

*NATURAL
PARK*

Destrelen

N1

Pointe-

Anse
Caraïbe

N1

Pet
Cul-de
Ma

Mahaut

2

D23

Route de la Traversée

Vernou

Petit-
Bourg

Malendure
*Pigeon
Island*

G

Bouillante

BASSE-TERRE

N1

Marigot

Vieux-
Habitants

La Soufrière

Matouba

St–Claude

Carbet

*Plage de
Rocroy*

D11

Basse-Terre ✪

Gourbeyre

N1

Banar

Caribbean Sea

Anse Turlet

D6

Trois-
Rivières

D6

Vieux-Fort

0   10 miles

0   15 km

Iles des Saintes
Terre-de-Haut

Terre-
de-Bas

Place

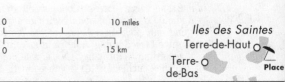

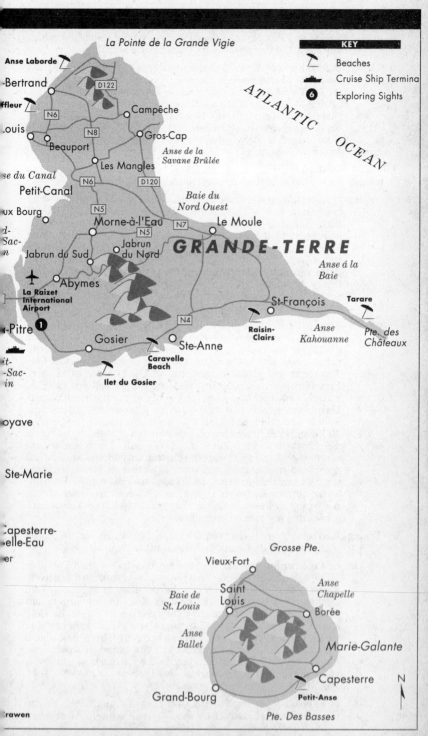

La Pointe de la Grande Vigie

KEY

Beaches

Cruise Ship Termina

6 Exploring Sights

ATLANTIC OCEAN

Anse Laborde

-Bertrand

D122

ffleur

N6

Campêche

Louis

N8

Gros-Cap

Beauport

Les Mangles

Anse de la
Savane Brûlée

se du Canal

N6

D120

Petit-Canal

Baie du
Nord Ouest

ux Bourg

N5

Morne-à-l'Eau

N7

Le Moule

d-
Sac-
n

N5

Jabrun du Sud

Jabrun
du Nord

GRANDE-TERRE

Anse á la
Baie

Abymes

La Raizet
International
Airport

N4

St-François

Tarare

-Pitre

1

**Raisin-
Clairs**

Anse
Kahouanne

Pte. des
Châteaux

Gosier

Ste-Anne

t-
-Sac-
in

**Caravelle
Beach**

Ilet du Gosier

oyave

Ste-Marie

apesterre-
elle-Eau
er

Grosse Pte.

Vieux-Fort

Anse
Chapelle

Baie de
St. Louis

Saint
Louis

Borée

Anse
Ballet

Marie-Galante

Capesterre

Grand-Bourg

Petit-Anse

N

rawen

Pte. Des Basses

Cascade aux Ecrevisses. Crayfish Falls is one of the loveliest and most popular spots on the island. There's a marked trail (it can be muddy and slippery) that leads to the splendid waterfall dashing down into the Corossol River—a good place for a dip.

Guided hikes for up to 12 people are arranged by **Organisation des Guides de Montagne de la Caraïbe** (Maison Forestière, Matouba, tel. 590/94–29–11) or by the **Office de Tourisme de Basse-Terre** (tel. 590/82–24–83). The acknowledged pros in the private sector are **Parfum d'Aventure** (1 Roche Blonval, St. Francois, tel. 590/88–47–62) or **Sport d'Av** (tel. 590/32–58–41) which both offer everything from four-wheel-drive safaris to sea-kayaking, hiking, and white-water canoeing trips.

Horseback Riding **La Manade** (Saint-Claude, tel. 590/81–52–21) on Basse-Terre offers half- or full-day rides through the rain forest.

Water Sports Windsurfing, waterskiing, and sailing are available at almost all beachfront hotels. The main windsurfing center is at the **UCPA** hotel club (tel. 590/88–64–80) in St-François. You can also rent equipment at **Holywind** (Résidence Canella Beach, Pointe de la Verdure, Gosier, tel. 590/90–44–00) and at the **Tropical Club Hotel** (tel. 590/93–97–97) at Le Moule, blessed with the constant Atlantic trade winds. For diving, head to Basse-Terre. The **Nautilus Club** (Plage de Malendure, tel. 590/98–89–08) is one of the island's top scuba operations and offers snorkeling trips to Pigeon Island, just offshore, as well as glass-bottom-boat trips.

Beaches Some of the island's best beaches of soft, white sand lie on the south coast of Grande-Terre from Ste-Anne to Pointe des Châteaux. For $5–$10 per passenger, hotels allow nonguests to use changing facilities, towels, and beach chairs. **Caravelle Beach,** just outside Ste-Anne, has one of the longest and prettiest stretches of sand. Protected by reefs, it's a fine place to snorkel, and you can rent water-sports gear from Club Med, at one end of the beach. **Raisin-Clairs,** just outside St-François, offers windsurfing, waterskiing, sailing, and other activities, with rentals arranged through the Méridien Hotel. **Tarare** is a secluded cove close to the tip of Pointe des Châteaux, where locals tan in the buff. There are several secluded coves around **Pointe des Châteaux,** where the Atlantic and Caribbean waters meet and crash against huge rocks, sculpting them into castlelike shapes. **La Grande Anse,** just outside Deshaies on the northwest coast of Basse-Terre, is a secluded beach of soft, beige sand sheltered by palms. The waterfront Karacoli restaurant serves rum punch and Creole dishes.

Dining Restaurants are legally required to include a 15% service charge in the menu price. No additional gratuity is necessary.

$$$ **Le Côte Jardin.** The marina between Bas-du-Fort and Pointe-à-Pitre, a 10-minute cab ride from the cruise ship terminal, is a lively venue with a dozen restaurants, bar lounges, and shops around the quay. You can take your pick from pizzas to hamburgers, but for something more formal, try the creative cuisine at Le Côte Jardin. The plant-filled restaurant is attractive, and the menu of haute French Creole lists dishes that range from basic lamb Provençal and baked red snapper to more exotic *escargots de la mer* (sea snails) with garlic butter. It's busy at lunch, so make sure you reserve a table. *La Marina, Bas-Du-Fort, tel. 590/90–91–28. AE, MC, V.*

$–$$ **Le Karacoli.** If you want to make a day out of it, aim for this charming beachfront restaurant on Basse-Terre's beautiful west coast.

From your table on the terrace, all you'll hear will be the splash of the waves and the rustling of coconut palms. The food is good Creole fare—such as goat *colombo* (curry) or *boudin* (blood sausage)—as well as the usual seafood dishes. For dessert, try the banana flambé, heavily perfumed with rum. *Grande-Anse, north of Deshaies, tel. 590/28–41–17. MC, V. No dinner.*

Jamaica

The third-largest island in the Caribbean, the English-speaking nation of Jamaica enjoys a considerable self-sufficiency based on tourism, agriculture, and mining. Its physical attractions include jungle mountains, clear waterfalls, and unforgettable beaches, yet the country's greatest resource may be its people. Although 95% of Jamaicans trace their bloodlines to Africa, their national origins also lie in Great Britain, the Middle East, India, China, Germany, Portugal, and South America, as well as in many other islands in the Caribbean. Their cultural life is a wealthy one; the music, art, and cuisine of Jamaica are vibrant with a spirit easy to sense but as hard to describe as the rhythms of reggae or the streetwise patois.

Don't let Jamaica's beauty cause you to relax the good sense you would use in your own hometown. Resist the promise of adventure should any odd character offer to show you the "real" Jamaica. Jamaica on the beaten track is wonderful enough, so don't take chances by wandering too far off it.

Currency Currency-exchange booths are set up on the docks at Montego Bay and Ocho Rios whenever a ship is in port. The U.S. dollar is accepted virtually everywhere, but change will be made in local currency. Check the value of the J$ on arrival—it fluctuates greatly. At press time the exchange rate was J$35 to U.S.$1. All prices given below are in U.S. dollars except where indicated.

Telephones Direct telephone services are available in communication stations at the ports. Because of recent fraud problems, some U.S. phone cards such as MCI will not accept credit card calls placed from Jamaica. Phones take phone cards, which are available from kiosks or variety shops.

Shore Excursions The following are good choices in Jamaica. They may not be offered by all cruise lines. Times and prices are approximate.

Natural Beauty **Prospect Plantation and Dunn's River Falls.** Visit the beautiful gardens of Prospect Plantation, with their bananas, cocoa, coffee, sugarcane, orchids, and other tropical foliage. Then stop at Dunn's River Falls to crawl and climb through the cool water. *4 hrs. Cost: $44.*

Rafting on the Martha Brae River. Glide down this pristine river in a 30-ft, two-seat bamboo raft, admiring the verdant plant life along the river's banks. *5 hrs. Cost: $54.*

Coming Ashore A growing number of cruise ships are using the city of Montego Bay (nicknamed "MoBay"), 108 km (67 mi) to the west of Ocho Rios, as their Jamaican port of call. The cruise port in Montego Bay is a $10 taxi ride from town. There's one shopping center within walking distance of the Montego Bay docks. The Jamaica Tourist Board office is about 5½ km (3½ mi) away on Gloucester Avenue on Doctor's Cave Beach.

In Montego Bay

In Ocho Rios Most cruise ships dock at this port on Jamaica's north coast, near the famous Dunn's River Falls. Less than 1.6 km (1 mi) from the Ocho Rios cruise ship pier are the Taj Mahal Duty Free Shopping

Jamaica

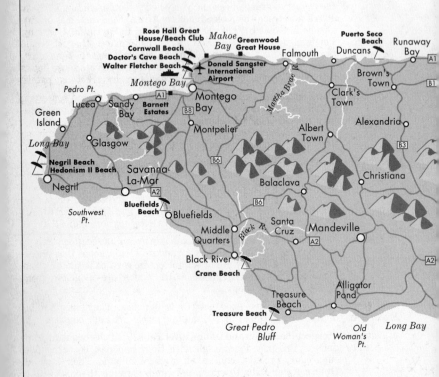

Rose Hall Great
House/Beach Club
Cornwall Beach
Doctor's Cave Beach
Walter Fletcher Beach

*Mahoe
Bay*
Greenwood
Great House
Falmouth

Puerto Seco
Beach
Duncans
Runaway
Bay

A1

Donald Sangster
International
Airport

Brown's
Town

B1

Pedro Pt.
Lucea
Sandy
Bay
Barnett
Estates

Clark's
Town

Alexandria

Montego Bay

A1
Montego
Bay

Albert
Town

B3

Green
Island

Montpelier

Christiana

Long Bay
Glasgow

B8

Martha Brae R.

Negril Beach
Hedonism II Beach

B6

Savanna-
La-Mar

Balaclava

Negril

A2

Mandeville

*Southwest
Pt.*

Bluefields
Beach
Bluefields

B6

Santa
Cruz

A2

Middle
Quarters

Black R.

A2

Black River

Alligator
Pond

Crane Beach

Treasure
Beach

Treasure Beach

*Great Pedro
Bluff*

*Old
Woman's
Pt.*

Long Bay

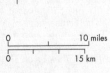

N

0   10 miles

0   15 km

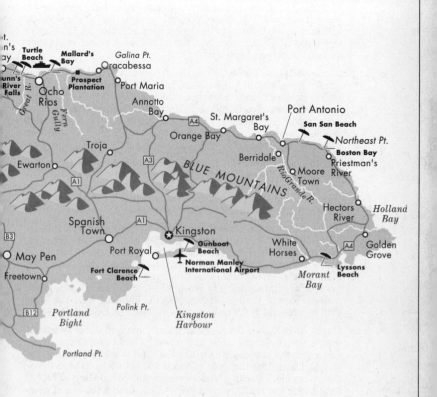

St.
nn's
ay

Turtle Beach
Mallard's Bay
Galina Pt.
Oracabessa
Prospect Plantation
Port Maria
unn's River Falls
Ocho Rios
Great R.
Fern Gully
Annotto Bay
St. Margaret's Bay
A4
Orange Bay
Troja
A3
BLUE MOUNTAINS
Berridale
Port Antonio
San San Beach
Northeast Pt.
Boston Bay
Priestman's River
Moore Town
Rio Grande R.
Ewarton
A1
Hectors River
Holland Bay
Spanish Town
A1
Kingston
Gunboat Beach
White Horses
A4
Golden Grove
B3
May Pen
Port Royal
Fort Clarence Beach
Norman Manley International Airport
Morant Bay
Lyssons Beach
Freetown
B12
Portland Bight
Polink Pt.
Kingston Harbour

Portland Pt.

Caribbean Sea

KEY
Beaches
Cruise Ship Terminal

Center and the Ocean Village Shopping Center, where the Jamaica Tourist Board maintains an office. Getting anywhere else in Ocho Rios will require a taxi.

Some of Jamaica's taxis are metered; rates are per car, not per passenger. You can flag cabs down on the street. All licensed and properly insured taxis display red Public Passenger Vehicle (PPV) plates. Licensed minivans also bear the red PPV plates. If you hire a taxi driver as a tour guide, be sure to agree on a price before the vehicle is put into gear.

Exploring
Jamaica
Montego Bay

Barnett Estates. Led by a charming guide in period costume who relates poetry and sings songs of the period as part of the presentation, this great-house tour is one of the best you'll find in Jamaica. The Kerr-Jarrett family has held the land here for 11 generations and still grows coconut, mango, and sugarcane on 3,000 acres; you'll get samples during the plantation tour by jitney. *Granville Main Rd., tel. 876/952–2382. Admission: $10. Open daily 9:30–10 (great house).*

Greenwood Great House, 24 km (15 mi) east of Montego Bay, has no spooky legend to titillate visitors, but it's much better than Rose Hall at evoking the atmosphere of life on a sugar plantation. Highlights of Greenwood include oil paintings of the family, china specially made for them by Wedgwood, a library filled with rare books, fine antique furniture, and a collection of exotic musical instruments. *Tel. 876/953–1077. Admission: $10. Open daily 9–6.*

One of the most popular excursions in Jamaica is rafting on the **Martha Brae River** (tel. 876/952–0889 for reservations), a gentle waterway filled with the romance of a tropical wilderness. Wear your swimsuit for a plunge at the halfway point of the 5-km (3-mi) river run. The ride costs less than $40 for two people.

Rose Hall Great House, perhaps the most impressive in the West Indies in the 1700s, enjoys its popularity less for its architecture than for the legend surrounding its second mistress. The story of Annie Palmer—credited with murdering three husbands and a plantation overseer who was her lover—is told in a novel sold everywhere in Jamaica: *The White Witch of Rose Hall* . The great house is east of Montego Bay, across the highway from the Rose Hall resorts. *Tel. 876/953–2323. Admission: $15. Open daily 9–6.*

Ocho Rios

Dunn's River Falls is 600 ft of cold, clear, mountain water splashing over a series of stone steps to the warm Caribbean. Don a swimsuit, climb the slippery steps, take the hand of the person ahead of you, and trust that the chain of hands and bodies leads to an experienced guide. The climb leaders are personable, reeling off bits of local lore while telling you where to step. Take a towel and wear tennis shoes. *Tel. 876/974–2857. Admission: $6. Open daily 8:30–4.*

The tour of **Prospect Plantation** is the best of several offerings that delve into the island's former agricultural lifestyle. It's not just for specialists; virtually everyone enjoys the beautiful views over the White River Gorge and the tour by jitney through a plantation with exotic fruits and tropical trees. Horseback riding through 1,000 acres is available, with one hour's notice, for about $20 per hour. *Tel. 876/994–1058. Admission: $12. Open daily 9–5. Tours Mon.–Sat. 10:30, 2, and 3:30; Sun. 11, 1:30, and 3:30.*

Shopping

Jamaican artisans express themselves in resort wear, hand-loomed fabrics, silk-screening, wood carvings, and paintings. Jamaican rum makes a great gift, as do Tia Maria (Jamaica's famous coffee liqueur) and Blue Mountain coffee. Cheap sandals are good buys (about $20 a pair).

Before visiting the crafts markets in Montego Bay and Ocho Rios, consider how much tolerance you have for pandemonium and price haggling. If you're looking to spend money, head for City Centre Plaza, Half Moon Village, Holiday Inn Shopping Centre, Montego Bay Shopping Center, St. James's Place, or Westgate Plaza in Montego Bay; in Ocho Rios, the shopping plazas are Pineapple Place, Ocean Village, the Taj Mahal, Coconut Grove, and Island Plaza. Some cruise lines run shore excursions devoted exclusively to shopping.

For Jamaican and Haitian paintings, head for the **Gallery of West Indian Art** (1 Orange La., Montego Bay, tel. 876/952–4547). A corner of the gallery is devoted to hand-turned pottery and beautifully carved birds and jungle animals. Eight kilometers (6 mi) east of the docks in Ocho Rios is **Harmony Hall** (tel. 876/975–4222), a huge house that has been converted into an art gallery, restaurant, and bar. Wares here include arts and crafts, carved items, ceramics, antiques, books, jewelry, fudge, spices, and Blue Mountain coffee.

Sports *Golf*	The best courses are at the **Half Moon Club** (tel. 876/953–2731), **Ironshore** (tel. 876/953–2800), and Tryall (tel. 876/956–5660) in Montego Bay or **Breezes Golf and Beach Resort** in Runaway Bay (tel. 876/973–2561) and **Sandal's Golf and Country Club** (tel. 876/975–0119) in Ocho Rios. Rates range from $25 to $50 for 18 holes at the Ocho Rios courses to $110 and higher at the Half Moon Club and Tryall.
Horseback *Riding*	**Chukka Cove** (St. Ann, tel. 876/972–2506), near Ocho Rios, is the best equestrian facility in the English-speaking Caribbean. Riding is also available at **Prospect Plantation** (Ocho Rios, tel. 876/994–1058) and **Rocky Point Stables** (Half Moon Club, Montego Bay, tel. 876/953–2286).
Beaches	**Doctor's Cave Beach** at Montego Bay is getting crowded: the 8-mi (5-mi) stretch of sugary sand has been spotlighted in so many travel articles and brochures that it's no secret to anyone anymore. Two other popular beaches near Montego Bay are **Cornwall Beach,** farther up the coast, which has food and drink options, and **Walter Fletcher Beach,** on the bay near the center of town. Fletcher offers protection from the surf on a windy day and has unusually calm waters for swimming. The **Rose Hall Beach Club,** east of central Montego Bay near Rose Hall Great House, is in a secluded area (far less crowded than beaches in town) and has changing rooms and showers, a water-sports center, volleyball and other beach games, and a beach bar and grill.

In Ocho Rios the busiest beach is **Turtle Beach,** not far from the cruise terminal. Several large resorts line the water, but the beach is public, so cruise passengers can enjoy an array of beach bars and grills and water-sports centers renting snorkel gear, small sailboats, Jet Skis, and other equipment.

Dining	Many restaurants add a 10% service charge to the bill. Otherwise, a tip of 10%–20% is customary.
$$–$$$	**Almond Tree.** This very popular restaurant offers a blend of Jamaican and European cuisines. The swinging rope chairs on the terrace bar and the tables perched above a lovely Caribbean cove are great fun. *83 Main St., Ocho Rios, tel. 876/974–2813. Reservations essential. AE, DC, MC, V.*

$$-$$$ **The Native.** This open-air stone terrace, shaded by a large poin-
ciana tree and overlooking Gloucester Avenue, specializes in
Jamaican and international dishes. To go native, start with
smoked marlin, move on to the Boonoonoonoos platter (a sampler
of local dishes), and round out the meal with coconut pie or *duck-
anoo* (a sweet dumpling of cornmeal, coconut, and banana
wrapped in a banana leaf and steamed). Caesar salad, seafood linguine, and shrimp kabobs are fine alternatives. *29 Gloucester Ave.,
Montego Bay, tel. 876/979–2769. AE, MC, V.*

$$-$$$ **Sugar Mill.** One of the finest restaurants in Jamaica, the Sugar Mill
serves seafood with flair on a terrace. Steak and lobster are usually garnished in a pungent sauce that blends Dijon mustard with
Jamaica's own Pickapeppa. *At Half Moon Golf Course, Montego
Bay tel. 876/953–2228. AE, MC, V.*

$–$$ **Evita's.** The setting is sensational: an 1860s gingerbread house
high on a hill overlooking Ocho Rios Bay (but also convenient from
Montego Bay). More than 30 kinds of pasta are served here, ranging from lasagna Rastafari (vegetarian) and fiery jerk spaghetti to
rotelle colombo (crabmeat with white sauce and noodles). There
are also excellent fish dishes from which to choose. *Mantalent
Inn, Eden Bower Rd., Ocho Rios, tel. 876/974–2333. AE, MC, V.*

$ **Ocho Rios Village Jerk Centre.** This blue-canopied, open-air eatery
is a good place to park yourself for frosty Red Stripe beer and
fiery jerk pork, chicken, or seafood. Milder barbecued meats, also
sold by weight (typically ¼ or ½ pound makes a good serving), also
turn up on the chalkboard menu that hangs on the wall. *DaCosta
Dr., Ocho Rios, tel. 876/974–2549. MC, V.*

Key West

The southernmost city in the Continental United States was originally a Spanish possession. Along with the rest of Florida, Key
West became part of American territory in 1821. During the late
19th century, Key West was Florida's wealthiest city per capita.
The locals made their fortunes from "wrecking"—rescuing people
and salvaging cargo from ships that foundered on nearby reefs.
Cigar making, fishing, shrimping, and sponge gathering also
became important industries.

Capital of the self-proclaimed "Conch Republic," Key West today
makes for a unique port of call for the 10 or so ships that visit each
week. A genuinely American town, it nevertheless exudes the
relaxed atmosphere and pace of a typical Caribbean island. Major
attractions for cruise passengers are the home of the Conch
Republic's most famous citizen, Ernest Hemingway; the birthplace of now-departed Pan American World Airways; and, if your
cruise ship stays in port late enough, the island's renowned sunset
celebrations.

Currency The U.S. dollar is the only currency accepted in Key West.

Telephones Public phones are found at the pier and on virtually every street
corner downtown. Local calls from a public phone cost 25¢.

Shore The following are good choices in Key West. They may not be
Excursions offered by all cruise lines. Times and prices are approximate.

Island Sights **Historic Homes Walking Tour.** You'll see three notable Key West
residences—the Harry S. Truman Little White House, the Don-
key Milk House, and the Audubon House and Gardens—on a short
guided stroll through the historic district. *2 hrs. Cost: $29.*

Undersea **Reef Snorkeling.** The last living coral reefs in Continental America
Creatures are your boat's destination. Changing facilities, snorkeling gear,
and unlimited beverages are included. *3 hrs. Cost: $40.*

Coming Cruise ships dock at Mallory Square or near Truman Annex. Both
Ashore are within walking distance of Duval and Whitehead streets, the
two main tourist thoroughfares. For maps and other tourism
information, the Chamber of Commerce (402 Wall St., tel. 305/294–
2587 or 800/527–8539) is found just off Mallory Square.

Because Key West is so easily explored on foot, there is rarely a
need to hire a cab. If you plan to venture beyond the main tourist
district, a fun way to get around is by bicycle or scooter. Key West
is a cycling town. In fact, there are so many bikes around that
cyclists must watch out for one another as well as for cars. Try
renting from **Keys Moped & Scooter** (tel. 305/294–0399) or **Moped
Hospital** (tel. 305/296–3344); both can be found on Truman Avenue.
Bike rentals begin at $4 for the day, scooters begin at $12 for three
hours. All rentals require a deposit on a credit card.

Two other ways to get around Key West are the **Conch Tour Train**
(tel. 305/294–5161) and the **Old Town Trolley** (tel. 305/296–6688).
The train provides a 90-minute, narrated tour of Key West that
covers 14 mi (22 km) of island sights. Board at the Front Street
Depot every half hour. The first train leaves at 9 AM and the last at
4:30 PM. The price is $15. The trolley operates trackless, trolley-
style buses for 90-minute, narrated tours of Key West. You may
get off at any of 12 stops and reboard later. The price is $16.

Exploring Key *Numbers in the margin correspond to points of interest on the*
West *Key West map.*

❶ **Mallory Square** is named for Stephen Mallory, secretary of the
Confederate Navy, who later owned the Mallory Steamship Line.
On nearby Mallory Dock, a nightly sunset celebration draws
street performers, food vendors, and thousands of onlookers.

❷ Facing Mallory Square is **Key West Aquarium,** which houses hundreds of brightly colored tropical fish and other fascinating sea
creatures from local waters. *1 Whitehead St., tel. 305/296–2051.
Admission: $8. Open daily 10–6; guided tours and shark feeding
at 11, 1, 3, and 4:30.*

❸ The **Mel Fisher Maritime Heritage Society Museum** symbolizes Key
West's salvaging past. On display are gold and silver bars, coins,
jewelry, and other artifacts recovered in 1985 from two Spanish
treasure ships that foundered in 1622. *200 Greene St., tel. 305/294–
2633. Admission: $6.50. Open daily 9:30–5.*

❹ At the end of Front Street, the **Truman Annex** is a 103-acre former
military parade ground and barracks. Also here is the Harry S.
Truman Little White House Museum, in the former president's
vacation home. *911 Front St., tel. 305/294–9911. Admission: $7.50.
Open daily 9–5.*

❺ The **Audubon House and Gardens** commemorates ornithologist
John James Audubon's 1832 visit to Key West. On display is a
large collection of the artist's engravings. *205 Whitehead St., tel.
305/294–2116. Admission: $7.50. Open daily 9:30–5.*

❻ At **301 Whitehead Street,** a sign proclaims the birthplace of Pan
American World Airways, the first U.S. airline to operate sched-
uled international air service. The inaugural flight took off from
Key West International Airport on October 28, 1927.

310

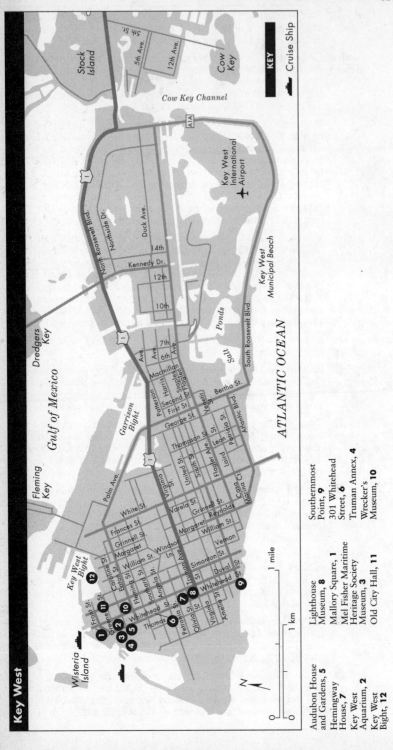

Key West

Audubon House
and Gardens, **5**
Hemingway
House, **7**
Key West
Aquarium, **2**
Key West
Bight, **12**

Lighthouse
Museum, **8**
Mallory Square, **1**
Mel Fisher Maritime
Heritage Society
Museum, **3**
Old City Hall, **11**

Southernmost
Point, **9**
301 Whitehead
Street, **6**
Truman Annex, **4**
Wrecker's
Museum, **10**

7 Built in 1851, **Hemingway House** was the first dwelling in Key West to have running water and a fireplace. Ernest Hemingway bought the place in 1931 and wrote eight books here. Descendants of Hemingway's cats still inhabit the grounds. Half-hour tours begin every 10 minutes. *907 Whitehead St., tel. 305/294–1575. Admission: $6.50. Open daily 9–5.*

8 Up the block from Hemingway House and across the street, behind a white picket fence, is the **Lighthouse Museum,** a 66-ft lighthouse built in 1847 and an adjacent 1887 clapboard house where the keeper lived. You can climb the 98 steps to the top for a spectacular view of the island. *938 Whitehead St., tel. 305/294–0012. Admission: $6. Open daily 9:30–5 (last admission 4:30).*

9 At the foot of Whitehead Street, a huge concrete marker proclaims this spot to be the **Southernmost Point** in the United States. Turn left on South Street. To your right are two dwellings that both claim to be the Southernmost House. Take a right onto Duval Street, which ends at the Atlantic Ocean, and you will be at the Southernmost Beach.

10 The **Wrecker's Museum** is said to be the oldest house in Key West. It was built in 1829 as the home of Francis Watlington, a sea captain and wrecker. It now contains 18th- and 19th-century period furnishings. *322 Duval St., tel. 305/294–9502. Admission: $4. Open daily 10–4.*

11 For a look at Key West as it was, visit the restored **Old City Hall** (510 Greene St.). Inside is a permanent exhibit of old Key West photographs, dating back to 1845.

12 **Key West Bight,** also known as Harbor Walk, remains the last funky area of Old Key West. Numerous charter boats and classic yachts call its slips home, and there's a popular waterfront bar called the Schooner Wharf (*see* Pub Crawling, *below*).

The **Reef Relief Environmental Center,** just a couple doors down from the Schooner Wharf bar, has videos, displays, and free information about the coral reef. *201 William St., tel. 305/294–3100. Open daily 9–5.*

Shopping Passengers looking for T-shirts, trinkets, and other souvenirs will find them all along Duval Street and around the cruise-ship piers. **Fast Buck Freddie's** (500 Duval St., tel. 305/294–2007) sells such novelties as banana leaf–shape furniture, fish-shape flatware, and battery-operated alligators that eat Muenster cheese. The **Paradise Gift Shop** (430 Duval St., tel. 305/292–8948) is noteworthy for its collection of flamingo items. **Jimmy Buffett's Margaritaville** (500B Duval St., tel. 305/296–3070) sells the music and books of the eponymous singer as well as activewear, housewares, and gadgets with the Buffett insignia. **Key West Island Bookstore** (513 Fleming St., tel. 305/294–2904) is the literary bookstore of the large Key West writers' community. **Lucky Street Gallery** (1120 White St., tel. 305/294–3973) carries the work of mainly keys artists.

Sports
Diving The excursions of **Captain's Corner** (0 Duval St. at the Ocean House Hotel, tel. 305/296–8865) last about four hours and leave at 9:30 and 1:30 (shallow reef diving) and at 10 (wreck and outer reef diving—for the more advanced).

Fishing and Boating The *Discovery* (tel. 305/293–0099) and *Fireball* (tel. 305/296–6293) are two glass-bottom boats designed for tours of the reef. The *Wolf* (tel. 305/296–9653) is a schooner that sails on day cruises with live music and bills itself as the "Flagship of the Conch Republic."

The ***Linda D III*** and ***Linda D IV*** (tel. 305/296–9798 or 800/299–9798), captained by third-generation Key West seaman Bill Wickers, run full- and half-day sportfishing outings. The Chamber of Commerce on Front Street, by the pier, has a full list of other operators.

Golf **Key West Golf Club** (tel. 305/294–5232) is an 18-hole course on the bay side of Stock Island. Passengers are charged $80 November 1–May 30 and $60 June 1 through October 31, which includes 18 holes and greens fees.

Snorkeling The northernmost living coral reef in the Americas and clear, warm Gulf of Mexico waters make Key West a good choice for getting your flippers wet (*see* Shore Excursions, *above*, and Beaches, *below*).

Beaches Facing the Gulf of Mexico, **Simonton Street Beach,** at the north end of Simonton Street and near the cruise-ship piers, is a great place to watch the boats come and go in the harbor. On the Atlantic Ocean, **Fort Zachary Taylor State Historic Site** has several hundred yards of beach near the western end of Key West. The beach is relatively uncrowded; snorkeling is good here. **Smathers Beach** features almost 2 mi (3 km) of coarse sand alongside South Roosevelt Boulevard. Vendors along the road will rent you rafts, Windsurfers, and other beach toys. **Southernmost Beach** is found at the foot of Duval Street (*see* Exploring, *above*).

Dining **Louie's Backyard.** If you're here on a clear day, there's no better
$$$ place to be than at Louie's—right on the water on a tiered terrace lit with tiny white lights in the evening. Come early for a drink at a table so close to the water you could lean over the rail and pick up some driftwood. The menu is a mix of Continental and Asian dishes: Try the venison with port, wild mushrooms, and goat cheese strudel or grouper with Thai peanut sauce. You'll need to take a cab from the cruise-ship pier. *700 Waddell Ave., tel. 305/294–1061. AE, DC, MC, V.*

$–$$ **Half Shell Raw Bar.** "Eat It Raw" is the motto, and even during the off-season this oyster bar keeps shucking. You eat at shellacked picnic tables in a pier setting with model ships, life buoys, and old license plates hung overhead. If shellfish isn't to your taste, try the broiled dolphinfish sandwich or linguine seafood marinara. *Land's End Marina, tel. 305/294–7496. Reservations not accepted. MC, V.*

Pub Crawling Three spots stand out for first-timers among the many local saloons frequented by Key West denizens. **Capt. Tony's Saloon** (428 Greene St.) is where Ernest Hemingway used to hang out when it was called **Sloppy Joe's.** The current **Sloppy Joe's** is found nearby at 201 Duval Street and has become a landmark in its own right. **Schooner Wharf** (Key West Bight; *see* Exploring Key West, *above*) is the most authentically local saloon, and it doesn't sell T-shirts. All are within easy walking distance of the cruise-ship piers.

Martinique

One of the most beautiful islands in the Caribbean, Martinique is lush with wild orchids, frangipani, anthurium, jade vines, flamingo flowers, and hundreds of hibiscus varieties. Trees bend under the weight of tropical treats such as mangoes, papayas, bright red West Indian cherries, lemons, and limes. Acres of banana plantations, pineapple fields, and waving sugarcane fill the horizon.

The towering mountains and verdant rain forest in the north lure hikers, while underwater sights and sunken treasures attract snorkelers and scuba divers. Martinique is also wonderful if your idea of exercise is turning over every 10 or 15 minutes to get an even tan, or if your adventuresome spirit is satisfied by a duty-free shop.

The largest of the Windward Islands, Martinique is 6,817 km (4,261 mi) from Paris, but its spirit and language are decidedly French, with more than a soupçon of West Indian spice. Tangible, edible evidence of that fact is the island's cuisine, a superb blend of classic French and Creole dishes.

Fort-de-France is the capital, but at the turn of the 20th century, St-Pierre, farther up the coast, was Martinique's premier city. Then, in 1902, volcanic Mont Pelée blanketed the city in ash, killing all its residents save for a condemned man in prison. Today, the ruins are a popular excursion for cruise passengers.

Currency
Legal tender is the French franc, which consists of 100 centimes. At press time, the rate was 5.65F to U.S.$1. Dollars are accepted, but if you're going to shop, dine, or visit museums on your own, it's better to convert a small amount of money into francs. There's an ATM, which accepts Visa, MasterCard, and Cirrus, at the Banc National de Paris (BNP) at the northern end of La Savane in Fort-de-France. All prices given below are in U.S. dollars except where indicated.

Telephones
You can't make collect calls from Martinique to the United States on the local phone system, but you can usually use an AT&T card. There are no coin phone booths on the island. If you must call home and can't wait until the ship reaches the next port, go to the post office and buy a telecarte, which looks like a credit card and is used in special booths marked TELECOM. Long-distance calls made with telecartes are less costly than operator-assisted calls.

Shore Excursions
The following is a good choice on Martinique. It may not be offered by all cruise lines. Time and price are approximate.

Island Sights
Martinique's Pompeii. By bus or taxi, drive through the lush green mountains, past picturesque villages, to St-Pierre, stopping at the museum there. This is one of the best island tours in the Caribbean. *4 hrs. Cost: $54.*

Coming Ashore
Cruise ships that dock call at the Maritime Terminal east of the city. The only practical way to get into town is by cab ($16 round-trip). To reach the Maritime Terminal tourist information office, turn right and walk along the waterfront. Ships that anchor in the Baie des Flamands (*see* Exploring Martinique, *below*) tender passengers directly to the downtown waterfront. A tourist office is just across the street from the landing pier in the Air France building. Guided walking tours ($15 for 1½ hrs) can be arranged at the nearby open-air marketplace.

Before hiring a taxi driver, especially for an island tour, make sure his English is good. Taxis are expensive. The minimum charge is 10F (about $2.90), but a journey of any distance can easily cost upwards of 50F. To get to the beaches and restaurants at Trois Islets will cost you well over 200F. A 40% surcharge is in effect between 8 PM and 6 AM and on Sunday. For a radio cab call 596/63–63–62 or 596/63–10–10.

Exploring Martinique
Numbers in the margin correspond to points of interest on the Martinique map.

Fort-de-   On the island's west coast, at the beautiful Baie des Flamands, lies
France   the capital city of **Fort-de-France.** Its narrow streets and pastel
 ❶   buildings with ornate wrought-iron balconies are reminiscent of
the French Quarter in New Orleans—but whereas New Orleans is
flat, Fort-de-France is hilly.

Bordering the waterfront is **La Savane,** a rather sad 12½-acre landscaped park filled with run-down gardens, tropical trees and broken fountains. It's a popular gathering place, though, and is the
setting for promenades, parades, and impromptu soccer matches.
Near the harbor is a marketplace where beads, baskets, pottery,
and straw hats are sold.

On rue de la Liberté, which runs along the west side of La Savane,
look for the **Musée Départementale de la Martinique.** Artifacts from
the pre-Columbian period include pottery, beads, and part of a
skeleton that turned up during excavations in 1972. One exhibit
examines the history of slavery; costumes, documents, furniture,
and handicrafts from the island's colonial period are on display. *9
rue de la Liberté, tel. 596/71–57–05. Admission: 15F. Open weekdays 8:30–1 and 2:30–5, Sat. 9–noon.*

Rue Schoelcher (pronounced shell-*cher*) runs through the center
of the capital's primary shopping district a six-block area bounded
by rue de la République, rue de la Liberté, rue Victor Sévère, and
rue Victor Hugo (*see* Shopping, *below*).

The **Romanesque St-Louis Cathedral** (west of rue Victor Schoelcher),
whose steeple rises high above the surrounding buildings, has
lovely stained-glass windows. A number of Martinique's former
governors are interred beneath the choir loft.

The **Bibliothèque Schoelcher,** a wildly elaborate Byzantine-Egyp-
tian-Romanesque public library, is named after Victor Schoelcher,
who led the fight to free the slaves in the French West Indies in
the 19th century. The eye-popping structure was built in 1887 and
exhibited at the 1889 Paris Exposition, after which it was disman-
tled, shipped to Martinique, and reassembled piece by piece.
Inside is a collection of ancient documents recounting Fort-de-
France's development. *Corner of rue de la Liberté, tel. 596/70–26–
67. Admission free. Open daily 8:30–6.*

The North   A nice way to see the lush island interior and St-Pierre is to take
the N3, which snakes through dense rain forests, north through
the mountains to Le Morne Rouge; then take the coastal N2 roadway back to Fort-de-France via St-Pierre. You can do the 64-km
(40-mi) round-trip in an afternoon.

The first stop along the N3 (also called the Route de la Trace) is
 ❷   **Balata** to see the Balata Church, an exact replica of Sacré-Coeur
Basilica in Paris, and the Jardin de Balata (Balata Gardens). Jean-
Phillipe Thoze, a professional landscaper and devoted horticultur-
ist, spent 20 years creating this collection of thousands of varieties
of tropical flowers and plants. There are shaded benches where
you can relax and take in the panoramic views of the mountains.
Rte. de Balata, tel. 596/72–58–82. Admission: 30F. Open daily 9–5.

 ❸   On the southern slopes of Mont Pelée along the N3 is **Le Morne
Rouge.** This town was, like St-Pierre, destroyed by the volcano
and is now a popular resort. Signs will direct you to the narrow
road that takes you halfway up the mountain—you won't really
have time to hike to the 4,600-ft peak, but this side trip gets you
fairly close and offers spectacular views.

④ A few kilometers south of Basse-Pointe, heading northeast on the N3 toward the Atlantic coast, is the flower filled village of **Ajoupa-Bouillon.** This 17th-century settlement in the midst of pineapple fields is a beautiful area, but skip it if you've never seen St-Pierre and are running out of time. From Le Morne Rouge, you'll need a good three hours to enjoy the coastal drive back to Fort-de-France.

⑤ If you opt to explore the northeast coast, head for **Macouba.** Its cliff-top location affords magnificent views. JM Distillery produces the best *rhum vieux* (aged rum) on the island. A tour and samples are free. *JM Distillery, on main road, Macouba, tel. 596/78–92–55. Admission free. Open weekdays 7–noon and 1:30–3:30.*

Macouba is also the starting point for another spectacular drive, the 10-km (6-mi) route to Grand-Rivière on the northernmost point. This is Martinique at its greenest. Groves of giant bamboo, cliffs hung with curtains of vines and 7-ft-high tree ferns that seem to grow as you watch them. At the end of the road is Grand-Rivière, a fishing village at the foot of high cliffs and, literally, the end of the road.

⑥ **St-Pierre** (southwest of Le Morne Rouge on the N2) is the island's oldest city. It was once called the Paris of the West Indies, but Mont Pelée changed all that in the spring of 1902, when it began to rumble and spit steam. By the first week in May, all wildlife had wisely vacated the area, but city officials ignored the warnings, needing voters in town for an upcoming election. On the morning of May 8, the volcano erupted, belching forth a cloud of burning ash with temperatures above 3,600°F. Within 3 minutes, Mont Pelée had transformed St-Pierre into Martinique's Pompeii. The entire town was annihilated, its 30,000 inhabitants calcified. There was only one survivor: a prisoner named Cyparis, who was saved by the thick walls of his underground cell. He was later pardoned and for some time afterward was a sideshow attraction at the Barnum & Bailey Circus.

You can wander through the site to see the ruins of the island's first church, built in 1640; the theater; the toppled statues; and Cyparis's cell. The *Cyparis Express* is a small tourist train that runs through the city, hitting the important sights with a running narrative (in French). *Tel. 596/55–50–92. Tickets: 30F. Train departs from pl. des Ruines du Figuier every 45 mins weekdays 9:30–1 and 2:30–5:30.*

While in St-Pierre, which now has only 6,000 residents, you might pick up some delicious French pastries to nibble on the way back after stopping in at the **Musée Vulcanologique.** Established in 1932 by American volcanologist Franck Perret, the collection includes photographs of the old town, documents, and excavated relics, including molten glass, melted iron, and contorted clocks stopped at 8 AM, the time of the eruption. *Rue Victor Hugo, tel. 596/78–15–16. Admission: 15F. Open daily 9–noon and 3–5.*

⑦ A short way south of St-Pierre is Anse Turin, where Paul Gauguin lived briefly in 1887 with his friend and fellow artist Charles Laval. The **Musée Gauguin** traces the history of the artist's Martinique connection through documents, letters, and reproductions of paintings he completed while on the island. *Tel. 596/77–22–66. Admission: 15F. Open daily 9–5:30.*

Shopping French products, such as perfume, wines, liquors, designer scarves, leather goods, and crystal, are all good buys in Fort-de-

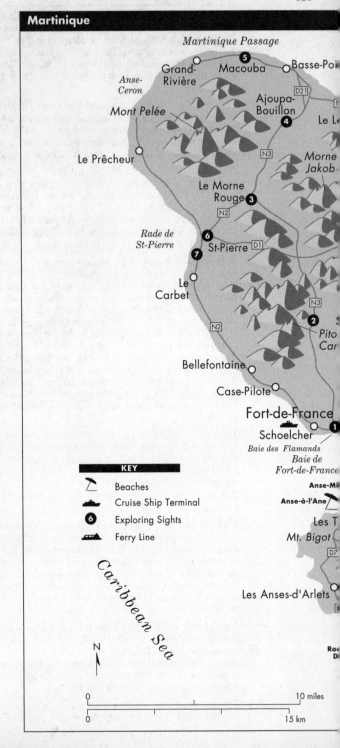

Martinique

Martinique Passage

Grand-Rivière

Macouba **5**

Basse-Poi

Anse-Ceron

Ajoupa-Bouillon **4**

D21

Le L

Mont Pelée

Le L

Le Prêcheur

N3

Morne Jakob

Le Morne Rouge **3**

N2

Rade de St-Pierre

6

7

St-Pierre

D1

Le Carbet

N3

2

Pito Car

N2

Bellefontaine

Case-Pilote

Fort-de-France

1

Schoelcher

Baie des Flamands

Baie de Fort-de-France

Anse-Mi

Anse-à-l'Ane

Les T

Mt. Bigot

D7

Les Anses-d'Arlets

Caribbean Sea

Ro
D

N

KEY

Beaches	
Cruise Ship Terminal	
6 Exploring Sights	
Ferry Line	

0 ——— 10 miles

0 ——— 15 km

France. In addition, luxury goods are discounted 20% when paid for with traveler's checks or major credit cards. Look for Creole gold jewelry; white and dark rums; and hand-crafted straw goods, pottery, and tapestries.

Small shops that sell luxury items are abundant around the cathedral in Fort-de-France, particularly on rue Victor Hugo, rue Moreau de Jones, rue Antoine Siger, and rue Lamartine. Look for Lalique, Limoges, and Baccarat at **Cadet Daniel** (72 rue Antoine Siger, tel. 596/71–41–48) and at **Roger Albert** (7 rue Victor Hugo, tel. 596/71–71–71), which also sells perfume. A wide variety of dolls, straw goods, tapestries, and pottery is available at the **Caribbean Art Center** (Centre de Métiers Art, opposite the tourist office, Blvd. Alfassa, tel. 596/70–32–16). The Galerie Arti-Bijoux (89 rue Victor Hugo, tel. 596/63–10–62) has some unusual and excellent Haitian art at reasonable prices.

Sports For charter excursions, contact **Bathy's Club** (Hôtel Méridien,
Fishing Anse-Mitan, tel. 596/66–00–00).

Golf **Golf de l'Impératrice Joséphine** (tel. 596/68–32–81) has an 18-hole Robert Trent Jones course with an English-speaking pro, a pro shop, a bar, and a restaurant. At **Trois-Ilets,** 1½ km (1 mi) from the Pointe du Bout resort area and 29 km (18 mi) from Fort-de-France, the club offers special greens fees for cruise ship passengers.

Hiking **Parc Naturel Régional de la Martinique** (Caserne Bouille, Fort-de-France, tel. 596/73–19–30) organizes inexpensive guided hiking tours. Information is available at the island tourist offices.

Horseback Excursions and lessons are available at the **Black Horse Ranch**
Riding (near La Pagerie in Trois-Ilets, tel. 596/68–37–69), **La Cavale** (near Diamant, tel. 596/76–22–94), and **Ranch Jack** (near Anse-d'Arlets, tel. 596/68–37–67).

Water Sports At hotel beach shacks, you can rent Hobie Cats, Sunfish, and Sailfish by the hour. If you're a member of a yacht club, show your club membership card and enjoy the facilities of **Club de la Voile de Fort-de-France** (Pointe Simon, tel. 596/70–26–63) and **Yacht Club de la Martinique** (blvd. Chevalier, Ste-Marthe, tel. 596/63–26–76). To explore the old shipwrecks, coral gardens, and other undersea sites, you must have a medical certificate and insurance papers. Among the island's dive operators are **Bathy's Club** (Hotel Méridien, Anse-Mitan, tel. 596/66–00–00) and the **Sub Diamant Rock** (Diamant-Novotel, tel. 596/76–42–42).

Beaches Topless bathing is prevalent at the large resort hotels. Unless you're an expert swimmer, steer clear of the Atlantic waters, except in the area of Cap Chevalier and the Caravelle Peninsula. **Pointe du Bout** has small, white-sand beaches, most of which are commandeered by resort hotels. **Anse-Mitan,** south of Pointe du Bout, is a white-sand beach with superb snorkeling. **Anse-à-l'Ane** offers picnic tables and a nearby shell museum; bathers cool off in the bar of the Calalou Hotel. **Grande-Anse** is less crowded—the preferred beach among people who know the island well. **Les Salines** is the best of Martinique's beaches, whether you choose to be with other sun worshipers or to find your own quiet stretch of sand. However, it's at least an hour's drive from Fort-de-France and 8 km (5 mi) beyond Ste-Anne.

Dining All restaurants include a 15% service charge in their menu prices.

$$ **Le Fromager.** If you're touring the north of the island, don't miss this beautiful restaurant perched high above St-Pierre, with

smashing views of the town's red roofs and the sea beyond. Superlative choices include crayfish colombo, marinated octopus, and duck fillet with pineapple. You may also opt for the 100F chef's choice menu, which might include avocado vinaigrette and sole *sauce pêcheur* (in a Creole sauce), as well as fruit or crème caramel. *On road to Fond St-Denis, tel. 596/78–19–07. AE, DC, MC, V.*

$$ **Le Ruisseau Restaurant at Leyritz Plantation.** Upon disembarking, negotiate a good price from a cab driver and treat yourself to the drive and lunch at this lovely restaurant in the northern portion of Martinique. It's an exhilarating trip full of hairpin curves and wonderful views of the island. At Le Ruisseau, you'll find roasted conch in the shell, fresh salads, red snapper, grilled lamb and assorted fruit. Stroll the gorgeous grounds before starting back. It's an excellent way to spend the day. *Basse-Pointe, tel. 596/78–53–92. Reservations essential. MC, V.*

$ **Le Marie Sainte.** Looking for a great lunch? Search no farther than a couple of blocks from your boat. Prix-fixe lunches start at 75F. Try the succulent *daube de poisson* (braised fish) or any specials of the day. *160 rue Victor Hugo, tel. 56/70–00–30, AE, MC, V. Closed Sun. No dinner.*

Nassau, The Bahamas

The 17th-century town of Nassau, the capital of the Bahamas, has witnessed Spanish invasions and hosted pirates, who made it their headquarters for raids along the Spanish Main. The new American Navy seized Ft. Montagu here in 1776, when they won a victory without firing a shot.

The cultural and ethnic heritage of old Nassau includes the Southern charm of British loyalists from the Carolinas, the African tribal traditions of freed slaves, and a bawdy history of blockade-running during the Civil War and rum-running in the Roaring Twenties. Over it all is a subtle layer of civility and sophistication, derived from three centuries of British rule.

Reminders of the island's British heritage are everywhere in Nassau. Court justices sport wigs and scarlet robes. The police wear colonial garb: starched white jackets, red-striped navy trousers, and tropical pith helmets. Traffic keeps to the left, and the language has a British-colonial lilt, softened by a slight drawl. Nassau's charm, however, is often lost in its commercialism. If you look past the duty-free shops, there are some interesting sights of historical significance worth seeing. And there's excellent shopping.

Shore Excursions The following are good choices in Nassau. They may not be offered by all cruise lines. Times and prices are approximate.

Undersea Creatures **Crystal Cay.** This excursion provides convenient transportation by ferry, where a 100-ft observation tower soars above the landscape, but the real views are of turtles, stingrays, and starfish below the water. Stay as long as you want—the ferry leaves the cruise-ship docks at 11, 1:30, 2:45, 3:15, and 4 PM. *Cost: $2 per trip; admission to Crystal Cay, $16.*

Dolphin Encounters (tel. 242/363–1653 or 242/363–1003). Close Encounter excursions ($30 per person) are offered on Blue Lagoon Island (Salt Cay), just east of Paradise Island. Sit on a platform with your feet in the water while dolphins play around you, or wade in the waist-deep water to get up close and personal with them. Trainers are available to answer questions. Swim-with-the-Dolphins ($85 per person) allows you to actually swim with these friendly creatures for about 30 minutes. Programs are educational, and each includes a 15-minute informational talk. They're also very popular, so make reservations as early as possible to avoid disappointment. Programs are available daily, 8 AM–5:30 PM.

Coming Ashore Cruise ships dock at one of three piers on Prince George's Wharf. Taxi drivers who meet the ships may offer you a $2 ride into town, but the historic government buildings and duty-free shops lie just outside the dock area. The one- or two-block walk takes five to 10 minutes. As you leave the pier, look for a tall pink tower: Diagonally across from here is the tourist information office. Stop in for maps of the island and downtown Nassau. On most days you can join a $4 per person 45-minute walking tour conducted by well-trained guides. Tours start every hour on the hour 11 AM–4 PM. Outside the office, an ATM dispenses U.S. dollars.

As you disembark from your ship you will find a row of taxis and luxurious air-conditioned limousines. The latter are Nassau's fleet of tour cars, useful and comfortable for a guided tour of the island. Taxi fares are fixed at $2 for the first ½ km (¼ mi), 30¢ each additional ½ km (¼ mi). Sightseeing tours cost about $20–$25 per hour.

Also along the wharf are surreys drawn by straw-hatted horses that will take you through the old city and past some of the nearby historic sites. The cost is $10 per person for two or more for 25 minutes, but verify prices before getting on.

For the more adventurous, scooters may be rented as you exit Prince George Wharf. Rates average $25 per half day, $40 per full day, plus $10 refundable deposit. Helmets are mandatory and provided.

To get to Paradise Island, take the ferry from the dock area ($4 each way).

Exploring Nassau *Numbers in the margin correspond to points of interest on the Nassau map.*

❶ As you leave the cruise wharf, you can't miss **Parliament Square.** Dating from the early 1800s and patterned after southern U.S. colonial architecture, this cluster of pink, colonnaded buildings with green shutters is striking. In the center of the square is a statue of the young Queen Victoria, and the Bahamas House of Parliament.

❷ For a great view (and a real workout), climb the **Queen's Staircase,** a famous Nassau landmark found at the head of Elizabeth Avenue. Its 66 steps, hewn from the coral limestone cliff by slaves in the late 18th century, were designed to provide a direct route between town and Ft. Fincastle at the top of the hill. The staircase was named more than a hundred years later, in honor of the 66 years of Queen Victoria's reign.

❸ **Ft. Fincastle** is easily recognized by its shape—it resembles the bow of a ship. Built in 1793, it never fired a shot in anger but served as a lookout and signal tower.

❹ For a really spectacular view of the island of New Providence, climb the 225 steps (or ride the elevator) to the top of the **Water Tower.** Rising to 126 ft, more than 200 ft above sea level, the tower is the highest point on the island.

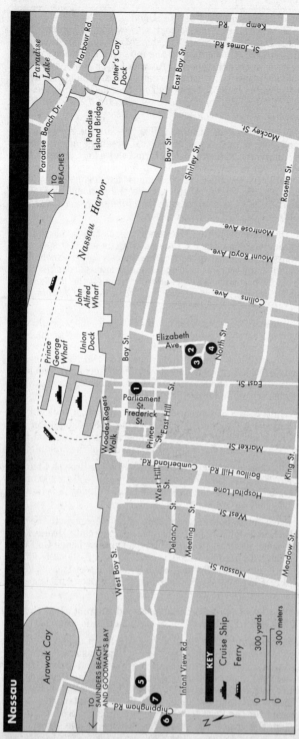

Nassau

Arawak Cay

TO SAUNDERS BEACH
AND GOODMAN'S BAY

Paradise Lake

Harbour Rd.

Paradise Beach Dr.

TO BEACHES

Nassau Harbour

Paradise Island Bridge

Potter's Cay Dock

East Bay St.

Kemp Rd.

St. James Rd.

Mackey St.

Bay St.

Shirley St.

Rosetta St.

Montrose Ave.

Mount Royal Ave.

Collins Ave.

North St.

East St.

Prince George Wharf

John Alfred Wharf

Union Dock

Bay St.

Elizabeth Ave.

Woodes Rogers Walk

Parliament St.

Frederick St.

Prince St.

East Hill St.

Market St.

King St.

Bailou Hill Rd.

Hospital Lane

Cumberland Rd.

West Hill St.

West St.

Delancy St.

Meeting St.

Nassau St.

Meadow St.

West Bay St.

Infant View Rd.

Chippingham Rd.

KEY

- Cruise Ship
- Ferry

0   300 yards

0   300 meters

N

Ardastra Gardens
and Zoo, **6**

Ft. Charlotte, **5**

Ft. Fincastle, **3**

Nassau Botanic
Gardens, **7**

Parliament Square, **1**

Queen's Staircase, **2**

Water Tower, **4**

⑤ The most interesting fort on the island is **Ft. Charlotte,** built in 1787 replete with a waterless moat, a drawbridge, ramparts, and dungeons. Like Ft. Fincastle, no shots were ever fired in anger from this fort. Ft. Charlotte is at the top of a hill and commands a fine view of Nassau Harbor and Arawak Cay, a small, man-made island that is home to the fish fry where you can pick up a delicious yet inexpensive lunch of conch salad or other native delicacies. *Off W. Bay St. at Chippingham Rd., tel. 242/322–7500. Admission free. Local guides conduct tours Mon.–Sat. 8:30–4.*

⑥ Passengers with a green thumb will appreciate the **Ardastra Gardens and Zoo,** with 5 acres of tropical greenery and flowering shrubs, an aviary of rare tropical birds, and exotic animals from different parts of the world. The gardens are renowned for the pink, spindly legged, marching flamingos that perform daily at 11, 2, and 4. The flamingo, by the way, is the national bird of the Bahamas. *Near Ft. Charlotte, off Chippingham Rd., tel. 242/323–5806. Admission: $10. Open daily 9–4:30.*

⑦ Across the street from the Ardastra Gardens and Zoo is the **Nassau Botanic Gardens.** On its 18-acre grounds are 600 species of flowering trees and shrubs; two freshwater ponds with lilies, water plants, and tropical fish; and a small cactus garden that ends in a grotto. The many trails wandering through the gardens are perfect for leisurely strolls. *Near Ft. Charlotte, off Chippingham Rd., tel. 242/323–5975. Admission: $1. Open daily 8–4.*

Shopping *Forbes* magazine once claimed that the two cities in the world with the best buys on wristwatches were Hong Kong and Nassau. Most of the stores selling these and other duty-free items are clustered along an eight-block stretch of Bay Street in Old Nassau or spill over onto a few side streets downtown. Most stores are open Monday–Saturday 9–5. The straw market is open seven days a week. Most shops accept major credit cards.

If you're interested in old-fashioned maps and prints, seek out **Balmain Antiques** (308 Bay St., tel. 242/323–7421). Though on Bay Street, it's a little hard to find: The doorway to the second-floor gallery is set off from the sidewalk on the side of the building.

Sports
Fishing Contact **Chubasco Charters** (tel. 242/322–8148) or **Brown's Charters** (tel. 242/324–1215). Boat charters range from $350 to $600 for a half-day, depending on the size of the boat. Full-day charters are double the half-day rate.

Golf Three excellent 18-hole championship courses are open to the public: **Cable Beach Golf Course** (opposite the Superclubs Breezes, tel. 242/327–6000; 800/222–7466 in the U. S.), **Paradise Island Golf Club** (eastern end of Paradise Island, tel. 242/363–3925; 800/321–3000 in the U. S.), and **South Ocean Beach & Golf Resort** (tel. 242/362–4391). Fees are $60–$135, depending on season, package, or whether you're a hotel guest.

Parasailing Parasailing is available from **Sea Sports Ltd.** (in front of the Nassau Beach Hotel, tel. 242/327–6058). A six-minute ride costs $30.

Beaches **Paradise Beach** stretches for more than 1½ km (1 mi) on the western end of Paradise Island. The $3 admission includes a welcome drink, towels, and the use of changing rooms and locker. On the ocean side of the awe-inspiring Atlantis Resort and Casino in the center of Paradise Island lies Cabbage beach, which is popular with locals and tourists alike. The **Western Esplanade** sweeps westward from the British Colonial Hotel on Bay Street (a 10-min walk from the cruise-ship pier). It's just across the street from shops and restaurants, and it has rest rooms, a snack bar, and changing facilities. A little farther west is **Saunders Beach. Goodman's Bay,** a bit farther west of Saunders, is popular with Bahamians for picnics and cookouts on weekends and holidays.

Dining **Graycliff.** Situated in a magnificent, 200-year-old colonial mansion,
$$$ Graycliff is filled with antiques and English country-house charm. The outstanding Continental and Bahamian menu includes beluga caviar, grouper *au poivre vert* (green-pepper sauce), and chateaubriand, with elegant pastries and flaming coffees for dessert. The wine cellar is excellent. Graycliff now offers its own hand-rolled cigars of Cuban tobacco—made on the premises. *W. Hill St., across from Government House, tel. 242/322–2796 or 800/ 633–7411. Reservations essential. Jacket required. AE, DC, MC, V.*

$$ **Green Shutters.** Shades of Fleet Street! This very British pub is a cozy place awash with wood paneling. Steak-and-kidney pie, bangers and mash (sausages and mashed potatoes), and shepherd's pie are featured alongside such island favorites as cracked conch and Bahamian crawfish tail. *48 Parliament St., tel. 242/325– 5702. AE, MC, V.*

$$ **Poop Deck.** A nautical air fills this favorite haunt of Nassau residents. Tables overlook the harbor and Paradise Island. Cuisine is exceptional Bahamian-style seafood, served in a festive, friendly atmosphere. The food is spicy, the wine list extensive. Save room for guava duff, a warm guava-layered local dessert, and a Calypso coffee, spiked with secret ingredients. *E. Bay St. (an 8-min cab ride from pier), tel. 242/393–8175. AE, DC, MC, V.*

$ **Crocodiles Waterfront Bar & Restaurant.** Watching the cruise ships come and go (hopefully, not your own) is just one of the attractions of this relaxing harborside restaurant. The tropical setting (thatched tiki huts) makes it fun for passengers of all ages. Bahamian dishes and burgers are the specialities of the house. *E. Bay St., tel. 242/323–3341. Reservations not accepted. MC, V.*

Nightlife Some ships stay late into the night or until the next day so that passengers can enjoy Nassau's nightlife. You'll find nonstop entertainment nightly along Cable Beach and on Paradise Island. All the larger hotels offer lounges with island combos for listening or dancing, and restaurants with soft guitar or piano background music.

Casinos The two casinos in New Providence—**Crystal Palace Casino** and **Paradise Island Resort and Casino**—open early in the day and remain active into the wee hours of the morning. Visitors must be 18 or older to enter a casino, 21 or older to gamble.

Nightclubs **Club Waterloo** (E. Bay St., tel. 242/393–7324) is one of Nassau's most swinging nightspots. Disco and rock can be heard nightly at **The Zoo** (Saunders Beach, tel. 242/322–7195)

Local **King & Knights** (tel. 242/327–5321), at the Nassau Beach Hotel
Entertainment showroom, is a native show featuring world-famous King Eric and his Knights. The show is the only one of its kind on the island with steel drums, unbelievable limbo feats, fire dancing, Bahamian music, song and dance. Dinner is at 7 PM, followed by two shows at 8:30 and 10:30, Tuesday through Saturday. One show is held Sunday and Monday at 8:30.

Panama Canal

Transit of the Panama Canal takes only one day. The rest of your cruise will be spent on islands in the Caribbean or at ports along the Mexican Riviera. Increasingly, Panama Canal itineraries include stops in Central America; some may also call along the northern coast of South America. Most Panama Canal cruises are one-way trips, part of a 10- to 14-day cruise between the Atlantic and Pacific oceans. Shorter loop cruises enter the canal from the Caribbean, sail around Gatún Lake for a few hours, and return to the Caribbean.

The Panama Canal is best described as a water bridge that "raises" ships up and over Central America, then down again, using a series of locks or water steps. Artificially created Gatún Lake, 85 ft above sea level, is the canal's highest point. The route is approximately 80 km (50 mi) long, and the crossing takes from eight to 10 hours. Cruise ships pay more than $100,000 for each transit, which is less than half of what it would cost them to sail around Cape Horn, at the southern tip of South America.

Just before dawn, your ship will line up with dozens of other vessels to await its turn to enter the canal. Before it can proceed, two pilots and a narrator will come on board. The sight of a massive cruise ship being raised dozens of feet into the air by water is so fascinating that passengers will crowd all the forward decks at the first lock. If you can't see, go to the rear decks, where there is usually more room and the view is just as intriguing. Later in the day you won't find as many passengers up front.

On and off throughout the day, commentary is broadcast over ship's loudspeakers, imparting facts and figures as well as anecdotes about the history of the canal. The canal stands where it does today not because it's the best route but because the railroad was built there first, making access to the area relatively easy. The railway had followed an old Spanish mule trail that had been there for more than 300 years.

St. Croix

St. Croix is the largest of the three U.S. Virgin Islands (USVI) that form the northern hook of the Lesser Antilles, and it's 64 km (40 mi) south of its sisters—St. Thomas and St. John. Christopher Columbus landed here in 1493, skirmishing briefly with the native Carib Indians. Since then, the USVI have played a colorful, if painful, role as pawns in the game of European colonialism. Theirs is a history of pirates and privateers, sugar plantations, slave trading, and slave revolt and liberation.

Through it all, Denmark had staying power; from the 17th to the 19th century, Danes oversaw a plantation slave economy that produced molasses, rum, cotton, and tobacco. Many of the stones you see in buildings or tread on in the streets were once used as ballast on sailing ships, and the yellow fort of Christiansted is a reminder of the value once placed on this island treasure.

Currency The U.S. dollar is the official currency of St. Croix.

Telephones Calling the United States from St. Croix works the same as within the states. Local calls from a public phone cost 25¢ for every 5 minutes.

Shore Excursions The following are good choices on St. Croix. They may not be offered by all cruise lines. Times and prices are approximate.

Island Sights **Bicycle Jaunt.** Ride along St. Croix's coast and through Frederiksted before heading along Northside Road. The 19-km (12-mi) trip will take you past ruins, historical sights, tropical forests, rolling hills, and ocean views. Bicycles and equipment are included. *3 hrs. Cost: $38.*

Tee Time **Golf at Carambola.** Robert Trent Jones designed this 18-hole, par-72 course, considered one of the Caribbean's finest. Cost includes shared golf cart and greens fees. *Half day. Cost: $70–$100.*

Coming Ashore Larger cruise ships dock in Frederiksted; smaller ships (fewer than 200 passengers) dock at Gallows Bay, outside Christiansted. You'll find information centers at both piers, and both towns are easy to explore on foot; beaches are nearby.

Taxis of all shapes and sizes are available at the cruise ship piers and at various shopping and resort areas. Remember, too, that you can hail a taxi that's already occupied. Drivers take multiple fares and sometimes even trade passengers at midpoints. Taxis don't have meters, so you should check the list of standard, official rates (available at the visitor centers or from the drivers themselves) and agree on a fare before you start. Try **St. Croix Taxi Association** (tel. 340/778–1088) or **Antilles Taxi Service** (tel. 340/773–5020).

Exploring St. Croix *Numbers in the margin correspond to points of interest on the St. Croix map.*

❶ Charming **Frederiksted** speaks to history buffs with its quaint Victorian architecture and historic fort. There's very little traffic, so this is the perfect place for strolling and shopping.

Ft. Frederik, completed in the late 18th century, sits adjacent to the cruise ship pier. Here, in 1848, the slaves of the Danish West Indies were freed by Governor Peter van Scholten.

Within walking distance of the pier are **St. Paul's Episcopal Church,** built in 1812, and **St. Patrick's Catholic Church,** built in 1843 of coral. Walk three blocks inland from the waterfront to reach Prince St. St. Patrick's is to the east, St. Paul's to the west.

❷ **Karl and Marie Lawaetz Museum.** This circa-1750 farm takes you on a trip back to the time when Denmark owned St. Croix. A Lawaetz family member shows you the four-poster bed where Karl and Marie slept and the china Marie hand-painted. The taxi fare from Frederiksted for two people runs $6. From Christiansted, the fare is $21. *Estate Little LaGrange, tel. 340/772-1539. Admission: $5. Open Tues.–Sat. 10–3.*

❸ **West End Salt Pond.** This remote pond is rife with mangroves and little blue herons. In the spring, large leatherback sea turtles clamber up the white sand across the road to lay their eggs. You will also see brown pelicans. Because the location is rather remote, for safety's sake, it's better to ask your taxi driver to include it on a tour rather than making it an excursion on its own.

❹ **Estate Whim Plantation Museum.** With its windmill, cookhouse, and other outbuildings, this lovingly restored estate gives a real sense of what life was like for the owners of St. Croix's sugar plantations in the 1800s. The great house, with a singular oval shape and high ceilings, features antique furniture and utensils, as well as a major apothecary exhibit. Note the house's fresh, airy atmosphere—the waterless moat was used not for defense but for gathering cooling air. A taxi trip for two from the Frederiksted pier will run $4. From Christiansted, the cost is $20.50. *Rte. 70, tel. 340/772–0598. Admission: $5. Open Mon.–Sat. 10–5.*

❺ **St. George Village Botanical Gardens.** With 17 acres of lush and fragrant flora to explore, this is a must for nature lovers. It sits amid

St. Croix

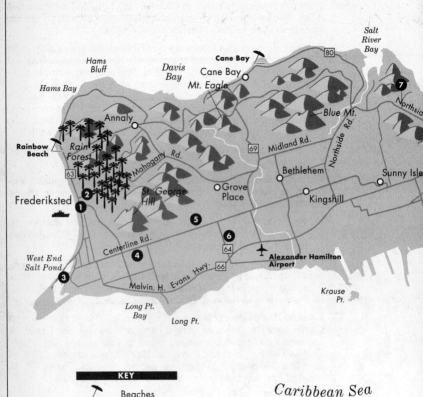

KEY

Beaches

Cruise Ship Terminal

6 Exploring Sights

Caribbean Sea

Buck Island

Buck Island Beach

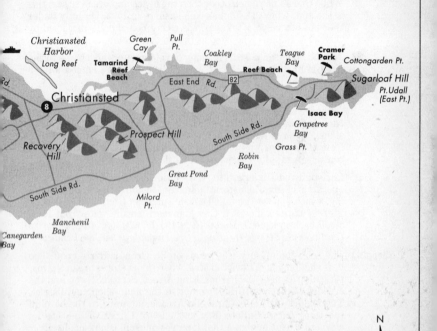

Christiansted Harbor
Long Reef

Green Cay

Pull Pt.

Tamarind Reef Beach

Coakley Bay

East End Rd. 82

Reef Beach

Teague Bay

Cramer Park

Cottongarden Pt.

Sugarloaf Hill

Pt. Udall (East Pt.)

Christiansted 8

Prospect Hill

Recovery Hill

South Side Rd.

South Side Rd.

Great Pond Bay

Milord Pt.

Robin Bay

Grass Pt.

Isaac Bay

Grapetree Bay

Manchenil Bay

Canegarden Bay

N

0   2 miles
0   3 km

the ruins of a 19th-century sugarcane plantation village. A taxi trip for two from the Frederiksted pier costs $6.50. From Christiansted, the cost is $15.50. *Tel. 340/692-2874. Admission: $5. Open daily 9–4.*

❻ Cruzan Distillery. The rum here is made with pure rainwater, making it (so they say) superior to any other. Visitors are welcome for a tour and a free rum-laced drink (the concoction changes daily). *West Airport Rd., tel. 340/692-2280. Admission: $4. Open daily 9–4.*

Salt River Bay National Historical Park and Ecological Preserve. While there's not much other than the beach and ocean to see, this is the spot where Columbus came ashore in 1493. Directly under the spot where your taxi parks is a ceremonial ball court used by the Carib Indians who lived at the site. *Rte. 80.*

❼ Judith's Fancy, an upscale housing development is also home to the circa 1750 ruins of a Danish sugar plantation. It's named after a woman who is buried on the property. *Rte. 751.*

❽ Christiansted. This charming historic town serves as St. Croix's commercial center. Trade here in the 1700s and 1800s was in sugar, rum, and molasses. Today the town is home to law offices, tourist shops, and restaurants, but many of the structures, which run from the harbor up into the gentle hillsides, date from the 18th century. A taxi for two from Frederiksted runs $20.

Christiansted Historic Site. The National Park Service oversees operation of several historic buildings, including the Steeple Building, which housed the first Danish Lutheran Church in St. Croix. Stop in at the yellow Ft. Christianvaern on the waterfront for a stroll back in time. *Hospital St., tel. 340/773-1460. Admission: $2 (includes the Steeple Building). Open weekdays 8–5, weekends 9–5.*

Shopping The selection of duty-free goods on St. Croix is fairly good. The best shopping is in **Christiansted,** where most stores are in the historic district near the harbor. King Street, Strand Street, and the arcades that lead off them comprise the main shopping district. The longest arcade is Caravelle Arcade, adjacent to the hotel of the same name. **Gallows Bay,** just east of Christiansted, has an attractive boutique area that features unusual island-made silver jewelry and gift items. In **Frederiksted,** a handful of shops face the cruise ship pier. Try **Island WeBe** for locally made products. They carry interesting double dolls, with a black face on one side and a white one on the other, tasty jams, and colorful island original art.

Sports The 18-hole course at the **Buccaneer** (tel. 340/773-2100) is close to
Golf Christiansted. More spectacular is the **Carambola Golf Course** (tel. 340/778-5638), designed by Robert Trent Jones, in a valley in the northwestern part of the island. The **Reef Club** (tel. 340/773-8844), in the northeast, has a 9-hole course. Rates for 18 holes range from $35 to $77.

Horseback At Sprat Hall, near Frederiksted, **Paul & Jill's Equestrian Stables**
Riding (tel. 340/772-2627) offer rides through the rain forest.

Scuba Diving **Dive Experience** (tel. 340/773-3307) is one of the island's best dive
and specialists. **Mile-Mark Charters** (tel. 340/773-2628) offers a full
Snorkeling range of water sports, including sailing, snorkeling, and scuba diving. Both are in Christiansted.

Beaches **Buck Island** and its reef can be reached only by boat from Christiansted but are well worth a visit. The beach is beautiful, but its finest treasures are those you see when you plop off the boat and adjust your face mask, snorkel, and flippers. At **Cane Bay,** a breezy north shore beach, the waters are not always gentle but the diving and snorkeling are wondrous, and there are never many people around. Less than 200 yards out is the drop-off, called Cane Bay Wall. Five kilometers (3 mi) north of Frederiksted you'll find **Rainbow Beach** where you can enjoy the sand, snorkel at a small nearby reef, and get a bite to eat at the bar. **Tamarind Reef Beach** is a small but attractive beach with good snorkeling east of Christiansted. Green Cay and Buck Island seem smack in front of you and make the view arresting.

Dining
$$

Le St. Tropez. A ceramic-tile bar and soft lighting add to the Mediterranean atmosphere at this pleasant bistro, tucked into a courtyard off Frederiksted's main thoroughfare. You can sit inside or on the adjoining patio to feast on French fare, including salads and grilled meats in delicate sauces. The menu changes daily, often taking advantage of fresh local seafood. The fresh basil, tomato, and mozzarella salad is heavenly. *67 King St., tel. 340/772–3000. AE, MC, V. Closed Sun.*

$

Java Mon. Christiansted's *in* spot for quick meals features 1950s decor that looks just like the Norman Rockwell magazine covers on the wall. The waterfront setting attracts a varied following of folks looking for take-out or eat-in "dreadlox" and bagels, roast pork Cubano sandwiches, black-cherry cheesecake, and cups of espresso or cappuccino. Sundried–tomato cream cheese provides an interesting addition to a pedestrian bagel. *59 Kings Wharf, tel. 340/773–2285. No credit cards. No dinner.*

St. Lucia

Lush St. Lucia—a ruggedly beautiful island, with towering mountains, dense rain forest, fertile green valleys, and hundreds of acres of banana plantations—lies in the middle of the Windward Islands. Nicknamed "the Helen of the West Indies" because of its natural beauty, St. Lucia is distinguished from its eastern Caribbean neighbors by its unique geological sites. The Pitons, twin peaks on the southwest coast that have become a symbol of this island, soar nearly a 1 km (½ mi) above the ocean floor. Nearby, just outside the French colonial town of Soufrière, is a "drive-in" volcano and bubbling sulfur springs with curative waters that have rejuvenated bathers for nearly three centuries.

Battles between the French and English over a 150-year period resulted in St. Lucia changing hands 14 times before 1814, when England ultimately won possession. In 1979, the island became an independent state within the British Commonwealth of Nations. The official language is English, although most people also speak a French Creole patois.

Currency

St. Lucia uses the Eastern Caribbean (EC) dollar. The exchange rate is about EC$2.70 to U.S.$1. Although U.S. dollars are readily accepted, you'll often get change in EC currency. Major credit cards and traveler's checks are also widely accepted. All prices given below are in U.S. dollars except where indicated.

Telephones

Telephone service from St. Lucia is excellent, and you can dial international numbers directly from pay phones and card phones. Telephone services are available at Pointe Seraphine, the cruise-ship port of entry and duty-free shopping complex. To charge an overseas call to a major credit card, dial 811; there's no surcharge.

Shore Excursions

The following is a good choice in St. Lucia. It may not be offered by all cruise lines. Time and price are approximate.

Natural **La Soufrière and the Pitons.** Travel the mountainous and winding
Beauty West Coast Road for a spectacular view of the Pitons on the way
to La Soufrière volcano and its sulfur springs, nearby Diamond
Falls and Mineral Baths, and the Botanical Gardens. Travel may
be by a combination of catamaran, bus, or minivan. A buffet lunch
is included. *6 to 8 hrs. Cost: $70.*

Coming Most cruise ships call at the capital city of Castries, on the island's
Ashore northwest coast. Either of two docking areas are used: Pointe
Seraphine, a port of entry and duty-free shopping complex, or
Port Castries, a commercial dock across the harbor. Ferry service
connects the two docking areas.

Smaller vessels call at Soufrière, on the island's southwest coast.
Ships calling at Soufrière usually anchor offshore and tender passengers to the wharf.

Tourist information offices are at Pointe Seraphine in Castries and
along the waterfront on Bay Street in Soufrière. Downtown Castries is within walking distance of the pier, and the produce market and adjacent craft and vendors' markets are the main
attractions. Soufrière is a sleepy West Indian town, but it's worth
a short walk around the central square just to view the authentic
French colonial architecture. Most of St. Lucia's sightseeing
attractions are found near Soufrière.

You can hire a taxi at the docks. Cabs are unmetered, but the government has issued a list of suggested fares that are posted at the
entrance to Pointe Seraphine. A 10–20 minute ride north from
Pointe Seraphine to Reduit Beach and Rodney Bay should cost
about $12. For sightseeing trips to Soufrière, at least a 1½-hour
drive south, expect to pay $20 per hour for up to four people and
plan an excursion of 6–8 hours, including lunch. A tour of the
entire island also takes about six hours and costs about $120.
Whatever your destination, negotiate the price with the driver
before you depart—and be sure that you both understand
whether the rate you've agreed upon is in EC or U.S. dollars.
Drivers appreciate a 10% tip.

Exploring St. *Numbers in the margin correspond to points of interest on the St.*
Lucia *Lucia map.*

Castries Area The **Castries Market** is at the corner of Jeremie and Peynier streets,
❶ just steps from the harbor. It's a typical, colorful, West Indian, open-
air market—although a good portion is now covered by bright
orange roofs as protection from the hot sun and occasional rain
shower. The market is open every day but most crowded on Saturday morning, when farm wives sell their produce. Behind it is the
craft market, where you can buy clay pottery, wood carvings, and
handwoven straw items. Across Peynier Street, at the Vendor's
Arcade, you can also buy souvenirs and handicrafts.

❷ **Derek Walcott Square** is a block of green space in downtown Castries, bordered by Brazil, Laborie, Micoud, and Bourbon streets.
Formerly Columbus Square, it was renamed for the hometown
poet who won the 1992 Nobel Prize in Literature. On the Laborie
St. Side of the square is a huge samaan tree estimated to be 400
years old.

Adjacent to the square, the Roman Catholic **Cathedral of the
Immaculate Conception,** built in 1897, looks rather somber from
the outside; inside the walls are decorated with colorful murals
painted by St. Lucian artist Dunstan St. Omer. *Facing Brazil St.,
downtown Castries.*

③ Rodney Bay, about 11 km (7 mi) north of Castries, is one of the Caribbean's busiest marinas. Reduit Beach is also here, a fine strip of white sand with a water-sports center (at the Rex St. Lucian Hotel). Several good lunch spots, offering a variety of cuisines, are within walking distance of the beach and/or marina.

According to island tales, pirate Jambe de Bois (Wooden Leg) **④** used **Pigeon Island,** off St. Lucia's northern tip, as his hideout. Now a national park, Pigeon Island has a beach, calm waters for swimming, restaurants, and picnic areas. On the grounds you'll see ruins of barracks, batteries, and garrisons dating from the French and British battles for control of St. Lucia. An excellent small museum has interactive and historical exhibits. The island is easily reached by a causeway. *St. Lucia Trust, tel. 758/450–8167. Admission: EC$10. Open daily 9–5.*

⑤ Heading south from Castries, a corkscrew road winds up **Morne Fortune** ("hill of good luck"). You'll see beautiful tropical foliage and flowers—frangipani, lilies, bougainvillea, hibiscus, and oleander—and get a splendid panoramic view of the city and harbor.

Ft. Charlotte, on the Morne, was begun in 1764 by the French as the Citadelle du Morne Fortune and completed and renamed by the British after 20 years of battling and changing hands. Its old barracks and batteries have been converted to government buildings and local educational facilities, but you can view the remains—redoubts, a guardroom, stables, and cells.

Soufrière It's a 1½-hour drive on the winding, West Coast Road from Cas-
Area tries to **Soufrière,** the French colonial capital named for the
⑥ nearby volcano. The mountainous region of St. Lucia is breathtakingly lush, and the road that snakes along the coast offers spectacular views of the Pitons, the rain forest, small bays and villages, and the Caribbean Sea. The town itself is small but charming in its authenticity, with architecture that dates back to the colonial period.

⑦ The **Diamond Botanical Gardens** has specimen tropical flowers and trees growing in their natural habitat. A pathway leads to Diamond Waterfall, where the mineral-rich cascade has created a multihued effect on the river rocks. If you wish, you can slip into your swimsuit and take a dip in the mineral baths, noted for their curative powers since 1713. *Soufrière Estate, tel. 758/452–4759. Admission: EC$7; Baths: outdoor EC$6.50, private EC$10. Open weekdays 10–5; Sun. and holidays 10–3.*

⑧ **La Soufrière,** the "drive-in" volcano, is southeast of the town of Soufrière. More than 20 pools of black, belching, sometimes smelly, sulfurous pools bubble, bake, and steam on the surface of this natural wonder. *Bay St., tel. 758/459–5500. Admission: EC$3, includes tour. Open daily 9–5.*

⑨ **Morne Coubaril Estate** is an historic 250-acre coconut and cocoa plantation that dates back to 1713. It still produces copra, manioc flour, and chocolate but mainly operates as a museum. On a 90-minute eco-tour, guides explain 18th-century plantation life, you explore a reconstructed village, and workers demonstrate early methods of production. A Creole buffet lunch is served (EC$25) by reservation only. *Soufrière, tel. 758/459–7340. Admission: EC$15, includes tour. Open daily 9–5.*

⑩ The **Pitons** have become the symbol of St. Lucia. These unusual pyramidal cones, covered with thick tropical vegetation, rise precipitously out of the cobalt sea just south of Soufrière Bay. Petit

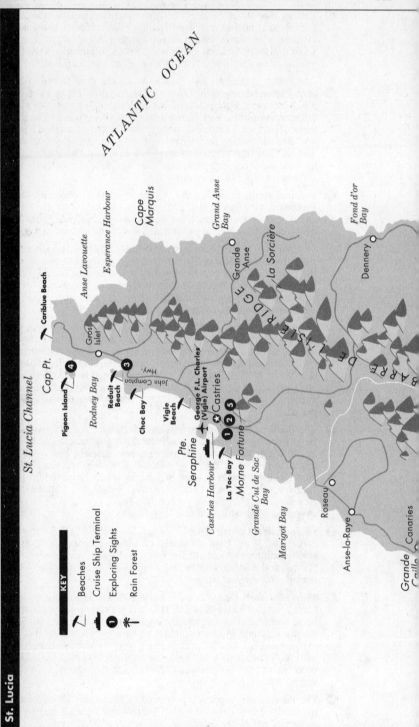

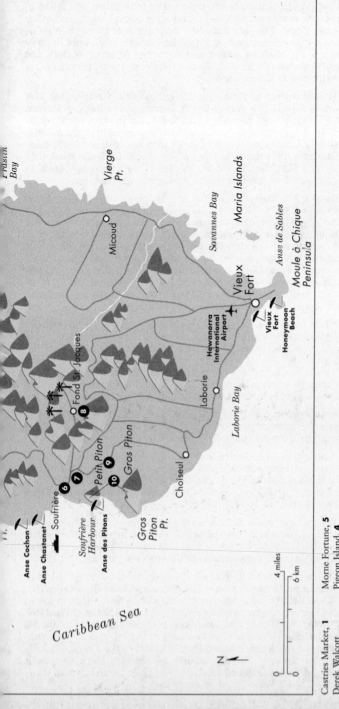

Frasin Bay

Vierge Pt.

Micoud

Savannes Bay

Maria Islands

Vieux Fort

Anse de Sables

Moule à Chique Peninsula

Hewanorra International Airport

Vieux Fort

Honeymoon Beach

Laborie

Laborie Bay

Fond St Jacques

Choiseul

8

Petit Piton

7

9

10

Gros Piton

6

Soufrière

Anse Cochon

Anse Chastanet

Soufrière Harbour

Anse des Pitons

Gros Piton Pt.

Caribbean Sea

N

0   4 miles

0   6 km

Castries Market, **1**
Derek Walcott Square, **2**
Diamond Botanical Gardens, **7**
La Soufrière volcano, **8**
Morne Coubaril Estate, **9**

Morne Fortune, **5**
Pigeon Island, **4**
The Pitons, **10**
Rodney Bay, **3**
Soufrière, **6**

Piton, at 2,619 ft, is taller than Gros Piton (2,461 ft), although Gros Piton is broader. This area is wonderfully scenic.

Shopping Local products include silk-screened or batik fabric and clothing, pottery, wood carvings, cocoa and spices, and baskets and other straw items. The only duty-free shopping is at Pointe Seraphine or La Place Carenage, both on the harborside. You'll want to experience the **Castries market** and scour the adjacent **vendor's and crafts markets** for handicrafts and souvenirs at bargain prices (*see* Exploring St. Lucia, *above*).

Artsibit (corner of Brazil and Mongiraud Sts., Castries, tel. 758/452–7865) sells the work of top St. Lucian artists. **Bagshaw Studios** (at Pointe Seraphine and on La Toc Rd., La Toc Bay, tel. 758/452–7570) sells clothing and household items created from unique silk-screened and hand-printed fabrics that are designed by Stanley Bagshaw and printed in the La Toc studio. **Caribelle Batik** (Old Victoria Rd., The Morne, tel. 758/452–3785) welcomes visitors to watch artisans creating batik clothing and wall hangings.

Eudovic Art Studio (Morne Fortune, 15 mins south of Castries, tel. 758/452–2747) sells trays, masks, and figures that are carved in the studio from native mahogany, red cedar, and eucalyptus wood. **Made in St. Lucia** (Gablewoods Mall, north of Castries, tel. 758/453–2788) sells only items made on the island—sandals, shirts, hot sauces, costume jewelry, carved wooden items, clay coal pots for cooking, original art, and more—all at reasonable prices. **Noah's Arkade** (Jeremie St. Castries and Pointe Seraphine, tel. 758/452–2523) has hammocks, straw mats, baskets and hats, and carvings, as well as island books and maps of St. Lucia.

Pointe Seraphine, the cruise ship terminal, is a modern, Spanish-style complex where dozens of shops sell designer perfume, china and crystal, jewelry, watches, leather goods, liquor, and cigarettes; to get the duty-free price, you must show your boarding pass or cabin key. Native crafts are also sold here. **La Place Carenage,** smaller than Pointe Seraphine but with many of the same shops, is on the opposite side of Castries Harbour.

Soufrière is not much of a shopping port, although there's a small arts and crafts center on the wharf and a batik studio at the Humming Bird Resort, along the waterfront at the north end of town.

Sports Among the sea creatures in these waters are dolphinfish, Spanish
Fishing mackerel, barracuda, kingfish, sailfish, and white marlin. For half- or full-day fishing excursions, contact **Captain Mike's** (Vigie Bay Marina, Castries, tel. 758/452–7044) or **Mako Watersports** (Rodney Bay Marina, tel. 758/452–0412).

Golf The golf courses on St. Lucia are scenic and good fun, but they're not quite world-class. **St. Lucia Golf and Country Club** (Cap Estate, tel. 758/452–8523) is a public nine-hole course that can be played as 18. A $49.50 package includes 18 holes of golf, cart, and club rental.

Hiking St. Lucia is laced with trails, but you should not attempt the challenging peaks on your own. The **Forest and Land Department** (tel. 758/450–2231) has established trails throughout the rain forest and can provide you with a guide. The **St. Lucia National Trust** (tel. 758/452–5005) maintains two hiking trails: one at Anse La Liberté, near Canaries on the Caribbean coast; the other is in the southwest, on the Atlantic coast, from Mandélé to the Fregate Islands Nature Reserve. Full-day excursions, including lunch, cost about $40 per person. **Pigeon Island** is a good place for an informal hike.

Horseback Riding	For trail rides in the north, contact **International Riding Stables** (Gros Islet, tel. 758/452–8139) or **Trim's Riding School** (Cas-en-Bas, tel. 758/452–8273); from Soufrière, contact **Trekker's** (Morne Coubaril Estate, tel. 758/459–7340). A half-hour ride runs about $35.
Scuba Diving	The coral reefs at Anse Cochon and Anse Chastanet, on the southwest coast, are popular dive sites. In the north, Pigeon Island is the most convenient site. For beach or boat dives, resort courses, underwater photography excursions, and day trips, contact: **Scuba St. Lucia** (Soufrière or Rodney Bay, tel. 758/459–7355); **Dolphin Divers** (Rodney Bay Marina, tel. 758/452–9485), Moorings Scuba Centre (tel. 758/451–4357), or **Frogs** (Windjammer Landing, tel. 758/452–0913).
Tennis	**St. Lucia Racquet Club** (adjacent to Club St. Lucia, Cap Estate, tel. 758/450–0551) is one of the top tennis facilities in the Caribbean. It has nine courts.
Beaches	All of St. Lucia's beaches are open to the public, but resorts are sometimes less than welcoming to cruise ship passengers. A good alternative for picnicking and swimming is **Pigeon Island**, admission EC$10, which has a white-sand beach and a small restaurant; it's about a 30-minute drive from Pointe Seraphine. **Reduit Beach,** 20 minutes north of Castries, is a long stretch of fine beige sand adjacent to Rodney Bay. Water-sports equipment can be rented at the Rex St. Lucian hotel.

Near Soufrière, **Anse Chastanet** is a gray-sand beach with a backdrop of green mountains, a view of the Pitons, and the island's best reefs for snorkeling and diving. A dive shop and bar are on the beach. **Anse des Pitons** lies directly between the Pitons and is accessible by boat from Soufrière. It, too, offers great snorkeling and diving. |
Dining	An 8% government tax is applicable to your bill, and some restaurants add a 10% service charge in lieu of tip.
$$–$$$	**Dasheene Restaurant.** The breathtaking view plus some of the best food on St. Lucia are reasons to make this open-air perch in the mountains your stop when touring in the area. Fresh-caught fish is always special, but there's an array of salads, sandwiches, and even a burger on the luncheon menu. *Ladera Resort, Soufrière, tel. 758/459–7323. AE, DC, MC, V.*
$$	**Jimmie's.** It's a 10- to 15-minute taxi ride from the ship, but worth it for the great views. Popular with locals as well as visitors, Jimmie's specializes in seafood—from Creole stuffed crab for an appetizer to the special seafood platter for an entrée. Dessert lovers had better be in a banana mood—everything from fritters to ice cream is made with St. Lucian "figs." *Vigie Marina, Vigie Cove, Castries, tel. 758/452–5142. Reservations not accepted. AE, MC, V.*
$$	**Lifeline Bar & Restaurant.** On the north side of town, within walking distance of the wharf, this cheerful waterfront bar and restaurant serves delicious French Creole cuisine. It is prepared by the Lifeline's award-winning chef, using fresh seafood or chicken flavored with local herbs. Sandwiches and salads are also available for a lighter lunch. After lunch, be sure to stop in at the proprietor's batik studio. *Humming Bird Beach Resort, Soufrière, tel. 758/459–7232. AE, D, MC, V.*
$$	**Still Plantation.** This attractive restaurant is a popular stop en route to Diamond Falls and La Soufrière volcano. The emphasis is on Creole cuisine, using local vegetables—christophenes, bread-

fruit, yams, callaloo—and seafood; but you'll also find pork and beef dishes on the menu. All fruits and vegetables used in the restaurant are produced organically on the estate. *Bay St., Soufrière, tel. 758/459–7224. MC, V.*

St. Martin/St. Maarten

St. Martin/St. Maarten: one tiny island, just 59 square km (37 square mi), with two different accents, and ruled by two separate nations. Here French and Dutch have lived side by side for hundreds of years, and when you cross from one country to the next there are no border patrols, no customs. In fact, the only indication that you have crossed a border at all is a small sign and a change in road surface.

St. Martin/St. Maarten epitomizes tourist islands in the sun, where services are well developed, but there's still some Caribbean flavor left. The Dutch side is ideal for people who like plenty to do. The French side has a more genteel ambience, more fashionable shopping, and a Continental flair. The combination of the halves makes an almost ideal port. On the negative side, the island has been thoroughly discovered and completely developed. There's gambling, but table limits are so low that high rollers will have a better time gamboling on the beach. It can be fun to shop, and you'll find an occasional bargain, but many goods (particularly electronics) are cheaper in the United States.

Though Dutch is the official language of St. Maarten, and French of St. Martin, almost everyone speaks English. If you hear a language you can't quite place, it's Papiamento, a Spanish-based Creole.

Currency Legal tender on the Dutch side is the Netherlands Antilles florin (guilder), written NAf; on the French side, it's the French franc (F). In general, the exchange rate is about NAf1.80 to U.S.$1, and 5F to U.S.$1. There's little need to exchange money, though, as dollars are accepted everywhere. All prices given below are in U.S. dollars except where indicated.

Telephones To phone from the Dutch side to the French side, dial 00–590 plus the local number. From the French side to the Dutch side, dial 00–5995 plus the local number. Remember that a call from one side to the other is an international call and not a local one.

At the Landsradio in Philipsburg, St. Maarten, there are facilities for overseas calls and an AT&T USADirect telephone. On the French side, it's not possible to make collect calls to the United States, but you can make credit-card calls from a phone on the side of the tourist office in Marigot. The operator will assign you a PIN number, valid for as long as you specify. Calls to the United States are about $4 per minute. To call from other public phones, you'll need to go to the special desk at Marigot's post office and buy a *telecarte*, which looks like a credit card.

Shore Excursions The following is a good choice in St. Martin/St. Maarten. It may not be offered by all cruise lines. Time and price are approximate.

Undersea Creatures **Orient Beach Sojourn.** Take a short bus ride to beautiful Orient Bay Beach on the French side of the island. The 1½-mi beach is often referred to as the French Riviera of the Caribbean, with its trendy, chic beachside restaurants and bars and colorful chaises longues and umbrellas. Lunch and drinks are included. *4½ hrs. Cost: $45.*

Coming Ashore

Except for a few vessels that stop on the French side, cruise ships drop anchor off the Dutch capital of Philipsburg or dock in the marina at the southern tip of the Philipsburg harbor. If your ship anchors, tenders will ferry you to the town pier in the middle of town, where taxis await passengers. If your ship docks at the marina, downtown is a 15-minute taxi ride away. The walk is not recommended. To get to major sights outside of Philipsburg or Marigot, your best bet is a taxi; negotiate the rate before you get in. A 2½-hour to 3-hour tour of the island for two people should be about $30, plus $10 each for extra persons. Nowhere on the island is more than a 30-minute drive from Marigot or Philipsburg.

Taxis are government-regulated and costly. Authorized taxis display stickers of the St. Maarten Taxi Association. Taxis are also available at Marigot.

Exploring St. Martin/ St. Maarten

Numbers in the margin correspond to points of interest on the St. Martin/St. Maarten map.

The Dutch Side

❶ The Dutch capital of **Philipsburg,** which stretches about 1½ km (1 mi) along an isthmus between Great Bay and Salt Pond, is easily explored on foot. It has three parallel streets: Front Street, Back Street, and Pond Fill. Little lanes called *steegjes* connect Front Street (which has been recobbled and its pedestrian area widened) with Back Street, which is considerably less congested because it has fewer shops. Altogether, a walk from one end of downtown to the other takes ½ hour, even if you stop at a couple of stores.

The first stop for cruise passengers should be Wathey Square, in the middle of the isthmus, which bustles with vendors, souvenir shops, and tourists. The streets to the right and left are lined with hotels, duty-free shops, restaurants, and cafés, most in West Indian cottages decorated in pastels with gingerbread trim. Narrow alleyways lead to arcades and flower-filled courtyards with yet more boutiques and eateries.

To explore beyond Philipsburg, start at the west end of Front Street. The road (which becomes Sucker Garden Road) leads north along Salt Pond and begins to climb and curve just outside town.

❷ The first right off Sucker Garden Road leads to **Guana Bay Point,** from which you get a splendid view of the island's east coast, tiny deserted islands, and little St. Barts in the distance.

❸ **Dawn Beach,** an excellent snorkeling beach, lies on the east coast of the island, just below Oyster Pond, and has an active sailing community.

The French Side

❹ Cruise ship passengers following the main road north out of Philipsburg will come first to Orléans. This settlement, also known as the **French Quarter,** is the island's oldest.

❺ North of Orléans is the French **Cul de Sac,** where you'll see the French colonial mansion of St. Martin's mayor nestled in the hills. From here the road swirls south through green hills and pastures, past flower-entwined stone fences.

❻ Past L'Espérance Airport is the town of **Grand Case,** known as the "Restaurant Capital of the Caribbean." Along its 1½-km-long (1-mi-long) main street are more than 20 restaurants serving French, Italian, Indonesian, and Vietnamese fare, as well as fresh

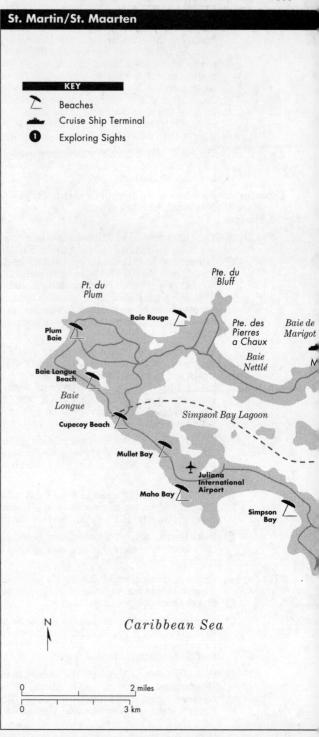

St. Martin/St. Maarten

KEY

> Beaches
> Cruise Ship Terminal
> ① Exploring Sights

Pt. du Plum

Pte. du Bluff

Baie Rouge

Plum Baie

Pte. des Pierres a Chaux

Baie de Marigot

Baie Nettlé

Baie Longue Beach

Baie Longue

Simpson Bay Lagoon

Cupecoy Beach

Mullet Bay

Juliana International Airport

Maho Bay

Simpson Bay

N

Caribbean Sea

0   2 miles

0   3 km

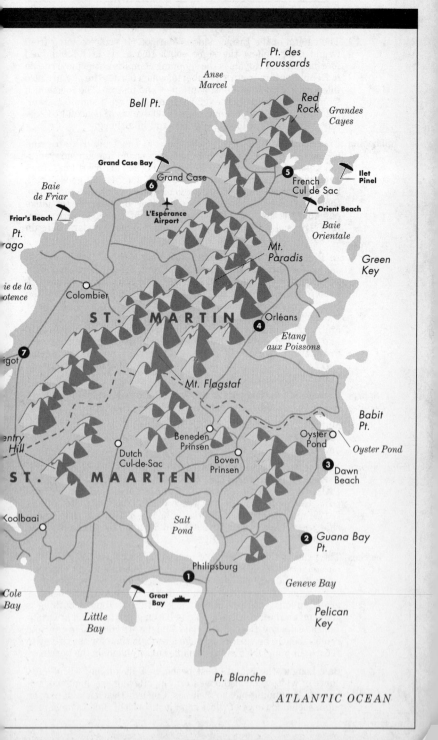

Pt. des
Froussards

Anse
Marcel

Bell Pt.

Red
Rock

Grandes
Cayes

Grand Case Bay

Grand Case

6

5

French
Cul de Sac

**Ilet
Pinel**

Baie
de Friar

L'Espérance
Airport

Orient Beach

Friar's Beach

Baie
Orientale

Pt.
rago

Mt.
Paradis

Green
Key

ie de la
otence

Colombier

ST.   MARTIN

Orléans

4

Etang
aux Poissons

Mt. Flagstaf

7

igot

Babit
Pt.

entry
Hill

Beneden
Prinsen

Oyster
Pond

Oyster Pond

ST.   MAARTEN

Dutch
Cul-de-Sac

Boven
Prinsen

3

Dawn
Beach

Koolbaai

Salt
Pond

2

Guana Bay
Pt.

Philipsburg

1

Cole
Bay

**Great
Bay**

Geneve Bay

Little
Bay

Pelican
Key

Pt. Blanche

ATLANTIC OCEAN

seafood. Along the shore, vendors known as *lolos* sell delicious barbecued chicken, beef on skewers, and other delicacies.

❼ The capital of the French side is **Marigot**. (If you're coming from Grand Case, follow the signs south to rue de la République.) Marina Port La Royale is the shopping complex at the port; rue de la République and rue de la Liberté, which border the bay, are also filled with duty-free shops, boutiques, and bistros. The road south from Marigot leads to the official border, where a simple marker, placed here in 1948, commemorates 300 years of peaceful coexistence. This road will bring you back to Philipsburg.

Shopping Prices can be 25%–50% below those in the United States and Canada for French perfume, liquor, cognac and fine liqueurs, crystal, linens, leather, Swiss watches, and other luxury items. However, it pays to know the prices back home; not all goods are a bargain. Caveat emptor: Although most merchants are reputable, there are occasional reports of inferior or fake merchandise passed off as the real thing–in particular, inferior cigars are sometimes passed off as genuine Havanas. When vendors bargain excessively, their wares are often suspect.

In Philipsburg, **Front Street** is one long strip of boutiques and shops; **Old Street,** near the end of Front Street, is packed with stores, boutiques, and open-air cafés. At Philipsburg's **Shipwreck Shop,** look for Caribelle batiks, hammocks, handmade jewelry, the local guava-berry liqueur, and herbs and spices. You'll find almost 100 boutiques in the **Mullet Bay** and **Maho** shopping plazas. In general, you'll find smarter fashions in Marigot than in Philipsburg. In Marigot, wrought-iron balconies, colorful awnings, and gingerbread trim decorate the shops and tiny boutiques in the **Marina Port La Royale** and on the main streets, **rue de la Liberté** and **rue de la République.**

Sports Contact **Sea Brat, Black Fin,** or **Pita** at Bobby's Marina, Philipsburg
Fishing (tel. 599/5–22366) for information on fishing charters.

Golf **Mullet Bay Resort** (tel. 599/5–52801) has an 18-hole championship course. Greens fees are $105 and club rental is $25 for 18 holes, $60 and $20 club rental for 9 holes.

Water Sports You can rent boats at **Caraibes Sport Boats** (tel. 590/87–89–38) and **Caribbean Watersports** (tel. 590/87–58–66). NAUI- , SSI- , and PADI-certified dive centers offer scuba instruction, rentals, and trips. On the Dutch side, try **Trade Winds Dive Center** (tel. 599/5–75176) and **St. Maarten Divers** (tel. 599/5–22446). On the French side, there's **Lou Scuba** (tel. 590/87-16-61) and **Blue Ocean** (tel. 590/87–89–73), both PADI-certified.

Beaches The island's 16 km (10 mi) of beaches are all open to cruise ship passengers. Those occupied by resort properties might charge a small fee (about $3) for changing facilities, and water-sports equipment can be rented at most hotels. Some of the 37 beaches are secluded; some are in the thick of things. Topless bathing is common on the French side. Nude bathing can be found at Orient Beach, Cupecoy Beach, and Baie Longue. If you take a cab to a remote beach, be sure to arrange a specific time for the driver to return for you. Don't leave valuables unattended on the beach.

Baie Longue, the island's best beach, is a 1½-km-long (1-mi-long) curve of white sand at the western tip, offering excellent snorkeling and swimming but no facilities. **Cupecoy Beach** is a narrower, more secluded curve of white sand just south of Baie Longue near the border. There are no facilities, but vendors sell drinks and rent beach chairs and umbrellas. This is a clothing optional beach.

Dining Restaurants on the French side often figure a service charge into the menu prices. On the Dutch side, most restaurants add 10%–15% to the bill. You can, if so moved by exceptional service, leave a tip.

$$$ **Le Poisson d'Or.** At this posh, popular restaurant in a stone house, the waters of the bay beckon from the 20-table terrace as you feast on hot foie gras salad in raspberry vinaigrette; smoked lobster boiled in tea with parsley cream sauce; or veal with Roquefort, hazelnut, and tarragon sauce. The young chef, François Julien, cooks with enthusiasm, but his cuisine must compete for attention with the striking setting. *Off rue d'Anguille, Marigot, St. Martin, tel. 590/87–72–45. AE, MC, V. No lunch Tues. in low season.*

$–$$ **Chesterfield's.** Burgers and salads are served at lunch, but menus are more elaborate for dinner on this indoor/outdoor terrace overlooking the marina. Specialties include French onion soup, roast duckling with fresh pineapple and banana sauce, and chicken Cordon Bleu. The Mermaid Bar is popular with yachtsmen. *Great Bay Marina, Philipsburg, St. Maarten, tel. 599/5–23484. No credit cards.*

$–$$ **Mini-Club.** This brightly decorated upstairs restaurant on the harbor in Marigot serves some of the island's best Creole and French cuisine. The chairs and madras tablecloths are a melange of sun-yellow and orange, and the whole thing is built, tree house–like, around the trunks of coconut trees. It's the place to be for Wednesday and Saturday's lunch buffet ($40), featuring roast pig, lobster, and roast beef. *Front de Mer, Marigot, St. Martin, tel. 590/87–50–69. AE, MC. No lunch Sun.*

$ **Shiv Sagar.** Authentic East Indian cuisine, emphasizing Kashmiri and Mogul specialties, is served in this small, mirrored room fragrant with cumin and coriander. Marvelous tandooris and curries are offered, but try one of the less-familiar preparations such as *madrasi machi* (red snapper cooked in a blend of hot spices). A large selection of vegetarian dishes is also offered. There's a friendly open-air bar out front. *3 Front St., Philipsburg, St. Maarten, tel. 599/5–22299. AE, D, DC, MC, V. Closed Sun.*

St. Thomas/St. John

St. Thomas is the busiest cruise port of call in the world. As many as a dozen ships may visit in a single day. Don't expect an exotic island experience: One of the three USVI (with St. Croix and St. John), St. Thomas is as American as any place on the mainland, complete with McDonald's franchises, and HBO. The positive side of all this development is that there are more tours to choose from here than anywhere else in the Caribbean, and every year the excursions get better. Of course, shopping is the big draw in Charlotte Amalie, the main town, but experienced travelers remember the days of "real" bargains. Today, so many passengers fill the stores that it's a seller's market. One of St. Thomas's best tourist attractions is its neighboring island, St. John, with its beautiful Virgin Islands National Park and beaches.

Currency The U.S. dollar is the official currency of St. Thomas and St. John.

Telephones It's as easy to call home from St. Thomas and St. John as from any city in the United States. In St. Thomas, public phones are easily found, and AT&T has a telecommunications center across from the Havensight Mall (*see* Coming Ashore, *below*). In St. John public phones are in front of the U.S. Post Office, east of the tender landing and at the ferry dock..

Shore The following are good choices in St. Thomas/St. John. They may
Excursions not be offered by all cruise lines. Times and prices are approximate.

Adventure **Helicopter Tour.** If you haven't taken a helicopter tour before, sign up for this exciting aerial tour of St. Thomas and surrounding islands. *1½ hrs, includes 40-min flight time. Cost: $99.*

Natural **St. John Island Tour.** Either your ship tenders you in to St. John in
Beauty the morning before docking at St. Thomas, or you take a bus from the St. Thomas docks to the St. John ferry. On St. John, an open-air safari bus winds through the national park to a beach for snorkeling, swimming, and sunbathing. (If you have the option, go to any beach but Trunk Bay.) Unless your ship is tied up in St. John for the day, all tours end with a ferry ride back to St. Thomas. *4½ hrs. Cost: $36.*

Undersea **Atlantis Submarine.** A surface boat ferries you out to a submarine
Creatures with large picture windows; the *Atlantis* dives to explore the underwater world, with good accompanying narrative. *1½ hrs. Cost: $69.*

Coki Beach Snorkeling. A good choice for novices who want to learn snorkeling (instruction and equipment usually are included) and see a variety of wildlife. *3 hrs. Cost: $25.*

Kayaking and Snorkeling Tour. Paddle on sit-atop kayaks through a marine sanctuary while a guide narrates both the on- and undersea scenes. *2½ hours. Cost: $50.*

Sailing and Snorkeling Tour. A romantic sail, a snorkeling lesson, and an attractive snorkeling site make this an excellent excursion for experiencing the true beauty of the Virgin Islands. The boat may be a modern catamaran, a single-hull sailing yacht, or a sailing vessel done up to look like a pirate ship. *3 hrs. Cost: $47.*

Scuba Diving. This excursion to one or two choice sites via boat or off a beach may be limited to certified divers, may be open to novices who have been taking lessons on the ship, or may include instruction for beginners. *3 hrs. Cost: $40.*

Coming Depending on how many ships are in port, cruise ships drop
Ashore anchor in the harbor at Charlotte Amalie and tender passengers directly to the waterfront duty-free shops, dock at the Havensight Mall at the eastern end of the crescent-shaped bay, or dock at Crown Bay Marina a few miles west of town. The distance from Havensight to the duty-free shops is 3 km (1½ mi), which can be walked in less than half an hour, or a taxi can be hired for $2.50 per person, one-way. Tourist information offices are at the Havensight Mall (across from Bldg. No 1) for docking passengers and downtown near Fort Christian (at the eastern end of the waterfront shopping area) for those coming ashore by tender. Both distribute free island and downtown shopping maps. From Crown Bay, it's also a half-hour walk or a $3 cab ride ($2.50 per cab-load for more than one passenger).

In St. John, your ship may pause outside Cruz Bay Harbor to drop you off or drop anchor if it's spending the day. You'll be tendered to shore at the main town of Cruz Bay. The shopping district starts just across the street from the tender landing. You'll find an eclectic collection of shops, cozy restaurants and myriad opportunities to people watch. The island has few organized sites. Your best bet is to take a tour of the Virgin Islands National Park offered by your ship or independently with a taxi driver who will meet your tender. The drive takes you past luscious beaches tucked under verdant hillsides and to a restored sugar plantation.

Exploring St. Thomas *Numbers in the margin correspond to points of interest on the St. Thomas map.*

Charlotte Amalie ❶ **Charlotte Amalie** is a hilly, overdeveloped shopping town. There are plenty of interesting historic sights here, and much of the town is quite pretty. So while you're shopping, take the time to see at least a few of the sights. For a great view of the town and the harbor, begin at the beautiful Spanish-style Hotel 1829, on Government Hill (also called Kongens Gade). A few yards farther up the road to the east is the base of the 99 Steps, a staircase "street" built by the Danes in the 1700s. Go up the steps (there are more than 99) and continue to the right to Blackbeard's Castle, originally Ft. Skytsborg. The massive five-story watchtower was built in 1679. It's now a dramatic perch from which to sip a drink and admire the harbor from the small hotel and restaurant. The terraces here make a perfect place to snap a photo of your ship.

Government House dates from 1867 and is the center of official life in the USVI. Inside are murals and paintings by Camille Pissarro. *Kongens Gade, tel. 340/774–0001. Open weekdays 8–5.*

Frederick Lutheran Church is the second-oldest Lutheran church in the Western Hemisphere. Its walls date to 1793. *Norre Gade, tel. 340/776–1315. Open Mon.–Sat. 9–4.*

Emancipation Garden honors the 1848 freeing of the slaves and features a smaller version of the Liberty Bell. *Between Tolbod Gade and Fort Christian.*

Ft. Christian protectively faces the harbor and bears the distinction of being St. Thomas's oldest standing structure (1672–80). The redbrick fortress has been used as a jail, governor's residence, town hall, courthouse, and church. Now designated as a U.S. national landmark, the building houses a museum filled with historical artifacts. *Waterfront Hwy. just east of shopping district, tel. 340/776–4566.*

The lime-green edifice on Kings Wharf is the **Legislature Building** (1874), seat of the 15-member USVI Senate since 1957. *Waterfront across from Ft. Christian, tel. 340/774–0880. Open daily 8–5.*

The South Shore and East End Route 32 brings you into **Red Hook,** which has grown from a sleepy little town, connected to the rest of the island only by dirt roads, into an increasingly self-sustaining village. There's luxury shopping at **American Yacht Harbor,** or you can stroll along the docks and visit with sailors and fishermen, stopping for a beer at Gunther's Spot or Tickles Dockside Pub. ❷

❸ **Coral World** has a three-level underwater observatory, the world's largest reef tank, and an aquarium with more than 20 TV-size tanks providing capsulized views of sea life. *Rte. 38, tel. 340/775–1555. Admission: $17. Open daily 9–5:30.*

❹ At **Tillett's Gardens** on Route 38 (*see* Shopping, *below*), local artisans craft stained glass, pottery, and ceramics. The late artist Jim Tillett's paintings and fabrics are also on display.

St. Thomas

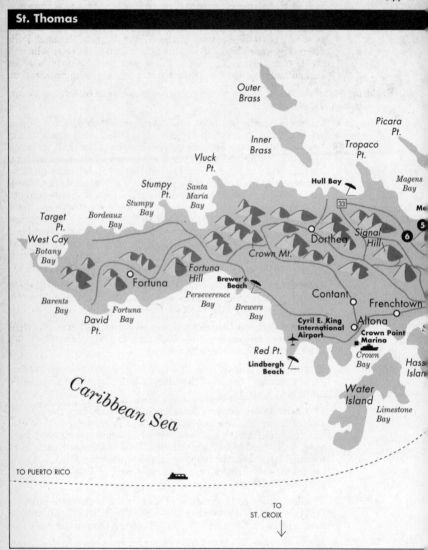

Outer
Brass

Picara
Pt.

Inner
Brass

Tropaco
Pt.

Vluck
Pt.

Magens
Bay

Stumpy
Pt.

Santa
Maria
Bay

Hull Bay

33

Me

Stumpy
Bay

5

Target
Pt.

Bordeaux
Bay

Dorthea

Signal
Hill

6

West Cay

Crown Mt.

Botany
Bay

Fortuna
Hill

Fortuna

**Brewer's
Beach**

Contant

Frenchtown

Barents
Bay

Perseverence
Bay

Brewers
Bay

**Cyril E. King
International
Airport**

Altona

David
Pt.

Fortuna
Bay

**Crown Point
Marina**

Red Pt.

Crown
Bay

Hass
Isla

**Lindbergh
Beach**

Caribbean Sea

Water
Island

Limestone
Bay

TO PUERTO RICO

TO
ST. CROIX

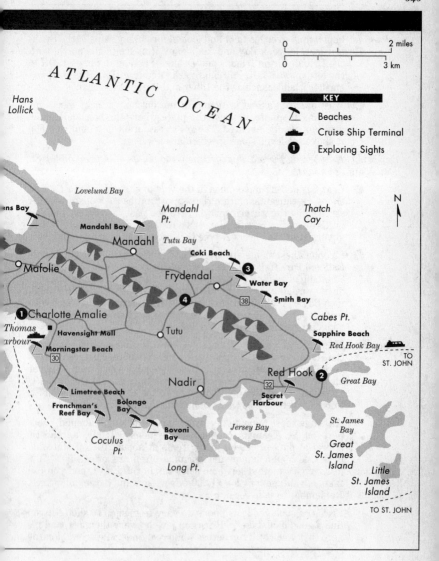

0   2 miles
0   3 km

KEY
Beaches
Cruise Ship Terminal
① Exploring Sights

ATLANTIC OCEAN

Hans
Lollick

N

Lovelund Bay

Mandahl
Pt.

Thatch
Cay

...ns Bay

Mandahl Bay

Mandahl

Tutu Bay

Coki Beach ③

Frydendal ④

Mafolie

Water Bay

38 **Smith Bay**

Charlotte Amalie ①

Thomas
...arbour

Havensight Mall

Tutu

Cabes Pt.

Sapphire Beach

Red Hook Bay

TO
ST. JOHN

Morningstar Beach

30

Nadir

Red Hook ②

Great Bay

Limetree Beach

32 **Secret
Harbour**

**Frenchman's
Reef Bay**

**Bolongo
Bay**

St. James
Bay

**Bovoni
Bay**

Jersey Bay

Great
St. James
Island

Coculus
Pt.

Little
St. James
Island

Long Pt.

TO ST. JOHN

North Shore/ In the heights above Charlotte Amalie is **Drake's Seat,** the moun-
Center tain lookout from which Sir Francis Drake was supposed to have
Islands kept watch over his fleet and looked for enemy ships of the Span-
5 ish fleet. Magens Bay and Mahogany Run are to the north, with
the British Virgin Islands and Drake's Passage to the east. Off to
the left, or west, are Fairchild Park, Mountain Top, Hull Bay, and
smaller islands, such as the Inner and Outer Brass islands.

6 West of Drake's Seat is **Mountain Top,** not only a tacky mecca for
souvenir shopping, but also the place where the banana daiquiri
was supposedly invented. There's a restaurant here and, at 1,500
ft above sea level, some spectacular views.

Exploring *Numbers in the margin correspond to points of interest on the St.*
St. John *John map.*

1 **Cruz Bay** doesn't have much in the way of sites. You'll mostly find
shops, restaurants, and myriad opportunities to people-watch. A
stroll along the waterfront will take you past the **Battery,** built on
an 18th-century fortification. It's now the seat of the island's small
government. You are welcome to wander around the grounds.

2 St. John's best sights are preserved in the sprawling **Virgin Islands
National Park** (tel. 340/776–6201), which covers most of the island.
Stunning vistas and gorgeous beaches can be reached on a taxi tour
or by renting a car. If you have the day to spend, head for Cinnamon Bay. This National Park Service campground has a beach with
water-sports equipment for rent, hiking just across the street, and
a modest restaurant and cool showers.

Shopping There are well over 400 shops in Charlotte Amalie alone, and near
the Havensight docks there are at least 60 more, clustered in converted warehouses. Even die-hard shoppers won't want to cover
all the boutiques, since a large percentage peddle the same T-
shirts and togs. Many visitors devote their shopping time on St.
Thomas to the stores that sell handicrafts and luxury items.

Although those famous "giveaway" prices no longer abound, shoppers on St. Thomas can still save money. Today, a realistic
appraisal puts prices on many items at about 20% off stateside
prices, although liquor and perfume often are priced 50%–70%
less. What's more, there's no sales tax in the USVI, and you can
take advantage of the $1,200-per-person duty-free allowance.
Remember to save receipts.

Prices on such goods as linens do vary from shop to shop—if you
find a good deal, take it. Prices on jewelry vary the most, and it's
here that you'll still run across some real finds. Major credit cards
are widely accepted.

Shopping The major shopping area is Charlotte Amalie, in centuries-old
Districts buildings that once served as merchants' warehouses and that, for
the most part, have been converted to retail establishments. Both
sides of **Main Street** are lined with shops, as are the side streets
and walkways between Main Street and the waterfront. These
narrow lanes and arcades have names like Drake's Passage, Royal
Dane Mall, Palm Passage, Trompeter Gade, Hibiscus Alley, and
Raadet's Gade. **Back Street,** also called Vimmelskaft Gade (1 block
north of Main St. off Nye Gade) and streets adjacent to it—Garden Street, Kongens Gade, and Norre Gade—are also very good
areas for browsing. At **Havensight Mall,** near the deep-water port,
you'll find branches of downtown stores, as well as specialty shops
and boutiques. Next door, at **Port of $ale,** factory outlets sell brand
names at bargain prices.

Charlotte
Amalie

Unless otherwise noted, the following stores have branches both downtown and in Havensight Mall and are easy to find. If you have any trouble, shopping maps are available at the tourist offices and often from your ship's shore-excursion desk. U.S. citizens can carry back a gallon, or six "fifths," of liquor duty-free.

A. H. Riise Gift & Liquor Shops: Waterford, Wedgwood, Royal Crown, and Royal Doulton china; jewelry, pearls, and watches; liquors, cordials, and wines, including rare vintage cognacs, Armagnacs, ports, and Madeiras; tobacco and imported cigars; fruits in brandy; barware from England; fragrances for men and women; and cosmetics. **Al Cohen's Discount Liquor** (Havensight Mall only): discount liquors. **Amsterdam Sauer:** one-of-a-kind fine jewelry. **Blue Carib Gems** (downtown only): Caribbean amber; black coral handcrafted in silver or gold. **Boolchand's:** cameras, audio-video equipment.

The **Caribbean Marketplace** (Havensight Mall only): Caribbean handicrafts, including Caribelle batiks from St. Lucia; bikinis from the Cayman Islands; Sunny Caribee spices, soaps, teas, and coffees from Trinidad. **Caribbean Print Gallery** (in A. H. Riise, downtown): old-fashioned maps and engravings of Caribbean scenes by MAPes MONDe Ltd. **Down Island Traders** (downtown only): hand-painted calabash bowls; jams, jellies, spices, and herbs; herbal teas made of rum, passion fruit, and mango; high-mountain coffee from Jamaica; Caribbean handicrafts. The **English Shop:** china and crystal from Spode, Limoges, Royal Doulton, Portmeirion, Noritaki, and others (Havensight only).

The Gallery (downtown only): Haitian and local oil paintings, metal sculpture, wood carvings, painted screens and boxes, figures carved from stone, oversize papier-mâché figures. **G'Day** (downtown only): umbrellas, artwork, sportswear. **H. Stern:** gems and jewelry. **Janine's Boutique** (downtown only): women's and men's apparel and accessories from European designers and manufacturers, including Louis Feraud, Valentino, Christian Dior, Pierre Cardin. **Leather Shop:** Fendi, Bottega Veneta, other fine leather goods. **Little Switzerland:** Lalique, Baccarat, Waterford, and other crystal; Wedgwood, Royal Doulton, and other china; Rolex watches. **Native Arts and Crafts Cooperative:** (downtown only): handmade dolls, quilts, art, jewelry, jams, teas, and hot sauces.

Pampered Pirate (downtown only): Caribbean handicrafts, spices, sauces, jams, and Jamaican coffee. **Pusser's Close-Out Store** (Havensight Mall only): discounted nautically themed clothing. **Royal Caribbean** (no affiliation with the cruise line): cameras, cassette players, audio-video equipment. **Tropicana Perfume Shoppes** (downtown only): fragrances for men and women.

Tillett's
Gardens

Tillett's Gardens and Craft Complex (Estate Tutu, tel. 340/775–1405) (*see* Exploring St. Thomas, *above*) is more than worth the cab fare to reach it. The late Jim Tillett's artwork is on display, and you can watch craftsmen and artisans produce watercolors, silk-screened fabrics, pottery, enamel work, candles, and other handicrafts.

St. John

In St. John, the small shopping district runs from **Wharfside Village** near the ferry landing to **Mongoose Junction,** just up the street from the cruise ship dock and tender landing, with lots of shops that carry an array of merchandise tucked in between.

Colombian Emeralds has two branches of its duty-free jewelry shops in St. John. Try either the main store at Mongoose Junction or its **Jewelers Warehouse** in Wharfside Village for emeralds, dia-

St. John

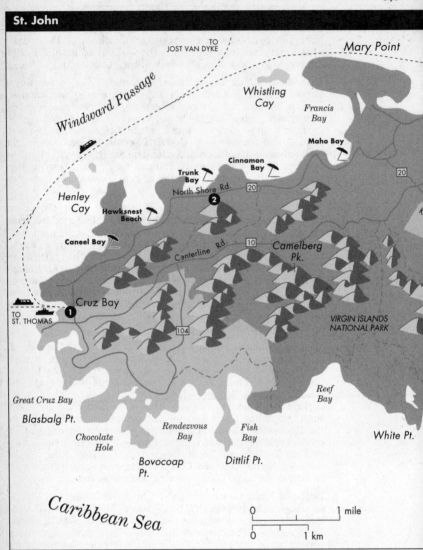

Cruz Bay, **1**
Virgin Islands
National Park, **2**

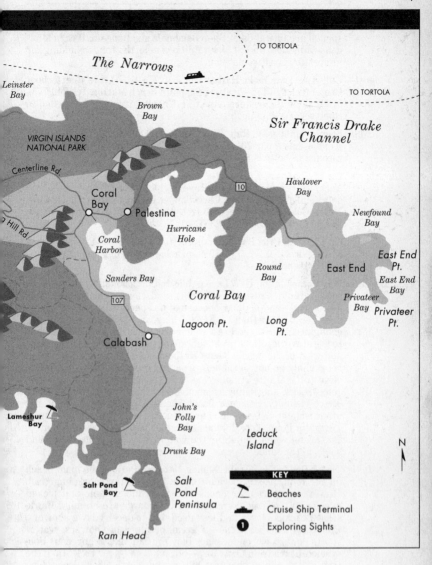

The Narrows

TO TORTOLA

TO TORTOLA

Leinster Bay

Brown Bay

Sir Francis Drake Channel

VIRGIN ISLANDS NATIONAL PARK

Centerline Rd

a Hill Rd

Coral Bay

Palestina

Hurricane Hole

Haulover Bay

Newfound Bay

Coral Harbor

Sanders Bay

Round Bay

East End

East End Pt.

East End Bay

107

Coral Bay

Lagoon Pt.

Long Pt.

Privateer Bay

Privateer Pt.

Calabash

John's Folly Bay

Leduck Island

Lameshur Bay

Drunk Bay

N

Salt Pond Bay

Salt Pond Peninsula

KEY

Beaches

Cruise Ship Terminal

1 Exploring Sights

Ram Head

monds, and other jewels. For interesting handcrafted jewelry try **Caravan Gallery. Heads Up** has unique watches with St. John spelled in nautical flags. Shop **Bamboula** and **Bougainvillea** in Mongoose Junction, and **St. John Editions** near the tender landing for interesting tropical clothing.

Sports Call **American Yacht Harbor** (tel. 340/775–6454), the **Charterboat**
Fishing **Center** (tel. 340/775–7990), or **Sapphire Beach Marina** (tel. 340/775–6100) all on the eastern end of St. Thomas, if you're interested in some serious angling.

Golf Scenic **Mahogany Run** (tel. 340/777–6006), north of Charlotte Amalie, has a par-70, 18-hole course and a view of the BVI. The rate for 18 holes is $90, cart included.

Water Sports On St. Thomas, **Underwater Safaris** (tel. 340/774–1350) is at the Yacht Haven Marina, near Havensight. Other reliable scuba and snorkeling operators are **Chris Sawyer Diving Center** (tel. 340/775–7320), **Coki Beach Dive Club** (tel. 340/775–4220), and **St. Thomas Diving Club** (tel. 340/776–2381).

On St. John, **Cruz Bay Watersports** (tel. 809/776–6234) and **Low Key Watersports** (tel. 340/776–8999) provide snorkeling and scuba trips to nearby reefs.

Beaches All beaches in the USVI are public, but occasionally you'll need to
St. Thomas stroll through a resort to reach the sand. Government-run **Magens Bay** is lively and popular because of its spectacular loop of white-sand beach, more than 1 km (½ mi) long, and its calm waters. Food, changing facilities, and rest rooms are available. **Coki Beach,** next to Coral World, offers great snorkeling among the reefs to the east and west of the beach. **Secret Harbour** is a pretty cove for superb snorkeling; go out to the left, near the rocks. **Morningstar Beach,** close to Charlotte Amalie, has a mostly sandy sea bottom with some rocks; snorkeling is good here when the current doesn't affect visibility. **Sapphire Beach** has a fine view of St. John and other islands. Snorkeling is excellent at the reef to the east, near Pettyklip Point, and all kinds of water-sports gear can be rented. Be careful when you enter the water; there are many rocks and shells in the sand.

St. John **Trunk Bay** in the Virgin Islands National Park is the main beach on St. John, mostly because of its underwater snorkeling trail. However, experienced snorkelers may find it tame and picked over, with too little coral or fish. Lifeguards are on duty. **Hawksnest Beach** is closer and less used, but it doesn't have showers. **Cinnamon Bay** has it all—a great beach, cool showers, water-sports equipment, and a snack bar. You can hike to gorgeous **Honeymoon Beach** from Cruz Bay—but it's a half-hour trek. Take the trail at the top of the first hill on the North Shore Road. The rangers at the national park visitor's center in Cruz Bay will point you in the right direction.

Dining Some restaurants add a 10%–15% service charge to the bill.

$$ **Fish Trap.** There are several rooms and terraces here, all open to the breezes. Chef Aaron Willis conjures up such tasty appetizers as conch fritters and Fish Trap chowder. The menu also includes an interesting pasta of the day, steak, chicken, and hamburgers. *Downtown Cruz Bay, St. John, tel. 340/693–9994. AE, D, MC, V. Closed Mon.*

$$ **Global Village Cuisine at Latitude 18.** Choose either the cozy but open-air dining room or the breezy bar-dining area. Hamburgers,

sandwiches, and salads make up the lunch menu. *Mongoose Junction, St. John, tel. 340/693–8677. AE, MC, V.*

$$ **Sun Dog Cafe.** Tucked under umbrellas at the upper reaches of Mongoose Junction, this nifty spot offers eclectic fare. The menu includes barbecue pork, cheese and veggies in phyllo dough, and even hot dogs. It's a great place to stop for a smoothie. *Mongoose Junction, St. John, tel. 340/693–8340. AE, MC, V. Closed Sun.*

$ **Beni Iguana's.** Sushi is served as an edible art in a charming Danish courtyard. A picture menu makes ordering easy by the piece, plate, or combination platter. *Grand Hotel Court, St. Thomas, tel. 340/777–8744. No credit cards.*

$ **Gladys' Cafe.** Owner Gladys Isles' welcoming smile will tempt you to try local favorites, such as whole panfried fish topped with a tangy Creole sauce, conch simmered with butter and onions, or chunks of Caribbean lobster served sandwich-style on a roll. For the less adventurous, the grilled chicken salad is a winner, too. *Royal Dane Mall, St. Thomas, tel. 340/774–6604. AE. No dinner.*

$ **Zorba's.** Greek dishes, like salads and Mediterranean-style seafood, are the specialties of the house at this converted 19th century residence. You can munch on freshly baked bread while looking out over the harbor—President Clinton and the First Family did over New Year's in 1997. *Government Hill near Hotel 1829, Charlotte Amalie, St. Thomas, tel. 340/776–0444. AE, MC, V.*

San Juan, Puerto Rico

Although Puerto Rico is part of the United States, few cities in the Caribbean are as steeped in Spanish tradition as San Juan. Old San Juan has restored 16th-century buildings, museums, art galleries, bookstores, 200-year-old houses with balustrade balconies overlooking narrow, cobblestone streets—all within a seven-block neighborhood. In contrast, San Juan's sophisticated Condado and Isla Verde areas have glittering hotels, flashy Las Vegas–style shows, casinos, and discos.

Out in the countryside is the 28,000-acre El Yunque rain forest, with more than 240 species of trees growing at least 100 ft high. You can also stretch your sea legs on dramatic mountain ranges, numerous trails, vast caves, coffee plantations, old sugar mills, and hundreds of beaches. No wonder San Juan is one of the busiest ports of call in the Caribbean.

Like any other big city, San Juan has its share of crime. Guard your wallet or purse, and avoid walking in the area between Old San Juan and the Condado.

Currency The U.S. dollar is the official currency of Puerto Rico.

Telephones Calling the United States from Puerto Rico works the same as calling within the states. Local calls from a public phone cost 25¢ for every 5 minutes. You can use the long-distance telephone service office in the cruise ship terminal, or call from any pay phone. You'll find a phone center by the Paseo de la Princesa.

Shore Excursions The following are good choices in San Juan. They may not be offered by all cruise lines. Times and prices are approximate.

Local Flavors **Bacardi Rum Distillery.** After seeing how it is made, you can sample and buy some Bacardi rum. *2 hrs. Cost: $18.*

San Juan Nightlife Tour. Several major hotels (like the Condado Plaza) have very exciting revues, especially those that feature flamenco or Latin dancers. Admission includes a drink or two. *1–2½ hrs. Cost: $34–$40.*

Natural **El Yunque Rain Forest.** A 45-minute drive heads east to the
Beauty Caribbean National Forest, where you can walk along various trails, see waterfalls, and climb the observation tower. Lunch at a country restaurant is included. *4½ hrs. Cost: $48.*

Coming Cruise ships dock within a couple of blocks of Old San Juan. The
Ashore Paseo de la Princesa, a tree-lined promenade beneath the city wall, is a nice place for a stroll; you can admire the local crafts and stop at the refreshment kiosks. A tourist information booth and long-distance telephone office are found in the cruise-terminal area. Major sights in the Old San Juan area are minutes, and mere blocks from the piers, but be aware that the streets are narrow and steeply inclined in places. A ride to anywhere else in the Old San Juan area costs $6; a 10- or 15-minute taxi ride to the Condado, Ocean Park, or Miramar in San Juan costs $10.

To get to Cataño and the Bacardi Rum Plant, take the 50¢ ferry that leaves from the cruise piers every half-hour. Your best bet, other than an organized ship excursion, to reach Bayamón and Caparra (still within the San Juan Metro area) is to take a taxi. Taxis line up to meet ships. Metered cabs authorized by the Public Service Commission charge an initial $1; after that, it works out to about 10¢ for each additional ⅓ mi. Waiting time is 10¢ for each 45 seconds. Insist that the meter be turned on, and pay only what is shown, plus a tip of 10%–15%. Be aware that you can negotiate with taxi drivers for specific trips, and you can hire a taxi for as little as $20 per hour for sightseeing tours.

If your feet fail you in Old San Juan, climb aboard the free open-air trolleys that rumble through the narrow streets. Take one from the docks or board anywhere along the route.

Exploring Old *Numbers in the margin correspond to points of interest on the Old*
San Juan *San Juan map.*

Old San Juan Old San Juan, the original city founded in 1521, lives up to its name with authentic and carefully preserved examples of 16th-and 17th-century Spanish colonial architecture. Graceful wrought-iron balconies decorated with lush green hanging plants extend over narrow, cobblestone streets. Seventeenth-century walls still partially enclose the old city. Designated a U.S. National Historic Zone in 1950, Old San Juan is packed with shops, open-air cafés, private homes, tree-shaded squares, monuments, plaques, pigeons, people, and traffic jams. It's faster to walk than to take a cab. Nightlife is quiet, even spooky during the low season; you'll find more to do in New San Juan, especially the Condado area.

❶ **San Cristóbal,** the 18th-century fortress that guarded the city from land attacks, is known as the Gibraltar of the West Indies. San Cristóbal is larger than El Morro (*see below*), and has spectacular views of both Old San Juan and the new city. *Calle Norzagaray, tel. 787/729–6960. Admission free. Open daily 9–5.*

❷ **Plaza de Armas** is the original main square of Old San Juan. The plaza has afountain with statues representing the four seasons.

❸ West of the main square stands **La Intendencia,** a handsome, three-story neoclassical building that was home to the Spanish Treasury from 1851 to 1898. Today it houses Puerto Rico's State Depart-

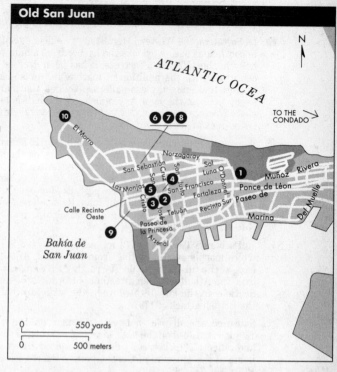

Old San Juan

ATLANTIC OCEA

N

TO THE CONDADO

El Morro

Norzagaray

San Sebastián

Sol

Luna

O'Donel

Muñoz

Rivera

Ponce de Léon

San Francisco

Fortaleza

Paseo de

Las Monjas

San José

Tetuán

Recinto Sur

Paseo de

Marina

Del Muelle

Calle Recinto Oeste

Paseo de la Princesa

Arsenal

Bahía de San Juan

0 ——— 550 yards

0 ——— 500 meters

---

ment. *Calle San José at Calle San Francisco, tel. 787/722-2121, ext. 230. Admission free. Open weekdays 8–noon and 1–4:30.*

4 On the north side of the Plaza de Armas is **City Hall,** called the *alcaldía.* Built between 1604 and 1789, it was fashioned after Madrid's city hall, with arcades, towers, balconies, and a lovely inner courtyard. An art gallery is on the first floor. *Tel. 787/724–7171, ext. 2391. Open weekdays 8–4.*

5 The remains of Ponce de León are in a marble tomb near the transept in the **San Juan Cathedral on Calle Cristo.** This great Catholic shrine of Puerto Rico had humble beginnings in the early 1520s as a thatch-top wood structure that was destroyed by a hurricane. It was reconstructed in 1540, when the graceful circular staircase and vaulted ceilings were added, but most of the work on the church was done in the 19th century. *153 Calle Cristo, tel. 787/722-0861. Admission free. Open daily 8:30–4.*

6 The **Pablo Casals Museum** exhibits memorabilia of the famed Spanish cellist, who made his home in Puerto Rico for the last 20 years of his life. *101 Calle San Sebastián, Plaza de San José, tel. 787/723–9185. Admission: $1. Open Tues.–Sat. 9:30–5:30.*

7 In the center of Plaza San José is the **San José Church.** With its series of vaulted ceilings, it is a fine example of 16th-century Spanish Gothic architecture. *Calle San Sebastián, tel. 787/725–7501. Admission free. Open Mon.–Sat. 8:30–4; Sun. Mass at 12:15.*

8 Next door to the San José Church is the 16th-century **Dominican Convent,** which houses an ornate 18th-century altar, religious manuscripts, artifacts, and art. *98 Calle Norzagaray, tel. 787/721–6866. Admission free. Chapel museum open Mon.–Sat. 9–5.*

❾ La Fortaleza, the Western Hemisphere's oldest executive mansion in continuous use, overlooks the harbor from a hilltop. Built originally in the 1500s as a fortress, it has been dressed up over the centuries with the addition of marble and mahogany, medieval towers, and stained-glass galleries. Guided tours are conducted every hour on the hour in English, on the half-hour in Spanish. *Calle Recinto Oeste, tel. 787/721–7000, ext. 2211. Admission free. Open weekdays 9–4.*

❿ San Juan's most famous sight is undoubtedly **El Morro (Fuerte San Felipe del Morro),** set on a rocky promontory on the northwestern tip of the old city. Rising 140 ft above the sea, the massive, six-level Spanish fortress is a labyrinth of dungeons, ramps, turrets, and tunnels. Built to protect the port, El Morro has a commanding view of the harbor and Old San Juan. Its small museum traces the history of the fortress. *Calle Norzagaray, tel. 787/729–6960. Admission free. Open daily 9–5.*

New San Juan In **Puerta de Tierra,** 1 km (½ mi) east of the pier, is Puerto Rico's white marble capitol, dating from the 1920s. Another kilometer east, at the tip of Puerta de Tierra, tiny Ft. San Jeronimo perches over the Atlantic like an afterthought. Added to San Juan's fortifications in the late 18th century, the structure barely survived the British attack of 1797.

Santurce, the district between Miramar on the west and the Laguna San José on the east, is a busy mixture of shops, markets, and offices. The classically designed Sacred Heart University is home of the Museum of Contemporary Puerto Rican Art (Barat Bldg., tel. 787/268–0049).

San Juan Environs The **Bacardi Rum Plant,** along the bay, conducts 45-minute tours of the bottling plant, museum, and distillery, which has the capacity to produce 100,000 gallons of rum a day—yes, you'll be offered a sample. A ferry to Cataño departs from the piers next to the cruise ship docks every half-hour from 6 AM until 10 PM, at a cost of 50¢. *Rte. 888, Km 2.6, Cataño, tel. 787/788–1500. Admission free. Tours every 30 mins Mon.–Sat. 9–10:30 and noon–4; closed holidays.*

Along Route 5 from Cataño to Bayamón, you'll find the **Barrilito Rum Plant.** The grounds include a 200-year-old plantation home and a 150-year-old windmill, which is listed in the National Register of Historic Places. *Rte. 5, Km 1.6, Bayamón, tel. 787/785-3490. Admission free. Open weekdays 8–11:30 and 1–4:30.*

About 6 km (4 mi) from San Juan on Route 2 West, you'll find the **Caparra Ruins,** where, in 1508, Ponce de León established the island's first settlement. Within the fort ruins is the small Museum of the Conquest and Colonization of Puerto Rico and its historic documents, exhibits, and excavated artifacts. *Rte. 2, Km 6.6, tel. 787/781–4795. Admission free. Open Tues.–Sat. 8:30–4:30.*

Past the Caparra Ruins, Route 2 brings you to **Bayamón,** about 11 km (7 mi) from central San Juan. In the Central Park, across from the city hall, are some historic buildings and a 1934 sugarcane train that runs through the park.

Shopping San Juan is not a free port, and you won't find bargains on electronics and perfumes. However, shopping for native crafts can be fun. Popular souvenirs and gifts include *santos* (small, hand-carved figures of saints or religious scenes), hand-rolled cigars, handmade lace, carnival masks, Puerto Rican rum, and fancy men's shirts called *guayaberas.*

Old San Juan is filled with shops, especially on calles **Cristo, La Fortaleza,** and **San Francisco.** You can get discounts on Hathaway shirts and clothing by Christian Dior and Ralph Lauren at **Hathaway Factory Outlet** (203 Calle Cristo, tel. 787/723–8946) and on raincoats at the **London Fog Factory Outlet** (156 Calle Cristo, tel. 787/722–4334). For one-of-a-kind local crafts, head for **Puerto Rican Arts & Crafts** (204 Calle La Fortaleza, Old San Juan, tel. 787/725–5596) or the **Haitian Gallery** (367 Calle Fortaleza, tel. 787/725–0986).

Sports

Golf There are four 18-hole courses shared by the **Hyatt Dorado Beach Hotel** and the **Hyatt Regency Cerromar Beach Hotel** (Dorado, tel. 787/796–1234, ext. 3238 or 3016). You'll also find 18-hole courses at **Wyndham Palmas del Mar Resort** (Humacao, tel. 787/852–6000), **Westin Rio Mar Resort and Country Club** (Río Grande, tel. 787/888–6000), **Punta Borinquén** (Aquadilla, tel. 787/890–2987), and **Bahia Beach Plantation** (Río Grande, tel. 787/256–5600).

Hiking Dozens of trails lace **El Yunque.** Information is available at the El Portal Tropical Forest Center (Route 191, tel. 787/888–1810). Admission is $3.

Water Sports Virtually all the resort hotels on San Juan's Condado and Isla Verde (*see* Beaches, *below*) strips rent paddleboats, Sunfish, and Windsurfers.

Beaches By law, all of Puerto Rico's beaches are open to the public (except for the Caribe Hilton's artificial beach in San Juan). The government runs 13 public *balnearios* (beaches), which have lockers, showers, and picnic tables; some have playgrounds and overnight facilities. *Admission free; parking $2. Open Tues.–Sun. 8–5 in summer, 9–6 in winter.*

Isla Verde is a white sandy beach close to metropolitan San Juan. Backed by several resort hotels, the beach offers picnic tables and good snorkeling, with equipment rentals nearby.

Dining *A 10%–15% tip is expected in restaurants.*

$$–$$$ **La Mallorquina.** The food here is basic Puerto Rican and Spanish fare, but the atmosphere is what recommends this spot. Said to date from 1848, this is the oldest restaurant in Puerto Rico, with pale pink walls and whirring ceiling fans, and a nattily attired and friendly wait staff. *207 Calle San Justo, tel. 787/722-3261. AE, MC, V. Closed Sun.*

$–$$ **Amadeus.** The atmosphere here is gentrified Old San Juan, with an ever-changing menu of appetizers, including plantain mousse with shrimp and Buffalo wings. Entrées on the nouvelle Caribbean menu range from Cajun-grilled mahimahi, to creamy pasta dishes, to chicken and steak sandwiches. *106 Calle San Sebastián, tel.787/722-8635. AE, MC, V. Closed Mon.*

Nightlife Almost every ship stays in San Juan late or even overnight to give passengers an opportunity to revel in the nightlife—the most sophisticated in the Caribbean.

Casinos By law, all casinos are in hotels. Alcoholic drinks are not permitted at the gaming tables, although free soft drinks, coffee, and sandwiches are available. The atmosphere is quite refined, and many patrons dress to the nines, but informal attire is usually fine. Casinos set their own hours, which change seasonally, but generally operate from noon to 4 AM. Casinos are in the following hotels: **Condado Plaza Hotel, Carib Inn, Clarion Hotel, El San Juan, Ramada, San Juan Marriott,** and **Sands.**

Discos   In Old San Juan, young people flock to **Lazer Videoteque** (251 Calle Cruz, tel. 787/721–4479). In Puerta de Tierra, Condado, and Isla Verde, the thirty-something crowd heads for **Amadeus** (El San Juan Hotel, tel. 787/791–1000), **Isadora's** (Condado Plaza Hotel, tel. 787/721–1000), and **Egipto** (Av. Robert Todd, Santurce, tel. 787/725–4664 or 787/725–4675) for live music and dancing.

Nightclubs   El San Juan's **Tropicoro** presents international revues and, occasionally, top-name entertainers. The Condado Plaza Hotel has the **Copa Room,** and its La Fiesta sizzles with steamy Latin shows.

Ports of Embarkation and Disembarkation

Miami   The Port of Miami is on Dodge Island, across from the downtown area via a five-lane bridge. Just before the bridge on the mainland is the large and attractive Bayside Marketplace, whose waterfront ambience, two stories of shops and restaurants, and street entertainers provide a pleasant alternative to the cruise terminals if you arrive before boarding begins.

Long-Term Parking   Street-level lots are right in front of the cruise terminals. Just leave your luggage with a porter, tip him, and park. The cost is $8 per day.

Port Canaveral   Florida's Port Canaveral is used primarily by ships that combine their sailings with a pre- or post-cruise package at an Orlando theme park. Walt Disney World, Magic Kingdom, Disney–MGM Studios, Epcot Center, Universal Studios, and Sea World are about an hour by car. Kennedy Space Center, also known as Space Port USA, is 15 mi (24 km) away and Cocoa Beach is nearby.

Long-Term Parking   An outdoor long-term parking lot is directly outside the terminal and costs $7 per day.

From the Airport   The Orlando airport is 45 minutes away from the docks. Taxi rates are very expensive, so try taking the $20-per-person **Cocoa Beach Shuttle** (tel. 800/633–0427) bus instead, but call first to make a reservation.

San Juan   Puerto Rico's capital has become a major port of embarkation for cruises to the "deep" or southern Caribbean.

From the Airport   The ride from the **Luis Muñoz Marín International Airport,** east of downtown San Juan, to the docks in Old San Juan takes about 20 minutes. The white "taxi turistico" cabs, marked by a logo on the door, have a fixed rate of $16 to the piers; there is a small fee for luggage. Other taxi companies charge by the mile, which can cost a little more. Be sure the taxi driver starts the meter, or agree on a fare beforehand.

Europe and the Mediterranean

For sheer diversity, there is no cruise destination quite like Europe. From the majesty of Norway's fjords to the ruins of ancient Greece, the Old World has more than one could possibly hope to see in a single cruise vacation. The hardest part of cruising in Europe is deciding what to see. Do you want to sail the Mediterranean, with ports of call in Greece, Turkey, Israel, Egypt, and Spain? Or would you prefer Northern Europe, perhaps including a few cities in the former Soviet Union? Or maybe Western Europe, with the glamorous beaches and resort cities of the French Riviera?

Select your ship as carefully as you choose your itinerary. Look especially at the mix of passengers: Are they all North Americans or a mix of Americans and Europeans? If the latter sounds interesting to you, *see* Chapter 2.

When to Go　Cruise lines sail in Europe from April to November. Peak season runs from May through August; the weather is usually at its best during this time, which means you will be joining the crowds. Early spring and late fall are a good time to visit if you want to avoid the fray—and get lower prices. Temperatures can be very comfortable, and it is possible to swim in the Mediterranean through early October. Some lines operate European itineraries year-round featuring the Canary Islands.

Currency　Currencies vary by country, and U.S. dollars are accepted at some ports. It is advisable to change only a small amount on your ship or ashore for purchasing trinkets or snacks. When making major purchases and eating at better restaurants, use credit cards, which offer the best exchange rate.

Passports and Visas　All U.S. citizens will need a passport to travel to Europe. Several countries, including Israel, Egypt, and Russia, require visas. Your cruise documents will specify whether visas are needed, and, generally, the line or your travel agent can obtain the visa for you for a fee.

What to Pack　A priority item for cruising Europe is a comfortable pair of shoes—walking is the best and sometimes only way really to explore in port. Wardrobes will be determined by your cruise itinerary. In the Mediterranean, casual summer wear will do. In countries such as Egypt, Turkey, and Morocco, women will want to dress conservatively, covering their arms and legs. Pack clothing that can be layered and that is suitable for hot days and cooler evenings.

Telephones and Mail　Unless money is no object, don't use the satellite phones aboard ship. At major ports where ships dock, there typically will be telephones at or near the pier. If your ship is tendering into port, ask at the shore-excursion office for the nearest calling center.

As a rule, cruise ships sell local stamps at the front desk, and you can send postcards from an onboard mailbox as well, eliminating the need to find a post office.

Shore Excursions　Due to its diversity and wealth of attractions, Europe is well suited to shore excursions, which are usually bus tours. However, depending on the port, you may want to explore on your own. Often, this is possible on foot. In larger ports, you can hire a local guide at the pier. A group of four to six will find this more economical and practical than will a couple or a single person. Renting

Reykjavik
ICELAND

NORWAY
Bergen

NORTHERN
IRELAND

SCOTLAND
Edinburgh

Skagerrak

North
Sea

DENMARK

Belfast

IRELAND   Irish   GREAT
          Sea
Dublin   BRITAIN

Hamburg

WALES   ENGLAND   HOLLAND
Cardiff   Amsterdam
        London   The Hague   GERM
                       Rotterdam

ATLANTIC   English Channel   Brussels   Bonn
OCEAN   BELGIUM   Frankfurt

                   Paris
                   LUXEMBOURG

           FRANCE   Zürich   Munich
                    Bern   Salzbur
                    SWITZERLAND
                    Lyon   LIECHTENSTEIN
                           Milan   Veni

PORTUGAL   Nice   Monaco
              Madrid   ANDORRA   Marseille   Florence
Lisbon   Corsica
        SPAIN   Barcelona

Seville   Granada   Balearic
                     Islands   Sardinia
                                        Tyrrheni
Gibraltar   Mediterranean Sea

MOROCCO   ALGERIA
        0   400 miles   TUNISIA
        0   600 km

a car is often more of a pain than a pleasure, given the limited time you have ashore. On some islands, motor scooters are an option—but they are notoriously dangerous. It's better to hire a car and driver. Ask your shore-excursions office for recommended companies in each port.

Amsterdam, The Netherlands

If you've come to Holland expecting to find its residents shod in wooden shoes, you're years too late; if you're looking for windmills at every turn, you're looking in the wrong place. The bucolic images that brought tourism here in the decades after World War II have little to do with the Netherlands of the '90s. Modern Holland is a marriage of economic power and cultural wealth, a mix not new to the Dutch: In the 17th century, for example, money raised through colonial outposts was used to buy or commission portraits and paintings by young artists such as Rembrandt, Hals, Vermeer, and van Ruisdael.

Amsterdam is the cultural focal point of the nation. Small and densely packed with fine buildings, many dating from the 17th century or earlier, it is easily explored on foot. The heart of the city consists of canals, with narrow streets radiating out like spokes of a wheel.

Currency The unit of currency in Holland is the guilder, written as NLG (for Netherlands guilder), Fl., or simply F. Each guilder is divided into 100 cents. At press time, the exchange rate for the guilder was 2.05 Fl. to the U.S. dollar.

Telephones The country code for the Netherlands is 31. All towns and cities have area codes that are used only when you are calling from outside the area. When dialing from outside the country, drop the initial zero in the local area code. All public phone booths require phone cards, which may be purchased from post offices, railway stations, and newsagents for Fl. 10 or Fl. 25. Pay phones in bars and restaurants take 25¢ or Fl. 1 coins. Dial 0800/0410 for an English-speaking operator. Direct-dial international calls can be made from any phone booth. To reach an **AT&T** long-distance operator, dial 0800/022–9111; for **MCI**, dial 0800/022–9122; for **Sprint**, dial 0800/022–9119.

Shore Excursions The following is a good choice in Amsterdam. It may not be offered by all cruise lines. Time and price are approximate.

City Tour Cruise. By motor coach and canal boat, you'll see Amsterdam's major sights, including the Royal Palace, New Church, and Rijksmuseum. The route also passes some of Amsterdam's architectural highlights, such as Mint Tower and Weeping Tower. *3 hrs. Cost: $36.*

Coming Ashore Ships dock at the cruise terminal; it's about a 10-minute drive to the main Dam Square. Central Station, the hub of the city, is the most convenient point to begin sightseeing. Across the street, in the same building as the Old Dutch Coffee House, is a tourist information center that offers helpful advice.

Getting Around Amsterdam is a small, congested city of narrow streets, which makes it ideal for exploring on foot. The most enjoyable way to get to know Amsterdam is by taking a boat trip along the canals. There are frequent departures from points opposite Central Station. Taxis are expensive: A 5-km (3-mi) ride costs around Fl. 15. Rental bikes are readily available for around Fl. 10 per day with a

Fl. 50–Fl. 200 deposit. Several rental companies are close to the central train station.

Exploring *Numbers in the margin correspond to points of interest on the*
Amsterdam *Amsterdam map.*

❶ The **Centraal Station** (Central Station), designed by P.J.H. Cuijpers, was built in 1884–89 and is a good example of Dutch architecture at its most flamboyant. It provides an excellent viewpoint for both the Beurs van Berlage and the Scheepvaartshuis, two of the city's best examples of early 20th-century architecture. The street directly in front of the station square is Prins Hendrikkade.

❷ The most important of Amsterdam's museums is the **Rijksmuseum** (State Museum), easily recognized by its towers. It was founded in 1808, but the current, rather lavish, building dates from 1885. The museum's fame rests on its unrivaled collection of 16th- and 17th-century Dutch masters. Of Rembrandt's masterpieces, make a point of seeing *The Nightwatch*, concealed during World War II in caves in Maastricht. The painting was misnamed because of its dull layers of varnish; in reality it depicts the Civil Guard in daylight. Also worth searching out are Frans Hals's family portraits, Jan Steen's drunken scenes, van Ruisdael's romantic but menacing landscapes, and Vermeer's glimpses of everyday life bathed in his usual pale light. *Stadhouderskade 42, tel. 020/6732121. Admission: Fl. 12.50. Open daily 10–5.*

❸ The not-to-be-missed **Rijksmuseum Vincent van Gogh** (Vincent van Gogh State Museum) contains the world's largest collection of the artist's works—200 paintings and nearly 500 drawings—as well as works by some 50 of his contemporaries. The museum will be renovated from fall 1998 through the end of 1999; the most important works will be shown in the South Wing of the Rijksmuseum (*see* above). *Paulus Potterstraat 7, tel. 020/5705200. Admission: Fl. 10. Open daily 10–5.*

❹ The **Stedelijk Museum** (Municipal Museum) has a stimulating collection of modern art and ever-changing displays of contemporary art. Before viewing the works of Cézanne, Chagall, Kandinsky, and Mondrian, check the list of temporary exhibitions in Room 1. Exhibits trace an artists' development rather than just showing a few masterpieces. *Paulus Potterstraat 13, tel. 020/5732911. Admission: Fl. 7.50. Open daily 11–5.*

❺ Arguably the most famous house in Amsterdam is **Anne Frankhuis** (Anne Frank House), which was immortalized by the poignant diary kept by the young Jewish girl from 1942 to 1944, when she and her family hid here from the German occupying forces. A small exhibition on the Holocaust can also be seen in the house. *Prinsengracht 263, tel. 020/5567100. Admission: Fl. 8. Open June–Aug., Mon.–Sat. 9–7, Sun. 10–7; Sept.–May, Mon.–Sat. 9–5, Sun. 10–5.*

The infamous *rosse buurt* (red-light district) is bordered by Amsterdam's two oldest canals (Oudezijds Voorburgwal and Oudezijds Achterburgwal). In the windows at canal level, women in sheer lingerie slouch, stare, or do their nails. Although the area can be shocking, with its sex shops and porn shows, it is generally safe. If you do decide to explore the area, take care; purse-snatchers and pickpockets are a problem.

❻ Dominating Dam Square is **Het Koninklijk Paleis te Amsterdam** (the Royal Palace at Amsterdam), a vast, well-proportioned structure that was completed in 1655. It is built on 13,659 pilings sunk

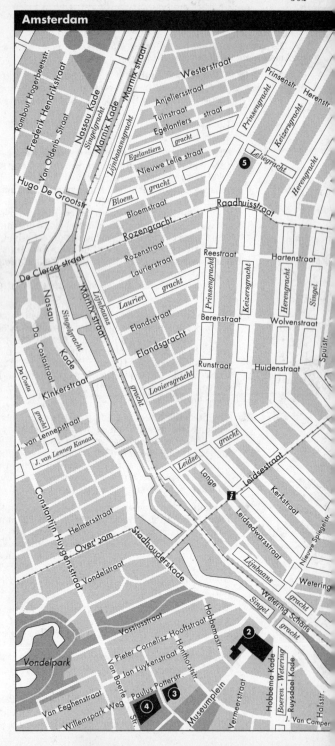

Amsterdam

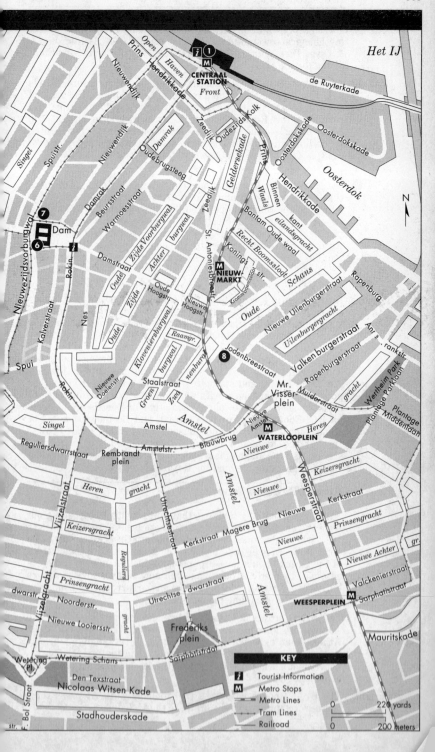

Het IJ

de Ruyterkade

Oosterdokskade

Oosterdok

Open Haven Front

Prins Hendrikkade

Nieuwendijk

CENTRAAL STATION

Zeedijk

Oudezijds Kolk

Geldersekade

Prins

Hendrikkade

Binnen Kant

Waals eilandsgracht

Oosterdokskade

Singel

Spuistr.

Damrak

Beursstraat

Warmoesstraat

Nieuwendijk

Oudebrugsteeg

Damrak

Oudebrugsteeg

Bantam Oude waal

Recht Boomssloot

Rapenburg

Dam

Nieuwezijdsvoorburgwal

Rokin

Damstraat

Zijds Voorburgwal

Achter burgwal

Oude

Zijds

Oude Hoogstr.

St. Antoniesbreestr.

Koningsstr.

Schans

NIEUW-MARKT

Krom Boomssloot

Oude

Nieuwe Uilenburgerstraat

Nieuwe Hoogstr.

Oude

Nieuwe

Uilenburgergracht

Valkenburgerstraat

Rapenburgerstraat

Rapenburg

Anjelierstr.

Nes

Kalverstraat

Spui

Rokin

Nieuwe Doelenstr.

Klovenlersburgwal

Groen burgwal

Raamgr.

nenburg

Jodenbreestraat

Mr. Visser-plein

Muiderstraat

gracht

Wertheim Park

Plantage Parklaan

Plantage Middenlaan

Plantage

Staalstraat

Zwa

Amstel

Amstel

Singel

Reguliersdwarrstraat

Vijzelstraat

Rembrandt plein

Amstelstr.

Heren

gracht

Keizersgracht

Reguliers

Prinsengracht

dwarstr.

Vijzelgracht

Noorderstr.

Nieuwe Looiersstr.

gracht

Weteging Pl.

F. Bol Straat

Wetering Scharrs

Den Texstraat

Nicolaas Witsen Kade

Stadhouderskade

Sarphatistraat

Frederiks plein

Blauwbrug

Amstel

WATERLOOPLEIN

Nieuwe

Nieuwe

Amstel

Nieuwe

Heren

Weesperstraat

Keizersgracht

Kerkstraat

Prinsengracht

Nieuwe Achter

gr.

Valckenierstraat

Sarphatistraat

WEESPERPLEIN

Mauritskade

Amstel

Nieuwe

Nieuwe

Kerkstraat

Magere Brug

Utrechtsestraat

Utrechtse dwarstraat

N

KEY

🛈 Tourist Information

Ⓜ Metro Stops

━ Metro Lines

⋯ Tram Lines

━ Railroad

0   220 yards

0   200 meters

into the marshy soil. The great pedimental sculptures are an allegorical representation of Amsterdam surrounded by Neptune and mythological sea creatures. *Dam, tel. 020/6248698. Admission: Fl. 5. Open Tues.–Thurs. 1–4; daily 12:30–5 in summer. Sometimes closed for state events.*

⑦ The **Nieuwe Kerk** (New Church), a huge Gothic structure, stands next to the royal palace on a corner of Dam Square. The original 16th-century structure was gutted by fire in the 17th century and rebuilt in the Renaissance style. As the national church, the Nieuwe Kerk is the site of all coronations; in democratic Dutch spirit, it also hosts special exhibitions and concerts. *Dam, tel. 020/ 6268168. Admission free, except for exhibitions. Daily 11–5.*

From 1639 to 1658, Rembrandt lived at Jodenbreestraat 4, now **⑧** the **Museum Het Rembrandthuis** (Rembrandt's House). For more than 20 years, the ground floor was used by the artist as living quarters; the sunny upper floor was his studio. It contains a superb collection of his etchings. The new, modern wing next door includes more exhibition space and an auditorium. From St. Antonies Sluis Bridge, just by the house, there is a canal view that has barely changed since Rembrandt's time. *Jodenbreestraat 4–6, tel. 020/6249486. Admission: Fl. 7.50. Open Mon.–Sat. 10–5, Sun. 1–5.*

Shopping Amsterdam is a cornucopia of interesting markets and quirky specialty shops selling antiques, art, and diamonds. The chief shopping districts, which have largely been turned into pedestrian-only areas, are the **Leidsestraat, Kalverstraat, Utrechtsestraat,** and **Nieuwendijk.** The **Rokin,** hectic with traffic, houses a cluster of diamond houses, boutiques, and renowned antiques shops selling 18th- and 19th-century furniture, antique jewelry, Art Deco lamps, and statuettes. The **Spiegelkwartier** is another good place for antiques, with a mix of collectors' haunts and old curiosity shops. Haute couture and other fine goods are at home on **P. C. Hooftstraat, Van Baerlestraat,** and **Beethovenstraat.** For trendy small boutiques and unusual crafts shops, locals browse through the **Jordaan.** For A-to-Z shopping in a huge variety of stores, visit the **Magna Plaza** shopping center, built inside the glorious old post office behind the Royal Palace.

Athens/Piraeus, Greece

Athens is essentially a village that outgrew itself, spreading out from the original settlement at the foot of the Acropolis. Back in 1834, when it became the capital of modern Greece, the city had a population of fewer than 10,000. Now it houses more than a third of the Greek population—around 4.3 million. A modern concrete city has engulfed the old village and now sprawls for 388 square km (244 square mi), covering almost all the surrounding plain from the sea to the encircling mountains.

The city is crowded, dusty, and overwhelmingly hot during the summer. It also has an appalling air-pollution problem. Still, Athens is an experience not to be missed. Its tangible vibrancy makes it one of the most exciting cities in Europe, and the sprawling cement has failed to overwhelm the few astonishing reminders of ancient Athens.

Currency The Greek monetary unit is the drachma (dr.). At press time, there were approximately 307 dr. to the U.S. dollar.

Telephones The country code for Greece is 30. When dialing Greece from outside the country, drop the first zero from the regional area code. Telephone kiosks are easy to find, although some can only be used for local calls. The easiest way to make a local or an international call is with a phone card, available at kiosks, convenience stores, or Hellenic Telecommunications Organization (OTE) offices. Go to an OTE office for convenience and privacy if you plan to make several international calls; there are several branches in Athens. For an **AT&T** long-distance operator, dial 00/800–1311; **MCI,** 00/800–1211; **Sprint,** 00/800–1411.

Shore Excursions The following are good choices in Athens. They may not be offered by all cruise lines. Times and prices are approximate.

Athens and the Acropolis. A must for the first-time visitor. Drive by motor coach to Athens, passing the Olympic Stadium, the former Royal Palace, and the Tomb of the Unknown Warrior on the way to the Acropolis, where a guide will lead an extensive walking tour. *4 hrs. Cost: $40.*

Agora and Plaka. The Acropolis, where Sophocles once taught, and Athens's old shopping district are the centerpieces of this half-day tour into historic Greece. *4 hrs. Cost: $38.*

Coming Ashore Cruise ships dock at Piraeus, 10 km (6 mi) from Athens's center. From Piraeus, you can take the nearby metro right into Omonia Square. The trip takes 20 minutes and costs 100 dr. Alternatively, you can take a taxi, which may well take longer due to traffic and will cost around 1,100 dr. Cruise lines nearly always offer bus transfers for a fee.

The central area of modern Athens is small, stretching from the Acropolis to Mt. Lycabettus, with its little white church on top. The layout is simple: Three parallel streets—Stadiou, Venizelou (a.k.a. Panepistimiou), and Akademias—link two main squares—Syntagma and Omonia. In summer, closing times often depend on the site's available personnel, but throughout the year, arrive at least 30 minutes before the official closing time to ensure you can buy a ticket.

Many of the sights you'll want to see, and most of the hotels, cafés, and restaurants, are within the central area of Athens, and it's easy to walk everywhere. Taxis are plentiful and heavily used. Although you'll eventually find an empty one, it's often faster to call out your destination to one carrying passengers; if the taxi is going in that direction, the driver will pick you up. Most drivers speak basic English and are familiar with the city center. The meter starts at 200 dr., and there is a basic charge of 58 dr. per km, which increases to 113 dr. between midnight and 5 AM. There is an additional 160 dr. charge for trips from the port. Some drivers overcharge foreigners; make sure they turn on the meter and use the high tariff ("Tarifa 2") only after midnight.

Exploring Athens *Numbers in the margin correspond to points of interest on the Athens map.*

❶ A steep, zigzag path leads to the **Akropolis** (Acropolis). After a 30-year building moratorium at the time of the Persian wars, the Athenians built this complex during the 5th century BC to honor the goddess Athena, patron of the city. It is now undergoing conservation as part of an ambitious 20-year rescue plan launched with international support in 1983 by Greek architects.

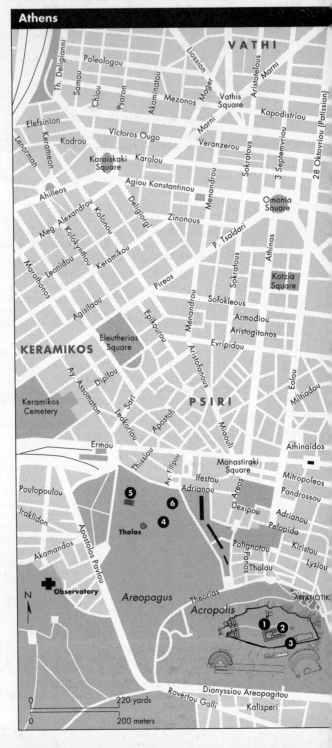

The first ruins you'll see are the Propylaea, the monumental gateway that led worshipers from the temporal world into the spiritual world of the sanctuary; now only the columns of Pentelic marble and a fragment of stone ceiling remain. Above, to the right, stands the graceful Naos Athenas Nikis or Apterou Nikis (Wingless Victory). The temple was mistakenly called the latter because common tradition often confused Athena with the winged goddess Nike. Athenians claimed the sculptor had purposely omitted the wings on the temple's statue to ensure Victory would never fly away from the city. The elegant and architecturally complex Erechtheion temple, most sacred of the shrines of the Acropolis and later turned into a harem by the Turks, has emerged from extensive repair work. Dull, heavy copies of the Caryatids (draped maidens) now support the roof. The Acropolis Museum houses five of the six originals, their faces much damaged by acid rain; the sixth is in the British Museum in London.

❷ The **Parthenonas** (Parthenon) dominates the Acropolis and indeed the Athens skyline. It was completed in 438 BC and is the most architecturally sophisticated temple of that period. Even with hordes of tourists wandering around the ruins, you can still feel a sense of wonder. The architectural decorations were originally painted in vivid red and blue, and the roof was of marble tiles, but time and neglect have given the marble pillars their golden-white shine, and the beauty of the building is all the more stark and striking. The British Museum houses the largest remaining part of the original 532-ft frieze (the Elgin Marbles). The building has 17 fluted columns along each side and eight at the ends, and these lean slightly inward and bulge to cleverly counterbalance the natural optical distortion. The Parthenon has had a checkered history: It was made into a brothel by the Romans, a church by the Christians, and a mosque by the Turks. The Turks also stored gunpowder in the Propylaea, and when this was hit by a Venetian bombardment in 1687, a fire raged for two days and 28 columns of the Parthenon were blown out, leaving the temple in its present condition. *Top of Dionyssiou Areopagitou, tel. 01/321–4172. Admission: 2,000 dr., joint ticket to Acropolis and museum. Open weekdays 8–6:30 (winter 8–4:30), weekends 8:30–2:30.*

❸ The **Museo Akropoleos** (Acropolis Museum), tucked into one corner of the Acropolis, contains some superb sculptures from the Acropolis, including the Caryatids and a large collection of colored *korai* (statues of women dedicated by worshipers to the goddess Athena, patron of the ancient city). *Tel. 01/323–6665. Admission: 2,000 dr., joint ticket to the Acropolis. Open Mon. 11–6:30 (11–4:30 in winter), Tues.–Fri. 8:30–6:30, weekends 8:30–2:30.*

On Areopagus, the rocky outcrop facing the Acropolis, St. Paul delivered his Sermon to the Unknown God. Legend also claims that Orestes was tried here for the murder of his mother. To the ❹ right stands the **Archaia Agora** (Ancient Agora) which means "marketplace," the civic center and focal point of community life in ancient Athens, where Socrates met with his students while merchants haggled over the price of olive oil.

The sprawling confusion of stones, slabs, and foundations at the Agora is dominated by the best-preserved temple in Greece, the ❺ **Hephaisteion** (often wrongly referred to as the Theseion), built during the 5th century BC. Like the other monuments, it is roped off, but you can walk around it to admire its 34 columns.

The impressive **Stoa Attalou** (Stoa of Attalos II), reconstructed by the American School of Classical Studies in Athens with the help of the Rockefeller Foundation, houses the **Museo tis Agoras** (Museum of the Agora Excavations), which offers a fascinating glimpse of everyday life in ancient Athens. *Three entrances: from Monastiraki, on Adrianou St.; from Thission, on Apostolos Pavlou St.; from Acropolis, on descent along Ag. Apostoli. Tel. 01/ 321–0185. Admission: 1,200 dr. Open Tues.–Sun. 8:30–2:45.*

The **Plaka** is almost all that's left of 19th-century Athens, a lovely quarter with winding lanes, neoclassical houses, and sights such as the Museo Ellinikis Laikis Technis (Greek Folk Art Museum; Kidathineon 17); the Aerides (Tower of the Winds), a 1st-century BC water clock near the Roman Agora; and the Mnimeio Lysikratous (Monument of Lysikrates; Herefondos and Lysikratous sts.). Above the Plaka, at the base of the Acropolis, is Anafiotika, the closest thing you'll find to a village in Athens. To escape the city bustle, take some time to wander among its whitewashed, bougainvillea-framed houses and its tiny churches. *Stretching east from the Agora.*

Make time to see the **Ethniko Archaiologiko Museo** (National Archaeological Museum). Despite being somewhat off the tourist route, a good 10-minute walk north of Omonia Square, it is well worth the detour. It houses one of the most exciting collections of antiquities in the world, including sensational archaeological finds made by Heinrich Schliemann at Mycenae; 16th-century BC frescoes from the Akrotiri ruins on Santorini; and the 6½-ft-tall bronze sculpture *Poseidon*, an original work of circa 470 BC, possibly by the sculptor Kalamis, which was found in the sea off Cape Artemision in 1928. *28 Oktovriou (Patission) 44, tel. 01/821–7717. Admission: 2,000 dr. Open Mon. 12:30–7 (10:30–4:45 in winter), Tues.– Fri. 8–7 (8:30–3 in winter), weekends and holidays 8:30–3.*

The **Goulandri Museo Kikladikis ke Archaias Technis** (Goulandris Museum of Cycladic and Ancient Art) collection spans 5,000 years, with nearly 100 exhibits of the Cycladic civilization (3000–2000 BC), including many of the slim marble figurines that so fascinated artists such as Picasso and Modigliani. *Neofitou Douka 4 or Irodotou 1, tel. 01/722–8321. Admission: 400 dr. Open Mon. and Wed.–Fri. 10–4, Sat. 10–3.*

Housed in an 1848 mansion built by an eccentric French aristocrat is the **Vizantino Museo** (Byzantine Museum). Since the museum is undergoing renovation, not all its pieces are on display, but it has a unique collection of icons, re-creations of Greek churches throughout the centuries, and the very beautiful 14th-century Byzantine embroidery of the body of Christ, in gold, silver, yellow, and green. Sculptural fragments provide an excellent introduction to Byzantine architecture. *Vasilissis Sofias 22, tel. 01/721–1027 and 01/723–1570. Admission: 500 dr. Open Tues.–Sun. 8:30–2:50.*

Shopping   Better tourist shops sell copies of traditional Greek jewelry, silver filigree, Skyrian pottery, onyx ashtrays and dishes, woven bags, attractive rugs (including *flokatis*—shaggy wool rugs, often brightly colored), worry beads called *koboloi* in amber or silver, and blue-and-white amulets to ward off the *mati* (evil eye). Prices for gold and silver are much lower in Greece than in many Western countries, and jewelry is of high quality. Some museums sell replicas of small items that are in their collections. The best handicrafts are sold in the **National Welfare Organization shop** (Vas.

Sofias 135, Platia Mavili; Ipatias 6 and Apollonos, Plaka) and the **Center of Hellenic Tradition** (Mitropoleos 59 or Pandrossou 36, Monastiraki). Other shops sell dried fruit, pistachios, and olives. Natural sponges and Greek coffee also make good gifts.

Barcelona, Spain

Barcelona, capital of Catalunya (Catalonia), thrives on its business acumen and industrial muscle. The hardworking citizens of this thriving metropolis are proud to have and use their own language—street names, museum exhibits, newspapers, radio programs, and movies are all in Catalan. An important milestone here was the city's long-awaited opportunity to host the Olympic Games, in summer 1992; the Olympics were of singular importance in Barcelona's modernization. Their legacy includes a vastly improved ring road and several other highways; four new beaches; and an entire new neighborhood in what used to be the run-down industrial district of Poble Nou. Few cities can rival the medieval atmosphere of the Gothic Quarter's narrow alleys, the elegance and distinction of the Moderniste (Art Nouveau) Eixample, or the many fruits of Gaudí's whimsical imagination.

Currency The unit of currency in Spain is the peseta (pta.). There are bills of 1,000, 2,000, 5,000, and 10,000 ptas. Coins are 1, 5, 25, 50, 100, 200, and 500 ptas. At press time, the exchange rate was about 152 ptas. to the U.S. dollar.

Telephones The country code for Spain is 34. When dialing Spain from outside the country, drop the initial 9 from the regional area code. Pay phones generally take the new, smaller 5- and 25-pta. coins; the minimum charge for short local calls is 25 ptas. Newer pay phones take only phone cards, which can be purchased at any tobacco shop in denominations of 1,000 or 2,000 ptas. International calls can be made from any pay phone marked TELÉFONO INTERNACIONAL. Use 50-pta. (or 100-pta. if the phone takes them) coins initially, then coins of any denomination to prolong your call. For lengthy international calls, go to the *telefónica*, a telephone office, where an operator assigns you a private booth and collects payment at the end of the call; this is the least expensive and by far the easiest way of phoning abroad. **AT&T** (tel. 900/99–00–11); **MCI** (tel. 900/99–00–14); **Sprint** (tel. 900/99–00–13).

Shore Excursions The following is a good choice in Barcelona. It may not be offered by all cruise lines. Time and price are approximate.

Barcelona Highlights. This comprehensive excursion winds its way from the pier to the Gothic Quarter. Along the way you'll see the unfinished Sagrada Familia cathedral and visit Montjuïc, one of the city's highest points, before reaching Plaza Catalunya for a walking tour of the Gothic Quarter. *3½ hrs. Cost: $30–$52.*

Coming Ashore Ships visiting Barcelona dock near the Gothic Quarter and the Columbus Monument, but it's too far to walk. Take the cruise-line bus.

Modern Barcelona above the Plaça de Catalunya is mostly built on a grid system, though there's no helpful numbering system as in the United States. The Gothic Quarter from the Plaça de Catalunya to the port is a warren of narrow streets, however, and you'll need a good map to get around. Most sightseeing can be done on foot—you won't have any other choice in the Gothic Quarter—but you'll need to use the metro or buses to link sightseeing areas. The subway is the fastest way of getting around, as well as the easiest to use. For both subways and city buses, you pay a flat fare of 150 ptas. or purchase a *tarjeta multiviatge*, good for 10 rides (780 ptas.). Taxis are black and yellow and when available for hire show a LIBRE sign in the daytime and a green light at night. The meter starts at 315 ptas., and there are small supplements for rides to the port. There are cab stands all over town; cabs may also be flagged down on the street.

Exploring Barcelona *Numbers in the margin correspond to points of interest on the Barcelona map.*

❶ At the Plaça de la Seu, step inside the magnificent Gothic **Catedral de la Seu** (cathedral) built between 1298 and 1450, though the spire and Gothic facade were not added until 1892. Highlights are the beautifully carved choir stalls, Santa Eulàlia's tomb in the crypt, the battle-scarred crucifix from Don Juan's galley in the Lepanto Chapel, and the cloisters. *Plaça de la Seu, tel. 93/315–1554. Admission free. Open daily 7:45–1:30 and 4–7:45.*

❷ Barcelona's most eccentric landmark is Gaudí's **Temple Expiatori de la Sagrada Família** (Expiatory Church of the Holy Family). Far from finished at his death in 1926—Gaudí was run over by a tram and died in a pauper's hospital—this striking creation will cause consternation or wonder, shrieks of protest or cries of rapture. In 1936, during the Spanish Civil War, Barcelona's Anarchists loved their crazy temple enough to spare it from the flames that engulfed so many other churches. An elevator takes visitors to the top of one of the towers for a magnificent view of the city. Gaudí is buried in the crypt. *C. de Sardenya between C. de Mallorca and C. de Provença, tel. 93/455–0247. Admission: 700 ptas. Open Sept.– May, daily 9–7; June–Aug., daily 9–9.*

❸ One of Barcelona's most popular attractions, the **Museu Picasso** (Picasso Museum) is actually two 15th-century palaces that provide a striking setting for the collections donated in 1963 and 1970, first by Picasso's secretary, then by the artist himself. The collection ranges from early childhood sketches to exhibition posters done in Paris shortly before his death. Of particular interest are his Blue Period pictures and his variations on Velázquez's *Las Meninas. Carrer Montcada 1519, tel. 93/319–6310. Admission: 650 ptas; Wed. ½ price, free 1st Sun. of month. Open Tues.–Sat. 10–8, Sun. 10–3.*

❹ **Santa Maria del Mar** (Saint Mary of the Sea) is Barcelona's best example of a Mediterranean Gothic church and is widely considered the city's loveliest. It was built between 1329 and 1383 in fulfillment of a vow made a century earlier by James I to build a church for the Virgin of the Sailors. Its simple beauty is enhanced by a stunning rose window and magnificent soaring columns. *Plaça Santa Maria. Open weekends 9–12:30 and 5–8.*

❺ An impressive square built in the 1840s in the heart of the Gothic Quarter, the **Plaça Sant Jaume** features two imposing buildings facing each other. The 15th-century Ajuntament, or City Hall, has an impressive black and gold mural (1928) by Josep María Sert and the famous Saló de Cent, from which the first European parliament, the Council of One Hundred, ruled the city from 1372 to 1714. You can wander into the courtyard, but to visit the interior, you will have to arrange an entrance with the protocol office. The Palau de la Generalitat, seat of the Catalan Regional Government, is a 15th-century palace open to the public on special days or by appointment. *Meeting of C. de Ferràn and C. Jaume I.*

372

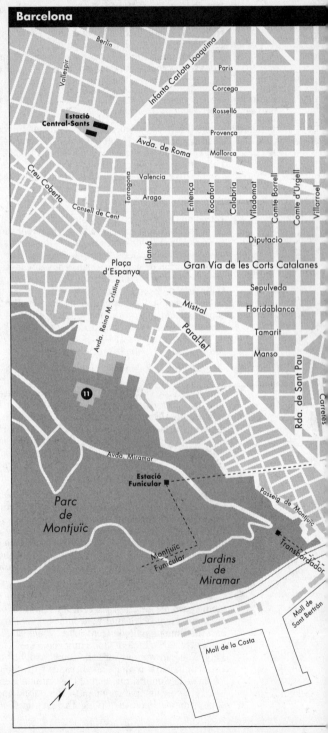

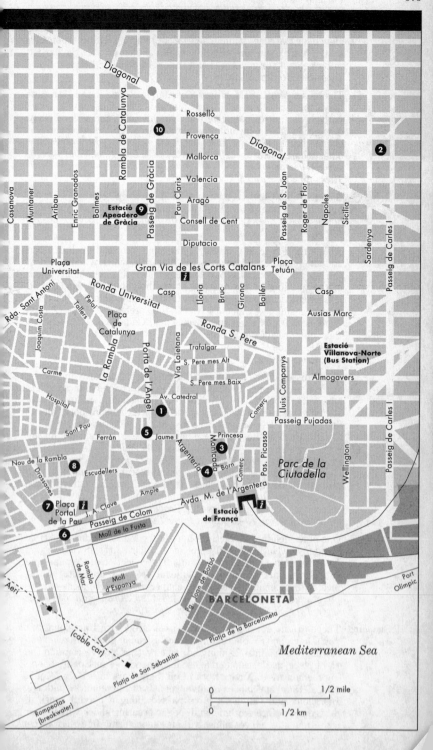

❻ Head to the bottom of Rambla and take an elevator to the top of the **Monument a Colom** (Columbus Monument) for a breathtaking view over the city. Columbus faces out to sea, pointing, ironically, east. (Nearby you can board the cable car that crosses the harbor to Barceloneta or goes up to Montjuïc.) *Admission: 300 ptas. Open Tues.–Sat. 10–2 and 3:30–6:30, Sun. 10–7.*

❼ The **Museu Marítim** (Maritime Museum) is housed in the 13th-century Drassanes Reiales (Royal Shipyards). The museum is packed with ships, figureheads, nautical paraphernalia, and several early navigation charts, including a map by Amerigo Vespucci and the oldest chart in Europe, the 1439 chart of Gabriel de Valseca, the oldest chart in Europe. *Plaça Portal de la Pau 1, tel. 93/318–3245. Admission: 350 ptas., Wed. 175 ptas., free 1st Sun. of month. Open Tues.–Sat. 10–2 and 4–7, Sun. 10–2.*

❽ Gaudí's **Palau Güell** mansion was built between 1885 and 1890 for his patron, Count Eusebi de Güell, and is the only one of Gaudí's houses that is open to the public. *Nou de la Rambla, 3. Admission: 350 ptas. Open Tues.–Sat. 10–1:30 and 4–7:30.*

Above the Plaça de Catalunya you come into modern Barcelona and an elegant area known as the **Eixample,** which was laid out in the late 19th century as part of the city's expansion scheme. Much of the building here was done at the height of the Moderniste movement, a Spanish and mainly Catalan offshoot of art nouveau, whose leading exponents were the architects Gaudí, Luís Domènech i Montaner, and Josep Puig i Cadafalch. The principal thoroughfares of the Eixample are the Rambla de Catalunya and the Passeig de Gràcia, on which stand some of the city's most elegant shops and cafés.

Moderniste houses are one of Barcelona's special drawing cards, ❾ so walk up Passeig de Gràcia until you come to the **Mançana de la Discòrdia** (Block of Discord), between Consell de Cent and Aragó. Its name is a pun on the word *mançana*, which means both "block" and "apple." The houses here are quite fantastic. At No. 43 is Gaudí's Casa Batlló. Farther along the street on the right, on the ❿ corner of Provença, is Gaudí's **Casa Milà** (Passeig de Gràcia 92), more often known as La Pedrera (Stone Quarry). Its remarkable curving stone facade with ornamental balconies actually ripples around the corner of the block. In the attic of La Pedrera is the superb Espai Gaudí, Barcelona's only museum dedicated exclusively to the architect's work. *Provença 261, tel. 93/484–5995. Open Tues.–Sun. 10–8; guided tours Tues.–Fri. 6 PM.*

⓫ One of the leading attractions here is the **Museu Nacional d'Art de Catalunya** (National Museum of Catalan Art) in the Palau Nacional atop a long flight of steps. The collection of Romanesque and Gothic art treasures—medieval frescoes and altarpieces, mostly from small churches and chapels in the Pyrénées—is simply staggering. *Montjuïc, tel. 93/423–7199. Admission: 650 ptas. Open Tues.–Sat. 10–7; Thurs. 10–9; Sun. 10–2:20.*

Shopping There are no special handicrafts associated with Barcelona, but you'll have no trouble finding typical Spanish goods anywhere in town. If you're into fashion and jewelry, then you've come to the right place, as Barcelona makes all the headlines on Spain's booming fashion front. **Xavier Roca i Coll** (Sant Pere mes Baix 24, just off Laietana) specializes in silver models of Barcelona's buildings. Barcelona and Catalonia have passed along a playful sense of design ever since Antoni Gaudí began creating shock waves over a century ago. Stores and boutiques specializing in design items (jewelry, furnishings, knickknacks) include **Bd** (Barcelona Design, at Mallorca 291–293) and **Dos i Una** (Rosselló 275).

Bullfighting Barcelona's bullring is the **Monumental** (Gran Via and Carles I), where bullfights are held on Sundays between March and October; check the newspaper for details. For tickets with no markup, go to the official ticket office (Muntaner 24, near Gran Via, tel. 93/453–3821). There's a **Bullfighting Museum** at the Monumental ring (open Mar.–Oct., daily 10–1 and 5:30–7).

Bergen, Norway

Norway has some of the most remote and dramatic scenery in Europe. Along the west coast, deep fjords knife into steep mountain ranges. In older villages, wooden houses spill down toward docks where Viking ships—and later, whaling vessels—once were moored. Norway is most famous for its fjords, which were formed during an ice age a million years ago. The entrances to most fjords are shallow, about 500 ft, while inland depths reach 4,000 ft.

Bergen is the gateway to the fjord region. The town was founded in 1070 and is now Norway's second-largest city; it will be the EU's European Culture Center for the year 2000. Bergen was a member of the medieval Hanseatic League and offered an ice-free harbor and convenient trading location on the west coast. Despite numerous fires in its past, much of medieval Bergen has remained. Seven surrounding mountains set off the weathered wooden houses, cobbled streets, and Hanseatic-era warehouses of Bryggen (the harbor area).

Currency The unit of currency in Norway is the krone, written as Kr. on price tags but officially written as NOK (bank designation), NKr, or kr. The krone is divided into 100 øre. Bills of NKr 50, 100, 200, 500, and 1,000 are in general use. Coins are in denominations of 50 øre and 1, 5, 10, and 20 kroner. The exchange rate at press time was NKr 7.6 to the U.S. dollar.

Telephones The country code for Norway is 47. Norway's phone system is not as expensive as one might fear. Public phones accept either coins or phone cards. Be sure to read the instructions; some phones require the coins to be deposited before dialing, some after. The minimum deposit is NKr 2 or NKr 3, depending on the phone. You can buy telephone cards at Narvesen kiosks or at the post office. International calls can be made from any pay phone. For calls to North America, dial 00–1, then the area code and number. You will need to dial 00 for an international connection. To reach an **AT&T** long-distance operator, dial 80019011.

Shore Excursions The following are good choices in Bergen. They may not be offered by all cruise lines. Times and prices are approximate.

City Tour. Head past the central harbor area to Bryggen, where rows of gabled merchants' houses line the streets. Stop at Troldhaugen, once the estate of composer Edvard Grieg, for a tour and concert. *3 hrs. Cost: $40.*

Viking History. Viking relics are the highlight of this short tour, which visits the Museum of Cultural History and the Maritime Museum. *3 hrs. Cost: $35.*

Coming Ashore Ships calling at Bergen dock at the harbor area at Bryggen. Seven surrounding mountains set off the weathered wooden houses, cobbled streets, and Hanseatic-era warehouses along the waterfront. Bergen is small and easily toured by foot.

Exploring Bergen
The best way to get a feel for Bergen's medieval trading heyday is to visit the **Hanseatisk Museum** on the Bryggen. One of the oldest and best-preserved of Bergen's wooden buildings, it is furnished in 16th-century style. *Bryggen, tel. 55316710. Admission: NKr 35. Open May–Aug., daily 10–4; Sept.–Apr., weekdays 11–3, Sat. noon–3, Sun. noon–4.*

On the western end of the Vågen is the Rosenkrantztårnet (Rosenkrantz tower), part of the **Bergenhus Festning** (Bergenhus Fortress), the 13th-century fortress guarding the harbor entrance. The tower and fortress were destroyed during World War II, but were meticulously restored during the 1960s and are now rich with furnishings and household items from the 16th century. *Bergenhus, tel. 55314380. Admission: NKr 15. Open mid-May–mid-Sept., daily 10–4; mid-Sept.–mid-May, Sun. noon–3, or upon request.*

From Ævregaten, the back boundary of Bryggen, you can walk through the meandering back streets to the popular **Fløybanen** (Fløyen Funicular). It climbs a steep 1,070 ft to the top of Fløyen, one of the seven mountains guarding the city. *vregt. Open May–Sept., weekdays every half hour 7:30 AM–11 PM, Sat. from 8 AM, Sun. from 9 AM until midnight .*

Shopping
Galleriet, on Torgalmenningen, is one of the best downtown shopping malls. Here you will find the more exclusive small shops along with all the chains, like Hennes & Mauritz and Lindex. **Prydkunst-Hjertholm** (Olav Kyrresgt. 7) is full of excellent, locally made glassware and pottery. **Husfliden** (Vågsalmenning 3) includes a department of traditional Norwegian costumes; also, don't miss the troll cave.

Canary Islands, Spain

Closer to North Africa than to mainland Spain, the ruggedly exotic Canary Islands are becoming a year-round destination for sun seekers and nature lovers alike. The Canaries lie 112 km (70 mi) off the coast of southern Morocco in the Atlantic Ocean and enjoy mild, sunny weather throughout the year, except for the north coast of Tenerife, which has above-average rainfall for the Canaries and below-average temperatures year-round. Each of the seven volcanic islands in the archipelago is distinct. Some have lush tropical vegetation, poinsettias as tall as trees, and banana plantations, while others are arid and resemble an exotic moonscape of lava rock and sand dunes. Mt. Teide (12,198 ft), Spain's highest peak, snowcapped for much of the year, is here. The islands are also home to national parks and dozens of other protected ecological zones in which visitors can hike through mist-shrouded forests of virgin laurel trees, climb mountains, eat food cooked by nature over volcanic craters, or scuba dive off long stretches of unspoiled coastline.

Currency
The unit of currency in the Canary Islands is the peseta (pta.). There are bills of 1,000, 2,000, 5,000, and 10,000 ptas. Coins are 1, 5, 25, 50, 100, 200, and 500 ptas. At press time, the exchange rate was about 152 ptas. to the U.S. dollar.

Telephones
The country code for Spain is 34. Pay phones generally take the new, smaller 5- and 25-pta. coins; the minimum charge for short local calls is 25 ptas. Area codes always begin with a 9 and are different for each province. If you're dialing from outside the country, drop the 9. Calling abroad can be done from any pay phone marked TELÉFONO INTERNACIONAL. Use 50-pta. (or 100-pta. if the

phone takes them) coins initially, then coins of any denomination to prolong your call. Newer pay phones take only phone cards, which can be purchased at any tobacco shop in denominations of 1,000 or 2,000 ptas. Dial 07 for international calls, wait for the tone to change, then dial 1 for the United States or 0101 for Canada. **AT&T** (tel. 900/99–00–11); **MCI** (tel. 900/99–00–14); **Sprint** (tel. 900/99–00–13).

Shore Excursions   The following are good choices in the Canary Islands. They may not be offered by all cruise lines. Times and prices are approximate.

In Tenerife   **Mt. Teide and Countryside.** A motor coach takes you through the Esperanza mountain range to Mt. Teide National Park with picturesque scenery along the way. *4½ hrs. Cost: $40.*

Botanical Gardens. This motor-coach excursion takes you to the Orotava Valley, with its banana plantations and views of Mt. Teide, before reaching the Botanical Gardens. *4¼ hrs. Cost: $33.*

In Lanzarote   **Timanfaya National Park and Winery Tour.** By motor coach, this tour visits the park of Timanfaya (fire mountains), before heading off to El Golfo, Los Hervideros, and Janubio, which feature a variety of different forms of volcanic activity. A visit to the La Geria vineyards includes a tasting. *4 hrs. Cost: $40.*

Coming Ashore   Ships dock in Tenerife at the Santa Cruz pier in the island's provincial capital.

Most visitors rent a car or Jeep—it is by far the best way to explore the countryside. **Hertz** and **Avis** have locations in both Tenerife and Lanzarote, though better rates can be obtained from the Spanish company **Cicar** (tel. 928/802790), located at airports.

Exploring the Canary Islands
Tenerife   Of all the Canary Islands, Tenerife is the most popular and has the greatest variety of scenery. Its beaches are small, though, with volcanic black sand or sand imported from the Sahara Desert. The **Museo Arqueológico Provincial** (Provincial Archeology Museum) in the island's capital, Santa Cruz, contains ceramics and mummies from the stone-age culture of the Guanches, the native people who inhabited the islands before they were conquered and colonized by the Spanish in the 15th century. The tourist office is just around the corner in the same building. *Bravo Murillo 5, tel. 922/24–20–90. Admission 400 ptas. Open Tues.–Sun. 10–8.*

The best thing to visit in Santa Cruz is the colorful weekday-morning market, **Mercado de Nuestra Señora de Africa** (Market of Our Lady of Africa), which sells everything from tropical fruits and flowers to canaries and parrots. *Av. de San Sebastín. Open Mon.–Sat. 5AM–noon.*

Inland, past banana plantations, almond groves, and pine forests, is the entrance to **Parque Nacional del Teide** (Mt. Teide National Park). The visitors' center, open daily 9–4, offers trail maps, guided hikes, educational videos, and bus tours. Before arriving at the foot of the mountain, you pass through a stark landscape called Las Cañadas del Teide, a violent jumble of rocks and minerals created by millions of years of volcanic activity. A cable car will take you within 534 ft of the top of Mt. Teide, where there are good views of the southern part of the island and neighboring Gran Canaria. *Cable car: Admission: 1,800 ptas. Open daily 9–5, last trip up at 4. Visitor center: Open daily 9–4.*

Also worth a visit are the north-coast towns of **Icod de los Vinos,** which boasts a 3,000-year-old, 57-ft-tall dragon tree once worshiped by the ancient Guanches and a plaza surrounded by typical wood-balconied Canarian houses; and, farther west, **Garachico,** the most peaceful and best-preserved village on this touristy isle.

Lanzarote Lanzarote is stark and dry, with landscapes of volcanic rock, good beaches, and tasteful low-rise architecture. The **Parque Nacional Timanfaya,** (Timanfaya National Park) popularly known as the fire mountains, takes up much of the southern part of the island. Here you can have a camel ride, take a guided coach tour of the volcanic zone, and eat lunch at one of the world's most unusual restaurants, El Diablo, where meat is cooked over the crater of a volcano using the earth's natural heat. *4 km (2½ mi) north of Yaiza, tel. 928/84–00–57. Admission: 900 ptas. Open daily 9–5.*

The **Jameos del Agua** (Water Cavern) is a natural wonder, created when molten lava streamed through an underground tunnel and hissed into the sea. Ponds in the caverns are home to a unique species of albino crab. The site also features an auditorium with fantastic acoustics for concerts and a restaurant-bar. *Rte. GC710, 21 km/13 mi north of Arrecife, tel. 928/835010. Admission: 1,200 ptas at night. Open Sun.–Mon., Wed.–Fri. 11–6:45; Tues. and Sat. 11 AM–3 AM.*

Shopping Tenerife is a free port, meaning no value-added tax is charged on
In Tenerife luxury items such as jewelry and electronics. The streets are packed with shops selling these items, but the prices do not represent a significant savings for Americans. The Canary Islands are famous for lacy, hand-embroidered tablecloths and place mats. The largest selection is available in Puerto de la Cruz at **Casa Iriarte** (San Juan 17). Contemporary crafts and traditional musical instruments can be found at the government-sponsored shop **Casa Torrehermosa** (Tomás Zerolo 27) in Orotava.

Beaches **Las Teresitas** beach, 7 km (4 mi) east of Santa Cruz, was con-
In Tenerife structed using white sand imported from the Sahara Desert and is popular with local families. **Playa de las Américas** is the newest, sunniest, and brashest beach area on Tenerife. The yellow sand is ringed with high-rise hotels, restaurants, and nightspots.

In Lanzarote Playa de la Garita is a wide bay with crystal-clear water that's great for snorkeling. The **Playa Blanca** resort area, reached by traveling down hard-packed dirt roads on Punta de Papagayo, features white-sand beaches. Bring your own picnic.

Copenhagen, Denmark

When Denmark ruled Norway and Sweden in the 15th century, Copenhagen was the capital of all three countries. Today it is still a lively northern capital, with about 1 million inhabitants. It's a city meant for walking, the first in Europe to recognize the value of pedestrian streets in fostering community spirit. As you stroll through the cobbled streets and squares, you'll find that Copenhagen combines the excitement and variety of big-city life with a small-town atmosphere. If there's such a thing as a cozy metropolis, you'll find it here.

You're never far from water, be it sea or canal. The city itself is built upon two main islands, Slotsholmen and Christianshavn, connected by drawbridges. The ancient heart of the city is intersected by two heavily peopled walking streets—part of the five such streets known collectively as Strøget—and around them curls a maze of cobbled streets packed with tiny boutiques, cafés, restaurants—all best explored on foot. In summer Copenhagen moves outside, and the best views of city life are from the sidewalk cafés in the sunny squares. The Danes are famous for their friendliness and have a word—*hyggelig*—for the feeling of well-being that comes from their own brand of cozy hospitality.

Currency   The monetary unit in Denmark is the krone (kr., DKr, or DKK), which is divided into 100 øre. At press time, the krone stood at about 6.9 kr. to the U.S. dollar.

Telephones   The country code for Denmark is 45. Pay phones take 1-, 2-, 5-, and 10-kr. coins. You must use area codes even when dialing a local number. Calling cards, which are sold at DSB stations, post offices, and some kiosks, cost DKr25, DKr50, or DKr100, and may be used at certain phones. For international calls dial 00, then the country code, the area code, and the number. To reach an **AT&T** long-distance operator, dial 8001–0010; **MCI**, 8001–0022; **Sprint**, 8001–0877.

Shore Excursions   The following are good choices in Copenhagen. They may not be offered by all cruise lines. Times and prices are approximate.

City Tour. This quick overview of the sights takes you to the Little Mermaid statue, Renaissance castle, City Hall Square, Tivoli Gardens, Christiansborg Palace, the Borsen Stock Exchange, the Canal District, and the courtyard of Amalienborg Palace. *3 hrs. Cost: $41.*

Royal Castle Tour. Castle aficionados can see two on this tour: Christiansborg Palace and Rosenborg Castle, as well as other sites. *3 hrs. Cost: $50.*

Coming Ashore   Ships visiting Copenhagen dock at Langelinie Pier, a short distance from the central part of the city.

Copenhagen is a city for walkers, not drivers. Attractions are relatively close together, and public transportation is excellent. Buses and suburban trains operate on a ticket system and divide Copenhagen and its environs into three zones. Tickets are validated on the time system: On the basic ticket, which costs 10 kr. for an hour, you can travel anywhere in the zone in which you started. The computer-metered taxis are not cheap. The base charge is DKr15, plus DKr8–DKr10 per km. You can either hail a cab (though this can be difficult outside the center) or pick one up at a taxi stand.

Exploring Copenhagen   *Numbers in the margin correspond to points of interest on the Copenhagen map.*

❶   Copenhagen's best-known attraction is **Tivoli.** In the 1840s, the Danish architect Georg Carstensen persuaded King Christian VIII that an amusement park was the perfect opiate for the masses, preaching that "when people amuse themselves, they forget politics." In the season from May to September, about 4 million people come through the gates. Tivoli is more sophisticated than a mere amusement park: It offers a pantomime theater and an open-air stage; elegant restaurants; a museum chronicling its own history; and numerous classical, jazz, and rock concerts. On weekends there are elaborate fireworks displays. In recent years Tivoli has also been opened a month before Christmas with a gift and decorations market and a children's theater, albeit in Danish. Try to see Tivoli at least once by night, when the trees are illuminated along with the Chinese Pagoda and the main fountain. *Vesterbrogade 3, tel. 33/15–10–01. Open May–mid-Sept., daily 11 AM–midnight.*

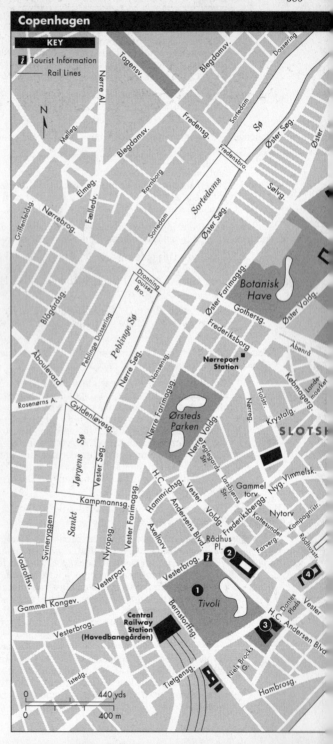

❷ The hub of Copenhagen's commercial district is Rådhus Pladsen which is dominated by the mock-Renaissance building **Københavns Rådhus** (city hall), completed in 1905. A statue of Copenhagen's 12th-century founder, Bishop Absalon, sits atop the main entrance. Inside, you can see the first World Clock, an astrological timepiece invented and built by Jens Olsen and put in motion in 1955. If you're feeling energetic, take a guided tour partway up the 350-ft tower for a panoramic view. *Rådhus Pladsen, tel. 33/66–25–82. Admission: tour 20 kr., tower 10 kr. Open Mon.–Wed. and Fri. 9:30–3, Thurs. 9:30–4, Sat. 9:30–1. Tours in English weekdays at 3, Sat. at 10. Tower tours Mon.–Sat. at noon; additional tours June–Sept. at 10 and 2.*

❸ The elaborately neoclassical **Ny Carlsberg Glyptotek** (New Carlsberg Sculpture Museum) has an impressive collection of works by Gauguin, Degas, and other Impressionists. The French, Egyptian, Greek, and Roman sculpture is noted as one of the most impressive collections of antiquities and sculpture in northern Europe. *Dantes Pl. 7, tel. 33/41–81–41. Admission free Wed. and Sun. Open Tues.–Sun. 10–4.*

❹ The city's **Nationalmuseet** (National Museum) houses extensive collections that chronicle Danish cultural history to modern times and displays Egyptian, Greek, and Roman antiquities. Viking enthusiasts may want to see the Runic stones in the Danish cultural-history section. *Ny Vestergade 10, tel. 33/13–44–11. Admission: 30 kr. Open Tues.–Sun. 10–5.*

❺ Castle Island is dominated by the massive gray **Christiansborg Slot** (Christiansborg Castle). The complex, which contains the Folketinget (Parliament House) and the Royal Reception Chambers, is on the site of the city's first fortress, built by Bishop Absalon in 1167. While the castle was being built at the turn of the century, the National Museum excavated the ruins beneath the site. *Christiansborg ruins, tel. 33/92–64–92. Admission: 15 kr. Open May–Sept., daily 9:30–3:30; Oct.–Apr., closed Mon., Wed., and Sat. Folketinget: tel. 33/37–55–00. Admission free. Tour times vary; call ahead. Reception Chambers: tel. 33/92–64–92. Admission: 28 kr. Opening and tour times vary; call ahead. Closed Jan.*

❻ The 19th-century Danish sculptor Bertel Thorvaldsen is buried at the center of the **Thorvaldsens Museum.** He was greatly influenced by the statues and reliefs of classical antiquity. In addition to his own works, there is a collection of paintings and drawings by other artists illustrating the influence of Italy on Denmark's Golden Age artists. *Porthusgade 2, tel. 33/32–15–32. Admission free. Open Tues.–Sun. 10–5.*

❼ With its steep roofs, tiny windows, and gables, the **Børsen,** the old stock exchange, is one of Copenhagen's treasures. It is believed to be the oldest building of its kind still in use—although it functions only on special occasions. It was built by the 16th-century monarch King Christian IV, a scholar, warrior, and architect of much of the city. The king is said to have had a hand in twisting the tails of the four dragons that form the structure's distinctive green copper spire. *Christiansborg Slotsplads. Not open to the public.*

❽ **Amalienborg** has been the principal royal residence since 1784. During the fall and winter, when the royal family returns to its seat, the Royal Guard and band march through the city at noon to change the palace guard. Among the museum's highlights are the study of King Christian IX (1818–1906) and the drawing room of his wife, Queen Louise. The collection also includes Rococo banquet silver, highlighted by a bombastic Viking-ship centerpiece, and a small costume collection. *Amalienborg Pl.; museum, tel. 33/ 12–21–86. Admission: 35 kr. Open May–late Oct., daily 11–4; late Oct.–Apr., Tues.–Sun. 11–4.*

❾ The **Frihedsmuseet** (Liberty Museum) in Churchillparken gives an evocative picture of the heroic Danish Resistance movement during World War II which managed to save 7,000 Jews from the Nazis by hiding them in homes and hospitals, then smuggling them across to Sweden. *Churchillparken, tel. 33/13–77–14. Admission free. Open Sept. 16–Apr., Tues.–Sat. 11–3, Sun. 11–4; May–Sept. 15, Tues.–Sat. 10–4, Sun. 10–5.*

❿ Near the Langelinie, which on Sunday is thronged with promenading Danes, is **Den Lille Havfrue** (Little Mermaid), the 1913 statue commemorating Hans Christian Andersen's lovelorn creation and the subject of hundreds of travel posters. *East on Langelinie.*

⓫ **Rosenborg Slot,** a Renaissance castle—built by Renaissance man Christian IV—houses the Crown Jewels, as well as a collection of costumes and royal memorabilia. Don't miss Christian IV's pearl-studded saddle. *Øster Voldgade 4A, tel. 33/15–32–86. Admission: 40 kr. Castle open late Oct.–Apr., Tues., Fri., and Sun. 11–2; treasury open daily 11–3. Both open May and Sept.–late Oct., daily 11–3; June–Aug., daily 10–4.*

The **Statens Museum for Kunst** (National Art Gallery) will reopen in the fall of 1999 with a complete refurbishment of the original 100-year-old building and a new, modern building that doubles the exhibition space. Though the collection remains the same—including works of Danish art from the Golden Age (early 19th century) to the present, as well as paintings by Rubens, Dürer, the impressionists, and other European masters—the space also includes a children's museum, an amphitheater, and other resources. *Sølvgade 48–50, tel. 33/91–21–26. Admission: 20 kr.–40 kr. (depending on exhibit). Open Tues.–Sun. 10–4:30, Wed. until 9 PM.*

Shopping Strøget's pedestrian streets are synonymous with shopping. Just off the street is Pistolstræde, a typical old courtyard that has been lovingly restored and is filled with intriguing boutiques. **Magasin** (Kongens Nytorv 13), one of the largest department stores in Scandinavia, offers everything in terms of clothing and gifts, as well as an excellent grocery. In **Illums Bolighus** (Amagertorv 10), designer furnishings, porcelain, quality clothing, and gifts are displayed in near-gallery surroundings. **Royal Copenhagen Porcelain** (Amagertorv 6) carries both old and new china and porcelain patterns and figurines. **Georg Jensen** (Amagertorv 4 and stergade 40) is one of the world's finest silversmiths and gleams with a wide array of silver patterns and jewelry. Don't miss the **Georg Jensen Museum** (Amagertorv 6, tel. 33/14–02–29), which showcases glass and silver beauties, ranging from tiny, twisted-glass shot glasses to an $85,000 silver fish dish.

Corfu, Greece

The northernmost of the seven major Ionian islands, Corfu has a lively history of conquest and counterconquest. All told, beginning with Classical times, Corfu has been ruled by the Corinthians, the tyrants of Syracuse, the kings of Epirus and of Macedonia, the Romans, the Norman and Angevin kings, the Venetians, and the British, and it was finally ceded to Greece in 1864. The climate of the island is rainy, which makes it green. Moderated by westerly winds, scored with fertile valleys, and punctuated by enormous, gnarled olive trees, the island is perhaps the most beautiful in Greece.

Currency The Greek monetary unit is the drachma (dr.). At press time, there were approximately 307 dr. to the U.S. dollar.

Telephones The country code for Greece is 30. When dialing Greece from outside the country, drop the first zero from the regional area code. Telephone kiosks are easy to find, although some can only be used for local calls. The easiest way to make a local or an international call is with a phone card, available at kiosks, convenience stores, or Hellenic Telecommunications Organization (OTE) offices. If you plan to make and pay for several international phone calls, go to an OTE office. For an **AT&T** long-distance operator, dial 00/800–1311; **MCI,** 00/800–1211; **Sprint,** 00/800–1411.

Shore Excursions The following are good choices in Corfu. They may not be offered by all cruise lines. Times and prices are approximate.

Paleokastritsa, Achilleion, and Corfu Town. Visit the pretty resort of Paleokastritsa and the 100-year-old Achilleion Palace, and drive past the major sights of the town. *3–4 hrs. Cost: $45–$50.*

City tour with Achilleion and Kanoni. Visit the famed and funky Achilleion Palace, the village of Kanoni, and enjoy a walking tour of Corfu. *4 hrs. Cost: $43.*

Coming Ashore Most cruise ships dock at Corfu Town.

Radio-dispatched taxis are available, and rates, set by the government, are reasonable. The bus network on the island is extensive, and buses tend to run fairly close to their schedules. Motorbike rentals are available, but caution is advised.

Exploring Corfu The **New Fortress** was built by the Venetians and added to by the French and the British. It was a Greek naval base until 1992, when it was opened to the public. Tourists can now wander through the fascinating maze of tunnels, moats, and fortifications. A classic British citadel stands at its heart, and there are stunning views of Corfu Town, the sea, and the countryside in all directions. The best times to come here are early morning and late afternoon. *Above the Old Port on north side of Corfu Town.*

The huge parade ground on the land side of the canal is the **Esplanade,** central to life in Corfu Town. It is bordered on the west by a street lined with a row of tall houses and arcades, called Liston, which was once the exclusive preserve of Corfiot nobility. Now the arcades are lively with cafés that spill out onto the square. Cricket matches are played on the northern side of the Esplanade.

The narrow streets that run west from the Esplanade lead to the medieval parts of the city, where Venetian buildings stand cheek-by-jowl with the 19th-century ones built by the British. This is a great shopping area—you can buy nearly anything on earth.

The **Archaeological Museum** displays artifacts from the excavation of Paleopolis. Note the Gorgon from the pediment of the 6th-century BC Temple of Artemis. *South of the Esplanade along Leoforos Dimokratias, tel. 0661/30680. Admission: 800 dr. Open daily 9–4:30.*

The village of **Analipis** crowns the site of the ancient town's Acropolis, and a path leads to a spring where Venetians watered their ships. Continue through the gardens and parks to the ruins of the Archaic Temple of Artemis and past the lagoon of Halikiopoulou to the tip of the peninsula, called Kanoni, one of the world's most beautiful spots.

The palace of **Achilleion** is a monument to bad taste redeemed by beautiful gardens stretching to the sea. The palace was built in the late 19th century by an Italian architect for Empress Elizabeth of Austria. The palace is a hodgepodge of a pseudo-Byzantine chapel, a pseudo-Pompeian room, and a pseudo-Renaissance dining hall, culminating in a hilariously vulgar fresco of *Achilles in His Chariot. 19 km/12 mi from Corfu Town, tel. 0661/56210. Admission: 700 dr. Open 8:30–7 in season.*

Shopping The downside of Corfu's popularity with tourists is that merchants have become greedy, at times charging outrageous prices in order to squeeze as much money as possible out of visitors. Ask your ship's cruise or shore-excursion director for the names of reputable shops.

Beaches The resort areas of Ermones and Glyfada, which are south of the popular resort area Paleokastritsa, offer good sunning. On the north coast, Roda and Sidari have good beaches.

Crete, Greece

The mountains, blue-gray and barren, split with deep gorges and honeycombed with caves, define both landscape and lifestyle in Crete. No other Greek island is so large and rugged. To Greeks, Crete is the Great Island, where rebellion was endemic for centuries—against Arab invaders, Venetian colonialists, Ottoman pashas, and German occupiers in World War II. Situated in the south Aegean, Crete was the center of Europe's earliest civilization, the Minoan, which flourished from about 2000 BC to 1200 BC. It was struck a mortal blow in about 1450 BC by some unknown cataclysm, now thought to be political.

Currency The Greek monetary unit is the drachma (dr.). At press time, there were approximately 307 dr. to the U.S. dollar.

Telephones The country code for Greece is 30. When dialing Greece from outside the country, drop the first zero from the regional area code. Telephone kiosks are easy to find, although some can only be used for local calls. The easiest way to make a local or an international call is with a phone card, available at kiosks, convenience stores, or Hellenic Telecommunications Organization (OTE) offices. Go to an OTE office for convenience and privacy if you plan to make several international calls. For an **AT&T** long-distance operator, dial 00/800–1311; **MCI,** 00/800–1211; **Sprint,** 00/800–1411.

Shore Excursions The following are good choices in Crete. They may not be offered by all cruise lines. Times and prices are approximate.

Knossos and the Museum. Minoan life is on display at the Archaeological Museum and Knossos, the largest Minoan palace. *4 hrs. Cost: $50.*

Chania and Akrotiri. This excursion explores the old town of Chania before heading to Akrotiri peninsula to see the tomb of Eleftherios Venizelos and the Ayia Triada Monastery. *Half day. Cost: $45.*

Coming Ashore Most ships dock at Heraklion. A few tie up at Souda Bay, which is about 15 minutes from Chania. Smaller vessels may dock at Ayios Nikolaos.

You can rent cars, Jeeps, and motorbikes in all the island's towns. Bus companies offer regular service between main towns.

Exploring Crete The most important Minoan remains are housed in the **archaeological museum** in Heraklion, Crete's largest (and least attractive) city. The museum's treasures include the frescoes and ceramics from Knossos and Agia Triada depicting Minoan life and the Phaestos disc. In 1996 an archaeologist proposed that its undecipherable scribblings are actually Greek in a code used by cult members, pushing the language's first appearance back another 200 years to 1700 BC. *Xanthoudidou 1, Platia Eleftherias, tel. 081/ 226–092. Admission: 1,000 dr. Open Mon. 12:30–7 (12:30–5 in winter), Tues.–Sun. 8–7 (8–5 in winter).*

The partly reconstructed **Palace of Knossos** will give you a feeling for the Minoan world. Note the simple throne room, which contains the oldest throne in Europe, and the bathrooms with their efficient plumbing. The palace was the setting for the legend of the Minotaur, a monstrous offspring of Queen Pasiphae and a bull, which King Minos confined to the labyrinth under the palace. *Tel. 081/231–940. Admission: 1,250 dr. Open daily 8–7 (8–5 in winter).*

The town of **Ayios Nikolaos** on the Gulf of Mirabellow was built just a century ago by Cretans and is good for an afternoon of strolling and shopping. *24 km/15 mi from Heraklion.*

Beaches In addition to archaeological treasures, Crete can boast of beautiful mountain scenery and a large number of beach resorts along the north coast. One is **Mallia,** which contains the remains of another Minoan palace and has good sandy beaches. Two other beach resorts, **Ayios Nikolaos** and the nearby **Elounda,** are farther east. The south coast offers good beaches that are quieter.

Dublin, Ireland

Europe's most intimate capital has become a boomtown—the soul of the new Ireland is in the throes of what is easily the nation's most dramatic period of transformation since the Georgian era. Dublin is riding the back of the Celtic Tiger (as the roaring Irish economy has been nicknamed) and massive construction cranes are hovering over both shiny new hotels and old Georgian houses. Travelers are coming to Dublin in ever-greater numbers, so don't be surprised if you stop to consult your map in Temple Bar—the city's most happening neighborhood—and are swept away by the ceaseless flow of bustling crowds. Literary Dublin can still be recaptured by those who want to follow the footsteps of Leopold Bloom's progress, as described in James Joyce's *Ulysses.* And Trinity College—alma mater of Oliver Goldsmith, Jonathan Swift, and Samuel Beckett, among others—still provides a haven of tranquillity.

Currency The unit of currency in Ireland is the pound, or punt (pronounced poont), written as IR£ to avoid confusion with the pound sterling. The currency is divided into 100 pence (written *p*). Although the Irish pound is the only legal tender in the republic, U.S. dollars and British currency are often accepted in large hotels and shops licensed as bureaux de change. The rate of exchange at press time was 70 pence to the U.S. dollar.

Telephones The country code for the Republic of Ireland is 353. When dialing from outside the country, drop the initial zero from the regional area code. There are pay phones in all post offices and most hotels and bars, as well as in street booths. Telephone cards are available at all post offices and most newsagents. Booths accepting cards are equally common as coin booths. For calls to the United States and Canada, dial 001 followed by the area code. To reach an **AT&T** long-distance operator, dial 1–800/550–000; **MCI**, 1–800/551–001; **Sprint,** 1–800/552–001.

Shore Excursions The following is a good choice in Dublin. It may not be offered by all cruise lines. Time and price are approximate.

City Tour. Two of Dublin's main attractions, St. Patrick's Cathedral and Trinity College, are the highlight of this excursion, which passes other city sights, such as St. Stephen's Square, Georgian Dublin, the River Liffey, and the Customs House. *3¼ hrs. Cost: $48.*

Coming Ashore Ships dock at the Ocean Pier in the city's industrial port area, about a 20-minute drive to downtown.

Dublin is small as capital cities go—the downtown area is positively compact—and the best way to see the city and soak in the full flavor is on foot. The River Liffey divides the city north and south. Official licensed taxis, metered and designated by roof signs, do not cruise; they are located beside the central bus station, at train stations, at O'Connell Bridge, at St. Stephen's Green, at College Green, and near major hotels. They are not of a uniform type or color. Make sure the meter is on. The initial charge is IR£2; the fare is displayed in the cab. A 1½-km (1-mi) trip in city traffic costs about IR£3.50.

Exploring Dublin *Numbers in the margin correspond to points of interest on the Dublin map.*

❶ O'Connell Bridge is the city's most central landmark. Look closely and you will notice a strange feature: The bridge is wider than it is long. The north side of O'Connell Bridge is dominated by an elaborate memorial to Daniel O'Connell, "the Liberator," erected as a tribute to the great 19th-century orator's achievement in securing Catholic emancipation in 1829.

Henry Street, to the left just beyond the General Post Office, is a pedestrian-only shopping area which leads to the colorful **Moore Street Market,** where street vendors recall their most famous ancestor, Molly Malone, by singing their wares—mainly flowers and fruit—in the traditional Dublin style. *Open Mon.–Sat. 9–6.*

❷ The **General Post Office,** known as the GPO, occupies a special place in Irish history. It was from the portico of its handsome classical facade that Padraig Pearse read the Proclamation of the Republic on Easter Monday 1916. You can still see the scars of bullets on its pillars from the fighting that ensued. The GPO remains the focal point for political rallies and demonstrations, and it is still a working post office, with an attractive two-story central gallery. *O'Connell St., tel. 01/872–8888. Open Mon.–Sat. 8–8, Sun. 10:30–6:30.*

❸ Charlemont House, whose impressive Palladian facade dominates the top of Parnell Square, now houses the **Hugh Lane Municipal Gallery of Modern Art.** Sir Hugh Lane, a nephew of Lady Gregory, who was Yeats's curious, high-minded aristocratic patron, was a keen collector of Impressionist paintings. The gallery also contains some interesting works by Irish artists, including Yeats's brother Jack. *Parnell Sq., tel. 01/874–1903. Admission free. Open Tues.–Thurs. 9:30–6, Fri.–Sat. 9:30–5, Sun. 11–5.*

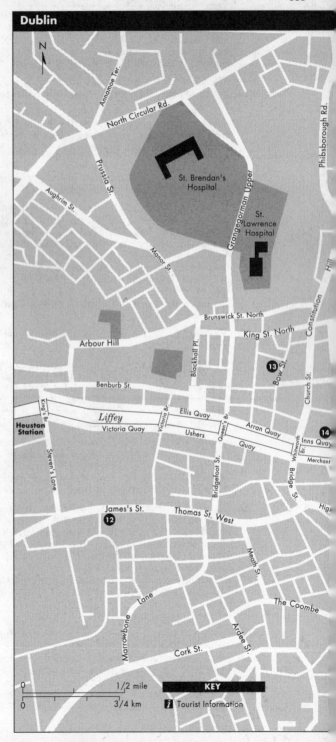

Dublin

N

Annamoe Ter.

North Circular Rd.

Phibsborough Rd.

Prussia St.

St. Brendan's
Hospital

Grangegorman Upper

St.
Lawrence
Hospital

Aughrim St.

Constitution Hill

Manor St.

Brunswick St. North

King St. North

Arbour Hill

Blackhall Pl.

Church St.

Bow St.

13

Benburb St.

14

King's Br.

Liffey

Ellis Quay

Arran Quay

Inns Quay

**Heuston
Station**

Victoria Quay

Ushers

Quay

Merchant

Steven's Lane

Bridgefoot St.

Queen's Br.

Victoria Br.

Whitworth Br.

Bridge St.

Hig

James's St.

Thomas St. West

12

Meath St.

The Coombe

Marrowbone Lane

Ardea St.

Cork St.

0   1/2 mile
0   3/4 km

KEY

i Tourist Information

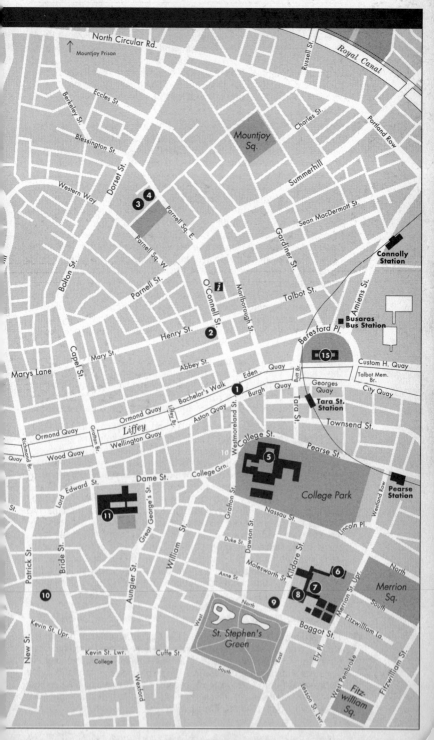

North Circular Rd.

↑ Mountjoy Prison

Royal Canal

Berkeley St.

Eccles St.

Blessington St.

Mountjoy Sq.

Western Way

Dorset St.

Parnell Sq. E.

Charles St.

Russell St.

Portland Row

Summerhill

Sean MacDermott St.

3 **4**

Parnell Sq. W.

Bolton St.

Parnell St.

O'Connell St.

Marlborough St.

Gardiner St.

Talbot St.

i

Connolly Station

Amiens St.

Henry St.

2

Capel St.

Mary St.

Abbey St.

Eden Quay

Beresford Pl.

Busaras Bus Station

Marys Lane

15

Custom H. Quay

Talbot Mem. Br.

City Quay

1

Bachelor's Walk

Burgh Quay

Georges Quay

Tara St. Station

Ormond Quay

Liffey Br.

Aston Quay

Liffey

Westmoreland St.

Townsend St.

Ormond Quay

Grattan Br.

Wellington Quay

Richmond Br.

Quay

Wood Quay

College St.

Pearse St.

10

5

College Grn.

Pearse Station

Lord Edward St.

Dame St.

11

Great George's St.

Grafton St.

Nassau St.

College Park

Lincoln Pl.

Westland Row

St.

Patrick St.

Bride St.

Aungier St.

William St.

Duke St.

Dawson St.

Anne St.

Molesworth St.

Kildare St.

6

North

Merrion Sq.

7

South

10

8

Merrion St. Upr.

New St.

Kevin St. Upr.

Kevin St. Lwr.

Cuffe St.

Wexford

St. Stephen's Green

North

West

East

South

9

Baggot St.

Ely Pl.

Fitzwilliam La.

Fitzwilliam St.

Lesson St. Lwr.

West Pembroke

Fitz-william Sq.

College

❹ The Parnell Square area is rich in literary associations. They are explained and illustrated in the **Dublin Writers Museum,** which opened in 1991 in two carefully restored 18th-century buildings. Paintings, letters, manuscripts, and photographs relating to Joyce, O'Casey, Shaw, Wilde, Yeats, Beckett, and others are on permanent display. There are also temporary exhibitions, lectures, and readings, as well as a bookshop. *18–19 Parnell Sq. N, tel. 01/872–2077. Admission: IR£2.75. Open Mon.–Sat. 10–5, Sun. 11–5.*

❺ A must for every visitor is a stop at **Trinity College.** The college, familiarly known as TCD, was founded by Elizabeth I in 1592 and offered a free education to Catholics—provided that they accepted the Protestant faith. As a legacy of this condition, right up until 1966, Catholics who wished to study at Trinity had to obtain a dispensation from their bishop or face excommunication. Today more than 70% of Trinity's students are Catholics, a clear indication of how far away those days seem to today's generation. The college's facade, built between 1755 and 1759, consists of a magnificent portico with Corinthian columns. The design is repeated on the interior, so the views from outside the gates and from the quadrangle inside are the same. On the sweeping lawn in front of the facade are statues of two of the university's illustrious alumni—statesman Edmund Burke and poet Oliver Goldsmith. Other famous students include the philosopher George Berkeley (who gave his name to the northern California city), Jonathan Swift, Thomas Moore, Oscar Wilde, John Millington Synge, Henry Grattan, Wolfe Tone, Robert Emmet, Bram Stoker, Edward Carson, Douglas Hyde, and Samuel Beckett.

The 18th-century building on the left, just inside the entrance, is the chapel. There's an identical building opposite, which is the Examination Hall. The oldest buildings are the library in the far right-hand corner and a row of redbrick buildings known as the Rubrics, which contain student apartments; both date from 1712.

Ireland's largest collection of books and manuscripts is housed in the **Trinity College Library.** There are 3 million volumes gathering dust here; about 1 km (½ mi) of new shelving has to be added every year to keep pace with acquisitions. The library is entered through the library shop. Its principal treasure is the Book of Kells, a beautifully illuminated manuscript of the Gospels, dating from the 8th century. Only a few pages from the 682-page, 9th-century gospel are displayed at a time, but there is an informative exhibit that reproduces many of them. At peak hours you may have to wait in line to enter the library. Apart from the many treasures it contains, the aptly named Long Room is impressive in itself, stretching for 213 ft and housing 200,000 of the library's volumes, mostly manuscripts and old books. Originally it had a flat plaster ceiling, but the perennial need for more shelving resulted in a decision to raise the level of the roof and add the barrel-vaulted ceiling and the gallery bookcases. *Tel. 01/677–2941. Admission: IR£3.50. Open Mon.–Sat. 9:30–4:45, Sun. noon–4:30.*

❻ The **National Gallery of Ireland** is the first in a series of important buildings on the west side of Merrion Square. It contains the country's finest collection of Old Masters—great treasures include Vermeer's incomparable *Woman Writing a Letter,* Gainsborough's *Cottage Girl,* and Caravaggio's recently rediscovered *The Arrest of Christ. Merrion Sq. (West), tel. 01/661–5133. Admission free. Open Mon.–Sat. 10–5:30, Thurs. until 8:30, Sun. 2–5.*

❼ **Leinster House,** seat of the Irish Parliament, is an imposing 18th-century building with two facades: Its Merrion Square facade is designed in the style of a country house, while the other facade, in Kildare Street, is in the style of a town house. Visitors may be shown the house when Dáil Eireann (pronounced dawl Erin), the Irish Parliament, is not in session. *Kildare St., tel. 01/678–9911. Tours: Mon., Fri. by prior arrangement. Dáil visitors' gallery: Access with an introduction from a member of Parliament.*

The **National Library's** collections include first editions of every major Irish writer. Temporary exhibits are held in the entrance hall, off the colonnaded rotunda. The recently renovated main reading room, opened in 1890, has a dramatic domed ceiling. *Kildare St., tel. 01/661–8811. Admission free. Open Mon. 10–9, Tues.–Wed. 2–9, Thurs.–Fri. 10–5, Sat. 10–1.*

❽ Situated on the other side of Leinster House from the National Library, the **National Museum** is most famous for its spectacular collection of Irish artifacts from 6000 BC to the present, including the Tara Brooch, the Ardagh Chalice, the Cross of Cong, and a fabled hoard of Celtic gold jewelry. *Kildare St., tel. 01/660–1117. Admission free. Open Tues.–Sat. 10–5, Sun. 2–5.*

❾ The **Genealogical Office**—the starting point for ancestor tracing—also incorporates the Heraldic Museum, which features displays of flags, coins, stamps, silver, and family crests that highlight the uses and development of heraldry in Ireland. *2 Kildare St., tel. 01/661–8811. Genealogical Office: Open weekdays 10–12:30, 2–4:30. Heraldic Museum: Admission free. Open Mon.–Wed., 10–8:30, Thurs.–Fri. 10–4:30, Sat. 10–12:30. Guided tours by appointment.*

❿ Legend has it that St. Patrick baptized many converts at a well on the site of **St. Patrick's Cathedral** in the 5th century. The building dates from 1190 and is mainly early English Gothic in style. At 305 ft, it is the longest church in the country. Its history has not always been happy. In the 17th century, Oliver Cromwell, dour ruler of England and no friend of the Irish, had his troops stable their horses in the cathedral. It wasn't until the 19th century that restoration work to repair the damage was begun. St. Patrick's is the national cathedral of the Protestant Church of Ireland and has had many illustrious deans. The most famous was Jonathan Swift, author of *Gulliver's Travels*, who held office from 1713 to 1745. Swift's tomb is in the south aisle, and Dean Swift's corner at the top of the north transept contains his pulpit, his writing table and chair, his portrait, and his death mask. Memorials to many other celebrated figures from Ireland's past line the walls of St. Patrick's. *Patrick St., tel. 01/475–4817. Admission: IR£2. Open Weekdays 9–5:15, Sat–Sun. 9–5.*

⓫ Guided tours of the lavishly furnished state apartments in **Dublin Castle** are offered every half hour and provide one of the most enjoyable sightseeing experiences in town. Only fragments of the original 13th-century building survive; the elegant castle you see today is essentially an 18th-century building. The state apartments were formerly the residence of the English viceroys and are now used by the president of Ireland to entertain visiting heads of state. The state apartments are closed when in official use, so phone first to check. *Off Dame St., tel. 01/677–7129. Admission: IR£2.50. Open weekdays 10–5, weekends 2–5.*

⓬ The **Guinness Brewery,** founded by Arthur Guinness in 1759 and covering 60 acres, dominates the area to the west of Christ Church. The brewery itself is closed to the public, but the Hop

Store, part-museum and part-gift-shop, puts on an 18-minute audiovisual show. After the show, visitors get two complimentary glasses (or one pint) of the famous black stout. *Guinness Hop Store, Crane St., tel. 01/453–3645. Admission: IR£4. Open Apr.— Sept., Mon.–Sat. 9:30–5, Sun. 10:30–4:30; Oct.–Mar., Mon.–Sat. 9:30–4, Sun. noon–4.*

⑬ Old Jameson Distillery is just behind St. Michan's. A 90-year-old warehouse has been converted into a museum to introduce visitors to the pleasures of Irish whiskey. You can watch an audiovisual presentation about the industry, tour the old distillery, and learn about distilling of whiskey from grain to bottle. There's also a free tasting. *Bow St., tel. 01/872–5566. Admission: IR£3.50. Open daily 10–5; tours every half-hour.*

Off the River Liffey are two of Dublin's most famous landmarks, both of them the work of 18th-century architect James Gandon **⑭** and both among the city's finest buildings. The first is the **Four Courts** surmounted by a massive copper-covered dome, giving it a distinctive profile. It is the seat of the High Court of Justice of Ireland. The building was completed between 1786 and 1802, then gutted during the "Troubles" of the 1920s; it has since been painstakingly restored. You will recognize the same architect's hand in **⑮** the **Custom House,** (closed to the public), farther down the Liffey. Its graceful dome rises above a central portico, itself linked by arcades to the pavilions at either end. *Four Courts: Inns Quay, tel. 01/872–5555. Open daily 10:30–4.*

Shopping   Although the rest of the country is well supplied with crafts shops, Dublin is the place to seek out more specialized items—antiques, traditional sportswear, haute couture, designer ceramics, books and prints, silverware and jewelry, and designer hand-knit items.

The city's most sophisticated shopping area is around **Grafton Street. St. Stephen's Green Center** contains 70 stores, large and small, in a vast Moorish-style glass-roof building on the Grafton Street corner. **Molesworth** and **Dawson streets** are the places to browse for antiques; **Nassau** and **Dawson streets,** for books; the smaller cross streets for jewelry, art galleries, and old prints. The pedestrian **Temple Bar** area, with its young, offbeat ambience, has a number of small art galleries, specialty shops (including music and books), and inexpensive and adventurous clothes shops. The area is further enlivened by buskers (street musicians) and street artists.

Tweeds and   Ready-made tweeds for men can be found at **Kevin and Howlin** (on
Woolens   Nassau St.), and at **Cleo Ltd.** (on Kildare St.). The **Blarney Woollen Mills** (on Nassau St.) has a good selection of tweed, linen, and woolen sweaters in all price ranges. The **Woolen Mills** (at Ha'penny Bridge) has a good selection of hand-knits and other woolen sweaters at competitive prices.

Edinburgh/Leith, Scotland

Scotland and England *are* different—and let no Englishman tell you otherwise. Although the two nations have been united in a single state since 1707, Scotland retains its own marked political and social character, with, for instance, legal and educational systems quite distinct from those of England (a division that will become even greater, now that Edinburgh is once again to be the seat of a Scottish Parliament). And by virtue of its commanding geographic position, on top of a long-dead volcano, and the survival of a large number of outstanding buildings carrying echoes of the nation's history, Edinburgh ranks among the world's greatest capital cities.

The key to understanding Edinburgh is to make the distinction between the Old and New Towns. Until the 18th century, the city was confined to the rocky crag on which its castle stands, straggling between the fortress at one end and the royal residence, the Palace of Holyroodhouse, at the other. In the 18th century, during a civilizing time of expansion known as the "Scottish Enlightenment," the city fathers fostered the construction of another Edinburgh, one a little to the north. This is the New Town, whose elegant squares, classical facades, wide streets, and harmonious proportions remain largely intact and are still lived in today.

Currency The British unit of currency is the pound sterling, divided into 100 pence (p). Bills are issued in denominations of 5, 10, 20, and 50 pounds (£). Coins are £1, £2, 50p, 20p, 10p, 5p, 2p, and 1p. Scottish banks issue Scottish currency, of which all coins and notes—with the exception of the £1 notes—are accepted in England. At press time, exchange rates were approximately US$1.65 to the pound.

Telephones The United Kingdom's country code is 44. When dialing from outside the country, drop the initial zero from the regional area code. Public telephones are plentiful; other than on the street, the best place to find a bank of pay phones is in a hotel or large post office. The workings of coin-operated telephones vary, but there are usually instructions in each unit. Most take 10p, 20p, 50p, and £1 coins. A Phonecard is also available; it can be bought in a number of retail outlets. Cardphones, which are clearly marked with a special green insignia, will not accept coins. The cheapest way to make an overseas call is to dial it yourself, but be sure to have plenty of coins or phone cards close at hand. After you have inserted the coins or card, dial 010 (the international code), then the country code—for the United States it is 1—followed by the area code and local number. To reach an **AT&T** long-distance operator, dial 0500890011; **MCI**, 0800890222; **Sprint**, 0800890877 (from a British Telecom phone) or 0500890877 (from a Mercury Communications phone). To make a collect or other operator-assisted call, dial 155.

Shore Excursions The following is a good choice in Edinburgh. It may not be offered by all cruise lines. Time and price are approximate.

City Tour. Survey Old Town and New Town, visiting Edinburgh Castle. Pass by sights such as Princes Street, St. Giles Cathedral, the Royal Mile, and Holyroodhouse Palace. *4 hrs. Cost: $48.*

Coming Ashore Ships dock at Leith, the port for Edinburgh. It is about a 15-minute drive to Edinburgh from the pier.

Walking is the best way to tour the old part of the city. It can be tiring, so wear comfortable shoes. Taxis are easily found; there are stands throughout the downtown area, most at the west end of Princes Street, South St. David Street and North St. Andrew Street (both just off St. Andrew Sq.), Waverley Market, Waterloo Place, and Lauriston Place.

Exploring Edinburgh *Numbers in the margin correspond to points of interest on the Edinburgh map.*

❶ **Edinburgh Castle,** the brooding symbol of Scotland's capital and the nation's martial past, dominates the city center. The castle's attractions include the city's oldest building—the 11th-century St.

Margaret's Chapel; the Crown Room, where the Regalia of Scotland are displayed; Old Parliament Hall; and Queen Mary's Apartments, where Mary, Queen of Scots, gave birth to the future King James VI of Scotland (who later became James I of England). In addition, military features of interest include the Scottish National War Memorial and the Scottish United Services Museum. The Castle Esplanade, the wide parade ground at the entrance to the castle, hosts the annual Edinburgh Military Tattoo—a grand military display staged during an annual summer festival. *Castlehill, tel. 0131/668–8800. Admission: £6. Open Apr.–Sept., daily 9:30–5:15; Oct.–Mar., daily 9:30–4:15.*

❷ **The Royal Mile,** the backbone of the Old Town, starts immediately below the Castle Esplanade. It consists of a number of streets, running into each other—Castlehill, Lawnmarket, High Street, and Canongate—leading downhill to the Palace of Holyroodhouse, home to the Royal Family when they visit Edinburgh. Tackle this walk in leisurely style; the many original Old Town "closes," narrow alleyways enclosed by high tenement buildings, are rewarding to explore and give a real sense of the former life of the city.

❸ **The Writers' Museum,** housed in Lady Stair's House, is a town dwelling of 1622 that recalls Scotland's literary heritage with exhibits on Sir Walter Scott, Robert Louis Stevenson, and Robert Burns. *Lady Stair's Close, Lawnmarket, tel. 0131/529–4901. Admission free. Open Mon.–Sat. 10–5, Sun. during festival 2–5.*

A heart shape set in the cobbles of High Street marks the site of
❹ the **Tolbooth,** the center of city life—and original inspiration for Sir Walter Scott's novel *The Heart of Midlothian*—until it was demolished in 1817.

❺ Near the former site of the Tolbooth stands the **High Kirk of St. Giles,** Edinburgh's cathedral; parts of the church date from the 12th century, the choir from the 15th. *High St. Suggested donation: £1. Open Mon.–Sat. 9–5 (7 in summer), Sun. 1–5 and for services.*

❻ The **Palace of Holyroodhouse,** still the Royal Family's official residence in Scotland, came into existence originally as a guest house for the Abbey of Holyrood, founded in 1128 by Scottish king David I. It was then extensively remodeled by Charles II in 1671. The state apartments, with their collections of tapestries and paintings, can be visited. *East end of Cannongate, tel. 0131/556–7371. Admission: £5.30. Open Apr.–Oct., daily 9:30–5:15; Nov.–Mar., daily 9:30–3:45; closed during royal and state visits.*

❼ The **National Gallery of Scotland,** on the Mound, the street that joins the Old and New Towns, contains works by the old masters and the French Impressionists and has a good selection of Scottish paintings. This is one of Britain's best national galleries and is small enough to be taken in easily on one visit. *The Mound, tel. 0131/556–8921. Admission free; charge for special exhibitions. Open Mon.–Sat. 10–5, Sun. 2–5. Print Room weekdays 10–noon and 2–4 by arrangement.*

❽ To the east along Princes Street is the unmistakable soaring Gothic spire of the 200-ft **Scott Monument,** built in the 1840s to commemorate Sir Walter Scott (1771–1832), the celebrated novelist of Scots history. The views from the top are well worth the 287-step climb. The monument is undergoing renovation, so it's best to call to make sure it's open. *Princes St., tel. 0131/529–4068. Open Apr.–Sept., Mon.–Sat. 9–6; Oct.–Mar., Mon.–Sat. 9–3.*

395

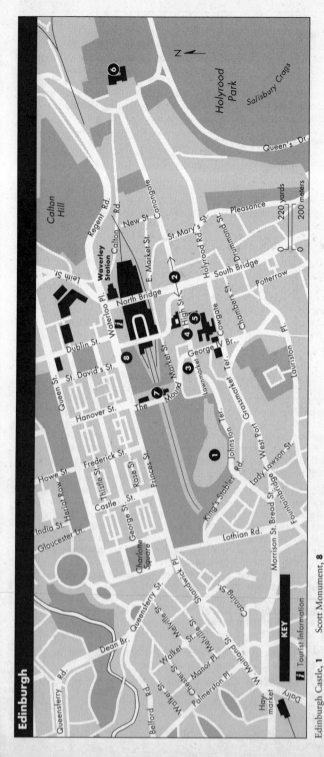

Edinburgh

Queensferry Rd.
Belford Rd.
Dean Br.
Queensferry St.
Walker St.
Chester St.
W. Maitland St.
Palmerston Pl.
Manor Pl.
Melville St.
Melville St.
Shandwick Pl.
Canning St.
Strandwick Pl.
Haymarket
Dalry
Morrison St.
Lothian Rd.
Bread St.
Fountainbridge St.
Lady Lawson St.
West Port
Grassmarket
Lauriston Pl.
Lauriston
Potterrow
Chambers St.
South Bridge
Pleasance
Queen's Dr.
Salisbury Crags
Holyrood Park
Holyrood Rd.
South Drummond St.
George IV Br.
Cowgate
Lawnmarket
High St.
The Mound
Market St.
North Bridge
E. Market St.
New St.
Canongate
Calton Rd.
Regent Rd.
Leith St.
Waterloo Pl.
Waverley Station
Calton Hill
St. Mary's St.
St. David's St.
Queen St.
Hanover St.
Frederick St.
Thistle St.
Rose St.
Princes St.
George St.
Castle St.
Charlotte Square
Howe St.
Heriot Row
India St.
Gloucester Ln.
King's Stables Rd.
Johnston Ter.
Dublin St.

N

0   220 yards
0   200 meters

KEY
🄸 Tourist Information

Edinburgh Castle, **1**
High Kirk of
St. Giles, **5**
National Gallery of
Scotland, **7**
Palace of
Holyroodhouse, **6**
The Royal Mile, **2**
Scott Monument, **8**
Tolbooth, **4**
The Writers'
Museum, **3**

Shopping **Princes Street** may have uninspiring architecture and a smattering of fast-food joints, but it's still one of the best places to shop for tweeds, tartans, and knits, especially if your time is limited. **Jenners** (4 Princes St.), opposite the Scott Monument, is Edinburgh's last independent department store; it has a wonderful Food Hall where you can find classic Scottish specialties like shortbreads and Dundee cakes. **George Street** is a good place to hit for smaller, upscale boutiques; the cross-streets Castle, Frederick, and Hanover are also well worth exploring.

Florence/Livorno, Italy

One of Europe's preeminent treasures, Florence is a venerable mecca for visitors from all over the world. A port call in Florence is a visit to the birthplace of the Italian Renaissance, and the city bears witness to the proud spirit and unparalleled genius of its artists and artisans. Founded by Julius Caesar, the city has the familiar grid pattern common to all Roman colonies. Except for the major monuments, which are appropriately imposing, the buildings are low and unpretentious. It is a small, compact city of ocher and gray stone and pale plaster; its narrow streets open unexpectedly into spacious squares populated by strollers and pigeons. At its best, it has a gracious and elegant air, though it can at times be a nightmare of mass tourism. Plan, if you can, to visit Florence in early spring or late fall to avoid the crowds. There is so much to see that it is best to savor a small part rather than attempt to absorb it all in a muddled vision.

Currency The unit of currency in Italy is the lira (plural, lire). There are bills of 1,000, 2,000, 5,000, 10,000, 50,000, 100,000, and 500,000 lire (this largest bill being almost impossible to change, except in banks); coins are worth 50, 100, 200, and 500 lire. In 1999 the euro will begin to be used as a banking currency, but the lire will still be the currency in use on a day-to-day basis. At press time, the exchange rate was about 1,770 to the U.S. dollar. When your purchases run into hundreds of thousands of lire, beware of being shortchanged, a dodge that is practiced at ticket windows and cashiers' desks, as well as in shops and even banks. Always count your change before you leave the counter.

Telephones The country code for Italy is 39. Most local calls cost 200 lire for two minutes. Pay phones take either 100-, 200-, or 500-lire coins or *schede telefoniche* (phone cards), purchased in bars, tobacconists, post offices, and TELECOM offices in either 5,000-, 10,000-, or 15,000-lire denominations. To place international calls, many travelers go to the Telefoni telephone exchange (usually marked TELECOM), where the operator assigns you a booth, can help place your call, and will collect payment when you have finished. To dial an international call, insert a phone card, dial 00, then the country code, area code, and phone number. For **AT&T USADirect,** dial access number tel. 172–1011; for **MCI Call USA,** access number tel. 172–1022; for **Sprint Express,** access number tel. 172–1877. You will be connected directly with an operator in the United States.

Shore Excursions The following is a good choice in Florence. It may not be offered by all cruise lines. Time and price are approximate.

City and Coastal Tour. See many of Florence's major civic and religous sights on this whirlwind day of sightseeing—plus a stop along the way to see the Leaning Tower of Pisa. *10 hrs. Cost: $145, including lunch.*

Coming Ashore Ships dock at Livorno, which is a little more than an hour from Florence. Most cruise lines sell bus transfers to Florence for independent sightseeing for about $70.

Once in the city, you can see most of Florence's major sights on foot, as they are packed into a relatively small central area. Wear comfortable shoes and wander to your heart's content: It is easy to find your way around in Florence. The system of street addresses is unusual, with commercial addresses (those with an *r* in them, meaning *rosso*, or red) and residential addresses numbered separately (32/r might be next to or a block away from plain 32).

Taxis wait at stands. Use only authorized cabs, which are white with a yellow stripe or rectangle on the door. The meter starts at 4,000 lire. To call a taxi, phone 055/4798 or 055/4390. The meter starts at 4,500 lire, with extra charges for nights, holidays, or radio dispatch.

Exploring Florence The best place to begin a tour of Florence is **Piazza del Duomo,** where the cathedral, bell tower, and baptistery stand in the rather cramped square.

The lofty **Duomo** (or Cattedrale of Santa Maria del Fiore) cathedral is one of the longest in the world. Begun by master sculptor and architect Arnolfo di Cambio in 1296, its construction took 140 years to complete. Inside, the church is cool and austere, a fine example of the architecture of the period. Among the sparse decorations, take a good look at the frescoes on the left wall and on the dome. However, these frescoes take second place to the dome itself, one of the world's greatest architectural and technical achievements. Faced with the cathedral's tremendous scale, the young architect Filippo Brunelleschi devised entirely new building methods; the result was one of the most important engineering breakthroughs of all time. It was the inspiration of such later domes as the one for St. Peter's in Rome and even the Capitol in Washington. Today, the dome stands for Florence in the same way that the Eiffel Tower symbolizes Paris. You can climb to the cupola gallery, 463 fatiguing steps up between the two skins of the double dome, for a fine view of Florence and the surrounding hills. *Piazza del Duomo, tel. 055/2302885. Admission to dome: 10,000 lire. Open weekdays 10–5 (1st Sat. of month 10–3:30), Sun. 1–5. Cupola (entrance in left aisle of cathedral) open weekdays 8:30–6:20, Sat. 9:30–5 (1st Sat. of month 9:30–3:20).*

Next to the Duomo is Giotto's 14th-century **Campanile** (bell tower), richly decorated with colored marble and sculpture reproductions (the originals are in the Museo dell'Opera del Duomo). The 414-step climb to the top is less strenuous than that to the cupola. *Piazza del Duomo. Admission: 8,000 lire. Open Apr.–Oct., daily 9–7:30; Nov.–Mar., daily. 9–5.*

In front of the cathedral is the **Battistero** (Baptistery), one of the city's oldest and most beloved edifices, where, since the 11th century, Florentines have baptized their children. The most famous of the baptistery's three portals is Ghiberti's east doors (facing the Duomo), dubbed the "gates of Paradise" by Michelangelo; gleaming copies now replace the originals, which have been removed to the Museo dell'Opera del Duomo (Cathedral Museum). *Admission: 5,000 lire. Open Apr.–Sept. 8–7:40; Oct.–Mar. 9–4:40.*

Along Via Calzaiuoli you'll come upon **Piazza della Signoria,** the heart of Florence and the city's largest square. In the center of the square a slab marks the spot of the 1497 "burning of the vanities," when reformist monk Savonarola urged the Florentines to burn their pictures, books, musical instruments, and other worldly objects. On the same spot, a year later, he was hanged and then burned at the stake as a heretic. Copies of several famous statues are found in the square or the adjoining loggia, including a copy of Michelangelo's *David* and a copy of Cellini's *Perseus Holding the Head of Medusa.*

The **Galleria degli Uffizi** (Uffizi Gallery) houses Italy's most important collection of paintings. The palace was built to house the administrative offices of the Medicis, onetime rulers of the city ("uffizi" is Italian for "offices"). Later their fabulous art collection was arranged in the Uffizi Gallery on the top floor, which was opened to the public in the 17th century—making this the world's first public gallery of modern times. The emphasis is on Italian art of the Gothic and Renaissance periods. Make sure you see the works by Giotto, and look for the Botticellis in Rooms X–XIV, Michelangelo's *Holy Family* in Room XXV, and the works by Raphael next door. In addition to its art treasures, the gallery offers a magnificent close-up view of Palazzo Vecchio's tower from the little coffee bar at the end of the corridor. Authorities have done wonders in repairing the damage caused by a bomb in 1993. *Loggiato Uffizi 6, tel. 055/23885. Admission: 12,000 lire. Open Tues.–Sat. 8:30–6:50, Sun. 8:30–1:50.*

The **Galleria dell'Accademia** (Accademia Gallery) houses Michelangelo's famous *David*. Skip the works in the exhibition halls leading to the main attraction; they are of minor importance, and you'll gain a length on the tour groups. Michelangelo's statue is a tour de force of artistic conception and technical ability, for he was using a piece of stone that had already been worked on by a lesser sculptor. Take time to see the forceful *Slaves*, also by Michelangelo; the rough-hewn, unfinished surfaces contrast dramatically with the highly polished, meticulously carved *David*. Michelangelo left the *Slaves* "unfinished" as a symbolic gesture: to accentuate the figures' struggle to escape the bondage of stone. *Via Ricasoli 60, tel. 055/2388609. Admission: 12,000 lire. Open Tues.–Sat. 8:30–6:50, Sun. 8:30–1:50.*

The remarkable **Cappelle Medicee** (Medici Chapels) contain the tombs of practically every member of the Medici family, and there were a lot of them, for they guided Florence's destiny from the 15th century to 1737. Cosimo I, a Medici whose acumen made him the richest man in Europe, is buried in the crypt of the Chapel of the Princes, and Donatello's tomb is next to that of his patron. The chapel upstairs is decorated in a dazzling array of colored marble. In Michelangelo's New Sacristy, his tombs of Giuliano and Lorenzo de' Medici bear the justly famed statues of *Dawn* and *Dusk*, and *Night* and *Day*. *Piazza Madonna degli Aldobrandini, tel. 055/2388602. Admission: 10,000 lire. Open daily 8:30–1:50. Closed 1st, 3rd, and 5th Mon. of month.*

Don't be put off by the grim look of Bargello, a fortresslike palace that served as residence of Florence's chief magistrate in medieval times, and later as a prison. It now houses Florence's **Museo Nazionale del Bargello** (National Museum), a treasure house of Italian Renaissance sculpture. In a historically and visually interesting setting, it displays masterpieces by Donatello, Verrocchio, Michelangelo, and many other major sculptors. This museum is on a par with the Uffizi, so don't shortchange yourself on time. *Via del Proconsolo 4, tel. 055/238–8606. Admission: 8,000 lire. Open daily 8:30–1:50. Closed 1st, 3rd, and 5th Sun. and 2nd and 4th Mon. of month.*

The **Ponte Vecchio** (Old Bridge) is Florence's oldest bridge. It seems to be just another street lined with goldsmiths' shops until you get to the middle and catch a glimpse of the Arno flowing below. Spared during World War II by the retreating Germans (who blew up every other bridge in the city), it also survived the 1966 flood. It leads into the Oltrarno District, which has its own charm and still preserves much of the atmosphere of old-time Florence, full of fascinating craft workshops. *East of Ponte Santa Trinita and west of Ponte alle Grazie.*

The church of **Santo Spirito** is important as one of Brunelleschi's finest architectural creations, and it contains some superb paintings, including a Filippino Lippi *Madonna*. Santo Spirito is the hub of a colorful neighborhood of artisans and intellectuals. An outdoor market enlivens the square every morning except Sunday; in the afternoon, pigeons, pet owners, and pensioners take over. *Piazza Santo Spirito. Open Thurs.–Tues. 8–noon and 4–6; Wed. 8–noon.*

Shopping Florence offers top quality for your money in leather goods, linens and upholstery fabrics, gold and silver jewelry, and cameos. Straw goods, gilded wooden trays and frames, hand-printed paper desk accessories, and ceramic objects make good inexpensive gifts. Many shops offer fine old prints.

The most fashionable streets in Florence are **Via Tornabuoni** and **Via della Vigna Nuova.** Goldsmiths and jewelry shops can be found on and around the **Ponte Vecchio.**

The **monastery of Santa Croce** houses a leather-working school and showroom (entrances at Via San Giuseppe 5/r, Piazza Santa Croce 16). The entire Santa Croce area is known for its leather workshops and inconspicuous shops selling gold and silver jewelry at prices much lower than those of the elegant jewelers near Ponte Vecchio.

Outside the Church of San Lorenzo, you'll find yourself in the midst of the sprawling **San Lorenzo Market,** dealing in everything and anything, including some interesting leather items. *Piazza San Lorenzo, Via dell'Ariento. Open Tues.–Sat. 8–7.*

French Riviera and Monte Carlo

Few places in the world have the same pull on the imagination as France's fabled Riviera, the Mediterranean coastline stretching from St-Tropez in the west to Menton on the Italian border. Cooled by the Mediterranean in the summer and warmed by it in winter, the climate is almost always pleasant. Avoid the area in July and August, however, unless you love crowds.

Although the Riviera's coastal resorts seem to live exclusively for the tourist trade and have often been ruined by high-rise blocks, the hinterlands remain relatively untarnished. The little villages perched high on the hills behind medieval ramparts seem to belong to another century. One of them, St-Paul-de-Vence, is the home of the Maeght Foundation, one of the world's leading museums of modern art. Artists, attracted by the light, have played a considerable role in popular conceptions of the Riviera, and their presence is reflected in the number of modern art museums: the Musée Picasso at Antibes, the Musée Renoir and the Musée d'Art Moderne Méditerranée at Cagnes-sur-Mer, and the Musée Jean Cocteau near the harbor at Menton. Wining and dining are special treats on the Riviera, especially if you are fond of garlic and olive

The French Riviera

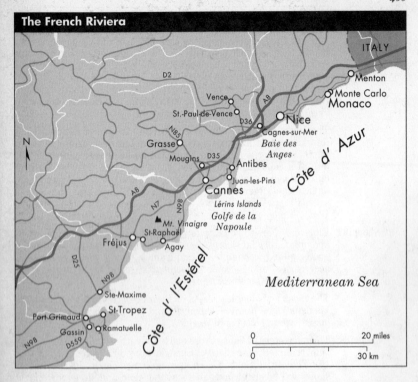

oil. Bouillabaisse, a spicy fish stew, is the most popular regional specialty.

The tiny principality of Monaco, which lies between Nice and Menton, is included in this section, despite the fact that it is a sovereign state. Although Monaco has its own army and police force, its language, food, and way of life are French.

Currency The unit of French currency is the franc (fr), subdivided into 100 centimes. Bills are issued in denominations of 50, 100, 200, and 500 francs (frs.); coins are 5, 10, 20, and 50 centimes and 1, 2, 5, 10, and 20 francs. The small, copper-color 5-, 10-, and 20-centime coins have considerable nuisance value, but they can be used for tips in bars and cafés. At press time the U.S. dollar bought 6 francs.

Telephones The country code for France is 33. French phone numbers have ten digits. All phone numbers have a two-digit prefix determined by zone; for the southeast, the code is 04. (Drop the zero if you are calling France from a foreign country.) Though there is no frontier between France and Monaco, Monaco is a different country; when dialing numbers from outside the country, even if calling from France, you must prefix the call with "377." Phone booths are plentiful; they are nearly always available at post offices and cafés. Some French pay phones take 1-, 2-, and 5-franc coins (1-fr. minimum), but most phones are now operated by *télécartes* (phone cards), which can be used for both local and international calls. The cards are sold in post offices, métro stations, and cafés sporting a red TABAC (tobacco) sign outside (cost: 40 frs. for 50 units; 96 frs. for 120 units). To call abroad, dial 19 and wait for the tone, then dial the country code, area code, and number. To reach an **AT&T** long-distance operator, dial 19–0011; **MCI,** 19–0019; **Sprint,** 19–0087. Dial 12 for local operators.

Shore Excursions The best way to spend time in the French Riviera is to wander the city streets, lunch at a café, or head to the beach. Depending on where you're docked, your cruise line may offer excursions to other nearby towns.

Coming Ashore Only small ships dock at St-Tropez or Monaco. Most larger ones will dock or drop anchor at Nice or Cannes, where you can hire a car, catch a train, or take a shore excursion to St-Tropez or Monaco.

Exploring the Riviera The towns of the French Riviera are easily and best seen on foot. Only if you wish to travel between towns will you need additional transportation.

St-Tropez Old money never came to St-Tropez, but Brigitte Bardot did—with her director Roger Vadim in 1956 to film *And God Created Woman.* The town has never been the same since. Off-season is the time to come, but even in summer there are reasons to stay. The soft, sandy beaches are the best on the coast, and the pastel houses make it a genuinely pretty town. Between the old and new ports is the **Musée de l'Annonciade,** set in a cleverly converted chapel, which houses paintings by artists drawn to St-Tropez between 1890 and 1940—including Paul Signac, Matisse, Derain, and Van Dongen. *Quai de l'Épi, tel. 04–94–97–04–01. Admission: 30 frs. Open June–Sept., Wed.–Mon. 10–noon and 3–7; Oct.–May, Wed.–Mon. 10–noon and 2–6.*

A long climb up to the **Citadelle** (citadel) is rewarded by a splendid view over the old town and across the gulf to Ste-Maxime, a quieter, more working-class family resort with a decent beach.

In Cannes Cannes is for relaxing—strolling along the seafront on the **Croisette** and getting tanned on the beaches. Near the eastern end of La Croisette is the Parc de la Roserie, where some 14,000 roses nod their heads in the wind.

The **Palais des Festivals** is where the famous film festival is held each May, and it is near the Cannes harbor.

Only a few steps inland is the old town, known as the **Suquet,** with its steep, cobbled streets and its 12th-century watchtower. To reach it, take a right turn off rue Félix Faure onto rue St-Antoine and continue spiraling up through rue du Suquet to the top of a 60-m (197-ft) hill.

In Nice The **place Masséna** is the logical starting point for an exploration of Nice. This fine square was built in 1815 to celebrate a local hero: one of Napoléon's most successful generals.

The **Promenade des Anglais,** built by the English community here in 1824, is only a short stroll past the fountains and the **Jardin Albert Ier.** It now carries heavy traffic but still forms a splendid strand between town and sea.

Just up rue de Rivoli is the **Palais Masséna,** a museum concerned with the Napoleonic era. *65 rue de France, tel. 04–93–88–11–34. Admission 25 frs. Open Tues.–Sun. 10–noon and 2–6.*

Farther west, along rue de France and right up avenue des Baumettes, is the **Musée des Beaux-Arts Jules-Chéret,** Nice's fine-arts museum, built in 1878 as a palatial mansion for a Russian princess. The rich collection of paintings includes works by Renoir,

Degas, and Monet; Oriental prints; sculptures by Rodin; and ceramics by Picasso. *33 av. des Baumettes, tel. 04–93–44–50–72. Admission: 25 frs. Open May–Sept., Tues.–Sun. 10–noon and 2–6; Oct.–April, Tues.–Sun. 10–noon and 2–5.*

The narrow streets in the old town are the prettiest part of Nice: Take the rue de l'Opéra to see the ornate **St-François-de-Paule** church (1750) and the **opera house.** At the northern extremity of the old town lies the vast **place Garibaldi**—all yellow-ocher buildings and formal fountains. Dominating Vieux Nice is the **Colline du Château** (Castle Hill), a romantic cliff fortified many centuries before Christ. It's fun to explore the ruins of the 6th-century castle and the surrounding garden; there's a lookout point on the stairs that gives you a stunning view of the bay.

The **Musée Chagall** (Chagall Museum) is just off the boulevard de Cimiez, near the Roman ruins. The museum was built in 1972 to house the Chagall collection, including the 17 huge canvases of *The Message of the Bible*, which took 13 years to complete. *Av. du Dr-Ménard, tel. 04–93–53–87–20. Admission: 30 frs. (38 frs. in summer). Open July–Sept., Wed.–Mon. 10–6; Oct.–June, Wed.–Mon. 10–5.*

A 17th-century Italian villa amid the Roman remains contains two museums: the **Musée Archéologique** (Archaeological Museum), with a plethora of ancient objects, and the renovated **Musée Matisse** (Matisse Museum) with paintings and bronzes by Henri Matisse (1869–1954). *164 av. des Arènes-de-Cimiez. Musée Matisse: tel. 04–93–81–08–08. Admission 25 fr. Open Apr.–Oct., Wed.–Mon. 10–6; Nov.–Mar., Wed.–Mon. 10–5. Musée Archéologique: tel. 04–93–81–59–57. Open Apr.–Sept., Tues.–Sun. 10–noon and 2–6; Oct.–Mar., Tues.–Sun. 10–1 and 2–5.*

In Monaco The Principality of Monaco covers just 473 acres and would fit comfortably inside New York's Central Park or a family farm in Iowa. The present ruler, Prince Rainier III, is part of the Grimaldi dynasty; back in the 1850s, a Grimaldi named Charles III made a decision that turned Monaco into a giant blue chip. He opened a casino, and while it took over a decade to catch on, it turned the principality into a glittering watering-hole for European society.

For more than a century Monaco's livelihood was centered in its splendid copper-roof **casino.** The oldest section dates from 1878 and was conceived by Charles Garnier, architect of the Paris opera house. It's as elaborately ornate as anyone could wish, bristling with turrets and gold filigree, and masses of interior frescoes and bas-reliefs. There are lovely sea views from the terrace, and the gardens out front are meticulously tended. The main activity is in the American Room, where beneath the gilt-edged ceiling, busloads of tourists feed the one-armed bandits. *Pl. du Casino. Persons under 21 not admitted. Jacket and tie are required in the back rooms. Open daily noon–4 AM.*

The **Musée National** (National Museum) has a compelling collection of 18th- and 19th-century dolls and mechanical figures, the latter shamelessly showing off their complex inner workings. It's magically set in a 19th-century seaside villa (designed by Garnier). *17 av. Princesse-Grace, tel. 93–30–91–26. Admission: 26 frs. Open daily except holidays: Easter–Aug., 10–6:30; Sept.–Easter, 10–12:15 and 2:30–6:30.*

Monaco Town, the principality's old quarter, has many vaulted passageways and exudes an almost tangible medieval feel. The magnificent **Palais du Prince** (Prince's Palace), a grandiose Italianate structure with a Moorish tower, was largely rebuilt in the last century. Here, since 1297, the Grimaldi dynasty has lived and ruled. The spectacle of the Changing of the Guard occurs each morning at 11:55; inside, guided tours take visitors through the state apartments and a wing containing the **Palace Archives** and **Musée Napoléon** (Napoleonic Museum). *Pl. du Palais, tel. 93–25–18–31. Palace admission: 35 frs. Open June–Oct., daily 9:30–12:30 and 2–6:30. Musée Napoléon and Palace Archives admission: 20 frs. Open June–Oct., daily 9:30–6:30.*

Next to the St-Martin Gardens—which contain an evocative bronze monument in memory of Prince Albert I (Prince Rainier's great-grandfather, the one in the sou'wester and flying oilskins, benignly guiding a ship's wheel)—is the **Musée Océanographique** (Oceanography Museum and Aquarium). This museum is also an internationally renowned research institute, founded by the very Prince Albert who is remembered outside as an eminent marine biologist; the late, great underwater explorer Jacques Cousteau directed it for years. The aquarium is the undisputed highlight, however, where a collection of the world's fish and crustacea—some colorful, some drab, some the stuff of nightmares—live out their lives in public. *Av. St-Martin, tel. 93–15–36–00. Admission: 60 frs. Open July–Aug., daily 9–8; Sept.–June, daily 9:30–7 (6 in winter).*

The Moneghetti area is the setting for the **Jardin Exotique** (Garden of Exotic Plants), where 600 varieties of cacti and succulents cling to the rock face, their improbable shapes and sometimes violent coloring further testimony that Mother Nature will try anything once. Your ticket also allows you to explore the caves next to the gardens and to visit the adjacent **Museum of Prehistoric Anthropology.** *Blvd. du Jardin Exotique, tel. 93–15–80–06. Admission: 38 frs. Open daily 9–7 (till dusk in winter).*

Beaches Many of Cannes's beaches are private, but that doesn't mean you
In Cannes can't use them, only that you must pay for the privilege. The Croisette offers splendid views of the Napoule Bay.

In St-Tropez The best beaches (*plages*) are scattered along a 5-km (3-mi) stretch reached by the route des Plages (beach road). Close to town are the family-friendly **Plage des Greniers** and the **Bouillabaisse,** but most people prefer a 10-km (6-mi) sandy crescent at **Les Salins** and **Pampellone.** These beaches are about 3 km (2 mi) from town.

Gibraltar

The Rock of Gibraltar acquired its name in AD 711 when it was captured by the Moorish chieftain Tarik at the start of the Arab invasion of Spain. It became known as Jebel Tariq (Rock of Tariq), later corrupted to Gibraltar. After successive periods of Moorish and Spanish domination, Gibraltar was captured by an Anglo-Dutch fleet in 1704 and ceded to the British by the Treaty of Utrecht in 1713. This tiny British colony, whose impressive silhouette dominates the straits between Spain and Morocco, is a rock just 5⅓ km (3⅜ mi) long, ¾ km (½ mi) wide, and 1,394 ft high.

Currency Gibraltar's official language is English and the currency is the British pound sterling. However, Spanish pesetas are generally accepted. At press time, exchange rates were approximately U.S.$1.65 to the pound.

Shore Excursions The following is a good choice in Gibraltar. It may not be offered by all cruise lines. Time and price are approximate.

The Rock. By taxi, you'll climb the 1,400-ft-high Rock of Gibraltar for a panoramic view of the town and harbor. Includes a visit to Ape's Den, home of Barbary apes. *1½ hrs. Cost: $32.*

Coming Ashore Cruise ships dock at Gibraltar's pier. From here, you can walk or take a taxi or shuttle to the center of town.

Since Gibraltar is just over 5 km (3 mi) long and only 1 km (½ mi) wide, getting around is not a major problem.

Exploring Gibraltar **Punta Grande de Europa** (Europa Point) is the Rock's most southerly tip. Stop here to admire the view across the Straits to the coast of Morocco, 22½ km (14 mi) away. You are standing on what in ancient times was called one of the two Pillars of Hercules. Across the water in Morocco, a mountain between the cities of Ceuta and Tangier formed the second pillar. Plaques explain the history of the gun installations here, and, nearby on Europa Flats, you can see the Nun's Well, an ancient Moorish cistern, and the Shrine of Our Lady of Europe, venerated by sailors since 1462.

Jews' Gate is an unbeatable lookout point over the docks and Bay of Gibraltar to Algeciras in Spain. From here you can gain access to the Upper Nature Preserve, which includes St. Michael's Cave (*see below*), the Apes' Den, the Great Siege Tunnel, and the Moorish Castle. *Engineer Rd. Admission to preserve, including all sights: £4.50, plus £2 per vehicle. Open daily 9:30–sunset.*

St. Michael's Cave, a series of underground chambers adorned with stalactites and stalagmites, provides an admirable setting for concerts, ballet, and drama.

Apes' Den, near the Wall of Charles V, is where you'll find the famous Barbary apes, a breed of cinnamon-colored, tailless monkeys, natives of the Atlas Mountains in Morocco. Legend holds that as long as the apes remain, the British will continue to hold the Rock. Winston Churchill himself issued orders for the maintenance of the ape colony when its numbers began to dwindle during World War II. *Old Queen's Rd.*

The **Great Siege Tunnel** (Old Queen's Rd.) is found at the northern end of the Rock. These huge galleries were carved out during the Great Siege of 1779–83. Here, in 1878, the governor, Lord Napier of Magdala, entertained former president Ulysses S. Grant at a banquet in St. George's Hall. From here, the Holyland Tunnel leads out to the east side of the Rock above Catalan Bay.

The recently refurbished **Gibraltar Museum**'s exhibits recall the history of the Rock throughout the ages. *Bomb House La., tel. 9567–74289. Admission: £2. Open weekdays 10–6, Sat. 10–2.*

Greek Islands

The islands of the Aegean have colorful legends—the Minotaur in Crete; the lost continent of Atlantis, which some believe was Santorini; and the Colossus of Rhodes, to name a few. Each island has its own personality. Mykonos has windmills, dazzling white-washed buildings, hundreds of tiny churches and chapels on golden hillsides, and small fishing harbors. Visitors to volcanic Santorini sail into what was once a vast volcanic crater and anchor near the island's forbidding cliffs. In Rhodes, a bustling modern town surrounds a walled town with a medieval castle.

Currency The Greek monetary unit is the drachma (dr.). At press time, there were approximately 307 dr. to the U.S. dollar.

Telephones The country code for Greece is 30. Telephone kiosks are easy to find, although some can only be used for local calls. The easiest way to make a local or an international call is with a phone card, available at kiosks, convenience stores, or Hellenic Telecommunications Organization (OTE) offices. Go to an OTE office for convenience and privacy if you plan to make several international calls; there are several branches in Athens. For an **AT&T** long-distance operator, dial 00/800–1311; **MCI**, 00/800–1211; **Sprint**, 00/800–1411.

Shore Excursions The following excursions are good choices in the Greek Islands. They may not be offered by all cruise lines. Times and prices are approximate.

In Mykonos The best way to explore Mykonos is on your own, wandering through the narrow whitewashed streets. Some lines may offer excursions to the neighboring island of Delos.

In Santorini **Akrotiri & Wine Tasting.** Visit the excavated town of Akrotiri, and then continue on your bus to a winery for a tasting. *4 hrs. Cost: $60.*

Oia. By motor coach, ride to the cliff-top village of Oia, where there will be time to wander through the town. *4 hrs. Cost: $30.*

In Rhodes **Mount Philerimos and Rhodes Town.** Visit the Church of Our Lady on the plateau of Philerimos and walk through the old walled portion of Rhodes Town to the Palace of Grand Masters. *4½ hrs. Cost: $49.*

Lindos. Drive 50 km (30 mi) to Lindos Village and up the summit of the Acropolis to see ruins and to shop in the village. *4 hrs. Cost: $45.*

In Lesbos **Island Tour.** Breeze through the island's highlights, including the Church of Taxiarches, Theofilos Museum, Theriade Museum, and Agiasso Village. *4 hrs. Cost: $36.*

Coming Ashore Depending on which Greek Islands your ship visits—and how many port calls it makes—you may dock, tender, or both.

In Mykonos Ships tender passengers to the main harbor area along the Esplanade in Mykonos Town.

In Santorini Ships drop anchor in the harbor off Thira or call at the port of Athinios. Passengers coming ashore below Thira can take the cable car to town, or, if you like a little more adventure, try the donkey service. Passengers who come ashore at Athinios will be met by buses and taxis. The bus ride into Thira takes about a half hour, and from there you can make connections to Oia.

In Rhodes Ships dock at Mandraki Harbor, once the ancient port of Rhodes. Rhodes Town stretches in front of the port.

In Lesbos Cruise ships visiting Lesbos tender passengers to the main town of Mytilini, where most of the town's sights are clustered.

Getting Around Most port cities in the Greek Islands are compact enough to explore on foot. There are, however, several outlying towns worth visiting; for these you'll need to hire a driver or rent a car.

In Mykonos Mykonos Town is well suited to walking. Taxis and buses will take you to other points of interest. Motorbikes also can be rented.

The Greek Islands

In Santorini Buses and taxis will take you around town. Many people rent mopeds, but they're not recommended as a safe means of traveling about the island.

In Rhodes It is possible to tour the island in one day only if you rent a car. Walking is advisable in Rhodes Town. Taxis can take you to other nearby sights and beaches.

In Lesbos A car is handy on Lesbos if you want to explore the island, and rentals cost around $60 a day. Bus service is relatively expensive and infrequent.

Exploring the Greek Islands
Mykonos Besides their sun-kissed beaches, the Greek Islands offer a diverse mix of historical, architectural, and cultural attractions. A visit to the **archaeological museum** is a good way to get a sense of the island's history; the most significant local find is a 7th-century BC *pithos* (storage jar) showing the Greeks emerging from the Trojan Horse. *North end of port, tel. 0289/22325. Admission: 400 dr. Open Tues.–Sun. 8:30–3.*

The most famous of the island's churches is the **Church of Paraportiani.** The sloping, whitewashed conglomeration of four chapels, mixing Byzantine and vernacular idioms, has been described as a "confectioner's dream gone mad," and its position on a promontory facing the sea sets off the unique architecture. *Anargon St.*

Venetia (Little Venice) is a neighborhood where a few old houses have been turned into bars. In the distance across the water are the famous windmills. *Southwest end of the port.*

The **Old Folk Museum** is housed in an 18th-century house and features one bedroom furnished and decorated in the fashion of the period. On display are looms and lace-making devices, Cycladic costumes, old photographs, and Mykoniot musical instruments. *Near Little Venice, tel. 0289/22591 or 0289/22748. Admission free. Open Mon.–Sat. 5:30–8:30, Sun. 6:30–8:30.*

About 40 minutes by boat from Mykonos and its 20th-century holiday pleasures is the ancient isle of **Delos**—the legendary sanctuary of Apollo. Its Terrace of the Lions, a remarkable group of nine Naxian marble sculptures from the 7th century BC, is a must. Worth seeing, too, are some of the houses of the Roman period, with their fine floor mosaics.

The best of the mosaics from Delos's ruins are in the island's **archaeological museum.** *Tel. 0289/22–259. Admission to archaeological site (including entrance to museum): 1,200 dr. Open Tues.– Sun. 8:30–3.*

Santorini Santorini's volcano erupted during the 15th century BC, destroying its Minoan civilization. At **Akrotiri,** on the south end of the island, the remains of a Minoan city buried by volcanic ash are being excavated. The site, believed by some to be part of the legendary Atlantis, should be a must on your sightseeing list. *13 km/8 mi from Fira, tel. 0286/81–366. Admission: 1,200 dr. Open Tues.– Sun. 8:30–3.*

Oia, the serene town at the northern tip, is charming and has spectacular views despite being packed with visitors in the summer. This is the place, if your time ashore allows, to watch the sunset. Oia, 14 km (8½ mi) from Thira, has the usual souvenir and handicrafts shops and several reasonably priced jewelry shops. Be sure to try the local wines. The volcanic soil produces a unique range of flavors, from light and dry to rich and aromatic.

The capital, **Fira,** midway along the west coast of the east rim, is no longer just a picturesque town but a major tourist center, overflowing with discos, shops, and restaurants.

At **Ancient Thira,** a cliff-top site on the east coast of the island, a well-preserved ancient town includes a theater and agora, houses, fortifications, and ancient tombs. *Take taxi partway up Mesa Vouna then hike to summit, no phone. Admission free. Open Tues.–Sun. 8:30–3.*

For an enjoyable but slightly unnerving excursion, take the short boat trip to the island's still-active small offshore volcanoes, called the **Kamenes** (Burnt Ones). You can descend into a small crater, hot and smelling of sulfur, and swim in the nearby water, which has been warmed by the volcano.

Rhodes The fascinating **old walled city,** near the harbor, was built by crusaders—the Knights of St. John—on the site of an ancient city. The knights ruled the island from 1309 until they were defeated by the Turks in 1522.

Within the fine medieval walls, on the Street of the Knights, stands the Knights' Hospital. Behind it, the **archaeological museum** houses ancient pottery and sculpture, including two famous statues of Aphrodite. *Platia Mouseou (Museum Square), reached by the wide staircase from the Hospital, tel. 0241/27–657. Admission: 800 dr. Open Tues.–Fri. 8:30–7, weekends and holidays 8:30–3.*

Another museum that deserves your attention is the restored and moated medieval **Palati ton Ippoton** (Palace of the Knights). Destroyed in 1856 by a gunpowder explosion, the palace was renovated by the Italians as a summer retreat for Mussolini. Note its splendid Hellenistic and Roman floor mosaics. *Street of the Knights, tel. 0241/23–359. Admission: 1,200 dr. Open Tues.–Fri. 8– 7, weekends 8:30–3.*

The walls of Rhodes's **Old Town** are among the greatest medieval monuments in the Mediterranean. For 200 years the knights strengthened them, making them up to 40 ft thick in places and curving the walls to deflect cannonballs. You can take a guided walk on about half of the 4-km (2½-mi) road along the top of the fortifications. *Old town, tel. 0241/21–954; 0241/23–359 tour information. Tours Tues. and Sat. 2:45 (arrive at least 15 mins early); departure from palace entrance.*

The enchanting village of **Lindos** is about 60 km (37 mi) down the east coast from Rhodes Town. Take a donkey from the village center and ride or put on your comfortable shoes and walk up the steep hill to the ruins of the ancient **Akropoli tis Archaias Lindou** (Acropolis of Lindos), which is slowly being restored. The sight of its beautiful colonnade with the sea far below is unforgettable. Look for little St. Paul's Harbor, beneath the cliffs of the Acropolis; seen from above, it appears to be a lake, as the tiny entrance from the sea is obscured by the rocks. *Above town, tel. 0244/31– 258. Admission: 1,200 dr. Open Tues.–Sun. 8:30–2:45.*

Lesbos   Above **Mytilini** looms the stone castle built by the Byzantines on a 600 BC temple of Apollo. It was repaired by Francesco Gateluzzi of the famous Genoese family. Inside there's only a crumbling prison and a Roman cistern, but a visit is worth it for the fine views. *Tel. 0251/27297. Admission: 400 dr. Open daily sunrise–sunset.*

One of Greece's best art museums is at **Varia**, home of the early 20th-century painter Theofilos. Eighty of his paintings can be seen. *4 km/2½ mi south of Mytilini, tel. 0251/28179. Admission: 250 dr. Open Tues.–Sun. 9–1 and 4:30–8.*

The **Theriade Library and Museum of Modern Art** includes Theriade's publications "Minotaure" and "Verved" and his collection of works, mostly lithographs, by Picasso, Matisse, Chagall, and Miró. *Next to Varia, tel. 0251/28179. Admission: 500 dr. Open Tues.– Sun. 9–2 and 5–8.*

The 18th-century monastery **Taxiarchis Michail** is famous for its black icon of Archangel Michael. Visitors used to make a wish and press a coin to the archangel's forehead; if it stuck, the wish would be granted. Owing to wear and tear on the icon, the practice is now forbidden. *In town of Mandamados, 37 km/23 mi northwest of Mytilini.*

At the foot of Mt. Olympos, the island's highest peak, sits **Agiassos** village. It remains a lovely settlement, with gray stone houses, cobblestone lanes, a medieval castle, and the church of Panayia Vrefokratousa. The latter was founded in the 12th century to house an icon believed to be the work of St. Luke.

In the main town of **Mytilini** there is a traditional Lesbos house, restored and furnished in 19th-century style, that people are permitted to visit. Call to arrange a time with owner Marika Vlachou. *Mitropleos 6, tel. 0251/28550. Admission free by appointment only.*

Shopping
In Mykonos Mykonos is the best of the Greek Islands for shopping. The main shopping street in Mykonos runs perpendicular to the harbor and is lined with jewelry stores, clothing, boutiques, cafés, and candy stores.

In Santorini For locally made items head to Oia, where you will find the best art galleries, antiques shops, craft shops, and stores that sell Byzantine reproductions. Boutiques abound in Thira as well.

In Rhodes Many attractive souvenir and handicrafts shops are in the Old Town, particularly on Sokratous Street, and just outside the walls vendors sell decorative Rhodian pottery, local embroidery, sea sponges, and relatively inexpensive jewelry.

In Lesbos Lesbos is famous for its chestnuts, olive oil, and ouzo. Agiassos is known for its wood crafts.

Beaches
In Mykonos Within walking distance of Mykonos Town are **Tourlos, Ayios Stefanos,** and **Ayios Ioannis. Psarou,** on the south coast, protected from wind by hills and surrounded by restaurants, offers a wide selection of water sports and is considered the finest beach.

In Santorini There is a red-sand beach below Akrotiri on the southwest shore. Long black-sand/volcanic beaches are found in Kamari and Perissa.

In Rhodes Rhodes town and the more sheltered east coast have exquisite stretches of beach, while the west side can be choppy. **Elli** beach in town has fine sand. Much of the coast is developed, so you can reach the best beaches only through the hotels that occupy them. There also is a long nice stretch of beach between Haraki and Vlicha Bay.

In Lesbos Some of the most spectacular beaches are sandy coves in the southwest, including the stretch from Skala Eressou to Sigri. **Vatera,** one of the island's best beaches, lies southwest of Agiassos on the southeast side of the island.

Helsinki, Finland

Helsinki is a city of the sea, built on peninsulas and islands along the Baltic shoreline. Streets curve around bays, bridges arch over the nearby islands, and ferries carry traffic to destinations farther offshore. The smell of the sea hovers over the city, while the huge ships that ply the Baltic constantly come and go from the city's harbors. Helsinki has grown dramatically since World War II, and now accounts for about one-sixth of the Finnish population. The city covers a total of 698 km (433 square mi) and includes 315 islands. Most of the city's sights, hotels, and restaurants, however, are on one peninsula—forming a compact hub of special interest to cruise passengers.

Currency The unit of currency in Finland is the Finnish mark, divided into 100 penniä. There are bills of FIM 20, 50, 100, 500, and 1,000. Coins are 10 and 50 penniä, and FIM 1, FIM 5, and FIM 10. At press time, the exchange rate was about FIM 5.5 to the U.S. dollar. Finland is prepared to be one of the "first wave" countries in the European Monetary Union project.

Telephones The country code for Finland is 358. Local calls can be made from public pay phones; have some FIM 1 and FIM 5 coins ready. Some pay phones only accept a phone card, the Tele kortti or HPY kortti, available at post offices, R-kiosks, and some grocery stores. They come in increments of FIM 30, 50, 100, and 150. You can dial

North America directly from anywhere in Finland. To make a direct international phone call from Finland, dial 00, or 999, or 990, then the appropriate country code and phone number. For an **AT&T** long-distance operator, dial 9800–10010; **MCI,** 9800–10280; **Sprint,** 9800–10284.

Shore Excursions
The following is a good choice in Helsinki. It may not be offered by all cruise lines. Time and price are approximate.

Heart of Helsinki. Take in the major sights, including the Senate Square, the Esplanade, and other Helsinki landmarks on this quick tour of the town. *2¼ hrs. Cost: $30.*

Coming Ashore
Ships calling at Helsinki dock harborside near Market Square. From here, you can easily spend the day exploring the city center on foot.

The center of Helsinki is compact and best explored on foot. If you want to use public transportation, your best buy is the *Helsinki Kortti* (Helsinki Card), which gives unlimited travel on city public transportation, as well as free entry to many museums, a free sightseeing tour, and a variety of other discounts. A one-day pass costs FIM 105; you can buy it at some hotels and travel agencies, Stockmann's department store, and the Helsinki City Tourist Office. Streetcars can be very handy and route maps and schedules are posted at most downtown stops. Single tickets are sold on board for FIM 7 (one ride without transfers) or FIM 9 (one ride with transfers). Taxis are all marked TAKSI. The meters start at FIM 30, with the fare rising on a kilometer basis. A listing of all taxi companies appears in the white pages under *Taksi*—try to choose one that is located nearby, because they charge from point of dispatch. The main phone number for taxi service is 700–700.

Exploring Helsinki
Numbers in the margin correspond to points of interest on the Helsinki map.

❶ The **Kauppatori** (Market Square) is frequented by locals and tourists alike. Under bright orange tents you'll find stalls selling everything from colorful, freshly cut flowers to ripe fruit to vegetables trucked in from the hinterland to handicrafts made in small villages. Look at the fruit stalls—mountains of strawberries, raspberries, blueberries, and, if you're lucky, cloudberries. Watching over it all is the unmissable, curvaceous Havis Amanda statue. *At South Harbor, harborside at Eteläranta and Pohjoisesplanadi. Open year-round, Mon.–Sat. 7–2, and also arts and crafts 3:30–8 June –Aug.*

❷ On the Pohjoisesplanadi (North Esplanade) is the **Presidentinlinna** (President's Palace), built as a private home in 1818 and converted for use by the czars in 1843. It was the official residence of Finnish presidents from 1919 to 1993. It still houses the presidential offices and is the scene of official receptions. It is not open to the public except for pre-arranged tours on Wednesdays and Sundays, 11 to 4. *Pohjoiseplanadi 1, tel. 09/641–200.*

At the district of **Katajanokka,** 19th-century brick warehouses are slowly being renovated to form a complex of boutiques, arts-and-crafts studios, and restaurants. You'll find innovative designs at these shops, and the restaurants tend to offer lighter fare, which can make this a tempting area in which to stop for lunch.

❸❹ **Senaatintori** (Senate Square), the heart of neoclassical Helsinki, is dominated by the domed **Tuomiokirkko** (Lutheran cathedral). The square is the work of Carl Ludvig Engel. The harmony created with the Tuomiokirkko, the main building of Helsinki University, and the State Council Building places you amid one of the purest styles of European architecture. Senaatintori has a dignified, stately air, enlivened in summer by sun worshipers who gather on the wide steps leading up to Tuomiokirkko and throughout the year by the bustle around the Kiseleff Bazaar on the square's south side. *North of City Hall. Tuomiokirkko open June–Aug., weekdays 9–5, Sat. 9–7, Sun. 9–8; Sept.–May, weekdays 10–4, Sat. 10–7, Sun. 10–4.*

⑤ Worth taking a look at is the old brick **Vanha Kauppahalli** (Old Market Hall)—with its voluminous displays of meat, fish, and other gastronomic goodies. *Eteläranta, along the South Harbor. Open weekdays 8–5, Sat. 8–2.*

⑥ The **Rautatieasema** (railway station) and its square form the bustling commuting hub of the city. The station's huge red-granite figures are by Emil Wikström, but the solid building they adorn was designed by Eliel Saarinen, one of the founders of the early 20th-century National Romantic style. *Kaivokatu, tel. 09/7071.*

⑦ The **Valtion Taidemuseo Ateneum** (Finnish National Gallery) houses both the Ateneum Museum of Finnish Art as well as major changing shows, an excellent bookshop, and a café. *Kaivokatu 2–4, tel. 09/173–361. Admission: FIM 20. Open Tues. and Fri. 9–6, Wed. and Thurs. 9–9, weekends 11–5.*

In front of the main post office, west of the railway station, is the **⑧** **Mannerheimin patsas** (statue of Marshal Mannerheim), gazing down Mannerheimintie, the major thoroughfare named in his honor. Perhaps no man in Finnish history is so revered as Baron Carl Gustaf Mannerheim, the military and political leader who guided Finland through much of the turbulent 20th century. When he died in Switzerland on January 28, 1951, his body was flown back to lie in state in the cathedral. For three days, young war widows, children, and soldiers filed past his bier.

⑨ The **Nykytaiteenmuseo** (Museum of Contemporary Art) makes a striking new backdrop for the Mannerheim statue; it is the latest addition to Helsinki's varied architectural catalogue. It opened to the public in spring 1998 to a mixed reaction: some praised the boldness of its curved steel shell, others condemned it for its encroachment on the sacred territory of the Mannerheim statue. Nevertheless, the wealth of Finnish art from the 1960s to the present it contains is undeniable. For opening times (still unavailable at press time) and other details of the museum, call the City Tourist Information office (tel. 09/169-3757). *Mannerheimintie.*

About 1 km (½ mi) along, past the colonnaded red-granite **⑩** **⑪** **Eduskantatalo** (Parliament House), stands **Finlandiatalo** (Finlandia Hall; tel. 09/40241), one of the last creations of Alvar Aalto, **⑫** and, a bit farther up Mannerheimintie, the **Suomen Kansallisooppera** (Finnish National Opera; tel. 09/4030–2350), a striking example of Scandinavian architecture. If you can't make it to a concert there, take a guided tour. Behind the hall and the opera house lies the inland bay of Töölönlahti, and almost opposite the hall stands **⑬** the **Suomen Kansallismuseo** (National Museum), another example of National Romantic exotica in which Eliel Saarinen played a part. The museum, which normally has international cultural exhibits, is closed for renovation until December 1999. *Mannerheimintie 34, tel. 09/405–0470.*

Helsinki

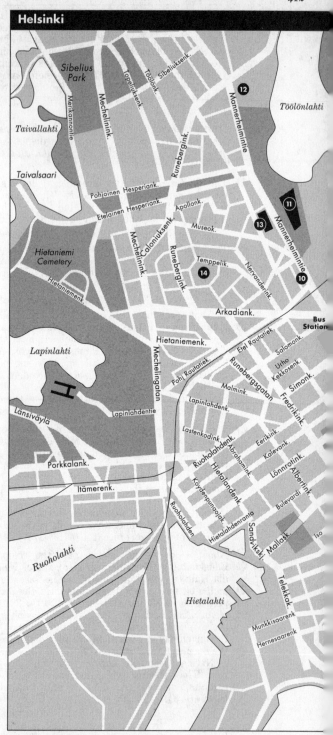

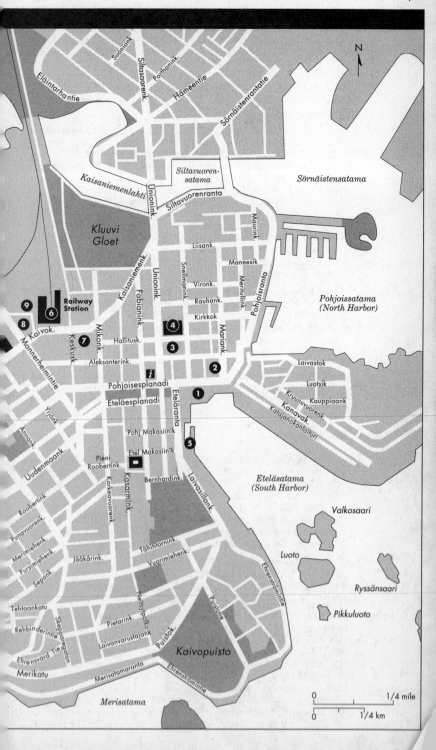

N

Suonionk.

Siltasaarenk.

Porthanink.

Eläintarhantie

Hämeentie

Sörnäistenrantatie

Kaisaniemenlahti

Unionink.

Siltavuoren-
satama

Siltavuorenranta

Sörnäistensatama

Kluuvi
Gloet

Liisank.

Maurink.

Katsaniemenk.

Unionink.

Snellmanink.

Maneesik.

Merikullink.

Pohjoisranta

Pohjoissatama
(North Harbor)

Vironk.

Rauhank.

**Railway
Station**

Fabianink.

Kirkkok.

Mariank.

⑨

⑥

⑧

Kaivok.

Keskusk.

Mikonk.

④

③

Hallitusk.

Aleksanterink.

Laivastok.

Mannerheimintie

⑦

Luotsik.

Kruununvuorenk.

Kauppiaank.

Pohjoisesplanadi

i

②

Eteläesplanadi

①

Kanavak.

Katajanokanlaituri

Yrjönk.

Eteläranta

Annank.

Pohj. Makasiink.

⑤

Eteläsatama
(South Harbor)

Uudenmaank.

Etel. Makasiink.

Pieni
Roobertink.

Roobertink.

Kasarmink.

Bernhardink.

Laivasillank.

Valkosaari

Punavuorenk.

Tähtitornink.

Luoto

Merimiehenk.

Jääkärink.

Vuorimiehenk.

Ryssänsaari

Pursimiehenk.

Ehrenströmintie

Sepank.

Pikluoto

Tehtaankatu

Neitsytpolku

Puistotie

Rehbinderintie

Pietarink.

Puistok.

Ehrensvärd Tie gatan

Laivanvarustajank.

Kaivopuisto

Merikatu

Merisatamaranta

Ehrenströmintie

Merisatama

0   1/4 mile

0   1/4 km

⑭ Tucked away in a labyrinth of streets to the west of the Opera is the strikingly modern **Temppeliaukion kirkko** (Temple Square Church). Carved out of solid rock and topped with a copper dome, this landmark is a center for church services and concerts. (From here it's only a short distance back to Mannerheimintie, where you can pick up any streetcar for the downtown area.) *Lutherinkatu 3, tel. 09/494–698. Open weekdays 10–8, Sat. 10–6, Sun. 11:30–1:45 and 3:20–5:30. Closed Tues. 12:45–2 PM and during concerts and services.*

Shopping Helsinki's prime shopping districts run along **Pohjoisesplanadi** (North Esplanade) and **Aleksanterinkatu** in the city center. Antiques shops cluster in the neighborhood behind Senate Square, called **Kruununhaka**. For one-stop shopping, hit **Stockmann's**, a huge store which fills an entire block bordered by Aleksanterinkatu, Keskuskatu, Pohjoisesplanadi, and Mannerheimintie. *Aleksanterinkatu 32, tel. 09/1211.* The **Forum** (Mannerheimintie 20) is a modern, multistory shopping center with a wide variety of stores, including clothing, gifts, books, and toys. Some shops in the **Kiseleff Bazaar Hall** (Aleksanterinkatu 22–28) sell handicrafts, toys, and knitwear; they are open on Sundays from noon to 4 in the summer. **Kalevala Koru** (Unioninkatu 25) has jewelry based on ancient Finnish designs.

Along Pohjoisesplanadi and on the other side Eteläesplanadi, you will find Finland's design houses. **Hackman Arabia** (Pohjoisesplanadi 25) sells Finland's well-known Arabia china, Iittala glass, and other items. **Pentik** (Pohjoisesplanadi 27) features artful leather goods. **Aarikka** (Pohjoisesplanadi 27 and Eteläesplanadi 8) offers wooden jewelry, toys, and gifts. **Artek** (Eteläesplanadi 18) is known for its Alvar Alto–designed furniture and ceramics. **Marimekko** (Pohjoisesplanadi 31 and Eteläesplanadi 14) sells women's clothing, household items, and gifts made from its famous textiles. **Design Forum Finland** (Eteläesplanadi 8) often hosts exhibits of the latest Finnish design innovations.

Ibiza, Spain

Settled by the Carthaginians in the 5th century BC, Ibiza in the 20th century has been transformed by tourism. From a peasant economy, it became a wild, anything-goes gathering place for the international jet set and for the hippies of the 1960s—only to enter the 1990s with its principal resort, Sant Antoni, regarded as one of the most boorish, noisy, and brash on the Mediterranean. Recently, however, ecology-minded residents have begun to make headway in their push for development restrictions.

Currency The unit of currency in Spain is the peseta (pta.). There are bills of 1,000, 2,000, 5,000, and 10,000 ptas. Coins are 1, 5, 25, 50, 100, 200, and 500 ptas. At press time, the exchange rate was about 152 ptas. to the U.S. dollar.

Telephones The country code for Spain is 34. Pay phones generally take the new, smaller 5- and 25-pta. coins; the minimum charge for short local calls is 25 ptas. Area codes always begin with a 9 and are different for each province. If you're dialing from outside the country, drop the 9. Calling abroad can be done from any pay phone marked TELÉFONO INTERNACIONAL. Use 50-pta. (or 100-pta. if the phone takes them) coins initially, then coins of any denomination to prolong your call. Newer pay phones take only phone cards, which can be purchased at any tobacco shop in denominations of 1,000 or 2,000 ptas. Dial 07 for international, wait for the tone to change, then dial 1 for the United States or 0101 for Canada. For lengthy international calls, go to the *telefónica,* a telephone office, where an operator assigns you a private booth and collects payment at the end of the call; this is the least expensive and by far the easiest way of phoning abroad. **AT&T** (tel. 900/99–00–11); **MCI** (tel. 900/99–00–14); **Sprint** (tel. 900/99–00–13).

Shore Excursions The following is a good choice in Ibiza. It may not be offered by all lines. Time and price are approximate.

Sanctuaries of Ibiza. Explore Ibiza's Old World treasures from a 15th-century church to the fortified upper town. *4 hrs. Cost: $40.*

Coming Ashore Ships calling at Ibiza dock in the harbor at Eivissa. You can explore the town on foot, but to see the outlying areas of the island you will need to take a taxi or bus.

Exploring Ibiza Once a quiet fisherman's quarter, **Sa Penya** is the part of the town of Eivissa that turned into a tourist mecca in the 1960s and it is full of restaurants and shops.

Dalt Vila, the walled upper town, is entered through Las Tablas, its main gate. On each side of the gate stands a statue, Roman in origin; both are now headless.

Inside the upper town, a ramp continues to the right and opens onto a long, narrow plaza lined with cafés. At the top of the hill lies the **cathedral,** which sits on the site of religious constructions from each of the cultures that have ruled Eivissa since the Phoenicians. Built in the 13th and 14th centuries and renovated in the 18th century, the cathedral has a Gothic tower and a baroque nave. The painted panels above a small vault adjoining the sacristy depict souls in purgatory being consumed by flames and tortured by devils while angels ascend to heaven. Go through the nave to the museum, which is well worth seeing. *At top of Carrer Major. Admission to museum: 300 ptas. Open Sun.–Fri. 10–1 and 4–6:30, Sat. 10–1.*

The **Museu Dalt Vila** (Museum of Archaeology) in the upper town has a collection of Phoenician, Punic, and Roman artifacts. *Plaça Catedral 3, tel. 971/30–12–31. Admission: 450 ptas. Open Mon.– Sat. 10–1.*

A passageway leads between the cathedral and castle to the **Bastion of Sant Bernardo.** (There's a great view here of the wide bay.)

A Punic necropolis, with more than 3,000 tombs, has been excavated at **Puig des Molins.** Many of the artifacts can be seen at the Museu Puig d'Es Molins (Punic Archaeological Museum), adjacent to the site. *Via Romana 31, tel. 971/30–17–71. Admission: 400 ptas. Open Mon.–Sat. 10–1.*

The **Museu d'Art Comtemporani** (Museum of Contemporary Art) is housed in the gateway's arch. *Ronda Pintor Narcis Putget s/n, tel. 971/30–27–23. Admission: 450 ptas. Open daily 10:30–1 and 6– 8:30.*

Irish Coast and Cork

Hilly Cork is Ireland's second-largest city. The road to Cork City passes through the beautiful wooded glen of Glanmire and along the banks of the River Lee. In the center of Cork, the Lee divides in two, giving the city a profusion of picturesque quays and bridges. The name Cork derives from the Irish *corcaigh* (pronounced corky), meaning a marshy place. The city received its first charter in 1185 and grew rapidly in the 17th and 18th centuries with the expansion of its butter trade. It is now the major metropolis of the south, with a population of about 133,250. The main business and shopping center of Cork lies on the island created by the two diverging channels of the Lee, and most places of interest are within walking distance of the center.

Currency The unit of currency in Ireland is the pound, or punt (pronounced poont), written as IR£ to avoid confusion with the pound sterling. The currency is divided into 100 pence (written *p*), Although the Irish pound is the only legal tender in the republic, U.S. dollars and British currency are often accepted in large hotels and shops licensed as bureaux de change. The rate of exchange at press time was 62 pence to the U.S. dollar and 95 pence to the British pound sterling.

Telephones The country code for the Republic of Ireland is 353. When dialing from outside the country, drop the initial zero from the regional area code. There are pay phones in all post offices and most hotels and bars, as well as in street booths. Telephone cards are available at all post offices and most newsagents. Booths accepting cards are equally common as coin booths. For calls to the United States and Canada, dial 001 followed by the area code. To reach an **AT&T** long-distance operator, dial 1–800/550–000; **MCI,** 1–800/551–001; **Sprint,** 1–800/552–001.

Shore Excursions The following are good choices in Cork. They may not be offered by all cruise lines. Times and prices are approximate.

Cork City and Blarney Tour. This is a good choice for passengers who want to visit Blarney. Upon reaching the village, you'll walk up the castle's steps to reach the famous Blarney stone. The tour also includes highlights of Cork city. *4 hrs. Cost: $58.*

Cobh Island and Whiskey Distillery. Drive through the seaside resort town of Cobh, the countryside, and Cork to reach Midleton for a visit to the Jameson Irish Whiskey Heritage Center. *4 hrs. Cost: $42.*

Coming Ashore Ships dock at the harbor of Cobh, which is around 24 km (15 mi) from the main district of Cork.

Once in the compact main district of Cork, the best way to see the city and soak in its full flavor is on foot.

Exploring Cork Patrick Street is the focal point of Cork and its major shopping district (*see below*). In the hilly area to the north is the famous 120-ft **Shandon Steeple,** the bell tower of St. Anne's Church. It is shaped like a pepper pot and houses the bells immortalized in the song *The Bells of Shandon.* Visitors can climb the tower; read the inscriptions on the bells; and, on request, have them rung over Cork. *Admission: IR£1, with bell tower IR£1.50. Open May–Oct., Mon.–Sat. 9:30–5; Nov.–Apr., Mon.–Sat. 10–3:30.*

Cobh is an attractive hilly town dominated by its 19th-century **cathedral.** It was the first and last European port of call for transatlantic liners, one of which was the ill-fated *Titanic.* Cobh has other associations with shipwrecks: It was from here that destroyers were sent out in May 1915 to search for survivors of the *Lusitania,* torpedoed by a German submarine with the loss of 1,198 lives.

Cobh's maritime past and its links with emigration are documented in a IR£2 million heritage center known as the **Queenstown Project,** which opened in the town's old railway station in

Irish Coast and Cork

1993. *Tel. 021/813–591. Admission: IR£3.50. Open Feb.–Nov., daily 10–6.*

Most visitors to Cork want to kiss the famous **Blarney Stone** in the hope of acquiring the "gift of the gab." Blarney itself, 8 km (5 mi) from Cork City, should not, however, be taken too seriously as an excursion. All that is left of Blarney Castle is its ruined central keep containing the celebrated stone. This is set in the battlements, and to kiss it, you must lie on the walk within the walls, lean your head back, and touch the stone with your lips. Nobody knows how the tradition originated, but Elizabeth I is credited with giving the word *blarney* to the language when, commenting on the unfulfilled promises of Cormac MacCarthy, Lord Blarney of the time, she remarked, "This is all Blarney; what he says, he never means." In Blarney village there are several good crafts shops, and the outing provides a good opportunity to shop around for traditional Irish goods at competitive prices. *Tel. 021/385–252. Admission: IR£3. Open Mon.–Sat. 9 to sundown, Sun. 9–5:30.*

Shopping Patrick Street is the main shopping area of Cork, and there you will find the city's two major department stores, **Roches** and **Cash's.** Cash's has a good selection of Waterford crystal. The liveliest place in town to shop is just off Patrick Street, to the west, near the city-center parking lot, in the pedestrian-only **Paul Street** area. **Mendows & Byrne** of Academy Street stocks the best in modern Irish design, including tableware, ceramics, knitwear, handwoven tweeds, and high fashion.

At the top of Paul Street is the **Crawford Art Gallery,** which has an excellent collection of 18th- and 19th-century views of Cork and mounts adventurous exhibitions by modern artists. *Emmet Pl., tel. 021/273–377. Admission free. Open weekdays 10–5, Sat. 9–1.*

Istanbul, Turkey

Turkey is one place to which the phrase "East meets West" really applies, both literally and figuratively. It is in Turkey's largest city, Istanbul, that the continents of Europe and Asia meet, separated only by the Bosporus, which flows 29 km (18 mi) from the Black Sea to the Sea of Marmara. For 16 centuries Istanbul, originally known as Byzantium, played a major part in world politics: first as the capital of the Eastern Roman Empire, when it was known as Constantinople, then as capital of the Ottoman Empire, the most powerful Islamic empire in the world, when it was renamed Istanbul.

Although most of Turkey's landmass is in Asia, Turkey has faced West politically since 1923, when Mustapha Kemal, better known as Atatürk, founded the modern republic. He transformed the remnants of the shattered Ottoman Empire into a secular state with a Western outlook. So thorough was this changeover—culturally, politically, and economically—that in 1987, 49 years after Atatürk's death, Turkey applied to the European Community (EC) for full membership. It has been a member of the North Atlantic Treaty Organization (NATO) since 1952.

Istanbul is noisy, chaotic, and exciting. Spires and domes of mosques and medieval palaces dominate the skyline. At dawn, when the muezzin's call to prayer rebounds from ancient minarets, many people are making their way home from the nightclubs and bars, while others are kneeling on their prayer rugs, facing Mecca. Day and night, Istanbul has a schizophrenic air to it. Women in jeans, business suits, or elegant designer outfits pass women wearing the long skirts and head coverings that villagers have worn for generations. Donkey-drawn carts vie with old Chevrolets and Pontiacs or shiny Toyotas and BMWs for dominance of the loud, narrow streets, and the world's most fascinating Oriental bazaar competes with Western boutiques for the time and attention of both tourists and locals.

Currency The monetary unit is the Turkish lira (TL), which comes in bank notes of 50,000, 100,000, 250,000, 500,000, 1,000,000 and 5,000,000. Coins come in denominations of 1,000, 2,500, 5,000, 10,000, 25,000 and 50,000. At press time, the exchange rate was 270,000 TL to the U.S. dollar. These rates are subject to wide fluctuation, so check close to your departure. Be certain to retain your original exchange slips when you convert money into Turkish lira—you will need them to reconvert the money. Because the Turkish lira is worth a lot less than most currencies, it's best to convert only what you plan to spend.

Telephones The country code for Turkey is 90. When dialing a number from outside the country, drop the initial zero from the local area code. All telephone numbers in Turkey have seven local digits plus three-digit city codes. Intercity calls are preceded by 0. Pay phones are yellow, push-button models. Most take *jetons* (tokens) although an increasing number, particularly in large cities, take phone cards. Tokens can be purchased for 7¢ at post offices and, for a couple of cents more, at street booths. Telephone cards are available at post offices. Multilingual directions are posted in phone booths. For all international calls dial 00, then dial the country code, area or city code, and the number. You can reach an international operator by dialing 132. To reach an **AT&T** long-distance operator, dial 00800-12277; **MCI,** 00800-1177; **Sprint,** 00800-14477.

Shore Excursions The following are good choices in Istanbul. They may not be offered by all lines. Times and prices are approximate.

Bazaar Sights. Visit the major city sights, including the Hippodrome, Blue Mosque, Hagia Sophia, and shop at the Grand Bazaar, which should be a must on anyone's list of things to do. *4½ hrs. Cost: $40.*

Coming Ashore Ships dock on the Bosporus in Istanbul on the European side of the city. Across the Galata Bridge lie the city's main attractions.

The best way to get around all the magnificent monuments in Sultanahmet in Old Istanbul is to walk. They're all within easy distance of one another. To get to other areas, you can take metered taxis, which are plentiful, inexpensive, and more comfortable than city buses. A tram system runs from Topkapí, via Sultanahmet, to Sirkeci. Nostalgic trams run the length of I stiklâl Caddesi from Taksim to Tünel and cost about 25¢.

Exploring Istanbul *Numbers in the margin correspond to points of interest on the Istanbul map.*

Old Istanbul (Sultanahmet) The number one attraction in Istanbul is **Topkapí Saray** (Topkapí Palace), on Seraglio Point in Old Istanbul, known as Sultanahmet.
❶ The palace, which dates from the 15th century, was the residence of a number of sultans and their harems until the mid-19th century. To avoid the crowds, try to get there by 9 AM, when the gates open. If you're arriving by taxi, tell the driver you want the Topkapí Saray in Sultanahmet, or you could end up at the remains of the former Topkapí bus terminal on the outskirts of town.

Sultan Mehmet II built the first palace during the 1450s, shortly after the Ottoman conquest of Constantinople. Over the centuries, sultan after sultan added ever more elaborate architectural fantasies, until the palace eventually ended up with more than four courtyards and some 5,000 residents, many of them concubines and eunuchs. Topkapí was the residence and center of bloodshed and drama for the Ottoman rulers until the 1850s, when Sultan Abdül Mecit moved with his harem to the European-style Dolmabahçe Palace, farther up the Bosporus coast.

❷ In Topkapí's outer courtyard are the **Aya Irini** (Church of St. Irene) open only during festival days for concerts, and the
❸ **Merasim Avlusu** (Court of the Janissaries), originally for members of the sultan's elite guard.

Adjacent to the ticket office is the **Bab-i-Selam** (Gate of Salutation), built in 1524 by Suleyman the Magnificent, who was the only person allowed to pass through it. In the towers on either side, prisoners were kept until they were executed beside the fountain outside the gate in the first courtyard.

In the second courtyard, amid the rose gardens, is the **Divan-i-Humayun,** the assembly room of the council of state, once presided over by the grand vizier (prime minister). The sultan would sit behind a latticed window, hidden by a curtain so no one would know when he was listening, although occasionally he would pull the curtain aside to comment.

Arkeoloji Müzesi, **4**
Aya Irini, **2**
Çiçek Pasaji, **10**
Dolmabahçe
Palace, **11**
Galata Tower, **9**
Hagia Sophia, **5**
Hippodrome, **7**
Merasim Avlusu, **3**
Sultan Ahmet Cami, **6**
Topkapí Saray, **1**
Türk Ve Islâm
Eserleri Müzesi, **8**

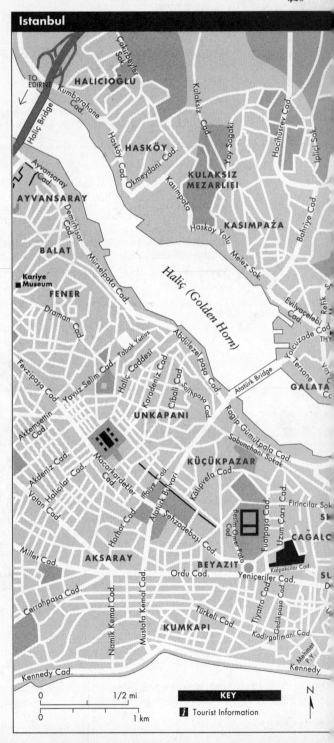

Istanbul

0   1/2 mi
0   1 km

KEY

ℹ Tourist Information

N

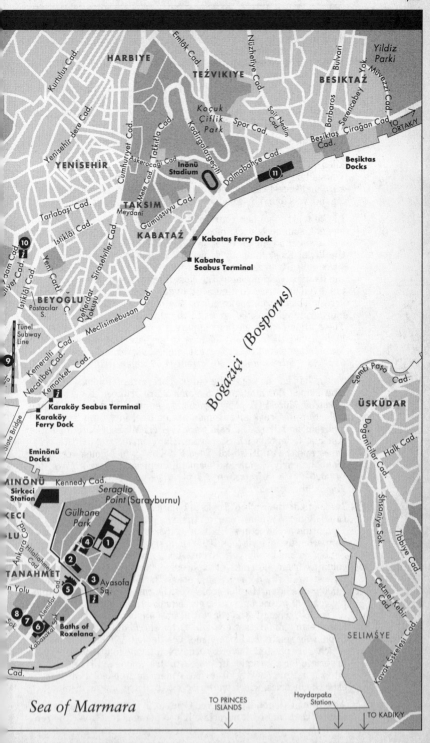

One of the most popular tours in Topkapí is the **Harem,** a maze of nearly 400 halls, terraces, rooms, wings, and apartments grouped around the sultan's private quarters on the west side of the second courtyard. Forty rooms are restored and open to the public. Next to the entrance are the quarters of the eunuchs and about 200 of the lesser concubines, who were lodged in tiny cubicles, as cramped and uncomfortable as the main rooms of the harem are large and opulent. Tours begin every half hour; because of the crowds during the height of the tourist season, buy a ticket for the harem tour soon after entering the palace.

In the third courtyard is the **Hazine Dairesi** (Treasury), four rooms filled with jewels, including two uncut emeralds, each weighing 3½ kilograms (7.7 pounds), that once hung from the ceiling. Here, too, you will be dazzled by the emerald dagger used in the movie *Topkapí* and the 84-carat "Spoonmaker" diamond, which according to legend, was found by a pauper and traded for three wooden spoons.

In the fourth and last courtyard of the Topkapí Palace are small, elegant summerhouses, mosques, fountains, and reflecting pools scattered amid the gardens on different levels. Here you will find the **Rivan Kiosk,** built by Murat IV in 1636 to commemorate the successful Rivan campaign. In another kiosk in the gardens, called the **Iftariye** (Golden Cage), the closest relatives of the reigning sultan lived in strict confinement under what amounted to house arrest. The custom began during the 1800s after the old custom of murdering all possible rivals to the throne had been abandoned. The confinement of the heirs apparently helped keep the peace, but it deprived them of any chance to prepare themselves for the formidable task of ruling a great empire. *Topkapí Palace, tel. 212/ 512–0480. Admission: $3.50, harem $1.50. Open Wed.–Mon. 9:30–5.*

To the left as you enter the outer courtyard of Topkapí Palace, a lane slopes downhill to three museums grouped together: the ➍ **Arkeoloji Müzesi** (Archaeological Museum), which houses a fine collection of Greek and Roman antiquities, including finds from Ephesus and Troy; the **Eski Şark Eserleri Müzesi** (Museum of the Ancient Orient), with Sumerian, Babylonian, and Hittite treasures; and the **Çinili Köşkü** (Tiled Pavilion), which houses ceramics from the early Seljuk and Osmanli empires. *Gülhane Park, tel. 212/520–7740. Admission: $2 includes all 3 museums. Open Tues.–Sun. 9:30–5.*

➎ Just outside the walls of Topkapí Palace is **Hagia Sophia** (Church of the Divine Wisdom), one of the world's greatest examples of Byzantine architecture. Built in AD 532 under the supervision of Emperor Justinian, it took 10,000 men six years to complete. Hagia Sophia is made of ivory from Asia, marble from Egypt, and columns from the ruins of Ephesus. The dome was the world's largest until the dome at St. Peter's Basilica was built in Rome 1,000 years later. Hagia Sophia was the cathedral of Constantinople for 900 years, surviving earthquakes and looting Crusaders until 1453, when it was converted into a mosque by Mehmet the Conqueror. Minarets were added by succeeding sultans. Hagia Sophia originally had many mosaics depicting Christian scenes, which were plastered over by Suleyman I, who felt they were inappropriate for a mosque. In 1935, Atatürk converted Hagia Sophia into a museum. Shortly after that, American archaeologists discovered the mosaics, which were restored and are now on display.

According to legend, the **Sacred Column,** in the north aisle, "weeps water" that can work miracles. It's so popular that, over the centuries, believers have worn a hole through the marble and brass column with their constant caresses. You can stick your finger in it and make a wish. *Ayasofya Meyd., Sultanahmet, tel. 212/522–1750. Admission: $4.50. Open Tues.–Sun. 9:30–4:30.*

6 Across from Hagia Sophia is the **Sultan Ahmet Cami** (Blue Mosque), with its shimmering blue tiles, 260 stained-glass windows, and six minarets, as grand and beautiful a monument to Islam as Hagia Sophia was to Christianity. Mehmet Ağa, also known as Sedefkar (Worker of Mother of Pearl) built the mosque during the reign of Sultan Ahmet I in eight years, beginning in 1609, nearly 1,100 years after the completion of Hagia Sophia. His goal was to surpass Justinian's masterpiece, and many believe he succeeded.

Press through the throngs and enter the mosque at the side entrance that faces Hagia Sophia. Remove your shoes and leave them at the entrance. Immodest clothing is not allowed, but an attendant will lend you a robe if he feels you are not dressed appropriately. *Sultanahmet Sq., no phone. Admission free. Open daily 9–5.*

The **Hünkar Kasri** (Carpet and Kilim museums) are in the mosque's stone-vaulted cellars and upstairs at the end of a stone ramp, where the sultans rested before and after their prayers. *Tel. 212/518–1330. Admission: $1.50. Call for hrs.*

7 The **Hippodrome** is a long park directly in front of the Blue Mosque. As a Roman stadium with 100,000 seats, it was once the focal point for city life, including chariot races, circuses, and public executions. Disputes between fans of rival chariot teams often degenerated into violence. In 531, 30,000 people died in the Hippodrome in what came to be known as the Nike riots. The monuments that can be seen today—the **Dikilitas** (Egyptian Obelisk), the **Örme Sütun** (Column of Constantinos), and the **Yilanli Sütun** (Serpentine Column) taken from the Temple of Apollo at Delphi in Greece—formed part of the central barrier around which the chariots raced. *Atmeydani, Sultanahmet. Admission free.*

On the western side of the Hippodrome is **Ibrahim Paşa Palace,** the grandiose residence of the son-in-law and grand vizier of Suleyman the Magnificent. Ibrahim Paşa was executed when he became too powerful for Suleyman's liking. The palace now houses the **8** **Türk Ve Islâm Eserleri Müzesi** (Museum of Turkish and Islamic Arts), which gives superb insight into the lifestyles of Turks of every level of society, from the 8th century to the present. *Şifahane Sok, across from the Blue Mosque, in line with the Serpentine Column, tel. 212/518–1385 or 212/518–1805. Admission: $2. Open Tues.–Sun. 9–4.*

New Town New Town is the area on the northern shore of the Golden Horn, the waterway that cuts through Istanbul and divides Europe from **9** Asia. The area's most prominent landmark is the **Galata Tower,** built by the Genoese in 1349 as part of their fortifications. In this century, it served as a fire lookout until 1960. Today it houses a restaurant and nightclub, and a viewing tower. *Büyük Hendek Cad., tel. 212/245–1160. Admission: $1. Open daily 9–8.*

10 North of the tower is the **Çiçek Pasaji** (Flower Arcade), off İ stiklâl Caddesi, a lively blend of tiny restaurants, bars, and street musicians. Strolling farther on İ stiklâl Caddesi is an experience in itself. The busy pedestrian road is lined with shops, restaurants, banks, and cafés in turn-of-the-century buildings. The restored original 19th-century tram still carries people from Tünel to Taksim Square. On the side streets you'll find Greek and Armenian churches, bars, and other establishments; in the narrow, poorer residential alleys, you'll see laundry hanging between the old buildings, as you dodge through the children at play.

⑪ The **Dolmabahçe Palace** was built in 1853 and, until the declaration of the modern republic in 1923, was the residence of the last sultans of the Ottoman Empire. It was also the residence of Atatürk, who died here in 1938. The palace, floodlit at night, is an extraordinary mixture of Hindu, Turkish, and European styles of architecture and interior design. Queen Victoria's contribution to the lavishness was a chandelier weighing 4½ tons. Guided tours of the palace take about 80 minutes. *Dolmabahçe Cad., tel. 212/258–5544. Admission: $10 for long tour, $5.50 for short tour. Open Tues., Wed., and Fri.–Sun. 9–4.*

Shopping The **Kapali Çarşişi** (Grand Bazaar) is what it sounds like: a smattering of all things Turkish—carpets, brass, copper, jewelry, textiles, and leather goods. A shopper's paradise, it lies about ½ km (¼ mi) northwest of the Hippodrome (*see* Exploring, *above*), a 15-minute walk or five-minute taxi ride. Also called the Covered Bazaar, this maze of 65 winding, covered streets hides 4,000 shops, tiny cafés, and restaurants. Originally built by Mehmet the Conqueror in the 1450s, it was ravaged by two modern-day fires, one in 1954 that virtually destroyed it, and a smaller one in 1974. In both cases, the bazaar was quickly rebuilt. It's filled with thousands of curios, including carpets, fabrics, clothing, brass ware, furniture, icons, and gold jewelry. *Yeniçeriler Cad. and Fuatpaşa Cad. Admission free. Open Apr.–Oct., Mon.–Sat. 8:30–7; Nov.– Mar., Mon.–Sat. 8:30–6:30.*

Tünel Square, a quick, short metro ride up from Karaköy, is a quaint group of stores with old prints, books, and artifacts.

Bargaining The best part of shopping in Turkey is visiting the *bedestans* (bazaars), all brimming with copper and brass items, hand-painted ceramics, alabaster and onyx goods, fabrics, richly colored carpets, and relics and icons trickling in from the former Soviet Union. The key word for shopping in the bazaars is "bargain." You must be willing to bargain, and bargain hard. It's great fun once you get the hang of it. As a rule of thumb, offer 50% less after you're given the initial price and be prepared to go up by about 25% to 30% of the first asking price. It's both bad manners and bad business to underbid grossly or to start bargaining if you're not serious about buying. Part of the fun of roaming through the bazaars is having a free glass of *çay* (tea), which vendors will offer you whether you're a serious shopper or just browsing. Outside the bazaars prices are usually fixed. Beware of antiques: Chances are you will end up with an expensive fake, but even if you do find the genuine article, it's illegal to export antiques of any type.

Limassol, Cyprus

The Mediterranean island of Cyprus was once a center for the cult of Aphrodite, the Greek goddess who is said to have risen naked and perfect from the sea near what is now the beach resort of Paphos. Wooded and mountainous, with a 751-km-long (466-mi-long) coastline, Cyprus lies just off the southern coast of Turkey.

Cyprus's strategic position in the eastern Mediterranean has made it subject to regular invasions by powerful armies. Greeks,

Phoenicians, Assyrians, Egyptians, Persians, Romans, Byzantines, Venetians, and British—all have ruled here and left their cultural mark.

Following independence from the British in 1960, the island became the focus of Greek-Turkish contention. Currently nearly 80% of the population are Greek Cypriots and 18% are Turkish Cypriots. Since 1974 Cyprus has been divided by a thin buffer zone—occupied by United Nations (UN) forces—between the Turkish Cypriot north and the Greek Cypriot south. The zone cuts right through the capital city of Nicosia. Talks aimed at uniting the communities into one bizonal federal state have been going on for years. The U.S. government is now involved in trying to resolve the dispute, and with the Republic of Cyprus anxious to join the European Union, governments from that organization's member countries are taking a greater interest, too.

Currency The monetary unit in the Republic of Cyprus is the Cyprus pound (C£), which is divided into 100 cents. There are notes of C£20, C£10, C£5, and C£1 and coins of 50, 20, 10, 5, 2, and 1 Cyprus cents. At press time the rate of exchange was C£0.52 to the U.S. dollar.

Telephones The country code for Cyprus is 357. Pay phones take either coins or Telecards; Telecards can be purchased at post offices, banks, souvenir shops, and kiosks. To reach an **AT&T** long-distance operator, dial 080–90010; **MCI**, 080–90000; **Sprint**, 080–90001. Public phones may require a deposit of a coin or phone card when you call these services.

Shore Excursions The following are good choices in Limassol. They may not be offered by all cruise lines. Times and prices are approximate.

Paphos Castle. A drive along the southwest of Cyprus leads to vineyards, coastal scenery, and the Paphos castle for a tour. *4½ hrs. Cost: $35.*

Kolossi Castle and Curium Ruins. Visit a Crusader castle and Cyprus's Greek and Roman ruins after a drive through the countryside. *3 hrs. Cost: $36.*

Village Tour. Journey through the country to explore three quaint villages—Omodos, Platres, and Lania. *3½ hrs. Cost: $36.*

Coming Ashore Ships dock at Limassol, a commercial port and wine-making center on the south coast. The city is a bustling, cosmopolitan town popular with tourists. Luxury hotels, apartments, and guest houses stretch along 12 km (7 mi) of seafront. The nightlife is lively. In central Limassol, the elegant modern shops of Makarios Avenue contrast with those of the old part of town, where you'll discover local handicrafts.

Shared taxis accommodate four to seven passengers and are a cheap, fast, and comfortable way of traveling. Seats must be booked by phone, and passengers may embark/disembark anywhere within the town boundaries. The taxis run every half hour; open Monday–Saturday 5:45 AM–6:30 PM. Sunday service is less frequent and rides must be booked one day ahead. Drivers are bound by law to use and display a meter. In-town journeys range from C£1.50 to about C£3.

Exploring Limassol Near the old port is **Limassol Fort,** a 14th-century castle built on the site of an earlier Byzantine fortification. According to tradition, Richard the Lionhearted married his future queen of England here in 1191. *Near old port.*

The **Cyprus Medieval Museum** at Limassol Fort displays a variety of medieval armor and relics. *Near old port, tel. 05/330132. Admission: 50¢. Open weekdays 7:30–5, Sat. 9–5, Sun. 10–1.*

For a glimpse of Cypriot folklore, visit the **Folk Art Museum** on St. Andrew's Street. The collection includes national costumes and fine examples of the island's crafts and woven materials. *St. Andrews St., tel. 05/362303. Admission: 30¢. Open Mon. and Wed.–Fri. 8:30–1:30 and 4–7 (winter 3–5:30), Tues. 8:30–1:30.*

The **Troodos Mountains,** north of Limassol, are popular in summer for their shady cedar and pine forests. Small, painted churches in the Troodos and Pitsilia foothills are rich examples of a rare indigenous art form. Asinou Church and St. Nicholas of the Roof, south of Kakopetria, are especially noteworthy. Be sure to visit the Kykko Monastery, whose prized icon of the Virgin is reputed to have been painted by St. Luke.

Curium (Kourion), west of Limassol, has numerous Greek and Roman ruins. There is an amphitheater, where actors occasionally present classical and Shakespearean drama. Next to the theater is the Villa of Eustolios, a summerhouse that belonged to a wealthy Christian. A nearby Roman stadium has been partially rebuilt. Three kilometers (2 miles) farther along the main Paphos road is the Sanctuary of Apollo Hylates (Apollo of the Woodlands), an impressive archaeological site. *Main Paphos Rd. Admission C£1. Open daily 7:30–sunset (winter 7:30–5:30).*

Other places to visit include **Kolossi Castle,** a Crusader fortress of the Knights of St. John, a 15-minute drive outside Limassol; and the fishing harbor of **Latchi** on the west coast, 32 km (20 mi) north of Paphos. Near Latchi are the **Baths of Aphrodite**, where the goddess of love is said to have seduced swains. The wild and undeveloped Akamas Peninsula is perfect for a hike.

Lisbon, Portugal

Portugal's capital presents unending treats for the eye. Its wide boulevards are bordered by black-and-white mosaic sidewalks made of tiny cobblestones called *calçada*. Modern, pastel-color apartment blocks vie for attention with art nouveau houses faced with decorative tiles. Winding, hilly streets provide scores of *miradouros*, natural vantage points that offer spectacular views of the river and the city. The city center stretches north from the spacious Praça do Comércio, one of the largest riverside squares in Europe, to the Rossío, a smaller square lined with shops and sidewalk cafés. This district, known as the Baixa (Lower Town), is one of the earliest examples of town planning on a large scale. The Alfama, the old Moorish quarter, lies just east of the Baixa, and the Bairro Alto—an 18th-century quarter of restaurants, bars, and clubs—just to the west. About 5 km (3 mi) northeast of the center, the riverside Expo site has the Lisbon Oceanarium—Europe's largest aquarium—as its major attraction.

Lisbon is a hilly city, and places that appear to be close to one another on a map are sometimes on different levels. Yet the effort is worthwhile—judicious use of trams, the funicular railway, and the majestic city-center vertical lift (also called the *elevador*) make walking tours enjoyable even on the hottest summer day.

Currency The unit of currency in Portugal is the escudo, which can be divided into 100 centavos. Escudos come in bills of 500$00, 1,000$00, 2,000$00, 5,000$00, and 10,000$00. (In Portugal the dollar sign stands between the escudo and the centavo.) Owing to the complications of dealing with millions of escudos, 1,000$00 is always called a *conto*, so 10,000$00 is referred to as 10 contos. Coins come in denominations of 1$00, 2$50, 5$00, 10$00, 20$00, 50$00, 100$00, and 200$00. At press time the exchange rate was about 184$00 to the U.S. dollar.

Telephones The country code for Portugal is 351. When dialing from outside the country, drop the initial zero from the regional area code. During the last two years or so Portugal has been updating its phone system, causing phone numbers to change throughout the country. The changes made up to press time (spring 1998) have been incorporated, but some 2% of the country's phone numbers are still slated to change. If you're trying to reach a number that has changed, your best bet is to get directory assistance through an international operator. Public telephones are easily found; older models accept coins, while PORTUGAL TELECOM card phones will accept plastic phone cards of 50 or 120 units (available at post and phone offices and most tobacconists and newsagents). International and collect calls can be made from most public telephones as well as from main post offices, which almost always have a supply of phone cabins—you'll be assigned a booth and payment will be collected at the end of the call. Access numbers to reach American long-distance operators are: for **AT&T,** 050–171288; **MCI,** 050–171234; **Sprint,** 050–171877.

Shore Excursions The following are good choices in Lisbon. They may not be offered by all cruise lines. Times and prices are approximate.

Lisbon Highlights. If you'd rather not do a lot of walking, sign up for this tour of Lisbon's many moods. *4 hrs. Cost: $40.*

Walking the City. Tour the Alfama district on foot, visiting St. George's Castle, Santa Justa Elevator, Rossio Square, and Black Horse Square. *3 hrs. Cost: $43.*

Coming Ashore Ships dock at the Fluvial terminal, adjacent to Praça do Comércio. Lisbon is a hilly city, and the sidewalks are paved with cobblestones, so walking can be tiring, even when you're wearing comfortable shoes.

Lisbon's sidewalks are paved with cobblestones, and there are many steep inclines, so walking can be tiring, even when you're wearing comfortable shoes. Luckily, Lisbon's tram service is one of the best in Europe and buses go all over the city. A Tourist Pass for unlimited rides on the tram, bus, metro, or the *elevador* (funicular railway system) costs 430$00 for one day's travel. Cabs can be easily recognized by a lighted sign on green roofs. There are taxi stands in the main squares, and you can usually catch one cruising by, though this can be difficult late at night. Taxis are metered and take up to four passengers at no extra charge. Rates start at 300$00.

Numbers in the margin correspond to points of interest on the Lisbon map.

Exploring Lisbon The Moors, who imposed their rule on most of the southern Iberian Peninsula during the 8th century, left their mark on Lisbon in many ways. The most visible examples are undoubtedly the imposing **Castelo de São Jorge** (St. George's Castle), set on one of the city's highest hills, and the Alfama, a district of narrow, twisting streets that wind their way up toward the castle. The best way to tour this area of Lisbon is to take a taxi to the castle and walk down.

Although the Castelo de São Jorge is Moorish in construction, it stands on the site of a fortification used by the Visigoths in the 5th century. The castle walls enclose the ruins of a Muslim palace that was the residence of the kings of Portugal until the 16th century; there is also a small village with a surviving church, a few simple houses, and souvenir shops. Inside the main gate are terraces offering panoramic views of Lisbon; be wary of slippery footing. *No phone. Admission free. Open Apr.–Sept., daily 9–9; Oct.–Mar., daily 9–7.*

② **Alfama,** a warren of streets below St. George's Castle, is a jumble of whitewashed houses, with their flower-laden balconies and red-tile roofs resting on a foundation of dense bedrock. It's a notorious place for getting lost, but it's relatively compact, and you'll keep coming upon the same main squares and streets.

③ The **Museu de Artes Decorativas** (Museum of Decorative Arts) is housed in an 18th-century mansion. More than 20 workshops teach rare handicrafts—bookbinding, ormolu, carving, and cabinetmaking. *Largo das Portas do Sol 2, tel. 01/886–2183. Admission: 500$00. Open Tues.–Sun. 10–5.*

④ The **Sé** (cathedral), founded in 1150 to commemorate the defeat of the Moors three years earlier, has an austere Romanesque interior enlivened by a splendid 13th-century cloister. *Largo da Sé, tel. 01/886–6752. Admission to cathedral free, cloister 100$00, sacristy 300$00. Open daily 9–noon and 2–6.*

⑤ **Rossío** (officially, Praça Dom Pedro IV), Lisbon's principal square, which in turn opens on its northwestern end into the Praça dos Restauradores, can be considered the beginning of modern Lisbon. Here the broad, tree-lined Avenida da Liberdade begins its northwesterly ascent, and ends just over 1½ km (1 mi) away at the green expanses of the Parque Eduardo VII.

⑥ In the **Parque Eduardo VII,** rare flowers, trees, and shrubs thrive in the *estufa fria* (cold greenhouse) and the *estufa quente* (hot greenhouse). *Parque Eduardo VII, tel. 01/388–2278. Admission to greenhouses: 75$00. Open Apr.–Sept., daily 9–6; Oct.–Mar., daily 9–5.*

⑦ The renowned **Fundação Calouste Gulbenkian** (Calouste Gulbenkian Foundation) is a cultural trust whose museum houses treasures collected by Armenian oil magnate Calouste Gulbenkian (1869–1955) and donated to the people of Portugal. There are superb examples of Greek and Roman coins, Persian carpets, Chinese porcelain, and paintings by such old masters as Rembrandt and Rubens, as well as impressionist and Pre-Raphaelite works. *Av. de Berna 45, tel. 01/795–0236. Admission: 200$00, free Sun. Open June–Sept., Tues., Thurs., Fri., and Sun. 10–5, Wed. and Sat. 2–7:30; Oct.–May, Tues.–Sun. 10–5.*

⑧ In the cozy, clublike lounge at the **Instituto do Vinho do Porto** (Port Wine Institute), visitors can sample from more than 300 types and vintages of Portugal's most famous beverage—from the extra-dry white varieties to the older ruby-red vintages. *Rua S. Pedro de Alcântara 45, tel. 01/342–3307. Admission free. Prices of tastings vary, starting at 200$00. Open Mon.–Sat. 10–10.*

⑨ The highly decorative **Igreja de São Roque** (Church of St. Roque) is best known for the flamboyant 18th-century Capela de São João Baptista (Chapel of St. John the Baptist), but it is nonetheless a showpiece in its own right. Adjoining the church is the Museu de Arte Sacra (Museum of Sacred Art). *Largo Trinidade Coelho, tel.*

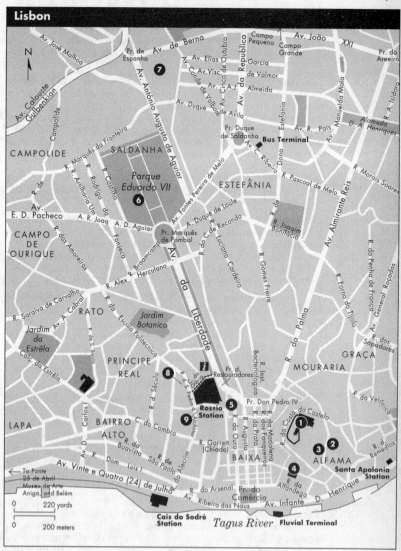

Lisbon

Alfama, **2**
Castelo de São
 Jorge, **1**
Fundação Calouste
Gulbenkian , **7**
Igreja de São
Roque, **9**
Instituto do Vinho do
Porto, **8**

Museu de Artes
Decorativas, **3**
Parque
Eduardo VII, **6**
Rossío, **5**
Sé, **4**

01/346–0361. Admission free. Church open daily 8:30–5; museum Tues.–Sun. 10–1 and 2–5.

To see the best examples of that uniquely Portuguese, late-Gothic architecture known as Manueline, head for **Belém**, at the far southwestern edge of Lisbon.

The **Mosteiro dos Jerónimos** (Jerónimos Monastery), in the Praça do Império, is an impressive structure conceived and planned by King Manuel I at the beginning of the 16th century to honor the discoveries of Vasco da Gama. Construction began in 1502 and was largely financed by treasures brought back from the so-called *descobrimentos*—the "discoveries" made by the Portuguese in Africa, Asia, and South America. Don't miss the stunning double cloister with its arches and pillars heavily sculpted with marine motifs. *Praça do Império, tel. 01/362–0034. Admission to church free, cloisters: 400$00, free Sun. Open June–Sept., Tues.–Sun. 10–6:30; Oct.–May, Tues.–Sun. 10–1 and 2:30–5.*

The **Museu de Marinha** (Maritime Museum) is at the west end of the Mosteiro dos Jerónimos monastery. Its huge collection reflects Portugal's long seafaring tradition, and exhibits range from early maps, model ships, and navigational instruments to entire fishing boats and royal barges. *Praça do Império, tel. 01/362–0010. Admission: 250$00, free Sun. 10–1. Open Tues.–Sun. 10–6.*

The **Torre de Belém** (Belém Tower) is another fine example of Manueline architecture, with openwork balconies, loggia, and domed turrets. Although it was built in the early 16th century on an island in the middle of the River Tagus, today the tower stands near the north bank—the river's course has changed over the centuries. *Av. de India, tel. 01/301–6892. Admission: 400$00 June–Sept., 250$00 Oct.–May. Open June–Sept., Tues.–Sun. 10–6:30; Oct.–May, Tues.–Sun. 10–1 and 2:30–5.*

The centerpiece of Expo '98 was the phenomenal Oceans Pavilion, renamed **Oceanário de Lisboa** (Lisbon Oceanarium) after the event. This stunning glass-and-stone structure is the largest aquarium in Europe. It contains 25,000 fish, seabirds, and mammals, and is the first aquarium to incorporate selected world ocean habitats (North Atlantic, Pacific, Antarctic, and Indian Ocean) within one complex. *Service details were unavailable at the time of writing; contact the tourist office for current details.*

Shopping The **Baixa** (Rua Augusta between the Rossío and the River Tagus), one of Lisbon's main shopping and banking districts, features a small crafts market, some of the best shoe shops in Europe, glittering jewelry stores, and a host of delicatessens selling anything from game birds to *queijo da serra*—a delicious mountain cheese from the Serra da Estrela range north of Lisbon.

Downtown restoration is best exemplified by the beautifully renovated **Eden** building (Av. da Liberdade), an Art Deco triumph containing a Virgin Megastore and a small shopping center.

The *Feira da Ladra* (flea market) is held on Tuesday morning and all day Saturday in the Largo de Santa Clara behind the Church of São Vicente, near the Alfama district.

London/Southampton, England

Southampton—a traditional terminal port for transatlantic crossings and the starting point for many historic voyages, including that of the *Mayflower*—is the port for ships calling at London, a city with a vibrant artistic, cultural, and commercial life. Modern London began to evolve in the Middle Ages, more than 600 years ago, and still standing is much of the work of Christopher Wren, the master architect chiefly responsible for reconstruction after the disastrous Great Fire of 1666. Traditionally London has been divided between the City, to the east, where its banking and commercial interests lie, and Westminster to the west, the seat of the royal court and of government. Today the distinction between the two holds good, and even the briefest exploration will reveal each area's distinct atmosphere. It is also in these two areas that you will find most of the grand buildings that have played a central role in British history: the Tower of London and St. Paul's Cathedral, Westminster Abbey and the Houses of Parliament, Buckingham Palace, and the older royal palace of St. James's.

Currency   The British unit of currency is the pound sterling, divided into 100 pence (p). Bills are issued in denominations of 5, 10, 20, and 50 pounds (£). Coins are £1, £2, 50p, 20p, 10p, 5p, 2p, and 1p. At press time,, exchange rates were approximately U.S.$1.65 to the pound.

Telephones   The United Kingdom's country code is 44. If calling the United Kingdom from abroad, drop the initial zero from the area code. Phone booths are not hard to find; other than on the street, the best place to find a bank of pay phones is in a hotel or large post office. The workings of coin-operated telephones vary, but there are usually instructions in each unit. Most take 10p, 20p, 50p, and £1 coins. Phonecards are also available; they can be bought in a number of retail outlets. Cardphones, which are clearly marked with a special green insignia, will not accept coins. The cheapest way to make an overseas call is to dial it yourself—but be sure to have plenty of coins or phone cards close at hand. After you have inserted the coins or card, dial 010 (the international code), then the country code—for the United States, it is 1—followed by the area code and local number. To reach an **AT&T** long-distance operator, dial 0500890011; **MCI,** 0800890222; for **Sprint,** 0800890877 (from a British Telecom phone) or 0500890877 (from a Mercury Communications phone). To make a collect or other operator-assisted call, dial 155.

Shore Excursions   Most cruise lines use Southampton as an embarkation or disembarkation point. Your best bet is to add a few days to your cruise to visit London. You can either arrange your own package or book a line's pre- or post-cruise package.

The following is a good choice should you want to tour sights near Southampton. It may not be offered by all cruise lines. Time and price are approximate.

Salisbury and Stonehenge. An hour from Southampton lies Salisbury Cathedral, which was built in AD 1220. After a walk through town and lunch, continue to Stonehenge. *Full day. Cost: $90.*

Coming Ashore   Ships dock at the Southampton terminal. Southampton's attractions are a short drive from the pier; London is about an hour and a half from Southampton by bus. Places such as Winchester, Stonehenge, Salisbury, and Bath are not far from Southampton.

London, although not simple of layout, is a rewarding walking city, and this remains the best way to get to know its nooks and crannies. If you want, you can take "the tube," London's extensive Underground system, which is by far the most widely used form of city transportation. Trains run both beneath and above the ground out into the suburbs, and all stations are clearly marked with the London Underground circular symbol. (A SUBWAY sign refers to an under-the-street crossing.)

There are 10 basic lines—all named. The Central, District, Northern, Metropolitan, and Piccadilly lines all have branches, usually taking you to the outlying sections of the city, so be sure to note which branch is needed for your particular destination. Begun in the Victorian era, the Underground is still being expanded and improved. The East London line, which runs from Shoreditch and Whitechapel south to New Cross, is due to reopen after major reconstruction in 1998. September 1998 is the latest date for the opening of the Jubilee line extension: This state-of-the-art subway will sweep from Green Park to Southwark, with connections to Canary Wharf and the Docklands and the much hyped Milennium Experience megadome, and on to the east at Stratford. A pocket map of the entire tube network is available free from most Underground ticket counters. One-day Travelcards are a good buy. These allow unrestricted travel on the tube, most buses, and British Rail trains in the Greater London zones and are valid weekdays after 9:30 AM, weekends, and all public holidays. The price is £3.50–£4.30

London's black taxis are famous for their comfort and for the ability of their drivers to remember the mazelike pattern of the capital's streets. Hotels and main tourist areas have ranks (stands) where you wait your turn to take one of the taxis that drive up. You can also hail a taxi if the flag is up or the yellow FOR HIRE sign is lighted. Fares start at £1.40; surcharges of 40p–60p are a tricky addition, used for extra passengers, bulky luggage, and the like. Note that fares are usually raised in April of each year. As for tipping, taxi drivers should get 10%–15% of the tab.

Exploring London *Numbers in the margin correspond to points of interest on the London map.*

Westminster is the royal backyard—the traditional center of the royal court and of government. Here, within a kilometer or so of one another, are virtually all of London's most celebrated buildings (St. Paul's Cathedral and the Tower of London excepted). Generations of kings and queens and their offspring have lived here since the end of the 11th century—including the current monarch. The queen resides at Buckingham Palace through most of the year; during summer periods when she visits her country estates, the palace is partially open to visitors.

❶ Trafalgar Square dates from about 1830. In short, it is London's most famous and festive square—permanently alive with people, Londoners and tourists alike, roaring traffic, and pigeons, it remains London's "living room." Great events, such as New Years, royal weddings, elections, and sporting triumphs, always see the crowds gathering. A statue of Lord Nelson, victor over the French in 1805 at the Battle of Trafalgar, at which he lost his life, stands atop a column. Huge stone lions guard the base of the column, which is decorated with four bronze panels depicting naval battles against France and cast from French cannons captured by Nelson. The bronze equestrian statue on the south side of the square is of the unhappy Charles I; he is looking down Whitehall toward the spot where he was executed in 1649.

❷ The **National Gallery** is generally ranked right after the Louvre as one of the world's greatest museums. Occupying the long neoclassical building on the north side of Trafalgar Square, it contains works by virtually every famous artist and school from the 14th to the 19th century. Its galleries overflow with masterpieces, including Jan van Eyck's *Arnolfini Marriage,* Leonardo da Vinci's *Burlington Virgin and Child,* Velásquez's *The Toilet of Venus* (known as "The Rokeby Venus"), and Constable's *Hay Wain.* The gallery is especially strong on Flemish and Dutch masters, Rubens and Rembrandt among them, and on Italian Renaissance works. The Sainsbury Wing houses the early Renaissance collection. *Trafalgar Sq., tel. 0171/839–3321; 0171/839–3526 recorded information. Admission free; charge for special exhibitions. Open Mon.–Sat. 10–6, Sun. 2–6; June–Aug., also Wed. until 8.*

❸ At the foot of Charing Cross Road is a second major art collection, the **National Portrait Gallery,** which contains portraits of well-known (and not so well-known) Britons, including monarchs, statesmen, and writers. *2 St. Martin's Pl., at foot of Charing Cross Rd., tel. 0171/306–0055. Admission free. Open weekdays 10–5, Sat. 10–6, Sun. 2–6.*

❹ **Buckingham Palace** is the London home of the queen and the administrative hub of the entire royal family. When the queen is in residence (normally on weekdays except in Jan., Aug., Sept., and part of June), the royal standard flies over the east front. Inside there are dozens of splendid state rooms used on such formal occasions as banquets for visiting heads of state. The private apartments of Queen Elizabeth and Prince Philip are in the north wing. Behind the palace lie some 40 acres of private gardens, a wildlife haven. The ceremony of the Changing of the Guard takes place in front of the palace at 11:30 daily, April through July, and on alternate days during the rest of the year. It's advisable to arrive early, since people are invariably stacked several deep along the railings, whatever the weather. Parts of Buckingham Palace are open to the public during August and September; the former chapel, bombed during World War II, rebuilt in 1961, and now the Queen's Gallery, shows paintings from the vast royal art collections. *Buckingham Palace Rd., tel. 0171/839–1377. Admission: £9. Open early Aug.–early Oct. (confirm specific dates, which are subject to the queen's mandate), daily 9:30–4. Queen's Gallery, tel. 0171/799– 2331. Admission: £3. Open Tues.–Sat. and bank holidays 10–5, Sun. 2–5.*

❺ **Parliament Square** is flanked, on the river side, by the Palace of Westminster. Among the statues of statesmen long since dead are those of Churchill, Abraham Lincoln, and Oliver Cromwell, the Lord Protector of England during the country's brief attempt at being a republic (1648–60).

❻ **Westminster Abbey** is the most ancient of London's great churches and the most important, for it is here that Britain's monarchs are crowned. The main nave is packed with atmosphere and memories, as it has witnessed many splendid coronation ceremonies, royal weddings, and more recently, the funeral of Diana, Princess of Wales. The abbey dates largely from the 13th and 14th centuries, although Henry VII's Chapel, an exquisite example of the heavily decorated late-Gothic style, was not built until the early 1600s, and the twin towers over the west entrance are an 18th-century addition. There is much to see inside, including the touching tomb of the Unknown Warrior, a nameless World War I soldier buried, in memory of the war's victims, in earth brought with his corpse from France; and the famous Poets' Corner, where England's great writers—Milton, Chaucer, Shakespeare, et al— are memorialized, and some are actually buried. Behind the high altar are the royal tombs, including those of Queen Elizabeth I;

London

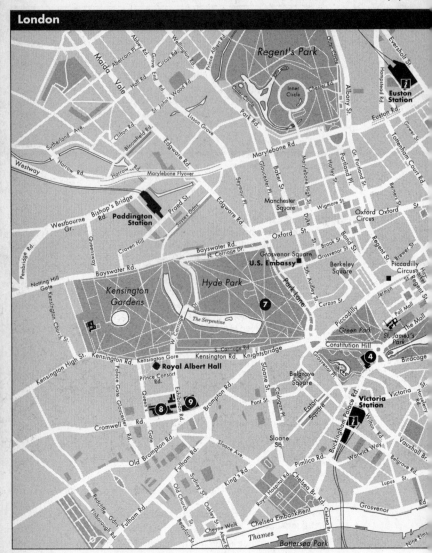

British Museum, **10**

Buckingham
Palace, **4**

Hyde Park, **7**

National Gallery, **2**

National Portrait
Gallery, **3**

Natural History
Museum, **8**

Parliament
Square, **5**

St. Paul's
Cathedral, **12**

Shakespeare's
Globe, **13**

Sir John Soane's
Museum, **11**

Tower of London, **14**

Trafalgar Square, **1**

Victoria and Albert
Museum, **9**

Westminster
Abbey, **6**

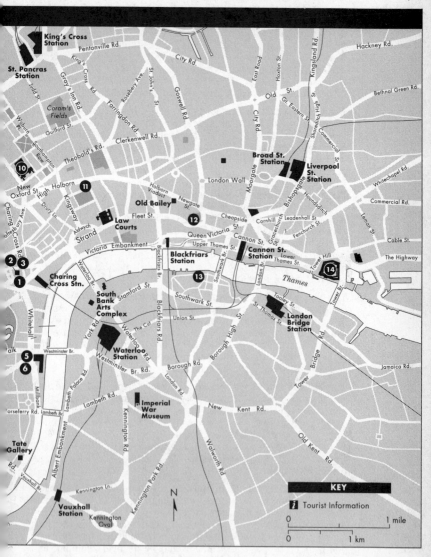

Mary, Queen of Scots; and Henry V. In the Chapel of Edward the Confessor stands the Coronation Chair. Among the royal weddings that have taken place here are those of the present queen and most recently, in 1986, the (ill-starred) duke and duchess of York. The abbey tends to be packed with crowds, so try to come early in the morning. *Broad Sanctuary, tel. 0171/222–5152. Admission £5. Open Mon., Tues., Thurs., and Fri. 9–4; Wed. 9– 7:45; Sat. 9–2 and 3:45–5; Sun. all day for services only.*

❼ Hyde Park, which covers about 340 acres, was originally a royal hunting ground. The sandy track along the south side of the park, is **Rotten Row.** It was Henry VIII's royal path to the hunt—hence the name, a corruption of *route du roi.* It's still used by the Household Cavalry, the queen's guard. You can see them leave, in full regalia, plumed helmets and all, at around 10:30, or await the return of the exhausted ex-guard about noon. The neighboring **Kensington Gardens** are a little more formal than Hyde Park. First laid out as palace grounds, they adjoin Kensington Palace. There is boating and swimming in the Kensington's Serpentine, an S-shape lake formed by damming a stream that used to flow here. Refreshments are served at the lakeside tearooms, and the Serpentine Gallery (tel. 0171/402–6075) holds noteworthy exhibitions of modern art. *Bounded by the Ring, Bayswater Rd., Park Lane, and Knightsbridge.*

❽ The **Natural History Museum** is housed in an ornate late-Victorian building with striking modern additions. As in the Science Museum, its displays on topics such as human biology and evolution are designed to challenge visitors to think for themselves. *Cromwell Rd., tel. 0171/938–9123, or 0142/692–7654 (recorded information). Admission: £6; free weekdays 4:30–5:50 and weekends 5–5:50. Open Mon.–Sat. 10–6, Sun. 2:30–6.*

❾ The **Victoria and Albert Museum** (or V&A) originated in the 19th century as a museum of decorative art. It has extensive collections of costumes, paintings, jewelry, and crafts from every part of the globe; don't miss the sculpture court, the vintage couture collections, and the great Raphael Room. *Cromwell Rd., tel. 0171/938– 8500 or 0171/938–8441 (recorded information). Admission: £5; free after 4:30, except Wed. Open Mon. noon–5:50, Tues., Thurs.– Sun. 10–5:50.; Wed. 10–9:30*

❿ The **British Museum** ("Mankind's attic") houses a vast and priceless collection of treasures, including Egyptian, Greek, and Roman antiquities; Renaissance jewelry; pottery; coins; glass; and drawings from virtually every European school since the 15th century. It's best to pick out one section that particularly interests you—to try to see everything would be an overwhelming and exhausting task. Some of the highlights are the Elgin Marbles, sculptures that formerly decorated the Parthenon in Athens; the Rosetta stone, which helped archaeologists interpret Egyptian script; and a copy of the Magna Carta, the charter signed by King John in 1215 to which is ascribed the origins of English liberty. *Great Russell St., tel. 0171/636–1555 or 0171/580–1788 (recorded information). Admission free. Open Mon.–Sat. 10–5, Sun. 2:30–6.*

⓫ **Sir John Soane's Museum,** on the border of London's legal district, is stuffed with antique busts and myriad decorative delights—it's an eccentric, smile-inducing 19th-century collection of art and artifacts in the former home of the architect of the Bank of England. *13 Lincoln's Inn Fields, tel. 0171/405–2107. Admission free. Open Tues.–Sat. 10–5.*

The City, the traditional commercial center of London, is the most ancient part of the capital, having been the site of the great Roman city of Londinium. Since those days, the City has been built and rebuilt several times and today, ancient and modern jostle each other elbow to elbow. The wooden buildings of the medieval City were destroyed in the Great Fire of 1666. There were further waves of reconstruction in the 19th century, and then again after World War II to repair the devastation wrought by air attacks. Modern developers in the 1980s contributed almost as much blight as the Blitz with the construction of ugly modern glass skyscrapers. Still, several of London's most famous attractions are here, along with the adjacent South Bank area, where Shakespeare's Globe has the starring role. Throughout all these changes, the City has retained its unique identity and character. The lord mayor and Corporation of London are still responsible for the government of the City, as they have been for many centuries. Commerce remains the lifeblood of the City, which is a world financial center rivaled only by New York, Tokyo, and Zurich. The biggest change has been in the City's population. Until the first half of the 19th century, many of the merchants and traders who worked in the City lived there, too. Today, despite its huge daytime population, scarcely 8,000 people live in the 677 acres of the City. Try, therefore, to explore the City on a weekday morning or afternoon. On weekends its streets are deserted, and many of the shops and restaurants, and even some of the churches, are closed.

⑫ **St. Paul's Cathedral** is London's symbolic heart. Its dome—the world's third largest—can be seen from many an angle in other parts of the city. Following the Great Fire, it was rebuilt by Sir Christopher Wren, the architect who was also responsible for designing 50 City parish churches to replace those lost in the disaster. St. Paul's is Wren's greatest work; fittingly, he is buried in the crypt under a simple Latin epitaph, composed by his son, which translates as: "Reader, if you seek his monument, look around you."

The greatest architectural glory of the cathedral is the dome. This consists of three distinct elements: an outer, timber-frame dome covered with lead; an interior dome built of brick and decorated with frescoes of the life of St. Paul by the 18th-century artist Sir James Thornhill; and, in between, a brick cone that supports and strengthens both. There is a good view of the church from the Whispering Gallery, high up in the inner dome. The gallery is so called because of its remarkable acoustics, whereby words spoken on one side can be clearly heard on the other, 107 ft away. *St. Paul's Churchyard, Paternoster Sq., tel. 0171/236–4128. Admission to cathedral free; ambulatory (American Chapel), crypt, and treasury: £4; galleries: £3.50; combined ticket: £6. Cathedral open for visits Mon.–Sat. 8:30–4:30; ambulatory, crypt, and galleries open Mon.–Sat. 9:30–4:15.*

⑬ The spectacular **Shakespeare's Globe** theater is a replica of Shakespeare's open-roofed Globe Playhouse (built in 1599; incinerated in 1613), where most of the playwright's great plays premiered. It stands 200 yards from the original site, overlooking the Thames. Built with authentic Elizabethan materials, down to the first thatched roof in London since the Great Fire, the theater stages its works in natural light (and sometimes rain), to 1,000 people on wooden benches in the "bays," plus 500 "groundlings," standing on a carpet of filbert shells and clinker, just as they did nearly four centuries ago. The theater season is only from June through September; throughout the year, you can tour the Globe through admission to the museum devoted to Shakespeare and his times on the premises. *New Globe Walk, Bankside (South Bank), tel. 0171/928–6406. Admission £5 for museum. Open daily 10–5. Call for performance schedule.*

⑭ The **Tower of London** is one of London's most famous sights and one of its most crowded, too. Come as early in the day as possible and head for the Crown Jewels, so you can see them before the crowds arrive. They are a breathtakingly splendid collection of regalia, precious stones, gold, and silver; the Royal Scepter contains the largest cut diamond in the world. The tower served the monarchs of medieval England as both fortress and palace.

Every British sovereign from William the Conqueror in the 11th century to Henry VIII in the 16th lived here, and it remains a royal palace, in name at least. The History Gallery is a walk-through display designed to answer questions about the inhabitants of the tower and its evolution over the centuries. Among other buildings worth seeing is the Bloody Tower. The little princes in the tower—the boy-king Edward V and his brother Richard, duke of York, supposedly murdered on the orders of the duke of Gloucester, later crowned Richard III—certainly lived in the Bloody Tower, and may well have died here, too. Look for the ravens whose presence at the tower is traditional. It is said that if they leave, the tower will fall and England will lose her greatness. *Tower Hill, tel. 0171/709–0765. Admission: £8.50. Open Mar.–Oct., Mon.–Sat. 9:30–6:30, Sun. 2–6; Nov.–Feb., Mon.–Sat. 9:30–5. Yeoman Warder guides conduct tours daily from Middle Tower, no charge, but tips are generally given. Subject to weather and availability of guides, tours are conducted about every 30 mins until 3:30 in summer, 2:30 in winter.*

Shopping Shopping is one of London's great pleasures. Different areas retain their traditional specialties. **Chelsea** centers on the King's Road; once synonymous with ultrafashion, it still harbors some designer boutiques, plus antiques and home-furnishings stores. **Covent Garden** is a something-for-everyone neighborhood, with clothing chain stores and top designers, stalls selling crafts, and shops selling gifts of every type—bikes, kites, herbs, beads, hats, you name it.

Regent Street has one of London's most pleasant department store, Liberty's, as well as Hamley's, the capital's toy mecca. In **St. James's** the English gentleman buys the rest of his gear: handmade hats, shirts, and shoes, silver shaving kits, and hip flasks. Here is also the world's best cheese shop, Paxton & Whitfield. Nothing in this neighborhood is cheap, in any sense.

Kensington's main drag, **Kensington High Street,** is lined with small, classy boutiques, with some larger stores at the eastern end. Neighboring **Knightsbridge** has Harrods, of course, but also Harvey Nichols, the top clothes stop, and many expensive designers' boutiques along Sloane Street, Walton Street, and Beauchamp Place.

Piccadilly is a busy street lined with some grand and very English shops (including Hatchards, the booksellers; Swaine, Adeney Brigg, the equestrian outfitters; and Fortnum and Mason, the department store that supplies the queen's groceries). **Jermyn Street,** south of Piccadilly, is famous for upscale shops that sell accessories for the gentleman's wardrobe, from handmade shoes to bespoke hats (his suits come from nearby Savile Row). Shops along **Duke Street** and **Bury Street** specialize in paintings, the former in old masters, the latter in early English watercolors. Don't be put off by the exclusive appearance of these establishments—anyone is free to enter, and there is no obligation to buy.

There are three special shopping streets in Mayfair, each with its own specialties. **Savile Row** is the home of gentlemen's tailors. Nearby **Cork Street** has many dealers in modern and classical art. **Bond Street** (divided into two parts, Old and New, though both are some 300 years old) is the classiest shopping street in London, the home of haute couture, with such famous names as Gucci, Hermès, and Chanel, and costly jewelry from such shops as Asprey, Tiffany, and Cartier.

North of Kensington Gardens is the lively **Notting Hill** district, where the lively Portobello Road antiques and bric-a-brac market is held each Saturday (arrive early in the morning for the best bargains). The street is also full of regular antiques shops that are open most weekdays.

Napoli Coast, Italy

Campania (the region of Naples, the Amalfi coast, and other sights) is where most people's preconceived ideas of Italy become a reality. You'll find lots of sun, good food that relies heavily on tomatoes and mozzarella, acres of classical ruins, and gorgeous scenery.

Currency The unit of currency in Italy is the lira (plural, lire). There are bills of 1,000, 2,000, 5,000, 10,000, 50,000, 100,000, and 500,000 lire (this largest bill being almost impossible to change, except in banks); coins are worth 50, 100, 200, and 500 lire. In 1999 the euro will begin to be used as a banking currency, but the lire will still be the currency in use on a day-to-day basis. At press time the exchange rate was about 1,770 to the U.S. dollar. When your purchases run into hundreds of thousands of lire, beware of being shortchanged, a dodge that is practiced at ticket windows and cashiers' desks, as well as in shops and even banks. Always count your change before you leave the counter.

Telephones The country code for Italy is 39. Most local calls cost 200 lire for two minutes. Pay phones take either 100-, 200-, or 500-lire coins or *schede telefoniche* (phone cards), purchased in bars, tobacconists, post offices, and TELECOM offices in either 5,000-, 10,000-, or 15,000-lire denominations. To place international calls, many travelers go to the Telefoni telephone exchange, where the operator assigns you a booth, can help place your call, and will collect payment when you have finished. Telefoni exchanges (usually marked TELECOM) are found in all cities. To dial an international call, insert a phone card, dial 00, then the country code, area code, and phone number. For **AT&T USADirect**, dial access number tel. 172–1011; for **MCI Call USA**, access number tel. 172–1022; for **Sprint Express**, access number tel. 172–1877. You will be connected directly with an operator in the United States.

Shore Excursions The following are good choices on the Napoli Coast. They may not be offered by all cruise lines. Times and prices are approximate.

In Naples **Pompeii.** It's a 45-minute motor-coach ride to the ruins at Pompeii, a place where time has stood still since AD 79 when Mount Vesuvius erupted. *4 hrs. Cost: $49.*

Heraculaneum and Naples. The well-preserved ruins at Heraklion and downtown Naples are the focus of this two-town tour. *3½ hrs. Cost: $49.*

In Sorrento **Excavations at Pompeii.** Here's another chance to see the ruins at Pompeii. *4½ hrs. Cost: $50.*

In Capri Capri is a place to wander, not tour. Cruise lines will arrange round-trip tickets on the public jetfoil for passengers wishing to visit Capri.

In Amalfi Cruise lines often offer excursions featuring the Amalfi coast, from Naples or Sorrento. You can also arrange to hire a car, often through the ship's tour desk.

Coming Ships calling on the Napoli Coast generally drop anchor offshore.
Ashore Nearby towns are easily reached from the major ports of call.

In Naples Ships calling at Naples tender passengers ashore from Naples Bay. You'll probably do a lot of walking in Naples, since the buses are crowded and taxis get stalled in traffic. Keep a firm grip on your pocketbook and camera.

In Sorrento Ships calling at Sorrento tender passengers to shore from the town's harbor. Sorrento is best explored on foot, since motor coaches must remain in designated areas.

In Capri The trip on the public jetfoil to Capri is about a 20-minute ride from Sorrento or about a 40-minute ride from Naples. A cog railway or bus service takes you up to the town of Capri from the marina.

In Amalfi Amalfi is within driving distance of Naples or Sorrento. Once in town, you will want to wander around on foot.

Exploring the The 17th-century **Palazzo Reale** (Royal Palace), built during the
Napoli Coast rule of the Bourbons, is still furnished in the lavish baroque style
Naples that suited the Bourbons so well. *Piazza del Plebiscito, tel. 081/ 580–8111. Admission: 8,000 lire. Open Apr.–Oct., Tues.–Sun. 9– 7:30; Nov.–Mar., Sun.–Tues. 9–1:30, Thurs.–Sat. 9–6.*

Also known as the Maschio Angioino, the massive stone **Castel Nuovo** was built by the city's Aragon rulers in the 13th century; inside, the city's **Museo Civico** comprises mainly local artworks from the 15th to the 19th centuries, and there are also regular exhibitions. The windows offer views over the piazza and the port below. *Castel Nuovo, Piazza Municipio. Admission: 10,000 lire. Open Mon.–Sat. 9–7, Sun. 9–1.*

A favorite Neapolitan song celebrates the quiet beauty of the church of **Santa Chiara,** which was built in the early 1300s in Provençal Gothic style. Directly across is the oddly faceted stone facade and elaborate baroque interior of the church of the **Gesù** (Via Benedetto Croce). *Piazza Gesù Nuovo. Admission free. Open daily 7–noon and 4–7 (until 6 in winter).*

The museum in the **Certosa di San Martino,** a Carthusian monastery restored in the 17th century, contains an eclectic collection of Neapolitan landscape paintings, royal carriages, and *presepi* (Christmas crèches). Check out the view from the balcony off Room 25. *Certosa di San Martino, tel. 081/578–1769. Admission: 8,000 lire. Open Tues.–Sun. 9–2.*

The **Museo Archeologico Nazionale** (National Archaeological Museum) is dusty, unkempt, and undergoes perpetual renovations, but it holds one of the world's great collections of antiquities.

Greek and Roman sculptures, vividly colored mosaics, countless objects from Pompeii and Herculaneum, and an equestrian statue of the Roman emperor Nerva are all worth seeing. *Piazza Museo, tel. 081/440166. Admission: 12,000 lire. Open Aug.–Sept., Mon.–Sat. 9–7, Sun. 9–1; Oct.–July, Wed.–Mon. 9–2.*

The **Museo di Capodimonte,** housed in an 18th-century palace built by Bourbon king Charles III, is surrounded by a vast park that affords sweeping view of the bay. The picture gallery is devoted to work from the 13th to the 18th centuries, including many familiar masterpieces by Dutch and Spanish masters, as well as by the great Italians. Other rooms contain an extensive collection of porcelain and majolica from the various royal residences, some produced in the Bourbons' own factory right here on the grounds. *Parco di Capodimonte, tel. 081/744–1307. Admission: 8,000 lire. Open Tues.–Sat 10–7, Sun. 10–2.*

Near Naples is **Pompeii,** where an estimated 2,000 residents were entombed on that fateful August day when Mt. Vesuvius erupted in AD 79. The ancient city of Pompeii was much larger than nearby Herculaneum, and excavations have progressed to a much greater extent (though the remains are not as well preserved, owing to some 18th-century scavenging for museum-quality artwork, most of which you are able to see at Naples's Museo Archeologico Nazionale; *see above*). This prosperous Roman city had an extensive forum, lavish baths and temples, and patrician villas richly decorated with frescoes. It's worth buying a detailed guide of the site to give meaning and understanding to the ruins and their importance. Be sure to see the Villa dei Misteri, whose frescoes are in mint condition. Perhaps that is a slight exaggeration, but the paintings are so rich with detail and depth:of color that one finds it difficult to believe that they are more than 1,900 years old. Have lots of small change handy to tip the guards at the more important houses so they will unlock the gates for you. *Pompeii Scavi, tel. 081/861–0744. Admission: 12,000 lire. Open daily 9–1 hr before sunset (ticket office closes 2 hrs before sunset).*

Sorrento Package tours have been stampeding here for years now, but truly, nothing can dim the delights of the marvelous climate and view of the Bay of Naples. The **Museo Correale,** an attractive 18th-century villa, houses an interesting collection of decorative arts (furniture, china, and so on) and paintings of the Neapolitan school. *Via Correale. Admission: 8,000 lire; gardens only 2,000 lire. Open Mar.–Oct., Mon. and Wed.–Sat. 9–12:30 and 5–7, Sun. 9–12:30; Nov.–Feb., Wed.–Mon. 9–1:30*

Capri No matter how many day-trippers crowd onto the island, no matter how touristy certain sections have become, Capri remains one of Italy's loveliest places. Incoming visitors disembark at Marina Grande, from where you can take some time out for an excursion to the **Grotta Azzurra** (Blue Grotto). Be warned that this must rank as one of the country's all-time great rip-offs: Motorboat, rowboat, and grotto admissions are charged separately, and if there's a line of boats waiting, you'll have little time to enjoy the grotto's marvelous colors. Once inside, though, you'll be surrounded by an astounding play of sapphire light. A cog railway or bus service takes you up to the deliberately commercial and self-consciously picturesque **Capri Town,** where you can stroll through the **Piazzetta,** a choice place from which to watch the action, and window-shop expensive boutiques.

To get away from the crowds, hike to **Villa Jovis,** one of the many villas that Roman emperor Tiberius built on the island, at the end of a lane that climbs steeply uphill. The walk takes about 45 minutes, with pretty views all the way and a final spectacular vista of the entire Bay of Naples and part of the Gulf of Salerno. *Villa Jovis, Via Tiberio. Admission: 4,000 lire. Open daily 9–1 hr before sunset.*

In Anacapri, the island's only other town, there is the little church of **San Michele,** off Via Orlandi, where a magnificent hand-painted majolica-tile floor shows you an 18th-century vision of the Garden of Eden. (You'll need to take a bus or open taxi to Anacapri from Capri town.) *Off Via Orlandi. Open Easter–Oct., daily 7–7; Nov.–Easter, daily 10–3.*

Villa San Michele is the charming former home of Swedish scientist-author Axel Munthe; it's filled with stunning statuary, including a sphinx that looks out across the azure sea. *Via Axel Munthe. Admission: 6,000 lire. Open May–Sept., daily 9–6; Nov.–Feb., daily 10:30–3:30; Mar., daily 9:30–4:30; Apr. and Oct., daily 9:30–5.*

Amalfi The main historical attraction is the **Duomo** or Cathedral of St. Andrew, which shows a mix of Moorish and early Gothic influences. The interior is a 10th-century Romanesque skeleton in an 18th-century baroque dress. *Admission free. Open Apr.–Sept. daily 7:30–9, Oct.–Mar. daily 7:30–noon and 4–6:30.*

The village of **Ravello,** 8 km (5 mi) north of Amalfi, is not actually on the coast, but on a high mountain bluff overlooking the sea. The road up to it is a series of switchbacks, and the village itself clings precariously on the mountain spur. The village flourished during the 13th century and then fell into a tranquillity that has remained unchanged for the past six centuries.

The 11th-century **Villa Rufolo** in Ravello is where the composer Richard Wagner once stayed, and there is a Wagner festival every summer on the villa's garden terrace. There is a Moorish cloister with interlacing pointed arches, beautiful gardens, an 11th-century tower, and a belvedere with a fine view of the coast. *Piazza del Duomo. Admission: 3,000 lire. Open summer, daily 9–8; winter, daily 9–6 or sunset.*

At the entrance to the **Villa Cimbrone** is a small cloister that looks medieval but was actually built in 1917, with two bas-reliefs: one representing nine Norman warriors, the other illustrating the seven deadly sins. Then, the long avenue leads through peaceful gardens scattered with grottoes, small temples, and statues to a belvedere and terrace, where, on a clear day, the view stretches out over the Mediterranean Sea. *Admission: 5,000 lire. Open daily 8:30–1 hr before sunset.*

Norwegian Coast and Fjords

Norway's Far North, land of the summertime midnight sun, offers picturesque scenery and quaint towns. The fjords continue northward from Bergen all the way to Kirkenes, at Norway's border with Finland and Russia. Norway's Far North is for anyone eager to hike, climb, fish, bird-watch for seabirds, see Samiland (land of the Sami, or "Lapps"), or experience the unending days of nighttime sun in June and July.

The major towns north of Bergen are Ålesund, Trondheim, Bodø, Narvik, Tromsø, Hammerfest, and Kirkenes. The best way to reach these places is by ship, whether cruise ship or coastal ferry (*see* Chapter 2).

Currency The unit of currency in Norway is the krone, written as Kr. on price tags but officially written as NOK (bank designation), NKr, or kr. The krone is divided into 100 øre. Bills of NKr 50, 100, 200, 500, and 1,000 are in general use. Coins are in denominations of 50 øre and 1, 5, 10, and 20 kroner. The exchange rate at press time was NKr 7.6 to the U.S. dollar.

Telephones The country code for Norway is 47. Public booths have either card phones or coin phones. Be sure to read the instructions; some phones require the coins to be deposited before dialing, some after. You can buy telephone cards at Narvesen kiosks or at the post office. The minimum deposit is NKr 2 or NKr 3, depending on the phone. International calls can be made from any pay phone. For calls to North America, dial 095–1, then the area code and number. You will need to dial 00 for an international connection. To reach an **AT&T** long-distance operator, dial 80019011.

Shore Excursions The following are good choices in the towns along Norway's coast. They may not be offered by all cruise lines. Times and prices are approximate.

In Trondheim **City Tour.** A visit to an open-air folk museum is the highlight of this tour, which also visits Nidaros Cathedral—built on the grave of St. Olav, who founded the city in AD 997. *3 hrs. Cost: $38.*

City View with Ringve Museum. You'll drive through the city on your way to the Ringve Museum of Musical Instruments, which is housed in a manor overlooking the fjord. *3 hrs. Cost: $45.*

In Bodø **Tour of Kjerringøy.** From Bodø, head off for Kjerringøy, which gained independence from Norway in 1800. Once there, you'll have time to wander the city's Central Square and streets. *Half day. Cost: $15.*

In Tromsø **Views of the City.** Tour the Tromsø Museum before driving around the island of Tromsø. Pass Lake Prestvatn, where the Northern Lights Observatory is located, to reach Tromsø Bridge for a visit to Tromsdalen Church, known as the Arctic Cathedral. The tour includes a ride on the cable car to Mt. Storsteinen for panoramic views of the city. *3 hrs. Cost: $34.*

Northern Lights. Visit the Northern Lights Planetarium, which opened in 1989, where you'll see a film on a 360-degree screen about, of course, the Aurora Borealis. A must for amateur astronomers. *3 hrs. Cost: $42.*

Coming Ashore Ships calling at Tromsø, Bodø, and Trondheim dock in the harbor, which is the lifeline of all the towns along the Norwegian coast.

Attractions are close by the pier, and the best way to explore these ports is on foot.

Exploring Trondheim This water-bound city has Scandinavia's two largest wooden buildings. One is the rococo **Stiftsgården** and the other is a student dormitory. Stiftsgården was built between 1774 and 1778 and became a royal palace in 1906. It is considered to be one of the highlights of Norwegian architecture although, strangely, the architect is unknown. *Tel. 73/52–13–11. Admission: NKr 30. Open June–mid-June, Tues.–Sat. 10–3, Sun. noon–5; late June–mid-Aug., Tues.–Sat. 10–5, Sun. noon–5; late Aug.–May, open one day per month.*

Construction of Scandinavia's largest medieval building, **Nidaros Domkirke** (cathedral), started in 1320 but was not completed until the early 1920s. For centuries, Niadaros Domkirke drew religious pilgrims. Norwegian kings were crowned here, and the crown jewels are still on display. *Kongsgården 2, tel. 73/53–84–80. Admission: NKr 12. Open mid-June–mid–Aug. weekdays 9–5:30, weekends 9–2; mid-Aug.–mid-Sept. weekdays 9–3; mid-Sept.– mid-Apr. weekdays noon–2:30, weekends 11:30–2; May–mid-June, weekdays 9–3, weekends 9–2.*

Exploring Bodø Bodø was bombed by the Germans in 1940. The stunning, contemporary **Bodø Cathedral,** its spire separated from the main building, was built after the war. Inside are rich, modern tapestries; outside is a war memorial.

The **Nordland County Museum** depicts the life of the Sami, as well as regional history. *Prinsengt. 116, tel. 75526128. Admission free. Open weekdays 9–3, weekends noon–3.*

Exploring Tromsø Be sure to see the spectacular **Ishavskatedral** (Arctic Cathedral), with its eastern wall made entirely of stained glass, across the long stretch of Tromsø bridge. Coated in aluminum, the bridge's triangular peaks make a bizarre mirror for the midnight sun. *Tel. 77/63–76–11. Admission: NKr 10. Open June–Aug., Mon.–Sat. 10– 6, Sun. 1:30–6. Times may vary according to church services.*

Be sure to walk around old Tromsø (along the waterfront) and to visit the **Tromsø Museum,** which concentrates on science, the Sami, and northern churches. *Lars Thøringsvei 10, Folkeparken, tel. 77645000; take Bus 27 or 22. Admission: NKr 10. Open June– Aug., daily 9–9; Sept.–May, weekdays 8:30–3:30, Sat. noon–3, Sun. 11–4.*

Oslo, Norway

Although it's one of the world's largest capital cities by land area, Oslo has only about 500,000 inhabitants. The foundations for modern Norwegian culture were laid here in the 19th century, during the period of union with Sweden, which lasted until 1905. Oslo blossomed at this time, and Norway produced its three greatest men of arts and letters: composer Edvard Grieg (1843–1907), dramatist Henrik Ibsen (1828–1906), and painter Edvard Munch (1863–1944). The polar explorers Roald Amundsen and Fridtjof Nansen also lived during this period.

In recent years the city has become more lively: Shops are open later, and pubs, cafés, and restaurants are crowded at all hours. The downtown area is compact, but the city limits include forests, fjords, and mountains, giving Oslo a pristine airiness that complements its urban dignity. Explore downtown on foot, or if you've been here before, venture beyond via bus, streetcar, or train.

Currency The unit of currency in Norway is the krone, written as Kr. on price tags but officially written as NOK (bank designation), NKr, or kr. The krone is divided into 100 øre. Bills of NKr 50, 100, 200, 500, and 1,000 are in general use. Coins are in denominations of 50 øre and 1, 5, 10, and 20 kroner. The exchange rate at press time was NKr 7.6 to the U.S. dollar.

Telephones The country code for Norway is 47. Public telephones accept small-denomination coins; for dialing instructions (in English), check the Oslo phone book. Public booths have either card phones or coin phones. Be sure to read the instructions; some phones require the coins to be deposited before dialing, some after. You can buy telephone cards at Narvesen kiosks or at the post office. The minimum deposit is NKr 2 or NKr 3, depending on the phone. International calls can be made from any pay phone. For calls to North America, dial 095–1, then the area code and number. You will need to dial 00 for an international connection. To reach an **AT&T** long-distance operator, dial 80019011.

Shore Excursions The following are good choices in Oslo. They may not be offered by all cruise lines. Times and prices are approximate.

Sculpture and Skiing. See how master sculpter Gutav Vigeland has populated Frogner park with human figures made of stone, iron, and bronze, and the ski jump where in winter some of the world's top athletes compete, and where in summer you can get a great view of Oslo and the fjords. *3 hrs. Cost: $36.*

Munch Museum and Scandinavian Design. Art lovers won't want to miss this tour, which takes in the Munch Museum and the Museum of Scandinavian Design, with its diverse collection of arts and crafts from AD 600 to the present. *3 hrs. Cost: $34.*

Coming Ashore Ships dock in Oslo's harbor. You can walk right into the main part of the city from the pier. The waterfront toward the central harbor is the heart of Oslo and head of the fjord. Aker Brygge, a quayside shopping and cultural center, with a theater, cinemas, and galleries among the shops, restaurants, and cafés, is a great place to hang out. You don't have to buy anything—just sit amid the fountains and statues and watch the activities.

A taxi is available if the roof light is on. There are taxi stands at Oslo Central Station and usually alongside Narvesen newsstands, or call 22388090; during peak hours, though, you may have to wait. The city also has a good bus and subway (T-bane) network. Tickets for either cost Nkr 18; you can buy them at the stops. For Nkr 40, the Tourist Kort (Tourist Ticket) gives 24 hours' unlimited travel on all public transportation.

Exploring Oslo *Numbers in the margin correspond to points of interest on the Oslo map.*

Oslo's main street, **Karl Johans Gate,** runs right through the center of town, from Oslo Central Station uphill to the Royal Palace. Half its length is closed to traffic, and it is in this section that you will find many of the city's shops and outdoor cafés.

❶ The **Slottet** (Royal Palace) is the king's residence. The neoclassical palace, completed in 1848, is as sober, sturdy, and unpretentious as the Norwegian character. The surrounding park is open to the public, though the palace is not. The changing of the guard happens daily at 1:30. When the king is in residence—signaled by a red flag—the Royal Guard strikes up the band. *Drammensvn. 1, tel. 22048700.*

❷ The **Universitet** (University) is made up of three big buildings. The main hall of the university is decorated with murals by Edvard Munch (1863–1944), Norway's most famous artist. The *aula* (hall) is open only during July. *Karl Johans gate 47. Admission to hall free. Open Last week of June–mid- Aug., weekdays 10–2:45.*

❸ **Nasjonalgalleriet** (the National Gallery) is Norway's largest public gallery. It has a small but high-quality selection of paintings by European artists, but of particular interest is the collection of works by Scandinavian Impressionists. Here you can see Edvard Munch's most famous painting, *The Scream;* however, most of his

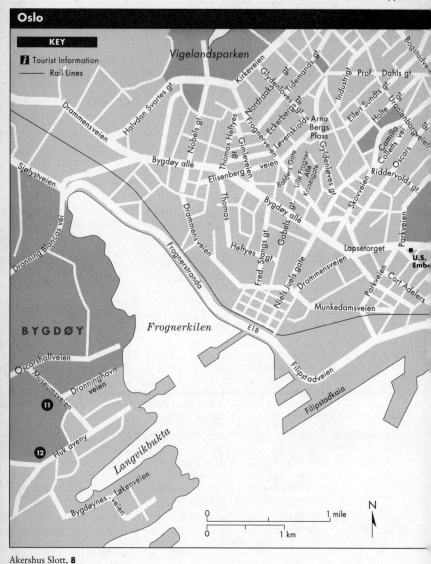

Oslo

KEY

i Tourist Information

Rail Lines

Vigelandsparken

Bogstadvei

Kirkeveien

Prof. Dahls gt.

Gyldenløves gt.

Nordraaks gt.

Tidemands gt.

Industrigt.

Eilert Sundts gt.

Holte

Uranienborgveien

Drammensveien

Halvdan Svartes gt.

Eckersbergs gt.

Arno Bergs Plass

Camilla

Colletts vei

Oscars

Nobels gt.

Thomas Heftyes

Frognerveien

Løvenskiolds gt.

Gyldenløves gt.

Riddervolds gt.

Bygdøy allé

Gimleveien

Elisenberg

veien

Bolårs Gate

Lille Frogner Allé

Skovveien

Parkveien

Sjølyststveien

Thomas

Bygdøy allé

Gabels gt.

Kristinagate

Lapsetorget

Heftyes

Fred. Stangs gt.

Drammensveien

Parkveien

U.S. Emb.

Dronning Blancas vei

Drammensveien

Niels Juels gate

Cort Adelers

Frognerstranda

Munkedamsveien

BYGDØY

Frognerkilen

E18

Oscarshallveien

Filipstadveien

Museumsveien

Dronninghavn veien

Filipstadkaia

11

12

Huk aveny

Langvikbukta

Løkenveien

Bygdøynes- veien

0 ——————— 1 mile

0 ——————— 1 km

N

Akershus Slott, **8**

Forsvarsmuséet and
Hjemmefrontmuséet, **9**

Historisk Museum, **4**

Munch-muséet, **13**

Nasjonalgalleriet, **3**

Nationaltheatret, **5**

Norsk
Folkemuseum, **11**

Oslo Domkirke, **7**

Rådhuset, **10**

Slottet, **1**

Stortinget, **6**

Universitet, **2**

Vikingskipshuset, **12**

Colletts gt.
Waldemar Thranes gt.
Akersbakken
Seilduksgt.
Helgesens gt.
Grüners gt.
Helgesens gt.
Sofienberggt.
Maridalsveien
Akerselva
Parkveien
Pilestredet
Ullevålsveien
Akersveien
Møllerveien
Nordregt.
Trondheimsveien
Jens Bjelkes gt.
Wessels gt.
Nordahl Bruns gt.
Hausmanns gt.
St. Olavsgt.
Holbergs gate
Frederiks gate
Universitetsgt.
Henrik Ibsens gt.
Møllergt.
Torggt.
Uregt.
13
Drammensveien
Karl
Johans
Rosenkrantz' gt.
Akersgata
Grubbegt.
Youngs-
torget
Storgt.
Brugt.
Norbygt.
Tøyengt.
Stortingsgt.
gate
Grensen
Stortorvet
Oslo
Spektrum
Løkkegata
Grønlandsleiret
Munkedamsveien
Amundsensgt.
Nedre Vollgt.
Slottsgt.
7
Oslo City
Schweigaards gt.
Dokkveien
Rådhusgt.
Nedre
Prinsens gt.
Central
Station
Nylandsveien
Pipervika
Akershusstranda
Tollbugata
Kirkegata
Dronningens gt.
Skippergt.
Fred Olsens gt.
Strandgt.
Bispegt.
E18
Mynt gt.
8
Akerselva
Bjørvika
Bispevika
9
Kongens gate
Skippergt.
SØRENGA
Oslo gt.
Oslofjorden
Mosseveien
Ekebergsletta

work is in the Munch Museum (*see below*). *Universitetsgt. 13, tel. 22/20–04–04. Admission free. Open Mon., Wed., Fri. 10–6, Thurs. 10–8, Sat. 10–4, Sun. 11–3.*

❹ The **Historisk Museum** (Historical Museum) is in back of the National Gallery. In addition to displays of daily life and art from the Viking period, the museum has an ethnographic section with a collection related to the great polar explorer Roald Amundsen, the first man to reach the South Pole. *Frederiksgt. 2, tel. 22/85–99–12. Admission free. Open Apr., daily 11–3:45; early May and Sept, daily 10–4:45; mid-May–mid-June, daily 9–5:45; mid-June–Aug., daily 9–6:45; Oct., daily 10–3:45; Nov.–Mar., weekdays 11–2:45, weekends 11–3:45.*

❺ The **Nationaltheatret** (National Theater) is watched over by the statues of Bjørnstjerne Bjørnson and Henrik Ibsen. Bjørnson was the nationalist poet who wrote Norway's anthem. Internationally lauded playwright Ibsen wrote *Peer Gynt* (he personally requested Edvard Grieg's musical accompaniment), *A Doll's House,* and *Hedda Gabler,* among others. He worried that his plays, packed with allegory, myth, and sociological and emotional angst, might not have appeal outside Norway. Instead, they were universally recognized and changed the face of modern theater. *Stortingsgt. 15, tel. 22/41–27–10.*

❻ The **Stortinget** (Parliament) is a bowfront, yellow-brick building that stretches across the block. It is open to visitors by request when Parliament is not in session: A guide will take you around the frescoed interior and into the debating chamber. *Karl Johans gt. 22, tel. 22/31–30–50. Admission free. Guided tours July–Aug. Call for hrs.*

❼ **Oslo Domkirke** (cathedral), consecrated in 1697, is modest by the standards of those in some other European capital cities, but the interior is rich with treasures, such as the baroque carved wooden altarpiece and pulpit. The ceiling frescoes by Hugo Lous Mohr were done after World War II. Behind the cathedral is an area of arcades, small restaurants, and street musicians. *Stortorvet 1. Admission free. Open weekdays 10–4.*

❽ **Akershus Slott,** a castle on the harbor, was built during the Middle Ages but restored in 1527 by Christian IV of Denmark—Denmark then ruled Norway—after it was damaged by fire. He then laid out the present city of Oslo (naming it Christiania, after himself) around his new residence; Oslo's street plan still follows his design. Some rooms are open for guided tours, and the grounds form a park around the castle. *Entrance from Festningspl, tel. 22/41–25–21. Guided tours of the castle, May–Sept., Mon.–Sat. 11, 1, and 3, Sun. 1 and 3.*

❾ On the grounds of Akershus Slott are the **Forsvarsmuséet** and **Hjemmefrontmuséet** (the Norwegian Defense and Resistance museums). Both give you a feel for the Norwegian fighting spirit throughout history and especially during the German occupation, when the Nazis set up headquarters on this site and had a number of patriots executed here. *Entrance from Festningspl., tel. 22/41–25–21. Admission: NKr 15. Forsvarsmuséet open June–Aug., weekdays 10–3, weekends 11–4; Sept.–May, weekdays 10–6, weekends 11–4. Hjemmefrontmuséett open mid-Apr.–mid-June, Mon.–Sat. 10–4, Sun. 11–4; mid-June–Aug., Mon., Wed., Sat. 10–5, Tues., Thurs. 10–6, Sun. 11–5; Sept., Mon.–Sat. 10–4, Sun. 11–4; Oct.–mid-Apr., Mon.–Sat. 10–3, Sun. 11–16.*

⑩ The large redbrick **Rådhuset** (city hall) is on the waterfront. Designed by architects Arnstein Arnesen and Magnus Paulsson it opened officially in 1950. Note the friezes in the courtyard, depicting scenes from Norwegian folklore, but the exterior is dull compared to the marble-floored inside halls, where murals and frescoes bursting with color depict daily life, historical events, and Resistance activities in Norway. The elegant main hall has been the venue for the Nobel Peace Prize Ceremony since 1991. *Rådhuspl., tel. 22/86–16–00. Admission free. Open May–Aug., Mon.–Sat. 9–5, Sun. noon–4; Sept.–Apr., Mon.–Sat. 9–3:30. Tours weekdays 10, noon, 2.*

From Pipervika Bay, you can board a ferry in the summertime for the seven-minute crossing of the fjord to the **Bygdøy** peninsula, where there is a complex of seafaring museums. *Ferries run May–Sept., daily every ½ hr 8:15–5:45.*

⑪ Take the ferry from Rådhusbryggen (City Hall Wharf) and walk up a well-marked road to see the **Norsk Folkemuseum** (Norwegian Folk Museum), a large park where centuries-old historic farmhouses have been collected from all over the country and reassembled. A whole section of 19th-century Oslo was moved here, as was a 12th-century wooden stave church. Look for the guides in period costume throughout the park, and on Sundays, there are displays of weaving and sheepshearing. *First ferry stop, Dronningen. Museumsvn. 10, tel. 22/12–37–00. Admission: NKr 50. Open Jan.–mid-May, Mon.–Sat. 11–3, Sun. 11–4; mid-May–mid-June, daily 10–5; mid-June–Aug., daily 10–6; early Sept., daily 10–5; mid-Sept.–Dec., Mon.–Sat. 11–3, Sun. 11–4.*

⑫ **Vikingskipshuset** (Viking Ship Museum) contains 9th-century ships used by Vikings as royal burial chambers, which have been excavated from the shores of the Oslofjord. Also on display are the treasures and jewelry that accompanied the royal bodies on their last voyage. The ornate craftsmanship evident in the ships and jewelry dispels any notion that the Vikings were skilled only in looting and pillaging. *Huk aveny 35, tel. 22/43–83–79. Admission: NKr 30. Open Nov.–Mar., daily 11–3; Apr. and Oct., daily 11–4; May–Aug., daily 9–6; Sept., daily 11–5.*

⑬ In 1940, four years before his death, Munch bequeathed much of his work to the city of Oslo; the **Munch-muséet** (Munch Museum) opened in 1963, the centennial of his birth. Although only a fraction of its 22,000 items—books, paintings, drawings, prints, sculptures, and letters—are on display, you can still get a sense of the tortured expressionism that was to have such an effect on European painting. *Tøyengt. 53 (from Rådhuset take Bus 29 or take the T-bane from the Nationaltheatret to Tøyen, an area in northeast Oslo), tel. 22/67–37–74. Admission: NKr 40. Open June–Sept. 15, Tues.–Sat. 10–6, Sun. noon–6; Sept. 16–May, Tues., Wed., Fri, Sat. 10–4, Thurs. 10–6, Sun. noon–6.*

Shopping Oslo has a wide selection of pewter, silver, glass, sheepskin, leather, and knitwear. Prices on handmade articles are government-controlled.

Many of the larger stores are between Stortinget and the cathedral; much of this area is for pedestrians only. The **Basarhallene**, at the back of the cathedral, is an art and handicrafts boutique center. Oslo's newest shopping area, **Aker Brygge**, was once a shipbuilding wharf. Right on the waterfront, it is a complex of booths, offices, and sidewalk cafés. Also check out **Bogstadveien/Hegdehaugsveien**, which runs from Majorstua to Parkveien.

Paris/Le Havre, France

Le Havre is the port city for Paris, one of Europe's most treasured and beautiful cities. Most cruise passengers will find a day far too short to truly explore the city. However, Paris is a compact city, and with the possible exception of the Bois de Boulogne and Montmartre, you can easily walk from one sight to the next. The city is divided in two by the River Seine, with two islands (Ile de la Cité and Ile St-Louis) in the middle. The south, or Left, Bank has a more intimate, bohemian flavor than the haughtier Right Bank. The east–west axis from Châtelet to the Arc de Triomphe, via the rue de Rivoli and the Champs-Elysées, is the principal thoroughfare for sightseeing and shopping on the Right Bank.

Currency The unit of French currency is the franc (fr.), subdivided into 100 centimes. Bills are issued in denominations of 50, 100, 200, and 500 francs (frs.); coins are 5, 10, 20, and 50 centimes and 1, 2, 5, 10, and 20 francs. The small, copper-color 5-, 10-, and 20-centime coins have considerable nuisance value, but they can be used for tips in bars and cafés. At press time, the U.S. dollar bought 6 francs.

Telephones The country code for France is 33. French phone numbers have ten digits. All phone numbers have a two-digit prefix determined by zone; for Paris and the Ile de France, the prefix is 01. (Drop the zero if you are calling France from a foreign country.) Phone booths are plentiful; they are nearly always available at post offices and cafés. Some French pay phones take 1-, 2-, and 5-franc coins (1-fr. minimum), but most phones are now operated by *télé-cartes* (phone cards), which can be used for both local and international calls. The cards are sold in post offices, métro stations, and cafés sporting a red TABAC (tobacco) sign outside (cost: 40 frs. for 50 units; 96 frs. for 120 units). To call abroad, dial 19 and wait for the tone, then dial the country code, area code, and number. To reach an **AT&T** long-distance operator, dial 0800–990011; **MCI**, 0800–9900; **Sprint**, 0800–990087. Dial 12 for local operators.

Shore Excursions The following is a good choice from Le Havre. It may not be offered by all cruise lines. Time and price are approximate.

Paris. Journey by coach to Paris, where you will tour the Cathedral of Notre Dame, the Eiffel Tower, Place de la Concorde, and have time to shop. Glimpse the tree-lined Champs-Elysées and Arc de Triomphe, Place de l'Opera, and Pont Neuf. Includes lunch. *12 hrs. Cost: $175.*

Coming Ashore Ships dock at Le Havre. The trip to Paris is approximately three hours each way. Cruise lines will typically sell transfers for around $100 to Paris for those who want to explore on their own.

Once you're in the city, you'll find that Paris's monuments and museums are within walking distance of one another. A river cruise is a pleasant way to get an overview. Even if you're stopping for a very short time, you may want to get a copy of the *Plan de Paris par Arrondissement*, a city guide available at most kiosks, with separate maps of each district, including the whereabouts of métro stations and an index of street names.

The most convenient form of public transportation is the *métro*; buses are a slower alternative, though they do allow you to see more of the city. Maps of the métro/RER network are available free from any métro station. There are 13 métro lines crisscrossing Paris and the nearby suburbs, and you are seldom more than a five-minute walk from the nearest station. It is essential to know the name of the last station on the line you take, since this name appears on all signs within the system. A connection (you can make as many as you please on one ticket) is called a *correspondance.* At junction stations, illuminated orange signs bearing the names of each line terminus appear over the corridors that lead to the various correspondances. Métro tickets cost 8 francs each, though a *carnet* (10 tickets for 46 frs.) is a far better value. Keep your ticket during your journey; you will need it to leave the RER system and in case you run into any green-clad inspectors when you are leaving the métro—they can be very nasty and will impose a big fine on the spot if you do not have a ticket.

Taxis are not terribly expensive but are not always easy to hail, either. There is no standard vehicle or color for Paris taxis, but all offer good value. Daytime rates (7 to 7) within Paris are about 2.80 fr. per km (½ mi), and nighttime rates are around 4.50 frs., plus a basic charge of 13 frs. Cruising cabs can be hard to find. There are numerous taxi stands, but these are not well marked. Cruise passengers should be aware that taxis seldom take more than three people at a time.

Exploring Paris *Numbers in the margin correspond to points of interest on the Paris map.*

➊ The most enduring symbol of Paris, and its historic and geographic heart, is the cathedral **Notre-Dame,** around the corner from Cité métro station. It was begun in 1163, making it one of the earliest Gothic cathedrals, although it was not finished until 1345. The south tower houses the great bell of Notre-Dame, as tolled by Quasimodo, Victor Hugo's fictional hunchback. The cathedral interior, with its vast proportions, soaring nave, and soft, multicolor light filtering through the stained-glass windows, inspires awe, despite the inevitable throngs of tourists. The 387-step climb up the towers is worth the effort for a perfect view of the famous gargoyles and the heart of Paris. *pl. du Parvis. Cathedral admission free. Towers admission: 32 frs. Open daily 8–7; tower daily (summer) 9:30–12:15 and 2–6, daily (winter) 10–5.*

➋ **Ste-Chapelle** (Holy Chapel) was built by Louis IX (1226–70) in the 1240s, to house what he believed to be Christ's Crown of Thorns, purchased from Emperor Baldwin of Constantinople. The lower chapel is low-ceilinged and brightly painted, while the upper one visually soars; its walls consist of little else but dazzling 13th-century stained glass. *In the Palais de Justice, Admission: 32 frs. Open daily 9:30–6:30; Oct.–Mar., daily 10–5.*

➌ The Hôtel de Cluny houses the **Musée National du Moyen-Age** (National Museum of the Middle Ages) a museum devoted to the late medieval and Renaissance periods. Look for the *Lady with the Unicorn* tapestries and the beautifully displayed medieval statues. *6 pl. Paul-Painlevé, tel. 01–53–73–78–00. Admission: 30 frs., 20 frs. on Sun. Open Wed.–Mon. 9:45–5:45.*

➍ **La Sorbonne,** Paris's ancient university, is where students used to listen to lectures in Latin, which explains why the surrounding area is known as the Quartier Latin (Latin Quarter). The Sorbonne is the oldest university in Paris—indeed, one of the oldest in Europe—and has for centuries been one of France's principal institutions of higher learning. You can visit the main courtyard on rue de la Sorbonne and peek into the main lecture hall, a major meeting point during the tumultuous student upheavals of 1968. *rue de la Sorbonne.*

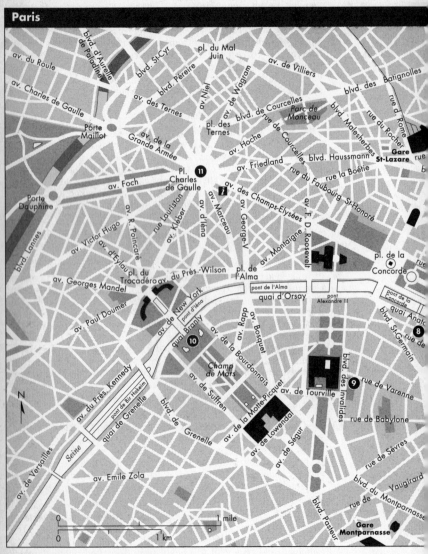

Paris

Arc de Triomphe, **11**

Jardin des Plantes, **6**

La Sorbonne, **4**

Louvre, **12**

Musée d'Orsay, **8**

Musée National du
Moyen-Age, **3**

Musée Rodin, **9**

Notre-Dame, **1**

Panthéon, **5**

St-Germain-
des-Prés, **7**

Ste-Chapelle, **2**

Tour Eiffel, **10**

❺ The **Panthéon,** with its huge dome and elegant colonnade, is reminiscent of St. Paul's in London but dates from a century later (1758–89). The Panthéon was intended to be a church, but during the French Revolution it was earmarked as a secular hall of fame. Its crypt contains the remains of such national heroes as Voltaire, Rousseau, and Zola. The interior is empty and austere, with principal interest centering on Puvis de Chavannes's late-19th-century frescoes, relating the life of Geneviève, patron saint of Paris. *pl. du Panthéon, tel. 01–44–32–18–00. Admission: 32 frs. Open daily 10–5:30.*

❻ Rue de Navarre and rue Lacépède lead to the **Jardin des Plantes** (Botanical Gardens), which have been on this site since the 17th century. The gardens have what is reputedly the oldest tree in Paris, an acacia Robinia (allée Becquerel) planted in 1636. Natural science enthusiasts will be in their element at the various museums, devoted to insects (Musée Entomologique), fossils and prehistoric animals (Musée Paléontologique), and minerals (Musée Minéralogique). The Grande Galerie de l'Evolution, with its collection of stuffed and mounted animals (some now extinct), is mind-blowing. *36 rue Geoffroy-St-Hilaire. Admission: 15–30 frs. Museums open Museums Wed.–Mon. 10–5; garden daily 7:30–sunset.*

❼ You can hardly miss the sturdy pointed tower of **St-Germain-des-Prés,** the oldest church in Paris (begun around 1160, though the towers date from the 11th century). Note the colorful nave frescoes by the 19th-century artist Hippolyte Flandrin, a pupil of Ingres. *Pl. St-Germain-des-Prés. Weekdays 8–7:30; weekends 8–9.*

❽ In a stylishly converted train station, the **Musée d'Orsay**—devoted to the arts (mainly French) spanning the period 1848–1914—is one of the city's most popular sights. The main artistic attraction is the Impressionists: Renoir, Sisley, Pissarro, and Monet are all well represented. The post-Impressionists—Cézanne, van Gogh, Gauguin, and Toulouse-Lautrec—are on the top floor, and thought-provoking sculptures lurk at every turn. *1 rue Bellechasse, tel. 01–40–49–48–14. Admission: 39 frs., 27 frs. on Sun. Open Tues., Wed., Fri., Sat. 10–5:30; Thurs. 10–9:30; Sun. 9–5:30.*

❾ The **Musée Rodin** (Rodin Museum) is among the most charming of Paris's individual museums. This 18th-century mansion is filled with the vigorous sculptures of Auguste Rodin (1840–1917). You'll doubtless recognize the seated *Le Penseur* (*The Thinker*), with his elbow resting on his knee, and the passionate *Le Baiser* (*The Kiss*). The garden also has hundreds of rosebushes, with dozens of different varieties. *77 rue de Varenne, tel. 01–44–18–61–10. Admission: 28 frs., 18 frs. Sun. Open Easter–Oct., Tues.–Sun. 10–6; Nov.–Easter, Tues.–Sun. 10–5.*

❿ No one will want to miss Paris's most famous landmark, the **Tour Eiffel** (Eiffel Tower). It was built by Gustave Eiffel for the World Exhibition of 1889. Such was Eiffel's engineering precision that even in the fiercest winds the tower never sways more than a few centimeters. Standing beneath it, you may have trouble believing that it nearly became 7,000 tons of scrap iron when its concession expired in 1909. Only its potential use as a radio antenna saved the day; it now bristles with a forest of radio and television transmitters. The view from 1,000 ft up will enable you to appreciate the city's layout and proportions. *quai Branly, tel. 01–44–11–23–23. Admission: by elevator to 2nd floor, 20 frs.; 3rd floor, 42 frs.; 4th* *floor, 57 frs. By foot: 2nd and 3rd floors only, 14 frs. Open July–Aug., daily 9 AM–midnight; Sept.–June, daily 9 AM–11 PM.*

11 Looming over place Charles-de-Gaulle, known to Parisians as "L'Étoile" (the Star), is the **Arc de Triomphe.** This 164-ft arch was planned by Napoléon to celebrate his military successes—but Napoléon had been dead for 15 years when the Arc de Triomphe was finally finished in 1836. From the top of the Arc you can see the "star" effect of Étoile's 12 radiating avenues and admire two special vistas: one down the Champs-Élysées toward place de la Concorde and the Louvre, and the other down avenue de la Grande Armée toward La Défense, a severe modern arch. France's Unknown Soldier is buried beneath the archway. Halfway up the Arc is a small museum devoted to its history. *Pl. Charles-de-Gaulle, tel. 01–43–80–31–31. Admission: 35 frs. Open daily 9:30 AM–11 PM; winter, daily 10–10.*

The **Champs-Elysées** is the site of colorful national ceremonies on July 14 and November 11; its trees are often decked with French tricolors and foreign flags to mark visits from heads of state. It is also where the cosmopolitan pulse of Paris beats strongest. The gracefully sloping 2-km (1¼-mi) boulevard was originally laid out in the 1660s by André Le Nôtre as a garden sweeping away from the Tuileries. There is not much sign of that as you stroll past the cafés, restaurants, airline offices, car showrooms, movie theaters, and chic arcades that occupy its upper half, although the avenue was spruced up in the early 1990s with wider sidewalks and an extra row of trees.

12 Once a royal palace, now the the world's largest and most famous museum, the **Louvre** has been given fresh purpose by a decade of expansion, renovation, and reorganization, symbolized by I. M. Pei's daring glass pyramid that now serves as the entrance to both the museum and an underground shopping arcade, the Carrousel du Louvre. The Louvre was begun as a fortress in 1200 (the earliest parts still standing date from the 1540s) and completed under Napoléon III in the 1860s. The museum's sheer variety can seem intimidating. The main tourist attraction is Leonardo da Vinci's *Mona Lisa* (known in French as *La Joconde*), painted in 1503. Be forewarned: her enigmatic smile is kept behind glass, invariably encircled by a mob of tourists. Turn your attention instead to some of the less-crowded rooms and galleries nearby, where Leonardo's fellow Italians are strongly represented: Fra Angelico, Giotto, Mantegna, Raphael, Titian, and Veronese. El Greco, Murillo, and Velázquez lead the Spanish; Van Eyck, Rembrandt, Frans Hals, Brueghel, Holbein, and Rubens underline the achievements of northern European art. English paintings are highlighted by works of Lawrence, Reynolds, Gainsborough, and Turner. Highlights of French painting include works by Poussin, Fragonard, Chardin, Boucher, and Watteau—together with David's *Coronation of Napoléon*, Géricault's *Raft of the Medusa*, and Delacroix's *Liberty Guiding the People.* Famous statues include the soaring *Victory of Samothrace* and the eternally fascinating *Venus de Milo. Palais du Louvre, tel. 01–40–20–51–51. Admission: 45 frs., 26 frs. after 3 PM and Sun; free 1st Sun. of the month. Open Thurs.–Sun. 9–6, Mon. and Wed. 9 AM–9:45 PM. Some sections open limited days.*

Shopping The shopping opportunities in Paris are endless and geared to every taste. Perfume and designer clothing are perhaps the most coveted Parisian souvenirs. The elegant **Avenue Montaigne** is a showcase of international haute-couture houses; Prada and Dolce & Gabbana have joined Chanel, Dior, Nina Ricci, Valentino, an other exclusive spots. Rue du Faubourg-St-Honoré and the place des Victoires are also good places to hit.

The area surrounding St-Germain-des-Prés on the Left Bank is a mecca for specialty shops and boutiques, and has recently seen an influx of the elite names in haute couture. If you're on a tight budget, search for bargains along the streets around the foot of Montmartre or in the designer discount shops (Cacharel, Rykiel, Dorotennis) along rue d'Alésia in Montparnasse. The most famous department stores in Paris are **Galeries Lafayette** and **Printemps**, on boulevard Haussmann. Others include **Au Bon Marché** on the Left Bank (métro: Sèvres-Babylone) and the **Samaritaine**, overlooking the Seine east of the Louvre (métro: Pont-Neuf).

Old prints are sold by *bouquinistes* (secondhand booksellers) in stalls along the Left Bank of the Seine. For state-of-the-art home decorations, the shop in the **Musée des Arts Décoratifs** in the Louvre (107 rue de Rivoli) is well worth visiting.

Reykjavik, Iceland

Iceland is anything but icy. Though glaciers cover about 10% of the country, summers are relatively warm, and winters are milder than those in New York. Coastal farms lie in green, pastoral lowlands, where cows, sheep, and horses graze alongside raging streams. Distant waterfalls plunge from heather-covered mountains with great spiked ridges and snowcapped peaks. Iceland's name can be blamed on Hrafna-Flóki, a 9th-century Norse settler who failed to plant enough crops to see his livestock through their first winter. Leaving in a huff, he passed a northern fjord filled with pack ice and cursed the country with a name that's kept tourism in cold storage for 1,100 years.

The second-largest island in Europe, Iceland is in the middle of the North Atlantic, where the warm Gulf Stream from the south meets cold currents from the north—just the right conditions for fish, which provide the nation with 80% of its export revenue. Beneath some of the country's glaciers are burning fires that become visible during volcanic eruptions—fires that heat the country's hot springs and geysers. The springs, in turn, provide warmth for the country's homes, hospitals, and public swimming pools, keeping the nation's air smokeless and smogless.

Currency The Icelandic monetary unit is the króna (plural, krónur), which is equal to 100 aurar and is abbreviated kr. locally and IKr internationally. At press time, the rate of exchange was IKr71 to the U.S. dollar.

Telephones The country code for Iceland is 354. All phone numbers in Iceland have seven digits; there are no city codes. Pay phones take IKr 10 and IKr 50 coins and are found in hotels, shops, bus stations, and post offices. Phone cards cost IKr 500 and are sold at post offices, hotels, and so on. For operator assistance with local calls dial 119; for information dial 118. For assistance with overseas calls, dial 115; for direct international calls dial 00. To reach a long-distance operator in the United States from Iceland, use the following international access codes: for **AT&T** dial 800–9001; **MCI**, 999–002; **Sprint**, 800–9003.

Shore Excursions The following are good choices in Iceland. They may not be offered by all cruise lines. Times and prices are approximate.

Golden Circle. Iceland's natural wonders are the focus of this tour, which visits Thingvellir National Park, Gulifoss (the Golden Waterfall), and Strokkur Geyser. You'll also see the second-largest glacier in Iceland and postglacial lava fields. *5 hrs. Cost: $75.*

City Sights. Reykjavík's naturally heated outdoor swimming pool is a highlight of a half day of sightseeing, which also visits the Arabaer Folk Museum and the National Museum and drives by the University, Old Town, the Parliament, the Cathedral, and residential areas. *3 hrs. Cost: $36.*

Coming Ashore Ships calling in Iceland berth at the dock in Reykjavík. The most interesting sights are in the city center, within easy walking distance of one another.

Getting Around The center of Reykjavík is served by two main bus stops: Brook Square and Hlemmur station. Buses run from 7 AM to midnight. The flat fare for Reykjavík and suburbs is IKr 120. Taxi rates start at about IKr 300; few in-town taxi rides exceed IKr 700. The best taxis to call are Hreyfill (tel. 588–5522), BSR (tel. 561–0000 or 561–1720), and Bæjarleiðir (tel. 553–3500).

Exploring Reykjavík The heart of Reykjavík is **Austurvöllur Square** (East Field), a small square in the center of the city. The 19th-century Alþingi (Parliament building), one of the oldest stone buildings in Iceland, faces the square. In the center of the square is a statue of Jón Sigurðsson (1811–79), the national hero who led Iceland's fight for independence, which it achieved fully in 1944.

Next to Alþingi is the **Dómkirkjan** (Lutheran cathedral), a small, charming stone church. Behind it is Tjörnin, a natural pond next to Reykjavík City Hall. One corner of the pond does not freeze; here thermal springs feed warm water, making it an attraction for birds year-round. *Austurvöllur Square (East Field), tel. 551–2113. Open Mon. and Tues.–Fri. 9–5, Wed. 10–5, unless in use for services.*

Overlooking Tjörnin stands the **Listasfn Íslands** (National Gallery), which houses a collection of Icelandic art. *Fríkirkjuvegur 7, tel. 562–1000. Admission: IKr 200. Open Tues.–Sun. noon–6.*

At Lækjartorg square, on the right, is the **Bernhöftstorfa** district, a small hill with colorful two-story wooden houses from the mid-19th century, where no modernizing efforts have been made. For a century and a half, the largest building has housed the oldest educational institution in the country, Menntaskólinn í Reykjavík, a college whose graduates have from the early days dominated political and social life in Iceland. *Corner of Amtmannsstígur and Lækjargata.*

Leading west out of Lækjartorg square is Austurstræti, a semi-pedestrian shopping street with the main post office on the right. From here you can take Bus 10 from the bus station for a 20-minute ride to the **Arbæjarsafn** (Open-Air Museum), a "village" of 18th- and 19th-century houses. *Árbær (Bus 10 at Hlemmur station), tel. 577–1111. Open June–Aug., Tues.–Sun. 10–6, and by appointment.*

At the **Ásmundur Sveinsson Sculpture Museum,** a few originals of this social realist sculptor are in the surrounding garden, which is accessible at all times free of charge. *v/Sigtún, tel. 553–2155. Admission: IKr 200. Open June–Sept., daily 10–4; Oct.–May, daily 1–4.*

The **Náttúrufræðistofnun** (Museum of Natural History) has one of the last great auks on display plus several exhibits on Icelandic natural history. *Hlemmtorg, Hverfisgata 116, tel. 562–9822. Admission free. Open Tues., Thurs., and weekends. 1:30–4.*

The **Hallgrímskirkja** (Hallgrim's Church) features a 210-ft gray-stone tower that dominates the city's skyline. The church, which took more than 40 years to build and was completed in the 1980s, is open to the public. The church tower offers a panoramic view of the city and its spacious suburbs. *Top of Skólavörðustígur, tel. 551–0745. Admission to tower: IKr 200. Open May–Sept., daily 9–6; Oct.–Apr., daily 10–6.*

The **National Gallery of Einar Jónsson** is devoted to the works of Iceland's leading early-20th-century sculptor. His monumental sculptures have a strong symbolic and mystical content. *Njarðar-gata, tel. 551–3797. Admission: IKr 200. Open June–mid-Sept., Tues.–Sun 1:30–4; weekends only mid-Sept.–Nov. and Feb.–May; closed Dec.–Jan. Sculpture garden always open.*

At the campus of the **University of Iceland** (founded 1911) is the outstanding Þjóðminjasafn (National Museum). On display are Viking artifacts, national costumes, weaving, wood carving, and silver works. *Suðurgata 41, tel. 552–8888. Small admission fee. Open Mid-May–mid-Sept., Tues.–Sun. 11–5; late Sept.–early May, Tues., Thurs., and weekends noon–5.*

Shopping Many of the shops that sell the most attractive Icelandic woolen goods and arts and crafts are on Aðalstræti, Hafnarstræti, and Vesturgata streets. The **Icelandic Handcrafts Center** (Falcon House, Hafnarstræti 3, tel. 551–1785) stocks Icelandic woolens, knitting and tapestry materials, and handmade pottery, glassware, and jewelry. At the **Handknitting Association of Iceland** (Skólavörðustígur 9, tel. 552–1890), you can buy high-quality hand-knitted items through a knitters' cooperative. **Rammagerðin** (Hafnarstræti 19, tel. 551–7910) stocks a wide range of Icelandic-made clothes, souvenirs, and books. On weekends, try the **flea market** (Harborside Kolaportið in the rear of the Customs House on Geirsgata) between 11 and 5.

Rome/Civitavecchia, Italy

Civitavecchia is the port city for Rome, where antiquity is taken for granted. Successive ages have piled the present on top of the past—building, layering, and overlapping their own particular segments of Rome's 2,500 years of history to form a remarkably varied urban complex. Most of the city's major sights are in a fairly small area known as the *centro*. At its heart lies ancient Rome, where the Forum and Colosseum stand. It was around this core that the other sections of the city grew up through the ages: medieval Rome, which covered the horn of land that pushes the Tiber toward the Vatican and extended across the river into Trastevere; and Renaissance Rome, which was erected upon medieval foundations and extended as far as the Vatican, creating beautiful villas on what was then the outskirts of the city.

Currency The unit of currency in Italy is the lira (plural, lire). There are bills of 1,000, 2,000, 5,000, 10,000, 50,000, 100,000, and 500,000 lire (this largest bill being almost impossible to change, except in banks); coins are worth 50, 100, 200, and 500 lire. In 1999 the euro will begin to be used as a banking currency, but the lire will still be the currency in use on a day-to-day basis. At press time, the exchange rate was about 1,770 lire to the U.S. dollar. When your purchases run into hundreds of thousands of lire, beware of being short-changed, a dodge that is practiced at ticket windows and cashiers' desks, as well as in shops and even banks. Always count your change before you leave the counter.

Telephones The country code for Italy is 39. Most local calls cost 200 lire for two minutes. Pay phones take either 100-, 200-, or 500-lire coins or *schede telefoniche* (phone cards), purchased in bars, tobacconists, post offices, and TELECOM offices in either 5,000-, 10,000-, or 15,000-lire denominations. To place international calls, you can go to the TELECOM telephone exchange, where the operator assigns you a booth, can help place your call, and collects payment when you have finished. TELECOM exchanges are found in all cities. To place an international call, insert a phone card, dial 00, then the country code, area code, and phone number. The cheaper and easier option, however, will be to use your AT&T, MCI, or Sprint calling card. For **AT&T USADirect,** dial access number tel. 172–1011; for **MCI Call USA,** access number tel. 172–1022; for **Sprint Express,** access number tel. 172–1877. You will be connected directly with an operator in the United States.

Shore Excursions Due to the limited amount of time you will have in the city and its wealth of sights, it is a good idea to select a tour in Rome. The following is a good choice in Rome. It may not be offered by all cruise lines. Time and price are approximate.

Highlights and History. An excellent choice for first-time visitors who want to span Rome's 2,500 years of history. Highlights include the Colosseum, the Vatican Museum, St. Peter's Basilica, and the Forum. Travel is by motor coach. *11 hrs. Cost: $160.*

Coming Ashore Ships dock at Civitavecchia, about one hour and 45 minutes to Rome by bus. Cruise lines usually will sell bus transfers to Rome for those who want to explore independently.

The layout of the centro is highly irregular, but several landmarks serve as orientation points to identify the areas that most visitors come to see: the Colosseo (Colosseum), the Pantheon and Piazza Navona, the Basilica di San Pietro (St. Peter's Church), the Scalinata di Piazza di Spagna (Spanish Steps), and Villa Borghese. You'll need a good map to find your way around; newsstands offer a wide choice. The important thing is to relax and enjoy Rome. Don't try to see everything, but do take time to savor its pleasures. If you are in Rome during a hot spell, do as the Romans do: Sightsee a little, take a break during the hottest hours, then resume sightseeing.

The best way to see Rome once you arrive is to choose an area or a sight that you particularly want to see, reach it by bus or metro, then explore the area on foot. Wear comfortable, sturdy shoes, preferably with thick rubber soles to cushion you against the cobblestones. You can buy transportation-route maps at newsstands and at ATAC (bus company) information and ticket booths. The metro provides the easiest and fastest way to get around, although its stops are limited. A BIG tourist ticket, valid for one day on all public transport, costs 6,000 lire. Taxis wait at stands and, for a small extra charge, can also be called by telephone. The meter starts at 4,500 lire. Use the yellow or the newer white cabs only, and be very sure to check the meter. To call a cab, phone 06/3570, 06/5551, 06/4994, or 06/88177.

Exploring Rome *Numbers in the margin correspond to points of interest on the Rome map.*

❶ In the valley below the Campidoglio is the **Foro Romano** (Roman Forum). Once only a marshy hollow, the forum became the political, commercial, and social center of Rome, studded with public meeting halls, shops, and temples. As Rome declined, these monuments lost their importance and eventually were destroyed by fire or the invasions of barbarians. Rubble accumulated (though much of it was carted off later by medieval home builders as construction material), and the site reverted to marshy pastureland; sporadic excavations began at the end of the 19th century. You don't really have to try to make sense of the mass of marble fragments scattered over the area of the Roman Forum. Just consider that 2,000 years ago this was the center of the Mediterranean world. Wander down the Via Sacra and climb the Palatine Hill, where the emperors had their palaces and where 16th-century cardinals strolled in elaborate Italian gardens. From the belvedere you have a good view of the Circus Maximus. *Entrances to Via Sacra on Via dei Fori Imperiali and Piazza Santa Maria Nova; entrances to Palatine on Via Sacra and and Via di San Gregorio, tel. 06/699–0110. Admission free. Open Apr.–Sept., Mon.–Sat. 9–6, Sun. 9–1; Oct.–Mar., Mon.–Sat. 9–3, Sun. 9–1.*

❷ Rome's most famous ancient ruin, the **Colosseo** (Colosseum), was inaugurated in AD 80 with a program of games and shows that lasted 100 days. On opening day alone 5,000 wild animals perished in the arena. The Colosseum could hold more than 50,000 spectators; it was faced with marble, decorated with stuccos, and had an ingenious system of awnings to provide shade. Gladiators would stand before the imperial box to salute the emperor, calling *"Ave, imperator, morituri te salutant"* (Hail, emperor, men about to die salute thee). Try to see it both in daytime and at night, when yellow floodlights make it a magical sight. The Colosseum, by the way, takes its name from a colossal, 118-ft statue of Nero that stood nearby. You must pay a fee to explore the upper levels. Some sections of the amphitheater may be closed off during ongoing restorations. *Piazza del Colosseo, tel. 06/700–4261. Admission 10,000 lire. Open Mon.–Sat. 9–2 hours before sunset, Sun. 9–1.*

❸ The **Terme di Caracalla** (Baths of Caracalla), numbered among ancient Rome's most beautiful and luxurious, were inaugurated by Caracalla in AD 217 and used until the 6th century. An ancient version of a swanky athletic club, the baths were open to the public; citizens could bathe, socialize, and exercise in huge pools and richly decorated halls and libraries, now towering ruins. *Via delle Terme di Caracalla. Admission: 8,000 lire. Open Apr.–Sept., Tues.–Sat. 9–6, Sun.–Mon. 9–1; Oct.–Mar., Tues.–Sat. 9–3, Sun.–Mon. 9–1.*

❹ The 200-year-old **Scalinata di Piazza di Spagna** (Spanish Steps), named for the Spanish Embassy to the Holy See (the Vatican), opposite the American Express office, are a popular rendezvous, especially for the young people who throng this area. The steps are banked with blooming azaleas from mid-April to mid-May. *Piazza di Spagna and Piazza Trinità dei Monti.*

❺ **Fontana di Trevi** (Trevi Fountain) is a spectacular fantasy of mythical sea creatures and cascades of splashing water. Legend has it that visitors must toss a coin into the fountain to ensure their return to Rome, but you'll have to force your way past crowds of tourists and aggressive souvenir vendors to do so. The fountain as you see it was completed in the mid-1700s, but there had been a drinking fountain on the site for centuries. Pope Urban VIII almost sparked a revolt when he slapped a tax on wine to cover the expenses of having the fountain repaired. *Piazza di Trevi.*

⑥ One of Rome's oddest sights is the crypt of the church of **Santa Maria della Concezione.** In four chapels under the main church, the skeletons and scattered bones of some 4,000 dead Capuchin monks are arranged in decorative motifs, a macabre practice peculiar to the baroque age. *Via Veneto 27, tel. 06/462850. Admission free, but donations encouraged. Open daily 9–noon and 3–6.*

Via della Conciliazione, the broad avenue leading to St. Peter's Basilica, was created by Mussolini's architects by razing blocks of old houses. This opened up a vista of the basilica, giving the eye time to adjust to its mammoth dimensions and thereby spoiling the effect Bernini sought when he enclosed his vast square (which is really oval) in the embrace of huge quadruple colonnades. In **⑦** **Piazza San Pietro** (St. Peter's Square), which has held up to 400,000 people at one time, look for the stone disks in the pavement halfway between the fountains and the obelisk. From these points the colonnades seem to be formed of a single row of columns all the way around.

When you enter St. Peter's Square (completed in 1667), you are entering Vatican territory. Since the Lateran Treaty of 1929, **Vatican City** has been an independent and sovereign state, which covers about 108 acres and is surrounded by thick, high walls. Its gates are watched over by the Swiss Guards, who still wear the colorful dress uniforms designed by Michelangelo. Sovereign of this little state is John Paul II, 264th pope of the Roman Catholic Church.

⑧ At noon on Sunday the pope appears at his third-floor study window in the **Vatican Palace,** to the right of the basilica, to bless the crowd in the square. (Note: Entry to St. Peter's, the Vatican Museums, and all other sites within Vatican City, e.g., the Gardens, is barred to those wearing shorts, miniskirts, sleeveless T-shirts, and otherwise revealing clothing. Women should carry scarves to cover bare shoulders and upper arms or wear blouses that come to the elbow. Men should dress modestly, in slacks and shirts.)

⑨ **Basilica di San Pietro** (St. Peter's Basilica) is one of Rome's most impressive sights. It takes a while to absorb the sheer magnificence of it, however, and its rich decoration may not be to everyone's taste. Its size alone is overwhelming, and the basilica is best appreciated when providing the lustrous background for ecclesiastical ceremonies thronged with the faithful. The original basilica was built in the early 4th century AD by the emperor Constantine, over an earlier shrine that supposedly marked the burial place of St. Peter. After more than a thousand years, the old basilica was so decrepit it had to be torn down. The task of building a new, much larger one took almost 200 years and employed the architectural genius of Alberti, Bramante, Raphael, Peruzzi, Antonio Sangallo the Younger, and Michelangelo, who died before the dome he had planned could be completed. Finally, in 1626, St. Peter's Basilica was finished. The basilica is full of extraordinary works of art. Among the most famous is Michelangelo's *Pietà* (1498), seen in the first chapel on the right just as you enter the basilica. Michelangelo has four *Pietàs* to his credit. The earliest and best known can be seen here. Two others are in Florence, and the fourth, the *Rondanini Pietà*, is in Milan.

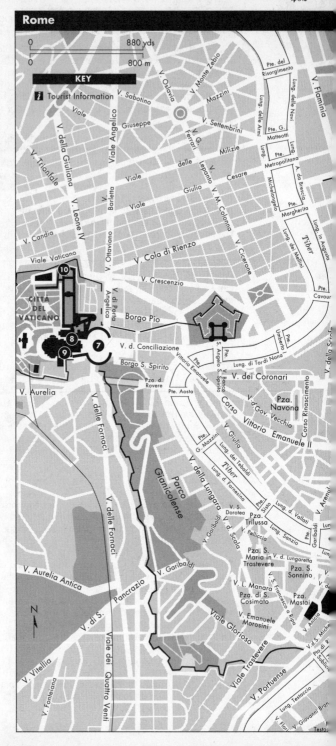

Rome

KEY

ℹ️ Tourist Information

At the end of the central aisle is the bronze statue of **St. Peter,** its foot worn by centuries of reverent kisses. The bronze throne above the altar in the apse was created by Bernini to contain a simple wood and ivory chair once believed to have belonged to St. Peter. Bernini's bronze *baldacchino* (canopy) over the papal altar was made with metal stripped from the portico of the Pantheon at the order of Pope Urban VIII, one of the powerful Roman Barberini family. His practice of plundering ancient monuments for material to implement his grandiose schemes inspired the famous quip, *"Quod non fecerunt barbari, fecerunt Barberini"* ("What the barbarians didn't do, the Barberini did").

As you stroll up and down the aisles and transepts, observe the fine mosaic copies of famous paintings above the altars, the monumental tombs and statues, and the fine stuccowork. Stop at the **Museo Storico** (Historical Museum), which contains some priceless liturgical objects.

The entrance to the so-called **Grotte Vaticane** (Vatican Grottoes), or crypt, is in one of the huge piers at the crossing. It's best to leave this visit for last, as the crypt's only exit takes you outside the church. The crypt contains chapels and the tombs of many popes. It occupies the area of the original basilica, over the necropolis, the ancient burial ground where evidence of what may be St. Peter's burial place has been found. To see the roof and dome of the basilica, take the elevator or climb the stairs in the courtyard near the exit of the Vatican Grottoes. From the roof you can climb a short interior staircase to the base of the dome for an overhead view of the interior of the basilica. Only if you are in good shape should you attempt the very long, strenuous, and claustrophobic climb up the narrow stairs to the balcony of the lantern atop the dome, where the view embraces the Vatican Gardens as well as all of Rome.

Free 60-minute tours of St. Peter's Basilica are offered in English daily (usually starting about 10 AM and 3 PM, and at 2:30 PM Sun.) by volunteer guides. They start at the information desk under the basilica portico. *St. Peter's Basilica, tel. 06/6988–4466. Open Apr.–Sept., daily 7–7; Oct.–Mar., daily 7–6. Treasury: entrance in Sacristy. Admission: 8,000 lire. Open Apr.–Sept., daily 9–6; Oct.–Mar., daily 9–5. Roof and dome: entrance in courtyard to the left as you leave basilica. Admission: 6,000 lire for elevator, 5,000 lire for stairs. Open Apr.–Sept., daily 8–6; Oct.–Mar., daily 8–5. Vatican Grottoes (Tombs of the Popes): entrance alternates among piers at crossing. Admission free. Open Apr.–Sept., daily 8–6; Oct.–Mar., daily 8–5.*

❿ The collections in the **Musei Vaticani** (Vatican Museums) cover nearly 8 km (5 mi) of displays. If you have time, allow at least half a day for Castel Sant'Angelo and St. Peter's and another half day for the museums. Posters at the museum entrance plot out a choice of four color-coded itineraries; the shortest takes about 90 minutes, the longest more than four hours, depending on your rate of progress.

No matter which tour you take, it will include the famed **Cappella Sistina** (Sistine Chapel). In 1508, Pope Julius II commissioned Michelangelo to fresco the more than 10,000 square ft of the chapel's ceiling. For four years Michelangelo dedicated himself to painting over fresh plaster, and the result was his masterpiece. Completed cleaning operations have removed centuries of soot and revealed its original and surprisingly brilliant colors. On the wall over the altar is Michaelangelo's *Last Judgement*, painted about 30 years after the ceiling was completed.

You can try to avoid the tour groups by going early or late, allowing yourself enough time before the closing hour. In peak season, the crowds definitely detract from your appreciation of this outstanding artistic achievement. To make sense of the figures on the ceiling, buy an illustrated guide or rent a taped commentary. A pair of binoculars and a mirror to reflect the ceiling also help.

The Vatican collections are so rich that unless you are an expert in art history, you will probably want only to skim the surface, concentrating on pieces that strike your fancy. Some of the highlights that might be of interest include the Egyptian collection and the *Laocoön*, the *Belvedere Torso*, and the *Apollo Belvedere*, which inspired Michelangelo. The Raphael Rooms are decorated with masterful frescoes, and there are more Raphaels in the *Pinacoteca* (Picture Gallery). At the Quattro Cancelli, near the entrance to the Picture Gallery, a rather spartan cafeteria provides basic nonalcoholic refreshments. *Viale Vaticano, tel. 06/69883041. Admission: 15,000 lire; free last Sun. of month. Open Easter wk and mid-Mar.–Oct., weekdays 8:45–3:45, Sat. 8:45–12:45; Oct.–mid-Mar. , Mon.–Sat. 8:45–12:45. Last Sun. of month 8:45–12:45. . Closed Sun., except last Sun. of month.*

⑪ Originally built in 27 BC by Augustus's general Agrippa and rebuilt by Hadrian in the 2nd century AD, the **Pantheon** is one of Rome's finest, best-preserved, and perhaps least appreciated ancient monuments. You don't have to look far past the huge columns of the portico and the original bronze doors to find the reason for its astounding architectural harmony: the diameter of the soaring dome is exactly equal to the height of the walls. The hole in the ceiling is intentional: the oculus at the apex of the dome signifies the "all-seeing eye of heaven." Romans and tourists alike pay little attention to it, and on summer evenings it serves mainly as a backdrop for all the action in the square. In ancient times the entire interior was encrusted with rich decorations of gilt bronze and marble. *Piazza della Rotonda, tel. 06/6830–0230. Admission: free. Open Mon.–Sat. 9–6:30, Sun. 9–1.*

Shopping Shopping is part of the fun of being in Rome. The best buys are leather goods of all kinds, from gloves to handbags and wallets to jackets; silk goods; and high-quality knitwear. Shops are closed on Sunday and on Monday morning; in July and August, they close on Saturday afternoon as well. **Via Condotti,** directly across from the Spanish Steps, and the streets running parallel to Via Condotti, as well as its cross streets, form the most elegant and expensive shopping area in the city. Romans themselves do much of their shopping along **Via Cola di Rienzo** and **Via Nazionale.** For minor antiques, **Via dei Coronari** and other streets in the Piazza Navona area are good. The most prestigious antiques dealers are situated in **Via del Babuino** and its environs. The open-air markets at **Campo dei Fiori** and in many neighborhoods throughout the city provide an eyeful of great local color.

Seville, Spain

Seville—Spain's fourth-largest city and capital of Andalucía—is one of the most beautiful and romantic cities in Europe. Here in this city of the sensuous Carmen and the amorous Don Juan, famed for the spectacle of its Holy Week processions and April Fair, you'll come close to the spiritual heart of Moorish Andalucía.

The downside to a visit to Seville is that petty crime, much of it directed against tourists, is rife. Take only the minimum amount of cash with you when going ashore. If you're unlucky, it's an equally depressing fact that the police have adopted a distinctly casual attitude to such thefts.

Currency The unit of currency in Spain is the peseta (pta.). There are bills of 1,000, 2,000, 5,000, and 10,000 ptas. Coins are 1, 5, 25, 50, 100, 200, and 500 ptas. At press time, the exchange rate was about 152 ptas. to the U.S. dollar.

Telephones The country code for Spain is 34. Pay phones generally take the new, smaller 5- and 25-pta. coins; the minimum charge for short local calls is 25 ptas. Area codes always begin with a 9 and are different for each province. If you're dialing from outside the country, drop the 9. Calling abroad can be done from any pay phone marked *teléfono internacional.* Use 50-pta. (or 100-pta. if the phone takes them) coins initially, then coins of any denomination to prolong your call. Newer pay phones take only phone cards, which can be purchased at any tobacco shop in denominations of 1,000 or 2,000 ptas. Dial 07 for international calls, wait for the tone to change, then 1 for the United States or 0101 for Canada. For lengthy international calls, go to the telefónica, a telephone office, where an operator assigns you a private booth and collects payment at the end of the call; this is the least expensive and by far the easiest way of phoning abroad. **AT&T** (tel. 900/99–00–11); **MCI** (tel. 900/99–00–14); **Sprint** (tel. 900/99–00–13).

Shore Excursions The following is a good choice in Seville. It may not be offered by all cruise lines. Time and price are approximate.

Survey of Seville. Travel through Seville's past and present on this comprehensive excursion that explores the city's religious, ethnic, and historical diversity. *8½ hrs. Cost: $124.*

Coming Ashore Ships dock at Cádiz for Seville. The drive to and from Seville is around two hours each way.

Once in the city, you can walk from some sights to others; hop a cab or even take a horse-drawn carriage to reach other areas.

Exploring Seville *Numbers in the margin correspond to points of interest on the Seville map.*

❶ A must is a visit to the **cathedral,** begun in 1402, a century and a half after St. Ferdinand delivered Seville from the Moors. This great Gothic edifice, which took just over a century to build, is traditionally described in superlatives. It's the biggest and highest cathedral in Spain, the largest Gothic building in the world, and the world's third-largest church after St. Peter's in Rome and St. Paul's in London. As if that weren't enough, it boasts the world's largest carved wooden altarpiece. Despite such impressive statistics, the inside can be dark and gloomy, with too many overly ornate baroque trappings. You may want to pay your respects to Christopher Columbus, whose mortal vestiges are said to be enshrined in a flamboyant mausoleum in the south aisle. Borne aloft by statues representing the four medieval kingdoms of Spain, it's to be hoped the great voyager has found peace at last, after the transatlantic quarrels that carried his body from Valladolid to Santo Domingo and from Havana to Seville. *Plaza Virgen de los Reyes, tel. 95/421–4971. Admission to cathedral and Giralda (see below): 600 ptas. Open Mon.–Sat. 10:30–5, Sun. 2–4, and mass.*

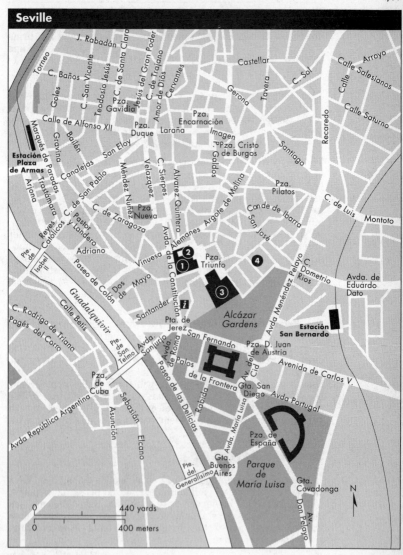

Seville

J. Rabadán · C. Baños · Goles · Torneo · C. San Vicente · Teodosia Jesús · C. de Santa Clara · Jesús del Gran Poder · Amor de Diós · C. de Trajano · Cervantes · Castellar · Calle Salesianos · Arroyo · C. Sol · Calle · Calle Saturno · Gerona · Tavera · Pza. Gavidia · Calle de Alfonso XII · Pza. Duque · Laraña · Pza. Encarnación · Imagen · Pza. Cristo de Burgos · Santiago · Recaredo · Marqués de Paradas · Gravina · Bailén · Canalejas · San Eloy · C. de San Pablo · Méndez Núñez · Velázquez · C. Sierpes · Álvarez Quintero · P.Pza. Galdos · Estación Plaza de Armas · Trastámara · Arjona · Reyes Católicos · C. y Landero · C. de Pastor · C. de Zaragoza · Pza. Nueva · Argote de Molina · Conde de Ibarra · Pza. Pilatos · C. de Luis Montoto · Adriano · Vinuesa · Avda. de la Constitución · Alemanes · Pza. Triunfo · San José · C Dometrio Rios · Avda. Menéndez Pelayo · Pte. de Isabel II · Paseo de Colón · Dos de Mayo · Santander · Pta. de Jerez · Alcázar Gardens · Avda. de Eduardo Dato · Guadalquivir · Calle Betis · C. Rodrigo de Triana · Pagés del Corral · Pte. de San Telmo · Avda. Sanjurio · Avd. de Roma · San Fernando · Pza. D. Juan de Austria · Estación San Bernardo · Avenida de Carlos V. · Pza. de Cuba · Sebastián Elcano · Asunción · Paseo de las Delicias · Avd. de Palos de la Frontera · Rabida · Gta. San Diego · Avda Portugal · Avda República Argentina · Avda. María Luisa · Pza. de España · Pte. del Generalísimo · Gta. Buenos Aires · Parque de María Luisa · Gta. Covadonga · Av. Don Pelayo

0 440 yards
0 400 meters

N

Every day the bell that summons the faithful to prayer rings out from a Moorish minaret, a relic of the Arab mosque whose admirable tower of Abu Yakoub the Sevillians could not bring themselves to destroy. Topped in 1565–68 by a bell tower and weather vane and called the **Giralda,** this splendid example of Moorish art is one of the marvels of Seville. In place of steps, 35 gently sloping ramps climb to the viewing platform 230 ft high. St. Ferdinand is said to have ridden his horse to the top to admire the view of the city he had conquered. Seven centuries later your view of the Golden Tower and shimmering Guadalquivir will be equally breathtaking. *Plaza Virgen de los Reyes, tel. 95/456–3321. Open Mon.–Sat. 11–5, Sun. 10–1:30 and 2–4.*

The high, fortified walls of the **Alcázar** belie the exquisite delicacy of the palace's interior. It was built by Pedro the Cruel—so known because he murdered his stepmother and four of his half-brothers—who lived here with his mistress María de Padilla from 1350 to 1369. Don't mistake this for a genuine Moorish palace, as it was built more than 100 years after the reconquest of Seville; rather, its style is Mudéjar—built by Moorish craftsmen working under orders of a Christian king. The palace centers around the beautiful **Patio de las Doncellas** (Court of the Damsels), whose name pays tribute to the annual gift of 100 virgins to the Moorish sultans whose palace once stood here. *Plaza del Triunfo, tel. 95/422–7163. Palace and gardens admission: 600 ptas. Open Tues.–Sat. 9:30–5, Sun. 9:30–1.*

The **Barrio de Santa Cruz,** with its twisting alleyways, cobbled squares, and whitewashed houses, is a perfect setting for an operetta. Once the home of Seville's Jewish population, it was much favored by 17th-century noblemen, and today boasts some of the most expensive properties in Seville. All the romantic images you've ever had of Spain will come to life here: Every house gleams white or deep ocher yellow, wrought-iron grilles adorn the windows, and every balcony and patio is bedecked with geraniums and petunias. Ancient bars nestle side by side with antiques shops.

Stockholm, Sweden

The city of Stockholm, built on 14 small islands among open bays and narrow channels, is a handsome, civilized place, full of parks, squares, and airy boulevards; yet it is also a bustling, modern metropolis. Glass-and-steel skyscrapers abound, but in the center you are never more than five minutes' walk from twisting, medieval streets and water views.

Currency The unit of currency in Sweden is the krona (plural, kronor), which is divided into 100 öre and is written as SKr, SEK, or kr. Coins come in values of 50 öre and 1, 5, or 10 kronor; bills in denominations of 20, 100, 500, and 1,000 kronor. At press time, the exchange rate was 7.99 SKr to the U.S. dollar.

Telephones The country code for Sweden is 46. When dialing from outside the country, drop the initial zero from the regional area code. Sweden has plenty of pay phones; to use them you'll need either SKr 1, SKr 5, or SKr 10 coins, since a local call costs SKr 2. You can also purchase a *telefonkort* (telephone card) from a Telebutik, hospital, or *Pressbyrån* store for SKr 35, SKr 60, or SKr 100. International calls can also be made from any pay phone. For calls to the United States and Canada, dial 009, then 1 (the country code), then wait for a second dial tone before dialing the area code and number. You can make calls from Telebutik offices. To reach an **AT&T** long-distance operator, dial 020/795611; **MCI**, 020/795922; **Sprint**, 020/799011.

Shore Excursions The following are good choices in Stockholm. They may not be offered by all lines. Times and prices are approximate.

City and Vasa Museum. Visit City Hall and Golden Hall, the site of the Nobel Prize banquet. Pass the Senate Building and Royal Opera House on the way to the Vasa Ship Museum. *3½ hrs. Cost: $44.*

Royal Palace and Millesgarden. A complete tour of the royal residence precedes a visit to Millesgarden, the home, studio, and gardens of Sweden's famous modern sculptor, Carl Milles. In between, you'll stroll the streets of Old Town and drive through Stockholm Center past the Royal Opera House. *3 hrs. Cost: $44.*

Coming Ashore Ships berth at Stockholm's pier within view of the Royal Palace in Old Town.

The most cost-effective way of getting around Stockholm is to buy a Stockholmskortet (the Key to Stockholm card). Besides unlimited transportation on city subway, bus, and rail services, it offers free admission to 70 museums and several sightseeing trips. The card costs SKr 199 for 24 hours. It is available from the tourist information centers at Sweden House and the Kaknäs TV tower, and at the Hotellcentralen accommodations bureau at the central train station.

Maps and timetables for all city transportation networks are available from the Stockholm Transit Authority (SL) information desks at Sergels Torg, the central train station, and at Slussen in Gamla Stan. You can also obtain information by phone (tel. 08/600–1000).

The subway system, known as T-banan, is the easiest and fastest way of getting around the city. Fares are based on zones, starting at SKr 14, good for travel within one zone, such as downtown, for one hour. You pay more if you travel in more than one zone. Single tickets are available at station ticket counters, but it is cheaper to buy the SL Tourist Card, which is valid on buses and the subway and also gives free admission to a number of sights and museums. It can be purchased at Pressbyrån newsstands and SL information desks and costs SKr 60 for 24 hours.

A 10-km (6-mi) taxi ride will cost SKr 97 between 9 AM and 4 PM on weekdays, SKr 107 on weekday nights, and SKr 114 on weekends. Major taxi companies are Taxi Stockholm (tel. 08/150000), Taxikurir (tel. 08/300000), and Taxi 020 (tel. 020/939393).

Exploring Stockholm *Numbers in the margin correspond to points of interest on the Stockholm map.*

Anyone in Stockholm with limited time should give priority to a tour of **Gamla Stan** (the Old Town), a labyrinth of narrow, medieval streets, alleys, and quiet squares on the island just south of the city center. Ideally, you should devote an entire day to this district. Be sure to spend at least a day visiting the large island of Djurgården. Although it's only a short walk from the city center, the most pleasant way to approach it is by ferry from Skeppsbron, in Gamla Stan.

❶ **Stadshuset** (city hall) was constructed in 1923; architect Ragnar Östberg's ornate facade has become a Stockholm landmark. Lav-

Stockholm

Gröna Lund, **4**
Kungliga Slott, **2**
Nordiska Museet, **5**
Skansen, **6**
Stadshuset, **1**
Vasamuseet, **3**

ÖSTERMALM

Sibyllegatan
Kommendörsgatan
Karlaplan
Banérgatan
Karlavägen
LADUGÅRDSGÄRDET
Narvavägen
Linnégatan
Oxenstiernsgatan
Gärdesgatan
Storgatan
Skärgårdsgatan
Artillerigatan
Skeppargatan
Greygatan
Styrmangatan
Riddargatan
Strandvägen
Linnégatan
Strandvägen

Djurgårdsbron

Djurgårdsbrunnsviken

Rosendalsvägen

SKEPPSHOLMEN

Svensksundsvägen

DJURGÅRDEN

Sirishovsvägen

Djurgårdsvägen
Alkärret
Falkenbergsg.
Allmänna Gränd
Djurgårds-
Slätten
Solliddsbacken
Singelbacken

KASTELL-
HOLMEN

Saltsjön

BECKHOLMEN

Baltic →

N

KEY

ℹ️ Tourist Information
— Rail Lines

0   500 yards
0   500 meters

ish mosaics adorn the walls of the Golden Hall, and the Prince's Gallery features a collection of large murals by Prince Eugen, brother of King Gustav V. Take the elevator halfway up, then climb the rest of the way to the top of the 348-ft tower for a magnificent view of the city. *Hantverkargatan 1, tel. 08/508–29000. Admission: SKr 30. Tours daily at 10 and noon; also at 11 and 2 in summer. Tower admission: SKr 15. Tower open May–Sept., daily 10–4:30.*

2 You should get to **Kungliga Slott** (Royal Palace), preferably by noon, when you can see the colorful changing-of-the-guard ceremony. The smartly dressed guards seem superfluous, as tourists wander at will into the palace courtyard and around the grounds. Several separate attractions are open to the public. Be sure to visit the Royal Armory, with its outstanding collection of weaponry and royal regalia. The Treasury houses the Swedish crown jewels, including the regalia used for the coronation of King Erik XIV in 1561. You can also visit the State Apartments, where the king swears in each successive government. *Gamla Stan, tel. 08/666–4466. Admission: SKr 45 for Armory; SKr 40 for Treasury; SKr 45 for State Apartments. Late Apr.–early Sept. Prices and hrs subject to change; call ahead.*

The *Vasa*, a restored 17th-century warship, is one of the oldest preserved war vessels in the world and has become Sweden's most popular tourist sight. It sank ignominiously in Stockholm Harbor on its maiden voyage in 1628, reportedly because it was not carrying sufficient ballast. Recovered in 1961, the ship has been restored to its original appearance and is housed in a spec- **3** tacular museum, **Vasamuseet.** It has guided tours, films, and displays. *Gälarvarvet, tel. 08/666–4800. Admission: SKr 45. Open Thurs.–Tues. 10–5, Wed. 10–8.*

4 **Gröna Lund,** Stockholm's only amusement park, is a family favorite, with traditional rides and new attractions on the waterfront each season. *Djurgårdesvägen, tel. 08/670–7600. Open late Apr.–early Sept. Call ahead for prices and hrs, as they are subject to change.*

5 **Nordiska Museet** (the Nordic Museum) provides insight into the way Swedish people have lived over the past 500 years. The collection includes displays of peasant costumes, folk art, and Sami culture. Families with children should visit the delightful "village life" play area on the ground floor. *Djurgårdsvägen 6–16, tel. 08/ 666–4600. Admission: SKr 50. Open Tues.–Sun. 11–5.*

6 More than 150 reconstructed traditional buildings from all over Sweden have been gathered at **Skansen,** an open-air folk museum with a variety of handicraft displays and demonstrations. There is a zoo, with native Scandinavian lynxes, wolves, and elks, as well as an aquarium and an old-style *tivoli* (amusement park). *Djurgårdsslätten 49–51, tel. 08/442–8000. Admission: Sept.–Apr., SKr30 weekdays, SKr40 weekends; May–Aug., SKr 50. Open Sept.–Apr., daily 9–5; May–Aug., daily 9 AM–10 PM. Prices and hours subject to change; call ahead.*

Shopping Shop till you drop means hitting the street **Hamngatan** with a vengeance. The **Gamla Stan** area is best for antiques shops, book shops, and art galleries. **Sturegallerian** (Stureg.) is an elegant covered shopping gallery built on the site of the former public baths at Stureplan. **Västerlånggatan,** one of the main streets in the Old Town, is a popular shopping area brimming with boutiques and antiques shops.

Turkish Coast and Kuşadası/Ephesus

Some of the finest reconstructed Greek and Roman cities, including the fabled Pergamum, Ephesus, Aphrodisias, and Troy, are found along the Aegean. Bright yellow road signs pointing to historical sites or to those currently undergoing excavation are everywhere here. There are so many Greek and Roman ruins, in fact, that some haven't yet been excavated and others are going to seed. Grand or small, all the sites are steeped in atmosphere and are best explored early in the morning or late in the afternoon, when there are fewer crowds. You can escape the heat of the day on one of the sandy beaches that line the coast.

Currency
The monetary unit is the Turkish lira (TL), which comes in bank notes of 50,000, 100,000, 250,000, 500,000, 1,000,000 and 5,000,000. Coins come in denominations of 1,000, 2,500, 5,000, 10,000, 25,000 and 50,000. At press time, the exchange rate was 270,000 to the U.S. dollar. These rates are subject to wide fluctuation, so check close to your departure. Be certain to retain your original exchange slips when you convert money into Turkish lira—you will need them to reconvert the money. Because the Turkish lira is worth a lot less than most currencies, it's best to convert only what you plan to spend.

Telephones
The country code for Turkey is 90. All telephone numbers in Turkey have seven local digits plus three-digit city codes. Intercity calls are preceded by 0. (If calling from outside the country, drop this zero when dialing.) Pay phones are yellow, push-button models. Most take *jetons* (tokens) although an increasing number, particularly in large cities, take phone cards. Tokens can be purchased for 7¢ at post offices and, for a couple of cents more, at street booths. Telephone cards are available at post offices. Multilingual directions are posted in phone booths. For all international calls dial 00, then dial the country code, area or city code, and the number. You can reach an international operator by dialing 132. To reach an **AT&T** long-distance operator, dial 00800-12277; **MCI**, 00800-11177; **Sprint,** 00800-14477.

Shore Excursions
The following are good choices along the Turkish coast. They may not be offered by all cruise lines. Times and prices are approximate.

In Izmir
City Tour. Visit the fairly well-preserved Velvet Fortress and Archeological Museum followed by a belly-dancing performance and a folkloric show. *3¾ hrs. Cost: $30.*

Ephesus. Drive 1 hour and 15 minutes to reach Ephesus, once the Roman Capital Asia Minor, where you'll tour the spellbinding ruins of Ephesus. Major sights include the Great Theater, the Library of Celsus, the Temple of Hadrian, and Curetes Street. *4¼ hrs. Cost: $45.*

In Kuşadası
Ancient Ephesus. This is the tour to take—it explores one of the best-preserved ancient cities of the world. Be prepared to do a lot of walking. *3 hrs. Cost: $41.*

In Bodrum
The Castle of Bodrum is easily explored on your own, and is within walking distance of the tender drop-off point.

Wooden Boat Ride. Sail one of the wooden boats that line Bodrum's harbor to small coves and bays for swimming and snorkeling. *4 hrs. Cost: $64.*

Coming
Ashore Whether your ship docks or drops anchor along the Turkish Coast, landing sites are conveniently located for independent exploration.

In Izmir Ships calling at Izmir's harbor dock along the waterfront boulevard called Kordon. Depending on what you want to see, you can walk, take a bus, or hire a taxi to explore the sights.

In Kuşadası Ships either dock or tender passengers ashore at Kuşadasi. Shops and restaurants are within walking distance of the port.

In Bodrum Ships calling at Bodrum tender passengers ashore in the main harbor. Walking Bodrum's streets is truly the best and most pleasurable way to explore local sights.

Exploring the Izmir, Turkey's third-largest city, is also its most Mediterranean
Turkish Coast in feel. Called Smyrna by the Greeks, it was a vital trading port
Izmir that was often ravaged by wars and earthquakes. The city was almost completely destroyed by a fire in 1922 during the final stages of Turkey's War of Independence against Greece. The center of the city is **Kültürpark,** which is a large green park that is the site of Izmir's industrial fair from late August until late September.

On top of Izmir's highest hill is the **Kadifekale** (Velvet Fortress), built in the 3rd century BC by Lysimachos. It is easily reached by dolmuş and is one of the few ancient ruins that was not destroyed in the fire of 1922.

At the foot of the hill is the restored **Agora,** the market of ancient Smyrna. The modern-day marketplace is in Konak Square, a maze of tiny streets filled with shops and covered stalls. *Open Mon.–Sat. 8–8.*

Kuşadası The major attraction near Kuşadasi is **Ephesus,** a city created by the Ionians in the 11th century BC and now one of the grandest reconstructed ancient sites in the world. It is the showpiece of Aegean archaeology. Ephesus was a powerful trading port and the sacred center for the cult of Artemis, Greek goddess of chastity, the moon, and hunting. The Ionians built a temple in her honor, one of the Seven Wonders of the Ancient World. During the Roman period, it became a shrine for the Roman goddess Diana. Today, waterlogged foundations are all that remain of the temple, but you can see the two-story **Library of Celsus**; nobleman's houses, with their terraces and courtyards; and a 25,000-seat amphitheater, still used today. The city is especially appealing out of season, when it can seem like a ghost town with its shimmering, long, white marble road grooved by chariot wheels. Allow yourself the full day for Ephesus. *4 km (2½ mi) west of Selçuk on Selçuk–Ephesus Rd., tel. 232/892–6402. Open daily 8:30–6 (summer), 8:30–5 (winter).*

Bodrum Sitting between two crescent-shape bays, Bodrum has for years been the favorite haunt of the Turkish upper classes. One of the outstanding sights in Bodrum is **Bodrum Kalesi**(Bodrum Castle), known as the Castle of St. Peter. Between the two bays, the castle was built by crusaders in the 11th century. It has beautiful gardens and the Museum of Underwater Archaeology. *Kale Cad., tel. 252/316–2516. Castle and museum admission: $3. Open Tues.–Sun. 8:30–noon and 1–5.*

The peninsula is downright littered with ancient Greek and Roman ruins, although getting to some of them involves driving over rough dirt roads. Five kilometers (3 miles) from Bodrum is

Halikarnas, a well-preserved 10,000-seat Greek amphitheater built in the 1st century BC and still used for town festivals. *Admission free. Open daily 8:30–sunset.*

Varna, Bulgaria

Bulgaria, a land of mountains and seascapes, of austerity and rustic beauty, lies in the eastern half of the Balkan peninsula. From the end of World War II until recently, it was the closest ally of the former Soviet Union and presented a rather mysterious image to the Western world. This era ended in 1989 with the overthrow of Communist party head Todor Zhivkov. Since then, Bulgaria has gradually opened itself to the West as it struggles along the path toward democracy and a free-market economy.

Founded in 681 by the Bulgars, a Turkic tribe from central Asia, Bulgaria was a crossroads of civilization even before that date. Archaeological finds in Varna, on the Black Sea coast, give proof of civilization from as early as 4600 BC. Bulgaria was part of the Byzantine Empire from AD 1018 to 1185 and was occupied by the Turks from 1396 until 1878. The combined influences are reflected in Bulgarian architecture, which has a truly Eastern feel. Five hundred years of Muslim occupation and nearly half a century of Communist rule did not wipe out Christianity, and there are many lovely, icon-filled churches to see.

Currency The unit of currency in Bulgaria is the lev (plural leva). There are bills of 100, 200, 500, 1,000, 2,000, 5,000, 10,000, 20,000, and 50,000 leva. Bills smaller than 100 still exist, but their use is illegal as of 1998, so don't accept change in 20 or 50 leva bills. Ask for coins. Although prices are sometimes quoted in dollars, all goods and services must be paid for in leva. All unspent leva must be exchanged before you depart the country, and you will need to present your official exchange slips to prove that the currency was legally purchased—so exchange only as much as you plan to spend. The value of the lev continues to fluctuate, and the exchange rate and price information quoted here may be outdated very quickly. At press time, the rate quoted by the Bulgarian State Bank is 1,790 leva to the U.S. dollar.

Telephones The country code for Bulgaria is 359. When dialing from outside the country, drop the initial zero from the regional area code. Local calls cost 2 leva and can be made from your hotel or from pay phones. Phone cards can be purchased at post offices, hotels, and street kiosks. Calls to the United States can be made from Bulfon or Betkom phones by using a local calling card to reach the international operator and then a long-distance calling card to reach the States. To place a call using an **AT&T USADirect** international operator, dial tel. 00–800–0010.

Shore Excursions The following is a good choice in Varna. It may not be offered by all cruise lines. Time and price are approximate.

Varna Tour. You'll see the city's major sites before visiting one of the area's renowned Black Sea spas. *Half day. Cost: $42.*

Coming Ashore Ships calling at Varna dock at the city harbor. Varna's main sights can be reached on foot. Buses are inexpensive; make sure to buy your ticket in advance from the kiosks near the bus stops.

The main sights in Varna are within easy walking distance of one another.

Exploring Varna Begin with the **Archeologicheski Musei** (Museum of Art and History), one of the great—if lesser-known—museums of Europe. The splendid collection includes the world's oldest gold treasures from the Varna necropolis of the 4th millennium BC, as well as Thracian, Greek, and Roman treasures, and richly painted icons. *41 bul. Osmi Primorski Polk, tel. 052/23–70–57. Open Tues.–Sat. 10–5.*

In Mitropolit Simeon Square, the monumental **Tsurkva Yspenie Bogorodichno** (Cathedral of the Assumption), 1880–86, is worth a look for its lavish murals. Opposite the cathedral, in the city gardens, is the **starata chasovnikuh kula** (Old Clock Tower), built in 1880 by the Varna Guild Association. *pl. Nezavisimost*

The 1602 **Tsurkva Sveta Bogoroditsa** (Church of the Holy Virgin) is worth a look for its beautifully carved iconostasis. *ul. Han Krum at ul. Knyaz Alexander Bwatenberg.*

Wander through the remains of the **Rimski Termi** (Roman Baths), dating from the 2nd to the 3rd century. Signs in English detail the various steps of the bath ritual. *ul. Han Krum just south of Tsurkva Sveta Bogoroditsa.*

The **Morski Muzei** (Marine Museum) displays the early days of navigation on the Black Sea and the Danube. *No. 2 Primorski Blvd., tel. 052/22–26–55. Open weekdays 8–4.*

In the extensive and luxuriant **Primorski Park** (Seaside Park) are restaurants, an open-air theater, and the fascinating Copernicus Astronomy Complex, near the main entrance. *Southern end of Primorski Blvd. Astronomy Complex: tel. 052/22–28–90. Open weekdays 8–noon and 2–5.*

Venice, Italy

For hundreds of years Venice—La Serenissima, the Most Serene—was the unrivaled mistress of trade between Europe and the Orient, and the staunch bulwark of Christendom against the tide of Turkish expansion. Though the power and glory of its days as a wealthy city-republic are gone, the art and exotic aura remain. The majority of its magnificent palazzi are slowly crumbling, but somehow in Venice the shabby, derelict effect is magically transformed into one of supreme beauty and charm. Hot and sultry in the summer, Venice is much more welcoming in early spring and late fall.

Currency The unit of currency in Italy is the lira (plural, lire). There are bills of 1,000, 2,000, 5,000, 10,000, 50,000, 100,000, and 500,000 lire (this largest bill being almost impossible to change, except in banks); coins are worth 50, 100, 200, and 500 lire. In 1999 the euro will begin to be used as a banking currency, but the lire will still be the currency in use on a day-to-day basis. At press time, the exchange rate was about 1,770 to the U.S. dollar. When your purchases run into hundreds of thousands of lire, beware of being shortchanged, a dodge that is practiced at ticket windows and cashiers' desks, as well as in shops and even banks. Always count your change before you leave the counter.

Telephones The country code for Italy is 39. Most local calls cost 200 lire for two minutes. Pay phones take either 100-, 200-, or 500-lire coins or *schede telefoniche* (phone cards), purchased in bars, tobacconists, post offices, and TELECOM offices in either 5,000-, 10,000-, or 15,000-lire denominations. To place international calls, many travelers go to the Telefoni telephone exchange (usually marked TELEcom), where the operator assigns you a booth, can help place your call, and will collect payment when you have finished. To dial an international call, insert a phone card, dial 00, then the country code, area code, and phone number. For **AT&T USADirect,** dial access number tel. 172–1011; for **MCI Call USA,** access number tel. 172–1022; for **Sprint Express,** access number tel. 172–1877. You will be connected directly with an operator in the United States.

Shore Excursions

The following are good choices in Venice. They may not be offered by all cruise lines. Times and prices are approximate.

Canals of Venice. See Venice from the water on this boat tour that glides down the bustling Grand Canal as well as some of the city's more intimate, narrow canals. Take time out for a visit to a glass factory. *3½ hrs. Cost: $52.*

Venice Tour. Visit St. Mark's Square and Cathedral, Doge's Palace, and the Bridge of Sighs. *2½ hrs. Cost: $42.*

Coming Ashore

Ships typically dock in Venice at the main port terminal, an unappealing building whose saving grace is its relative nearness to St. Mark's Square.

Cruise passengers may find that getting around Venice presents some unusual problems: the complexity of its layout (the city is made up of more than 100 islands, all linked by bridges); the bewildering unfamiliarity of waterborne transportation; the apparently illogical house numbering system and duplication of street names in its six districts; and the necessity of walking whether you enjoy it or not. It's essential to have a good map showing all street names and water-bus routes; buy one at any newsstand, and count on getting lost more than once.

Walking is the only way to reach many parts of Venice, so wear comfortable shoes. ACTV water buses run the length of the Grand Canal and circle the city. There are several lines, some of which connect Venice with the major and minor islands in the lagoon. **Line 1** is the Grand Canal local, calling at every stop, and continuing via San Marco to the Lido. (It takes about 45 minutes from the station to San Marco.) **Line 52** runs from the railway station to San Zaccaria via Piazzale Roma and Zattere, and continues to the Lido. **Line 52/** (note the difference) goes along the same route, but makes stops along the Giudecca instead of Zattere, and continues to Fondamente Nuove (where boats leave for the islands of the northern Lagoon) and Murano. **Line 82** runs in a loop from San Zaccaria to Giudecca, Zattere, Piazzale Roma, the train station., Rialto, (with fewer stops along the Grand Canal than Line 1) and back to San Zaccaria (and out to the Lido in the afternoon). The fare is 4,500 lire on all lines. A 24-hour tourist ticket costs 15,000 lire. Timetables are posted at every landing stage, but there is not always a ticket booth operating. You may get on a boat without a ticket, but you will have to pay a higher fare on the boat. For this reason, it may be useful to buy a *blochetto* (book of tickets) in advance. Landing stages are clearly marked with name and line number, but check before boarding, particularly with the 52 and 82, to make sure the boat is going in your direction.

If you mustn't leave Venice without treating yourself to a gondola ride, take it in the quiet of the evening when the churning traffic on the canals has died down and at high tide, when the palace windows are illuminated, and the only sounds are the muted splashes of the gondolier's oar. Make sure he understands that you want to see the *rii,* or smaller canals, as well as the Grand Canal. There's supposed to be a fixed minimum rate of about 120,000 lire for 50 minutes, and a nighttime supplement of 30,000. Come to terms with your gondolier *before* stepping into his boat.

Motoscafis, or water "taxis," are excessively expensive, and the fare system is as complex as Venice's layout. A minimum fare of about 50,000 lire gets you nowhere, and you'll pay three times as much to get from one end of the Grand Canal to the other. Always agree on the fare before starting out.

Few tourists know about the two-man gondolas that ferry people across the Grand Canal at various fixed points. It's the cheapest and shortest gondola ride in Venice, and it can save a lot of walking. The fare is 700 lire, which you hand to one of the gondoliers when you get on. Look for TRAGHETTO signs.

Exploring Venice *Numbers in the margin correspond to points of interest on the Venice map.*

❶ Even the pigeons have to fight for space on **Piazza San Marco,** the most famous piazza in Venice, and pedestrian traffic jams clog the surrounding byways. Despite the crowds, San Marco is the logical starting place for exploring Venice. Napoléon called this "the most beautiful drawing room in all of Europe."

❷ The **Basilica di San Marco** (St. Mark's Basilica) was begun in the 11th century to hold the relics of St. Mark the Evangelist, the city's patron saint, and its richly decorated facade is surmounted by copies of the four famous gilded bronze horses (the originals are in the basilica's upstairs museum). Inside, golden mosaics sheathe walls and domes, lending an extraordinarily exotic aura: half Christian church, half Middle Eastern mosque. Be sure to see the Pala d'Oro, an eye-filling 10th-century altarpiece in gold and silver, studded with precious gems and enamels. From the atrium, climb the steep stairway to the museum: The bronze horses alone are worth the effort. *Piazza San Marco. Basilica open Mon.–Sat. 9:30–5:30 (5 in winter), Sun. 2–5:30 (5 in winter); free admission. Pala d'Oro and Treasury, tel. 041/522–5205; opening hours same as basilica, last entry 30 min. before closing. Gallery and Museum: hours same as basilica, last entry 30 min. before closing.*

❸ During Venice's heyday, the **Palazzo Ducale** (Doge's Palace) was the epicenter of the Serene Republic's great empire. More than just a palace, it was a combination White House, Senate, Supreme Court, torture chamber, and prison. The building's exterior is striking; the lower stories consist of two rows of fragile-seeming arches, while above rests a massive pink-and-white marble wall, whose solidity is barely interrupted by its six great Gothic windows. The interior is a maze of vast halls, monumental staircases, secret corridors, and the sinister prison cells and torture chamber. The palace is filled with frescoes, paintings, and a few examples of statuary by some of the Renaissance's greatest artists. Don't miss the famous view from the balcony, overlooking the piazza and St. Mark's Basin and the church of San Giorgio Maggiore across the lagoon. *Piazzetta San Marco, tel. 041/522–4951. Admission: 14,000 lire. Open Apr.–Oct., daily 9–7; Nov.–Mar., daily 9–5. Last entry 1 1/2 hrs before closing time.*

❹ For a pigeon's-eye view of Venice take the elevator up to the top of the **Campanile di San Marco** (St. Mark's bell tower) in Piazza San Marco, a reconstruction of the 1,000-year-old tower that collapsed one morning in 1912, practically without warning. Fifteenth-century clerics found guilty of immoral acts were suspended in wooden cages from the tower, sometimes to live on bread and water for as long as a year, sometimes to die of starvation and exposure. Look for them in Carpaccio's paintings of the square, which hang in the Accademia (*see below*). *Piazza San Marco, tel. 041/522–4064. Admission: 5,000 lire. Open daily 9:30– 3:45, with slightly longer hours in summer. Closed for maintenance for two weeks in Jan.*

❺ The **Galleria dell'Accademia** (Accademia Gallery) is Venice's most important picture gallery and a must for art lovers. Try to spend at least an hour viewing this remarkable collection of Venetian art, which is attractively displayed and well lighted. Works range from 14th-century Gothic to the Golden Age of the 15th and 16th centuries, including oils by Giovanni Bellini, Giorgione, Titian, and Tintoretto, and superb later works by Veronese and Tiepolo. *Campo della Carità, tel. 041/522–2247. Admission: 12,000 lire. Open Mon.–Sat. 9–7, Sun. 9–2, longer hours in summer.*

❻ The church of Santa Maria Gloriosa dei Frari—known simply as the **I Frari**—is one of Venice's most important churches, a vast, soaring Gothic building of brick. Since it is the principal church of the Franciscans, its design is suitably austere to reflect that order's vows of poverty, though paradoxically it contains a number of the most sumptuous pictures in any Venetian church. Chief among them are the magnificent Titian altarpiece, the immense *Assumption of the Virgin*, over the main altar. Titian was buried here at the ripe old age of 88, the only one of 70,000 plague victims to be given a personal church burial. *Campo dei Frari, tel. 041/ 522–2637. Admission: 3,000 lire. Open Mon.–Sat. 9–noon and 3–6, Sun. 3–6.*

Just off Piazzetta di San Marco (the square in front of the Doge's Palace) you can catch Vaporetto 1 at either the San Marco or San Zaccaria landing stages (on Riva degli Schiavoni), to set off on a boat tour along the **Grand Canal.** Serving as Venice's main thoroughfare, the canal winds in the shape of an S for more than 3½ km (2 mi) through the heart of the city, past some 200 Gothic-Renaissance palaces. Although restrictions have been introduced to diminish the erosive effect of wash on buildings, this is still the route taken by vaporetti, gondolas, water taxis, mail boats, police boats, fire boats, ambulance boats, barges carrying provisions and building materials, bridal boats, and funeral boats. Your vaporetto tour will give you an idea of the opulent beauty of the palaces and a peek into the side streets and tiny canals where the Venetians go about their daily business. *Vaporetto 1. Cost: 3,500 lire.*

❼ The **Ca' Rezzonico**—the most spectacular palace in all of Venice— was built between the mid-17th and 18th centuries and is now a museum of sumptuous 18th-century Venetian paintings and furniture. The Ca' Rezzonico is the best chance to glimpse Venetian splendor and is a must-see; its magnificent ballroom hosted the grandest Venetian costume balls, the last given for Elizabeth Taylor and Richard Burton during the 1960s. At press time, only the first floor was open. *Fondamenta Rezzonico, S. Barnaba, tel. 041/ 2410100. Open Sat.–Thu. 10–4. Admission: 12,000 lire.*

Shopping Venetian glass is as famous as the city's gondolas, and almost every shop window displays it. There's a lot of cheap glass for sale; if you want something better, try Carlo Moretti's chic, contemporary designs at **L'Isola** (Campo San Moisè 1468, near Piazza San Marco). On the island of Murano, where prices are generally no

Venice

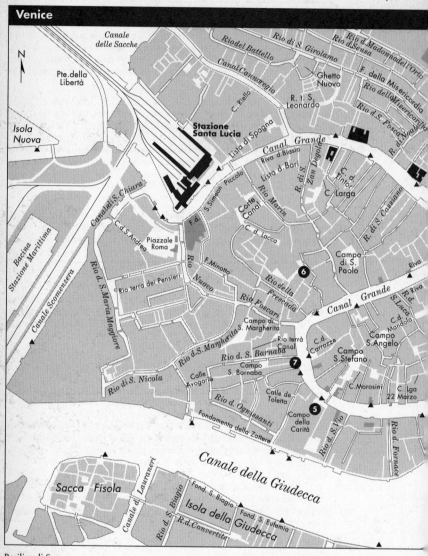

Basilica di San
Marco, **2**

Ca' Rezzonico, **7**

Campanile di San
Marco, **4**

Galleria
dell'Accademia, **5**

I Frari, **6**

Palazzo Ducale, **3**

Piazza San Marco, **1**

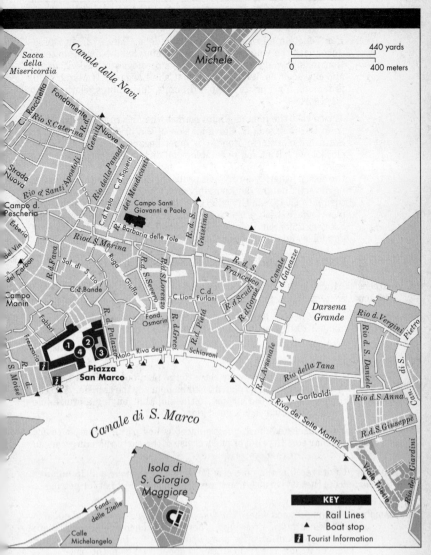

Sacca
della
Misericordia

Canale delle Navi

San
Michele

0 ——————— 440 yards
0 ——————— 400 meters

Fondamente
Rachetta
C.d.
Rio S.Caterina
R.d.
Gesuiti Nuove

Strada
Nuova
Rio d'Santi Apostoli
Rio della Panada
C.d.Squero
C.d.Testa
R. dei Mendicanti

Campo d.
Pescheria
Erberia
Campo Santi
Giovanni e Paolo
R. Barbaria delle Tole
R.d.S.
Giustina

del Vin
del Carbon
Rio d.S.Marina
Ruga
Giuffa
R.d.S.Severo
R.d.S.Lorenzo
R.d.S.
Francesco
Canale
d.Galeazze

Campo
Manin
R.d.Fava
Sal.di S.Lio
C.d.Bande
C.Lion
C.d.
Furlani
R.d'Scudi
R.d'Corpie

Fabbri
R.d.Palazzo
Fond.
Osmarin
R.d.Greci
R.d.Pietà
Schiavoni
R.d.Arsenale

Darsena
Grande
Rio d.Vergini
Rio d.S.Danièle
Pietro
Cau.S.

Frezzeria
R. d.
S.Moise
del Moise

1
2
4
3
Molo
Riva degli
Schiavoni
Rio della Tana
R.d.Arsenale
V. Garibaldi
Rio d.S.Anna

**Piazza
San Marco**

Riva dei Sette Martiri
R.d.S.Giuseppe
Viale Trieste
Rio dei Giardini

Canale di S. Marco

Isola di
S. Giorgio
Maggiore

Ci

Fond.
delle Zitelle
Calle
Michelangelo

KEY
—— Rail Lines
▲ Boat stop
i Tourist Information

lower than those in Venice, **Domus** (Fondamenta dei Vetrai) has a good selection.

For Venetian fabrics, **Norelene** (Calle della Chiesa 727, in Dorso-duro, near the Guggenheim) has stunning hand-painted material that makes wonderful wall hangings or elegantly styled jackets and chic scarves. **Venetia Studuim** (Calle Larga XXII Marzo 2430) is famous for Fortuny-inspired lamps, furnishings, clothes, and accessories.

Try to visit the famous **Rialto market** when it's in full swing (start from the Salizzada S. Giovanni side of the bridge on Tuesday to Saturday mornings; Monday is quiet because the fish market is closed), with fruit and vegetable vendors hawking their wares in a colorful and noisy jumble of sights and sounds. Not far beyond is the fish market, where you'll probably find sea creatures you've never seen before (and possibly won't want to see again). A left turn into Ruga San Giovanni and Ruga del Ravano will bring you face to face with scores of shops: At **La Scialuppa** (Calle delle Saoneri, 2695 San Polo) you'll find hand-carved wooden models of gondolas and their graceful oar locks known as *forcole*.

Ports of Embarkation and Disembarkation

**Athens/
Piraeus**
Athens is the gateway for cruises to the Greek Islands and to the eastern Mediterranean, including cruises of the Black Sea.

*From the
Airport*
Piraeus lies 10 km (6 mi) from Athens. You can take a taxi for about 1,100 dr. or buy a transfer from the cruise line in advance.

Istanbul
Istanbul is a major jumping off point for cruises of the eastern Mediterranean.

*From the
Airport*
Atatürk Airport lies very close to the pier, but traffic in Istanbul is notoriously bad, so plan on half an hour for the transfer. You can take a cab from the airport to the ship, but buying a cruise-line transfer in advance is a good idea.

**Rome/Civitave
cchia**
For reasons as much geographical as historical, Rome is a very popular port to begin or end a cruise of the eastern Mediterranean or the western Mediterranean.

*From the
Airport*
Civitavecchia, the port city for Rome, is an hour and 15 minutes from the city. Cruise-line transfers are your best bet for getting to the ship.

Southampton
Southampton is where the *Queen Elizabeth 2* arrives and departs on transatlantic crossings. There's not much in the immediate vicinity except a coffee shop and berths for ferries going to the Isle of Wight. The train station is about ¼ mi from the pier.

*From the
Airport*
Southampton is 90 km (56 mi) southwest of London. The trip by BritRail takes an hour and 40 minutes from central London's Waterloo Station. Driving from London to Southampton takes less than two hours.

4   Itineraries

Sailing Schedules

Itineraries begin with fall 1998 and run through summer 1999. Ship deployments and itineraries are subject to change; ports of call may also vary with departure date. Check with your cruise line or travel agent.

Abercrombie & Kent

Explorer **Fall:** 32-night **South America/Atlantic Ocean** cruise from Santa Cruz de Tenerife (Canary Islands) to Port Stanley (Falkland Islands). **Mid-fall–winter:** 10- and 15-night **Antarctica** cruises sail round-trip from Ushuaia (Argentina) or between Ushuaia and Port Stanley. **Spring:** 7- to 16-night **Amazon** loops from Iquitos (Peru) and between Iquitos and Belém (Brazil). **Summer:** 11- to 14-night **northern Europe** cruises between Aberdeen (Scotland) and Reykjavík (Iceland), between Aberdeen and Spitsbergen (Norway), and between Aberdeen and Plymouth (England).

Alaska Sightseeing/Cruise West

Spirit of Alaska **Fall:** 7-night **Columbia and Snake River** loops from Portland (Oregon). **Winter:** No cruises scheduled. **Early spring:** 7-night **Columbia and Snake River** loops from Portland. 10-night **Inside Passage** cruise from Seattle to Juneau. **Mid-spring–summer:** 3- and 4-night **Prince William Sound** loops from Whittier.

Spirit of Columbia **Fall:** 7-night **British Columbia** loops from Seattle. **Winter:** No cruises scheduled. **Spring–summer:** 7-night **British Columbia** loops from Seattle. 12-night **British Columbia** cruise from Seattle to Juneau. 7-night **Inside Passage** cruises between Juneau and Ketchikan.

Spirit of Discovery **Fall:** 7-night **Columbia and Snake River** loops from Portland (Oregon). **Winter:** No cruises scheduled. **Spring–summer:** Same as fall. 7-night **Inside Passage** cruises between Juneau and Ketchikian.

Spirit of Endeavour **Fall:** 3- and 4-night **California Wine Country** loops from San Francisco. **Winter–early spring:** 7-night **Baja Mexico** cruises from Cabo San Lucas. **Spring–summer:** 7-night **Inside Passage** cruises between Seattle and Juneau.

Spirit of Glacier Bay **Fall:** 7-night **Puget Sound** loops from Seattle. **Winter:** No cruises scheduled. **Spring–summer:** 3- and 4-night **Prince William Sound** loops from Whittier.

Spirit of '98 **Fall:** 3- and 4-night **California Wine Country** loops from San Francisco. **Winter–early spring:** 7-night **Baja Mexico** cruises from Cabo San Lucas. **Spring–summer:** 7-night **Inside Passage** cruises between Seattle and Juneau.

Alaska's Glacier Bay Tours & Cruises

Executive Explorer **Fall–winter:** No cruises scheduled. **Spring–summer:** 9-night **Inside Passage** cruises between Seattle and Juneau. 7-night **Inside Passage** cruises between Ketchikan and Juneau.

Wilderness Adventurer **Fall:** No cruises scheduled. **Winter:** 6-night **Baja California** loops from La Paz (Mexico). **Spring–summer:** 10-night **Inside Passage** cruises between Seattle and Juneau. 6-night **Inside Passage** loops from Juneau.

Wilderness **Fall:** No cruises scheduled. **Winter:** 6-night **Baja California** loops
Discover from La Paz (Mexico). **Spring–summer:** 10-night **Inside Passage**
cruises between Seattle and Juneau. 6-night **Alaska** cruises to be
announced.

Wilderness **Fall–winter:** No cruises scheduled. **Spring–summer:** 10-night **Inside**
Explorer **Passage** cruises between Seattle and Juneau. 3-, 4- , and 5-night
Inside Passage cruises from Juneau.

American Canadian Caribbean Line

Grande **Fall:** 12-night **New England and Canada** cruises sail between War-
Caribe ren (Rhode Island) and Québec City. 14-night **eastern seaboard**
cruises from Warren to Palm Beach Gardens (Florida). **Winter–**
early spring: 11-night **Panama** cruises between Panama City and
Colón or Balboa (Panama). 11-night **Central America** cruise
between Balboa and Belize City. **Mid-spring–summer:** Same as fall.
15-night **New England and Canada** loops from Warren.

Grande **Fall:** Same as Grande Caribe. **Winter:** 11-night **Virgin Islands**
Mariner cruises between Ponce (Puerto Rico) and St. Thomas, and loops
from St. Thomas. 11-night **Venezuela** cruise between St. Lucia and
Trinidad, loop from Trinidad, and cruise between Trinidad and
Curaçao.14-night Central America cruise from Panama City to
Belize City. **Spring–summer:** Same as fall. 12-night **Canada** cruises
from Massena (New York) to Corner Brook (Newfoundland).

Niagara **Fall:** 15-night **Great Lakes** cruise between Chicago and Warren
Prince (Rhode Island). 14-night **mid-America** cruise between Chicago and
New Orleans. 12-night **southern America** cruises between New
Orleans and Nashville. **Winter–early spring:** 11-night **Central Amer-**
ica cruises between Belize City and Roatan (Honduras). 14-night
Central America loops from Belize City. **Spring–summer:** Same as
fall. 6-night **New England** loops from Warren. 12-night **New**
England canals cruises between Warren and Buffalo (New York).

American Hawaii Cruises

Independence **Year-round:** 7-night **Hawai'i** loops from Honolulu.

Carnival Cruise Lines

Carnival **Year-round:** 7-night **eastern Caribbean** or **western Caribbean** loops
Destiny from Miami.

Celebration **Fall:** 7-night **western Caribbean** loops from Tampa or New Orleans.
Winter–summer: 7-night **western Caribbean** loops from New
Orleans.

Elation **Year-round:** 7-night **Mexican Riviera** loops from Los Angeles.

Ecstasy **Year-round:** 3-night **Bahamas** loops from Miami. 4-night **western**
Caribbean loops from Miami.

Fantasy **Year-round:** 3- and 4-night **Bahamas** loops from Port Canaveral.

Fascination **Year-round:** 7-night **southern Caribbean** loops from San Juan.

Holiday **Year-round:** 3- and 4-night **Baja Mexico** loops from Los Angeles.
Early winter: 10- and 11-night **Mexican Riviera** loops from Los
Angeles.

Imagination **Fall:** 7-night **western Caribbean** loops from Miami. **Winter–summer:**
7- **Fall:** 7-night **western Caribbean** or **eastern Caribbean** loops from
Miami.

Inspiration **Year-round:** 7-night **southern Caribbean** loops from San Juan.

Jubilee **Fall–winter:** 16-night **Panama Canal** transit from San Diego to Miami. 11-night **Panama Canal** transits from Miami. 10- and 11-night **southern Caribbean** loops from Miami. **Spring–summer:** 12-night **Hawai'i** cruises between Ensenada (Mexico) and Honolulu and between Honolulu and Vancouver. 7-night **Alaska** cruises between Vancouver and Seward (Alaska).

Sensation **Fall:** 7-night **eastern Caribbean** loops from Miami. **Winter–summer.** 7-night **western Caribbean** cruises from Tampa.

Tropicale **Year-round:** 4- and 5-night **western Caribbean** cruises from Tampa.

Celebrity Cruises

Century **Fall–spring:** 7-night **eastern Caribbean** loops from Fort Lauderdale. 7-night **western Caribbean** loops from Fort Lauderdale. **Summer: Europe** cruises to be announced.

Galaxy **Fall–spring:** 7-night **southern Caribbean** loops from San Juan. **Summer:** 11-night **Inside Passage** cruise from Los Angeles to Vancouver. 7-night **Inside Passage** loops from Vancouver.

Horizon **Fall–spring:** 10- and 11-night **Caribbean** loops from Fort Lauderdale. **Spring–summer:** 7-night **Bermuda** loops from New York.

Mercury **Fall–spring:** 7-night **western Caribbean** loops from Fort Lauderdale. **Spring–summer:** 10-night **Inside Passage** cruise from Los Angeles to Vancouver. 7-night **Inside Passage** loops from Vancouver. 7-night **Inside Passage/Gulf of Alaska** cruises between Vancouver and Seward (Alaska).

Zenith **Fall–early spring:** 13-night **Panama Canal** transit from New York and Acapulco. 10- and 11-night **Panama Canal** transits between San Juan and Acapulco and between Acapulco and Fort Lauderdale. 15-night **Panama Canal** transit from Acapulco to New York. **Spring–summer:** 7-night **Bermuda** loops from New York.

Clipper Cruise Line

Nantucket Clipper **Fall:** 7- to 11-night **Hudson River and Chesapeake Bay** or **eastern seaboard** cruises from Boston to New York, loops from New York, cruises between New York and Alexandria (Virginia), or cruises between Alexandria and Jacksonville (Florida). **Winter:** 7-night **Virgin Islands** loops from St. Thomas. **Spring:** 7- to 14-night **eastern Seaboard** cruises between Jacksonville and Charleston (South Carolina), Jacksonville and Alexandria, Alexandria and Baltimore, and Alexandria and Halifax (Nova Scotia). **Summer:** 7- and 14-night **Canada and New England** cruises between Halifax and Rochester (New York), and between Rochester and Québec City. 14-night **Great Lakes** cruises between Québec City and Chicago.

Yorktown Clipper **Fall:** 10-night **Pacific Northwest** cruises between Seattle and Portland (Oregon). 5-night **northern California** loops from San Francisco. **Winter–mid-spring:** 10-night **southern Caribbean and Orinoco River (Venezuela)** cruises between Curaçao and Trinidad. 7-night **southern Caribbean** cruises between Grenada and St. Kitts. 6-night **Costa Rica/Panama Canal** cruises between Colón (Costa Rica) and Puerto Caldera (Costa Rica). 7-night **Sea of Cortez** loops from La Paz (Mexico). **Summer:** 10- and 11-night **Inside Passage** cruises between Seattle and Juneau. 7-night **Inside Passage** cruises between Juneau and Ketchikan and loops from Juneau.

Clipper Adventurer **Fall:** 15-night **Venezuela/Amazon** cruise from St. Kitts to Manaus (Brazil). 14-night **Amazon/Brazil** cruise from Manaus to Rio de Janeiro. 16-night **South America** cruise from Rio de Janeiro to Santiago. **Late fall–early spring:** 13- and 14-night **South America/ Antarctica** cruises between Santiago to Buenos Aires. 14-night **South American** cruise between Ushuaia (Argentina) and Rio de Janeiro. 13-night **Brazil/Amazon** cruise from Rio de Janeiro to Manaus. 13-night **Amazon/Orinoco River (Venezuela)/Caribbean** cruise from Manaus to Barbados. **Mid-spring–summer:** 11-night **Mediterranean** cruises between Lisbon and Civitavecchia/Rome. 15-night **northern Europe** cruise between Lisbon and Dartmouth (England). 13-night **northern Europe** cruise from Dartmouth to Edinburgh (Scotland). 14-night **northern Europe** cruise from Edinburgh to Sondrestromfjord (Greenland). 12-night **Northwest Passage** cruises between Sondrestromfjord and Resolute Bay (Alaska). 14-night **Canada** cruise from Sondrestromfjord to Halifax (Nova Scotia).

Crystal Cruises

Crystal Harmony **Fall:** 8-night **Hawaiʻi** cruise from Vancouver to Honolulu. 11-night **Hawaiʻi** cruise from Honolulu to Yokohama (Japan). 12- to 19-night **Asia** cruises from Yokohama to Beijing/Tianjin, from Beijing/Tianjin to Hong Kong, and from Hong Kong to Sydney (Australia). 11- and 14-night **South Pacific** cruises between Sydney and Auckland (New Zealand), from Auckland to Honolulu, and from Honolulu to Acapulco. **Winter–spring:** 10- and 11-night **Panama Canal** transits between Acapulco and San Juan, Barbados, New Orleans, or Fort Lauderdale. 16-night **South America** cruise from Barbados to Buenos Aires. 14-night **South America** cruise from Buenos Aires to San Juan. 8-night **Mexican Riviera** cruise from Acapulco to San Francisco. **Late spring–summer:** 12-night **Inside Passage** loops from San Francisco.

Crystal Symphony **Fall:** 12- and 10-night **Mediterranean** cruises from Rome to Athens, Athens to Venice, Venice to Barcelona, and Barcelona to Lisbon. 10-night westbound **transatlantic crossing** from Lisbon to Barbados. 10- and 11-night **Panama Canal** transits between Acapulco and San Juan, Barbados, or Fort Lauderdale. **Winter–early spring:** 13-night **Panama Canal** transit from Fort Lauderdale to Los Angeles. 99-night **world** cruise includes a 17-night westbound **Pacific crossing** from Los Angeles to Auckland (New Zealand); a 15-night **Southeast Asia** segment between Auckland and Cairns (Australia); a 15-night **Southeast Asia** segment from Cairns to Hong Kong; a 12-night **Southeast Asia** segment from Hong Kong to Singapore; an 11-night **Asia** segment from Singapore to Mumbai (India); a 16-night **Arabian Sea/Red Sea/Mediterranean** segment from Mumbai to Athens/Piraeus; and a 13-night **Mediterranean/northern Europe** segment from Athens/Piraeus to Lisbon. **Late spring–summer:** 10-night **northern Europe/Mediterranean** cruise from Barcelona to London. 12-night **Mediterranean** cruises between Lisbon and Rome/ Civitavecchia, Rome/Civitavecchia and Athens/Piraeus, and Athens/ Piraeus and Barcelona. 12-night **northern Europe** cruises between London and Copenhagen. 13-night **northern Europe** cruise from London to Rouen (France). 12-night **Mediterranean** cruise from Rouen to Rome/Civitavecchia.

Delta Queen Steamboat Company

American Queen **Year-round:** 3- to 7-night river cruises on the **Mississippi River system** from New Orleans, Memphis, St. Louis, St. Paul, Cincinnati, and Pittsburgh.

Delta Queen **Year-round:** 3- to 14-night river cruises on the **Mississippi River system** from New Orleans, Memphis, St. Louis, St. Paul, Cincinnati, Nashville, Pittsburgh, Chattanooga, Ottawa, and Galveston.

Mississippi Queen **Year-round:** 3- to 14-night river cruises on the **Mississippi River system** from New Orleans, Memphis, St. Louis, St. Paul, Cincinnati, Nashville, Pittsburgh, and Chattanooga.

Disney Cruise Line

Disney Magic **Year-round:** 3- and 4-night **Bahamas** loops from Port Canaveral.

Disney Wonder **Year-round:** 3- and 4-night **Bahamas** loops from Port Canaveral.

Holland America Line

Maasdam **Fall–winter:** 13- to 17-night **Panama Canal** transit from Vancouver, Seattle, or Los Angeles to Fort Lauderdale. 10-night **Panama Canal** transits between Fort Lauderdale and Acapulco. **Spring–summer:** 10-night eastbound **transatlantic crossing** from Fort Lauderdale to Lisbon. 12-night **Mediterranean** cruises between Lisbon and Venice, Istanbul and London, and London and Venice; loops from Venice. 12-night **northern Europe** cruises between London and Copenhagen.

Nieuw Amsterdam **Fall–winter:** 11-night **Pacific Ocean** cruise from Vancouver to Osaka (Japan). 14-night **Asia** cruise from Osaka to Hong Kong. 15-night **Southeast Asia** cruises between Hong Kong and Singapore. 17-night **Southeast Asia/Australia** cruises between Singapore and Sydney. 14- to 16-night **Australia/New Zealand** cruises between Auckland (New Zealand) and Sydney. **Spring:** 15-night **Southeast Asia** cruise from Singapore to Hong Kong. 14-night **Asia** cruises between Osaka and Hong Kong. 11-night **Pacific Ocean** cruise from Osaka to Vancouver. **Spring–summer:** 7-night **Inside Passage** loops from Vancouver.

Noordam **Fall:** 10- to 18-night **Panama Canal** transit from Vancouver, San Diego, or Acapulco to Tampa. 7-night **western Caribbean** loops from Tampa. **Winter:** 14-night **southern Caribbean** loop from Tampa. 16-night **South America** cruise from Tampa to Rio de Janeiro. 16-night **South America** cruises between Rio de Janeiro and Valparaiso (Chile). **Spring–summer:** 16-night **South America** cruise from Rio de Janeiro to Fort Lauderdale. 10-night **Caribbean** loop from Fort Lauderdale. 19-night **Panama Canal** transit from Fort Lauderdale to Vancouver. 7-night **Inside Passage/Gulf of Alaska** cruises between Vancouver and Seward (Alaska). 7-night **Inside Passage** loops from Vancouver.

Rotterdam **Fall:** 12-night **Mediterranean** cruise from Kusadasi (Turkey) to Venice, from Venice to Istanbul, from Kusadasi to Valletta (Malta), from Katakolon (Greece) to Naples (Italy), and from Valletta to Casablanca (Morocco). 10-night westbound **transatlantic crossing** from Casablanca to Nassau (Bahamas). 10-night **southern Caribbean** loop from Nassau. **Winter–spring:** 14-night **Panama Canal** transit from Fort Lauderdale to Los Angeles. 98-night **world** cruise from Los Angeles to Fort Lauderdale or New York. 9-night eastbound **transatlantic crossing** from New York to Lisbon. **Mid-spring–**

summer: 12-night **Mediterranean and northern Europe** cruises from Lisbon to Rome/Civitavecchia, from Rome to London, from London to Copenhagen, from Rome to Athens/Piraeus; loops from Venice.

Ryndam **Early fall:** 10- to 17-night **Panama Canal** transit from Vancouver, San Francisco, or Acapulco to Fort Lauderdale. **Winter–early spring:** 7-night **eastern Caribbean** loop from Fort Lauderdale. 10-night **southern Caribbean** loops from Fort Lauderdale. **Spring–summer:** 19-night **Panama Canal** transit from Fort Lauderdale to Vancouver. 7-night **Inside Passage/Gulf of Alaska** cruises between Vancouver and Seward (Alaska). 7-night **Inside Passage** loops from Vancouver.

Statendam **Fall:** 10- and 19-night **Hawai'i** cruises between San Diego and Honolulu or from Vancouver to Honolulu; a loop from Los Angeles. **Late fall–winter:** 13- to 24-night **Panama Canal** transit from Honolulu, Los Angeles, or Puerto Vallarta to Fort Lauderdale. 10-night **southern Caribbean** loops from Fort Lauderdale. **Spring–summer:** 16-night **Hawai'i** loops from San Francisco and from San Francisco to Vancouver. 7-night **Inside Passage/Gulf of Alaska** cruises between Vancouver and Seward (Alaska). 7-night **Inside Passage** loops from Vancouver.

Veendam **Early fall:** 10-night **New England and Canada** cruises between New York and Montréal. 10-night **New England/Bermuda** loops from New York. **Mid-fall–early spring:** 7-night **western Caribbean** or **eastern Caribbean** loops from Fort Lauderdale. **Spring–summer:** 7-night **Inside Passage** loops from Vancouver.

Volendam **Mid-fall–spring:** 10-night **southern Caribbean** loops from Fort Lauderdale.

Westerdam **Early fall:** 12- to 21-night **Panama Canal** transits from Vancouver, Los Angeles, or Acapulco to Fort Lauderdale. **Fall:** 7-night **eastern Caribbean** loops from Fort Lauderdale. **Winter:** 7-night **western Caribbean** loops from Fort Lauderdale. 7-night **eastern Caribbean** loops from Fort Lauderdale. **Spring–summer:** 18-night **Panama Canal** transit from Fort Lauderdale to Vancouver. 7-night **Inside Passage** loops from Vancouver.

Orient Lines

Marco Polo **Fall:** 11-night **Mediterranean** cruises between Athens/Piraeus and Istanbul. 22-night **Red Sea/Africa** cruise from Athens/Piraeus to Mombasa (Kenya). 15-night **Africa** loop from Mombasa. 17-night **Africa** cruise from Mombasa to Cape Town (South Africa). **Winter:** 30-night **transatlantic crossing/Antarctica** cruise from Cape Town to Ushuaia (Argentina) or 17 nights from Cape Town to Buenos Aires. 8- to 23-night **Antarctica** cruise-tour from Buenos Aires to Ushuaia, loop from Ushuaia, or cruise from Ushuaia to Christchurch (New Zealand). 34-night **Antarctica/New Zealand** cruise from Ushuaia to Auckland (New Zealand). **Late winter–early spring:** 11-night **South Pacific** cruise from Christchurch to Auckland. 18-night **South Pacific** cruise from Auckland to Sydney. 22-night **Southeast Asia** cruise from Sydney to Singapore. **Spring–summer:** 16-night **Southeast Asia/India** cruise from Singapore to Mumbai (India). 21-night **India/Mediterranean** cruise from Mumbai to Istanbul. 32-night **Southeast Asia/Mediterranean** cruise from Singapore to Istanbul. 10- to 17-night **Mediterranean** cruises between Istanbul and Athens/Piraeus, Barcelona and Istanbul, Athens/Piraeus and Barcelona, Lisbon and Athens/Piraeus,

Rome/Civitavecchia and Istanbul, and Rome/Civitavecchia and Barcelona.

Princess Cruises

Crown Princess
Early fall: 10-night **Hawai'i** cruise from Vancouver to Honolulu.12-night **Hawai'i** cruises between Honolulu and Papeete (Tahiti). 9-night **Hawai'i** cruise from Honolulu to Ensenada (Mexico). **Mid-fall–winter:** 12-night **Costa Rica** cruises between San Diego and Puerto Caldera (Costa Rica) and between Puerto Caldera and Los Angeles; loops from Los Angeles. 10-night **Mexican Riviera** loops from Los Angeles. **Spring:** Same as Early fall. **Late Spring–summer:** 7-night **Inside Passage/Gulf of Alaska** cruises between Vancouver and Seward (Alaska).

Dawn Princess
Early fall: 7-night **Mexican Riviera** cruise from Los Angeles to Acapulco. 11-night **Panama Canal** transit from Acapulco to San Juan. **Fall–spring:** 7-night **southern Caribbean** loops from San Juan. **Late Spring–summer:** 7-night **Inside Passage/Gulf of Alaska** cruises between Vancouver and Seward (Alaska).

Grand Princess
Fall–spring: 13-night westbound **transatlantic crossing** from Barcelona to New York. 7-night **eastern Caribbean** loops from Fort Lauderdale. **Mid-spring–summer:** 12-night **Europe/Mediterranean** cruises between Venice and Barcelona.

Island Princess
Early fall: 65-night **world** cruise from San Francisco to Rome. **Fall:** 14-night **Mediterranean** cruises between Rome/Civitavecchia and Istanbul. **Winter:** 23-night **Mediterranean/Red Sea/Africa** cruise between Istanbul and Cape Town (South Africa). 14-night **Africa** cruises between Cape Town and Nairobi/Mombasa (Kenya). 14-night **Africa/India** cruises between Nairobi/Mombasa and Mumbai (India). **Early spring–summer:** 24-night **Africa/Red Sea/Mediterranean** cruise from Cape Town to Athens/Piraeus. **Europe/Mediterranean** cruises to be announced.

Pacific Princess
Fall: 14-night **Mediterranean** cruises between Rome/Civitavecchia and Istanbul. **Winter:** 25-night **Mediterranean/Africa** cruise from Istanbul to Cape Town (South Africa). 14-night **Africa** cruises between Cape Town and Nairobi/Mombasa (Kenya). **Spring–summer:** 23-day **Africa/Mediterranean** cruise from Cape Town to Rome/Civitavecchia. **Europe/Mediterranean** cruises to be announced.

Regal Princess
Fall–early spring: 15-night **Panama Canal** transit from San Francisco to Fort Lauderdale. 10-night **Panama Canal** transit loops from Fort Lauderdale. 16-night **Panama Canal** transit from Fort Lauderdale to Los Angeles. **Mid-spring–summer:** 7-night **Inside Passage/Gulf of Alaska** cruises between Vancouver and Seward (Alaska).

Royal Princess
Early fall: 10-night **New England and Canada** cruises between New York and Montréal. **Mid-fall–early spring:** 17-night **South America** cruise from Fort Lauderdale to Santiago. 14-night **South America** cruises between Buenos Aires and Santiago. 14-night **South America/Amazon** cruise between Buenos Aires and Manaus (Brazil). 11-night **South America/Amazon** cruise between Manaus and San Juan. 17-night **Panama Canal/South America** cruise from San Juan to Santiago. 19-night **South America/Africa** cruise from Buenos Aires to Barcelona. **Mid-spring–summer: Europe/Mediterranean** cruises to be announced.

Sea Princess **Fall:** 7-night **western Caribbean** loops from Fort Lauderdale. **Mid-spring–summer:** 7-night **Inside Passage/Gulf of Alaska** cruises between Vancouver and Seward (Alaska).

Sky Princess **Fall:** 19-night **Alaska/Far East** cruise from Vancouver to Xingang/Beijing. 13-night **Southeast Asia** cruises between Xingang/Beijing and Hong Kong. 16-night **Southeast Asia** cruise from Xingang/Beijing to Bangkok. 14-night **Southeast Asia** cruises between Bangkok and Hong Kong. **Winter:** 19-night **Southeast Asia/Australia** cruise from Bangkok to Sydney. 14-night **South Pacific** cruises between Sydney and Auckland. **Spring:** 16-night **South Pacific** cruise from Sydney to Papeete (Tahiti). 12-night **Hawai'i/French Polynesia** cruise from Papeete (Tahiti) to Honolulu. 10-night **Hawai'i** cruise from Honolulu to Vancouver. **Mid-spring–summer:** 11-night **Inside Passage** loops from San Francisco.

Sun Princess **Early fall:** 7-night **Mexican Riviera** cruise from Los Angeles to Acapulco. **Fall–spring:** 10- and 11-night **Panama Canal** transits between Acapulco and San Juan. **Mid-spring–summer:** 7-night **Inside Passage** loops from Vancouver.

Radisson Seven Seas Cruises

Hanseatic **Fall:** 13-night **Canada** cruise from Sondrestromfjord (Greenland) to Québec City. 10-night **Canada and New England** cruise from New York to Québec City. 7-night **South America** cruise from Puerto Montt (Chile) to Ushuaia (Argentina). **Winter:** 10- , 11- , and 17-night **Antarctica** loop from Ushuaia (Argentina). 20-night eastbound **transatlantic crossing** cruise from Ushuaia to Cape Town (South Africa). **Spring–Summer:** To be announced.

Radisson Diamond **Fall:** 7-night **Mediterranean** cruises between Istanbul and Athens/Piraeus. 7-night **Mediterranean** cruise from Istanbul to from Rome/Civitavecchia. 10-night **Mediterranean/Canary Islands** cruise from Rome/Civitavecchia to Madeira (Spain). 18-night westbound **transatlantic crossing** from Rome/Civitavecchia to Barbados. 8-night eastbound **transatlantic crossing** from Madeira to Barbados. 6-night **Caribbean** cruise from Barbados to San Juan. 5-night **Caribbean** loop from San Juan. 7-night **Caribbean** cruise from San Juan to Aruba. 7-night **Caribbean** cruise from Aruba to Puerto Limón (Costa Rica). 8-night **Caribbean** cruise from Puerto Limón to Fort Lauderdale. 11-night **Panama Canal** transit from Fort Lauderdale to Puerto Caldera (Costa Rica). **Winter:** 7- , 9- , and 10-night **Panama Canal** transits between Cozumel and Puerto Caldera, Puerto Caldera and Fort Lauderdale, and Puerto Caldera and Aruba. **Late winter–spring:** 4- and 5-night **Caribbean** loops from San Juan. 9-night eastbound **transatlantic crossing** from San Juan to Madeira (Spain). **Late spring:** 7- and 11-night Mediterranean cruises from Madeira to Cannes (France), Rome/Civitavecchia to Istanbul, Istanbul to Rome/Civitavecchia, Rome/Civitavecchia to Barcelona, Barcelona to Cannes, and Cannes to Dover/London. **Summer:** 11-night **northern Europe** cruise from Dover/London to Stockholm. 7-night **northern Europe** cruises between Stockholm and Copenhagen.

Song of Flower **Fall:** 7- and 8-night **Mediterranean** cruises between Athens/Piraeus and Istanbul. 10-night **Mediterranean/Red Sea** cruise from Istanbul to Aqaba (Jordan). 11-night **Red Sea** cruise from Aqaba to Dubai. 9-night **Indian Ocean** cruise from Dubai to Mumbai (India). 14-night **Southeast Asia** cruise from Mumbai to Singapore. 6- , 11- , and 12-night **Southeast Asia** cruises between Singapore and Bali. **Winter:** 8-night **Southeast Asia** cruises between Bali and Phuket (Thailand). 11- and 13-night **Southeast Asia** cruises from Bali to Singapore, from Singapore to Hong Kong, and from Hong Kong to Phuket. 8-night **Southeast Asia/Indian Ocean** cruise from Phuket to Mumbai (India). **Spring:** 9-night **Indian Ocean** cruise from Mumbai to Dubai. 13-night **Red Sea** cruise from Dubai to Aqaba. 9-night **Mediterranean** cruise from Aqaba to Athens/Piraeus. **Late spring–summer:** 7- , 8- , and 9-night **Mediterranean** cruises between Athens/Piraeus and Istanbul, from Istanbul to Venice, from Venice to Monte Carlo, and from Monte Carlo to Lisbon. 9-night **western Europe** cruises from Lisbon to Rouen (France), and from Rouen to Edinburgh (Scotland). 10-night **northern Europe** cruise from Edinburgh to Stockholm. 7-night **northern Europe** cruises between Stockholm and Copenhagen. 12-night **western Europe** cruise from London to Monte Carlo. 8-night **Mediterranean** cruise from Monte Carlo to Venice. 7-night **Mediterranean** cruises between Istanbul and Athens/Piraeus.

Paul Gauguin   **Year-round:** 7-night **French Polynesia** loops from Tahiti.

Royal Caribbean International

Enchantment of the Seas   **Year-round:** 7-night **eastern Caribbean** loops from Miami. 7-night **western Caribbean** loops from Miami.

Grandeur of the Seas   **Year-round:** 7-night **eastern Caribbean** loops from Miami.

Legend of the Seas   **Early fall:** 10- and 11-night **Hawai'i** cruises between Vancouver and Honolulu or Honolulu and Ensenada (Mexico). **Fall–mid-spring:** 10- and 11-night **Mexican Riviera** loops from San Diego. 14-night **Panama Canal** transits between San Diego and Fort Lauderdale. **Mid-spring–summer:** 7-night **Mediterranean** loops from Barcelona.

Majesty of the Seas   **Year-round:** 7-night **western Caribbean** loops from Miami.

Monarch of the Seas   **Year-round:** 7-night **southern Caribbean** loops from San Juan.

Nordic Empress   **Fall–spring:** 3- and 4-night **southern Caribbean** loops from San Juan. **Summer:** 7-night **Bermuda** loops from New York.

Rhapsody of the Seas   **Fall–spring:** 11-night **Hawai'i** cruise from Vancouver to Honolulu and from Honolulu to Ensenada (Mexico). 13-night **Panama Canal** transit from San Diego to San Juan. 7-night **southern Caribbean** loops from San Juan. **Late spring–summer:** 7-night **Inside Passage** loops from Vancouver.

Song of America   **Fall–winter:** 7-night **Mexican Riviera** loops from Los Angeles. A 14-night **Panama Canal** transit from Los Angeles to Miami.

Sovereign of the Seas   **Year-round:** 3- and 4-night **Bahamas** loops from Miami.

Splendour of the Seas   **Early fall:** 12-night **Mediterranean** loops from Barcelona. 14-night westbound **transatlantic crossing** from Barcelona to Miami. **Late fall–spring:** 10- and 11-night **Caribbean** loops from Miami. 13-night eastbound **transatlantic crossing** from Miami to Barcelona. **Summer:** 12-night **northern Europe/Mediterranean** cruises between Barcelona and Harwich (England), loops from Barcelona, and loops from Harwich. 12-night **British Isles** loop from Harwich.

Viking Serenade   **Year-round:** 3- and 4-night **West Coast** loops from Los Angeles.

Vision of the Seas **Early fall:** 10-night **New England and Canada** loops from Boston. 8-night **eastern Caribbean** cruise from Boston to San Juan. **Late fall–early spring:** 10- and 11-night **Panama Canal** transits between Acapulco and San Juan. **Mid-spring–summer:** 7-night **Inside Passage** loops from Vancouver.

Royal Olympic Cruises

Odysseus **Fall:** 3- and 4-night **Mediterranean** loops from Athens/Piraeus. 21-night westbound **transatlantic crossing** from Athens/Piraeus to Rio de Janeiro. **Winter:** 12- and 14-night **South America** cruises between Rio de Janeiro and Buenos Aires (Argentina). 14-night **Straits of Magellan** cruises between Puerto Montt (Chile) and Buenos Aires. **Spring:** 7-night **South America** cruise from Buenos Aires and Rio de Janeiro. 15-night eastbound **transatlantic crossing** from Rio de Janeiro to Lisbon. 12-night **Mediterranean** cruises between Lisbon and Athens/Piraeus. **Summer:** 10- and 14-night **Mediterranean/Baltic/northern Europe** cruises.

Olympic **Fall:** 3- and 4-night **Mediterranean** loops from Athens/Piraeus. **Winter:** No cruises scheduled. **Spring–summer:** Same as fall.

Olympic Countess **Fall:** 7-night **Mediterranean** loops from Athens/Piraeus. **Winter:** 13-night **Caribbean/Orinoco River (Venezuela)** loop from San Juan. 10- and 11-night **Caribbean/Orinoco River** loops from San Juan. **Early spring:** 21-night eastbound **transatlantic crossing/Mediterranean cruise** from San Juan to Athens/Piraeus. **Summer:** Same as fall.

Orpheus **Fall:** 7-night **Mediterranean** loops from Athens/Piraeus. **Winter:** No cruises scheduled. **Spring–summer:** Same as fall.

Stella Oceanis **Fall:** 3- , 4- , and 7-night **Mediterranean** loops from Athens/Piraeus. **Winter:** No cruises scheduled. **Spring:** Same as fall. **Summer:** 12-night **Mediterranean** loops from Athens/Piraeus.

Stella Solaris **Fall:** 7-night Mediterranean loops from Athens/Piraeus. **Winter:** 21-night **Mediterranean/westbound transatlantic** crossing from Athens/Piraeus to Fort Lauderdale. 13- , 14- , or 16-night **Caribbean/Amazon** cruises between Fort Lauderdale or Galveston (Texas) and Manaus. 27-night **Caribbean/Amazon** loop from Fort Lauderdale. 13-night **South America** cruise from Rio de Janeiro to Manaus. 11-night **western Caribbean** loop from Galveston or 14-night **western Caribbean** cruise from Fort Lauderdale to Galveston. **Spring:** 12-night **Panama Canal** transit loop from Galveston or 15-night **Panama Canal** transit from Galveston to Fort Lauderdale. 22- or 25-night eastbound **transatlantic crossing** from Galveston or Fort Lauderdale to Athens/Piraeus. **Late spring–summer:** Same as fall.

Triton **Fall:** 3- and 4-night **Mediterranean** loops from Athens/Piraeus. **Winter:** No cruises scheduled. **Spring–summer:** Same as fall.

World Renaissance **Fall:** 3- and 7-night **Mediterranean** loops from Athens/Piraeus. **Winter:** No cruises scheduled. **Spring–summer:** Same as fall.

Seabourn Cruise Line

Seabourn Legend **Early fall:** 10–night **Mediterranean** cruises between Nice and Rome, Rome and Monte Carlo, Monte Carlo and Barcelona, and Barcelona and Lisbon. **Fall–early spring:** 18-night westbound **transatlantic crossing** from Lisbon to Fort Lauderdale. 3-night **Florida** loop from Fort Lauderdale. 14-night **Panama Canal** transits between Fort Lauderdale and Puerto Caldera (Costa Rica). 16-night **Caribbean** loop from Fort Lauderdale. 12-night **Caribbean** cruise from Tampa to San Juan. 7-night **Caribbean** loops from San Juan. 7-night **Caribbean** cruise from San Juan to Barbados, and from Barbados to St. Thomas. 8-night **Caribbean** cruise from St. Thomas to Fort Lauderdale. 10-night **Caribbean** loops from Fort Lauderdale. **Spring–summer:** 12- and 14-night **Mediterranean** cruises from Lisbon, Monte Carlo, Nice, Amsterdam, London, and Copenhagen.

Seabourn Pride **Fall:** 14-night **New England and Canada** loops from New York. 12-night **eastern seaboard** cruise from New York to Nassau. 10- to 16-night **eastern Caribbean** and **western Caribbean** loops from Fort Lauderdale. **Winter–early spring:** 18-night **Panama Canal/South America** cruises between Fort Lauderdale and Valparaiso (Chile). 23-night **South America** cruises between Valparaiso and Rio de Janeiro. 15-night **Amazon** cruises between Rio de Janeiro and Manaus (Brazil). 15-night **Amazon/Caribbean** cruise from Manaus to Fort Lauderdale. 12-night **Panama Canal** transit from Fort Lauderdale to San José (Costa Rica). **Spring–summer:** 10-night **Caribbean** cruise from San José to San Juan. 6-night **eastern Caribbean** cruise from San Juan to Fort Lauderdale. 13-night eastbound **transatlantic crossing** from Fort Lauderdale to Lisbon. 12-night **Mediterranean/Canary Islands** loop from Lisbon. 14-night **western Europe** cruise from Lisbon to Amsterdam and from Amsterdam to London. 12- and 14-night **northern Europe** cruises between Copenhagen to London, loops from London, and loops from Copenhagen. 17-night westbound **transatlantic crossing** from Copenhagen to New York.

Seabourn Spirit **Fall:** 7-night **Mediterranean** loop from Istanbul and from Athens to Haifa (Israel). 7- to 16-night **Africa/Seychelles** cruises from Haifa to Mombasa (Kenya), Mombasa to Singapore; loop from Mombasa. **Winter–early spring:** 7- to 16-night **Southeast Asia** cruises between Singapore and Hong Kong, Singapore and Bali, Hong Kong and Bali, Hong Kong and Bangkok, Shanghai and Hong Kong, and Hong Kong and Singapore. 12-night **Southeast Asia** cruise from Singapore to Mumbai (India). 13-night **Arabian Sea/Red Sea** cruise from Mumbai to Haifa. **Spring–summer:** 10- and 14-night **Mediterranean** cruises between Haifa and Istanbul, Istanbul and Athens/ Piraeus, Istanbul and Rome/Civitavecchia; loop from Istanbul. 7-night **French Riviera** cruises between Rome/Civitavecchia and Monte Carlo, and Monte Carlo and Nice. 7-night loop from Nice.

Silversea Cruises

Silver Cloud **Fall:** 10-night **New England and Canada** cruise from Montréal to New York. 10-night **eastern seaboard/Caribbean** cruise from New York to Nassau. 8-night **eastern Caribbean** cruise from Nassau to Barbados. 7- to 18-night **South America** cruises from Barbados to Rio de Janeiro, Rio de Janeiro to Buenos Aires, Buenos Aires to Valparaiso (Chile), Buenos Aires to Ushuaia (Argentina), Ushuaia to Valparaiso, and Valparaiso to Acapulco. 8-night **Mexican Riviera** cruise from Acapulco to Los Angeles. 3-night **California** loop from Los Angeles. 16-night **Hawai'i/South Pacific** cruise from Los Angeles to Papeete (Tahiti). **Winter:** 10-night **South Pacific** cruises from Papeete to Lautoka (Mooréa) and from Lautoka to Auckland (New Zealand). 16-night **South Pacific** cruise from Auckland to Sydney. 14-night **South Pacific** cruise from Sydney to Bali. 14-night **Southeast Asia** cruise from Bali to Hong Kong. 12-night **Southeast Asia** cruise from Hong Kong to Singapore. 14-night **Indian Ocean** cruise from Singapore to Mumbai (India). 16-night **Indian Ocean/Red Sea/Mediterranean** cruise from Mumbai to Athens/Piraeus. **Spring–summer:** 11- and 12-night **Mediterranean/**

northern Europe cruises from Athens/Piraeus, Rome/Civitavec-
chia, Barcelona, Lisbon, London, Copenhagen, Stockholm, and
Edinburgh (Scotland).

Silver Wind **Fall:** 7- to 9-night **Mediterranean** cruises from Lisbon to Barcelona,
Barcelona to Monte Carlo, and Monte Carlo to Athens/Piraeus. 14-
night **Red Sea** cruise from Haifa (Israel) to Mombasa (Kenya). 10-,
11-, and 15-night **Africa** cruises from Mombasa to Cape Town
(South Africa), Cape Town to Durban (South Africa), and Durban
to Mahé (Seychelles). 14-night **Indian Ocean/Southeast Asia** cruise
from Mahé to Singapore. **Winter:** 12-night **Southeast Asia** cruise
from Singapore to Bangkok. 12- and 14-night **Southeast Asia**
cruises from Bangkok to Hong Kong, and from Hong Kong to Bali.
13-night **Southeast Asia** cruise from Bali to Sydney (Australia). 14-
night **Australia/New Zealand** cruise between Sydney and Auckland (New Zealand). 14-night **South Pacific** cruise from Auckland
to Papeete (Tahiti). 16-night **South Pacific** cruise from Papeete to
San Diego. **Spring:** 3-night **California** loop from San Diego. 8-night
Mexican Riviera cruise from San Diego to Acapulco. 16-night
Panama Canal transit from Acapulco to West Palm Beach
(Florida). 3-night **Florida** loop from West Palm Beach. 7-night
Caribbean cruise from West Palm Beach to Barbados. 14-night
eastbound **transatlantic/Mediterranean** cruise from Barbados to
Rome/Civitavecchia. **Summer:** 7-, 10-, 11-, 12-, and 14-night
Mediterranean cruises from Istanbul, Athens/Piraeus, Rome/Civi-
tavecchia, Monte Carlo, Barcelona, Lisbon, or Malta.

Special Expeditions

Polaris **Year-round:** 7-night **Galápagos Islands** cruises.

Sea Bird, Sea **Fall:** 6-night **Pacific Northwest** cruises sail between Vancouver and
Lion Seattle. 6-night **Columbia and Snake River** loops from Portland
(Oregon). **Winter:** 7- and 8-night **Baja California** whale-watching
cruises. **Spring–summer:** 6-night **Columbia and Snake River** loops
from Portland. 7-night **Inside Passage** cruises between Juneau and
Sitka. 10-night **Alaska/British Columbia** cruises between Juneau
and Seattle.

Caledonian **Fall:** 13-night **Mediterranean** cruise from Lisbon to Malta. 14-night
Star **Mediterranean** cruise from Italy to Istanbul. 18-night westbound
transatlantic crossing from Lisbon to Salvador (Brazil). **Winter:** 18-
night **Antarctica** loops from Santiago. 18-night **Madagascar and
Seychelles** cruise. 19-night **Red Sea/Mediterranean** cruise Aqaba
(Jordan) to Lisbon. **Spring–summer:** 7-night **Sweden** loops from
Stockholm. 12-night **British Isles** cruises between Edinburgh
(Scotland) and Dartmouth (England).

Star Clippers

Star Clipper **Fall–early spring:** 28-night westbound **transatlantic crossing** from
Cannes to Antigua. 7-night **eastern Caribbean** loop from Antigua.
7-night. **Mid-spring–summer:** 28-day eastbound **transatlantic crossing** from Antigua to Cannes (France). 7-night **Mediterranean** loops
from Cannes.

Star Flyer **Fall–early spring:** 42-day **Indian Ocean crossing** from Safaga
(Egypt) to Phuket (Thailand). 7-day **Southeast Asia** loops from
Phuket. **Mid-spring–summer:** 35-night **Indian Ocean crossing** from
Phuket to Athens/Piraeus. 7-night **Mediterranean** loops from
Kuşadasi (Turkey).

Windstar Cruises

Wind Song **Fall:** 7-night **Mediterranean** loops from Rome/Civitavecchia. 14-night westbound **transatlantic crossing** from Lisbon to Barbados. 14-night **Panama Canal** transit from Barbados to Puerto Caldera (Costa Rica), or 7-night **Caribbean** cruises from Barbados to Aruba, and Aruba to Puerto Caldera. **Late fall–winter:** 7-night **Costa Rica** loops from Puerto Caldera. **Spring:** 14-night **Panama Canal** transit from Puerto Caldera to Barbados. 14-night eastbound **transatlantic crossing** from Barbados to Lisbon. 7- and 14-night **Mediterranean** cruises from Lisbon to Barcelona, Barcelona to Rome/Civitavecchia, and Lisbon to Rome/Civitavecchia. **Summer:** 7-night **Mediterranean** cruises between Rome/Civitavecchia and Athens/Piraeus and between Athens/Piraeus and Istanbul.

Wind Spirit **Early fall:** 7-, 8-, 13-, and 14-night **Mediterranean** cruises from Athens/Piraeus, Istanbul, Rome/Civitavecchia, Barcelona, and Lisbon. **Late fall–early spring:** 7- and 14-night **Caribbean** loops from St. Thomas. **Spring–summer:** 14-night eastbound **transatlantic crossing** from St. Thomas to Lisbon. 7- and 14-night **Mediterranean** cruises from Lisbon to Nice (France), Nice to Rome/Civitavecchia, and Lisbon to Rome/Civitavecchia. 7-night **Mediterranean** cruises between Rome/Civitavecchia and Athens/Piraeus or Istanbul.

Wind Star **Early fall:** 7-night **Mediterranean** cruises between Athens/Piraeus and Istanbul. **Late fall–summer:** 5-night **Indian Ocean** cruise from Salalah (Oman) to Mumbai (India). 18-night **Indian Ocean/Southeast Asia** cruise from Mumbai to Singapore. **Winter:** 10- and 11-night **Southeast Asia** cruises between Singapore and Bali. **Spring–summer:** 7-night **Southeast Asia** cruises between Singapore and Phuket (Thailand) or Singapore and Bangkok.

Wind Surf **Fall:** 15-night **Mediterranean** cruise from Nice (France) to Lisbon. 14-night westbound **transatlantic crossing** from Lisbon to Barbados. **Late fall–early spring:** 7-night **Caribbean** loops from Barbados. **Spring–summer:** 14-night eastbound **transatlantic crossing** from Barbados to Lisbon. 7-, 8-, and 15-night **Mediterranean** cruises from Lisbon to Barcelona, Barcelona to Nice, and Lisbon to Nice. 7-night **Mediterranean** loops from Nice, cruises between Nice and Rome/Civitavecchia and cruises between Rome/Civitavecchia and Venice.

World Explorer Cruises

Universe Explorer **Winter:** No cruises. **Late spring–summer:** 14-night **Inside Passage** loops from Vancouver. 9-night **Inside Passage/Gulf of Alaska** loops from Vancouver.

Index

NOTES

NOTES

NOTES

NOTES

NOTES

NOTES

NOTES

Fodor's Travel Publications

Available at bookstores everywhere. For descriptions of all our titles, a key to Fodor's guidebook series, and on-line ordering, visit http://www.fodors.com/books/

Gold Guides

U.S.

Alaska

Arizona

Boston

California

Cape Cod, Martha's Vineyard, Nantucket

The Carolinas & Georgia

Chicago

Colorado

Florida

Hawai'i

Las Vegas, Reno, Tahoe

Los Angeles

Maine, Vermont, New Hampshire

Maui & Lāna'i

Miami & the Keys

New England

New Orleans

New York City

Oregon

Pacific North Coast

Philadelphia & the Pennsylvania Dutch Country

The Rockies

San Diego

San Francisco

Santa Fe, Taos, Albuquerque

Seattle & Vancouver

The South

U.S. & British Virgin Islands

USA

Virginia & Maryland

Washington, D.C.

Foreign

Australia

Austria

The Bahamas

Belize & Guatemala

Bermuda

Canada

Cancún, Cozumel, Yucatán Peninsula

Caribbean

China

Costa Rica

Cuba

The Czech Republic & Slovakia

Denmark

Eastern & Central Europe

Europe

Florence, Tuscany & Umbria

France

Germany

Great Britain

Greece

Hong Kong

India

Ireland

Israel

Italy

Japan

London

Madrid & Barcelona

Mexico

Montréal & Québec City

Moscow, St. Petersburg, Kiev

The Netherlands, Belgium & Luxembourg

New Zealand

Norway

Nova Scotia, New Brunswick, Prince Edward Island

Paris

Portugal

Provence & the Riviera

Scandinavia

Scotland

Singapore

South Africa

South America

Southeast Asia

Spain

Sweden

Switzerland

Thailand

Toronto

Turkey

Vienna & the Danube Valley

Vietnam

Special-Interest Guides

Adventures to Imagine

Alaska Ports of Call

Ballpark Vacations

The Best Cruises

Caribbean Ports of Call

The Complete Guide to America's National Parks

Europe Ports of Call

Family Adventures

Fodor's Gay Guide to the USA

Fodor's How to Pack

Great American Learning Vacations

Great American Sports & Adventure Vacations

Great American Vacations

Great American Vacations for Travelers with Disabilities

Halliday's New Orleans Food Explorer

Healthy Escapes

Kodak Guide to Shooting Great Travel Pictures

National Parks and Seashores of the East

National Parks of the West

Nights to Imagine

Orlando Like a Pro

Rock & Roll Traveler Great Britain and Ireland

Rock & Roll Traveler USA

Sunday in San Francisco

Walt Disney World for Adults

Weekends in New York

Wendy Perrin's Secrets Every Smart Traveler Should Know

Worlds to Imagine

Fodor's Special Series

Fodor's Best Bed & Breakfasts

America
California
The Mid-Atlantic
New England
The Pacific Northwest
The South
The Southwest
The Upper Great Lakes

Compass American Guides

Alaska
Arizona
Boston
Chicago
Coastal California
Colorado
Florida
Hawai'i
Hollywood
Idaho
Las Vegas
Maine
Manhattan
Minnesota
Montana
New Mexico
New Orleans
Oregon
Pacific Northwest
San Francisco
Santa Fe
South Carolina
South Dakota
Southwest
Texas
Underwater Wonders of the National Parks
Utah
Virginia
Washington
Wine Country
Wisconsin
Wyoming

Citypacks

Amsterdam
Atlanta
Berlin
Boston
Chicago
Florence
Hong Kong
London
Los Angeles
Miami
Montréal
New York City
Paris

Prague
Rome
San Francisco
Sydney
Tokyo
Toronto
Venice
Washington, D.C.

Exploring Guides

Australia
Boston & New England
Britain
California
Canada
Caribbean
China
Costa Rica
Cuba
Egypt
Florence & Tuscany
Florida
France
Germany
Greek Islands
Hawai'i
India
Ireland
Israel
Italy
Japan
London
Mexico
Moscow & St. Petersburg
New York City
Paris
Portugal
Prague
Provence
Rome
San Francisco
Scotland
Singapore & Malaysia
South Africa
Spain
Thailand
Turkey
Venice
Vietnam

Flashmaps

Boston
New York
San Francisco
Washington, D.C.

Fodor's Cityguides

Boston
New York
San Francisco

Fodor's Gay Guides

Amsterdam
Los Angeles & Southern California
New York City
Pacific Northwest
San Francisco and the Bay Area
South Florida
USA

Karen Brown Guides

Austria
California
England B&Bs
England, Wales & Scotland
France B&Bs
France Inns
Germany
Ireland
Italy B&Bs
Italy Inns
Portugal
Spain
Switzerland

Pocket Guides

Acapulco
Aruba
Atlanta
Barbados
Beijing
Berlin
Budapest
Dublin
Honolulu
Jamaica
London
Mexico City
New York City
Paris
Prague
Puerto Rico
Rome
San Francisco
Savannah & Charleston
Shanghai
Sydney
Washington, D.C.

Languages for Travelers (Cassette & Phrasebook)

French
German
Italian
Spanish

Mobil Travel Guides

America's Best Hotels & Restaurants
Arizona

California and the West
Florida
Great Lakes
Major Cities
Mid-Atlantic
Northeast
Northwest and Great Plains
Southeast
Southern California
Southwest and South Central

Rivages Guides

Bed and Breakfasts of Character and Charm in France
Hotels and Country Inns of Character and Charm in France
Hotels and Country Inns of Character and Charm in Italy
Hotels and Country Inns of Character and Charm in Paris
Hotels and Country Inns of Character and Charm in Portugal
Hotels and Country Inns of Character and Charm in Spain
Wines & Vineyards of Character and Charm in France

Short Escapes

Britain
France
Near New York City
New England

Fodor's Sports

Golf Digest's Places to Play (USA)
Golf Digest's Places to Play in the Southeast
Golf Digest's Places to Play in the Southwest
Skiing USA
USA Today The Complete Four Sport Stadium Guide

Fodor's upCLOSE Guides

California
Europe
France
Great Britain
Ireland
Italy
London
Los Angeles
Mexico
New York City
Paris
San Francisco

With guidebooks for every kind of travel—from weekend getaways to island hopping to adventures abroad—it's easy to understand why smart travelers go with **Fodor's**.

At bookstores everywhere.
www.fodors.com

Smart travelers go with **Fodor's**™

WHEREVER YOU TRAVEL, *H*ELP IS NEVER FAR AWAY.

From planning your trip to

providing travel assistance along

the way, American Express®

Travel Service Offices are

always there to help

you do more.

Travel

http://www.americanexpress.com/travel